Lecture Notes in Computer Science 8333

Commenced Publication in 1973
Founding and Former Series Editors:
Gerhard Goos, Juris Hartmanis, and Jan van Leeuwen

Editorial Board

Reinhard Klette   Mariano Rivera
Shin'ichi Satoh (Eds.)

Image and Video Technology

6th Pacific-Rim Symposium, PSIVT 2013
Guanajuato, Mexico, October 28 – November 1, 2013
Revised Selected Papers

 Springer

Volume Editors

Reinhard Klette
The University of Auckland
1142 Auckland, New Zealand
E-mail: r.klette@auckland.ac.nz

Mariano Rivera
Centro de Investigación en Matematicas A.C.
36000 Guanajuato, Mexico
E-mail: mrivera@acimat.mx

Shin'ichi Satoh
National Institute of Informatics
Tokyo 101-8430, Japan
E-mail: satoh@nii.ac.jp

ISSN 0302-9743   e-ISSN 1611-3349
ISBN 978-3-642-53841-4   e-ISBN 978-3-642-53842-1
DOI 10.1007/978-3-642-53842-1
Springer Heidelberg New York Dordrecht London

Library of Congress Control Number: 2013956520

CR Subject Classification (1998): H.5.1, H.5, I.4-5, I.2.10, I.3, H.3-4, E.4

LNCS Sublibrary: SL 6 – Image Processing, Computer Vision, Pattern Recognition, and Graphics

Typesetting: Camera-ready by author, data conversion by Scientific Publishing Services, Chennai, India

Printed on acid-free paper

Springer is part of Springer Science+Business Media (www.springer.com)

Preface

The 2013 Pacific-Rim Symposium on Image and Video Technology took place at the geographic center of Mexico. The beautiful town of Guanajuato is on the UNESCO world heritage list. It represents various challenges for video and image technologies. How to represent a road map which needs to be 3-dimensional because of the amazing geometry and topology of this historic city? What about vision-based driver-assistance systems in this unique environment? How to use panoramic imaging for representing the various outlooks on the colorful city with its narrow valleys and roads and steep hills? Which vision technologies are appropriate to accompany the diversity of arts present in the hometown of *Cervantino*, the most significant cultural festival in Latin America?

The PSIVT Steering Committee decided, after Chile, for the second time to have one of the editions of PSIVT in America. The four previous editions of PSIVT were held in Asia, namely, in Taiwan, Japan, Singapore, and South Korea. The series takes place in countries sharing a coast line with the Pacific Ocean.

PSIVT 2013 attracted 90 submissions to the main conference, and more than half of this number again to the four workshops that accompanied the symposium. Submissions came from all over the world, and the 43 accepted papers published in these proceedings demonstrate that image and video technology is a very vivid research area, which takes its problems from real-world demands.

For this 2013 issue of PSIVT, we had three keynote speakers. Uwe Franke (Daimler Research & Development) reported about research on computer vision at Daimler A.G., and how this research resulted in recent successes such as the introduction of stereo vision into cars, and also into the first 100-km fully autonomous drive of a Mercedes car through diverse traffic situations in Germany. Kenichi Kanatani (Okayama University) provided an overview of optimization techniques for geometric estimation, an area where the computer vision community valued his contributions very highly, and PSIVT 2013 commemorated his achievements with a dedicated workshop on the occasion of his retirement. Yasuyuki Matsushita (Microsoft Research Asia) lectured on a photometric approach for achieving high-fidelity 3D reconstruction; how recovered surface normals can help to fill in the fine surface details. There were also three tutorials, a demo session, and invited lectures at the four accompanying workshops.

Three program co-chairs and 30 area chairs finalized the decision on the selection of 19 oral presentations and 24 short-oral/poster presentations. During the reviewing process we made sure that each paper was reviewed by at least three reviewers, we added a rebuttal phase for the first time in PSIVT, and finalized the non-trivial acceptance decision-making process based on recommendations of the area chairs. Program co-chairs were not allowed to be a co-author of any paper submitted to PSIVT 2013.

Our sponsors were CIMAT Guanajuato, Chiba University, and the Université Paris-Est at Marne la Vallée. The symposium was endorsed by the International Association for Pattern Recognition (IAPR), which also sponsored the best paper award.

We wish to acknowledge a number of people for their invaluable help in putting this conference together. Many thanks to the Organizing Committee for their excellent logistical management, the area chairs for their rigorous evaluation of papers, the Program Committee members as well as external reviewers for their considerable time and effort, and the authors for their outstanding contributions.

For the local organizers, we thank Norma Cortes and the events staff from CIMAT, Jose Angel Chavarra and the design staff from CIMAT, Claudia Esteves (Universidad de Guanajuato), Alonso Ramirez Manzanares (Universidad de Guanajuato), and, last but not least Jean-Bernard Hayet (CIMAT), who was often the one who had everything under control. We also thank the pool of volunteer students from CIMAT and Universidad de Guanajuato.

PSIVT 2013 was a very enjoyable conference. We hope that the next PSIVT meeting in November 2015 in Auckland, New Zealand, attracts even more high-quality submissions.

November 2013

Reinhard Klette
Mariano Rivera
Shin'ichi Satoh

Organization

Steering Committee

Kap Luk Chan	Nanyang Technological University, Singapore
Yung-Chang Chen	National Tsing Hua University, Taiwan
Yo-Sung Ho	Gwangju Institute of Science and Technology, Korea
Qingming Huang	Chinese Academy of Sciences, China
Reinhard Klette	University of Auckland, New Zealand
Wen-Nung Lie	National Chung Cheng University, Taiwan
Domingo Mery	Pontificia Universidad Católica, Chile
Mariano Rivera	Centro de Investigación en Matemáticas, México
Akihiro Sugimoto	National Institute of Informatics, Japan

Honorary Chair

José Antonio de la Peña	Centro de Investigación en Matemáticas, México

General Chairs

José Luis Marroquín	Centro de Investigación en Matemáticas, México
Tieniu Tan	Chinese Academy of Sciences, China

Program Chairs

Reinhard Klette	University of Auckland, New Zealand
Mariano Rivera	Centro de Investigación en Matemáticas, México
Shin'ichi Satoh	National Institute of Informatics, Japan

Local Organization Chairs

Jean-Bernard Hayet	Centro de Investigación en Matemáticas, México
Alonso Ramírez-Manzanares	Universidad de Guanajuato, México
Claudia Esteves	Universidad de Guanajuato, México

Workshop Chairs

Fay Huang   Ilan University, Yi-Lan, Taiwan
Akihiro Sugimoto   National Institute of Informatics, Japan

Tutorial Chair

Petra Wiederhold   CINVESTAV, México

Demo Chairs

Sandino Morales   University of Auckland, New Zealand
Flavio Vigueras   Universidad Autónoma de San Luis Potos,
                             México

Publicity Chairs

Domingo Mery   Universidad Católica, Chile
Rachid Deriche   Inria, France
Jim Little   University of British Columbia, Canada
Chia-Yen Chen   NUK, Taiwan
Thierry Peynot   ACFR, Australia

Area Chairs

Miguel Carrasco   Universidad Diego Portales, Chile
L. Enrique Sucar   INAOE, México
Julian Fierrez   Universidad Autónoma de Madrid, Spain
Edel Garcia Reyes   Cenatav, Cuba
Rogelio Hasimoto   Centro de Investigación en Matemáticas,
                             México
Shinsaku Hiura   Hiroshima City University, Japan
Shuqiang Jiang   Institute of Computing Technology, Chinese
                             Academy of Sciences, China
Xiaoyi Jiang   Münster University, Germany
Ramakrishna Kakarala   Nanyang Technical University, Singapore
Shang-Hong Lai   National Tsing Hua University, Taiwan
Jaejoon Lee   Samsung Electronics, Korea
Chia-Wen Lin   National Tsing Hua University, Taiwan
Huei-Yung Lin   National Chung Cheng Uiversity, Taiwan
Jim Little   University of British Columbia, Canada
Qingshan Liu   Nanjing University of Information Sciences and
                             Technology, China
Brendan McCane   Otago University, New Zealand
Yasuhiro Mukaigawa   Osaka University, Japan

Paul Pang	Unitec, New Zealand
Luis Pizarro	Imperial College, UK
Antonio Robles-Kelly	NICTA, Canberra, Australia
Peter Schenzel	Halle University, Germany
Mingli Song	Zhejiang University, China
Yu-Wing Tai	KAIST, Korea
Gang Wang	Nanyang Technological University, Singapore
Lei Wang	University of Wollongong, Australia
Jianxin Wu	Nanyang Technological University, Singapore
Changsheng Xu	Chinese Academy of Sciences, China
Shuicheng Yan	National University of Singapore, Singapore
Weiqi Yan	Auckland University of Technology, New Zealand
Junsong Yuan	Nanyang Technological University, Singapore

Program Committee

Hajime Nagahara	Juan Carlos Sanmiguel Avedillo
Atsushi Nakazawa	Wei-Ta Chu
Dong Zhao	Y.W. Guo
Daisuke Iwai	Lu Fang
Chunhua Shen	Wei-Yang Lin
Lingqiao Liu	Michael Greenspan
Yi Wu	Siohoi Ieng
Jen Shin Hong	Damon Shing-Min Liu
Gangqiang Zhao	Jean-Bernard Hayet
Yang Cong	Masayuki Tanaka
Lei Qin	Guangyu Zou
Yonghong Tian	John Zelek
Yin Li	Yezhou Yang
Li Cheng	Steven Mills
Liu Xiao	Brendon Woodford
Lu Jiwen	Stephen Marsland
Miguel Angel Romero	Francois Rousseau
Vassilios Vonikakis	Peng Yang
Lei Xie	Yu-Bin Yang
Yuxin Peng	Philip Ogunbona
Hao Yang	Itaru Kitahara
Jun Zhou	Luping Zhou
Liu Wenyu	Min Xu
Akinobu Maejima	Zhang Tianzhu
Chen-Kuo Chiang	Rui Huang
Guo-Shiang Lin	Philippe Giguère
Huiyu Zhou	Kwang Moo Yi
Yu-Chiang Frank Wang	Yen-Yu Lin

Felix Calderon
Anali Alfaro
Billy Peralta
Oscar Dalmau
Paulo Menezes
Ivan Lillo
Anko Boerner
Björn Fröhlich
Bok-Suk Shin
Paulo Menezes
Olaf Hellwich
Jinwei Jiang
Ricardo Legarda-Saenz
Arturo Espinosa Romero

Kaori Yoshida
Ryszard Kozera
Carlos Brito Loeza
Francisco Madrigal
Gisela Klette
Miguel Arias
Paulo Menezes
Eduardo Bayro Corrochano
Jes'us Ariel Carrasco Ochoa
Luis Eduardo Falc'on Morales
Pierre Kornprobst
Kaihua Zhang
Yu Zhang

Additional Reviewers

Tao Ban
Aaron Chen
Heng-Chou Chen
Dario Di Fina
Fan Huijie
Svebor Karaman
Xiao-Jiao Mao
Kaushik Mitra
Ling-Yan Pan

Yiming Peng
Aswin Sankaranarayanan
Chunwei Song
Hakaru Tamukoh
Rafael Tibaes
Tiberio Uricchio
Jiu-Yang Zhao
Pengfei Zhu

PSIVT 2013 Best Paper Award Committee

José Antonio de la Peña   Centro de Investigación en Matemáticas,
                           México
José Luis Marroquín   Centro de Investigación en Matemáticas,
                           México
Tieniu Tan   Chinese Academy of Sciences, China

Sponsors of PSIVT 2013

Main Sponsor: CIMAT Guanajuato

Gold Sponsors: Chiba University
                  Université Paris-Est at Marne la Vallée

Best Paper: International Association for Pattern
                  Recognition (IAPR)

Best Paper Prize PSIVT 2013

"Wide-Baseline Dense Feature Matching for Endoscopic Images"

by Gustavo Puerto-Souza and Gian-Luca Mariottini

Best Student Paper Prize PSIVT 2013

"Joint Dictionary and Classifier Learning for Categorization of Images Using a Max-margin Framework"

by Hans Löbel, Álvaro Soto, René Vidal, and Domingo Mery

Table of Contents

Gamut Mapping through Perceptually-Based Contrast Reduction

Syed Waqas Zamir, Javier Vazquez-Corral, and Marcelo Bertalmío

Department of Information and Communication Technologies, Universitat Pompeu
Fabra, Barcelona, Spain
{waqas.zamir,javier.vazquez,marcelo.bertalmio}@upf.edu

Abstract. In this paper we present a spatial gamut mapping algorithm
that relies on a perceptually-based variational framework. Our method
adapts a well-known image energy functional whose minimization leads
to image enhancement and contrast modification. We show how by varying the importance of the contrast term in the image functional we are
able to perform gamut reduction. We propose an iterative scheme that
allows our algorithm to successfully map the colors from the gamut of
the original image to a given destination gamut while preserving the colors' perception and texture close to the original image. Both subjective
and objective evaluation validate the promising results achieved via our
proposed framework.

Keywords: Gamut Mapping (GM), Gamut Mapping Algorithm (GMA),
color contrast, variational methods.

1 Introduction

The color gamut of a device is the set of colors that this device is able to reproduce. Different display systems have different color gamuts, making a process
called gamut mapping (GM) essential: GM transforms colors from an input to
an output gamut with the intention that a viewer watching the same image in
different displays perceives the same colors. Intensive research has been carried
out in the GM area; however, it is still an open field due to the difficulty of the
challenges involved. One of the major tasks is to retain the perceived quality of
the original image into the gamut mapped image and most of the algorithms in
the literature lack in this regard.

A plethora of Gamut Mapping Algorithms (GMAs) exists in the literature and
the interested reader is referred to the excellent book by Morovič [19]. In general,
gamut mapping algorithms are classified into two broader categories. The first
category consists of global (also called non-local or non-adaptive) GMAs [9], [11],
[21], [22] that involve point-to-point mapping of colors (usually a predefined
lookup table) from source to destination gamut. The standard non-local GM
algorithm, Hue Preserving Minimum ΔE (HPMINDE), was proposed by Murch
and Taylor [21] where, in order to reproduce the image, the out-of-gamut colors
are clipped to closest points on the target gamut boundary along the lines of hue.

R. Klette, M. Rivera, and S. Satoh (Eds.): PSIVT 2013, LNCS 8333, pp. 1–11, 2014.

The non-adaptive GMAs involve either clipping or compression and completely ignore the spatial color configuration in the source image. In contrast, the second category involves the GMAs that take into account the spatial color information of the original image whilst fitting the color gamut of an image into the gamut of a given device [1], [2], [3], [12], [18], [20], [23]. However, these algorithms are often computationally expensive, or based on many assumptions and may report halo artifacts. McCann [16], [17] proposed a Retinex-inspired framework that performs spatial comparisons to reproduce the image while preserving the local gradients at all scales as in the original image. A similar multi-resolution GM approach that adapts to the original image content is suggested by Farup et al. [10]. A cluster based approach is defined in [14] for the optimization of GM. Alsam and Farup [2] proposed an iterative GMA that at iteration level zero gives the result identical to gamut clipping. However, by increasing the number of iterations, the solution approaches spatial gamut mapping. Unlike the global GMAs, the potential of spatial GM methods is to preserve the color gradient between two out-of-gamut colors instead of mapping them to the same in-gamut color. Another fundamental motivation behind spatial gamut mapping, in order to emulate the color perception properties of the Human Visual System (HVS), is the need to formulate a strategy where two out-of-gamut colors with identical lightness and chromaticity map to two different in-gamut colors depending on their spatial context in the image [12].

One of the major problems in GM is the evaluation of GMAs. Usually, subjective comparisons are performed [6], [8]. The most common subjective method is the pair comparison, where observers are asked to choose which of two different gamut-mapped versions of an image is more faithful to the original. However, subjective measures are time consuming, involve complexities, and do not provide clear cues to improve the given GMA. Recently, a perceptually-based color image difference metric [15] has been proposed that particularly emphasises on the assessment of gamut-mapped images. It is based on predicting the distortions in lightness, hue, chroma, contrast and structure of the gamut-mapped images by performing the comparison with the original images.

The contribution of this paper is to propose a perceptually inspired GMA where gamut reduction is achieved through contrast reduction, by adapting a framework [5], [4] that is inspired by the properties of contrast perception in the HVS and closely related to the Retinex theory of color vision [13]. Our method outperforms state of the art techniques ([2], [14]) both subjectively and according to the aforementioned perceptually-based metric of [15].

This paper is organized as follows; first, the image energy functional presented in [5] for the perceptually inspired contrast enhancement is described in section 2. Then, in section 3, the contrast enhancement model is adapted to obtain our GM method. In section 4, experiments and results are discussed. Finally, the paper is concluded in section 5.

2   Image Energy Functional

Bertalmío et al. proposed an image enhancement model in [5], where the image energy functional is defined as

$$
E(I) = \frac{\alpha}{2} \int_{\mathfrak{J}} \left(I(x) - \frac{1}{2} \right)^2 dx + \frac{\beta}{2} \int_{\mathfrak{J}} (I(x) - I_0(x))^2 dx
$$
$$
- \frac{1}{2} \int_{\mathfrak{J}^2} \int w(x,y)|I(x) - I(y)|dxdy
$$
(1)

where $\alpha \geq 0, \beta > 0$, I is a color channel (R, G or B), $w(x,y)$ is a normalized Gaussian kernel of standard deviation σ, and $I(x)$ and $I(y)$ are two intensity levels at pixel locations x and y respectively.

This functional has two competing parts. The positive competing terms are global: the first one controls the dispersion from the middle gray value, which is assumed to be $1/2$ as described in the gray-world hypothesis [7], whereas the second term in the functional penalizes the departure from the original image I_0. The negative competing term represents the local contrast. Therefore, by minimizing the image energy $E(I)$, the aim is to maximize the contrast, while not departing too much from the original image, and to preserve the gray-world hypothesis. It is formulated in [5] that the steady state of the energy $E(I)$ can be achieved using the evolution equation

$$
I^{k+1}(x) = \frac{I^k(x) + \Delta t \left(\frac{\alpha}{2} + \beta I_0(x) + \frac{1}{2} R_{I^k}(x) \right)}{1 + \Delta t(\alpha + \beta)}
$$
(2)

where the initial condition is $I^{k=0}(x) = I_0(x)$. The function $R_{I^k}(x)$ indicates the contrast function:

$$
R_{I^k}(x) = \frac{\sum_{y \in \mathfrak{J}} w(x,y)s_m\left(I^k(x) - I^k(y) \right)}{\sum_{y \in \mathfrak{J}} w(x,y)}
$$
(3)

where x is a fixed image pixel and y varies across the image. We define the slope function s_m for a real constant $m > 1$, when $d = I^k(x) - I^k(y)$, as follows

$$
s_m(d) = \begin{cases} -1, & \text{if } -1 \leq d \leq -\frac{1}{m} \\ m \cdot d, & \text{if } -\frac{1}{m} < d < \frac{1}{m} \\ +1, & \text{if } \frac{1}{m} \leq d \leq 1 \end{cases}
$$
(4)

In [4] it is shown that the presented model is related to the Retinex theory of color vision proposed by Land [13] and that the model can be adapted to perform contrast reduction by just changing the sign of the contrast term. In the next section we will explain how we can use this contrast reduction property for gamut mapping.

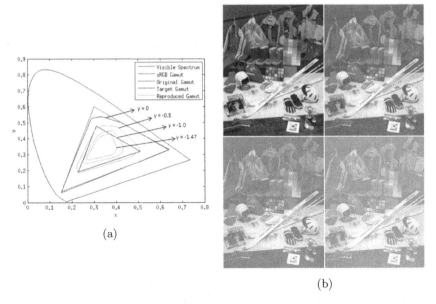

(a)

(b)

Fig. 1. Perceptual GM Approach. (a): Gamuts on chromaticity diagram. (b): Top left: original image. Top right: $\gamma = -0.50$. Bottom left: $\gamma = -1.0$. Bottom right: $\gamma = -1.47$.

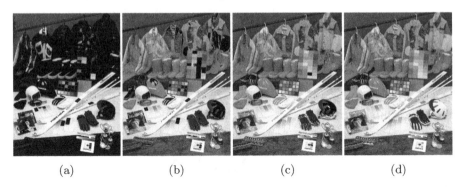

(a)   (b)   (c)   (d)

Fig. 2. Gradual mapping of colors. Out-of-gamut colors (in black) when (a): $\gamma = 0$, (b): $\gamma = -0.50$, (c): $\gamma = -1.0$, (d): $\gamma = -1.47$.

3   Gamut Mapping Framework

In this section, we adapt the image energy functional defined in Eq. (1) to perform gamut mapping from the gamut of the original image to the target gamut of a given device. In order to control the strength of the contrast modification, we add the contrast coefficient γ in the image energy functional $E(I)$. Recall that α controls the dispersion around middle gray. Since, in the case of gamut

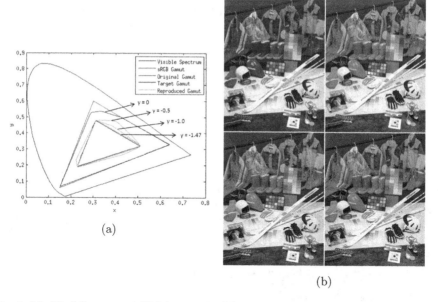

(a)

(b)

Fig. 3. Modified Perceptual GM Approach. (a): Gamuts on chromaticity diagram. (b): Top left: original image. Top right: $\gamma = -0.50$. Bottom left: $\gamma = -1.0$. Bottom right: $\gamma = -1.47$.

mapping, the HVS adapts to the luminance of the environment instead of the luminance of the stimulus, we set $\alpha = 0$ and the image energy model defined in Eq. (1) becomes

$$E(I) = \frac{\beta}{2} \int_{\mathfrak{J}} \left(I(x) - I_0(x)\right)^2 dx - \frac{\gamma}{2} \int \int_{\mathfrak{J}^2} w(x,y)|I(x) - I(y)|dxdy \qquad (5)$$

and subsequently the evolution equation (2) reduces to

$$I^{k+1}(x) = \frac{I^k(x) + \Delta t \left(\beta I_0(x) + \frac{\gamma}{2} R_{I^k}(x)\right)}{1 + \beta \Delta t} \qquad (6)$$

whereas, being $\gamma \in \mathbb{R}$ positive or negative depends on whether we want to maximize or minimize the contrast, respectively [4]. In this paper, γ will always be negative, since our goal is to reduce the contrast in order to perform GM.

The evolution equation (6) has a steady state for each particular set of values for β, Δt and γ. For example, in Fig. 1a, a chromaticity diagram is shown with different gamuts (visible spectrum, sRGB gamut, original gamut, target gamut and reproduced gamut). It can be seen that when $\gamma = 0$ the steady state of the evolution equation is equivalent to the original image. In the same figure we show that as γ decreases, the steady state of Eq. (6) has a gamut which is gradually smaller. Fig. 1a shows that, just by selecting an enough small gamma

  (a) original image   (b) $\sigma = 25$ (c) $\sigma = 100$ (d) $\sigma = 200$

Fig. 4. Effect of standard deviation(σ)

Fig. 5. Original sRGB images. Row 3; images 1, 2, 3, and Row 4; image 5 are from CIE [8]. Rest of the images are courtesy of Kodak.

($\gamma = -1.47$ in this case) we are already performing a gamut mapping algorithm. However, in this case, colors that were originally inside the target gamut move inwards too much, and the appearance of the image becomes washed-up, as Fig. 1b shows.

In order to improve the previous result, we present an iterative method in terms of the contrast coefficient γ. At iteration 1, we set $\beta = 1$ and $\gamma = 0$, and therefore the original image is obtained as the steady state. We leave untouched the pixels that are inside the destination gamut, and we move to iteration 2, where we decrease γ (for example, setting $\gamma = -0.05$) and run Eq. (6) to steady

Fig. 6. Gamut mapping results. Column 1: original images. Columns 2: output of HPMINDE clipping [21]. Column 3: output of Lau et al. [14]. Column 4: output of Alsam et al. [2]. Column 5: output of our algorithm.

state. In this second iteration, we check whether any of the points that were outside the gamut at the previous iteration have been moved inside the destination gamut. If this is the case, we leave them untouched for the following iterations. We keep iterating by decreasing γ until all the out-of-gamut colors come inside the destination gamut. An example of this iterative procedure is shown in Fig. 2, where black pixels represent out-of-gamut pixels left in that iteration. It can be seen in Fig. 3a, that the reproduced gamut is covering a much wider range of colors than previously. It is shown in Fig. 3b that the colors are better preserved as compared to the previous example (see Fig. 1b).

4 Experiments

We work in the RGB domain by fixing the parameters $\beta = 1, \Delta t = 0.10$ and iterate by decreasing the parameter γ ($\gamma \leq 0$) until the colors of the original image come inside the target gamut. For each value of γ we run Eq. (6) to steady state, which we assume that has been reached when the difference between two consecutive steps falls below 0.5%. We have noticed that the standard deviation σ of the Gaussian kernel w is of great importance; we observe in Fig. 4 that a small value of σ leads to the preservation of colors but introduces artifacts, whereas for the larger values of σ each color pixel is strongly influenced from the surrounding colors. Therefore, we compute the gamut mapped images $\mathcal{I}_\sigma$

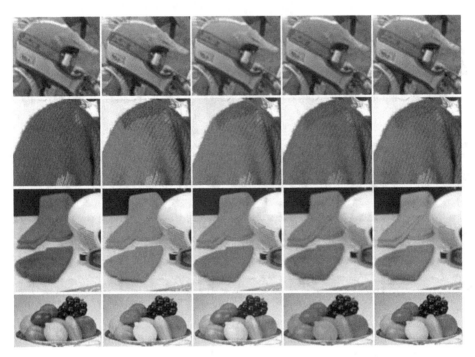

Fig. 7. Preserving details, all images are cropped from Fig. 6. Column 1: original cropped images. Column 2: output of HPMINDE [21]. Column 3: output of Lau et al. [14]. Column 4: output of Alsam et al. [2]. Column 5: output of our algorithm.

by using four different values of standard deviations $\sigma \in \{50, 100, 150, 200\}$. Subsequently, in order to obtain a final gamut mapped image $\mathcal{I}_{final}$, we combine all the outcomes $\mathcal{I}_\sigma$ with respect to the original image $\mathcal{I}_{orig}$, in Lab color space, by using the Delta-E measure.

$$\mathcal{I}_{final}(x) = \arg\min_{\mathcal{I}_\sigma} \left(Lab(\mathcal{I}_\sigma(x)) - Lab(\mathcal{I}_{orig}(x)) \right)^2, \quad \sigma \in \{50, 100, 150, 200\}$$

(7)

We are confident that varying these parameters according to the application and image characteristics would give better results. However, our choice of parameters is the same for all the results shown in this paper.

4.1 Qualitative Results

In this section, we apply our method on a rather challenging target gamut as shown in Fig. 1a. The original sRGB images used are illustrated in Fig. 5. Given an image in sRGB, our algorithm maps the gamut of the original image into the destination gamut. The results presented in Fig. 6 show that our proposed

Table 1. Quality assessment: perceptual difference measure [15]

	HPMINDE Clipping [21]	Lau et al. [14]	Alsam et al. [2]	Our Algorithm
Caps Image	0.1027	0.1022	0.0821	**0.0711**
Raft Image	0.0772	0.0747	0.0857	**0.0471**
Barn Image	0.0268	0.0242	0.0134	**0.0088**
Girl Image	0.0825	0.0695	0.0359	**0.0209**
Birds Image	0.1829	0.1119	**0.0923**	0.1086
Motorbikes Image	0.0330	0.0396	0.0322	**0.0155**
Boat Image	0.0255	0.0187	0.0035	**0.0008**
Beach Image	0.0168	0.0151	0.0077	**0.0046**
Party Image	0.0569	0.0878	0.0487	**0.0280**
Portrait Image	0.0235	0.0393	0.0209	**0.0104**
Picnic Image	0.0954	0.0954	**0.0448**	0.0638
Window Image	0.0514	0.0591	0.0443	**0.0326**
Woman with Hat Image	0.1313	0.0882	0.0528	**0.0410**
Sailing Boats Image	0.0183	0.0287	0.0195	**0.0130**
Statue Image	0.0025	0.0061	0.0053	**0.0020**
Model Image	0.0292	0.0736	0.0398	**0.0390**
Ski Image	0.1899	0.1964	0.1734	**0.1040**

Table 2. Quality assessment: statistical data

	Mean	Median	RMS
HPMINDE Clipping [21]	0.0674	0.0514	0.0873
Lau et al. [14]	0.0665	0.0695	0.0807
Alsam et al. [2]	0.0472	0.0398	0.0627
Our Algorithm	**0.0360**	**0.0280**	**0.0485**

framework works well in preserving the colors, texture and color gradients from the out-of-gamut regions while staying faithful to the perception of the original image. For example, in Fig. 7, rows 1 and 4, it can be seen that the colors reproduced by our GM algorithm (fifth column) are much more saturated than those of HPMINDE [21] (second column), and the state of the art algorithms of Lau et al. [14] (third column) and Alsam et al. [2] (fourth column). Similarly, in Fig. 7, row 2, our algorithm not only reproduces the color efficiently but also preserves a great amount of texture. In Fig. 7, row 3, we can see our method accurately represents the difference in the lightness of identical hue (see the pink socks and pink beanie). Results show that our algorithm outperforms not only the widespread method [21] but also the state of the art algorithms [2], [14].

4.2   Objective Quality Assessment

Visually, the results presented so far underline the good performance of our GMA in terms of visual quality. This subjective outcome is backed by using the perceptual color quality measure presented in [15]: the Color Image Difference (CID) metric estimates the perceptual differences given by the changes, from one image to the other, in features such as hue, lightness, chroma, contrast and structure.

Comparisons using the CID metric are provided in Table 1. In this table we can see that our algorithm outperforms the other methods in 15 out of 17 test images. Moreover, the statistical data (mean, median and root mean square) is also presented in Table 2. These results show that our method produces a gamut mapped image which is, perceptually, more faithful to the original image as compared with the other methods.

5   Conclusions

In this paper, we have presented a gamut mapping algorithm based on a perceptually inspired variational framework. We have shown how to modify the variational framework in order to perform gamut mapping reduction. The main advantage of our method is its perceptual inspiration, that allows us to mimic some basic properties of the HVS while performing the mapping, and this is corroborated by the good scores we obtain with a perceptual metric for color and contrast distortion.

One subject left untreated in this paper is the need to develop a GMA that is capable of mapping colors from a smaller gamut to a larger gamut. In this direction, we are currently working on adapting our formulation to the problem of gamut extension.

Acknowledgement. This work was supported by the European Research Council, Starting Grant ref. 306337, and by Spanish grants ref. TIN2011-15954-E and ref. TIN2012-38112. The authors would like to thank Jan Morovič, Ivar Farup and Ali Alsam for their comments, suggestions and source codes. Many thanks go to Cheryl Lau for running experiments on a set of images.

References

1. Alsam, A., Farup, I.: Colour Gamut Mapping as a Constrained Variational Problem. In: Proc. 16th Scandinavian Conference on Image Analysis, pp. 109–118 (2009)
2. Alsam, A., Farup, I.: Spatial Colour Gamut Mapping by Orthogonal Projection of Gradients onto Constant Hue Lines. In: Proc. 8th International Symposium on Visual Computing, pp. 556–565 (2012)
3. Bala, R., Dequeiroz, R., Eschbach, R., Wu, W.: Gamut Mapping to Preserve Spatial Luminance Variations. Journal of Imaging Science and Technology, 122–128 (2001)
4. Bertalmío, M., Caselles, V., Provenzi, E.: Issues About Retinex Theory and Contrast Enhancement. International Journal of Computer Vision 83(1), 101–119 (2009)
5. Bertalmío, M., Caselles, V., Provenzi, E., Rizzi, A.: Perceptual Color Correction Through Variational Techniques. IEEE Transactions on Image Processing 16(4), 1058–1072 (2007)

6. Bonnier, N., Schmitt, F., Brettel, H., Berche, S.: Evaluation of Spatial Gamut Mapping Algorithms. In: Proc. 14th Color Imaging Conference (2006)
7. Buchsbaum, G.: A Spatial Processor Model for Object Colour Perception. Journal of the Franklin Institute 310(1), 1–26 (1980)
8. CIE: Guidelines for the evaluation of gamut mapping algorithms. Technical Report (2004)
9. Ebner, F., Fairchild, M.D.: Gamut mapping from below: Finding minimum perceptual distances for colors outside the gamut volume. Color Research and Application, 402–413 (1997)
10. Farup, I., Gatta, C., Rizzi, A.: A multiscale framework for spatial gamut mapping. IEEE Transactions on Image Processing, 2423–2435 (2007)
11. Katoh, N., Ito, M., Ohno, S.: Three-dimensional gamut mapping using various color difference formulae and color spaces. Journal of Electronic Imaging 4(8), 365–379 (1999)
12. Kimmel, R., Shaked, D., Elad, M., Sobel, I.: Space-Dependent Color Gamut Mapping: A Variational Approach. IEEE Transactions on Image Processing, 796–803 (2005)
13. Land, E.H., McCann, J.J.: Lightness and Retinex Theory. Journal of the Optical Society of America, 1–11 (1971)
14. Lau, C., Heidrich, W., Mantiuk, R.: Cluster-based color space optimizations. In: Proc. IEEE International Conference on Computer Vision, pp. 1172–1179 (2011)
15. Lissner, I., Preiss, J., Urban, P., Lichtenauer, M.S., Zolliker, P.: Image-Difference Prediction: From Grayscale to Color. IEEE Transactions on Image Processing 22(2), 435–446 (2013)
16. McCann, J.J.: Lessons Learned from Mondrians Applied to Real Images and Color Gamuts. In: Proc. Color Imaging Conference, pp. 1–8 (1999)
17. McCann, J.J.: A Spatial Colour Gamut Calculation to Optimize Colour Appearance. Colour Image Science: Exploiting Digital Media, 213–233 (2002)
18. Meyer, J., Barth, B.: Color Gamut Matching for Hard Copy. In: Proc. SID Digest, pp. 86–89 (1989)
19. Morovič, J.: Color gamut mapping. John Wiley & Sons (2008)
20. Morovič, J., Wang, Y.: A Multi-Resolution, Full-Colour Spatial Gamut Mapping Algorithm. In: Proc. Color Imaging Conference, pp. 282–287 (2003)
21. Murch, G.M., Taylor, J.M.: Color in Computer Graphics: Manipulating and Matching Color. In: Eurographics Seminar: Advances in Computer Graphics V, pp. 41–47 (1989)
22. Stone, M.C., Cowan, W.B., Beatty, J.C.: Color gamut mapping and the printing of digital color images. ACM Transactions on Graphics 7(4), 249–292 (1988)
23. Zolliker, P., Simon, K.: Retaining Local Image Information in Gamut Mapping Algorithms. IEEE Transactions on Image Processing 16(3), 664–672 (2007)

Precise Correction of Lateral Chromatic Aberration in Images

Victoria Rudakova and Pascal Monasse

Université Paris-Est, LIGM (UMR CNRS 8049),
Center for Visual Computing, ENPC, F-77455 Marne-la-Vallée
{rudakovv,monasse}@imagine.enpc.fr

Abstract. This paper addresses the problem of lateral chromatic aberration correction in images through color planes warping. We aim at high precision (largely sub-pixel) realignment of color channels. This is achieved thanks to two ingredients: high precision keypoint detection, which in our case are disk centers, and more general correction model than what is commonly used in the literature, radial polynomial. Our setup is quite easy to implement, requiring a pattern of black disks on white paper and a single snapshot. We measure the errors in terms of geometry and of color and compare our method to three different software programs. Quantitative results on real images show that our method allows alignment of average 0.05 pixel of color channels and a residual color error divided by a factor 3 to 6.

Keywords: chromatic aberration, image warping, calibration, polynomial model, image enhancement.

1 Introduction

In all optical systems refraction causes the color channels to focus slightly differently. This phenomenon is called chromatic aberration (hereafter CA). When the digital image is obtained, the color channels are misaligned with respect to each other and therefore the phenomenon manifests itself as colored fringes at image edges and high contrast areas. With the increase of sensor resolution for many consumer and scientific cameras, the chromatic aberration gets amplified. For high precision applications, when usage of color information becomes important, it is necessary to accurately correct such defects. Figure 1 shows the effect of our CA correction on real image. CA is classified into two types: axial and lateral. The former occurs when different wavelengths focus at different distances from the lens - in digital images it produces blurring effect since blue and red channels are defocused (assuming the green channel is in focus). A lateral defect occurs when the wavelengths focus at different points on the focal plane and thus geometrical color plane misalignments occur.

In order to define a magnitude of high precision correction, a visual perception experiment was done for different misalignment levels (in pixel units). A synthetic disk was generated on a large image with misalignment between channels

R. Klette, M. Rivera, and S. Satoh (Eds.): PSIVT 2013, LNCS 8333, pp. 12–22, 2014.
© Springer-Verlag Berlin Heidelberg 2014

Fig. 1. Cropped and zoomed-in image from camera Canon EOS 40D, before (left) and after (right) chromatic aberration correction by our method. Notice the attenuated color fringes at edges between left and right images.

introduced, then the image was blurred in order to avoid aliasing, and downsampled. A part of the downsampled image was cropped and zoomed-in in Figure 2. It can be noted that 0.1 pixel misalignment is a borderline when aberration becomes just-noticeable, while misalignments of 0.3 pixel and higher are quite perceptible.

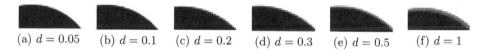

(a) $d = 0.05$ (b) $d = 0.1$ (c) $d = 0.2$ (d) $d = 0.3$ (e) $d = 0.5$ (f) $d = 1$

Fig. 2. Visual perception tests for chromatic aberration on synthetic disk image for different values of displacements d (in pixels). Note that a displacement value of 0.1 pixel is just noticeable, while 0.3 pixel displacement is quite perceptible.

Rare papers propose to compensate both axial and lateral CA. The optical solutions [1,2] try to overcome this effect, but they can be quite expensive and not always effective for the zones farther from the optical center. Another example [3] proposes an active lens system based on modification of the camera settings (magnification, focus, sensor shifting) for each color channel. Such approach may not be practical since it requires taking three pictures for each channel under different camera settings. Kozubek and Matula [4] show how to correct for both types of aberrations in the environment of fluorescent microscopy; however, this method cannot be applied for camera imaging systems.

As most other approaches, we address the lateral CA only but require a single image. Like Boult and Wolberg [5], we formulate the correction as an image warping problem, which means re-aligning color channels digitally. However, Bould and Wolberg [5] do not use any aberration model, interpolating the correction of control points, whereas all other warping methods assume radial nature of the distortion. Matsuoka *et al.* [6] provide an evaluation of the state of art correction methods, all of which use different ways to model the radial distortion [7,8,9].

However, it is important to note that not all cameras can be satisfactorily corrected by the same radial model. We will see that more accurate results could be achieved with a more general bivariate polynomial model.

Our lateral CA correction is achieved through realigning the red and blue color planes to the reference green plane. Accurate keypoints (which are centers of disks from a circle pattern) are extracted in each channel independently as described by Section 2. The geometric displacements between color planes is then modelled by bivariate polynomials in Section 3. Section 4 exposes the quantitative results in terms of both color and geometry misalignments, compares to other software and provides real scene examples. We draw some conclusions in Section 5.

2   Keypoint Detection

The calibration pattern is made of disks whose centers are used as keypoints. A disk is a filled black circle of fixed radius. High precision requires accounting for a tilt of the camera with respect to the pattern plane normal, thus the disks are viewed as slightly elliptic shapes. We are thus interested in precise ellipse center detection, which is obtained by an adjustment of a parametric model simulating the CCD response using an iterative optimization process. The parametric model takes into account both geometry and intensity.

The geometric model, describing the relationship between model point (x, y) of the filled circle and image point (x', y'), is represented by a local affine transform:

$$\begin{pmatrix} x \\ y \\ 1 \end{pmatrix} = \begin{pmatrix} \lambda_1 \cos\theta & -\lambda_2 \sin\theta & 0 \\ \lambda_1 \sin\theta & \lambda_2 \cos\theta & 0 \\ 0 & 0 & 1 \end{pmatrix} \cdot \begin{pmatrix} x' - t_u \\ y' - t_v \\ 1 \end{pmatrix}, \tag{1}$$

depending on the five geometry parameters, (t_u, t_v) (subpixel ellipse center position, the parameters we are interested in), λ_1, λ_2 the elongation factors of major and minor axes, and θ the angle between the major axis and x axis.

The intensity model assumes constant intensity in the disk center and in the periphery with a linear transition between both. For luminance level L_1 at the disk center and L_2 at its periphery ($L_1 < L_2$), the luminance transition is represented by three line segments as in Figure 3, the gradient part being linear with slope k. The distances $-\frac{1}{k}$ and $\frac{1}{k}$ define the border of the disk, gradient, and periphery areas.

At a model point (x, y) of (1), the corresponding image point (x', y') has luminance level $L(x', y')$ according to Figure 3. We use the Levenberg-Marquardt algorithm to minimize the sum of squared differences of the gray levels between each pixel (x', y') of the elliptic patch in the image I and point (x, y) of the theoretical CCD model L, with respect to the 8 parameters $\{\lambda_1, \lambda_2, \theta, t_u, t_v, k, L_1, L_2\}$:

$$\arg\min_{\lambda_1, \lambda_2, \theta, t_u, t_v, k, L_1, L_2} \sum_{x', y'} (I(x', y') - L(x, y))^2. \tag{2}$$

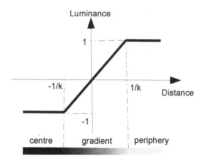

Fig. 3. The luminance transition model for one disk, of parameter k

Only the resulting subpixel center coordinates (t_u, t_v) are used for color channel alignment.

The process is the following: in each color channel, R, G and B, a simple thresholding gives rough disk locations. Each one is refined through the above minimization and keypoints of R and B channels are paired to nearest keypoint in G channel. This provides a discrete alignment at keypoints of these two channels to the green one. We use the green channel as reference as it is the most represented in the standard Bayer pattern.

3   Correction Model

Lateral CA can be considered as geometric distortion between color channels. Assuming the distortion field is smooth by nature, the main idea is to model each distortion field, one for red and one for blue channels, by bivariate polynomials in x and y, while keeping one channel as a reference (the green one). The polynomial model, when compared to many other distortion models (radial, division, rational functions), is general and can perfectly approximate the former models [10]. To achieve high precision the degree 11 was chosen for both x and y. Experimentally the error stabilizes for polynomials of degrees 7 to 11 [10].

The keypoints are represented in pixel coordinates as (x_f, y_f) for a certain color plane f, red (r), blue (b) or green (g). The lateral misalignments between the red (or blue) and the green planes are corrected by identifying the parameters of polynomials p_{fx}, p_{fy} approximating at best the equations

$$x_{gi} = p_{fx}(x_{fi}, y_{fi})$$
$$y_{gi} = p_{fy}(x_{fi}, y_{fi}), \tag{3}$$

with the target colors $f = r$ or $f = b$ and i describing keypoint index.

The polynomial model p_{fx} of degree m and polynomial coefficients $\{p_{x_0},$ $p_{x_1}, \cdots, p_{x_{\frac{(m+1)(m+2)}{2}-1}}\}$ can be expanded as:

$$
\begin{aligned}
x_g =& p_{x_0} x_f^m + p_{x_1} x_f^{m-1} y_f + p_{x_2} x_f^{m-2} y_f^2 + p_{x_m} y_f^m + p_{x_{m+1}} x_f^{m-1} + \cdots \\
&+ p_{x_{m+2}} x_f^{m-2} y_f + p_{x_{2m}} y_f^{m-1} + p_{x_{\frac{(m+1)(m+2)}{2}-3}} x_f + \cdots \\
&+ p_{x_{\frac{(m+1)(m+2)}{2}-2}} y_f + p_{x_{\frac{(m+1)(m+2)}{2}-1}}.
\end{aligned}
$$

The unknowns are the parameters of polynomials p_{fx} and p_{fy}. These are $(m+1)(m+2)/2 = 78$ for degree $m = 11$ for each polynomial. Our pattern is composed of about 1000 disks (we show below that we can pack so many disks of small diameter on our pattern without deterioration of precision), and it also means there is no risk of overfitting because the number of control points is far higher than the number of unknowns. For a number K of keypoints $(x_{fi}, y_{fi}), i = 1, \cdots, K$ distributed all over the image, the polynomial coefficients are computed by minimizing the difference of displacements between the reference and distorted channels:

$$
E = \sum_{i=1}^{K} (p_{fx}(x_{fi}, y_{fi}) - x_{gi})^2 + (p_{fy}(x_{fi}, y_{fi}) - y_{gi})^2. \tag{4}
$$

The solution vector p of this least square problem satisfies a linear system $Ap = v$ with A the coefficient matrix built from the x_{fi}, y_{fi}. For favorable numerical conditioning of A, these pixel coordinates need to be normalized between 0 and 1 by application of a global scale.

After the calibration is done, it is straightforward to perform the correction for any image which was taken under the same fixed camera settings. The polynomials p_{fx} and p_{fy} calculate the corrected pixel coordinates for each distorted pixel coordinate (x_f, y_f) as in (3), and then the color is obtained by interpolation from the corrected coordinates.

4   Experiments

A set of experiments are performed to measure the ellipse center detection accuracy at different ellipse sizes against noise and aliasing. To evaluate the CA correction method we use two types of metrics: geometry and color. Comparison to existing commercial software is done.

4.1   Keypoint Detection Accuracy

Synthetic disk (filled circle) 8-bit images were generated on a large image, blurred, downsampled with scale $s = 20$ and finally Gaussian noise were added. Subpixel disk center location is used as ground truth and compared to detected disk center. Figure 4 shows the performance of the algorithm against Gaussian

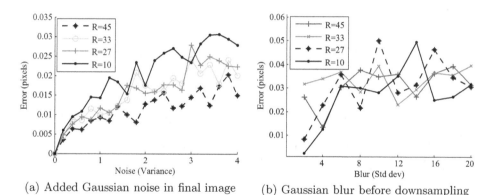

(a) Added Gaussian noise in final image   (b) Gaussian blur before downsampling

Fig. 4. Keypoint detection precision for varying disk radii, R (pixels) and downsampled rate $s = 20$

noise level added to the images (median error out of 25 iterations) and amount of blur for different disk radii.

It can be observed that in all cases the error is less than 0.05 pixel, even for small disk radius (10 pixels). That allows us to pack more keypoints in a given pattern area. As expected, the error increases roughly linearly with noise level. However, it remains constant under blur. This is important because in a Bayer pattern image, red and blue channels are notoriously aliased. Figure 4 (b) shows that this does not affect the disk centers detection.

4.2   Geometry Misalignment

The calibration pattern is printed on an $A3$ format paper. It is composed of $37 \times 26 = 962$ black disks of radius $0.4cm$ and separation of $1.1cm$ between consecutive disks. Three digital reflex cameras with interchangeable lenses are used to capture the images: Canon EOS 5D, Canon EOS 40D and Sony DSLR A200. They are noted hereafter 'cam 1', 'cam 2' and 'cam 3'. RAW images are separated in their three channels. The green channel is kept at original resolution of the raw image by bilinear interpolation of missing pixels in the Bayer pattern. Red and blue channels are in (aliased) half-dimension images.

The color planes keypoint displacements are presented in Table 1. Significant reduction is observed after correction. It can be noted that the residuals are of similar magnitude as the keypoint detection, which emphasizes the importance of having precise keypoints.

Further details on keypoint displacements are presented for one case (cam 1 with $f_1 = 24mm$, blue channel) in Figure 5. From the histograms it can be seen that error distribution decreases and stays within 0.05 pixel; this numerical result holds for most of our tests. The vector fields show how the character of the displacement field had changed: before correction it has a fairly radial nature, after correction it is less structured.

Table 1. Keypoint displacements between color planes in the format "RMSE (maximum)" distances in pixels before and after correction at two focal lengths for each camera

	Uncorrected		Corrected	
Cameras	Red/Green	Blue/Green	Red/Green	Blue/Green
cam 1				
$f_1 = 24mm$	0.191 (0.763)	1.606 (3.615)	0.029 (0.088)	0.025 (0.131)
$f_2 = 70mm$	0.488(0.835)	1.347 (1.584)	0.032 (0.113)	0.040 (0.134)
cam 2				
$f_1 = 18mm$	0.654 (0.978)	1.419 (3.358)	0.029 (0.113)	0.058 (0.153)
$f_2 = 55mm$	0.459 (0.879)	1.524 (2.496)	0.044 (0.123)	0.039 (0.092)
cam 3				
$f_1 = 18mm$	0.9106 (1.1422)	1.5371 (3.4125)	0.0344 (0.1037)	0.0373 (0.0882)
$f_2 = 70mm$	0.2502 (0.5382)	1.7066 (2.4355)	0.0492 (0.1249)	0.0429 (0.1502)

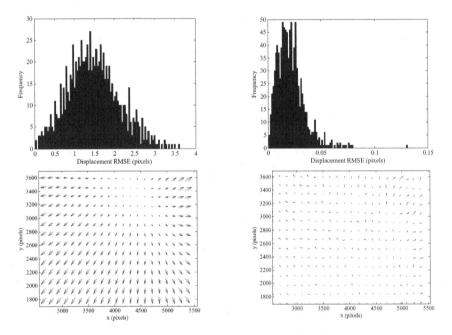

Fig. 5. Histograms (top row) and vector fields (bottom row) of Euclidean displacements of keypoints of the calibration image for blue channel with respect to green channel taken by cam 1 with $f_1 = 24mm$ before (left column) and after (right column) correction

Three software solutions were chosen to perform a comparison with our method: DxO Optics Pro (noted as 'DxO') [11], Canon DPP ('DPP') [12] and Jaliko lenstool ('JLT') [13]. The first two use lab-computed calibration database for each camera and each lens, and perform correction based on the database, with possibility of manual readjustment for each image. The CA correction by JLT method is fully automatic and for any kind of camera (no database) but requires several images. Cam 2 was chosen for this experiment and the keypoint displacement results are shown in Figure 6 for different focal lengths. The results demonstrate that only our method achieves precision where defects are not visible anymore (see Figure 2): the mean always stays within $0.05 - 0.1$ pixel while for other methods the average remains around 0.4 pixels.

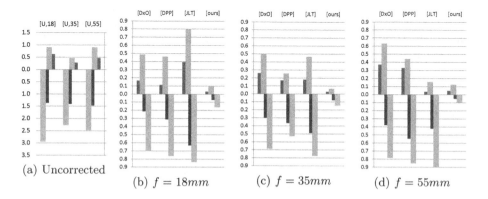

Fig. 6. Comparison of our method to other software for cam 2 and different focal lengths f, the comparison is in terms of mean (dark colored bars) and maximum (light colored bars) misalignments for both red (positive axis) and blue (negative axis) channels. (a) provides information on the initial uncorrected keypoint displacements for the same focal lengths (notice the different scale).

4.3   CA Correction: Color Misalignment

To visualize the effect of CA correction, color based $3D$ point cloud is built for the calibration image. Since we use a black and white pattern, it is expected that $3D$ color cloud of the calibration image would lie along the gray line connecting black and white spots. If chromatic aberration is present, color channels are not aligned and occurring blue-red hues come out at significant distance from the gray line, thus creating a bulged $3D$ color cloud. Figure 7 shows two color clouds built in RGB space before and after the correction for cam 1 at $f_1 = 24mm$.

To get a quantitative evaluation of the color cloud, we use statistics on the distances d_x from each color point to a local gray line. To compensate the absence of white balance in the RAW image, we use the local gray line, representing $3D$ regression of the point cloud (obtained by eigen decomposition of the variance-covariance matrix of the color cloud). Figure 8 shows the frequency histogram of

Fig. 7. $3D$ color clouds of the calibration image before (left) and after (right) correction

color pixels in the calibration image. Obviously, the majority of pixels belong to the regions of the local black and white spots and these have naturally almost vanishing error. To get more significant statistics, we eliminate all those majority pixels. The distances of the remaining points to the local gray line are used to get a quantitative measure:

$$S = \sqrt{\frac{\sum_x d_x^2}{N}}. \tag{5}$$

Assuming the gray line passes through two points $X_1^{(g)}$, $X_2^{(g)}$, the distance from

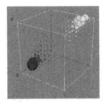

Fig. 8. Frequency histogram representation

a color point x to the gray line is expressed as: $d_x = \dfrac{\left| (x - X_1^{(g)}) \ (x - X_2^{(g)}) \ e_3 \right|}{\| X_2^{(g)} - X_1^{(g)} \|}$, with the numerator being a determinant of a 3×3 matrix whose third column is the vector $e_3 = (0\ 0\ 1)^T$. Table 2 shows the RMSE and maximum distances for the calibration image and two cameras. The color misalignment can be reduced up to 6 times, depending on the camera. The plot of color error around two disks of the pattern image for cam 1 is shown in Figure 9 as gray level values (white is maximum, black is zero). After correction, the error magnitude for chromatic aberration is comparable with noise level, as opposed to the plot before correction, where noise is masked by the amplitude of color error.

4.4   Visual Improvement for Real Scenes

To see the improvement in image quality, a zoomed-in crops of outdoor images are shown Figure 10 and Figure 11. Red and blue fringes can be seen in original images. They disappear after correction. The same effect can be observed in Figure 1.

Table 2. Error measures of color distribution in RMSE (maximum distance) format

Camera	Uncorrected, $S_u(d_{u,max})$	Corrected, $S_c(d_{c,max})$	Ratio, $\frac{S_u}{S_c}(\frac{d_{u,max}}{d_{c,max}})$
cam 1			
$f_1 = 24mm$	41.54 (78.21)	6.91 (22.87)	6.01 (3.41)
$f_2 = 70mm$	30.74 (68.98)	5.92 (18.33)	5.19 (3.76)
cam 2			
$f_1 = 18mm$	32.35 (66.07)	9.46 (34.08)	3.41 (1.93)
$f_2 = 55mm$	36.48 (78.73)	7.35 (31.32)	4.96 (2.51)
cam 3			
$f_1 = 18mm$	19.99 (50.18)	5.75 (24.45)	3.47 (2.05)
$f_2 = 70mm$	28.51 (94.54)	7.22 (76.76)	3.94 (1.23)

Fig. 9. Error distances (5) to the local gray line for the calibration image of cam 1, before (left) and after (right) correction

Fig. 10. Cropped and zoomed-in image from camera 1, before (left) and after (right) correction

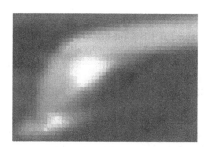
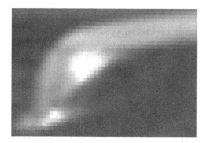

Fig. 11. Cropped and zoomed-in image from camera 3, before (left) and after (right) correction

5 Conclusion

We have proposed a high precision chromatic aberration correction method, using a single snapshot of a pattern of black disks. Their centers are used as keypoints and aligned between different channels. A dense correction vector field is then deduced by a general polynomial model. Though already quite accurate, the precision is limited by the keypoint location detection. Comparison tests showed that our method outperforms existing software solutions by a significant margin. Further work includes comparison with a pattern made of pure noise, producing numerous SIFT [14] keypoints. Whereas their precision is likely to be lower, their number could compensate that and may improve the overall correction.

Acknowledgments. This work was carried out in IMAGINE, a joint research project between École des Ponts ParisTech (ENPC) and the Scientific and Technical Centre for Building (CSTB). Part of this work was funded by the Agence Nationale de la Recherche, Callisto project (ANR-09-CORD-003).

References

1. Farrar, N.R., Smith, A.H., Busath, D.R., Taitano, D.: In-situ measurement of lens aberrations. In: Optical Microlithography, vol. XIII (2000)
2. Millán, M.S., Otón, J., Pérez-Cabré, E.: Dynamic compensation of chromatic aberration in a programmable diffractive lens. Optics Express 14, 9103–9112 (2006)
3. Willson, R., Shafer, S.: Active lens control for high precision computer imaging. In: Proc. IEEE ICRA, vol. 3, pp. 2063–2070 (April 1991)
4. Kozubek, M., Matula, P.: An efficient algorithm for measurement and correction of chromatic aberrations in fluorescence microscopy. Journal of Microscopy 200(3), 206–217 (2000)
5. Boult, T.E., Wolberg, G.: Correcting chromatic aberrations using image warping. In: 1992 IEEE Computer Society Conference on Computer Vision and Pattern Recognition, Proceedings CVPR 1992, pp. 684–687. IEEE (1992)
6. Matsuoka, R., Asonuma, K., Takahashi, G., Danjo, T., Hirana, K.: Evaluation of correction methods of chromatic aberration in digital camera images. In: ISPRS Photogrammetric Image Analysis, vol. I-3 (2012)
7. Kaufmann, V., Ladstdter, R.: Elimination of color fringes in digital photographs caused by lateral chromatic aberration. In: CIPA XX International Symposium (2005)
8. Luhmann, T., Hastedt, H., Tecklenburg, W.: Modelling of chromatic aberration for high precision photogrammetry. In: Proc. of the ISPRS Commission V Symp. on Image Engineering and Vision Metrology, vol. 36, pp. 173–178 (2006)
9. Mallon, J., Whelan, P.F.: Calibration and removal of lateral chromatic aberration in images. Pattern Recognition Letters 28(1), 125–135 (2007)
10. Tang, Z.: High accuracy measurement in 3D stereo reconstruction. PhD thesis, ENS Cachan, France (2011)
11. DxO: DxO Optics Pro, http://www.dxo.com/intl/photography/dxo-optics-pro
12. Canon: Digital Photo Professional, http://www.canon.com/
13. Dunne, A., Mallon, J.: Jaliko LensTool (2010), http://www.jaliko.com/
14. Lowe, D.G.: Distinctive image features from scale-invariant keypoints. Int. J. Comput. Vision 60(2), 91–110 (2004)

High Accuracy Optical Flow for 3D Medical Image Registration Using the Census Cost Function

Simon Hermann[1,2] and René Werner[3]

[1] Department of Computer Science, The University of Auckland, New Zealand
[2] Department of Computer Science, Humboldt University of Berlin, Germany
[3] Department of Computational Neuroscience,
University Medical Center Hamburg-Eppendorf, Germany

Abstract. In 2004, Brox et al. described how to minimize an energy functional for dense 2D optical flow estimation that enforces both intensity and gradient constancy.

This paper presents a novel variant of their method, in which the census cost function is utilized in the data term instead of absolute intensity differences. The algorithm is applied to the task of pulmonary motion estimation in 3D computed tomography (CT) image sequences. The performance evaluation is based on DIR-lab benchmark data for lung CT registration. Results show that the presented algorithm can compete with current state-of-the-art methods in regards to both registration accuracy and run-time.

Keywords: Medical image registration, census cost function, pulmonary motion estimation, 4D CT, gradient constancy.

1 Introduction

Accurate motion estimation of anatomical and pathological structures is beneficial in many clinical applications. A typical scenario is radiation therapy of lung cancer patients, where the challenge is to apply a high radiation dose to the tumor while keeping the exposure to surrounding healthy tissue to a minimum. The planning process of the radiation treatment is usually based on one static 3D CT scan, which leads to breathing-induced uncertainties concerning position and shape of the tumor and surrounding structures.

With the introduction of 4D (3D + time) CT imaging protocols, it is possible to acquire a sequence of 3D lung CT images that captures the different breathing phases of the patient. Estimated motion patterns can be incorporated into the treatment planning process and the effects of lung movement on the dose distribution can be analyzed prior to the actual radiation treatment [19]. The reliability of the extracted information, such as dosimetric motion effects, depends to a great extent on the accuracy of the applied registration algorithm that recovers the motion information. In other words, there is a great need for accurate, robust and fast non-linear registration algorithms.

R. Klette, M. Rivera, and S. Satoh (Eds.): PSIVT 2013, LNCS 8333, pp. 23–35, 2014.
© Springer-Verlag Berlin Heidelberg 2014

The objective of this paper is to show that the well known algorithm for 'high accuracy optical flow estimation', as proposed by Brox et al. [1], yields the potential to fulfill all of these requirements. It minimizes an L_1 energy in combination with a total variation (TV) regularization term. One of the most notable contributions of [1] is to include a gradient constancy assumption into the energy formulation, which is based on the gradient end point error (EPE). This is especially interesting because gradient information have only very recently been successfully exploited for pulmonary motion estimation [15,8]. However, the gradient-based constraints in [15,8] are entirely based on differences in gradient orientations. In other words, they estimate image similarities based on the gradient angular error and not, as presented in [1], on the EPE.

With the exception of [14], we are not aware of any literature that employs and evaluates the EPE in combination with the solution scheme of Brox et al. for the purpose of lung CT image registration. Unfortunately, the paper [14] contains only preliminary evaluation results, based on only one single 4D CT data set. Additionally, Heinrich et al. [7] presented a solution scheme to minimize a TV-L_1 energy similar to [1] – but without enforcing gradient constancy.

Considering application background and related literature, this paper describes two novel contributions.

First, a formulation for arbitrary dimensions of the algorithm following Brox et al. [1] is presented, which includes the census cost function in the data term. This is in line with Müller et al. [13], who introduced the census cost function for coupled convex approaches following the TV-L_1 solution scheme as proposed by Zach et al. [21].

Second, a straight forward 3D implementation of the presented algorithm is evaluated for pulmonary motion estimation in 4D CT data, with a focus on the quantification of the influence of the gradient constancy assumption and the census cost function on the registration accuracy.

The evaluation is based on DIR-lab data for 4D lung CT registration [3,4], a publicly available data base, which is commonly used to benchmark registration errors in the given application context.

The remainder of this paper is structured as follows. Section 2 introduces the energy formulation and the numerical scheme of the method, followed by implementation details of the 3D algorithm. The evaluation is described in Section 3, followed by a discussion in Section 4. Section 5 concludes this paper.

2   General Formulation of High Accuracy Optical Flow

The structure of this section follows Brox et al. [1]. However, the formulation of the energy itself and the resulting equation systems are derived for arbitrary dimensions. Furthermore, we replace the energy part that enforces intensity constancy with an arbitrary residual, similar to Müller et al., who introduced such a term for coupled convex optical flow approaches [13]. The basic notation is taken from [10].

2.1   Basic Notation

The input of the algorithm are two single channel images I_0 and I_1, defined on an n-dimensional image domain $\Omega \subset \mathbb{R}^n$ with $I : \Omega \longrightarrow \mathbb{R}$. A point $\mathbf{x} \in \Omega$ describes a position within the image domain and $I(\mathbf{x})$ refers to the intensity of an image I at $\mathbf{x}$.

The output is an n-dimensional vector field $\mathbf{u} : \Omega \longrightarrow \mathbb{R}^{m \ln}$, with $\mathbf{u} = (u_1, ..., u_m, 0_{m+1}, ..., 0_n)$, that describes the displacement from the reference image I_0 to the match or target image I_1. Here, m refers to the degrees of freedom of the elements of the vector field. A typical example for $m < n$ is the case of stereo estimation for rectified image pairs, where $n = 2$ but $m = 1$. For the task of 3D medical image registration we have $n = m = 3$.

2.2   The Energy Functional

The energy to be minimized is the weighted sum

$$E(\mathbf{u}) = E_D(\mathbf{u}) + \alpha E_S(\mathbf{u}) \tag{1}$$

where the data term is defined by

$$E_D(\mathbf{u}) = \int_{\Omega} \Gamma\left(\chi \left|\rho(\mathbf{x}, \mathbf{u})\right|^2 + \gamma \left|\nabla I_1(\mathbf{x} + \mathbf{u}) - \nabla I_0(\mathbf{x})\right|^2\right) d\mathbf{x} \tag{2}$$

The term $\rho(\mathbf{x}, \mathbf{u})$ refers to a generic residual with $\rho := \rho_{I_0, I_1} : \Omega \times \mathbb{R}^{m \ln} \longrightarrow \mathbb{R}$, which is evaluated between I_0 and I_1 at position $\mathbf{x}$ under consideration of $\mathbf{u}(\mathbf{x})$. The second term enforces gradient constancy by minimizing the end point error of the intensity gradient. Each part of the data term is coupled with a weighting factor (χ and γ). This makes it possible to omit the contribution of the individual data terms in order to evaluate their impact on the registration result separately. The smoothness term of the energy reads

$$E_S(\mathbf{u}) = \int_{\Omega} \Gamma\left(\sum_{b=1}^{m} \left|\nabla u_b(\mathbf{x})\right|^2\right) d\mathbf{x} \tag{3}$$

The function Γ is given as $\Gamma(s^2) = \sqrt{s^2 + \varepsilon^2}$, with $\varepsilon = 0.0001$, which results in an approximate L_1 energy for both the data and the regularization term.

2.3   Euler-Lagrange Equations

With the set Θ of following abbreviations (for $a = 1, ..., n$, and $b = 1, ..., m$)

$$\rho_t := \rho(\mathbf{x}, \mathbf{u}) \tag{4}$$

$$\rho_b := \partial_b \rho(\mathbf{x}, \mathbf{u}) \tag{5}$$

$$I_{at} = I_{ta} := \partial_a I_1(\mathbf{x} + \mathbf{u}) - \partial_a I_0(\mathbf{x}) \tag{6}$$

$$I_{ab} = I_{ba} := \partial_{ab} I_1(\mathbf{x} + \mathbf{u}) \tag{7}$$

we get the m Euler-Lagrange equations for $b = 1, ..., m$

$$0 \stackrel{!}{=} \mathcal{D} \cdot \left[\chi \rho_b \rho_t + \gamma \sum_{a=1}^{n} I_{ab} I_{at} \right] - \alpha \, \text{div} \left[\mathcal{S} \cdot \nabla u_b(\mathbf{x}) \right] \tag{8}$$

with the constant terms

$$\mathcal{D} = \Gamma' \left(\chi \rho_t^2 + \gamma \sum_{a=1}^{n} I_{at}^2 \right) \text{ and } \mathcal{S} = \Gamma' \left(\sum_{b=1}^{m} |\nabla u_b(\mathbf{x})|^2 \right) \tag{9}$$

for all m equations.

2.4 Numerical Approximation

The Euler-Lagrange equations from Eq. (9) are nonlinear in $\mathbf{u}$ due to the non-quadratic penalizers and the non-linearized data constraints [2]. In order to linearize these equations, Brox et al. [1] employ two nested fixed point iterations. The outer fixed point iteration runs over the index k. With the iteration variable $\mathbf{u}^k$ and $\mathbf{u}^0 = \mathbf{0}$, $\mathbf{u}^{k+1}$ is, for $b = 1, ..., m$, the solution of

$$0 \stackrel{!}{=} \mathcal{D}^{k+1} \cdot \left[\chi \rho_b^k \rho_t^{k+1} + \gamma \sum_{a=1}^{n} I_{ab}^k I_{at}^{k+1} \right] - \alpha \, \text{div} \left[\mathcal{S}^{k+1} \cdot \nabla u_b^{k+1}(\mathbf{x}) \right] \tag{10}$$

First order Taylor expansions are used to remove non-linearities in the data constraints. The Taylor expansions read for $a = 1, ..., n$

$$\rho_t^{k+1} =: \mathcal{T}_t^k \approx \rho_t + \sum_{b=1}^{m} \rho_b^k du_b^k \tag{11}$$

$$I_{at}^{k+1} =: \mathcal{T}_{at}^k \approx I_{at} + \sum_{b=1}^{m} I_{ab}^k du_b^k \tag{12}$$

with $\mathbf{u}^{k+1} = \mathbf{u}^k + d\mathbf{u}^k$. The unknown $\mathbf{u}^{k+1}$ is composed of the solution from the previous iteration step $\mathbf{u}^k$ and unknown updates $d\mathbf{u}^k$. Let $\overline{\mathcal{D}}$ refer to the term $\mathcal{D}$ of Eq. (9) with substitution of the respective Taylor approximations, we then get for $b = 1, ..., m$

$$0 \stackrel{!}{=} \overline{\mathcal{D}}^k \cdot \left[\chi \rho_b^k \mathcal{T}_t^k + \gamma \sum_{a=1}^{n} I_{ab}^k \mathcal{T}_{at}^k \right] - \alpha \, \text{div} \left[\mathcal{S}^k \cdot \nabla (u_b^k(\mathbf{x}) + du_b^k(\mathbf{x})) \right] \tag{13}$$

In order to remove the remaining non-linearity due to Γ', an inner fixed point iteration is performed over the unknown flow updates $d\mathbf{u}^k$. Dropping the iteration index k for better readability and introducing a new iteration index l, the final linear system of equations reads for $b = 1, ..., m$

$$0 \stackrel{!}{=} \overline{\mathcal{D}}^l \cdot \left[\chi \rho_b \mathcal{T}_t^{l+1} + \gamma \sum_{a=1}^{n} I_{ab} \mathcal{T}_{at}^{l+1} \right] - \alpha \, \text{div} \left[\mathcal{S}^l \cdot \nabla (u_b(\mathbf{x}) + du_b^{l+1}(\mathbf{x})) \right] \tag{14}$$

The discretized linear system of equations is solved by successive over-relaxation (SOR), which is known for its fast convergence and suitability to be implemented on parallel hardware architectures [6,17].

2.5   The Census Cost Function as Data Residual

The census transform was introduced by Zabih and Woodfill [20] in 1994. It assigns a binary signature vector to an image position $\mathbf{x}$, which is calculated based on the ordinal characteristic of $I(\mathbf{x})$ in relation to intensities within a defined neighborhood $\mathcal{N}_{\mathbf{x}}$ of $\mathbf{x}$. The binary signature vector $C[\mathbf{x}]$ at $\mathbf{x}$ is generated as follows:

$$C[\mathbf{x}] = \left\{ \Upsilon\left[I(\mathbf{x}) \geq I(\mathbf{y})\right] \right\}_{\mathbf{y} \in \mathcal{N}_{\mathbf{x}}} \tag{15}$$

where $\Upsilon[\cdot]$ returns 1 if true, and 0 otherwise. The residual $\rho(\mathbf{x}, \mathbf{u})$ is the Hamming distance of two signature vectors. Formally, we write

$$\rho(\mathbf{x}, \mathbf{u}) = \Xi\left\{ C_0[\mathbf{x}] \oplus C_1[\mathbf{x} + \mathbf{u}] \right\} \tag{16}$$

where C_0 and C_1 refer to census signatures of images I_0 and I_1, respectively. $\Xi\{\cdot\}$ is an operator that counts the 1's of the binary string in the argument. For efficiently counting of 1's in bit strings, we refer to Warren's 'Hackers Delight' [18].

2.6   Implementation Details

Before the input images are processed by the algorithm, their dynamic is mapped into a floating point intensity domain of $[0, 255]$, using a scale factor that is based on the maximum intensity of both images. In order to restrict the focus during the registration process on a specific region of interest, the algorithm takes binary lung segmentation masks $S_0, S_1 : \Omega \rightarrow \{0, 1\}$ as optional input data. In case that such segmentation masks are provided, the input images are cropped accordingly and the evaluation of the data term is omitted where $S_0(\mathbf{x}) = 0$. For the specific application at hand, this provides a way of coping with motion discontinuities near the lung borders, which are the consequence of the lungs sliding along the inner part of the chest wall. It additionally speeds up the run-time of the algorithm.

The numerical scheme from section 2.4 is embedded into a coarse-to-fine approach, a common technique to overcome local minima. Image pyramids with arbitrary scale factors and with a fixed number of L pyramid levels are employed, where $\ell = 1$ refers to the finest and $\ell = L$ refers to the coarsest level. The pyramids are configured via target resolutions r_x, r_y, r_z for the coarsest level of each dimension. As a consequence, a scale factor is defined for each dimension based on the number L of pyramid levels and the respective target resolution. In case that the input images exhibit an anisotropic spatial resolution (CT data usually offer high in-plane resolution when compared to the slice thickness; cf. Section 3.1), the following common strategy is followed, see for example [15,12]: In a first step, images are scaled down only along the image axes with a high resolution until the pixel spacing is almost identical for all image dimensions.

---

input : Images I_0 and I_1

ouput: Displacement field **u**

Initialization of image pyramids based on L, r_x, r_y, r_z.

Set $\mathbf{u}^L = \mathbf{0}$

for $\ell \leftarrow L$ **to** 1 **do**

    for $w \leftarrow 1$ **to** η **do**

        Set $\mathbf{du}_w^\ell = \mathbf{0}$

        Warp $I_1^\ell \xrightarrow{\mathbf{u}^\ell} I_0^\ell$, by means of trilinear interpolation

        Initialize Θ^ℓ according to Eq.(4-7), using central differences

        for $o \leftarrow 1$ **to** ϑ **do**

            With $\mathbf{u}^\ell$, $\mathbf{du}_w^\ell$, and Θ^ℓ calculate: $\overline{\mathcal{D}}$ and $\mathcal{S}$

            for $i \leftarrow 1$ **to** κ **do**

                Perform SOR iteration [on Eq.(14)] to update $\mathbf{du}_w^\ell$

            end

        end

        Update $\mathbf{u}^\ell \leftarrow \mathbf{u}^\ell + \mathbf{du}_w^\ell$

        Smooth $\mathbf{u}^\ell$ with a Gauss filter (ψ, σ)

    end

    if $\ell > 1$ **then**

        Initialize $\mathbf{u}^{\ell-1}$ with $\mathbf{u}^\ell$

    else

        Set output: $\mathbf{u} = \mathbf{u}^1$

    end

end

Algorithm 1. Structure of the proposed algorithm

The following downscaling steps are then performed along all image axes and are subsequently referred to as 'isotropic levels'.

At the coarsest level, the displacement field is initialized with zero, and the result of each level is propagated to the next finer level.

Each level consists of a fixed number η of warps, of ϑ outer iterations and of κ SOR iterations. At the end of each warping iteration, the intermediate solution is filtered using a Gauss filter with a fixed window size ψ and a fixed σ. The scheme is summarized in Algorithm 1.

The implementation is C++-based, and the algorithm is executed on an Intel®Core™ i7 Quad-Core Processor with 2.4 GHz. OpenMP is employed to utilize hyper-threading.

3 Experiments

The performance of the algorithm was evaluated on ten thoracic 4D CT data sets, provided by the DIR-lab[1] of the University of Texas M.D. Anderson Cancer Center (Houston, USA) [3,4].

3.1 Image Data

Each 4D CT data set of the DIR-lab data pool consists of a sequence of 3D CT images acquired at ten different breathing phases. The dimension of the sequences varies between $256 \times 256 \times 94$ and $512 \times 512 \times 136$ pixel, the spatial resolution between $0.97 \times 0.97 \times 2.5$ mm^3 and $1.16 \times 1.16 \times 2.5$ mm^3. To be in line with most of the related publications, we focus on the registration of the end-inspiration (EI, reference image) and end-expiration (EE, target image) scans for evaluation purposes. These are the scan pairs with the largest motion amplitudes.

For each EI and EE scan pair, 300 anatomical landmark pairs within the lungs at prominent bifurcations of the bronchial or vessel trees have been annotated and are provided together with the CT data. The landmark pairs serve as ground truth information for quantitative evaluation of the registration accuracy. Therefore, let $\hat{\mathbf{x}}_{I_0}$ be a landmark position in the reference image, $\hat{\mathbf{x}}_{I_0,\mathbf{u}} := \hat{\mathbf{x}}_{I_0} + \mathbf{u}\left(\hat{\mathbf{x}}_{I_0}\right)$ its transformed position, and $\hat{\mathbf{x}}_{I_1}$ the true landmark position in the target image. Following the DIR-lab, the registration error for that landmark is then computed as Euclidean distance between $\hat{\mathbf{x}}_{I_1}$ and the center $\hat{\mathbf{x}}_{I_0,\mathbf{u}}^{\times}$ of the pixel that is closest to $\hat{\mathbf{x}}_{I_0,\mathbf{u}}$. This strategy is referred to as 'snap-to-pixel' evaluation and ensures that the comparison of the 'detected' landmark positions $\hat{\mathbf{x}}_{I_1}$ (detected by a human observer) and $\hat{\mathbf{x}}_{I_0,\mathbf{u}}^{\times}$ (registration result) is based on positions defined on the same grid.

3.2 Algorithm Configuration and Evaluation Setup

For the evaluation, the following default parametrization of the algorithm is used. The census transform is calculated for a $5 \times 5 \times 5$ neighborhood on isotropic and $5 \times 5 \times 3$ on anisotropic levels. The motivation for reducing the kernel in z-direction on anisotropic levels is to compensate for the coarser spatial resolution along the z-axis of the DIR-lab data. Values calculated by ρ are scaled to the domain $[0, 21] \in \mathbb{R}$. Furthermore, the number of warps is set to $\eta = 7$, $\vartheta = 2$ outer iterations are employed and the equation system is sloved with $\kappa = 4$ SOR iterations. The weights that control the contribution of each data term are set to $\chi = 1$ (for the census cost function) and $\gamma = 8.5$ (for the EPE). In order to exclude one of the energy terms from the registration, the respective weight is set to zero. The regularization term is weighted by $\alpha = 1.25$. The image pyramids are initialized with 16 levels and a target resolution of $r_x = 16, r_y = 16, r_z = 16$,

---

[1] http://www.dir-lab.com

Table 1. Published landmark-based registration error values for the registration of the end-inspiration and -expiration images of the DIR-lab 4D CT data sets; values given in mm (snap-to-pixel evaluation). 'Our approach' refers to masked registration and combined use of census-based and EPE data term.

	Our approach	CCW+ [5][1]	HSS+ [11][2]	HW [10]	RHK+ [15]	w / o registration
01	0.80 (0.92)	0.85 (1.00)	0.98 (1.00)	0.78 (0.92)	**0.78 (0.91)**	3.89 (2.78)
02	0.77 (0.92)	0.74 (0.99)	0.83 (1.02)	0.78 (0.92)	**0.74 (0.87)**	4.34 (3.90)
03	**0.92 (1.10)**	0.93 (1.07)	1.08 (1.15)	0.93 (1.09)	0.94 (1.07)	6.94 (4.05)
04	**1.22 (1.24)**	1.33 (1.51)	1.45 (1.53)	1.24 (1.30)	1.26 (1.26)	9.83 (4.86)
05	1.21 (1.47)	**1.14 (1.25)**	1.55 (1.75)	1.22 (1.43)	1.22 (1.48)	7.48 (5.51)
06	**0.90 (1.00)**	1.04 (1.05)	1.52 (1.28)	0.94 (0.99)	0.97 (1.03)	10.89 (6.97)
07	0.98 (1.01)	1.03 (1.01)	1.29 (1.22)	1.01 (0.96)	**0.91 (1.00)**	11.03 (7.43)
08	1.16 (1.45)	1.11 (1.18)	1.75 (2.40)	1.11 (1.28)	**1.07 (1.24)**	14.99 (9.01)
09	1.00 (0.97)	1.04 (1.00)	1.22 (1.07)	**0.98 (1.00)**	1.03 (1.01)	7.92 (3.98)
10	0.99 (1.28)	1.05 (1.10)	1.47 (1.68)	**0.94 (1.03)**	0.98 (1.10)	7.30 (6.35)
$\varnothing_{err}$	0.99 (1.13)	1.03 (1.12)	1.31 (1.41)	**0.99 (1.09)**	0.99 (1.10)	8.46 (6.58)
$\varnothing_{time}$	**46 s**	192 s[4]	55/73 min[3]	110 s	104 s	-

[1] Ranked 1st on DIR-lab homepage; please note that the 300 freely available landmark correspondences, which are used throughout our paper, are only a subset of the landmarks used for evaluation by the DIR-lab.
[2] Ranked 2nd on DIR-lab homepage; see above note on the used landmark sets.
[3] Times for balanced flow; format: cases 01-05 / 06-10 (after additional preprocessing).
[4] Sum of mean times of grid search and filtering as given in table 5 of [5].

Gauss smoothing of the flow field at the end of each warp iteration is performed with $(\psi, \sigma) = (5, 1)$.

The methodological approach for the evaluations is as follows. First, a baseline for an optimal performance is established when both data terms are employed. In order to quantify the individual impact of each data term, the algorithm is then evaluated once with $\chi = 0$ (EPE only), once with $\gamma = 0$ (census only). All setups are evaluated with and without lung segmentation masks supporting the registration process (cf. Section 2.6).

3.3 Results

The identified optimal baseline configuration, described in the previous section 3.2, leads to registration errors that are currently amongst the lowest published values on the DIR-lab benchmark. The results are listed in Table 1, along with a few of the best reported error values that can be found in recent literature. Minimum error values are marked by a gray background and bold letters. In case of two identical mean values, the minimum is determined by the standard deviation, found in brackets behind each error value. The rightmost column of Table 1 refers to the registration error when no registration was performed, i.e.

$\mathbf{u} = \mathbf{0}$. Those values give an indication of the mean motion amplitudes of the data sets. All those values correspond to the 'snap-to-pixel evaluation' concept and with lung masks supporting the registration.

It is, however, important to mention that although the application of binary lung masks leads to significantly better registration results, it also leads to invalid motion patterns outside the specified regions of interest. Although this is not acceptable in several clinical applications [16], error values for unmasked registration are only rarely found in literature, and are therefore not included in Table 1.

The results of the comparative evaluation of the impact of the individual data terms on the registration accuracy are summarized in Table 2. A few examples of the registration results are visualized in Figure 1. If we consider the registration results obtained with binary lung masks, we see that the algorithm with the isolated EPE data term outperforms the configuration with the isolated census data term – the combination of both data terms, however, performs better than any of them individually.

This observation is in partial disagreement to registration results obtained without lung segmentation masks. For this particular evaluation setup, only 60% of the error minima are scored by the combined data term configuration. Furthermore, the isolated census data term is often superior over the EPE data term. This is especially apparent for CT data that features large motion amplitudes (see w/o registration columns of Table 1), such as data set 08. The behavior seems to be reversed for data with only small motion amplitudes (data sets 01-03).

4   Discussion

Comparison to State-of-the-art Approaches. If we compare the registration errors listed in Table 1, we see that the presented algorithm can compete with current state-of-the-art methods in the field of pulmonary motion estimation in 4D CT data. With an average run-time of 46 seconds per data set, we may consider the presented approach to be of interest for actual clinical applications that require close to real-time performance.

Comparison of Census and Gradient Data Term. The strong registration performance of a combination of census-based and EPE data term when using lung masks indicates that both terms provide, in general, complementary information when applied to pulmonary motion estimation. The interpretation of registration results obtained without lung masks is, however, more difficult.

We assume that the EPE lacks robustness at strong motion discontinuities that occur at the transition of inner and outer lung structures (cf. Section 2.6), which is likely to have a major impact on registration errors of landmarks which are located close to lung borders. Providing lung segmentation masks is one way

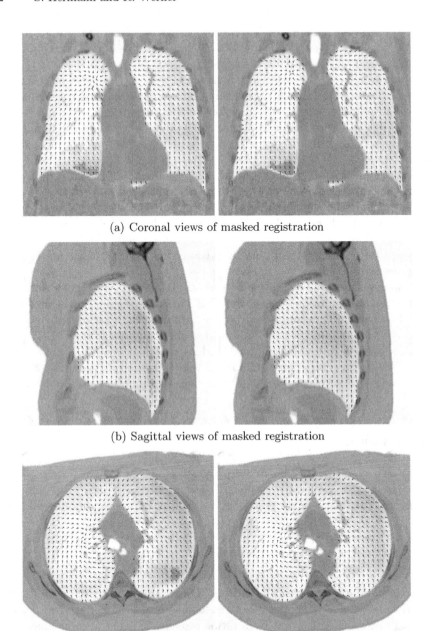

(a) Coronal views of masked registration

(b) Sagittal views of masked registration

(c) Axial view of masked registration

Fig. 1. Illustration of registration results for the DIR-lab case 08, performing a masked registration. Left: Results of census-based registration. Right: Results of gradient-based registration; estimated motion between EI and EE; the color-coded visualization uses the hue color channel to encode orientation (also highlighted by normalized arrows) and the saturation channel to encode the motion magnitude. Rows from top to bottom: 2D views of the registration results in (a) coronal, (b) sagittal, and (c) axial views.

Table 2. Mean landmark distances and corresponding standard deviations after registration with the proposed algorithm variants. All values in mm.

#	with lung masks			w/o lung masks		
	Census	EPE	combined	Census	EPE	combined
01	0.87 (0.94)	**0.76 (0.91)**	0.80 (0.92)	0.86 (0.97)	**0.79 (0.88)**	0.81 (0.91)
02	1.00 (1.01)	0.79 (0.92)	**0.77 (0.92)**	0.96 (1.06)	0.81 (0.94)	**0.80 (0.94)**
03	1.14 (1.13)	0.94 (1.09)	**0.92 (1.10)**	1.19 (1.11)	0.94 (1.10)	**0.93 (1.10)**
04	1.42 (1.33)	1.25 (1.24)	**1.22 (1.24)**	1.49 (1.37)	1.26 (1.29)	**1.25 (1.27)**
05	1.38 (1.42)	1.25 (1.48)	**1.21 (1.47)**	1.33 (1.51)	1.42 (1.82)	**1.28 (1.58)**
06	1.25 (1.06)	0.92 (0.96)	**0.90 (1.00)**	1.36 (1.23)	1.43 (2.20)	**1.19 (1.50)**
07	1.29 (1.06)	1.00 (1.05)	**0.98 (1.01)**	**1.74 (2.68)**	3.64 (5.85)	3.03 (5.26)
08	1.34 (1.55)	1.55 (2.80)	**1.16 (1.45)**	**2.62 (4.93)**	5.39 (7.64)	3.52 (5.94)
09	1.23 (1.11)	1.01 (1.00)	**1.00 (0.97)**	1.26 (1.28)	1.20 (1.27)	**1.16 (1.23)**
10	1.19 (1.19)	1.01 (1.31)	**0.99 (1.28)**	**1.29 (1.82)**	1.35 (2.24)	1.52 (2.17)
$\varnothing_{err}$	1.21 (1.18)	1.05 (1.28)	**0.99 (1.13)**	**1.41 (1.79)**	1.82 (2.52)	1.52 (2.17)

to cope with the effects (although resulting motion fields are only valid inside the lungs; cf. Section 3.3). In case that no lung masks are applied, we assume that the EPE responds to the strong intensity gradients at the lung borders and the resulting high energy is propagated into the lungs by the regularization term.

Thus, in areas where the dominating intensity gradients of the lung borders and the motion patterns of the poorly contrasted inner lung structures are not aligned, larger registration errors occur for the EPE. It appears, that the ordinal character of the census cost function leads to a relatively robust performance, because it compensates, to a certain degree, the misbalance of the high intensity contrast at the lung borders and the low contrast of inner lung structures. This leads to very low registration errors for census-based unmasked registration, which is comparable to those reported by Heinrich et al. [9]. They employ a discrete method without lung segmentation information, that results in a mean error of 1.43 mm for the DIR-lab data.

To support this interpretation, we additionally consider the algorithms ALMI and STORM, which are described in another work by Heinrich et al. [8]. Both represent gradient orientation-based registration methods, which are also evaluated on DIR-lab data without the use of lung segmentation masks. Their results are very similar to the EPE-based registration results, i.e. we see that both methods perform excellent on data sets with small displacements, while they tend to fail when large motion amplitudes are present. We therefore assume that our gradient-based registration results, without the application of lung segmentation masks, are state-of-the-art – and consequently conclude that census-based registration must be very robust for this particular task.

5 Conclusions

This paper shows that the presented 3D variant of the 'high accuracy optical flow' algorithm is as accurate and fast as the currently best performing state-of-the-art methods. Its robust behavior that results from the inclusion of the census cost function was demonstrated based on registration results of unsegmented CT scans. We therefore conclude that this algorithm has the potential to meet the requirements for real-world clinical application.

Acknowledgments. The authors thank Dr. Gisela Klette for thoroughly proof reading this paper.

References

1. Brox, T., Bruhn, A., Papenberg, N., Weickert, J.: High Accuracy Optical Flow Estimation Based on a Theory for Warping. In: Pajdla, T., Matas, J(G.) (eds.) ECCV 2004. LNCS, vol. 3024, pp. 25–36. Springer, Heidelberg (2004)
2. Brox, T.: From Pixels to Regions: Partial Differential Equations in Image Analysis. PhD thesis, Saarland University (2005)
3. Castillo, R., Castillo, E., Guerra, R., Johnson, V.E., McPhail, T., et al.: A framework for evaluation of deformable image registration spatial accuracy using large landmark point sets. Phys. Med. Biol. 54, 1849–1870 (2009)
4. Castillo, R., Castillo, E., Martinez, J., Guerrero, T.: Ventilation from four-dimensional computed tomography: density versus Jacobian methods. Phys. Med. Biol. 55, 4661–4685 (2010)
5. Castillo, E., Castillo, R., White, B., Rojo, J., Guerrero, T.: Least median of squares filtering of locally optimal point matches for compressible flow image registration. Phys. Med. Biol. 57, 4827–4833 (2012)
6. Gwosdek, P., Bruhn, A., Weickert, J.: High Performance Parallel Optical Flow Algorithms on the Sony Playstation 3. In: Proc. Vision, Modeling, and Visualization - VMV, pp. 253–262 (2008)
7. Heinrich, M.P., Jenkinson, M., Brady, M., Schnabel, J.A.: Discontinuity preserving regularisation for variational optical-flow registration using the modified Lp norm. In: Med. Image Anal. Clinic: A Grand Challenge, pp. 185–194 (2010)
8. Heinrich, M.P., Jenkinson, M., Gleeson, F.V., Brady, M., Schnabel, J.A.: Deformable multimodal registration with gradient orientation based on structure tensors. Annals of the BMVA, 1–11 (2011)
9. Heinrich, M.P., Jenkinson, M., Brady, M., Schnabel, J.A.: MRF-based deformable registration and ventilation estimation of lung CT. IEEE Trans. Medical Imaging 32, 1239–1248 (2013)
10. Hermann, S., Werner, R.: TV-L_1-based 3D Medical Image Registration with the Census Cost Function. In: Klette, R., Rivera, M., Satoh, S. (eds.) PSIVT 2013. LNCS, vol. 8333, pp. 149–161. Springer, Heidelberg (2014)
11. Hoog, A.C.B., Singh, T., Singla, P., Podgorsak, M.: Evaluation of advanced Lukas-Kanade optical flow on thoracic 4D-CT. J. Clin. Monit. Comput. 27, 433–441 (2013)
12. Kabus, S., Lorenz, C.: Fast Elastic Image Registration. Medical Image Analysis for the Clinic: A Grand Challenge, 81–89 (2010)

13. Müller, T., Rabe, C., Rannacher, J., Franke, U., Mester, R.: Illumination-Robust Dense Optical Flow Using Census Signatures. In: Mester, R., Felsberg, M. (eds.) DAGM 2011. LNCS, vol. 6835, pp. 236–245. Springer, Heidelberg (2011)
14. Negahdar, N., Amini, A.A.: A 3D Optical Flow Technique based on Mass Conservation for Deformable Motion Estimation from 4-D CT Images of the Lung. In: SPIE Medical Imaging 2012: Biomedical Applications in Molecular, Structural, and Functional Imaging. SPIE, vol. 8317, p. 83171F (2012)
15. Rühaak, J., Heldmann, S., Kipshagen, T., Fischer, B.: Highly Accurate Fast Lung CT Registration. In: SPIE Medical Imaging: Image Processing. SPIE, vol. 8669, p. 86690Y (2013)
16. Schmidt-Richberg, A., Werner, R., Handels, H., Ehrhardt, J.: Estimation of slipping organ motion by registration with direction-dependent regularization. Med. Image Anal. 16, 150–159 (2012)
17. Sundaram, N., Brox, T., Keutzer, K.: Dense Point Trajectories by GPU-Accelerated Large Displacement Optical Flow. In: Daniilidis, K., Maragos, P., Paragios, N. (eds.) ECCV 2010, Part I. LNCS, vol. 6311, pp. 438–451. Springer, Heidelberg (2010)
18. Warren, H.S.: Hacker's Delight, pp. 65–72. Addison-Wesley Longman, Amsterdam (2002)
19. Werner, R., Ehrhardt, J., Schmidt-Richberg, A., Albers, D., Frenzel, T., et al.: Towards accurate dose accumulation for Step-&-Shoot IMRT: Impact of weighting schemes and temporal image resolution on the estimation of dosimetric motion Eeffects. Z. Med. Phys. 22, 109–122 (2012)
20. Zabih, R., Woodfill, J.: Non-parametric Local Transforms for Computing Visual Correspondence. In: Eklundh, J.-O. (ed.) ECCV 1994. LNCS, vol. 801, pp. 151–158. Springer, Heidelberg (1994)
21. Zach, C., Pock, T., Bischof, H.: A Duality Based Approach for Realtime TV-L1 Optical Flow. In: Hamprecht, F.A., Schnörr, C., Jähne, B. (eds.) DAGM 2007. LNCS, vol. 4713, pp. 214–223. Springer, Heidelberg (2007)

Non-rigid Multimodal Image Registration Based on the Expectation-Maximization Algorithm

Edgar Arce-Santana*, Daniel U. Campos-Delgado, Flavio Vigueras-Gómez,
Isnardo Reducindo **, and Aldo R. Mejía-Rodríguez ***

Facultad de Ciencias, Universidad Autónoma de San Luis Potosí,
Av. Salvador Nava Mtz. S/N, Zona Universitaria, 78290,
San Luis Potosí, SLP, México
arce@uaslp.mx

Abstract. In this paper, we present a novel methodology for multimodal non-rigid image registration. The proposed approach is formulated by using the Expectation-Maximization (EM) technique in order to estimate a displacement vector field that aligns the images to register. In this approach, the image alignment relies on hidden stochastic random variables which allow to compare the intensity values between images of different modality. The methodology is basically composed of two steps: first, we provide an initial estimation of the the global deformation vector field by using a rigid registration technique based on particle filtering, obtaining, at the same time, an initial estimation of the joint conditional intensity distribution of the registered images; second, we approximate the remaining deformations by applying an iterative EM-technique approach, where at each step, a new estimation of the joint conditional intensity distribution and the displacement vector field are computed. The proposed algorithm was tested with different kinds of medical images; preliminary results show that the methodology is a good alternative for non-rigid multimodal registration.

1 Introduction

Image registration is an important task in digital image processing, for example in medical imaging [1, 2] where it can be used in several processes like: characterization of the anatomical changes in the heart during a cardiac cycle, quantification of the gradual atrophy of the brain by ageing, modeling the evolution of anatomic structures during medical treatment, tissue segmentation through medical atlases, correction of artifacts caused by movement in fetal images, among many other [2–4]. According to the analysed deformations, image registration can be divided into two philosophies: rigid registration or parametric, and elastic or non-rigid. In the literature, the problem of rigid registration has been studied extensively [2], where basically a cost function related to the

---

* This work was supported by CONACYT through grants No. 168140.
** I. Reducindo was supported by CONACyT doctoral scholarship No. 218513.
*** A. Mejía-Rodríguez was supported by CONACyT doctoral scholarship No. 213579.

R. Klette, M. Rivera, and S. Satoh (Eds.): PSIVT 2013, LNCS 8333, pp. 36–47, 2014.

registration accuracy is minimized that depends on a small set of parameters of a rigid transformation (affine or perspective [5]). The goal of these methods is to obtain the set of parameters describing a geometric transformation between the target and source images that optimizes the similarity metric (e.g. Mutual Information) [3], examples of these algorithms are those based on gradient descent [6], or more recent approaches based on global optimization techniques, such as particle filtering (PF) or genetic algorithms [7–9].

On the other hand, the non-rigid registration is, as expected, a more complex and involved problem, especially for multimodal images; however it has a greater number of applications in medical imaging [4]. In the literature, the most common method to solve the elastic registration is by means of splines, where a family of functions are used to approximate the complex non-rigid deformations by seeking their best parameters that optimize a similarity metric; but the main drawback of these methods is their complexity and their high computational cost [10–12]. Meanwhile, some proposals from the literatures are inspired on the optical flow (OF) equations for non-rigid registration [13]. One of these methods is presented in [14], where a non-parametric non-rigid registration modeled as a diffusion process is described. This method, called Demons, alternates between the computation of a force vector related to the variational derivative of the similarity metric, and a regularization process by a simple Gaussian smoothing. Similarly, in [15], it was proposed a non-parametric diffeomorphic registration method based on Demons algorithm. The key idea behind Diffeomorphic Demons (DiffDemons) is to restrict the entire space of deformations vector fields optimized by Demons algorithm to a space of diffeomorphic transformations by combining a recently developed Lie algebra framework on diffeomorphisms, and an optimization procedure for Lie groups. In order to apply these two algorithms (Demons and DiffDemons) for multimodal registration, an histogram matching was performed by normalizing the grayscale values of a source image based on the grayscale values of the reference one at a specified number of quantile values [16]. A most recent proposal to solve the non-rigid registration problem is based on an iterative OF framework in order to find the deformation vector field, after conducting an initial rigid registration using the PF [17]; this method has shown promising results in [18] and [19]. Nonetheless, the problem of this algorithm is its restriction to unimodal images or the necessity of an injective intensity transference function between the target and source images, which is not the case in multimodal medical image registration. In [20], a new proposal is based on mapping the images into a common space, using local variability measures (LVM), where their intensities can be compared, and then to apply an iterative OF in scale space [21], but the problem with this technique is the strong dependence on textures and contrast with respect to the background in the images.

In this context, we propose a new methodology to address the problem of multimodal non-rigid registration under the framework of the Expectation-Maximization (EM) technique [22]. The expectation step is formulated by using an estimation of the joint intensity distribution between the target image and the aligned source image in each iteration of the EM procedure. Next, this distribution is used to find a new approximation to the deformation vector field whose goal is to improve the registration accuracy between the target and source images. The results in the paper show that the new methodology improved the state of the art algorithms (Demons and DIffDemons) for multimodal non-rigid registration. The paper is organized as follows. In section 2, the non-rigid multimodal image registration based on EM is presented, where the analytical derivations are described in subsections 2.1 and 2.2. Experiments and results are shown in section 3. Finally, in section 4 some conclusions are drawn about this work, as well as directions for future research.

2   Methodology

2.1   EM-Approach

Let $\mathcal{L}$ be a pixel grid where the images to register I_1 and I_2 are observed, such that the observation model for each pixel $\mathbf{i}_k \in \mathcal{L}$ in the image I_1 is given by

$$F[I_1(\mathbf{i_k})] = I_2(\mathbf{i_k} + \mathbf{d}(\mathbf{i_k})) + \eta(\mathbf{i_k}) \quad k = 1, \ldots, N, \tag{1}$$

where $N = \text{card}(\mathcal{L})$ is the number of pixels in the images, $\mathbf{d}(\mathbf{i}_k)$ is the displacement vector field that aligns the two images (I_1, I_2) at each pixel $\mathbf{i}_k$, $\eta(\mathbf{i}_k)$ is Gaussian noise with known probability distribution P_η (e.g. $\eta(\mathbf{i}_k) \ \forall \mathbf{i}_k \in \mathcal{L}$ are i.i.d. samples of a normal random variable with zero mean and standard deviation $\sigma_{\mathbf{i}_k}$), and $F[\cdot]$ is a relation which allows to compare the intensity values of the pixels in both images. In fact, one major obstacle in multimodal non-rigid registration is an accurate characterization of $F[\cdot]$. However, as will be described in this section, the EM can overcome this limitation by the assignation of hidden variables [22].

Therefore, to estimate the displacement vector field $\mathbf{d}(\cdot)$ in (1), it is convenient to use a probabilistic approach based on the EM algorithm [22], and establish as hidden variables $Y(\mathbf{i}_k) \triangleq F[I_1(\mathbf{i}_k)] \ \forall \mathbf{i}_k \in \mathcal{L}$, in such a way that we can write the a posteriori probability distribution over the while pixel grid $\mathcal{L}$ as

$$P(\mathbf{d}|I_1, \tilde{I}_2, Y) = P(\mathbf{d}|\tilde{I}_2, Y), \tag{2}$$

where $\tilde{I}_2(\mathbf{i}_k) \triangleq I_2(\mathbf{i}_k + \mathbf{d}(\mathbf{i}_k))$. Notice that given Y, this probability distribution only depends on intensity values of the transformed image $\tilde{I}_2$. Now, by using the Bayes' theorem, we can rewrite (2) as

$$P(\mathbf{d}|\tilde{I}_2, Y) = \frac{P(\tilde{I}_2, Y|\mathbf{d})P(\mathbf{d})}{P(\tilde{I}_2, Y)}, \tag{3}$$

but since $P(\tilde{I}_2, Y)$ is a joint intensity distribution that does not depends on $\mathbf{d}$, then it acts a normalizing constant in (3). Thus we can rewrite the previous equation as

$$P(\mathbf{d}|\tilde{I}_2, Y) = \frac{1}{Z}P(\tilde{I}_2, Y|\mathbf{d})P(\mathbf{d}). \tag{4}$$

where $Z \triangleq P(\tilde{I}_2, Y)$. If we assume that each pixel in $\mathcal{L}$ is independent, then the a posteriori probability distribution in (2) can be expressed as

$$P(\mathbf{d}|\tilde{I}_2, Y) = \prod_{k=1}^{N} P(\mathbf{d}(\mathbf{i}_k)|\tilde{I}_2(\mathbf{i}_k), Y(\mathbf{i}_k))$$

$$= \prod_{k=1}^{N} \frac{1}{Z(\mathbf{i}_k)} P(I_2(\mathbf{i}_k + \mathbf{d}(\mathbf{i}_k)), Y(\mathbf{i}_k)|\mathbf{d}(\mathbf{i}_k)) P(\mathbf{d}(\mathbf{i}_k)). \qquad (5)$$

Therefore, by analyzing the a posteriori distribution in (5), the EM framework can be applied by considering the displacement vector field at each pixel $\mathbf{d}(\mathbf{i}_k)$ as the unknown parameters, $Y(\mathbf{i}_k)$ as the hidden variables, and the information of the registered images $(I_1(\mathbf{i}_k), I_2(\mathbf{i}_k))$.

2.2 The Expectation Step (E)

Now, the cost function for the expectation step with respect to the hidden variables $Y(\mathbf{i}_k)$ can be written as

$$Q(\mathbf{d}, \mathbf{d}^{(t-1)}) = \mathcal{E}\left[\log\left\{\prod_{k=1}^{N} \frac{P(I_2(\mathbf{i}_k + \mathbf{d}(\mathbf{i}_k)), Y(\mathbf{i}_k)|\mathbf{d}(\mathbf{i}_k))}{Z(\mathbf{i}_k)} P(\mathbf{d}(\mathbf{i}_k))\right\}\middle| I_1, I_2, \mathbf{d}^{(t-1)}\right],$$

$$(6)$$

$$= \sum_{k=1}^{N} \mathcal{E}\left[\log P(I_2(\mathbf{i}_k + \mathbf{d}(\mathbf{i}_k)), Y(\mathbf{i}_k)|\mathbf{d}(\mathbf{i}_k))| I_1, I_2, \mathbf{d}^{(t-1)}\right]$$

$$+ \sum_{k=1}^{N} \mathcal{E}\left[\log P(\mathbf{d}(\mathbf{i}_k))| I_1, I_2, \mathbf{d}^{(t-1)}\right] - \sum_{k=1}^{N} \mathcal{E}\left[\log Z(\mathbf{i}_k)| I_1, I_2, \mathbf{d}^{(t-1)}\right]$$

where $\mathbf{d}^{(t-1)}$ is an estimate of displacement vector field at a given iteration $(t-1)$ in the EM-algorithm. Moreover, if Y only takes integer values in the set $\mathcal{I} = \{0, ..., 255\}$, the cost function $Q(\mathbf{d}, \mathbf{d}^{(t-1)})$ can be expressed as

$$Q(\mathbf{d}, \mathbf{d}^{(t-1)}) = \underbrace{\sum_{Y \in \mathcal{I}}\left\{\sum_{k=1}^{N} \log P(I_2(\mathbf{i}_k + \mathbf{d}(\mathbf{i}_k)), Y(\mathbf{i}_k)|\mathbf{d}(\mathbf{i}_k))\right\} P(Y|I_1, I_2, \mathbf{d}^{(t-1)})}_{\Gamma(\mathbf{d}, \mathbf{d}^{(t-1)})} \quad (7)$$

$$+ \underbrace{\sum_{k=1}^{N} \log P(\mathbf{d}(\mathbf{i}_k))}_{R(\mathbf{d})} + \underbrace{\left(-\sum_{k=1}^{N} \log Z(\mathbf{i}_k)\right)}_{K_1} \qquad (8)$$

$$= \Gamma(\mathbf{d}, \mathbf{d}^{(t-1)}) + R(\mathbf{d}) + K_1,$$

As a result, the term $\Gamma(\mathbf{d}, \mathbf{d}^{(t-1)})$ is commonly called the data term, while $R(\mathbf{d})$ is known as the regularization term. Next, by the observation model in (1), conditional intensity distribution related to the hidden variables can be simplified as follows

$$P(Y|I_1, I_2, \mathbf{d}^{(t-1)}) = P(Y|I_1, \mathbf{d}^{(t-1)}) \tag{9}$$

Furthermore, if we assume that each element of Y is independent, then the data term can be written as

$$\Gamma(\mathbf{d}, \mathbf{d}^{(t-1)}) = \sum_{Y \in \mathcal{I}} \left\{ \sum_{k=1}^{N} \log P(I_2(\mathbf{i}_k + \mathbf{d}(\mathbf{i}_k)), Y(\mathbf{i}_k)|\mathbf{d}(\mathbf{i}_k)) \right\}$$
$$\times \prod_{m=1}^{N} P(Y(\mathbf{i}_m)|I_1(\mathbf{i}_m), \mathbf{d}(\mathbf{i}_m)^{(t-1)}) \tag{10}$$

$$= \sum_{Y(\mathbf{i}_1)=0}^{255} \cdots \sum_{Y(\mathbf{i}_N)=0}^{255} \sum_{k=1}^{N} \{\log P(I_2(\mathbf{i}_k + \mathbf{d}(\mathbf{i}_k)), Y(\mathbf{i}_k)|\mathbf{d}(\mathbf{i}_k))\}$$
$$\times \prod_{m=1}^{N} P(Y(\mathbf{i}_m)|I_1(\mathbf{i}_m), \mathbf{d}(\mathbf{i}_m)^{(t-1)}) \tag{11}$$

$$= \sum_{Y(\mathbf{i}_1)=0}^{255} \cdots \sum_{Y(\mathbf{i}_N)=0}^{255} \sum_{k=1}^{N} \sum_{l=0}^{255} \delta(l - Y(\mathbf{i}_k)) \{\log P(I_2(\mathbf{i}_k + \mathbf{d}(\mathbf{i}_k)), l|\mathbf{d}(\mathbf{i}_k))\}$$
$$\times \prod_{m=1}^{N} P(Y(\mathbf{i}_m)|I_1(\mathbf{i}_m), \mathbf{d}(\mathbf{i}_m)^{(t-1)}) \tag{12}$$

$$= \sum_{k=1}^{N} \sum_{l=0}^{255} \{\log P(I_2(\mathbf{i}_k + \mathbf{d}(\mathbf{i}_k)), l|\mathbf{d}(\mathbf{i}_k))\}$$
$$\times \underbrace{\sum_{Y(\mathbf{i}_1)=0}^{255} \cdots \sum_{Y(\mathbf{i}_N)=0}^{255} \delta(l - Y(\mathbf{i}_k)) \prod_{m=1}^{N} P(Y(\mathbf{i}_m)|I_1(\mathbf{i}_m), \mathbf{d}(\mathbf{i}_m)^{(t-1)})}_{\Theta}, \tag{13}$$

where $\mathbf{i}_m \in \mathcal{L}$ for all $m = 1, \ldots, N$, and $\delta(\cdot)$ represents the Kronecker delta function. In addition, since $P(Y(\mathbf{i}_m)|I_1(\mathbf{i}_m), \mathbf{d}(\mathbf{i}_m)^{(t-1)})$ represents the conditional distribution of $Y(\mathbf{i}_m)$ given $I_1(\mathbf{i}_m)$, this distribution can be estimated by using the joint histogram of intensities between the images I_1, $\tilde{I}_2$ using the displacement vector field $\mathbf{d}^{(t-1)}$. Now, we can simplify the term Θ by observing that it can be rewritten as

$$\Theta = \left(\sum_{Y(\mathbf{i}_1)=0}^{255} \cdots \sum_{Y(\mathbf{i}_N)=0}^{255} \delta(l - Y(\mathbf{i}_k)) \prod_{m=1, m \neq k}^{N} P(Y(\mathbf{i}_m)|I_1(\mathbf{i}_m), \mathbf{d}(\mathbf{i}_m)^{(t-1)}) \right)$$
$$\times P(l|I_1(\mathbf{i}_k), \mathbf{d}(\mathbf{i}_k)^{(t-1)}) \tag{14}$$

$$= \prod_{m=1, m \neq k}^{N} \left(\sum_{Y(\mathbf{i}_m)=0}^{255} P(Y(\mathbf{i}_m)|I_1(\mathbf{i}_m), \mathbf{d}(\mathbf{i}_m)^{(t-1)}) \right) P(l|I_1(\mathbf{i}_k), \mathbf{d}(\mathbf{i}_k)^{(t-1)}), \tag{15}$$

and since $\sum_{Y(\mathbf{i}_m)=0}^{255} P(Y(\mathbf{i}_m)|I_1(\mathbf{i}_m), \mathbf{d}(\mathbf{i}_m)^{(t-1)}) = 1$ for any $\mathbf{i}_m \in \mathcal{L}$, then the data term in (10) is given now by

$$\Gamma(\mathbf{d}, \mathbf{d}^{(t-1)}) = \sum_{k=1}^{N} \sum_{l=0}^{255} \log \{P(I_2(\mathbf{i}_k + \mathbf{d}(\mathbf{i}_k)), l|\mathbf{d}(\mathbf{i}_k))\} P(l|I_1(\mathbf{i}_k), \mathbf{d}(\mathbf{i}_k)^{(t-1)}).$$

(16)

If we define

$$P(I_2(\mathbf{i}_k + \mathbf{d}(\mathbf{i}_k)), l|\mathbf{d}(\mathbf{i}_k)) = \frac{1}{\sqrt{2\pi}\sigma_{\mathbf{i}_k}} \exp \left\{ -\frac{(l - I_2(\mathbf{i}_k + \mathbf{d}(\mathbf{i}_k)))^2}{2\sigma_{\mathbf{i}_k}^2} \right\}, \quad (17)$$

where $\sigma_{\mathbf{i}_k}$ is the standard deviation of the conditional distribution $P(l|I_1(\mathbf{i}_k), \mathbf{d}(\mathbf{i}_k)^{(t-1)})$, then

$$\log \{P(I_2(\mathbf{i}_k + d(\mathbf{i}_k)), l|\mathbf{d}(\mathbf{i}_k))\} = \log \frac{1}{\sqrt{2\pi}\sigma_{\mathbf{i}_k}} - \frac{(l - I_2(\mathbf{i}_k + \mathbf{d}(\mathbf{i}_k)))^2}{2\sigma_{\mathbf{i}_k}^2}. \quad (18)$$

Hence we can rewrite equation (16) as

$$\Gamma(\mathbf{d}, \mathbf{d}^{(t-1)}) = K_2 - \sum_{k=1}^{N} \frac{1}{2\sigma_{\mathbf{i}_k}^2} \sum_{l=0}^{255} (l - I_2(\mathbf{i}_k + \mathbf{d}(\mathbf{i}_k)))^2 P(l|I_1(\mathbf{i}_k), \mathbf{d}(\mathbf{i}_k)^{(t-1)}) \quad (19)$$

where $K_2 \triangleq -256 \sum_{k=1}^{N} \log(\sqrt{2\pi}\sigma_{\mathbf{i}_k})$. Moreover, this term can be simplified as

$$\Gamma(\mathbf{d}) = K_2 - \sum_{k=1}^{N} \frac{1}{2\sigma_{\mathbf{i}_k}^2} \{\sigma_{\mathbf{i}_k}^2 + (\bar{l} - I_2(\mathbf{i}_k + \mathbf{d}(\mathbf{i}_k)))^2\}$$

$$= K_2 + K_3 - \sum_{k=1}^{N} \frac{1}{2\sigma_{\mathbf{i}_k}^2} (\bar{l} - I_2(\mathbf{i}_k + \mathbf{d}(\mathbf{i}_k)))^2$$

$$= K - \sum_{k=1}^{N} \frac{1}{2\sigma_{\mathbf{i}_k}^2} (\bar{l} - I_2(\mathbf{i}_k + \mathbf{d}(\mathbf{i}_k)))^2,$$

where $K_3 \triangleq -N/2$, and $K \triangleq K_2 + K_3$ is a constant value. It is worth noting that the data term Γ now depends only on $\mathbf{d}$, since its dependence on $\mathbf{d}^{(t-1)}$ is appended on the average value $\bar{l}$ and variance $\sigma_{\mathbf{i}_k}^2$, both evaluated with respect the conditional distribution $P(l|I_1(\mathbf{i}_k), \mathbf{d}(\mathbf{i}_k)^{(t-1)})$. Therefore, we can write an equivalent expression for the cost function Q as

$$Q(\mathbf{d}) = K - \sum_{k=1}^{N} \frac{1}{2\sigma_{\mathbf{i}_k}^2} (\bar{l} - I_2(\mathbf{i}_k + \mathbf{d}(\mathbf{i}_k)))^2 - \lambda \sum_{<k,m>} ||\mathbf{d}(\mathbf{i}_k) - \mathbf{d}(\mathbf{i}_m)||_2^2, \quad (20)$$

that only depends on the vector field $\mathbf{d}$, and its information regarding the previous estimation $\mathbf{d}^{(t-1)}$ is inherited in the first and second order statistics $\bar{l}$ and $\sigma_{\mathbf{i}_k}^2$. Here, we have used a Gibbs distribution [23] for the regularization term $R(\mathbf{d}) = \lambda \sum_{<k,m>} ||\mathbf{d}(\mathbf{i}_k) - \mathbf{d}(\mathbf{i}_m)||_2^2$, where $\lambda > 0$ is a parameter which controls the homogeneity of the displacement vector field $\mathbf{d}$, and $< k, m >$ stands for the nearest neighbours.

2.3   The Maximization Step (M)

At the maximization step (M), it is possible to estimate the vector field $\mathbf{d}$ at t-iteration by an optimization process

$$\mathbf{d}^{(t)*} = \arg\min_{\mathbf{d}} \bar{Q}(\mathbf{d}), \qquad (21)$$

where

$$\bar{Q}(\mathbf{d}) = \sum_{k=1}^{N} \frac{1}{2\sigma_{\mathbf{i}_k}^2} (\bar{l} - I_2(i + \mathbf{d}(\mathbf{i}_k)))^2 + \lambda \sum_{<k,m>} ||\mathbf{d}(\mathbf{i}_k) - \mathbf{d}(\mathbf{i}_m)||_2^2. \qquad (22)$$

It is important to point out that the optimization problem in (22) is non-linear and to derive a feasible solution, we approximate the non-linear terms by using a first order Taylor's expansion [6]

$$I_2(\mathbf{i}_k + \mathbf{d}(\mathbf{i}_k)) \approx I_2(\mathbf{i}_k) + \nabla I_2(\mathbf{i}_k)^T \mathbf{d}(\mathbf{i}_k), \qquad (23)$$

where $\nabla(\cdot)$ and $(\cdot)^T$ denote the gradient and transpose operators, respectively. Once expanded the data term, the equation (22) can be approximated by

$$\bar{Q}(\mathbf{d}) \approx \sum_{k=1}^{N} \frac{1}{2\sigma_{\mathbf{i}_k}^2} (\bar{l} - I_2(\mathbf{i}_k) - \nabla I_2(\mathbf{i}_k)^T \mathbf{d}(\mathbf{i}_k))^2 + \lambda \sum_{<k,m>} ||\mathbf{d}(\mathbf{i}_k) - \mathbf{d}(\mathbf{i}_m)||_2^2, \qquad (24)$$

where the optimality stationary conditions are derived with respect to the displacements $\mathbf{d}(\mathbf{i}_k)$. Due to the quadratic structure of the cost function $\bar{Q}(\mathbf{d})$, the resulting system of equations is linear and it can be solved by using the Gauss-Seidel algorithm. However, this approximation is accurate only if the displacement vector field $\mathbf{d}(\mathbf{i}_k)$ is small; thus it is suggested to apply first a global parametric multimodal rigid registration; in this work, we use an algorithm based on the Particle Filter (PF) described in [8], in order to obtain a first estimation of the displacement vector field.

In summary, the proposed method to solve the non-rigid multimodal image registration can be described by the next algorithm:

1. Compute a multimodal rigid registration by finding the parameters of an affine transformation through the PF. This affine transformation is used to calculate a first approximation of displacements vector field $\mathbf{d}^{(0)}$.
2. Find the vector field $\mathbf{d}^{(n)}$ in an iterative form departing from the previous estimations $\mathbf{d}^{(0)} + \mathbf{d}^{(1)} + \ldots + \mathbf{d}^{(n-1)}$, by applying the EM-algorithm with the cost function

$$\bar{Q}(\mathbf{d}^{(n)}, \mathbf{d}^{(n-1)}) \approx \sum_{k=1}^{N} \frac{1}{2\sigma_{\mathbf{i}_k}^2} (\bar{l} - \tilde{I}_2^{(n-1)}(\mathbf{i}_k) - \nabla \tilde{I}_2^{(n-1)}(\mathbf{i}_k) \mathbf{d}^{(n)}(\mathbf{i}_k)^T)^2$$

$$+ \lambda \sum_{<k,m>} ||\mathbf{d}^{(n)}(\mathbf{i}_k) - \mathbf{d}^{(n)}(\mathbf{i}_m)||_2^2 \qquad (25)$$

until a convergence criterion on the magnitude of $\mathbf{d}^{(n)}$ is satisfied; here $\tilde{I}_2^{(n-1)}(\mathbf{i}_k) \triangleq I_2\left(\mathbf{i}_k + \sum_{l=0}^{n-1} \mathbf{d}^{(l)}(\mathbf{i}_k)\right) \forall \mathbf{i}_k \in \mathcal{L}$, and $\bar{l} = \mathcal{E}\{l|I_1(\mathbf{i}_k), \sum_{l=0}^{n-1} \mathbf{d}^{(l)}(\mathbf{i}_k)\}$.

3. If the convergence condition is met, then the resulting displacement vector field is given by $\mathbf{d} = \mathbf{d}^{(0)} + \mathbf{d}^{(1)} + \ldots + \mathbf{d}^{(n)}$ and stop, else $n = n + 1$ and go to step 2.

3   Experiments and Results

The following three experiments show the capacity of the proposed algorithm to register images having different gray intensities. For these examples, the regularization parameter λ is fixed to 150. In the proposed approach, the stopping condition in the iterative procedure is defined in terms of the average value of the Euclidean norm of the displacement vector field $\mathbf{d}^{(n)}$; then, the algorithm stops when this value is less than 10^{-3}.

3.1   Elastic Image Registration with Intensity Variation

In the first example, we use two MRI images having not only gray intensity differences, but also different brain structures morphology, as it is shown in pictures 1.(a) (source) and 1.(b) (target). The images resolution is 256×256. In order to visualize the misalignments between the original images, the source image is shown in green and the target image in red, both in Fig. 1.(c).

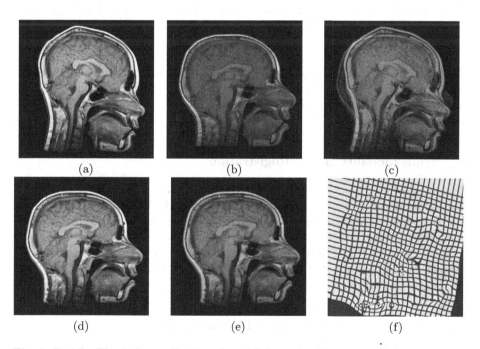

(a)   (b)   (c)

(d)   (e)   (f)

Fig. 1. Test for Elastic Image Registration with Intensity Variation: (a) Source image, (b) target image, (c) superimposed images, (d) registered source image, (e) superimposed images after registration, and (f) deformation grid field

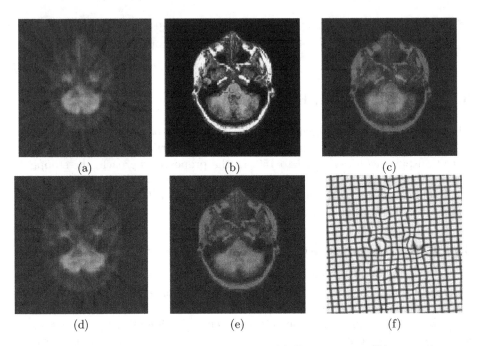

Fig. 2. Test for Multimodal Image Registration: (a) Source image, (b) target image, (c) superposition of the source and target images, (d) transformed source image after registration, (e) superimposed images after registration, and (f) deformation grid field

The experiment aims to align both MRI images by using our approach. We can observe in Figures 1.(d) and 1.(e) how despite of the differences in structure and gray intensities, the proposed algorithm achieves a very accurate non-rigid multimodal registration.

3.2 Multi-modality Image Registration

The second experiment also involves the registration of two images acquired with different techniques: anatomic (MRI) and functional (PET). These images come from very different devices, and by analyzing both images for a specific patient, it is useful to detect functional deficiencies in anatomical structures. The images resolution is 162×162. The result of the registration process for this experiment is shown in Fig. 2. Note that although the information from the images is very different, qualitatively, the algorithm is able to register them.

3.3 Registration with Synthetic Deformations

In order to compare numerically our proposal with recently published algorithms, we performed four experiments where non-rigid image registration algorithms are applied to two MRI images: T1 and T2. In these experiments, we use four

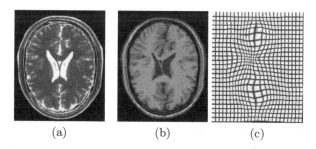

(a)   (b)   (c)

Fig. 3. Test with Synthetic Deformations: (a) Source T2-image; (b) target T1-image; (c) deformation grid field for GT4

Table 1. Vector field error with respect to the ground truths (Euclidean norm) after non-rigid registration

Method	Vector Field Error			
	Average (mm)			
	GT1	GT2	GT3	GT4
LVM	2.0592	1.6432	2.0613	2.4284
Demons	3.7906	4.8985	5.0919	6.3559
DiffDemons	3.8772	6.5214	4.9879	6.9309
EMNRR	**1.2212**	**1.3246**	**1.9011**	**2.1722**
EMNRRMS	**0.7198**	**0.9167**	**1.82312**	**1.2998**

synthetic and known vector fields to deform the T1-image, such that each synthetic field represents a ground truth deformation (named GT1, GT2, GT3, and GT4). Fig. 3.(a) illustrates the original T2-weighted source image; Fig. 3.(b) shows one of the four T1-weighted test images, and Fig. 3.(c) shows its deformation grid field (corresponding to GT4). The images resolution is 217×180. Table 1 presents the numerical results obtained for 4 non-rigid registration algorithms: Local Variability Measures (LVM) [20], Demons [14], DiffDemons [15], and our proposed approach for EM-non-rigid registration (EMNRR). This table shows the mean error of the displacement vector field estimated for each algorithm. In these results we can notice that, among the four approaches, the best performance in terms of the mean error is given by EMNRR.

Furthermore, it is still possible to improve the results obtained with EMNRR by using a multi-scale framework. For this purpose, the target and source images were sub-sampled at two levels (each dividing the image size by two), and the vector field is firstly estimated at the coarsest scale; the solution at this scale is then used as an initial vector field (multiplying each vector by 2) for solving the non-rigid registration problem at each finer scale. The average errors of the estimated vector fields for the multi-scale version (EMNRRMS) are shown in the fifth row of Table 1, illustrating that the multi-scale version of our proposal EMNRRMS still improves its original version EMNRR.

4 Conclusions and Future Work

We propose in this work a new methodology for non-rigid multimodal image registration based on the Expectation-Maximization approach. The mathematical derivations of our proposal were presented in detail in the paper, where the resulting algorithm is based on quadratic optimization and an estimation of the joint conditional intensity distribution of the registering images. The experiments and results showed a remarkable performance to register different kinds of images. We evaluated the algorithm primarily with medical imaging, where it was highlighted as a good alternative for multimodal elastic medical image registration.

For future work, it is pursued to carry out an adaptation strategy of the algorithm parameters in order to increase its performance, for example by modifying spatially the regularization term in order to derive a piecewise smooth vector field, which is more consistent with the behaviour of deformations in medical imaging. Also, a more detailed evaluation of the EMNRR and EMNRRMS algorithms is necessary by using medical index errors. Finally, an implementation for volume registration will be also pursued.

References

1. Zitová, B., Flusser, J.: Image registration methods: a survey. Image and Vision Computing 21, 977–1000 (2003)
2. Pluim, J.P., Fitzpatrick, J.M.: Image registration. IEEE Transactions on Medical Imaging 22(11), 1341–1343 (2003)
3. Pluim, J.P., Maintz, J.B.A., Viergever, M.A.: Mutual-information-based registration of medical images: a survey. IEEE Transactions on Medical Imaging 22(8), 986–1004 (2003)
4. Rueckert, D., Aljabar, P.: Nonrigid registration of medical images: Theory, methods, and applications. IEEE Signal Processing Magazine 27(4), 113–119 (2010)
5. Gonzalez, R.C., Woods, R.E., Eddins, S.L.: Digital Image Processing Using MATLAB, 2nd edn. Gatesmark Publishing (2009)
6. Nocedal, J., Wright, S.J.: Numerical Optimization, 2nd edn. Springer (2006)
7. Das, A., Bhattacharya, M.: Affine-based registratiom of ct and mr modality images of human brain using multiresolution approaches: comparative study on genetic algorithm and particle swarm optimization. Neural Computing and Applications
8. Arce-Santana, E.R., Campos-Delgado, D.U., Alba, A.: Affine image registration guided by particle filter. IET Image Processing 6(5), 455–462 (2002)
9. Reducindo, I.: Registro rígido de imágenes guiado por filtro de partículas. Master's thesis, Universidad Autónoma de San Luis Potosí (December 2010)
10. Xuan, J., Wang, Y., Freedman, M.T., Adali, T., Shields, P.: Nonrigid medical image registration by finite-element deformable sheet-curve models. International Journal of Biomedical Imaging, 1–9 (2006)
11. Serifović-Trbalić, A., Demirović, D., Prljaca, N., Szekely, G., Cattin, P.C.: Intensity-based elastic registration incorporating and isotropic landmark erros and rotational information. International Journal of Computer Assisted Radiology and Surgery 4(5), 463–468 (2009)

12. Klein, A., Andersson, J., Ardekani, B.A., Ashburner, J., et al.: Evaluation of 14 nonlinear deformation algorithms applied to human brain mri registration. Neuroimage 46(3), 786–802 (2009)
13. Horn, B.K., Schunck, B.G.: Determining optical flow, Artificial Intelligence 17
14. Thirion, J.P.: Image matching as a diffusion process: an analogy with maxwells demons. Med. Image Anal. 2(3), 243–260 (1998)
15. Vercauteren, T., Pennec, X., Perchant, A., Ayache, N.: Idiffeomorphic demons: efficient non-parametric image registration. Neuroimage 45(1), 561–572 (2009)
16. Laszlo, G.N., Xuan, K.U.: New variants of a method of mri scale standardization. IEEE Tran. on Med. Imaging 19(2), 143–150 (2000)
17. Arce-Santana, E., Campos-Delgado, D.U., Alba, A.: A non-rigid multimodal image registration method based on particle filter and optical flow. In: Bebis, G., et al. (eds.) ISVC 2010, Part I. LNCS, vol. 6453, pp. 35–44. Springer, Heidelberg (2010)
18. Reducindo, I., Arce-Santana, E.R., Campos-Delgado, D.U., Alba, A.: Evaluation of multimodal medical image registration based on particle filter. In: Int. Conf. on Electrical Eng., Computing Science and Automatic Control
19. Mejia-Rodriguez, A., Arce-Santana, E., Scalco, E., Tresoldi, D., Mendez, M., Bianchi, A., Cattaneo, G., Rizzo, G.: Elastic registration based on particle filter in radiotherapy images with brain deformations. In: 2011 Annual International Conference of the IEEE on Engineering in Medicine and Biology Society (EMBC), pp. 8049–8052 (2011), http://dx.doi.org/10.1109/IEMBS.2011.6091985, doi:10.1109/IEMBS.2011.6091985
20. Reducindo, I., Arce-Santana, E.R., Campos-Delgado, D.U., Vigueras-Gómez, F.: Non-rigid multimodal image registration based on local variability measures and optical flow. In: 2012 Annual International Conference of the IEEE on Engineering in Medicine and Biology Society, EMBC (2012)
21. ter Haar Romeny, B., Florack, L., Koenderink, J., Viergever, M.: Scale space: Its natural operators and differential invariants. In: Colchester, A.C.F., Hawkes, D.J. (eds.) IPMI 1991. LNCS, vol. 511, pp. 239–255. Springer, Heidelberg (1991)
22. Dempster, A.P., Laird, N.M., Rubin, D.B.: Maximum likelihood from incomplete data via the em algorithm. Journal of the Royal Statistical Society Series b 39(1), 1–38 (1977)
23. Geman, D., Geman, S.: Stochastic relaxation, gibbs distribution and the bayesian restoration of images. IEEE Trans. Pattern Analysis and Machine Learning Intelligence 6(6), 721–741 (1984)

Wide-Baseline Dense Feature Matching
for Endoscopic Images

Gustavo A. Puerto-Souza and Gian-Luca Mariottini

Dept. of Computer Science and Engineering,
Univ. of Texas at Arlington, 500 UTA Blvd., 76019 Texas, USA
gustavo.puerto@mavs.uta.edu
gianluca.mariottini@uta.edu

Abstract. Providing a feature-matching strategy to accurately recover
tracked features after a fast and large endoscopic-camera motion or a
strong organ deformation, is key in many endoscopic-imaging applications, such as augmented reality or soft-tissue shape recovery. Despite
recent advances, existing feature-matching algorithms are characterized
by limiting assumptions, and have not yet met the necessary levels of
accuracy, especially when used to recover features in distorted or poorly-
textured tissue areas. In this paper, we present a novel feature-matching
algorithm that accurately recovers the position of image features over the
entire organ's surface. Our method is fully automatic, it does not require
any explicit assumption about the organ's 3-D surface, and leverages
Gaussian Process Regression to incorporate noisy matches in a probabilistically sound way. We have conducted extensive tests with a large
database of more than 100 endoscopic-image pairs, which show the improved accuracy and robustness of our approach when compared to current state-of-the-art methods.

1 Introduction

Providing a reliable solution for the recovery of tracked image features [1] that
were lost after a sudden endoscopic-camera motion, or strong organ deformation,
is key in order to guarantee long-term performances in many endoscopic-imaging
applications, such as augmented reality (AR) [2–4], structure and camera-motion
estimation [5–7], and soft-tissue shape recovery [8–10].

Feature matching (or "tracking-by-detection") [11, 12] is a promising technique, as it deals with retrieving corresponding features between two distinct
images, even when separated by a wide baseline. Differently from feature tracking [5, 13–16], feature matching does not make any temporal assumption about
the two images, about the camera pose [17], or about the 3-D geometry of the
observed scene (e.g., known organ motion due to periodic breathing).

Despite recent advances [18–20], existing feature-matching algorithms are
characterized by limiting assumptions and, most important, have not yet met
the necessary levels of accuracy, especially when used to recover features in distorted or poorly-textured areas. Figure 1(a) illustrates an example obtained by

R. Klette, M. Rivera, and S. Satoh (Eds.): PSIVT 2013, LNCS 8333, pp. 48–59, 2014.

using the HMA feature-matching approach [21] (a toolbox is publicly available at [22]). Even if this method recovers a larger number of correct matches (inliers) when compared to existing methods, HMA exhibits a large error (green lines) when used to recover the position of features on the organ's boundaries (green circles). These large errors are caused by the absence of supporting geometric constraints (the colored polygons correspond to affine mappings [23]) in such highly-distorted or textureless areas.

Other regularization methods have been proposed to recover the non-rigid object's shape, such as Finite Element Methods (FEM) [24, 25], and point-set methods (such as Thin-Plate Splines - TPS) [26, 27]. However, FEM-based regularization approaches require an explicit 3-D mesh representation of the organ's surface, and cannot properly describe sharp surface boundaries. Point-set methods are computationally intensive and few of them can be applied to point sets extracted from real endoscopic images.

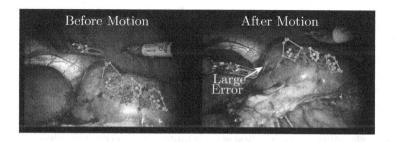

(a) State-of-the-art HMA Method

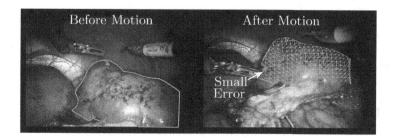

(b) Our Method

Fig. 1. (a) The recent feature-matching HMA method works accurately when used to predict the position of features near-by the supporting affine transformations (colored polygons), but exhibits large pixel errors (green line) when used to the feature position on organ's boundaries. (b) Our proposed strategy *accurately and densely* recovers the position of image features over the *entire* organ's surface.

In [28] the authors adopt a TPS warping coupled with bending constraints that gives robustness to self-occlusions. This deformable model is used as geometric constraint to remove outliers based on their reprojection error. While some effort have been shown for applying this method in an AR surgical application [29], it is distant from a clinical use due to its computational complexity and the sensitivity to outliers; moreover, there is no reported quantitative analysis about its accuracy and robustness in real clinical cases. A different approach is followed in [25] where Gaussian Processes (GP) [30] are used to model the deformable mapping between images. The authors interleaved the GP estimation with an iterative noise-level thresholding to retain only the most certain matches. These filtered matches are used as training data for a weighted-GP regression that estimates the deformable mapping. However, this method tends to eliminate potential correct matches, especially those ones away from the majority of the inliers (e.g. on the object borders). Furthermore, this algorithm has not been evaluated on endoscopic scenarios and it usually fails in cases of large change of view and strong deformations, which are very usual in endoscopic images.

In this paper, we present a novel feature-matching algorithm that *accurately and densely* recovers the position of image features over the *entire* organ's surface. Our method is fully automatic, and it does not require any explicit assumption about the organ's 3-D surface. We adopt Gaussian Process Regression to incorporate noisy matches in a probabilistically sound way. A qualitative example of the performance of our method is illustrated in Fig. 1(b), which shows the dense mapping and the decreased reprojection error. Furthermore, this is the first work that uses GP for dense feature matching in real endoscopic images which are more challenging than the in-lab scenarios tested in [25]. We have conducted extensive tests using a large database with more than 100 endoscopic-image pairs showing the improved accuracy and robustness of our approach when compared to the current state-of-the-art HMA algorithm [21] and the other GP method in [25].

The paper is organized as follows: Sect. 2 presents our dense feature-matching algorithm. Sect. 3 illustrates the results of our extensive experimental evaluation and discusses the algorithms' performance. Finally, Sect. 4 draws the conclusions of this work.

2   Methods

In this section we present our dense feature-matching algorithm that uses as input a training (or template) image, $\mathcal{I}^t$, and a query (or output) image $\mathcal{I}^q$ (e.g., the one before and after a complete occlusion, respectively) and returns a dense mapping between them.

Our strategy consists of two phases: in the first *Sparse Feature-Matching* phase, a set of n sparse matches $\mathcal{M} = \{(\mathbf{x}_i, \mathbf{y}_i)\}_{i=1}^{n}$ are obtained by processing a set of appearance-based (e.g., SIFT) initial matches extracted from $\mathcal{I}^t$ and $\mathcal{I}^q$. In this first phase, we adopt the state-of-the-art HMA algorithm [21], which returns a set of accurate matches $\mathcal{M}$, as well as a collection of *rigid* (affine) mappings between both images. As mentioned in Sect. 1, we observed that HMA can easily lead to large errors when these rigid mappings are used to predict the position of some features located in an organ's area no associated to a specific affine mapping (e.g., on the organ's boundaries where only a few SIFT features are found due to high distortions).

In the second phase, the feature matches from HMA are used as input to a *Gaussian Process (GP) regression*. The goal of this GP phase is to find a latent dense mapping function $f(\mathbf{x})$ that models the *non-rigid motion* of any image point $\mathbf{x}_* \in \mathcal{I}^t$ to the corresponding point $\mathbf{y}_* = f(\mathbf{x}_*)$ in $\mathcal{I}^q$. This second phase also outputs a *dense* set of correspondences that adapt more appropriately to the shape of the organ. The GP phase is described in detail in the next section.

2.1 Gaussian Process Regression Phase

In this phase, the sparse image matches in $\mathcal{M} \triangleq \{(\mathbf{x}_i, \mathbf{y}_i)\}_{i=1}^n$ are used to estimate the *non-rigid and dense* function $f(\mathbf{x})$ that maps any image point $\mathbf{x}_* \in \mathcal{I}^t$ to its corresponding image point $\mathbf{y}_* \in \mathcal{I}^q$. $f(\mathbf{x})$ can be written as, $\mathbf{y}_* = f(\mathbf{x}_*) + \epsilon$, where $\epsilon \sim \mathcal{N}(\mathbf{0}, \sigma^2 \mathbf{I})$ is an additive Gaussian noise with zero mean and standard deviation σ. Each knot in the mesh-grid in Fig. 1(b)-right, corresponds to each predicted point $\mathbf{y}_*$ on $\mathcal{I}^q$.

The HMA matches in $\mathcal{M}$ are used as input to a Gaussian Process [30], which describes the posterior distribution of the latent function f as, $p(f|\mathcal{M}) \propto p(\mathcal{M}|f)p(f)$, where $f(\mathbf{p}) \sim \mathcal{GP}(\mu(\mathbf{p}), k(\mathbf{p}, \mathbf{q}))$, $\mathbf{p}$ and $\mathbf{q}$ being two generic vectors. Since a GP is completely determined by its mean and covariance matrix, we define, $\mu(\mathbf{p}) = \mathbf{p}$, as the deterministic mean of the non-rigid function f [25]. The GP covariance matrix is defined as, $k(\mathbf{p}, \mathbf{q}) = \lambda exp\left(-\frac{\|\mathbf{p}-\mathbf{q}\|^2}{2\rho^2}\right)$, where λ is the amplitude of the process variance and ρ is the length of the process variation.

Note that $p(f|\mathcal{M})$ captures the interaction between the *observed* correspondences and the latent function f, while $p(f)$ represents the *a-priori* knowledge about the non-rigid mapping in terms of the given mean and covariance of the GP.

We denote as $\mathbf{X} \in \mathbb{R}^{n \times 2}$ and $\mathbf{Y} \in \mathbb{R}^{n \times 2}$ the matrices containing all the n 2-D HMA matches in $\mathcal{I}^t$ and $\mathcal{I}^q$, respectively. The matrix $\mathbf{X}_* \in \mathbb{R}^{m \times 2}$ contains the m features to be predicted, and $\mathbf{Y}_* \in \mathbb{R}^{m \times 2}$ all the corresponding predicted points, so that $\mathbf{y}_{*i} = f(\mathbf{x}_{*i}) + \epsilon$. Then, the joint distribution of both the observed values, $\mathbf{Y}$, and of the target values, $\mathbf{Y}_*$, under the prior is given by,

$$\begin{bmatrix} \mathbf{Y} \\ \mathbf{Y}_* \end{bmatrix} \propto \mathcal{N}\left(\begin{bmatrix} \mathbf{X} \\ \mathbf{X}_* \end{bmatrix}, \begin{bmatrix} \mathbf{K}(\mathbf{X}, \mathbf{X}) + \sigma^2 \mathbf{I} & \mathbf{K}(\mathbf{X}, \mathbf{X}_*) \\ \mathbf{K}(\mathbf{X}_*, \mathbf{X}) & \mathbf{K}(\mathbf{X}_*, \mathbf{X}_*) \end{bmatrix}\right),$$

where each (i, j) entry for the matrices $\mathbf{K}(\mathbf{X}, \mathbf{X}) \in \mathbb{R}^{n \times n}$, $\mathbf{K}(\mathbf{X}_*, \mathbf{X}) \in \mathbb{R}^{m \times n}$, and $\mathbf{K}(\mathbf{X}_*, \mathbf{X}_*) \in \mathbb{R}^{m \times m}$ is defined as $k(\mathbf{x}_i, \mathbf{x}_j)$ for row vectors $\mathbf{x}_i$ and $\mathbf{x}_j$ belonging, respectively, to $\mathbf{X}$ or $\mathbf{X}_*$.

Then, the points predicted by the non-rigid function [30] corresponding to $\mathbf{X}_*$ are given by:

$$\mathbf{Y}_* = \mathbf{X}_* + \mathbf{K}(\mathbf{X}_*, \mathbf{X})(\mathbf{K}(\mathbf{X}, \mathbf{X}) + \sigma^2 \mathbf{I})^{-1}(\mathbf{Y} - \mathbf{X}). \tag{1}$$

Note that each entry $k(\cdot, \cdot)$ varies according to the values of its *hyper-parameters* λ and ρ. In order to improve the performance of the GP, we iteratively selected these parameters by maximizing the marginal log-likelihood of the model with respect to the hyper-parameters. The marginal log-likelihood of the model given the n training matches is given by: $\log\left(p(\mathbf{Y}|\mathbf{X}, \sigma, \boldsymbol{\theta})\right) = \sum_{i=1}^{2} -0.5(\mathbf{Y}_i - \mathbf{X}_i)^T \boldsymbol{\alpha}_i - 0.5 \log |\mathbf{K}(\mathbf{X}, \mathbf{X}) + \sigma^2 \mathbf{I}| - 0.5\, n \log 2\pi$, where $\boldsymbol{\theta} \triangleq [\theta_1, \theta_2]^T = [\rho, \lambda]^T$, $\boldsymbol{\alpha}_i = (\mathbf{K}(\mathbf{X}, \mathbf{X}) + \sigma^2 \mathbf{I})^{-1}(\mathbf{Y}_i - \mathbf{X}_i)$ and $\mathbf{Y}_i$ and $\mathbf{X}_i$ represent the i-th column of $\mathbf{Y}$ and $\mathbf{X}$, respectively. The gradients of this marginal log-likelihood over each component of the hyper-parameter vector are:

$$\frac{\partial \log\left(p\left(\mathbf{Y}|\mathbf{X}, \sigma, \boldsymbol{\theta}\right)\right)}{\partial \theta_j} = \frac{1}{2}\mathrm{tr}\left(\left(\boldsymbol{\alpha}_i \boldsymbol{\alpha}_i^T - \left(\mathbf{K} + \sigma^2 \mathbf{I}\right)^{-1}\right)\frac{\partial \mathbf{K}}{\partial \theta_j}\right).$$

This log-likelihood is maximized by using its gradients into a non-linear optimization method.

3   Experimental Results and Discussion

We present here our experimental validation conducted on a large and publicly-available benchmark containing: an *In-lab* dataset, with 18 image-pairs of a textured non-planar object, subject to controlled rotations and deformations, and a *Surgical-Image* dataset with more than 100 cases extracted from real partial-nephrectomy surgeries [18]. Figure 2 illustrates some representative examples of the adopted benchmark.

This benchmark is particularly appealing for our method as it contains manually-annotated (ground-truth) correspondences, thus allowing us to quantitatively assess the performances of our proposed algorithm and compare them with other state-of-the-art methods by measuring the pixel reprojection error. We compared the accuracy of our algorithm with respect to Zhu's method [25] and HMA [18]. In the case of Zhu and HMA, the training data consists of a set of appearance-based matches (SIFT). The parameters in Zhu and HMA were selected based on the reported values on their respective papers with slight changes in order to maximize their accuracy.

In our method, SIFT features were extracted and the set of sparse correspondences are obtained by means of the HMA Toolbox (publicly available at [22]). In our experimental validation, we propose to increase the number of correspondences, $\mathcal{M}$, by using the affine transformation mappings provided by HMA and by also including those initial SIFT matches with a pixel reprojection error below to fifteen pixels. This choice is based on the ROC analysis reported in [21] which shows that increasing this threshold introduces other correct matches that were not captured by the affine model and few slightly incorrect matches. These extra matches are useful to allow other image features on the entire organ's surface (in particular in the organ's boundaries) to become a support for the GP estimation phase. Also note that the noise introduced by those erroneous matches is already modeled by σ in the GP. The correspondences $\mathcal{M}$ were then used as the training data $\mathbf{X}$ and $\mathbf{Y}$ for the GP regression phase. Based on the precision of HMA's

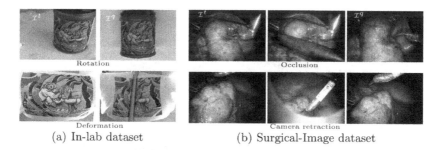

(a) In-lab dataset   (b) Surgical-Image dataset

Fig. 2. *Datasets used in our experiments. (a)* Some of the images of the rotation and deformation cases for the In-lab dataset. The left image was fixed as training image, while the object in the query images was rotated or deformed. *(b)* Some of the images in the Surgical image dataset. The training images (left) were acquired before sudden occlusions, camera retraction or strong changes of illumination (center), while the query images (right) were obtained after such events.

affine transformations (set at 5 pixels), we set the noise as $\sigma = \frac{5}{3}$ pixels; the hyper-parameters λ and ρ are estimated as described in Sect. 2. For a better numerical stability, we center each column of $\mathbf{X}$ and $\mathbf{Y}$ to have mean zero and standard deviation one, as well as appropriately scaling σ by the inverse of the larger standard deviation of the columns of $\mathbf{Y}$.

3.1   In-lab Dataset

This dataset includes 7 image-pairs of a rotated textured object whose rotation angles range from -30 to $+30$ degrees [1], as well as 11 cases of a controlled object deformation divided as small, medium and strong deformations. Fig. 2(a) shows some representative examples of this dataset. The image resolution of these images is 640×480, and the number of ground-truth correspondences is in average 55 for the rotation, and 30 for the deformation cases.

Our results are reported in Table. 1: the columns show the mean and standard deviation of the reprojection errors for different object's rotation angles, and object's deformations for our proposed approach, HMA and Zhu's algorithm.

Table 1. *In-lab dataset:* Rotation and Deformation Sets

Method	$-30°$	$-20°$	$-10°$	$0°$	$10°$	$20°$	$30°$	Small Def.	Med. Def.	Str. Def.
Our meth.	5.2±6.6	2.8±3.2	2.2±2.4	1.6±1.9	1.7±1.4	2.4±3.3	2.3±3.6	2.7±4.3	2.2±2.4	2.5±2.7
HMA	9.3±10.3	6.7±6.4	3.7±4.3	3.2±3.8	3.3±3.7	3.6±4.2	4.0±5.5	4±4.5	5.9±10.6	6.5±3.8
Zhu	19.6±14.3	17.6±12.7	13.4±11.15	13.7±9.7	12.6±8.7	13.8±11.6	14.2±12.8	10.9±8.01	21.1±14.0	23.9±14.3

From the results of Table 1 we can observe the enormous improvement of our method over Zhu and HMA. This improvement of our algorithm with respect to Zhu's method is also evident in the qualitative examples shown in Fig. 3. An example of the rotation case is shown in Fig. 3(a) which shows that our method

---

[1] These angles were chosen to guarantee a good percentage of reliable SIFT matches [31].

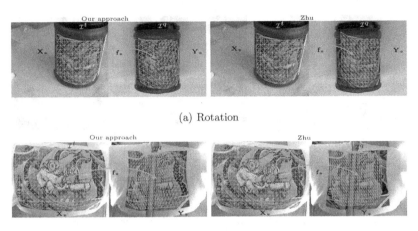

(a) Rotation

(b) Deformation

Fig. 3. *Qualitative comparison*: *(a)* Estimated correspondences $\mathbf{X}_*$ and $\mathbf{Y}_*$ using our approach and Zhu's method, for image pair 4 of the rotation set of the In-lab dataset. *(b)* Estimated correspondences for image pair 6 of the deformation set of the In-lab dataset.

can successfully match the features between images (blue meshes). Conversely, Zhu has problems to match the boundaries due to the lack of matches in that area and the reduced robustness to outliers of their adaptive thresholding approach. As a result, the estimated mapping for these features is very similar to their original position in the training image. Moreover, Fig. 3(b) shows the resulting example for a strong deformation. Note that our approach obtains a very precise mapping as noticeable in the borders of the (blue) warped mesh. On the other hand, Zhu shows problems in the borders. We observed that Zhu is in fact very conservative when filtering its training data; as a result, those matches on the borders are usually removed or strongly penalized when there is a large viewpoint change or a strong deformation between images.

3.2 Surgical-Images Dataset

This dataset contains 100 images extracted before and after camera occlusions, organ deformation, camera retraction/re-insertion, and large changes of illumination, as shown in the examples of Fig. 2(b).

A qualitative comparison between our approach and Zhu's method is presented in the challenging examples of Figs. 4 and 5, which illustrate two cases of very poor textured and highly-cluttered images. Figures 4(a) show the mapping (blue meshes) between the images for both algorithms. Note that our approach results in a higher accurate mapping (e.g., see the organ boundaries indicated by the yellow arrows). In particular, our approach achieves better results than Zhu because it uses more informative training data (this can be observed in Figs. 4(b) which show the matches used as training data). Note that, even if both methods used the *same set* of input appearance-based matches, Zhu's adaptive thresholding

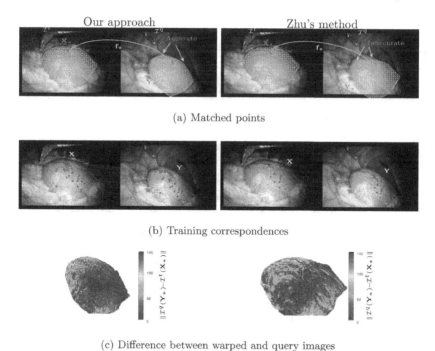

(a) Matched points

(b) Training correspondences

(c) Difference between warped and query images

Fig. 4. *Qualitative comparison*: *(a)* Estimated correspondences $\mathbf{X}_*$ and $\mathbf{Y}_*$ using our approach and Zhu's method, for image pair 10 of the Surgical-Image database. *(b)* Set of sparse matches used as training data for both methods (dashed lines). *(c)* Absolute pixel difference between the warped and the reference regions.

removes a large number of matches, in particular those on the organ's boundaries. As a result, the estimated mapping has large errors. This is a very common issue for GP where the uncertainty in the prediction quickly grows on the borders of the training data. We also evaluate, in Figs. 4(c), the quality of the mapping by computing the difference of intensities between the warped ($\mathcal{I}^t(\mathbf{X}_*)$) and the corresponding query ($\mathcal{I}^q(\mathbf{Y}_*)$) images. Despite illumination changes, observe that the areas with large similarity (blue areas) between warped and query images are more evident with our approach than with Zhu.

Moreover, Figs. 5(a) show a case where Zhu fails to prune the noisy appearance-based matches due to high clutter of the images and because Zhu's tight constraints remove the matches on the top and left-parts of the organ. Conversely, our algorithm is able to estimate a very precise mapping because of its capacity to deal with noisy matches. This is evident from Figs. 5(b) which show the matches used as training sets by each algorithm. As a result, the intensity similarities between warped and query images are significantly lower for our approach than Zhu. Note that for our method, the similarity errors, in Figs. 5(c), are mostly caused by illumination changes between views.

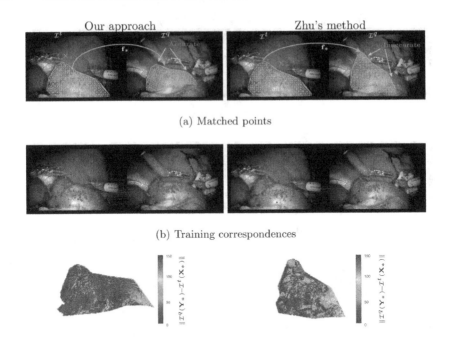

(a) Matched points

(b) Training correspondences

(c) Difference between warped and query images

Fig. 5. *Qualitative comparison*: *(a)* Estimated correspondences $\mathbf{X}_*$ and $\mathbf{Y}_*$ using our approach and Zhu's method, for image pair 15 of the Surgical-Image database. *(b)* Set of sparse matches used as training data for both methods (dashed lines). *(c)* Absolute pixel difference between the warped and the reference regions.

To provide a quantitative comparison, we decided to partition the dataset in three categories according to their percentage of correct matches[2] as: less than 15% (very hard), between $15-40\%$ (hard) and more than 40% (regular) correct matches. Table 2 summarizes the results of the reprojection errors (mean and standard deviation) through the three categories.

Table 2. *Surgical-Image dataset:* Average errors (pixels) over the 100 image pairs

Algorithm	Avg.Err. [pixels] 0 − 15% inliers	Avg.Err. [pixels] 15 − 40% inliers	Avg.Err. [pixels] 40 − 100% inliers	Failures
Our method	**4.49±4.68**	**3.4±3.23**	**1.84±1.66**	**5**
HMA	5.89±6.27	4.59±4.79	2.26±2.29	5
Zhu	16.07±9.39	9.43±7.11	7.07±4.63	9

The results in Table 2 show a 70% error reduction of our approach with respect to Zhu, thus supporting the observations from the qualitative examples. Moreover, Zhu tends to fail in almost twice number of cases due to convergence problems. In addition to providing a dense mapping, our proposed approach has an accuracy improvement of approximately 23% when compared to HMA.

---

[2] The appearance-based matches and the percentage of final correct matches (inliers) were provided from the dataset.

4   Conclusions

We presented a feature-matching algorithm that accurately and densely recovers the position of image features over the entire organ's surface. Our method is fully automatic, it does not require any explicit assumption about the organ's 3-D surface, and it combines sparse feature-matching with the probabilistic modeling of Gaussian Process Regression. We demonstrated the effectiveness of our algorithm under a highly-controlled in-lab dataset, and a large endoscopic dataset with more than 100 images of challenging scenarios. We measured the reprojection errors with respect to manually annotated ground-truth and observed that one of the main advantages of our proposed algorithm is its higher accuracy when compared to state-of-the-art methods, in particular for features closer to the tissue's boundaries. This happens because our algorithm can leverage the extra information provided from (initially-discarded and noisy) SIFT matches, thanks to the probabilistic noise modeling of Gaussian Processes and the hyperparameters' estimation.

References

1. Shi, J., Tomasi, C.: Good features to track. In: IEEE Computer Society Conference on Computer Vision and Pattern Recognition, pp. 593–600 (June 1994)
2. Cohen, D., Mayer, E., Chen, D., Anstee, A., Vale, J., Yang, G.Z., Darzi, A., Edwards, P.: Augmented reality image guidance in minimally invasive prostatectomy. In: Prostate Cancer Imaging. Computer-Aided Diagnosis, Prognosis, and Intervention, pp. 101–110 (2010)
3. Su, L.M., Vagvolgyi, B.P., Agarwal, R., Reiley, C.E., Taylor, R.H., Hager, G.D.: Augmented reality during robot-assisted laparoscopic partial nephrectomy: Toward real-time 3D-CT to stereoscopic video registration. Urology 73(4), 896–900 (2009)
4. Higgins, E.W., Helferty, P.J., Lu, K., Merritt, A.S., Lav, R., Kun-Chang, Y.: 3d ct-video fusion for image-guided bronchoscopy. Computerized Medical Imaging and Graphics 32(3), 159–173 (2008)
5. Mountney, P., Yang, G.-Z.: Motion compensated SLAM for image guided surgery. In: Jiang, T., Navab, N., Pluim, J.P.W., Viergever, M.A. (eds.) MICCAI 2010, Part II. LNCS, vol. 6362, pp. 496–504. Springer, Heidelberg (2010)
6. Mountney, P., Stoyanov, D., Yang, G.Z.: Three-dimensional tissue deformation recovery and tracking. IEEE Signal Processing Magazine 27(4), 14–24 (2010)
7. Hu, M., Penney, G.P., Rueckert, D., Edwards, P.J., Bello, F., Casula, R., Figl, M., Hawkes, D.J.: Non-rigid reconstruction of the beating heart surface for minimally invasive cardiac surgery. In: Proc. of the 12th Int. Conf. on Med. Image Comp. and Comp.-Ass. Int., pp. 34–42 (2009)
8. Lo, B.P.L., Visentini-Scarzanella, M., Stoyanov, D., Yang, G.Z.: Belief propagation for depth cue fusion in minimally invasive surgery. In: Proc. of the 11th Int. Conf. on Med. Image Comp. and Comp.-Ass. Int, pp. 104–112 (2008)
9. Visentini-Scarzanella, M., Mylonas, G.P., Stoyanov, D., Yang, G.Z.: i-brush: A gaze-contingent virtual paintbrush for dense 3d reconstruction in robotic assisted surgery. In: Proc. of the 12th Int. Conf. on Med. Image Comp. and Comp.-Ass. Int., pp. 353–360 (2009)

10. Totz, J., Mountney, P., Stoyanov, D., Yang, G.Z.: Dense surface reconstruction for enhanced navigation in MIS. In: Proc. of the 14th Int. Conf. on Med. Image Comp. and Comp.-Ass. Int., pp. 89–96 (2011)

11. Lepetit, V., Fua, P.: Monocular model-based 3-d tracking of rigid objects: A survey. Foundations and Trends in Computer Graphics and Vision 1, 1–89 (2005)

12. Puerto-Souza, G.A., Mariottini, G.L.: A comparative study of correspondence-search algorithms in mis images. In: Proc. of the 15th Int. Conf. on Med. Image Comp. and Comp.-Ass. Int., pp. 625–633 (2012)

13. Stoyanov, D., Mylonas, G., Deligianni, F., Darzi, A., Yang, G.Z.: Soft-tissue motion tracking and structure estimation for robotic assisted mis procedures. In: Proc. of the 8th Int. Conf. on Med. Image Comp. and Comp.-Ass. Int., pp. 139–146 (2005)

14. Richa, R., Bo, A.P., Poignet, P.: Towards robust 3d visual tracking for motion compensation in beating heart surgery. Medical Image Analysis 15(3), 3012–3315 (2010)

15. Giannarou, S., Visentini-Scarzanella, M., Yang, G.Z.: Probabilistic tracking of affine-invariant anisotropic regions. In: IEEE Transactions on Pattern Analysis and Machine Intelligence (2012)

16. Yip, M., Lowe, D., Salcudean, S., Rohling, R., Nguan, C.: Real-time methods for long-term tissue feature tracking in endoscopic scenes. In: Information Processing in Computer-Assisted Interventions, pp. 33–43 (2012)

17. Tola, E., Lepetit, V., Fua, P.: Daisy: An efficient dense descriptor applied to wide-baseline stereo. IEEE Transactions on Pattern Analysis and Machine Intelligence 32(5), 815–830 (2010)

18. Puerto-Souza, G.A., Mariottini, G.L.: Hierarchical multi-affine (HMA) algorithm for fast and accurate feature matching in minimally-invasive surgical images. In: Proc. IEEE/RSJ Int. Conf. Intel. Robots Syst., pp. 2007–2012 (October 2012)

19. Del Bimbo, A., Franco, F., Pernici, F.: Local shape estimation from a single keypoint. In: Proc. Comp. Vis. Patt. Rec. Workshops, pp. 23–28 (2010)

20. Cho, M., Lee, J., Lee, K.M.: Feature correspondence and deformable object matching via agglomerative correspondence clustering. In: Proc. 9th Int. Conf. Comp. Vis., pp. 1280–1287 (2009)

21. Puerto-Souza, G.A., Mariottini, G.L.: A Fast and Accurate Feature-Matching Algorithm for Minimally-Invasive Endoscopic Images. IEEE Transactions on Medical Imaging (in Press, 2013)

22. HMA feature-matching toolbox (Web),
    http://ranger.uta.edu/~gianluca/feature_matching/

23. Hartley, R., Zisserman, A.: Multiple view geometry in computer vision. Cambridge Univ. Press (2000)

24. Pilet, J., Lepetit, V., Fua, P.: Fast Non-Rigid Surface Detection, Registration and Realistic Augmentation. International Journal of Computer Vision 76(2) (2008)

25. Zhu, J., Hoi, S., Lyu, L.: Nonrigid shape recovery by gaussian process regression. In: IEEE Conference on Computer Vision and Pattern Recognition, pp. 1319–1326 (2009)

26. Belongie, S., Malik, J., Puzicha, J.: Shape Matching and Object Recognition Using Shape Contexts. IEEE Transactions on Pattern Analysis and Machine Intelligence 24, 509–522 (2001)

27. Myronenko, A., Song, X.: Point Set Registration: Coherent Point Drift. IEEE Transactions on Pattern Analysis and Machine Intelligence 32(12), 2262–2275 (2010)

28. Pizarro, D., Bartoli, A.: Feature-based deformable surface detection with self-occlusion reasoning. International Journal of Computer Vision 97(1), 54–70 (2012)
29. Kim, J.-H., Bartoli, A., Collins, T., Hartley, R.: Tracking by detection for interactive image augmentation in laparoscopy. In: Dawant, B.M., Christensen, G.E., Fitzpatrick, J.M., Rueckert, D. (eds.) WBIR 2012. LNCS, vol. 7359, pp. 246–255. Springer, Heidelberg (2012)
30. Rasmussen, C., Williams, C.: Gaussian processes for machine learning, vol. 1. MIT press, Cambridge (2006)
31. Mikolajczyk, K., Schmid, C.: A performance evaluation of local descriptors. IEEE Transactions on Pattern Analysis and Machine Intelligence 27(10), 1615–1630 (2005)

Vehicle Detection Based on Multi-feature Clues and Dempster-Shafer Fusion Theory

Mahdi Rezaei[1] and Mutsuhiro Terauchi[2]

[1] The University of Auckland, New Zealand
m.rezaei@auckland.ac.nz
[2] Hiroshima International University, Japan
mucha@he.hirokoku-u.ac.jp

Abstract. On-road vehicle detection and rear-end crash prevention are demanding subjects in both academia and automotive industry. The paper focuses on monocular vision-based vehicle detection under challenging lighting conditions, being still an open topic in the area of driver assistance systems. The paper proposes an effective vehicle detection method based on multiple features analysis and Dempster-Shafer-based fusion theory. We also utilize a new idea of *Adaptive Global* Haar-like (AGHaar) features as a promising method for feature classification and vehicle detection in both daylight and night conditions. Validation tests and experimental results show superior detection results for day, night, rainy, and challenging conditions compared to state-of-the-art solutions.

Keywords: Vehicle detection, Monocular vision, Collision detection, Line and corner features, Dempster-Shafer theory, Data fusion.

1 Introduction

According to a recent report in 2012 by [12], rear-end crashes contribute in 33% of collisions as the highest rate among 18 types of crash studied. By maintaining early vehicle detection and warning, it is possible to provide more time for a distracted driver to take an appropriate safe maneuver to resolve driving conflicts, and consequently to decrease the possibility of rear-end crashes.

Vision-based driver assistance research addresses subjects such as vehicle detection based on analysing shadow underneath a vehicle [1,6], stereo vision to estimate distances between *ego-vehicle* (i.e. the car the system is operating in) and obstacles [24], optical flow-based methods [2], the utilization of local binary patterns (LBP) [15,17], or of Haar-like features [11,13,26].

The use of Haar and triangle features is proposed in [7]. Reported results indicate improvements compared to a standard detector using Haar features only. However, no validation tests and experiments have been considered for night conditions as well as for challenging lighting situations. Thresholding for red and white colours [16] also appears as one option to detect vehicles' taillights. However, this approach only works for night conditions, and the second weakness is that the method only works for the detection of lead vehicles which are levelled

R. Klette, M. Rivera, and S. Satoh (Eds.): PSIVT 2013, LNCS 8333, pp. 60–72, 2014.

to the ego-vehicle; a tilted vehicle (e.g. due to a road ramp, road surface at a curve, or when turning at a round about) cannot be detected by this approach.

Shadow based vehicle detection is discussed in [1,6]. However, shadows only are unreliable indicators for the existence of a vehicle. A vehicle's shadow varies in size and position, depending on sun position.

Stereo vision and a genetic algorithm [14], or stereo vision and 3-dimensional (3D) features [24] take the advantage of depth information, represented in a disparity map, and apply inverse perspective mapping. However, the reported feature detection does not support accurate distinguishing of vehicles from other obstacles (i.e. false-positives) at night or in complicated road scenes.

A recent proposal represents a fusion technique using radar and optical flow information [5]. While the radar sensor can have multiple detections for the same vehicle, the optical flow technique can only detect overtaking vehicles with considerable velocity differences compared to the ego-vehicle.

Although we use only a monocular vision sensor for the research reported in this paper, we introduce an accurate, real-time, and effective vehicle detection algorithm to prevent imminent accidents in both day and night conditions. As a fundamental idea of this paper, we hypothesize that despite of vehicles' make, model, or colour, all vehicles have some similar features and appearances in common, including occlusion edges between vehicle and road background, different light reflectance patterns on the rear windshield compared to the body of a vehicle, a tendency towards a rectangular shape of the vehicle, and a visible shadow bar around the vehicle's rear bumper;

The paper proposes a data fusion based approach using multiple clue detection by a single camera sensor with substantial improvement in true-positive detection rate, and a lower false-positive alarm rate.

Different to other work that puts more effort into a single solution for vehicle detection, we offer a data fusion approach using a novel boosted classifier called *adaptive global Haar classification* (AGHaar) in conjunction with corner and line features to effectively detect vehicles in far and close distance as well as day and night.

The paper is organized as follows: Application of a new variant of Haar features for vehicle detection is introduced in Section 2. Section 3 discusses on line and corner feature analysis for refining initial detection results. In Section 4, a comprehensive multi-data fusion solution model is provided for robust vehicle detection based on the Dempster-Shafer theory. Section 5 provides experimental results, and Section 6 concludes.

2 Adaptive Global Haar Classifier

As an extension for standard Haar-like features, in this section we review on a recently introduced idea of *global Haar features* [21] which will be integrated in training phase of our vehicle classifier. We also improve our classifier to be *adaptive* to intensity changes to ensure robust vehicle detection at day, night, or challenging lighting conditions.

Global Haar Features. Following Viola and Jones [25], Haar features are widely used for solving various object detection problems (e.g., see [19,26]). The value of such a Haar feature is defined by a weighted difference of image values in *white* or *black* adjacent rectangular patches, efficiently calculated by using an integral image [3].

In contrast to standard Haar features that consider adjacent black and white regions (we call them local features), here [21] as our recent work, for the first time we introduced *global Haar features*, to be used in conjunction with local features. Despite we initially used global Haar features for face detection in noisy and challenging condition, however, these features can be utilized for many other object detection purposes. Global Haar features provide global intensity information in a given sliding window, which can represent, for example, nearly uniform intensities on a road surface (i.e. when there is no other object shown in the reference window), or a nearly constant intensity of a vehicle (i.e. if a vehicle overlaps the reference window). Figure 1 represents the extraction of two global Haar-features from a given standard (local) Haar feature.

Classifier's Parameter Adaptation. Extending another recent work on eye detection under various lighting conditions [20], we try to have our vehicle classifier to be adaptive for day and night condition.

In addition to parameters that affect the training phase of a classifier (such as training feature set), there are parameters which need to be tuned during the application phase. The main parameters are: sliding window size (SWS), scale factor (SF) which specifies the rate by which SWS increases in each new iteration of the search, and the minimum number of neighbours (MNN) which is required to confirm multiple neighbour detections as a single object. Although most of research consider some fixed optimum values for these parameters, we experienced these parameters can be highly variable depending on the intensity changes of road scene. In our solution we dynamically revise and change these parameters based on road and sky intensity variation to pursue an efficient vehicle detection both in day or night conditions; see Fig. 2 for an illustration.

Instead of assigning fixed values for SWS, SF and MNN, we decide having those parameters to be time variant and adaptive, depending on the overall intensity of

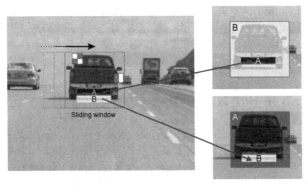

Fig. 1. *Left*: A sliding window with three local Haar features. *Right*: Extension of a given local feature into two global features.

current input frame and temporal information. For example for low light conditions, the MNN should have a smaller value than for ideal lighting conditions, because a classifier has a reduced chance of multiple object detections in dark conditions than for day light conditions. The question to be answered remains that what should be our reference for measuring the overall light intensity in an input frame?

Figure 2 illustrates pixel sampling from expected sky and road background regions, to estimate lighting conditions. We apply a 4-patch hybrid intensity averaging at expected sky and road regions, shown as S_l and S_r, and R_l and R_r; we use $w/20 \times 20$ and $20 \times h/20$ patches where w and h is width and height of the frame, respectively. Then, based on the identified lighting situation, we adaptively adjust the classifier parameters for more efficient vehicle detection.

Since a strong reflection spot, street lights, or a very dark shadow may fall in one or some of those four patches, we apply a heuristic intensity averaging including standard *mean* and *mode* (Mo) averaging to make sure we are measuring a balance of actual intensity in the whole scene as per below:

$$
I_s(\lambda) = \frac{1}{2}\left[\left(\lambda \cdot \text{Mo}(S_l) + \frac{(1-\lambda)}{m}\sum_{i=1}^{m}S_l^i\right) + \left(\lambda \cdot \text{Mo}(S_r) + \frac{(1-\lambda)}{n}\sum_{j=1}^{n}S_r^j\right)\right]
$$

where $I_s(\lambda)$ is the hybrid intensity value of the *sky* region, and m and n are the total numbers of pixels in the S_l and S_r regions.

Figure 2, on the right side, demonstrates an "acceptable" segmentation of sky and road areas. Dark and light blue segments are detected based on mean intensity measurements of S_l and S_r, with a variation of ± 10. Similarly, the green segments show the road surface based on R_l and R_r. In the shown example of a night scene (bottom, left), bright pixels occur in the S_l region; this influenced our mean-intensity measurement of the left part of the sky; consequently, dark

Fig. 2. Dynamic averaging for ground and sky region under day or night conditions

blue segments (bottom, right) show regions around the street lights, instead of being light blue as the sky in general.

However, on the other hand, measurement in S_r supported the acceptable segmentation of the sky shown as a light-blue segment.

The *mode pixel value* (i.e. the pixel value with the highest frequency of repetition in $S_l \cup S_r$) determines which of the resulting segments (light blue or dark blue) is a better representative of the sky intensity. By assigning $\lambda=0.66$, we consider a *double importance factor* for the detected mode intensity compared to a standard mean; this consequently reduces the negative impact of any inappropriate segmentation. In other words, for the night scene shown at the bottom of Fig. 2, the final value of $I_s(\lambda)$ is automatically much closer to the intensity of light blue segments rather than to that of the dark blue segments. A similar approach is applied for road background intensity evaluation, $I_r(\lambda)$, which is shown by dark and light green segments.

As a final stage for defining the adaptive Haar-feature based detector, we experimentally adjust ten sets of optimum values for classifier parameters SWS, SF, and MNN based on values of $I_s(\lambda)$ and $I_r(\lambda)$ for the upper and lower part of the input video sequence. This parameter adaptation is then extended for the whole intensity range of 0-255 based on a cubic interpolation, as outlined in [20].

3   Line and Corner Features

The described AGHaar classifier provides us an *initial* vehicle detection. Although the proposed classifier clearly outperforms LBP and standard Haar classifiers, we still consider those detections by AGHaar as being vehicle *candidates* or *RoIs* only. In order to have more accurate results (i.e. less false-positives) we continue our evaluation by analysing line and corner features before confirming a RoI as being a vehicle.

Horizontal Edges. Instead of (e.g.) shadow analysis like [1], we take parallel horizontal edges into account as a more reliable feature for pointing to a possible existence of a vehicle in a RoI. Our hypothesis is that horizontal edge features can be perceived due to depth differences between bumper and body of a vehicle, edges around a vehicle's registration plate, or horizontal borders of windshields.

We apply the *progressive probabilistic Hough transform* (PPHT) [10] for fast and real-time detection of horizontal lines only. The PPHT was designed following the *standard Hough transform* (SHT) as introduced by Duda and Hart [4]: a line L in the xy coordinate system can be represented by polar coordinates (θ, ρ) as follows: $\rho = x \cdot cos\ \theta + y \cdot sin\ \theta$. Detected edge pixels $P_i = (x_i, y_i)$ in xy-space are transformed into curves in $\theta\rho$-space, also known as *Hough space*, or, in its discrete version, as *accumulator space*. In case of the PPHT, a voting scheme is applied to tackle with the high computational cost of SHT. While in SHT all edge pixels are mapped into the accumulator space, PPHT only votes based on a fraction of randomly selected pixels. There is one voting bin for each line candidate, and a minimum number of pixels (i.e. of votes) is considered as

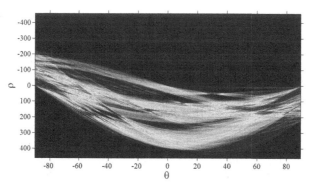

Fig. 3. Edge pixels of a sample road scene mapped into $\theta\rho$-space. The accumulator values are shown using a colour key where dark blue is for zero, red is for high values, and light blue for low positive values.

a threshold for detecting a line. For shorter lines a higher spatial density of supporting pixels is required, while for longer lines less spatial density of supporting pixels is sufficient. Overall, the PPHT ensures much faster line detection with results being about equal in accuracy with those obtained by SHT [8]. Figure 3 shows an accumulator space graph, obtained from a real world road scene. The figure illustrates that high accumulator values are close to the leftmost or rightmost borders at $-90°$ or $+90°$. This confirms for a road scene that the number of horizontal lines is considerably higher than for other slopes. In order to aim for horizontal lines $y \approx const$ we define two *ranges of interest* for θ:

1. $\quad 90° - \tau \leq \theta \leq 90°$
2. $\quad -90° < \theta \leq -90° + \tau$

Note that because ρ is considered in PPHT for positive and negative values, θ is only in the range between $-90°$ to $+90°$.

Mapping back from Hough space to Cartesian space, Figure 4-right shows detected horizontal lines for the road scene already used for Figure 3.

As illustrated, we can expect detection of one or more horizontal lines per vehicle, for any vehicle in a road scene, either for short distances or far vehicles.

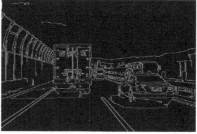

Fig. 4. Horizontal line detection by our customized PPHT

Corner Detection. Figure 4, right, also illustrates that there might be a few more horizontal lines which do not belong to vehicles, for example due to shadows of vehicles, trees, clouds, or rectangular traffic signs (e.g. large boards). However, shaded regions or traffic signs usually have a plain or simple texture. In order to avoid false detections, we also analyse corners in the scene. Our experimental studies clearly indicate that vehicle regions have typically a higher density of corner points than road, sky, or other background regions (see Fig. 5). The visual complexity of a car's rear-view is defined by combinations of a registration plate, taillights, a bumper, and the vehicle body. This complexity defines typically significant corners for a vehicle, especially at regions down the rear windshield.

We decided for using the *Shi-Tomasi method* [23] for detecting "appropriate" corner points due to its performance in our application context. A corner is defined by larger intensity differences to adjacent pixels in comparison to non-corner image regions. In this method, an $m \times n$ subwindow W_p is considered which slides through the input image I, defined by the reference pixel $p = (x, y)$ in the upper left corner. (For example, m and n is chosen between 10 and 20.) The weighted difference between window W_p and an adjacent window of the same size, and at reference point $p + (u, v)$, is measured as follows:

$$D_p(u, v) = \sum_{i=1}^{m} \sum_{j=1}^{n} w_{ij} [I(x_i + u, y_j + v) - I(x_i, y_j)]^2 \tag{1}$$

where $0 \le u \le m/2$ and $0 \le v \le n/2$, for $x_i = x + i$ and $y_j = y + j$; w_{ij} are the used weights at window positions (i, j); they are either identical 1, or a sampled Gauss function. Using the linear terms of the Taylor expansion of those differences only, it follows that

$$D_p(u, v) \approx \sum_{i=1}^{m} \sum_{j=1}^{n} w_{ij} [u \cdot I_x(x_i, y_j) + v \cdot I_y(x_i, y_j)]^2$$

$$= \sum_{i=1}^{m} \sum_{j=1}^{n} w_{ij} \left(u^2 I_x^2 + 2uv I_x I_y + v^2 I_y^2 \right) \tag{2}$$

where I_x and I_y stand for the derivatives of I in $x-$ and $y-$direction, respectively. By converting into matrix format, and not including arguments (x_i, y_j), we have that

$$D_p(u, v) \approx [u \; v] \left(\sum_{i=1}^{m} \sum_{j=1}^{n} w_{ij} \begin{bmatrix} I_x^2 & I_x I_y \\ I_x I_y & I_y^2 \end{bmatrix} \right) \begin{bmatrix} u \\ v \end{bmatrix} = [u \; v] \, \mathbf{M} \begin{bmatrix} u \\ v \end{bmatrix} \tag{3}$$

where $\mathbf{M}$ is short for the matrix defined in Equ. (3). Let λ_1 and λ_2 be the eigenvalues of $\mathbf{M}$, representing the differences between original and moved window, and $R = \min\{\lambda_1, \lambda_2\}$. Corner points are selected by comparing R with a given threshold; if R is greater than this threshold then the centre pixel of W_p is selected as being a corner point; see [23].

The corner points shown in Figure 5 have been detected this way. This method provides the expected results of higher corner point densities in lower parts of

Fig. 5. Detected corner points are more dense in vehicle's back-side regions

the vehicles' rear view, especially around the registration plate, the bumper, taillights, or tires.

4   Data Fusion and Temporal Information

The AGHaar method alone is robust enough in a majority of road scenarios but not for challenging lighting conditions. However, in order to ensure an even more reliable technique we apply data fusion for all the available information clues.

As possible approaches for data fusion, we considered the Bayesian or the Dempster-Shafer [22] framework. The Bayesian method interprets weights of input entities as probabilities. The Dempster-Shafer theory (also called *theory of belief*, or *D-S theory* for short) assigns "masses" based on human expertise which only approximate the concept of probabilities. Since the Bayesian approach is based on "pure" statistical analysis, you also need to be "pure" (i.e. very accurate) on providing all statistical data for each source of information. This, consequently, comes with the requirement of a comprehensive initial database analysis among a wide range of recorded videos from different roads scenes. If not doing so, resulting inaccurate weight assignments can cause completely wrong outcomes of data fusion [9].

The D-S theory is well-known for its effectiveness to express uncertain judgments of experts by serving as an alternative method of modelling evidence and uncertainty compared to the Bayesian probabilistic approach. The D-S theory is based on two ideas: *(1)* Define a degree of belief to identify "subjective probabilities" for a related question, and *(2)* Dempster's rule to combine degrees of belief from independent items of evidence.

Using D-S theory for data fusion for vehicle detection, we not only consider two categories of "vehicle" and "no-vehicle" but also we assign a degree of belief for an "unknown" status. Considering a mass for the "unknown" status we are adding a safety margin to avoid potential wrong decisions. This automatically takes us to more rational decisions based on a combination of information consensus and human expertise; whereas in the Bayesian technique, we only have two probability values (for "existing" or "not existing"), but not a combination of both.

Table 1. Mass assignments for three sources of information

Status	Source 1 (m_1) AGHaar	Source 2 (m_2) Corner features	Source 3 (m_3) Horizontal lines
T	75%	55%*	65%*
NT	15%	15%	20%
U	10%	20%	15%
Total	100%	100%	100%

* Maximum mass value if features match with threshold τ.

In the considered context we experienced that a D-S theory-based fusion approach leads to more acceptable results, especially if we have incompleteness of information and a situation where the accuracy of each information source cannot be assured individually.

Let $\Theta = \{T, NT\}$ be the set representing the state of vehicle detection from each of the three available information sources described in Sections 2 and 3 (i.e. AGHaar, corner features, and horizontal lines) where T represents that target (vehicle) is detected, and NT stands for non-target. Each element in the power set $2^\Theta = \{ \varnothing, \{T\}, \{NT\}, \{T, NT\} \}$ is considered to be a proposition concerning the actual state of the vehicle detection system.

Based on the theory of evidence, a mass m_i is assigned for each element in 2^Θ, where $1 \leq i \leq 3$ stands for the considered information source. Value $i = 1$ is for AGHaar, $i = 2$ for corner features, and $i = 3$ for horizontal lines. Those three functions m_i are also called *basic belief assignments for information sources* 1, 2, and 3, satisfying $m_i : 2^\Theta \to [0, 1]$ with the two properties

$$m_i(\varnothing) = 0 \quad \text{and} \quad \sum_{A \in 2^\Theta} m_i(A) = 1$$

The mass $m_i(A)$ represents the ratio of all relative and available evidences that support the validity of state A from the ith information source.

For example, considering AGHaar as our main sources of vehicle detection, we consider $m_1(T) = 0.75$, $m_1(NT) = 0.15$, and $m_1(U) = 0.1$ which means that we have a belief into the true detection rate by AGHaar in 75% of all cases, we also have a 15% belief for false detections, and have no opinion in 10% of the cases (unknown assignment) due to lack of knowledge or incompleteness of analysis. Table 1 summarizes the masses defined for the three information sources.

Depending on size and distance of rectangular regions selected by AGHaar as vehicle candidates, we expect a number of corners and horizontal lines that fall into the lower part of the RoI if the candidate is actually a true positive (a vehicle).

The closer to the chosen threshold τ (as defined above) the more the possibility of being confirmed as a vehicle. In other words, if the numbers of detected corners and horizontal lines are less than the defined threshold then we decrease our level of belief by appropriately decreasing the default masses of $m_2(\mathrm{T})$ and $m_3(\mathrm{T})$, and, on the other hand, by increasing $m_2(NT)$ and $m_3(NT)$ to reject the false candidates in the fusion process. However, $m_2(U)$ and $m_3(U)$ remain unchanged.

Also, in order to prevent incorrect updates of m_2 and m_3 due to noise, we apply weighted averaging on the masses by considering the masses allocated for n (e.g., $n = 5$) past frames to utilize temporal information as well:

$$\overline{m}_i = \frac{\sum_{t=1}^{n} \delta_t \, m_i}{\sum_{t=1}^{n} \delta_t} \tag{4}$$

In case $n = 5$ we choose, for example, $\delta_5 = 0.5$ and $\delta_1 \ldots \delta_4$ are set to be 0.2.

Considering 30 frame processing per second, in our 3.2 GHz Corei7 platform, the masses in the past few frames should remain almost close to the actual updated values as per previous step, or just having a 'smooth' change. If a sudden change happens in the current frame due to considerable noise (e.g. intense light) then the weighted averaging contributes to the masses from temporal information to maintain a moderated mass for the current frame.

Considering the masses m_i as being the confidence in each element of 2^Θ, we measure the combined confidence value $m_{1,2,3}(Z)$ by fusing information from Sources 1 to 3 following Dempster's rule of combination:

$$m_{1,2,3}(Z) = (m_1 \oplus m_2 \oplus m_3)(Z) = \frac{\sum_{A \cap B \cap C = Z} m_1(A) \cdot m_2(B) \cdot m_3(C)}{1 - \sum_{A \cap B \cap C = \emptyset} m_1(A) \cdot m_2(B) \cdot m_3(C)} \tag{5}$$

where $\oplus$ denotes the orthogonal sum which is defined by summing the mass product over all elements in the numerator part whose intersections are $A \cap B \cap C = Z$, and the denominator applies normalization in the range of $[0, 1]$.

5   Experimental Results

In order to validate the proposed method we used the iROADS dataset [18] that includes a diverse set of road scenes, recorded in day, night, under various weather and lighting conditions. Figures 6 and 7 show sample results and *receiver operating characteristic* (ROC) curves for situation *day*. LBP based classification shows the lowest detection rate and the highest rate of false positives. While AGHaar alone performs better than LBP and Standard Haar detector, the D-S fusion-based method outperforms the best results with a smaller rate of false alarms. Figures 8 provide samples of results for rainy night conditions. In contrast to results for situation *day*, for situation *night* the AGHaar method did not perform visibly better than standard Haar. This is mainly due to reflections of street lights on rain droplets (see Fig. 8, top) which lead to false alarms. However, the D-S fusion method shows still a high true detection rate, similar to situations *day*, with only a minor increase in false alarms (raised from 10 to 19) which is a very small portion considering the total number of true detections in our test database.

Fig. 6. Vehicle detection for situation *day* light. *Top row*: Left to right: LBP based detections, standard Haar-like classification, improved detections based on AGHaar method. *Bottom row*: Left to right, Detected corner features in road scene. Horizontal edges detected, Fusion-based detection based on AGHaar RoI, corner and edges clues.

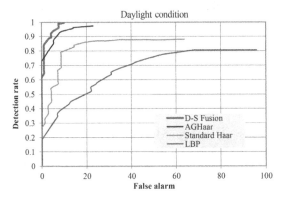

Fig. 7. Performance evaluation for situation *day*

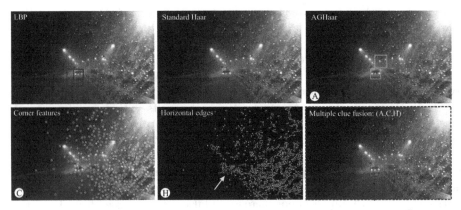

Fig. 8. Vehicle detection in situation *night*. Description of images as in Fig. 6.

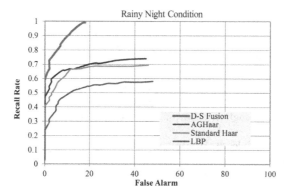

Fig. 9. Performance evaluation for situation *night*

6   Concluding Remarks

The paper outlined an efficient proposal for monocular vehicle detection using only camera data recorded in a driving vehicle. Experimental results proved a superior performance based on the AGHaar classifier and multiple feature clue fusion, compared to the well known methods of LBP or standard Haar-like classifier.

Low computational cost of the implemented D-S fusion technique allowed us to keep maintaining real-time processing while taking the advantages of Multi-source data, extracted from only a single camera.

Validation tests on the comprehensive iROADS dataset also confirmed the robustness of the method across diverse lighting and weather conditions.

Acknowledgment. The authors thank professor Reinhard Klette for discussions and comments on the paper.

References

1. Ali, A., Afghani, S.: Shadow based on-road vehicle detection and verification using Haar wavelet packet transform. In: Proc. IEEE Int. Conf. Information Communication Technologies, pp. 346–350 (2005)
2. Choi, J.: Realtime on-road vehicle detection with optical flows and Haar-like feature detectors. Technical Report, CS Department, University of Illinois at Urbana-Champaign (2006)
3. Crow, F.: Summed-area tables for texture mapping. Computer Graphics 18, 207–212 (1984)
4. Duda, R.O., Hart, P.E.: Use of the Hough transformation to detect lines and curves in pictures. Communication ACM 15, 11–15 (1972)
5. Garcia, F., Cerri, P., Broggi, A., Escalera, A., Armingo, J.M.: Data fusion for overtaking vehicle detection based on radar and optical flow. In: Proc. IEEE Intelligent Vehicles Symposium, pp. 494–499 (2012)
6. Han, S., Han, Y., Hahn, H.: Vehicle detection method using Haar-like feature on real time system. In: Proc. World Academy of Science, Engineering and Technology, pp. 455–459 (2009)

7. Haselhoff, A., Kummert, A.: A vehicle detection system based on Haar and triangle features. In: Proc. IEEE Intelligent Vehicles Symposium, pp. 261–266 (2009)
8. Kiryati, N., Eldar, Y., Bruckstein, A.M.: A probabilistic Hough transform. Pattern Recognition 24, 303–316 (1991)
9. Koks, D., Challa, S.: An introduction to Bayesian and Dempster-Shafer data fusion. Technical report DSTO-TR-1436, DSTO Systems Sciences Laboratory (2005)
10. Matas, J., Galambos, C., Kittler, J.V.: Robust detection of lines using the progressive probabilistic Hough transform. Computer Vision Image Understanding 78, 119–137 (2000)
11. Moutarde, F., Stanciulescu, B., Breheret, A.: Real-time visual detection of vehicles and pedestrians with new efficient AdaBoost features. In: Proc. Workshop Planning Perception Navigation Intelligent Vehicles (2008)
12. National Highway Traffic Safety Administration. Traffic safety facts, U.S. Department of Transportation (2012)
13. Nguyen, T.T., Grabner, H., Bischof, H., Gruber, B.: On-line boosting for car detection from aerial images. In: Proc. IEEE Int. Conf. Research Innovation Vision Future, pp. 87–95 (2007)
14. Nguyen, V.D., Nguyen, T.T., Nguyen, D.D., Jeon, J.W.: Toward real-time vehicle detection using stereo vision and an evolutionary algorithm. In: Proc. Vehicular Technology Conf., pp. 1–5 (2012)
15. Ojala, T., Pietikäinen, Mäenpää, T.: Multiresolution grey-scale and rotation invariant texture classification with local binary patterns. IEEE Trans. Pattern Analysis Machine Intelligence 24, 971–987 (2002)
16. O'Malley, R., Jones, E., Glavin, M.: Rear-lamp vehicle detection and tracking in low-exposure colour video for night conditions. IEEE Trans. Intelligent Transportation Systems 11, 453–462 (2010)
17. Qian, Z., Shi, H., Yang, J.: Video vehicle detection based on local features. Advanced Materials Research 186, 56–60 (2011)
18. Rezaei, M., Terauchi, M.: iROADS dataset (Intercity Roads and Adverse Driving Scenarios). Available in enpeda image sequence analysis test site – EISATS (September 10, 2013), http://www.mi.auckland.ac.nz/EISATS
19. Rezaei, M., Klette, R.: Simultaneous analysis of driver behaviour and road condition for driver distraction detection. Int. J. Image Data Fusion 2, 217–236 (2011)
20. Rezaei, M., Klette, R.: Adaptive Haar-like classifier for eye status detection under non-ideal lighting conditions. In: Proc., Image Vision Computing, New Zealand, pp. 521–526 (2012)
21. Rezaei, M., Ziaei Nafchi, H., Morales, S.: Global Haar-like Features: A New Extension of Classic Haar Features for Efficient Face Detection in Noisy Images. In: 6th Pacific-Rim Symposium on Image and Video Technology (2013)
22. Shafer, G.: A Mathematical Theory of Evidence. Princeton University Press (1976)
23. Shi, J., Tomasi, C.: Good features to track. In: Proc. Computer Vision Pattern Recognition, pp. 593–600 (1994)
24. Toulminet, G., Bertozzi, M., Mousset, S., Bensrhair, A., Broggi, A.: Vehicle detection by means of stereo vision-based obstacles features extraction and monocular pattern analysis. IEEE Trans. Image Processing 15, 2364–2375 (2006)
25. Viola, P., Jones, M.: Rapid object detection using a boosted cascade of simple features. In: Proc. Computer Vision Pattern Recognition, pp. 511–518 (2001)
26. Wen, X., Yuan, H., Yang, C., Song, C., Duan, B., Zhao, H.: Improved Haar wavelet feature extraction approaches for vehicle detection. In: Proc. IEEE Intelligent Transportation Systems Conf., pp. 1050–1053 (2007)

UHDB11 Database for 3D-2D Face Recognition

George Toderici[1], Georgios Evangelopoulos[1], Tianhong Fang[1]
Theoharis Theoharis[2,1], and Ioannis A. Kakadiaris[1]

[1] Computational Biomedicine Lab, Department of Computer Science,
University of Houston, Houston, TX 77204, USA
[2] IDI, Norwegian University of Science and Technology (NTNU), Norway

Abstract. Performance boosts in face recognition have been facilitated by the formation of facial databases, with collection protocols customized to address challenges such as light variability, expressions, pose, sensor/modality differences, and, more recently, uncontrolled acquisition conditions. In this paper, we present database UHDB11, to facilitate 3D-2D face recognition evaluations, where the gallery has been acquired using 3D sensors (3D mesh and texture) and the probes using 2D sensors (images). The database consists of samples from 23 individuals, in the form of 2D high-resolution images spanning six illumination conditions and 12 head-pose variations, and 3D facial mesh and texture. It addresses limitations regarding resolution, variability and type of 3D/2D data and has demonstrated to be statistically more challenging, diverse and information rich than existing cohorts of 10 times larger number of subjects. We propose a set of 3D-2D experimental configurations, with frontal 3D galleries and pose-illumination varying probes and provide baseline performance for identification and verification (available at `http://cbl.uh.edu/URxD/datasets`).

Keywords: face recognition, face databases, 3D-2D facial data, illumination, face pose, verification, identification, computer vision.

1 Introduction

Databases for face recognition focus either on the shortcomings of conventional 2D images (*e.g.*, acquisition conditions, inter-person variability) or on the benefits of using alternative sensors and modalities (*e.g.*, 3D scans and facial models). In addition, both modalities are traditionally employed in multimodal, 2D+3D systems [4] where shape and texture features are combined to compute face similarity. Databases that contain both types of data (*i.e.*, 2D and 3D), apart from the 2D texture of a 3D face [11], were designed in order to primarily explore the merits of 3D-3D versus 2D-2D or multi-view 2D-2D recognition when both gallery (or target) and probe (or query) sets originate from the same modality.

A different paradigm for face recognition, proposed to combine the detail captured by 3D data with the practical applicability of a 2D recognition system, is a 3D-2D, cross-modal framework, where the probe and gallery sets are acquired from different sensors. One of the conjectures posed and tested by the Face Recognition Grand Challenge [11] involved the effectiveness of high-resolution 2D images versus 3D scans for recognition. By combining the two in an asymmetric, cross-sensor framework, efficient,

R. Klette, M. Rivera, and S. Satoh (Eds.): PSIVT 2013, LNCS 8333, pp. 73–86, 2014.
© Springer-Verlag Berlin Heidelberg 2014

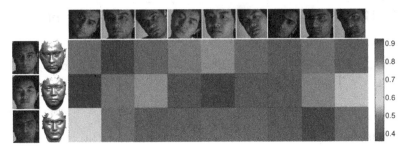

Fig. 1. 3D-2D face recognition using 3D samples for the gallery and 2D probes. Color represents similarity values in $[0, 1]$.

discriminative and practical systems and methods can arise for face verification or face identification (Fig. 1).

By inter-changing the type of data for the enrollment and recognition sessions, different practical scenarios can be formulated. A 3D-2D framework, where the need for 3D acquisition hardware is restricted to enrollment only, can facilitate the acquisition, storage and distribution of highly-descriptive databases of 3D models. On a 2D-3D framework, the abundance of existing face databases, composed primarily of 2D data, can provide reference enrollment sets for matching 3D facial scans. 3D-2D (or 2D-3D) face recognition is distinct from *asymmetric* recognition, where shape features are matched against texture features (heterogeneous 3D FR), *3D-aided* recognition, where real or reconstructed 3D models are used for registration or normalization (3D-aided 2D FR), or *multi-modal* recognition, where shape and texture data are fused on a single facial signature (3D+2D FR).

Research on 3D-2D face recognition has been focusing primarily on methods, whose performance is evaluated on existing 3D databases, with a subset of the registered textures of the 3D data used as 2D input. However, a realistic 3D-2D configuration may involve different resolutions, sensors, and acquisition sessions between enrollment and recognition sets. To facilitate research on 3D-2D and 3D-aided 2D face recognition, we created database UHDB11 (University of Houston Database 11), that aims to address 3D-2D database requirements and limitations related to high-resolution data, full-face 3D data and identity-independent variability in pose and lighting conditions. In spite of the small identity sample size, compensated by the relatively large number of probe instances per individual (approx. 70) and the roughly-quantized head-pose (12) and illumination variations (6), database UHDB11 provides challenging data instances for pairwise comparisons and complements the limited (in number) available 3D-2D databases such as FRGC v2.0 [11].

Why is UHDB11 database useful? (i) It provides a 3D+2D modality, asymmetric 3D/2D probe-gallery matches, and data from three modalities per subject (3D shape, 3D texture, 2D image), (ii) it covers different acquisition conditions (posed subjects apart from light conditions), (iii) it simulates realistic application scenarios (3D enrollment and uncontrolled 2D recognition), and (iv) it is statistically more challenging, diverse and information rich than evaluation cohorts of 10 times larger number of subjects [3].

Fig. 2. Sample 2D image and 3D mesh data from the UHDB11 database

Table 1. Databases for 2D-2D and 3D-3D face recognition with variations in: **P** : Pose, **V**: Viewpoints, **I**: Illumination, **E**: Expressions, **M**: Multiple instances/captures, **T**: Time-lapse, **S**: Sessions, **O**: Occlusions, **AU**: Action Units (the levels of variation are given in parentheses).

Database	Ref.	Year	Type	# Subjects	Variation	# Samples
FERET	[10]	2000	2D-2D	1,199	T, M	14,126
CMU PIE	[15]	2002	2D-2D	68	V (13), E (4), I (43)	>41,000
FRGC v2.0	[11]	2005	2D-2D	466	M, I (Controlled/Uncontrolled)	24,042
LFiW	[9]	2007	2D-2D	5,749	Uncontrolled	13,233
CMU Multi-PIE	[7]	2008	2D-2D	337	V (15), E (6), I (19), S (4)	>750,000
GBU	[12]	2011	2D-2D	437	I (Outdoor, Indoor Ambient)	6,510
FRGC v2.0	[11]	2005	3D-3D	466	E (7)	4,007
BU-3DFE	[18]	2006	3D-3D	100	E (7)	2,500
UND ND-2006	[5]	2007	3D-3D	888	M, E (6)	13,450
Bosphorus	[14]	2008	3D-3D	105	P (13), E (6), AU (28), O (4)	4,652
3D TEC	[17]	2011	3D-3D	214	Twins, E (2)	428

The rest of this paper is organized as follows: In Sec. 2, we provide a brief overview of existing databases for 2D-2D and 3D-3D face recognition along with reference cohorts previously used for 3D-2D experiments. In Sec. 3, we outline the purpose and potential use of the proposed 3D-2D database. The data specifications and six potential experimental configurations for 3D-2D benchmarking are presented in Sec. 4, while a baseline evaluation using a system for 3D-2D face recognition is provided in Sec. 5. Limitations and extensions of UHDB11 are discussed in Sec. 6.

2   Face Recognition Databases

The type and variation in existing face recognition databases depends on the challenges aimed to be addressed by each one [6]. Categories include facial expressions [13], uncontrolled acquisition conditions [9], illumination and viewpoints [15,7], different sensors and resolutions [11,4], identity mismatches due to different sessions [12] and even twin subjects [17]. Although a comprehensive review of available databases is out of the scope of this paper, we provide a brief overview of well-established sets (Table 1) in order to highlight their targeted challenges and contrast them to UHDB11.

2.1   Databases for 2D-2D Recognition

The FERET database [10] was one of the first systematically collected sets for large scale 2D face recognition evaluations. It contains 14,126 images of 1,199 individuals, with time-lapse and multiple sessions for some of the subjects (365 duplicate sets). The average inter-pupil distance (IPD) in the FERET faces is 68 pixels with a standard deviation of 8.7 pixels. Controlled light conditions were also used in the CMU PIE database [15], which in addition included viewpoint variations, resulting in different head poses, using a fixed camera grid and a still subject. Data are color images of dimension 640 × 486 pixels. The extended CMU Multi-PIE [7] increased the number of subjects (337), acquisition sessions and resolution of the collected images to 3,072 × 2,048, with an IPD typically more than 400 pixels. The Face Recognition Grand Challenge [11] defined recognition frameworks on the 2D sets of FRGC v2.0 (Experiments 1 and 4) on probe sets of size 16,028 and 8,014 for controlled and uncontrolled (*e.g.*, outdoor) conditions. Multiple viewpoints or sessions per subject were also provided for multi-still recognition (Experiment 2). High-resolution, frontal images, of average IPD 175 ± 36 pixels, from the uncontrolled set of the FRVT 2006 Notre Dame data were grouped in three partitions of increasing difficulty (easy, average and hard matching pairs) on the GBU database [12]. Labeled Faces in the Wild (LFiW) [9] was proposed as a large scale, unconstrained recognition benchmark, where both probe and gallery faces can vary considerably with respect to non-identity or imaging factors. The images are of resolution 250 × 250 pixels and were collected for 5,749 subjects using face detection on web data.

2.2   Databases for 3D-3D Recognition

FRGC v2.0 is a multi-modal database which was designed to explore the independent and comparative role of high resolution images, multiple captures, and 3D facial imagery for face recognition [11]. The size of the FRGC v2.0 3D set is 4,007 samples, corresponding to 1-22 instances for each of 466 subjects. Samples are range data of resolution 640 × 480 obtained from a structured light sensor, with a registered texture image of the same dimensions and an average IPD of 160 pixels. Four facial landmarks are provided as meta-data. The largest database of 3D facial data is UND ND-2006 [5], originally proposed for multi-instance gallery and facial component studies, containing 13,450 scans for 888 subjects. Variations of identity among twins are captured in the 3D TEC [17] database that contains the 3D facial data for 107 pairs of identical twins.

BU-3DFE [18] was the first 3D database developed for facial expression analysis. It includes facial meshes for 100 subjects, under a neutral and six prototypical expressions, on four intensity levels. The 3D model data were acquired using the 3dMD system [2], cropped to an effective facial region size of $13K - 21K$ polygons, with an associated texture of 512 × 512 pixels. The locations of 83 facial points are also specified per sample. Similarly, the Bosphorus database [14] consists of 3D data captured using a structured-light 3D sensor, for the study of multi-expression, multi-pose 3D recognition. Data variability includes facial expressions from six prototypical emotions and 28 groups of similar action units (lower, upper and combinations), pose variations in pitch and yaw angles and occlusions. The texture images are of relatively high resolution $(1,600 \times 1,200$ pixels) and the segmented 3D facial areas correspond to approximately 35K vertices. A set of 24 manually labeled facial landmarks is provided as meta-data.

Table 2. Databases and experimental cohorts for 3D-2D face recognition

	Source	Subj.	Gallery Size	Probe Size	Probe Type	Resolution
FRGC-Exp 5 [11]	FRGC v2.0	466	4,007	16,028	2D Image	1,200 × 1,600
FRGC-Exp 6 [11]	FRGC v2.0	466	4,007	8,014	2D Image	2,272 × 1,704
Huang *et al.* [8]	FRGC v2.0	466	466	3,541	2D Texture	640 × 480
Al-Osaimi *et al.* [3]	FRGC v2.0	250	250	470	2D Texture	640 × 480
GBU/FRGC	GBU, FRGC v2.0	437	186	(set) 2,170	2D Image	3,008 × 2,000
UHDB11-Exp. 1	UHDB11	23	23	1,602	2D Image	3,888 × 2,592

2.3 Cohorts for 3D-2D Recognition

Several partitions or combinations of existing sets with 2D and 3D data can be employed for 3D-2D experiments (Table 2). Two of the configurations for FRGC v2.0 [11] specify a 3D-2D scenario, where the gallery is the full set of 3D data (4,007) and each probe is a single 2D image. For controlled (Experiment 5) and uncontrolled (Experiment 6) acquisition, the probe set size is 16,028 and 8,014, of pixel resolution 1,200 × 1,600 and 2,272 × 1,704 respectively.

Huang *et al.* [8] designed an asymmetric 3D-2D recognition configuration from the 4,007 3D samples of FRGC v2.0 that correspond to 466 subjects. The first neutral-expression instance from each subject was used to form a 3D gallery of 466, and the texture images of the remaining 3,541 instances, cropped to an effective size of 175 × 190, form the 2D probe set. Evaluations involve 2D-2D (texture-based), 3D-2D (asymmetric) and fused matching. Similarly, Al-Osaimi *et al.* [3] used 470 textures as probes, matched against 250 3D galleries in an open recognition cohort, for studying illumination normalization. Alternative cohorts can be formed through the overlap of subject identity sets for databases originating from the same Institutes. For example, using the 2D images from GBU [12] (2,170 per partition) and the corresponding 3D data from FRGC v2.0, following the identity naming convention of the UND data, a 3D-2D experiment of 186 3D targets and 2,170 probes can be defined for the difficult set.

Compared to these cohorts, UHDB11 proposes to address limitations regarding resolution, variability and type of 3D/2D data. FRGC v2.0, for example, offers a large-scale framework, however with: (i) frontal-only 2D probes, (ii) lower resolution, (iii) no 2D images available for the 3D gallery (3D/2D same session) and (iv) no quantization of the space of (illumination) variations that can facilitate condition-specific quantitative analysis. With respect to [3], empirical statistical evidence from 3D-2D and 2D-2D recognition suggests that UHDB11 (i) provides richer information (higher pairwise score variance) from less subjects, and (ii) is more challenging (in terms of verification performance and match-non-match score separability).

3   UHDB11 Intended Purpose and Uses

The intended use of the developed database is primarily the performance and robustness evaluation of 3D-2D face recognition algorithms under sample variability related

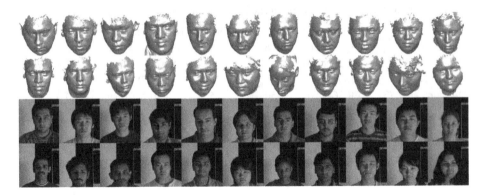

Fig. 3. Database samples acquired with single light (3) and frontal pose (5) as raw 3D (top), cropped in a sphere of radius 150 units centered at the tip of the nose, and 2D textures (bottom). The samples correspond to the gallery set of the full UHDB11 3D-2D cohort (Exp. 1).

to pose and/or lighting. The enrollment set, referred also as gallery or target, is the collection of data with known identity and the recognition set, referred as probe or query, is the collection of samples of unknown identity that are acquired off- or on-line. The recognition set can be restricted to the gallery identities (closed set) or include previously unseen samples (open set). For *face verification*, where a claimed identity is verified on the set of gallery identities, a decision for a positive match is obtained on a one-to-one matching basis. For *face identification*, the closest ranking identity is retrieved after one-to-many matching.

In a 3D-2D recognition setting the gallery data are 3D and the probe data 2D. If the gallery is represented by both 2D and 3D modalities, template face signatures can be extracted using any aspect of face appearance (texture and/or shape). Conversely, a 2D-3D setting yields comparisons of 3D probes to 2D gallery images. By specifying close-set data partitions and inter-changing the role and number of probe and gallery instances, both settings can be explored through the proposed database. In terms of acquisition conditions, UHDB11 can be used to quantify the effects of pose (head rotation in 2D views) and illumination (intensity, direction, shadows) on recognition performance. Different cohorts can be formed adapted to pose, lighting or their combinations. In addition, methods developed for multiple gallery instances, for enhancing the target set or normalizing score values, can be assessed since multiple captures per subject are available. A suggested list of experimental configurations is provided in Sec. 4.2.

With both 3D and 2D data available, the comparison of 3D-2D frameworks to their 2D-2D or 3D-3D counterparts on the same data is advocated [11,16]. We use the following definitions: *Image* refers to a 2D still obtained via a photographic camera, *shape* refers to the 3D data component acquired by a 3D scanner and *texture* to the corresponding 2D component, registered to the 3D. UHDB11 can be used to evaluate image-image algorithms for conventional 2D face recognition and 3D model-based, image-image methods for 3D-aided 2D face recognition. Likewise, it can assist benchmarking of asymmetric (*e.g.*, texture-image, shape-image) [8] or multimodal schemes (shape/texture-image) [4] for performance evaluation across features and modalities.

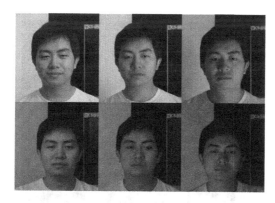

Fig. 4. Illumination variations in 2D images. Rows correspond to light arrays positioned left and right from the subject respectively. Columns correspond to lower, middle, upper positioned lights. Different lights are indexed 1-6, from upper left to lower right.

4   Database Description

4.1   Acquisition and Specifications

Three-dimensional data were captured using a 3dMD two-pod optical scanner [2] and 2D data using a commercial Canon DSLR camera. Lighting condition variations were obtained using multiple diffuse lights, from incandescent light bulbs with approximate color temperature of $2,800K$. Both 3D and 2D data were acquired from 23 subjects of different ethnic groups and gender, under all combinations of six illumination conditions and twelve head poses, four yaw and three roll rotations, resulting in 72 different pose/light variations per subject. From the 23×72 pool, 31 instances have been removed due to inconsistent specifications or corrupted data, yielding 1,625 samples across subjects and acquisition conditions.

Six directional lights (indexed by 1-6) were positioned on the sides of the camera pair in two stacked, vertical arrays (lights 1-3 left and lights 4-6 right), simulating directional light conditions on the face, apart from the ambient room light. Figure 4 illustrates the lighting conditions formed on a frontal face from the left (top row) and the right (bottom row) light arrays. For each illumination condition, a subject was asked to face four different points in the room, generating rotations on the Y axis (yaw angles). For each rotation on Y, three images with rotations on the Z axis (roll angles) were acquired, assuming a coordinate system with the Z axis pointing towards the camera. In Fig. 5, rows correspond to yaw and columns to roll pose variations.

Table 3. UHDB11 face sizes (inter-pupil distance in units)

	Min	Max	Mean	Median	Std. Dev.
Gallery (3D)	61	70	66	66	2
Gallery (2D)	349	440	404	406	25
Probe (2D)	253	511	402	400	34

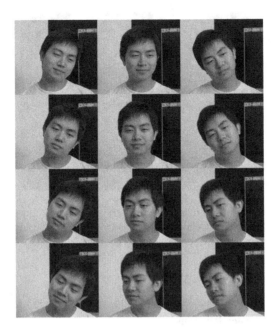

Fig. 5. Head pose variations in 2D images. Rows correspond to yaw and columns to roll rotations. Different poses are indexed 1-12 (upper left to lower right).

Since poses in images are the result of actual head movement (*i.e.*, camera configuration is fixed) as opposed to varying the camera viewpoints (as in most 2D databases), precise ground truth for yaw and roll degrees is not available (*e.g.*, through camera information and pose from calibration parameters). Poses are quantized with respect to the virtual positions and instructions given to subjects during acquisition. A finer distribution of the rotation angles can be obtained through automatic pose estimation using 3D-2D landmark correspondences.

The 2D images are high-resolution color JPEGs of size $3{,}888 \times 2{,}592$ pixels, and the textures for the 3D facial meshes are bitmaps (BMP) of dimension $2{,}732 \times 1{,}948$ pixels. The raw 3D data include the upper torso and subject head, whereas the head area corresponds roughly to $10K - 15K$ vertices and $20K - 30K$ triangles, depending on head size. Data pre-processing can include isolating the 3D facial area by defining a sphere around the most extruded facial location (tip of nose). The resulting 3D sets (Fig. 3,7) range from $9.5K$ (min) to $17.5K$ (max) vertices and $18K$ to $35K$ triangles, depending on face size.

Mesh data were reconstructed from the stereo pair as a single point cloud, triangulated in a polygonal mesh. The 3dMD acquisition system is composed from two stereo cameras (pods), under different viewpoints and provides a $180°$ face coverage (ear-to-ear), with approximately 1.5 *ms* capture speed at the highest resolution. Data are captured as a single point cloud from the stereo pair with a surface accuracy of less than 0.2 *mm* RMS [2].

Table 4. UHDB11 database evaluation configurations and experiments

Setting	Type	Gallery		Probes	
		# Instances (per subject)	# Light - # Pose	# Instances	# Light - # Pose
Exp. 1	Full	23 (1)	1-1	1602	6-12
Exp. 2	Multi-sample	138 (6)	6	1487	6-12
Exp. 3	Light Var.	23 (1)	1-1	115	5-1
Exp. 4	Pose Var.	23 (1)	1-1	250	1-11
Exp. 5	Yaw Var.	23 (1)	1-1	382	6-3
Exp. 6	Op. Light	23 (1)	1-1	814	3-12

Fig. 6. Sample 3D data with head pose, corresponding to the single-subject poses of the multi-sample gallery (Exp. 2 in Table 4)

4.2   Cohorts and 3D-2D Experiments

The multitude of illumination/pose conditions on UHDB11 enables the specification of different 3D-2D verification and identification tasks. As a reference, we define six experimental settings (Table 4), for which the verification rate at 10^{-3} false acceptance rate and rank-1 identification rate can be used, at a minimum, as performance metrics for benchmark comparisons.

Exp. 1 - Full set, frontal galleries. The default 3D-2D configuration is designed as a closed-set experiment, with 23 gallery datasets (3D mesh/texture, 2D image), shown in Fig. 3, and 1,602 2D probe images. The gallery is composed of a single scan, texture and image per subject, of frontal pose and unique light condition (3). The remaining, multiple 2D images per subject are used for the probe set.

Exp. 2 - Multi-sample galleries: For the effect of multi-instance enrollment, a configuration with multiple 3D data for each of the 23 subjects is used as gallery. Six unique pose-light instances per subject are used as gallery data, forming a total set of 138. Figure 6 depicts an example of multi-sample 3D data for a single subject. The remaining 1,487 samples are used as a closed 2D probe set.

Exp. 3 - Light variation: To verify resilience in illumination variations, the probe set is composed by the 2D subset with frontal pose, across the five lighting conditions (1,2,4-6) that are not in the default gallery set (Exp. 1).

Exp. 4 - Pose variation: To isolate the influence of pose, the probe set is composed by the 2D subset with gallery light conditions (3), across the non-frontal pose variations (1-4, 6-12) that are not in the default gallery set (Exp. 1).

Exp. 5 - Yaw variation: For the influence of the more common, yaw-only viewpoint variations, the zero-roll poses (2, 8, 11) at the gallery light condition (3) are used for the probe set, with the default, frontal-pose gallery (Exp. 1).

Fig. 7. The reference UHLS9 facial landmark set (nine points on eyes, mouth and nose) annotated on 3D meshes and 2D images

Exp. 6 - Light direction: For the influence of opposing illumination conditions, the probe set is formed from the frontal pose instances (5), illuminated from an opposite to the default gallery (Exp. 1) light direction (4, 5, 6).

4.3 Facial Landmarks

The locations of nine facial point landmarks are provided as a reference with UHDB11 for the purpose of landmark detection, registration or pose estimation. Landmarks have been manually annotated by experts for both 3D and 2D data, examples of which are shown in Fig. 7 superimposed on 3D meshes and 2D images. The reference set (UHLS9) consists of the outer and inner eye corners, nose tip and nose inner corners and mouth corners. For 3D, both the mesh and overlaid texture have been used for accurate localization. Hidden points due to self-occlusions have been excluded from the 2D sets, with the final valid number of landmarks varying from four to nine across the database.

5 Baseline Performance Evaluation

As baseline evaluation, we report recognition performance on the UHDB11 experiments using a reference 3D-2D system [16], where the tested conjecture was that 3D-2D surpasses 2D-2D and can approximate shape-based 3D-3D recognition. Results are reported using light normalization through a bidirectional relighting module Raw similarity matrices have been normalized using Z-score normalization, although improved results have been reported using a Multi-Dimensional Scaling projection of the distance matrix.

5.1 System Description

For gallery processing, raw 3D data are fitted to a 3D deformable face model and model-registered images for the texture components are generated using the model surface parametrization. For recognition, a 2D probe is transformed to a geometry texture image, given a fitted gallery model and the 3D-2D landmark correspondence between image and mesh. The 3D-2D projection parameters are estimated for each probe-gallery pair, so that a mapping between mesh and image points is defined. To match the illumination of the probe texture, the gallery texture is bidirectionally relit using an analytic

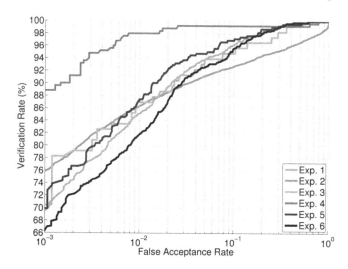

Fig. 8. ROC curves (in logarithmic FAR range) for 3D-2D face verification using the reference system, on the different experiments of UHDB11 database

skin reflectance model and an iterative optimization scheme. The final similarity score is based on the correlation of the gradient orientations of the pose and light-normalized texture pair.

5.2 Verification and Identification

Performance for 3D-2D face recognition is reported for the tasks of verification and identification using receiver operating characteristics (ROC) curves that show verification rate (VR) at varying false acceptance rates (FAR) (Fig. 8), and cumulative match characteristics (CMC) curves that show rank-k recognition rate (RRk) (Fig. 9). For quantitative comparisons we report the following curve-extracted measures in Table 5: VR at FAR = 0.001 and FAR = 0.01, equal error rate (EER), *i.e.*, the point where false accept equals false reject rate, area under curve (AUC) for verification and rank-1 recognition rate (RR1) for identification.

The specified UHDB11 experiments (Table 4) constitute configurations of different sizes, thus different number of total comparisons for ROCs, ranging from 2,645 (Exp. 3) to 36,846 (Exp. 1). For all experiments the verification rate is above 66% at 0.001 and 81% at 0.01 FAR. In addition, AUC values are very high (above 0.98 in every case), and the EER are low (below 0.07 in all cases). For the full UHDB11 3D-2D set (Exp. 1), verification performance is 69.5% at 0.001 and 85.1% at 0.01 FAR, with a set size that is two to 10 times larger than experiments 3-6. This performance is superior to 2D-2D FR systems [16] and can be additionally enhanced by more sophisticated score normalization algorithms.

A relative evaluation of the different experiments allows for observations on the challenges of the proposed database, as seen by the reference system. Overall best performance, with a 88.8% VR at 0.001 FAR, is achieved in Exp. 4 (23×250) where the light

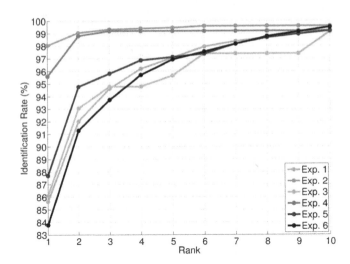

Fig. 9. CMC curves (ranks 1-10) for 3D-2D face identification using the reference system, on the different experiments of UHDB11 database

conditions are the same in probe and gallery sets. This indicates the anticipated decrease in performance when imposing illumination inconsistencies in the 2D images and an increased pose-resilience of the reference system. Analogously, Exp. 3 (23×115) where frontal pose is used in both sets, demonstrates a 10.5% lower verification rate. Experiments 5 and 6 involve combinations of pose and light variations, similar to Exp. 1, but constrain the type of head-pose and light direction variation respectively. Differences due to opposing lighting directions, captured by Exp. 6 (23×814), attain the lowest relative performance, possibly due to asymmetric shadows and specularities.

Identification baselines for the different 3D-2D experiments, shown in Fig. 9 for rank 1-10 out of the 23 gallery identities, are all above 84% and up to 96% rank - 1 rate. With the main baseline (Exp. 1) at 85.6%, Exp. 5 ranks second best to Exp. 4, along with Exp. 3. Since it is not clear if this performance ordering of the six configurations is due to the reference system or the challenges in the database, the results of competing 3D-2D algorithms will further rate the difficulty of each set.

Table 5. Face recognition results using the reference 3D-2D system on UHDB11 database

Method	Size	Verification				RR1(%)
		@ 10^{-3} FAR	@ 10^{-2} FAR	EER	AUC	
Exp. 1	$23 \times 1,602$	0.695	0.851	0.056	0.986	85.6
Exp. 2	$138 \times 1,487$	0.759	0.864	0.078	0.960	98.1
Exp. 3	23×115	0.783	0.870	0.062	0.983	86.1
Exp. 4	23×250	0.888	0.980	0.016	0.994	95.6
Exp. 5	23×382	0.728	0.874	0.051	0.988	87.7
Exp. 6	23×814	0.663	0.817	0.067	0.985	83.8

6   Limitations and Extensions

Database UHDB11 is a systematic approach to bridge the availability gap between 3D-2D and symmetric 3D or 2D facial database benchmarks. The main source of limitation of the current distribution relates to the small subject number, which is restricted compared to existing 2D or 3D datasets (Table 1) or formed 3D-2D cohorts (Table 2). However UHDB11 was formed in order to facilitate the development of 3D-2D systems in the presence of non-identity variations, and contains multiple captures of the same subject. In that respect, it can be useful for evaluating light and pose normalization algorithms, on a restricted identity set, with multiple samples per subject on the probe or gallery sets.

Some additional limitations concern the type and variability of acquisition conditions. More challenging and even extreme poses are required for real-life recognition conditions, and these can include unconstrained head rotations, self-occlusions and change in camera viewpoint. UHDB11 involves a single, fixed camera and approximate head rotations in roll and yaw angles. Extensions will include pitch rotations, yaw rotations above $30°$ and multiple viewpoints for combined face/camera position variation and ground-truth. The acquired, indoor illumination conditions, simulate a small range of lighting conditions and can be further enhanced to include outdoor captures, multiple light sources and varying intensity.

Our on-going efforts focus on addressing these limitations by complementing the database with additional captures, an increased subject and sample size and more challenging acquisition conditions. This involves outdoor sessions with natural lighting conditions and sessions from a custom 21 3D/2D camera acquisition system with multiple reference viewpoints, reconstructions from posed or partial 3D data and an increased subject number (5-10 times) of multiple captures, age groups and ethnic groups.

7   Conclusions

We presented a database and evaluation framework for 3D-2D and 2D-3D face recognition, where the gallery and recognition sets have data from different facial sensing modalities. UHDB11 is publicly available [1] and aims to address data requirements regarding face resolution in 2D and 3D and identity-independent variability, in the form of lighting conditions and facial pose. For performance benchmarking under different light/pose combinations, a set of database cohorts and experiments has been designed, on which we provided a 3D-2D face identification and verification baseline at demanding operational conditions (0.001 FAR). The database may additionally be useful for asymmetric, model-based or multimodal face recognition.

References

1. UHDB11 face database (2013), http://cbl.uh.edu/URxD/datasets
2. 3dMD. 3D Imaging Systems and Software (November 2012)
3. Al-Osaimi, F.R., Bennamoun, M., Mian, A.S.: Illumination normalization of facial images by reversing the process of image formation. Machine Vision and Applications 22(6), 899–911 (2011)

4. Bowyer, K., Chang, K., Flynn, P.: A survey of approaches and challenges in 3D and multi-modal 3D+2D face recognition. Computer Vision and Image Understanding 101(1), 1–15 (2006)
5. Faltemier, T.C., Bowyer, K.W., Flynn, P.J.: Using multi-instance enrollment to improve performance of 3D face recognition. Computer Vision and Image Understanding 112(2), 114–125 (2008)
6. Gross, R.: Face databases. In: Li, S.Z., Jain, A.K. (eds.) Handbook of Face Recognition, pp. 301–327. Springer, New York (2005)
7. Gross, R., Matthews, I., Cohn, J., Kanade, T., Baker, S.: Multi-PIE. Image and Vision Computing 28(5), 807–813 (2010)
8. Huang, D., Ardabilian, M., Wang, Y., Chen, L.: Oriented gradient maps based automatic asymmetric 3D-2D face recognition. In: Proc. 5th IAPR International Conference on Biometrics, New Delhi, India, March 29-April 1, pp. 125–131 (2012)
9. Huang, G.B., Mattar, M., Berg, T., Learned-Miller, E.: Labeled faces in the Wild: A database for studying face recognition in unconstrained environments. In: ECCV Workshop on Faces in 'Real-Life' Images: Detection, Alignment, and Recognition, Marseille, France, October 17-20 (2008)
10. Phillips, P.J., Moon, H., Rizvi, S., Rauss, P.J.: The FERET evaluation methodology for face recognition algorithms. IEEE Trans. Pattern Analysis and Machine Intelligence 22(10), 1090–1104 (2000)
11. Phillips, P.J., Flynn, P.J., Scruggs, T., Bowyer, K.W., Chang, J., Hoffman, K., Marques, J., Min, J., Worek, W.: Overview of the Face Recognition Grand Challenge. In: Proc. IEEE Conference on Computer Vision and Pattern Recognition, San Diego, CA, June 20-25 (2005)
12. Phillips, P.J., Beveridge, J.R., Draper, B.A., Givens, G., O'Toole, A.J., Bolme, D.S., Dunlop, J., Lui, Y.M., Sahibzada, H., Weimer, S.: An introduction to the Good, the Bad, and the Ugly face recognition challenge problem. In: 9th IEEE International Conference on Automatic Face and Gesture Recognition, Santa Barbara, CA, March 21-25 (2011)
13. Sandbach, G., Zafeiriou, S., Pantic, M., Yin, L.: Static and dynamic 3D facial expression recognition: A comprehensive survey. Image and Vision Computing 30(10), 683–697 (2012)
14. Savran, A., Alyüz, N., Dibeklioğlu, H., Çeliktutan, O., Gökberk, B., Sankur, B., Akarun, L.: Bosphorus database for 3D face analysis. In: Schouten, B., Juul, N.C., Drygajlo, A., Tistarelli, M. (eds.) BIOID 2008. LNCS, vol. 5372, pp. 47–56. Springer, Heidelberg (2008)
15. Sim, T., Baker, S., Bsat, M.: The CMU pose, illumination, and expression database. IEEE Transactions on Pattern Analysis and Machine Intelligence 25(12), 1615–1618 (2003)
16. Toderici, G., Passalis, G., Zafeiriou, S., Tzimiropoulos, G., Petrou, M., Theoharis, T., Kakadiaris, I.A.: Bidirectional relighting for 3D-aided 2D face recognition. In: Proc. IEEE Conf. on Computer Vision and Pattern Recognition, San Francisco, CA, June 13-18 (2010)
17. Vijayan, V., Bowyer, K., Flynn, P., Huang, D., Chen, L., Ocegueda, O., Shah, S., Kakadiaris, I.A.: Twins 3D face recognition challenge. In: Proc. International Joint Conference on Biometrics, Washington, DC, October 11-13 (2011)
18. Yin, L., Wei, X., Sun, Y., Wang, J., Rosato, M.: A 3D facial expression database for facial behavior research. In: Proc. 7th IEEE International Conference on Automatic Face and Gesture Recognition, Southampton, UK, April 2-6, pp. 211–216 (2006)

Joint Dictionary and Classifier Learning for Categorization of Images Using a Max-margin Framework

Hans Lobel[1], René Vidal[2], Domingo Mery[1], and Alvaro Soto[1]

[1] Department of Computer Science, Ponficia Universidad Católica de Chile
[2] Center for Imaging Science, Johns Hopkins University

Abstract. The Bag-of-Visual-Words (BoVW) model is a popular approach for visual recognition. Used successfully in many different tasks, simplicity and good performance are the main reasons for its popularity. The central aspect of this model, the visual dictionary, is used to build mid-level representations based on low level image descriptors. Classifiers are then trained using these mid-level representations to perform categorization. While most works based on BoVW models have been focused on learning a suitable dictionary or on proposing a suitable pooling strategy, little effort has been devoted to explore and improve the coupling between the dictionary and the top-level classifiers, in order to generate more discriminative models. This problem can be highly complex due to the large dictionary size usually needed by these methods. Also, most BoVW based systems usually perform multiclass categorization using a one-vs-all strategy, ignoring relevant correlations among classes. To tackle the previous issues, we propose a novel approach that jointly learns dictionary words and a proper top-level multiclass classifier. We use a max-margin learning framework to minimize a regularized energy formulation, allowing us to propagate labeled information to guide the commonly unsupervised dictionary learning process. As a result we produce a dictionary that is more compact and discriminative. We test our method on several popular datasets, where we demonstrate that our joint optimization strategy induces a word sharing behavior among the target classes, being able to achieve state-of-the-art performance using far less visual words than previous approaches.

1 Introduction

Bag-of-Visual-Words (BoVW) [1] is currently one of the most popular approaches for solving visual recognition problems, like scene or object detection and categorization. BoVW models encode information using a mid-level representation based on a dictionary of visual words, which encodes appearance information from local patches [2]. To perform categorization, these models are combined with top-level supervised classifiers that are trained using the mid-level representations. Spatial information is also usually incorporated into these models by concatenating information from different spatial areas [10].

The construction of the visual dictionary is one the most important aspect of these models. Commonly, it is built using generative approaches that minimize errors in patch

R. Klette, M. Rivera, and S. Satoh (Eds.): PSIVT 2013, LNCS 8333, pp. 87–98, 2014.

reconstruction, such as vector quantization [1] or sparse coding [3] techniques, In these cases dictionary construction is decoupled from the training of top-level classifiers [1,4]. As an alternative, discriminative dictionary construction strategies have also been proposed but mostly considering a weak link to the training of top-level classifiers [6,10].

Regarding the categorization process, BoVW models generally use a one-versus-all classification strategy. Unfortunately, this scheme does not considers relevant correlations among classes. Furthermore, they usually employ a visual dictionary for each target class, an aspect that turns out to be critical when the number of classes increases.

In this work we introduce a novel approach for visual recognition that presents two main contributions. Our first contribution is a method that jointly learns a suitable BoVW representations and top-level classifiers using a multiclass max-margin approach. The mathematical formulation behind this method is very general, however, we focus on a BoVW representation using a Spatial Pyramid Matching scheme. In contrast to previous works, we model dictionary words as linear SVMs [11] using a direct multiclass scheme. This allow us to pose our formulation as an energy minimization problem. Furthermore, we combine the responses of these discriminative dictionary words using a max-pooling strategy, as several recent works have shown the superiority of max-pooling over alternative polling strategies [12,13].

Our second contribution is a direct result of our learning scheme. By using a joint optimization strategy, we are able to induce word sharing among target classes. This allows us to achieve state-of-the-art categorization performance in several common benchmarks datasets, using an order of magnitude less words than previous approaches. We believe that word sharing is a critical issue to the scalability of visual recognition algorithms.

2   Related Work

BoVW model has remained throughout the last years as one of the the most common strategies for visual recognition, mainly for its simplicity and good results [1,4]. At the heart of this strategy lies the visual dictionary, which is used to quantize descriptor vector extracted from images. Dictionary learning is generally performed using an unsupervised method, like *K-Means*, to cluster the extracted descriptors [1,5,6,7,8,9,10].

In order to increase BoVW performance, sparse coding techniques have also been used as a method for learning a visual dictionary and to quantize feature descriptors. A remarkable example of this is [12], where sparse coding, max-pooling, and linear SVMs are used to achieve excellent categorization performance. Discriminative sparse representations have also been proposed [14], mostly building particular dictionaries for each class. In [13,15], the coupling of dictionary and classifier learning is explored. Altough similar in spirit to our work, here we explore a stronger form of coupling, consisting of a shared dictionary of linear SVMs and a multiclass classifier, instead of the standard one-vs-all framework. Also, they use different methods to obtain the visual words and to build the mid-level representation used by the top-level classifier.

Deep belief networks (DBN) [16,17] applied to visual recognition also present some similarities to our work, mainly regarding spatial pooling schemes and intermediate representations based on linear filters. As a consequence of a multi-layered generic structure, DBNs have many parameters and they are usually difficult to train. This presents a main difference to our work, as we embed semantic knowledge to our model by explicitly considering compositional relations among low level visual features, mid-level visual words, and top-level classifiers, leading to a more meaningful and simpler architecture. Also, the Hinge loss function used in our work leads to a different mathematical formulation.

Max-margin schemes have also been successfully used for visual recognition. Currently, one of the most used schemes is the one presented in [18], where a latent SVM is used to learn a mixture of multiscale deformable part models for binary classification. Also, in the area of action recognition, [19] proposes an extension to the method of [18] that uses a multiclass classification scheme. Although our discriminative BoVW model is also based on a max-margin approach, our hierarchical formulation, mid-level pooling scheme, and training scheme are highly different that the ones used by part-based approaches. In particular, our formulation is able to scale to cases that involve hundreds of parts, while part-based approaches are designed to operate with a reduced set of parts.

3   Model Description

3.1   Image Representation

We assume that visual descriptors [20,21] are extracted from images, either centered at interest points or by using a dense sampling scheme, and that each of these descriptors has size T. Also, inspired by the work of [22], we define a visual dictionary Θ of K words,

$$\Theta = [\theta_1\ \theta_2\ \theta_3\ \ldots\ \theta_K] \in \mathbb{R}^{(T+1) \times K}, \tag{1}$$

where each word θ_k is represented as a linear classifier with bias:

$$\theta_k = [\theta_{k,1}, \theta_{k,2}, \ldots, \theta_{k,T}, b_k]^T \in \mathbb{R}^{T+1}. \tag{2}$$

To encode each descriptor, we use an encoding scheme based on the classification score obtained by each dictionary word, similar to the one presented in [23]. More specifically, if v is a descriptor vector, its coding based on the dictionary Θ, $c_\Theta(v)$, is defined as:

$$c_\Theta(v) = [v^T \theta_1,\ \ldots,\ v^T \theta_K] = v^T \Theta \tag{3}$$

In order to use dictionary words with a bias term as defined above, every descriptor vector v has a constant 1 appended at the end. Intuitively, if the visual words are sufficiently discriminative, the descriptor v should be similar to only a few words from the dictionary. Therefore, we expect the vector $c_\Theta(v)$ to have only a few values greater than zero.

Given a dictionary Θ and a spatial pyramidal decomposition of the image into L regions, we represent the image using *max spatial pooling*. For each region l, $l \in [1, L]$, let $v_{l,j}$ be its j-th descriptor vector, where $j \in [1, N_l]$ and N_l is the number of descriptors extracted from region l. Given a dictionary Θ, we encode region l using *max spatial pooling* as:

$$x_{l,\Theta} = [\max_{j=1}^{N_l} v_{l,j}^T \theta_1,\ \max_{j=1}^{N_l} v_{l,j}^T \theta_2,\ \ldots,\ \max_{j=1}^{N_l} v_{l,j}^T \theta_K]^T \in \mathbb{R}^K. \tag{4}$$

As we are working in a discriminative setting instead of a generative one, like sparse coding generated dictionaries, our scheme assigns negative weights instead of a zero-weight to dictionary words with low similarity. As this can potentially lead to overfitting issues, we assume that each region l contains a null feature vector $\mathbf{0}$, whose classification score is equal to zero for any of the dictionary words. Using this trick, if in a given region none of the extracted feature vectors obtains a positive score, the max score over the region will be obtained by the null feature vector, thus putting a zero weight on the region descriptor.

Finally, the complete descriptor of an image I given a dictionary Θ, $x_\Theta(I)$, is obtained by concatenating the descriptors of its L regions, *i.e.*,

$$x_\Theta(I) = [x_{1,\Theta}, x_{2,\Theta}, \dots, x_{L,\Theta}]^T \in \mathbb{R}^{KL}. \tag{5}$$

Figure 1 shows a diagram of the creation of the coding of an image region.

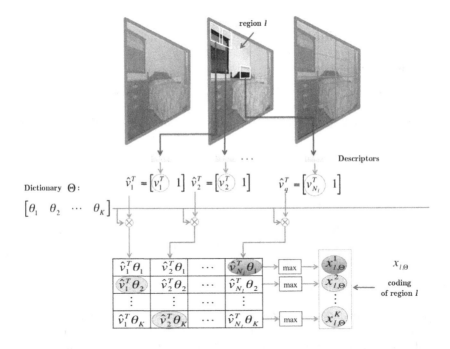

Fig. 1. Diagram of the coding of an image region l

3.2   Image Classification

Given a descriptor for image I, $x_\Theta(I)$, we define an image classification score, or energy function, for an image I as:

$$E(I, y, \Theta, W) = w_y^T x_\Theta(I). \tag{6}$$

Here, $w_y \in \mathbb{R}^{KL}$ represents the parameters of a classifier learnt for object class $y \in \{1, 2, \dots, M\}$ and

$$W = [w_1 \ w_2 \ \cdots \ w_M] \in \mathbb{R}^{KL \times M} \qquad (7)$$

represents all the object classifier parameters.

If w_y is divided in L sub-vectors of size K, each one assigned to a different region, we can rewrite the energy in the following form:

$$E(I, y, \Theta, W) = \sum_l^L \sum_k^K w_{y,l,k} \cdot \max_{j=1}^{N_l}(v_{l,j}^T \theta_k). \qquad (8)$$

where $w_{y,l,k}$ refers to the k-th element of the l-th sub-vector of w_y. This formulation makes explicit the fact that the total energy of an image is a linear combination of max functions. It can also be seen, that the energy function shows a linear dependence on the weights w_y, but a nonlinear one on the dictionary words. Figure 2 shows a schematic view the construction of the energy function.

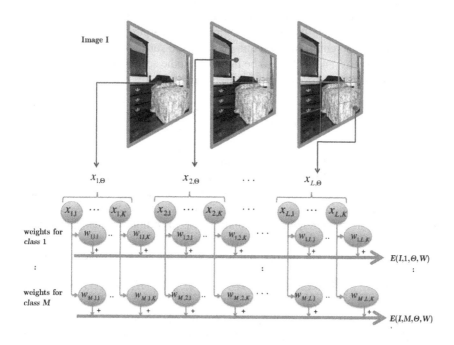

Fig. 2. Schematic view the construction of the energy function

Given the parameters of the classifiers for the different object categories, W, and the parameters of the classifiers for the different visual words, Θ, we classify an image I as follows

$$y^* = \underset{y}{\operatorname{argmax}} E(I, y, \Theta, W) \qquad (9)$$

4   Learning

The model described in the previous section depends on two sets of parameters: the object classifiers W and the visual words classifiers Θ. Rather than first learning the visual words and then learning the object classifiers, our goal is to learn both of them simultaneously so that the visual words are discriminative for the visual classification task.

More specifically, given a set of training examples $\{I_i, y_i\}_{i=1}^N$, where I_i is the i-th image and y_i is its class, we propose to find Θ and W by solving the following regularized max-margin learning problem:

$$\min_{W,\Theta,\{\xi_i\}} \frac{1}{2}\|W\|_F^2 + \frac{C_1}{2K}\|\Theta\|_F^2 + \frac{C_2}{N}\sum_{i=1}^N \xi_i \tag{10}$$

$$\text{s.t. } E(I_i, y_i, \Theta, W) - E(I_i, y, \Theta, W) \geq \Delta(y_i, y) - \xi_i,$$
$$\forall i \in \{1, \ldots, N\} \wedge \forall y \in \{1, \ldots, M\}.$$

The objective function encourages the construction of visual words that behave like linear SVMs, *i.e.*, classifiers that jointly maximize the margin and minimize the loss. On the other hand, the constraints encourage the score for an image according to its ground truth label, $E(I_i, y_i, \Theta, W)$, to be higher than the score according to any other label, $E(I_i, y, \Theta, W)$, by a loss function $\Delta(y_i, y)$ given by

$$\Delta(y_1, y_2) = \begin{cases} 0 & \text{if } y_1 = y_2 \\ 1 & \text{otherwise} \end{cases}. \tag{11}$$

The slack variables $\xi_i \geq 0$ allow for a violation of these constraints.

At first sight, one could think that the formulation in (10) is a particular case of Structural SVM (S-SVM) [24]. However, this is not the case due to two fundamental differences. First, the constraints are not linear in Θ, while in S-SVMs the constraints are always linear in the parameters. Second, the optimization problem is not jointly convex on Θ and W.

To see the latter, notice that the optimal solution for the slack variables is given by

$$\xi_i^*(\Theta, W) = \max_y (E(I_i, y, \Theta, W) + \Delta(y_i, y)) - E(I_i, y_i, \Theta, W) \tag{12}$$

and recall that the point-wise maximum of convex functions is convex. Therefore, given $W \geq 0$, the energy in (8) is convex in Θ because it is the weighted sum of convex functions with nonnegative weights. By the same argument, the first term in (12) is convex, however the second one is concave. As a consequence, the objective function for Θ given $W \geq 0$ is the sum of a convex and a concave function in Θ. Otherwise, the cost function is generally non-convex. On the other hand, notice that given Θ, the objective function is convex in W, because the first term of (12) is a maximum of convex functions, while the second term is linear in W.

Motivated by the above analysis, we propose to solve the problem in (10) using an alternating minimization approach where we alternate between the computation of W

given a fixed Θ and the computation of Θ given a fixed W. Due to the non-convexity of the cost function, there is no theoretical analysis guaranteeing its convergence. However, our experiments show that for suitable selection of the parameters, our procedure does converge in practice.

Given $\Theta = \Theta^{(t)}$ at iteration t, the computation of W reduces to a standard multiclass SVM problem, which can be efficiently solved, *e.g.*, with a cutting-plane algorithm [24]. Such methods typically produce a solution for both the classifier parameters $W^{(t)}$ and the slack variables $\xi_i^{(t)}$.

Given $W = W^{(t)}$ at iteration t, the computation of Θ requires solving the following problem

$$\min_{\Theta} \frac{C_1}{2K}\|\Theta\|_F^2 + \frac{C_2}{N}\sum_i^N E(I_i, \hat{y}_i, \Theta, W^{(t)}) + \Delta(y_i, \hat{y}_i) - E(I_i, y_i, \Theta, W^{(t)}) \quad (13)$$

where

$$\hat{y}_i = \underset{y}{\operatorname{argmax}}\, E(I_i, y, \Theta, W) + \Delta(y_i, y). \quad (14)$$

As stated before, the optimization problem in (13) is not convex, hence we can not guarantee that we find a global minimizer. We find an approximate solution by using an interior point method [25] applied to an approximation of a modified version of (13). The modification consists of solving the problem in (13) subject to the additional constraints

$$E(I_i, y, \Theta, W^{(t)}) - E(I_i, y_i, \Theta, W^{(t)}) + \Delta(y_i, y) \leq \xi_i^{(t)}$$
$$\forall i \in \{1, \ldots, N\} \wedge \forall y \in \{1, \ldots M\}. \quad (15)$$

These additional constraints ensure that the new slack variables (after modifying Θ) are at most equal to the slack variables at the previous iteration (obtained after modifying W). The approximation consists of replacing the max-pooling function by a *soft-max* approximation to ensure differentiability. Specifically, we use the *log-sum-exponential* (LSE) approximation,

$$\max_{i=1}^N (z_i) \approx \frac{1}{r}\log(\sum_i^N \exp(rz_i)) \quad (16)$$

which preserves the convexity of the point-wise maximum operation. The parameter r controls the sharpness of the approximation, where larger values generate better approximations. The energy function finally becomes:

$$E(I, y, \Theta, W) \approx \sum_l^L \sum_k^K \frac{w_{y,l,k}}{r} \log(\sum_j^{N_l} \exp(r \cdot \hat{v}_{l,j}^T \theta_k)). \quad (17)$$

Te solve the approximate optimization problem we require the partial derivatives of the objective function and the partial derivatives of the constraints, both of which are straightforward to obtain from (17).

5   Experiments

We performed evaluations on 3 different datasets (Caltech 101, 15 Scene Categories, and MIT67 Indoor) and analyzed the potential performance gains delivered by the dictionary update step and classification performance compared to other methods. We obtain as main results i) state-of-the-art performance on 2 datasets when compared to other similar methods and ii) the generation of a unique dictionary of discriminative patches shared among target classes, with an order of magnitude less visual words than similar approaches.

5.1   Implementation Details

- **Feature extraction:** Images are downsized to no more than 300 pixels in each direction. Local HOG-LBP descriptors [26] are then extracted from each image using a dense grid of regions of 16x16 pixels, with a spacing of 8 pixels in each direction. We use a spatial pyramidal decomposition with 21 regions (depth 2).
- **Initial dictionary:** To obtain the initial dictionary, we sample 100.000 descriptors from training images and cluster them with *K-Means*. After this process, a linear SVM is trained for each centroid, using as positive examples the ones belonging to that centroid and as negative examples descriptors belonging to the other centroids.
- **Nonlinear optimization:** To implement the gradient descent step for the dictionary estimation, we use the interior point solver Ipopt (Interior Point OPTimizer) [25]. This solver is optimized for large scale constrained nonlinear problems as our case.

5.2   Datasets Details

- **Caltech101:** This dataset is formed by 101 object categories plus a background class. We use 10 random splits of the data, keeping 30 images for training and the rest for testing.
- **15 Scene Categories:** This dataset contains 15 diferent natural scene categories. We use 10 random splits of the data, keeping this time 100 images for training and the rest for testing.
- **MIT67 Indoor:** This dataset contains 67 different indoor scene categories, with a very high intra-class variation. We use the standard evaluation procedure, using 80 images per class for training and 20 for testing.

5.3   Behavior of Dictionary Words

The purpose of this experiment is to visually appreciate some dictionary words before and after the dictionary update process. Figure 3 shows a group of patches from 15 Scene Categories that initially obtain high response for a dictionary word that encourages diagonal lines. The six patches on the left obtain a high score before and after the dictionary update, while the four patches on the right obtain a high score before the update, but after it obtain a very low score, using the same dictionary word.

The set of patches on the left in Figure 3 show a more homogeneous appearance than the ones on the right. Despite also showing diagonal lines, the presence of noise in the

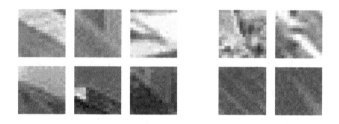

Fig. 3. The dictionary update step gradually reduces the score of noisy patches (right)

rightmost patches, makes them more prone to be confused with other patches that show structures diferent than the one represented by that dictionary word. Our algorithm, using the max-pooling and the classifier weights, its able to progresively reduce the score of these patches, by updating the dictionary words accordingly.

5.4   Classification Performance

As we mentioned, we test our method using three datasets: Caltech101, 15 Scene Categories, and MIT67 Indoor. Table 1 shows our first experiment designed to evaluate performance evolution as a function of the number of dictionary words. There is a

Table 1. Performance evolution as a function of the number of dictionary words

Dataset	\multicolumn{3}{c}{Number of Words}
	50	100	200
Caltech101	63.1 ± 0.8	72.0 ± 0.5	73.1 ± 0.5
15 Scenes	72.2 ± 0.5	83.7 ± 0.2	84.8 ± 0.2
MIT67 Indoor	31.2	38.3	39.9

masive performance gain when dictionary size grows from 50 to 100 words. After that, the gain is less significant but clearly measurable. Unfortunately, due to memory requirements associated to our current implementation, it was not possible to test with a higher number of words.

The next experiment compares our results against methods using only a BoVW scheme, without the aid of global features [27] or object models [18], and a fixed spatial pyramid matching scheme with at most depth 2, *i.e.* 21 pooling regions. Table 2 shows the results. We also include a baseline method in the comparison, consisting in only solving the problem in 10 with a fixed Θ.

We can observe that we achieve state-of-the-art performance in 15 Scene Categories and MIT67 Indoor, while obtaining competitive results in Caltech101. An important aspect of our results is that we use only 200 dictionary words, where other methods use more than thousand. In particular, in the case of Caltech101, we believe that our current

Table 2. Our proposed method achieves state-of-the-art performance in 2 out of 3 datasets using only 200 words

Method	# Words	Dataset		
		Caltech101	15 Scenes	MIT67
Baseline	200	63.9 ± 0.6	78.1 ± 0.3	33.2
SPM [8]	400	64.6 ± 0.8	81.4 ± 0.5	-
LLC [28]	2048	**73.4**	80.5 ± 0.6	-
LCSR [29]	1024	73.2 ± 0.8	82.7 ± 0.5	-
ScSPM [12]	1024	73.2 ± 0.5	80.3	-
Max-margin [15]	5250	-	82.7 ± 0.5	-
Object Bank [23]	200	-	80.9	37.6
Reconfigurable Models [30]	200	-	78.6 ± 0.7	37.9
Discriminative Patches [31]	14070	-	-	38.1
Proposed	200	73.1 ± 0.5	**84.8 ± 0.2**	**39.9**

dictionary size might be hurting performance, as the high number of categories might require a larger dictionary size for better results.

6   Conclusions and Future Work

BoVW models are commonly based on two main steps: first learning the dictionary and then learning classifiers that use this dictionary. In this work we present a novel method for jointly learning a dictionary of discriminative visual words and a top-level classifier using a multiclass max-margin approach. Our formulation is highly general an can be adapted to various spatial decompositions of images. In particular, when we compare several techniques based on a spatial pyramid matching scheme, our method achieves state-of-the-art performance on two of the three datasets considered in our experiments (15 Scenes and MIT67).

Regarding the resulting dictionary, the proposed joint learning scheme produces a strong sharing of visual words among the target classes. In practice, this allows us to use a dictionary that has an order of magnitude less visual words than previous BoVW methods, but without reducing recognition performance. As the number of target object classes increases in practical applications, word sharing will become a relevant issue, since time spent obtaining responses for different linear classifiers (at the level of dictionary words and top-level classifier) will be a major processing bottleneck.

Future work will focus on using multiscale patches to enrich our hypothesis space, thus allowing us to search for suitable dictionary words that represent more meaningful visual structures. We also plan to improve running time and memory use, in order to be able to evaluate performance on new larger datasets [32].

Acknowledgment. This work was partially funded by FONDECYT grant 1120720, NSF grant 11-1218709, and the Sloan Research Foundation.

References

1. Sivic, J., Zisserman, A.: Video google: A text retrieval approach to object matching in videos. In: ICCV (2003)
2. Lowe, D.: Distinctive image features from scale-invariant keypoints. IJCV 60(2), 91–110 (2004)
3. Yang, L., Jin, R., Sukthankar, R., Jurie, F.: Unifying discriminative visual codebook generation with classifier training for object category reorganization. In: CVPR (2008)
4. Niebles, J.C., Wang, H., Li, F.: Unsupervised learning of human action categories using spatial-temporal words. IJCV 79(3), 299–318 (2008)
5. Csurka, G., Dance, C.R., Fan, L., Willamowski, J., Bray, C.: Visual categorization with bags of keypoints. In: In Workshop on Statistical Learning in Computer Vision, ECCV (2004)
6. Winn, J., Criminisi, A., Minka, T.: Object categorization by learned universal visual dictionary. In: ICCV, pp. 1800–1807 (2005)
7. Jurie, F., Triggs, B.: Creating efficient codebooks for visual recognition. In: ICCV (2005)
8. Lazebnik, S., Schmid, C., Ponce, J.: Beyond bags of features: Spatial pyramid matching for recognizing natural scene categories. In: IEEE Conference on Computer Vision and Pattern Recognition (CVPR), pp. 2169–2178 (2006)
9. Moosmann, F., Triggs, B., Jurie, F.: Fast discriminative visual codebooks using randomized clustering forests. In: Neural Information Processing Systems, NIPS (2007)
10. Lazebnik, S., Raginsky, M.: Supervised learning of quantizer codebooks by information loss minimization. PAMI 31(7), 1294–1309 (2009)
11. Singaraju, D., Vidal, R.: Using global bag of features models in random fields for joint categorization and segmentation of objects. In: IEEE Conference on Computer Vision and Pattern Recognition, CVPR (2011)
12. Yang, J., Yu, K., Gong, Y., Huang, T.: Linear spatial pyramid matching using sparse coding for image classification. In: CVPR (2009)
13. Boureau, Y., Bach, F., LeCun, Y., Ponce, J.: Learning mid-level features for recognition. In: CVPR (2010)
14. Mairal, J., Bach, F., Ponce, J., Sapiro, G., Zisserman, A.: Supervised dictionary learning. In: Advances in Neural Information Processing Systems, vol. 21, pp. 1033–1040 (2008)
15. Lian, X.-C., Li, Z., Lu, B.-L., Zhang, L.: Max-margin dictionary learning for multiclass image categorization. In: Daniilidis, K., Maragos, P., Paragios, N. (eds.) ECCV 2010, Part IV. LNCS, vol. 6314, pp. 157–170. Springer, Heidelberg (2010)
16. Hinton, G., Osindero, S.: A fast learning algorithm for deep belief nets. Neural Computation 18, 2006 (2006)
17. Krizhevsky, A., Sutskever, I., Hinton, G.: Imagenet classification with deep convolutional neural networks. In: NIPS (2012)
18. Felzenszwalb, P., Girshick, R., McAllester, D., Ramanan, D.: Object detection with discriminatively trained part based models. IEEE Transactions on Pattern Analysis and Machine Intelligence 32(9), 1627–1645 (2010)
19. Wang, Y., Mori, G.: Hidden part models for human action recognition: Probabilistic versus max margin. PAMI 33(7), 1310–1323 (2011)
20. Dalal, N., Triggs, B.: Histograms of oriented gradients for human detection. In: IEEE Computer Society Conference on Computer Vision and Pattern Recognition (CVPR 2005), vol. 1, pp. 886–893 (2005)
21. Ahonen, T., Hadid, A., Pietikainen, M.: Face description with local binary patterns: Application to face recognition. IEEE Transactions on Pattern Analysis and Machine Intelligence 28(12), 2037–2041 (2006)

22. Jain, A., Zappella, L., McClure, P., Vidal, R.: Visual dictionary learning for joint object categorization and segmentation. In: Fitzgibbon, A., Lazebnik, S., Perona, P., Sato, Y., Schmid, C. (eds.) ECCV 2012, Part V. LNCS, vol. 7576, pp. 718–731. Springer, Heidelberg (2012)

23. Li, L., Su, H., Xing, E., Fei-Fei, L.: Object bank: A high-level image representation for scene classification & semantic feature sparsification. In: Neural Information Processing Systems (NIPS), Vancouver, Canada (December 2010)

24. Tsochantaridis, I., Hofmann, T., Joachims, T., Altun, Y.: Support vector machine learning for interdependent and structured output spaces. In: ICML (2004)

25. Waechter, A., Biegler, L.: On the implementation of an interior-point filter line-search algorithm for large-scale nonlinear programming. Mathematical Programming 106, 25–57 (2006)

26. Wang, X., Han, T.X., Yan, S.: An hog-lbp human detector with partial occlusion handling. In: IEEE International Conference on Computer Vision (ICCV), pp. 32–39 (2009)

27. Oliva, A., Torralba, A.: Modeling the shape of the scene: A holistic representation of the spatial envelope. International Journal of Computer Vision 42, 145–175 (2001)

28. Wang, J., Yang, J., Yu, K., Lv, F., Huang, T., Gong, Y.: Locality-constrained linear coding for image classification. In: IEEE Conference on Computer Vision and Pattern Recognition, CVPR (2010)

29. Shabou, A., Le-Borgne, H.: Locality-constrained and spatially regularized coding for scene categorization. In: CVPR (2012)

30. Parizi, S., Oberlin, J., Felzenszwalb, P.: IEEE Conference on Computer Vision and Pattern Recognition (CVPR), pp. 2775–2782 (2012)

31. Singh, S., Gupta, A., Efros, A.A.: Unsupervised discovery of mid-level discriminative patches. In: Fitzgibbon, A., Lazebnik, S., Perona, P., Sato, Y., Schmid, C. (eds.) ECCV 2012, Part II. LNCS, vol. 7573, pp. 73–86. Springer, Heidelberg (2012)

32. Deng, J., Dong, W., Socher, R., Li, L.-J., Li, K., Fei-Fei, L.: ImageNet: A Large-Scale Hierarchical Image Database. In: IEEE Conference on Computer Vision and Pattern Recognition, CVPR (2009)

Multibit Embedding Algorithm
for Steganography of Palette-Based Images

Shoko Imaizumi and Kei Ozawa

Graduate School of Advanced Integration Science, Chiba University
1–33 Yayoicho, Inage-ku, Chiba-shi, Chiba 263-8522, Japan
imaizumi@chiba-u.jp

Abstract. We propose a high-capacity data hiding scheme for palette-based images that does not seriously degrade the image quality in this paper. The proposed scheme can embed a multiple-bit message within the unit of a pixel matrix by using Euclidean distance, while some conventional schemes can embed only a one-bit message per pixel. The stego-images created by using our scheme offer a better quality compared to those by the conventional scheme. Moreover, we have obtained these results with low implementation cost. The experimental results show that the proposed scheme is efficient.

Keywords: Steganography, data hiding, palette-based image, Euclidean distance, pixel matrix.

1 Introduction

Steganography [1,2] is a data hiding scheme that communicates a secret messages by imperceptibly embedding them into a cover data, such as an image or audio, etc. When the cover data is an image, the image is called a cover image. A cover image that possesses a secret message actually forms a stego-image. The stego-image can be transmitted through open channels without suspicion since the secret message is generally embedded into the cover image without creating noticeable artifacts. The authorized recipient can extract the embedded message from the stego-image, while others are unaware of the existence of the message behind the stego-image.

Palette-based images, which generally use no more than 256 palette entries (simply called entries hereafter), are frequently used as cover images. This is because palette-based images can be conveniently distributed and found through communication channels, even if the channel is quite narrow. Entries that compose palette-based images are stored in the palette. Each pixel in a palette-based image possesses an index that points to the entry.

There are two types in steganographic schemes for palette-based images embedding a message by controlling entries in the palette. One of them changes the colors of the entries in order to embed a message with only slight degradation [3–6]. Niimi's scheme [3], for instance, embeds a message based on the Green values of the colors for the target pixels. The other retains the colors of

R. Klette, M. Rivera, and S. Satoh (Eds.): PSIVT 2013, LNCS 8333, pp. 99–110, 2014.

the entries and may reorder the entries in the palette [7–13]. EZ stego scheme [7] sorts the palette by luminance and embeds message bits into the LSBs of the indices. Fridrich [8] presented a steganographic scheme for hiding message bits into the parity bit of close colors. The former schemes [3–6] create some new entries in the palette, and removes the same number of entries as the new entries. Thus, the schemes should increase the computational cost of the calculation for adding and removing entries. Our scheme adopts the latter schemes [7–13].

We propose a high-capacity steganographic scheme for palette-based images in this paper. The proposed scheme can embed a multiple-bit message within the unit of a pixel matrix, while some conventional schemes can embed only a one-bit message per pixel. This scheme forms better quality stego-images using simple implementation than the conventional scheme. A performance analysis validated our scheme.

2   Related Work

We review three conventional steganographic schemes for palette-based images [7, 8, 13] in this section.

2.1   EZ Stego Scheme [7]

EZ stego scheme is one of the most famous steganographic schemes for embedding a one-bit message within the unit of a pixel by changing its entry. Assume that there are X entries in the palette and that the length of the embedded message is Γ bits. This scheme embeds a secret message using the following steps.

Step 1 Sort entries E_i $(i = 0, 1, \ldots, X)$ in the palette in ascending order according to the luminance L_i, which is represented as

$$L_i = 0.299r_i + 0.587g_i + 0.144b_i, \tag{1}$$

where r_i, g_i, and b_i are the red, green, and blue values of an entry E_i, respectively.

Step 2 Select the γ-th target pixel $(\gamma = 1, 2, \ldots, \Gamma)$ containing index i of entry E_i from the cover image.

Step 3 Find index i' of entry E_i in the reordered palette.

Step 4 Replace the LSB of index i' with the γ-th one-bit message to be embedded, and then obtain index i'_n of the neighboring entity E_{i_n}. Note that if the one-bit message is equal to the LSB of index i', leave index i' unchanged and return to **Step 2**.

Step 5 Find index i_n of entry E_{i_n} in the original palette.

Step 6 Replace index i in the target pixel with index i_n.

Step 7 Repeat **Steps 2** to **6** until $\gamma = \Gamma$.

The recipient should only collect the LSBs by using the location map when extracting the message. However, EZ stego may occasionally replace an entry in a pixel with a totally different entry, because it reorders the palette entries according to the luminance given by Eq. (1).

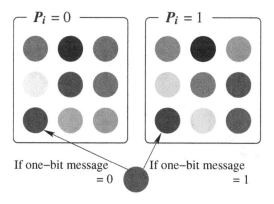

Fig. 1. Embedding one-bit message bit into parity in Fridrich's scheme [8]

2.2   Fridrich's Scheme [8]

To solve the problem of EZ stego scheme, Fridrich proposed another scheme that embeds a Γ-bit message into the parities of close entries. The embedding procedure is described as follows.

Step 1 Calculate parities P_i for all entries $E_i\,(r_i, g_i, b_i)$ in the palette, which is defined as

$$P_i = (r_i + g_i + b_i) \quad \mathrm{mod}\ 2,$$
$$i = 0, 1, \ldots, X. \tag{2}$$

Step 2 Select the γ-th target pixel $(\gamma = 1, 2, \ldots, \Gamma)$ with entry E_i, whose parity is P_i, in the cover image. Note that if the γ-th one-bit message M_γ to be embedded is equal to P_i, leave the γ-th pixel unchanged and repeat **Step 2**.

Step 3 Find the closest entry E_{i_c} to the entry E_i of the target pixel in the set of entries whose parities $p\,(p = 0\ \text{or}\ 1)$ are equal to M_γ, by using the Euclidean distance D_{i_0, i_1}, as shown in Fig. 1. The D_{i_0, i_1} between two entries $E_{i_0}\,(r_{i_0}, g_{i_0}, b_{i_0})$ and $E_{i_1}\,(r_{i_1}, g_{i_1}, b_{i_1})$ is given by

$$D_{i_0, i_1} = \sqrt{\left(\Delta r_{i_0, i_1}\right)^2 + \left(\Delta g_{i_0, i_1}\right)^2 + \left(\Delta b_{i_0, i_1}\right)^2}. \tag{3}$$

Step 4 Replace entry E_i of the target pixel with the closest entry E_{i_c}.
Step 5 Repeat **Steps 2** to **4** until $\gamma = \Gamma$.

The message can be easily recovered by collecting the parity bits for the entries of the target pixels according to the location map. Although this scheme can avoid replacing the colors of the target pixels with completely different ones, it can only embed a one-bit message per pixel.

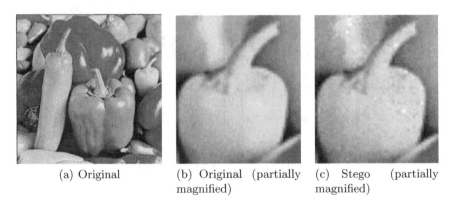

(a) Original   (b) Original   (partially   (c) Stego   (partially
                        magnified)   magnified)

Fig. 2. Example of message embedding using Tanaka's scheme [13]

2.3   Tanaka's Scheme [13]

Tanaka presented a high-capacity steganography that is based on Fridrich's scheme. This scheme can embed a k-bit message per pixel without increasing the degradation of the image quality compared to that for Fridrich's scheme. The main contribution of this scheme is assigning a k-bit parity to each of X entries. Parity P_i is assigned to entry E_i using the following steps.

Step 1 Find initial entry E_{i_0}, that is

$$E_{i_0} = \arg \min_{i} \left(256^2 r_i + 256^1 g_i + 256^0 b_i \right). \tag{4}$$

Assign 0 to parity P_{i_0} for entry E_{i_0}.
Step 2 Find entry E_{i_x}, that is

$$E_{i_x} = \arg \min_{i \in \alpha} D_{i_{x-1},i}, \tag{5}$$

where D is defined by Eq. (3). Note that α is a set of i in which each entry E_i has not been assigned a parity yet.
Step 3 Set parity $P_{i_x} = P_{i_{x-1}} + 1$.
Step 4 Repeat **Steps 2** and **3** until $x = 2^k - 1$.
Step 5 Find entry E_{i_x}, which is given by Eq. (5).
Step 6 Find the 2^k closest entries $E_{i_c^{(p)}}$ to E_{i_x} in the sets $\alpha^{(p)}$ on each parity p $\left(p = 0, 1, \ldots, 2^k - 1 \right)$, which are given by

$$E_{i_c^{(p)}} = \arg \min_{i^{(p)} \in \alpha^{(p)}} D_{i_x, i^{(p)}}. \tag{6}$$

Step 7 Set parity P_{i_x} as

$$P_{i_x} = \arg \max_{p} D_{i_x, i_c^{(p)}}. \tag{7}$$

Step 8 Repeat **Steps 5** to **7** until $x = X - 1$.

The embedding procedure is the same as that for Fridrich's scheme. When a message is embedded into an cover image as shown in Fig. 2(a), part of the image, such as that shown in Fig. 2(b), for instance, is degraded like that shown in Fig 2(c). If the entry of the target pixel has no close entries in the palette, the target pixel is changed to a totally different color, and the stego-image is seriously damaged.

3   Proposed Scheme

In this section, we present a high-capacity steganographic scheme for palette-based images that has less degradation than the conventional scheme. Our scheme is composed of simple operations. This scheme is based on embedding the message into the parities. The new approach uses 3×3 pixel matrices to inhibit the serious degradation of a stego-image. Note that the arbitrary size of the matrix can be adopted to the proposed scheme.

3.1   Reordering Palette Entries

Assume that we embed a k-bit message, where $k = 1, 2$, or 3, into each 3×3 pixel matrix. First, we reorder all X entries in the palette for a cover image using following steps.

Step 1 Find initial entry E_{i_0} in the original palette using the following equation.

$$E_{i_0} = \arg \min_{i} \ \left(256^2 r_i + 256^1 g_i + 256^0 b_i\right). \tag{8}$$

Step 2 Set index $I_0 = 0$ to E_{i_0}.
Step 3 Find entry E_{i_x}, that is

$$E_{i_x} = \arg \min_{i \in \alpha} \ D_{i_{x-1}, i}, \tag{9}$$

where D is defined by Eq. (3). Note that α is a set of i, where each entry E_i has not been assigned an index yet.

Table 1. Reordered palette in proposed scheme

Index I_x	Entry E_{i_x}
0	$\arg \min_i \left(256^2 r_i + 256 g_i + b_i\right)$
1	$\arg \min_{i \in \alpha} D_{i,0}$
2	$\arg \min_{i \in \alpha} D_{i,1}$
. . .	. . .
$X - 2$	$\arg \min_{i \in \alpha} D_{i, X-3}$
$X - 1$	$E_i \, (i \in \alpha)$

$t_{0(\beta)}$	$t_{1(\beta)}$	$t_{2(\beta)}$
$t_{3(\beta)}$	$t_{4(\beta)}$	$t_{5(\beta)}$
$t_{6(\beta)}$	$t_{7(\beta)}$	$t_{8(\beta)}$

Fig. 3. Pixels $t_{j(\beta)}$ in 3×3 matrix

Step 4 Set index $I_x = x$ to E_{i_x}.
Step 5 Repeat **Steps 2** and **4** until $x = X - 1$.

The neighboring entries possess similar colors to each other when using the above mentioned steps. The reordered palette is formed in the way shown in Table 1.

3.2 Embedding Procedure

We divide embedded message M into B of k-bit blocks, whose values are represented as M_β ($M_\beta = 0, 1, \ldots, 2^k - 1$ and $\beta = 1, 2, \ldots, B$). The k-bit message M_β is embedded into the pixels $t_{j(\beta)}$ ($j = 0, 1, \ldots, 8$) in the β-th 3×3 matrix, which are shown in Fig. 3. The embedding procedure is as follows.

Step 1 Select the β-th target matrix with nine pixels $t_{j(\beta)}$ ($j = 0, 1, \ldots, 8$).
Step 2 Take summation S_β over nine indices $I_{j(\beta)}$ of $t_{j(\beta)}$.

$$S_\beta = \sum_{j=0}^{8} I_{j(\beta)}. \tag{10}$$

Step 3 Calculate parity P_β for the β-th pixel matrix given as

$$P_\beta = S_\beta \mod 2^k, \tag{11}$$

where $k = 1, 2,$ or 3.
Step 4 Calculate minimal error R_β between M_β and P_β, as shown in Fig. 4.

$$R_\beta = \begin{cases} \min\left(P_\beta - M_\beta, M_\beta - P_\beta + 2^k\right), & \text{if } M_\beta < P_\beta \\ \min\left(M_\beta - P_\beta, P_\beta - M_\beta + 2^k\right), & \text{if } M_\beta > P_\beta. \end{cases} \tag{12}$$

If $R_\beta = 0$, i.e., $M_\beta = P_\beta$, leave the β-th matrix unchanged and return to **Step 1**.
Step 5 Extract the R_β of pixels $t_{j(\beta)}$ in ascending order corresponding to the Euclidean distance $D_{j(\beta)}$ between entry $E_{j(\beta)}$ $\left(E_{j(\beta)} = E_{i_x}\right)$ for pixel $t_{j(\beta)}$ and entry $E_{i_{x-1}}$ or $E_{i_{x+1}}$, which is given as

$$D_{j(\beta)} = \begin{cases} D_{i_x, i_{x-1}}, & \text{if } R_\beta < 0 \\ D_{i_x, i_{x+1}}, & \text{if } R_\beta > 0. \end{cases} \tag{13}$$

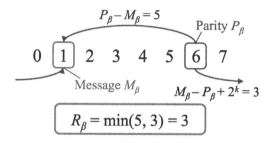

Fig. 4. Decision of minimal error R_β ($k = 3$)

Step 6 Replace the R_β of indices $I_{j(\beta)}$ $\left(I_{j(\beta)} = I_x\right)$ of target pixels $t_{j(\beta)}$ to I_{x_i-1} or I_{x_i+1}.

Step 7 Repeat **Steps 1** to **6** until $\beta = B$.

3.3 Extracting Procedure

The algorithm for extracting the embedded message is quite simple. After reordering the palette entries according to Section 3.1, the extracting procedure works in the following way.

Step 1 Select the β-th target matrix with nine pixels $t_{j(\beta)}$ ($j = 0, 1, \ldots, 8$) according to the location map.

Step 2 Take summation S_β over nine indices $I_{j(\beta)}$ of $t_{j(\beta)}$.

$$S_\beta = \sum_{j=0}^{8} I_{j(\beta)}. \tag{14}$$

Step 3 Calculate parity P_β for the β-th pixel matrix given as

$$P_\beta = S_\beta \mod 2^k, \tag{15}$$

where $k = 1, 2,$ or 3.

Step 4 Assign P_β to M_β.

Step 5 Repeat **Steps 1** to **Step 4** until $\beta = B$.

Step 6 Concatenate the B of the k-bit messages M_β in ascending order of β, and read the extracted message M.

Note that the recipient has to receive the location map in order to extract the message.

4 Experimental Results

We present the experimental results of the proposed scheme and compare them with those of Tanaka's scheme [13]. We performed our experiments on 11

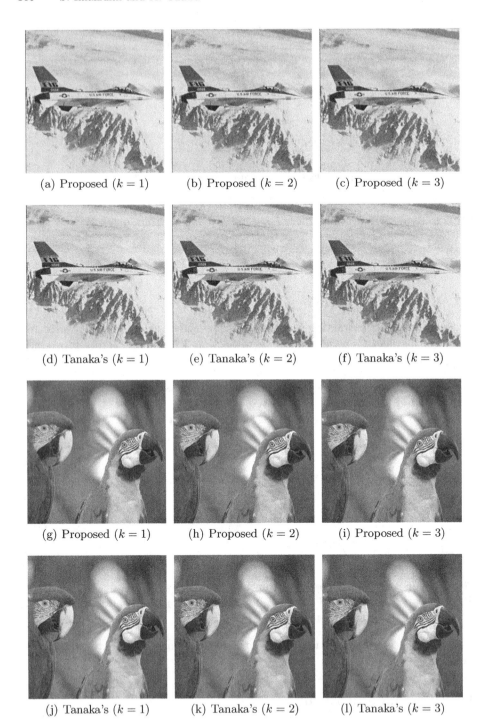

(a) Proposed ($k = 1$)   (b) Proposed ($k = 2$)   (c) Proposed ($k = 3$)

(d) Tanaka's ($k = 1$)   (e) Tanaka's ($k = 2$)   (f) Tanaka's ($k = 3$)

(g) Proposed ($k = 1$)   (h) Proposed ($k = 2$)   (i) Proposed ($k = 3$)

(j) Tanaka's ($k = 1$)   (k) Tanaka's ($k = 2$)   (l) Tanaka's ($k = 3$)

Fig. 5. Stego-images with a $7,000 \times k$-bit message (Airplane and Parrots)

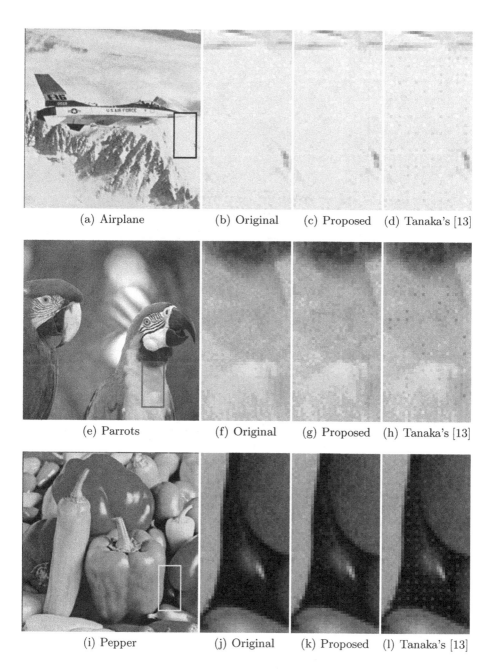

(a) Airplane   (b) Original   (c) Proposed   (d) Tanaka's [13]

(e) Parrots   (f) Original   (g) Proposed   (h) Tanaka's [13]

(i) Pepper   (j) Original   (k) Proposed   (l) Tanaka's [13]

Fig. 6. Comparisons of stego-images between proposed scheme and Tanaka's scheme [13]

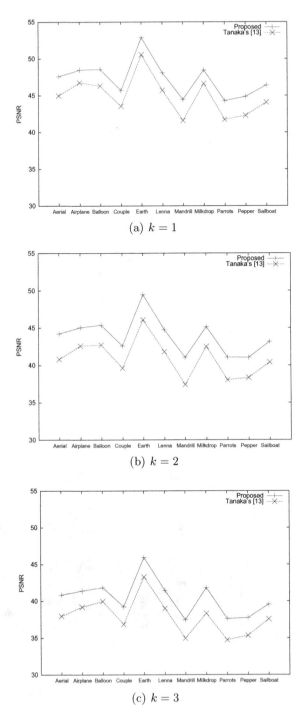

(a) $k = 1$

(b) $k = 2$

(c) $k = 3$

Fig. 7. Comparisons of PSNRs between proposed scheme and Tanaka's scheme [13]

Table 2. PSNRs of stego-images

	$k = 1$		$k = 2$		$k = 3$	
	Proposed	Tanaka's [13]	Proposed	Tanaka's [13]	Proposed	Tanaka's [13]
Aerial	47.57	44.98	44.22	40.81	40.84	37.97
Airplane	48.47	46.75	45.04	42.59	41.39	39.20
Balloon	48.58	46.31	45.37	42.72	41.85	39.97
Couple	45.69	43.54	42.58	39.62	39.23	36.86
Earth	52.86	50.53	49.47	46.07	45.95	43.30
Lenna	48.08	45.72	44.75	41.81	41.44	39.02
Mandrill	44.46	41.58	41.04	37.40	37.46	34.96
Milkdrop	48.46	46.62	45.14	42.50	41.83	38.33
Parrots	44.30	41.72	41.07	38.05	37.62	34.73
Pepper	44.85	42.27	41.03	38.34	37.74	35.34
Sailboat	46.41	44.08	43.16	40.41	39.56	37.57

palette-based images from SIDBA [14], that were 256×256 pixels, and embedded a $7,000 \times k$-bit message into each image.

Fig. 5 shows the stego-images of Airplane and Parrots from SIDBA with a $7,000 \times k$-bit message, where $k = 1, 2$, or 3, using the proposed scheme and Tanaka's scheme [13], respectively. Figs. 6(b), (f), and (j) are parts of the original images, which are enclosed by the squares in Figs. 6(a), (e), and (i), respectively. Figs. 6(c) and (d), Figs. 6(g) and (h), and Figs. 6(k) and (l) are the same parts of the stego-images when using the proposed scheme and Tanaka's scheme [13], respectively.

We summarized the evaluation using PSNR for the stego-images embedded by the proposed scheme in Table 2 and Fig. 7 to compare them with those for Tanaka's scheme [13]. The maximum difference between those two schemes is 3.64 and the minimum difference is 1.72. These results validate the proposed scheme.

5   Conclusion

We have proposed a high-capacity steganographic scheme for palette-based images that are only slightly degraded. The proposed scheme embeds a multiple-bit message within the unit of a pixel matrix to improve the quality of stego-images, while some conventional schemes can embed only a one-bit message within the unit of a pixel. The implementation of this scheme is simple and straightforward. A performance analysis proved the effectiveness of our scheme. Our future work involves improvement of the way to reorder the entries in the palette.

Acknowledgments. This work was supported by JSPS KAKENHI Grant Number 23800010.

References

1. Kahn, D.: The history of steganography. In: Anderson, R. (ed.) IH 1996. LNCS, vol. 1174, pp. 1–5. Springer, Heidelberg (1996)
2. Chandramouli, R., Kharrazi, M., Memon, N.D.: Image Steganography and Steganalysis: Concepts and Practice. In: Kalker, T., Cox, I., Ro, Y.M. (eds.) IWDW 2003. LNCS, vol. 2939, pp. 35–49. Springer, Heidelberg (2004)
3. Niimi, M., Noda, H., Kawaguchi, E., Eason, R.O.: High capacity and secure digital steganography to palette-based images. In: Proc. of IEEE ICIP, pp. II-917–II-920 (2002)
4. Wu, M.-Y., Ho, Y.-K., Lee, J.-H.: An iterative method of palette-based image steganography. Pattern Recognition Letters 25(3), 301–309 (2004)
5. Wang, X., Yao, Z., Li, C.-T.: A palette-based image steganographic method using colour quantisation. In: Proc. of IEEE ICIP, pp. II-1090–II-1093 (2005)
6. Zhao, H., Wang, H., Khan, M.K.: Steganalysis for palette-based images using generalized difference image and color correlogram. Signal Processing 91(11), 2595–2605 (2011)
7. Machado, R.: EZ Stego, Stego Online (1997), http://www.stego.com
8. Fridrich, J.: A new steganographic method for palette-based image. In: Proc. of IS&T PICS, pp. 285–289 (1999)
9. Tzeng, C.-H., Yang, Z.-F., Tsai, W.-H.: Adaptive data hiding in palette images by color ordering and mapping with security protection. IEEE Trans. Commun. 52(5), 791–800 (2004)
10. Zhang, X., Wang, S., Zhou, Z.: Multibit assignment steganography in palette images. IEEE Signal Proc. Lett. 15, 553–556 (2008)
11. Kim, S.-M., Cheng, Z., Yoo, K.-Y.: A new steganography scheme based on an index-color image. In: Proc. of International Conference on Information Technology: New Generations, pp. 376–381 (2009)
12. Wang, C.-T., Liao, C.-H., Chen, R.-M.: High Capacity Image Data Hiding Scheme for Grouping Palette Index. In: Proc. of International Conference on Multimedia and Ubiquitous Engineering, pp. 197–204 (2009)
13. Tanaka, G., Suetake, N., Uchino, E.: A steganographic method realizing high capacity data embedding for palette-based images. In: Proc. of International Workshop on Smart Info-Media Systems in Asia, pp. 92–95 (2009)
14. Onoe, M., Sasaki, M., Inamoto, Y.: SIDBA Standard Image Data Base. MIPC Report 79-1 (1979)

A Statistical Method
for Peak Localization in Hough Space
by Analysing Butterflies

Zezhong Xu[1,2] and Bok-Suk Shin[1]

[1] Department of Computer Science, The University of Auckland
Auckland, New Zealand
[2] College of Computer Information Engineering, Changzhou Institute of Technology
Changzhou, Jiangsu, China
zxu531@aucklanduni.ac.nz, b.shin@auckland.ac.nz

Abstract. The Hough transform is an efficient method for extracting lines in images. Precision of detection relies on how to find and locate accurately the peak in Hough space after the voting process. In this paper, a statistical method is proposed to improve peak localization by considering quantization error and image noise, and by considering the coordinate origin selection. The proposed peak localization is based on butterfly analysis: statistical standard variances and statistical means are computed and used as parameters of fitting and interpolation processes. We show that accurate peak parameters are achieved. Experimental results compare our results with those provided by other peak detection methods. In summary, we show that the proposed peak localization method for the Hough transform is both accurate and robust in the presence of quantization error and image noise.

Keywords: Hough transform, peak detection, mean, variance.

1 Introduction

The *Hough transform* (HT) [5,11] is an efficient method for extracting geometric features in an image containing noisy, missing, and extraneous data. However, without further considerations, the HT requires a heavy computational load. In order to improve its efficiency, many proposals have been published, such as *fast HT* [16], *adaptive HT* [12], or special architectures [1] aiming at reducing the amount of computation and storage for real-time implementations. The *probabilistic HT* [15] and the *randomized HT* [24] only use selected sampling pixels for voting in the Hough space (also known as *accumulator array*). In addition, image noise and parameter quantization cause peak spreading in the Hough space.

Numerous methods are focused on peak enhancement in the accumulator array; the emphasis is here on generated distinct peaks and finding of those peaks. By modifying the HT voting scheme, peaks in the accumulator array are enhanced, and peak detection becomes easier. Edge information [3,9,17] and image preprocessing techniques [7,10,20] are used to guide the voting process.

R. Klette, M. Rivera, and S. Satoh (Eds.): PSIVT 2013, LNCS 8333, pp. 111–123, 2014.

By assigning different weights to votes, peaks becomes more distinct and peak finding becomes easier.

After finding a peak, there are two kinds of common methods to compute accurate peak parameters: simply select the absolute peak cell (θ,ρ) as potential solution, or take a weighted average [14,22] also including adjacent cells (θ_i,ρ_i). Two alternative accurate peak localization methods are presented in [18,19], where two different smoothing windows are employed. Weighted averaging is used to compute the θ value, and linear interpolation for the ρ value.

Recently, the *butterfly distribution* [8] in the accumulator array attracted attention. Several methods are motivated by the butterfly shape of a peak in Hough space. The butterfly shape was used for complete line segment detection in [2,4,23]. By analysing a butterfly pattern, the parameters of a line segment are extracted from the *butterfly's characteristics*; a local operator method [13] for peak enhancement proves to be more robust to image noise.

This paper proposes a novel statistical method for locating peaks in Hough space. The image centre is selected as the coordinates origin. After voting, the cell distribution is analysed around a peak in Hough space. By considering image noise and quantization error, the statistical mean and standard variance are computed and used to estimate a peak's parameters. An accurate peak is finally computed by fitting and interpolation.

The rest of the paper is organized as follows. Section 2 introduces an analysis of peak distribution in Hough space. Section 3 describes our peak finding and peak localization method based on statistical mean and variance. Section 4 compares by providing experimental results. Section 5 concludes.

2   Analysis of Peak Distribution

After voting, distribution of cells with voting values around a peak in Hough space resemble the shape of a butterfly. See Fig. 1. Those *butterfly patterns* (*butterflies* for short) have been analysed widely [8] in terms of shape and direction, also for understanding the width and length of the corresponding line segment.

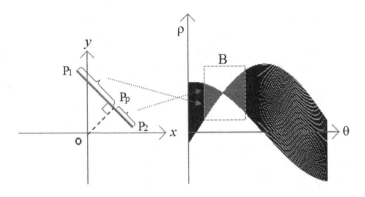

Fig. 1. Pixel contributions to cells. *Left*: Image space. *Right*: Hough space.

ρ_j

4	4	4	3	2	3	1	0	0	3	1	3	1	4	3
1	3	2	2	3	2	1	1	1	0	3	0	1	1	3
2	3	5	3	1	2	4	0	0	1	0	4	2	2	6
2	1	3	4	5	0	0	2	1	0	2	0	5	11	11
5	3	4	5	2	6	4	4	2	2	0	6	13	14	10
1	3	1	0	4	1	2	3	7	4	12	18	15	11	11
6	6	4	4	1	3	3	3	2	21	25	18	13	11	9
8	9	10	12	16	18	13	10	43	36	22	18	13	10	10
9	10	13	13	15	21	40	67	35	26	25	16	15	13	10
7	8	10	14	15	22	28	5	1	2	5	11	12	11	8
8	8	9	13	19	21	3	2	6	1	1	2	2	6	11
9	10	11	14	16	3	1	5	0	2	0	1	2	0	3
10	10	12	12	4	3	4	0	3	3	2	2	3	3	1
7	9	11	6	2	2	1	0	2	3	5	2	1	2	2
8	11	6	2	3	2	2	3	0	1	1	2	2	3	0
8	7	5	2	4	4	2	2	3	3	3	3	3	3	4
9	4	2	4	0	0	4	2	2	1	2	3	3	2	4

θ_i

Fig. 2. Voting values for a noisy line segment in an image, with a peak at value 67

The technique presented in this paper is based on analysing the statistical structure of a butterfly.

Hough Space. A pixel in image space votes for many cells in Hough space. Let H_{ij} be the voting value at cell (i, j) in Hough space, i.e. at $\theta = i$ and $\rho = j$, where i and j are increments along ρ and θ coordinates. A *peak* at a cell (i, j) is formed by having a set of approximately collinear pixels voting for the same cell. See Fig. 2.

Although collinear pixels all contribute to the same peak, different pixels on a line also contribute to different parts around a peak in Hough space. Figure 1 illustrates that pixels left of the perpendicular point P_P contribute to the left-bottom part and the right-upper part from the peak in the butterfly region B. Pixels right of the perpendicular point P_P contribute to the left-upper part and the right-bottom part from the peak in the butterfly region B.

Butterfly Distribution around a Peak. When mapping one noise-free and zero-thickness line segment into Hough space with infinitesimal quantization, an *ideal butterfly* is produced which has two wings. The two wings are symmetrical and connect at the *symmetric point* or peak $(\theta_{peak}, \rho_{peak}) = \lambda$. Within an ideal butterfly, the sum $\sum_j H_{ij}$, i.e. for a variation in ρ-coordinates, remains identical, but the value of cell is changed in the same sum $\sum_j H_{ij}$. A program for analysing the Hough space needs to detect the symmetric point.

However, in the presence of image and quantization noise, *valid* (i.e. generated by the corresponding noisy line segment) voting values around a peak do not form an ideal symmetric point. For every column around a peak, sums of valid values in cells are only approximately equal. A butterfly is composed of column intervals of length $c_i^{wing} = c_i$ containing valid values $H_{ij}^{wing} = H_{ij}$, or of length c^{peak} (i.e. only in a single column i) with valid values H^{peak}, satisfying

$$c_i^{wing} > c^{peak} \quad \text{and} \quad H_{ij}^{wing} < H^{peak} \tag{1}$$

Values c_i^{wing}, H_{ij}^{wing}, c^{peak}, and H^{peak} depend on the number of pixels in the image in the corresponding noisy line segment.

Since the sum of valid values is approximately identical for every column around a peak, the standard variance σ is selected for measuring the *degree of voting scatter* of each column. The smaller the standard variance is, the *more clustered* the voting is. The butterfly's symmetric point is defined by the minimum σ in all contributing columns.

Selection of the Origin in Image Space. Let M and N be width and height of the image space, respectively. In standard Hough transform, the origin in image space is selected to be at a corner of the image, identified with the origin of the coordinate system as used for representing image data. In this case, the range of ρ in the Hough space is from $-\sqrt{M^2 + N^2}$ to $\sqrt{M^2 + N^2}$, and the range of θ is $[0,\ 180°)$.

If the image centre is selected to be the origin, the range of ρ changes into the interval

$$[-\frac{\sqrt{M^2 + N^2}}{2},\ \frac{\sqrt{M^2 + N^2}}{2}]$$

Thus, it is reduced to half of its previous size.

The Hough transform equation is then as follows:

$$\rho = (u - \frac{M}{2}) \cos\theta + (v - \frac{N}{2}) \sin\theta \tag{2}$$

where (u, v) is a pixel coordinate in image space. The location of the origin in the image influences the distance from the perpendicular point P_p to the line segment. By practical experience, this translation of the origin causes a smaller butterfly-like region of valid values of one peak.

Suppose that a line is far away from its perpendicular point; then the butterfly distribution is totally different with respect to either the image corner O or the image centre O'. In case of selecting O as the origin of the image, peak and both wings may not be very distinct in Hough space; several columns may have only one valid cell with the same maxima. The likelihood of such a case is reduced by

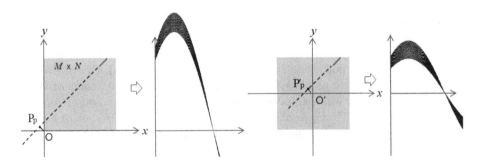

Fig. 3. Butterfly distribution for different coordinate origins. *First and second, from the left*: Image corner as origin, and butterfly in HT space. *Third and fourth*: Same line segment and image centre as origin, and corresponding butterfly in HT space.

selecting O' as the coordinate origin. In general, if O' is the origin, a butterfly region is more distinctly defined by two wings and a symmetrical point.

Figure 3 shows butterfly region distributions for both origin options. In case of the image corner origin, the perpendicular point is far away from the line segment; column interval at the peak has a similar width as column intervals at the ends of the wings in the butterfly region B. It is difficult to detect the peak. In case of the image centre origin, the distance from P_p to line segment is reduced; column intervals in wings of the butterfly are wider, thus defining a more distinct peak.

3   Peak Detection

In this paper, the proposed peak detection procedure combines *finding* of a peak ("roughly") with *localizing* it precisely. After voting for all cells in the accumulator array, the first step is to find a possible peak in the Hough space. Then, for peak localization, accurate peak parameters are estimated by considering peak spreading in the accumulator cells around a found peak.

Peak Finding. The most common method [13] for peak finding is to determine a global threshold first, and to select cells that received more votes than the threshold. Another methods is to identify a peak as a local maxima.

In this paper, a combined local-global method is used for finding an initial peak λ^0, to be accurately localized in the following. The initial peak λ^0 is decided by using the sum of all the nine voting values in a sliding 3×3 window over the whole accumulator array; the window having the maximum sum contains the initial peak λ^0 at its central cell.

Peak Localization. We aim to detect a final peak $\widehat{\lambda}$ as the symmetrical point of the butterfly (identified by λ^0) through our proposed peak localization method which allows us to detect a symmetrical point (as defined above) not only by cell coordinates but even at subcell accuracy (i.e. in real coordinates). The size of a cell is defined by the applied quantization of the Hough space. Our method aims at overcoming the accuracy limitations defined by the quantization setting. Figure 4 illustrates a symmetrical point of a butterfly at subcell accuracy, which identifies a location between adjacent cells, in general with real coordinates.

Let W denote a chosen window, symmetric to λ^0, for approximating the butterfly region B. In our experiments we decided for an 11×11 window W.

We compute the coordinates θ_{peak} and ρ_{peak} of the peak $\widehat{\lambda}$ by using fitting and interpolation techniques. Regarding fitting, we fit a curved function with the σ_i-values for the column intervals in window W; the θ_{peak}-value is defined by the minimum. Regarding interpolation, we compute all m_i-values of the column intervals in window W for computing ρ_{peak} at the obtained θ_{peak}-value.

Statistical means m and variances σ are used as input parameters for those two fitting or interpolation processes. For completeness we provide the basic formulas for the statistical mean m_i and variance σ_i of column intervals symmetric to the found initial peak λ^0:

$$m_i = \sum_W [H_{ij} \cdot \rho_j] / \sum_W H_{ij} \tag{3}$$

$$\sigma_i = \sqrt{\sum_W [H_{ij} \cdot (\rho_j - m_i)^2] / \sum_W H_{ij}} \tag{4}$$

Window W defines the range of i- and j-values in those sums.

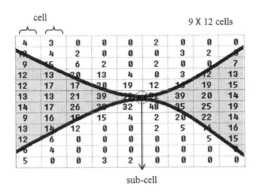

Fig. 4. The symmetric point of a butterfly with subcell accuracy

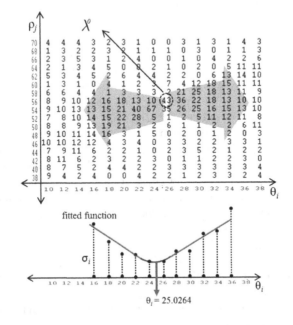

Fig. 5. Function fitting for an 11×11 window W symmetric to the initial peak

Fitting for θ_{peak}. Around λ^0, the localization of the θ-value of the peak is where the voting is "most clustered", as defined by our model in (1).

Since the statistical variance can measure the degree of voting scatter for each θ column, the standard derivation of every column in W, i.e. symmetric to the found peak λ^0, is computed. The θ_{peak}-value at subcell accuracy is computed by fitting a curved function to these standard variances:

1. Compute statistical standard variances σ_i for each column interval left and right of λ^0 within window W.
2. Fit a curved function f with the θ_i and σ_i values:

$$f : \sigma = f(\theta)$$

3. Detect θ_{peak} where this fitted function f has its minima.

$$\theta_{peak} = \theta | f'(\theta) = 0$$

A result is illustrated in Fig. 5. The initial peak λ^0 was found at $(\theta, \rho) = (26, 56)$ with the described peak finding method, and the σ_i-values shown in the bottom part are computed for the shaded cells symmetric to λ^0. A curved function is fitted to those values, the minimum of the function f at $\theta_{peak} = 25.0264$ is of real type, thus not located at a cell but of subcell accuracy.

Interpolation for ρ_{peak}. We calculate the statistical means of θ_i-values in W, i.e. in column intervals left and right of λ^0. The final ρ_{peak} is computed by intersection an interpolated line with the vertical line $\theta_{peak} = 25.0264$:

1. Compute statistical means m_i, for each column interval left and right of λ^0 in window W.

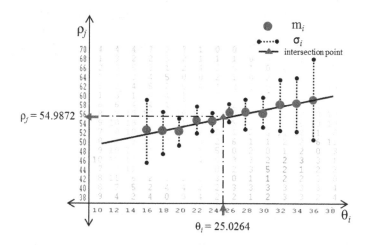

Fig. 6. Linear interpolation for detecting the ρ-value at subcell accuracy

2. Fit a line g with the computed statistical means m_i as follows:

$$g : \rho = g(\theta) \triangleq b_1\theta + b_0$$

3. Compute ρ_{peak} corresponding to the intersection point with the interpolated line:

$$\rho_{peak} = g(\theta_{peak})$$

A result is illustrated in Fig. 6. The computed m_i-values are used for fitting a line, an intersection point is decided then with the defined vertical line at θ_{peak}. The ρ coordinate of the intersection point is the final ρ_{peak}-value. In the shown example, the interpolated ρ_{peak}-value equals 54.9872, and is again a real type for subcell accuracy. The final peak $\widehat{\lambda} = (\theta_{peak}, \rho_{peak})$ is thus detected at $(25.0264, 54.9872)$.

4   Experimental Results

In this section, the proposed peak detection method for the Hough transform is applied at first to a set of simulated data to test the accuracy of line detection. Then we apply the method for real-world data, and selected the detection of lane borders in image sequences recorded for driver assistance purposes.

Test on Simulated Images. We generate $M \times N = 200 \times 200$ binary images that contain 500 randomly generated black pixels as noise. The four endpoint coordinates of one line segment are also produced randomly, and line parameters (θ, ρ) are computed and recorded as ground truth. Black pixels on the line are generated by moving a pixel randomly (i.e. not exactly on the line) by 1 pixel along its normal. A simulated image is shown in Fig. 7, left.

The image centre is selected as the coordinate origin. The accumulator array is quantized by using steps $(\triangle\theta, \triangle\rho) = (2, 2)$. Each pixel votes for all possible cells in the Hough space. After voting, the line parameters are detected with the proposed peak finding and peak localization method. A detection result is shown in Fig. 7, right.

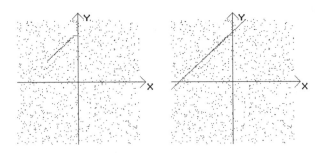

Fig. 7. Line segment detection in simulated images. *Left*: Input image. *Right*: Detected line.

Table 1. Comparison of detection errors

	Detection errors		
	SHT	LSF	F&I
Mean error	(0.633, 0.656)	(0.063, 0.056)	(0.169, 0.119)
Error variance	(0.802, 0.797)	(0.082, 0.075)	(0.210, 0.150)

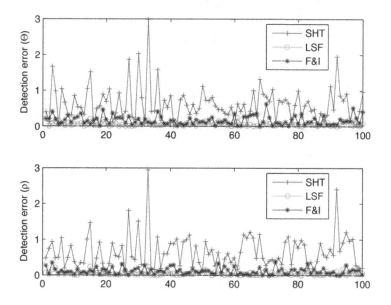

Fig. 8. Comparison of results for 100 generated images

In order to test the detection accuracy, we compare the detection results with the proposed peak localization method (*F&I*) with results obtained either by applying a standard HT (*SHT*), which takes the absolute peak (i.e. with its cell coordinates) as line parameters, or by applying a least-square fit (*LSF*) to the generated line segment pixels, which is regarded as the optimal solution.

For a test for 100 random line segments we report mean error and the error variance. To be precise, the error is measured for both parameters separately, and it is the difference between ground truth value and calculated value. See Table 1. Figure 8 also shows the detection results for the different methods for the 100 input images.

The standard HT is very sensitive to parameter quantization and image noise. Detection errors are larger. By using the fitting and interpolation techniques, we achieve subcell accuracy. By using statistical mean and variance as discussed above, we ensured robustness to image noise. Detection results with the proposed method are actually very close to results obtained by least-square fitting to the

Fig. 9. F&I lane detection results for four frames of real world images

randomly digitized line segments, even under the given coarse quantization and image noise of the reported experiment.

Real World Test. We use image sequences for testing, published in Set 3 of EISATS [6]. These are publicly available long sequences of traffic scenes recorded in Denmark, where lane borders appear to be mostly straight.

One sequence contains 800 frames. When processing these images for line detection, images are first resized to $M \times N = 320 \times 256$, then the image centre is selected as the coordinate origin, and only pixels in the 60% lower part are processed because lane borders are located at the bottom of the whole image. Lane detection results for four images of this data set are shown in Fig. 9.

In a given image, the existence of multiple lines leads to overlays of multiple butterflies in Hough space. We applied multiple-line detection in order to detect accurately every line. The process is as follows: First, a peak $(\theta_{peak}, \rho_{peak})$ is detected by our proposed method, second, a set of pixels contributing to this peak is selected in image space by considering the line parameters and a line thickness, third, the votes of those pixels are removed in accumulator space by decreasing the value in corresponding cells by 1. Then the next peak is found, and so forth until the voting value of the found peak is smaller than a given threshold.

Results show that lane markings are accurately detected if they are "dominantly straight" in the recorded image. With the proposed method, providing

Fig. 10. SHT lane detection results for the same four frames as shown in Fig. 9

subcell accuracy of lane parameters, wide lane markings are identified by two
lines (left and right borders).[1]

Lane detection results of the standard HT are also shown in Fig. 10. Some
lane borders are missing and there are some spurious lane borders detected. If
parameters of a lane border are not matching the used space quantizations then
SHT detection results are inaccurate in this case.

5   Conclusions

Peak localization is an important component for any Hough transform procedure.
By analysing the butterfly distribution of a peak in Hough space, a statistical
mean and variance-based method is proposed to compute accurately the peak
parameters. Peak spreading and coordinate origin selection are also considered.

Detection accuracy of the proposed method is compared with that of a standard HT peak detection procedure and an ideal least-squares fitting method.
Results show that by fitting and interpolation based on statistical mean and
variance, the proposed peak localization method is accurate and robust to parameter quantization and image noise.

---

[1] An actually operative solution for lane detection could have this as a sub-procedure,
combined with temporal reasoning between frames and adaptive curved-line detection at places where straight segments depart from the lane marking in the image.
However, we do not aim at presenting a complete lane detection algorithm in this
paper; this application is only chosen for illustration of the proposed peak detection
technique. For a current review on lane detection methods, see [21].

Acknowledgments. The authors would like to thank Reinhard Klette for his comments and kind support. The first author thanks Jiangsu Overseas Research & Training Program for University Prominent Young & Middle-aged Teachers and President for granting a scholarship to visit and undertake research at The University of Auckland.

References

1. Albanesi, M.G., Ferretti, M., Rizzo, D.: Benchmarking Hough transform architectures for real-time. Real-Time Imaging 6(2), 155–172 (2000)
2. Atiquzzaman, M., Akhtar, M.W.: Complete line segment description using the Hough transform. Image Vision Computation 12(5), 267–273 (1994)
3. Ballard, D.H.: Generalizing the Hough transform to detect arbitrary shapes. Pattern Recognition 13(2), 111–122 (1981)
4. Du, S., Tu, C., van Wyk, B.J., Ochola, E.O., Chen, Z.: Measuring straight line segments using HT butterflies. PLoS ONE 7(3), e33790 (2012)
5. Duda, R.O., Hart, P.E.: Use of the Hough transformation to detect lines and curves in pictures. Comm. ACM 15(1), 11–15 (1972)
6. EISATS:enpeda. image sequence analysis test site (2013), http://www.mi.auckland.ac.nz/EISATS
7. Fernandes, L.A.F., Oliveira, M.: Real-time line detection through an improved Hough transform voting scheme. Pattern Recognition 41(1), 299–314 (2008)
8. Furukawa, Y., Shinagawa, Y.: Accurate and robust line segment extraction by analysing distribution around peaks in Hough space. Computer Vision Image Understanding 92(1), 1–25 (2003)
9. Guerreiro, R.F.C., Aguiar, P.M.Q.: Connectivity-enforcing Hough transform for the robust extraction of line segments. IEEE Trans. Image Processing. 21(12), 4819–4829 (2012)
10. Guo, S., Pridmore, T., Kong, Y., Zhang, X.: An improved Hough transform voting scheme utilizing surround suppression. Pattern Recognition Letters 30, 1241–1252 (2009)
11. Hough, P.V.C.: Methods and means for recognizing complex patterns. U.S. Patent 3.069.654 (1962)
12. Illingworth, J., Kittler, J.: The adaptive Hough transform. IEEE Trans. Pattern Analysis Machine Intelligence 9(5), 690–698 (1987)
13. Ji, J., Chen, G., Sun, L.: A novel Hough transform method for line detection by enhancing accumulator array. Pattern Recognition Letters 32(11), 1503–1510 (2011)
14. Kiryati, N., Bruckstein, A.M.: Antialiasing the Hough transform. Graphical Models Image Processing 53, 213–222 (1991)
15. Kiryati, N., Eldar, Y., Bruckstein, A.M.: A probabilistic Hough transform. Pattern Recognition 24(4), 303–316 (1991)
16. Li, H., Lavin, M.A., LeMaster, R.J.: Fast Hough transform: A hierarchical approach. Computer Vision Graphics Image Process 36(2-3), 139–161 (1986)
17. Leavers, V.F., Sandler, M.B.: An efficient Radon transform. In: Int. Conf. Pattern Recognition, pp. 380–389 (1988)
18. Niblack, W., Petkovic, D.: On improving the accuracy of the Hough transform: Theory, simulation, and experiments. In: IEEE Conf. Computer Vision Pattern Recognition, pp. 574–579 (1988)

19. Niblack, W., Petkovic, D.: On improving the accuracy of the Hough transform. Machine Vision Applications 3, 87–106 (1990)
20. Palmer, P.L., Kittler, J., Petrou, M.: An optimizing line finder using a Hough transform algorithm. Computer Vision Image Understanding 67(1), 1–23 (1997)
21. Shin, B.-S., Xu, Z., Klette, R.: Visual lane analysis - a concise review. Technical report MItech-TR-84, The University of Auckland (2013)
22. Tsai, D.M.: An improved generalized Hough transform for the recognition of over-lapping objects. Image Vision Computing 15, 877–888 (1997)
23. Tu, C., Du, S., van Wyk, B.J., Djouani, K., Hamam, Y.: High resolution Hough transform based on butterfly self-similarity. Electronics Letters 47(25), 1360–1361 (2011)
24. Xu, L., Oja, E., Kultanen, P.: A new curve detection method: Randomized Hough transform (RHT). Pattern Recognition Letters 11(5), 331–338 (1990)

Efficiency Analysis of POC-Derived Bases for Combinatorial Motion Estimation

Alejandro Reyes*, Alfonso Alba**, and Edgar Arce-Santana

Facultad de Ciencias, Universidad Autónoma de San Luis Potosí,
Av. Salvador Nava Mtz. S/N, Zona Universitaria, 78290,
San Luis Potosí, SLP, México
rey_es@ymail.com, fac@fc.uaslp.mx, arce@fciencias.uaslp.mx

Abstract. Motion estimation is a fundamental problem in many computer vision applications. One solution to this problem consists in defining a large enough set of candidate motion vectors, and using a combinatorial optimization algorithm to find, for each point of interest, the candidate which best represents the motion at the point of interest. The choice of the candidate set has a direct impact in the accuracy and computational complexity of the optimization method. In this work, we show that a set containing the most representative maxima of the phase-correlation function between the two input images, computed for different overlapping regions, provides better accuracy and contains less spurious candidates than other choices in the literature. Moreover, a pre-selection stage, based in a local motion estimation algorithm, can be used to further reduce the cardinality of the candidate set, without affecting the accuracy of the results.

1   Introduction

The problem of optical flow estimation consists in finding the apparent (projected) motion of each object in a sequence of images [1]. This motion does not always correspond to the true displacement of the object in the tri-dimensional scene. As an example, consider an object that moves towards the viewer along the camera axis. As the object approaches, it will appear larger in size and thus the optical flow field will resemble a radial pattern where each pixel seems to be moving outwards from the center of the object. Nevertheless, the estimation of optical flow has numerous applications in computer vision, robot vision, robot and vehicle navigation, non-parametric (smooth) image registration and morphing, video encoding and video stabilization. It is also often used, along with stereo disparity estimation, as the grounds for 3D motion estimation, which is also called *scene flow* [2].

Formally, a given point in a moving object is projected to a point $x = (x(t), y(t))$ in the 2D frame, where t denotes time. The optical flow is thus defined as $v(x, t) = dx/dt$. Since t is usually discrete, one can alternatively write

---

* A. Reyes was supported by CONACyT scholarship No. 327373.
** This work was partially supported by CONACyT grant 154623.

R. Klette, M. Rivera, and S. Satoh (Eds.): PSIVT 2013, LNCS 8333, pp. 124–135, 2014.

$v(x, t) \approx x(t + 1) - x(t)$. Therefore, the problem consists in estimating $v(x, t)$ from a given sequence of video frames $I(x, t)$. In some cases, one is interested in estimating the optical flow only at specific points, which typically correspond to recognizable image features such as edges or corners. In general, one may want to estimate the flow field densely, that is, estimate $v(x, t)$ for each pixel x.

Many algorithms for the estimation of optical flow have been proposed in the literature. For a comprehensive review of the most relevant methods, please refer to [1, 3]. Most state of the art methods for the estimation of dense optical flow are based on the variational approach proposed by Horn and Schunck [4]. The approach followed by these methods is based on the *optical flow constraint* which states that the color intensity of a given point $x(t)$ does not vary (or varies very smoothly) across time, and the solution usually requires minimizing a energy function $U(v) = M(v) + R(v)$ where $M(v)$ is a matching term which penalizes the differences between $I(x(t), t)$ and $I(x(t+1), t+1)$ (thus enforcing the optical flow constraint), and $R(v)$ is a regularization term which penalizes abrupt spatial changes in v (thus reducing the effects of noise). The energy function originally proposed by Horn and Schunck is quadratic, resulting in a convex optimization problem whose solution can be efficiently found using linear algebra iterative methods, such as Gauss-Seidel. However, this method usually leads to oversmooth solutions where the edges and details of the objects are not well preserved. More recent proposals rely on more complex energy functions which provide accurate estimations, but require non-linear optimization techniques whose implementation is more difficult and computationally expensive.

Other methods follow a combinatorial approach, where a large enough set of plausible motion vectors $\mathcal{D} = \{v_1, \ldots, v_N\}$ is defined, and then a discrete optimization algorithm is used to assign the most adequate base vector to each pixel. We call such a set $\mathcal{D}$ a *basis*, although it is not a basis in the linear algebra sense, since the base vectors are not linearly independent. The optimization process which assigns a candidate vector to each pixel can be performed locally or globally. In a local approach, one usually estimates a cost function $C_k(x)$ which measures how adequately the base vector v_k describes the motion at pixel x. For example, the classic block matching (BM) method uses the sum of absolute differences (SAE) or the sum of squared differences (SSD) of intensities between a window centered at $I(x, t)$ and an equally-sized window centered at $I(x + v_k, t + 1)$. Since both SAE and SSD can be computed very efficiently, for example, by using the integral images [5] or aggregate cost techniques, the local approach adapts very well to realtime applications, as long as the size of the basis N is relatively small. On the other hand, global combinatorial approaches are similar to variational methods in the sense that one usually has to minimize an energy function $U(e)$, where $e(x)$ is a field of labels (often modeled as a Markov Random Field) which indicate the base vector assigned to each pixel (i.e., the vector assigned to pixel x is $v_{e(x)}$); however, the minimization of $U(e)$ is a combinatorial problem which usually requires computationally expensive methods such as graph-cuts [6], or belief propagation [7]. In both approaches, local and global, computational complexity increases directly with respect to the number N of vectors in the basis. Moreover, the presence of spurious vectors in the basis; that is, vectors which do not correspond to the motion of any of the objects in the scene and should not be assigned to any pixel, may increase the uncertainty and have a negative impact in the accuracy of the estimations. For these reasons, it is desirable to choose a basis that is small yet represents well the true motions of the objects, with the least possible amount of spurious vectors.

Various algorithms have been proposed to obtain a good basis for a given input scene. As a first approach, one could define the basis to contain all vectors with integer coordinates within a certain range, for example, from $-D$ to D, forming a regular grid of size $(2D + 1) \times (2D + 1)$. Clearly, even for small values of D the size of the basis will be relatively large, and will likely contain many spurious candidates. Another choice is to use a polar grid, where the basis vectors are uniformly spaced in angle and magnitude, and with magnitude up to D [8]. For example, for a displacement range of $D = 4$ pixels, the rectangular grid approach would define a basis with 81 vectors, whereas the polar grid approach with 8 different angles (at intervals of $\pi/4$ radians) would yield 33 candidates, including the vector $(0, 0)$. Both of these approaches typically yield relatively large bases and are severely limited by the displacement range D. Another solution consists in performing, in a first stage, a crude estimation of the optical flow with a very large set of candidates, for instance, a rectangular grid with a large enough D, using a fast local method such as block matching; then, an heuristic is used to form a reduced basis for each pixel, containing the most likely candidates which resulted from the previous stage, and the reduced bases are used in a slower global optimization method [9]. One disadvantage of this method is that any spurious candidates that may have been wrongly chosen for a given pixel during the local matching stage will also form part of the reduced basis; another disadvantage is that this reduction technique has limited use in realtime implementations.

Recently, another method was proposed to obtain a reduced basis with very little computational overhead [10]. This method is based on the estimation of the phase-only correlation (POC) function, which for two 1D discrete-time signals $f(x)$ and $g(x)$ is defined as

$$r(x) = \mathcal{F}^{-1} \left\{ \frac{F(k)G^*(k)}{|F(k)G^*(k)|} \right\}, \tag{1}$$

where F and G are the Fourier transforms of f and g, respectively, G^* denotes the complex conjugate of G, and $\mathcal{F}^{-1}$ is the inverse Fourier transform. It is easy to show that if g is a shifted version of f, i.e., $g(x) = f(x - d)$, then $r(x) = \delta(x + d)$, where $\delta(x) = 1$ if $x = 0$ and $\delta(x) = 0$ otherwise; therefore, one can estimate the displacement between f and g as $\hat{d} = \arg\max_x\{r(x)\}$. A more general case is when $g(x)$ can be modeled as a version of $f(x)$ where different segments suffer different displacements; in other words, when $g(x) = f(x - d(x))$ where $d(x)$ is a piece-wise constant function, then the POC function is a sum of distorted delta functions, centered at the locations which corresponds to the displacement values that the function $d(x)$ can take (see [10] for details). This result can be extended to 2D signals (images) and higher-dimensional signals. In the context of combinatorial motion estimation, the locations of the maxima of the 2D POC between the input images form an adequate basis for computationally efficient implementations.

This work focuses exclusively on combinatorial motion estimation methods which rely on a finite candidate vector set (a basis) from which pixel velocities can be selected, and presents an in-depth evaluation of the bases that can be obtained by finding multiple maxima in the POC function, in terms of (1) the accuracy with which they can represent the true motions in the scene, and (2) their computational cost (mainly given by the cardinality of the basis). Using these criteria, we also present a comparison against the bases obtained using typical rectangular and polar grids, and applying a heuristic to reduce the size of the bases using a block matching stage. Finally, we assess the accuracy of an actual estimation of the optical flow field with each of the bases under study using state-of-the-art Quadratic Markov Measure Field models [11]. The results from these analyses demonstrate that the POC-derived bases have a significant positive impact on the computational efficiency, without sacrificing the accuracy of the estimated motions.

2   Methodology

2.1   Basis Estimation

Let $f(\boldsymbol{x})$ and $g(\boldsymbol{x})$ be the input images (e.g., two consecutive frames in a video sequence), where $\boldsymbol{x}$ denotes the position of a pixel. Let $N_x \times N_y$ be the size of the images (in pixels) and let L be the lattice where the image is defined; i.e., $L = [0, \ldots, N_x - 1] \times [0, \ldots, N_y - 1]$.

To prevent interference between too many peaks in the POC function, the input images are divided in overlapping square regions of size $W \times W$, where W is chosen as a power of two so that FFTs can be computed efficiently. In our tests, we have obtained the best results using $W = 128$. The overlap between adjacent regions can be as small as the largest displacement $D_{\max}$ one wants to find. With this consideration, the image is divided horizontally in M_x and vertically in M_y regions, where

$$M_x = \left\lceil \frac{N_x - W}{W - D_{\max}} \right\rceil + 1, \quad M_y = \left\lceil \frac{N_y - W}{W - D_{\max}} \right\rceil + 1, \tag{2}$$

and the horizontal and vertical spacing between regions is thus given by $s_x = (N_x - W)/(M_x - 1)$ and $s_y = (N_y - W)/(M_y - 1)$, respectively. Therefore, region (i, j) is defined by the sub-lattice $L_{ij} = [is_x, \ldots, is_x + W - 1] \times [js_y, \ldots, js_y + W - 1]$ for all $i = 0, \ldots, M_x - 1$ and $j = 0, \ldots, M_y - 1$.

For each region (i, j), the POC function $r_{ij}(\boldsymbol{d})$ is computed between the sub-images of $f(\boldsymbol{x})$ and $g(\boldsymbol{x})$ defined at $\boldsymbol{x} \in L_{ij}$. Then, the set $\mathcal{D}_{ij} = \{\boldsymbol{d}_{ij}^1, \ldots, \boldsymbol{d}_{ij}^P\}$, which contains the locations of the P most significant maxima of r_{ij}, is found. We have obtained good results with P between 5 and 8. The vectors $\boldsymbol{d}_{ij}^q$ represent

likely displacements for the objects observed in region (i, j). One can also define
the set of likely displacements for the full image as $\mathcal{D} = \cup_{i,j} \mathcal{D}_{ij} = \{d_1, \ldots, d_K\}$,
where K is the cardinality of this set.

It is also useful to estimate a candidate subset $\mathcal{D}_x$ for each pixel x. To do this,
one can build, for each candidate $d_k \in \mathcal{D}$, a mask image $m_k(x)$ which indicates
if d_k is an adequate candidate for pixel x as follows:

$$m_k(x) = \begin{cases} 1 & \text{if } \exists i, j \, : \, x \in L_{ij}, \ d_k \in D_{ij}, \\ 0 & \text{otherwise.} \end{cases} \tag{3}$$

Then, the subset $\mathcal{D}_x$ of candidates for pixel x is given by $\mathcal{D}_x = \{d_k \in \mathcal{D} \, : \, m_k(x) = 1\}$.

2.2   Basis Reduction

Following the idea in [9], given a basis $\mathcal{D}$, one can obtain a reduced basis $\hat{\mathcal{D}}$
by performing a fast local optical flow estimation (such as block-matching),
and eliminating any motion vectors that were not assigned to any pixel during
this process. Formally, the estimated motion $v(x)$ for a pixel x is obtained by
minimizing the sum of a given cost function c over a window centered at x, over
the set of candidate motion vectors:

$$v(x) = \arg \min_{d \in \mathcal{D}_x} \left\{ \sum_{r \in W} c(f(x + r) - g(x + r + d)) \right\}, \tag{4}$$

where W is a moving window of size $(2w + 1) \times (2w + 1)$, defined by $W = [-w, \ldots, w] \times [-w, \ldots, w]$. The size w of the window represents a trade-off between noise reduction and detail preservation; however, in this stage we are not
interested in the preservation of borders and details, so it is recommendable to
use a large window to avoid noisy estimations that could let spurious candidates
to be included in the reduced basis. In our tests, we have obtained the best
results with $w = 14$ (a 29×29 window). The cost function c is usually chosen to
be the absolute value $c(x) = |x|$, or the square $c(x) = x^2$. For color images, the
cost can be defined in terms of the L_2 norm. In our tests, we have chosen a trun-
cated absolute value, given by $c(x) = \min\{|x|, \epsilon\}$, which is slightly more robust
to outliers. The value of ϵ is chosen as a proportion of the full dynamic range of
the non-truncated cost function; for instance, $\epsilon = \kappa R$, where R is the dynamic
range of the images (i.e., the difference between the maximum and minimum
intensity values). In our tests, we have obtained the best average results with
$\kappa = 0.03$.

Once the optical flow $v(x)$ has been estimated, one can define the reduced
basis $\hat{\mathcal{D}}$ as the set of motion vectors used in v; that is, $\hat{\mathcal{D}} = \{v(x) \, : \, x \in L\}$. It is
also possible to find a reduced candidate set $\hat{\mathcal{D}}_x$ for each pixel x as $\hat{\mathcal{D}}_x = \hat{\mathcal{D}} \cap \mathcal{D}_x$.

2.3   Optimal Ground Truth Reconstruction

To evaluate the quality of a given basis, one could use any combinatorial method
for the estimation of the optical flow for a scene with a known ground truth

$w(x)$, and compare the estimated flow field against the ground truth. However, the quality of the results will strongly depend on the accuracy of the optical flow method and may not reflect the adequateness of the basis itself. One alternative consists in measuring how well the basis vectors can represent the ground truth, regardless of the method used for the actual estimation of the optical flow. To do this, one can obtain an optimal reconstruction of the ground truth, for a given basis $\mathcal{D} = \{d_1, \ldots, d_k\}$, by taking, for each pixel x, the candidate which is closer to the true motion vector at x. In other words, the optimal ground truth reconstruction $w_{\mathcal{D}}$ for a given basis $\mathcal{D}$ is computed as $w_{\mathcal{D}}(x) = \arg\min_{d \in \mathcal{D}} \{\|d - w(x)\|\}$.

From this reconstruction, one can compute the average end-point error (AEE) and average angular error (AAE) with respect to the ground truth w, as defined in [3]. Note that, for a given basis $\mathcal{D}$, the optimal reconstruction $w_{\mathcal{D}}$ is designed to minimize the AEE, and in this sense represents the best possible estimation one can obtain.

It is also interesting to find which, and how many, of the candidates are actually useful for reconstructing the ground truth. These are given by $\mathcal{D}_{GT} = \{w_{\mathcal{D}}(x) \; : \; x \in L\}$. We define the *efficiency* $E_{\mathcal{D}}$ of a given basis $\mathcal{D}$ as the percentage of basis vectors which are used in the optimal reconstruction; that is, $E_{\mathcal{D}} = (|\mathcal{D}_{GT}|/|\mathcal{D}|) \times 100\%$.

2.4   Optical Flow Estimation with a QMMF Model

We have also implemented a state-of-the-art global optimization algorithm based on an Entropy-Controlled Quadratic Markov Measure Field model (EC-QMMF) [11]. Under this model, one estimates the probabilities $b_k(x) = P(v(x) = d_k \mid f, g, \mathcal{D})$, where f and g are the input images and $\mathcal{D} = \{d_1, \ldots, d_K\}$ is a given basis. Note that, in order for $b(x) = (b_1(k), \ldots, b_K(x))$ to be a proper probability measure, it is necessary that $b_k(x) \geq 0$ and $\sum_k b_k(x) = 1$. Once the measure field b is known, once can compute an estimator for $v(x)$ as the central tendency of $b(x)$. For instance, using the mode as central tendency measure, the flow field could be estimated by $v(x) = d_{e(x)}$, $e(x) = \arg\max_k\{b_k(x)\}$, while using the mean as central tendency measure, the optical flow estimation is given by

$$v(x) = \sum_{k=1}^{K} b_k d_k. \tag{5}$$

Note that the mean estimator given by (5) can take values outside of the candidate set $\mathcal{D}$ and is therefore able to produce smoother optical flow fields. However, if the measures $b(x)$ are highly entropic (i.e., approximately uniform), then the mean estimator given by (5) will approach a constant vector (the average of the candidates) for all x. The EC-QMMF models attempt to avoid this problem by imposing both smoothness and entropy constraints to the measure field b. Under this model, the optimal b is obtained by minimizing the energy function $U(b)$ given by

$$U(b) = \sum_{x \in L} \sum_{k=1}^{K} b_k^2(x)[-\log \hat{b}(x) - \mu] + \lambda \sum_{x \in L} \sum_{y \in \mathcal{N}_x} \beta_{x,y} ||b(x) - b(y)||^2, \quad (6)$$

subject to

$$b_k(x) \geq 0, \ \forall x \in L, k \in \{1, \ldots, K\} \quad (7)$$

$$\sum_{k=1}^{K} b_k(x) = 1, \ \forall x \in L. \quad (8)$$

Here, $\hat{b}(x) = \left(\hat{b}_1(x), \ldots, \hat{b}_K(x) \right)$ is a normalized likelihood measure, which in our case is given by

$$\hat{b}_k(x) = \exp\{-c(f(x) - g(x + d_k))\}, \quad (9)$$

where $c(x)$ is the truncated absolute cost function used in Section 2.2, the set $\mathcal{N}_x$ is a neighborhood of x, which in our case consists of all pixels whose distance to x is less or equal than 1, and the variables λ and μ are hyperparameters that control, respectively, the degree of smoothing and the entropy penalization (for details on the probabilistic framework from which the energy function $U(b)$ is derived, please see [11]). Finally, the coefficients $\beta_{x,y}$ measure the likelihood of pixels x and y belonging to the same object, in order to preserve detail at the edges of the objects in the reference image. These coefficients are given by $\beta_{x,y} = \exp\{-\frac{\gamma}{R}||f(x) - f(y)||\}$, where the hyperparameter γ controls the awareness of the algorithm to edges and R is the dynamic range of the image [12].

Since $U(b)$ is quadratic, it can be minimized very efficiently by solving a linear system with constraints. Constraint (8) can be handled by introducing the corresponding Lagrange multipliers so that the system remains linear, while constraint (7) is handled by a simple projection method: each time a measure $b(x)$ is updated, any negative components $b_k(x)$ are set to zero, and $b(x)$ is renormalized. Our implementation uses the Gauss-Seidel method to solve the unconstrained linear system, and the proposed projection method.

3   Results and Discussion

Several tests were performed to assess the quality of the bases obtained using the proposed method and compare them with other methods in the literature. The test scenes were obtained from the Middlebury optical flow database; there are eight training scenes with known ground truth: Dimetrodon, Grove2, Grove3, Hydrangea, RubberWhale, Urban2, Urban3 and Venus. A technical description of each scene and the challenges they present can be found in [3].

All tests were performed in a computer with a quad-core 3.1 GHz Intel Core i5 CPU and 8 Gb of RAM; however, our implementations have not been thoroughly

Table 1. Number of candidates in each of the bases under study, for each test scene

	Dimetrodon	Grove2	Grove3	Hydrangea	Rubberwhale	Urban2	Urban3	Venus
$\mathcal{D}_{\text{POC5}}$	21	20	65	40	19	52	55	29
$\mathcal{D}_{\text{POC5-R}}$	14	13	61	37	13	46	52	22
$\mathcal{D}_{\text{POC8}}$	39	35	81	65	34	77	86	50
$\mathcal{D}_{\text{POC8-R}}$	21	23	74	53	18	55	75	29
$\mathcal{D}_{\text{RGRID}}$	625	625	625	625	625	625	625	625
$\mathcal{D}_{\text{RGRID-R}}$	34	77	222	65	40	378	315	105
$\mathcal{D}_{\text{PGRID}}$	385	385	385	385	385	385	385	385
$\mathcal{D}_{\text{PGRID-R}}$	31	89	167	77	52	131	227	114

optimized and do not run in multiple cores. The reported results are meant to serve only as an additional characterization of the different bases under study and do not necessarily demonstrate the full potential of the proposed methods in terms of accuracy and computational efficiency.

3.1 Test Bases

For each scene, we construct four different bases:

- $\mathcal{D}_{\text{POC5}}$ - A basis obtained using the proposed POC method with $P = 5$ candidates per region, and regions of size 128×128.
- $\mathcal{D}_{\text{POC8}}$ - A basis obtained using the proposed POC method with $P = 8$ candidates per region, and regions of size 128×128.
- $\mathcal{D}_{\text{RGRID}}$ - A rectangular grid with a displacement range $D = 12$; that is, $\mathcal{D}_{\text{RG}} = [-12, \ldots, 12] \times [-12, \ldots, 12]$. This basis contains 625 candidate vectors.
- $\mathcal{D}_{\text{PGRID}}$ - A polar grid with range $D = 24$ and 16 different angles (at intervals of $\pi/8$). That is, $\mathcal{D}_{\text{RG}} = \{(d\cos(a\pi/8), d\sin(a\pi/8)) : d \in \{0, \ldots, 24\}, a \in \{0, \ldots, 15\}\}$. This basis contains 385 vectors.

For each of these bases, we also perform the reduction stage described in Section 2.2 to obtain the reduced bases $\mathcal{D}_{\text{POC5-R}}$, $\mathcal{D}_{\text{POC8-R}}$, $\mathcal{D}_{\text{RGRID-R}}$ and $\mathcal{D}_{\text{PGRID-R}}$, respectively. The exact number of candidates contained in each base, for each one of the test scenes, is shown in Table 1. Note that the cardinality of the POC-derived bases is considerably smaller than the cardinality of the grid bases.

3.2 Optimal Ground Truth Reconstruction Error

Table 2 shows the average and standard deviation (over the eight Middlebury training scenes) of the AEE and AAE between the ground truth and the optimal reconstruction with each of the bases under study. The efficiency (percentage of base vectors used in the reconstruction) is also shown. Note that the lowest AEE is achieved with the POC-derived bases. This is probably due to the fact that the displacement range in the grid bases is limited, particularly in the case of

Table 2. Evaluation of the different bases under study with respect to the optimal ground truth reconstruction that can be obtained with each basis. The columns show the mean and standard deviation (SD) of the average end-point error (AEE, in pixels), average angular error (AAE, in degrees) and Efficiency percentage, measured over the eight test scenes. Values shown in bold face correspond to the best case.

	Mean AEE	SD AEE	Mean AAE	SD AAE	Mean Eff	SD Eff
$\mathcal{D}_{POC5}$	0.372	0.092	4.859	2.401	73.620	18.180
$\mathcal{D}_{POC5\text{-}R}$	0.373	0.091	4.861	2.401	**86.553**	**13.215**
$\mathcal{D}_{POC8}$	0.360	0.091	4.724	2.432	55.738	23.356
$\mathcal{D}_{POC8\text{-}R}$	**0.360**	**0.090**	4.723	2.431	73.778	22.308
$\mathcal{D}_{RGRID}$	0.641	0.773	4.699	2.781	6.920	5.509
$\mathcal{D}_{RGRID\text{-}R}$	0.642	0.773	4.701	2.781	39.064	34.023
$\mathcal{D}_{PGRID}$	0.454	0.254	**4.309**	**2.177**	10.584	6.754
$\mathcal{D}_{PGRID\text{-}R}$	0.455	0.254	**4.309**	**2.177**	40.462	27.321

the rectangular grid. One could increase this range, however, it would result in a very large number of candidates that would be impractical in many cases. On the other hand, the lowest AAE is achieved with the polar grid approach. This is possibly because the other methods (POC and rectangular grid) only produce candidates with integer coordinates, and thus fail to accurately represent the direction of short movements.

It is also worth noting that the reduction stage using block matching considerably reduces the cardinality of the basis, and increases its efficiency, but has a neglible impact in the reconstruction accuracy. This suggests that the proposed reduction stage does eliminate a fair amount of spurious candidates.

One could question if *any* of these bases is adequate for the estimation of the optical flow between the two input images. One way to answer this question is to determine if a given basis $\mathcal{D}$ is better than a random basis $\mathcal{D}_{rand}$, in terms of the accuracy and efficiency with which the ground truth can be reconstructed. To do this, one can generate a R random bases (where R is large enough), and for each case, compute the ground truth reconstruction and estimate the accuracy of the reconstruction (by means of the AEE and AAE) and its efficiency. With this data, one can construct the empirical distributions of the accuracy and efficiency for random bases and test if the results for a given basis $\mathcal{D}$ could be drawn from these distributions. The empirical distributions can be obtained, for instance, using kernel density estimation with a bandwidth given by Silverman's rule of thumb [13]. For a given scene, the random bases are constructed by choosing vectors with a uniformly random direction, and an uniformly random magnitude between 0 and a displacement range $D = 24$. For a given scene, the cardinality of all the random bases is chosen to be equal to $|\mathcal{D}_{POC8}|$, which is the largest cardinality of the POC-derived bases. Figure 1 shows the distributions (both as histograms and kernel density estimators) for AAE, AEE and efficiency for two different scenes: Rubberwhale and Urban3, and the positions where the bases under study lie within these distributions. Note that, in most cases, the scores obtained with the test bases lie near or completely outside the tails of

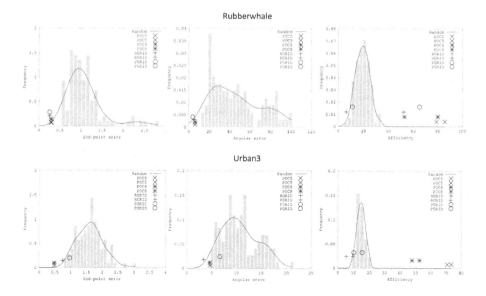

Fig. 1. Distributions of AEE, AAE and Efficiency between the ground truth and the optimal reconstruction using a random basis, for two of the Middlebury scenes: Rubberwhale and Urban3. The black marks indicate where the results obtained with non-random bases lie within the corresponding distributions.

the distributions (left tail for AEE and AAE, right tail for efficiency), which supports the notion that these bases are adequate for the estimation of the optical flow.

3.3 Optical Flow Estimation Error

For the final test presented in this paper, we estimated the optical flow for six of the eight Middlebury training scenes using the EC-QMMF model. For this test, we used only the reduced bases, since the reduction stage does not seem to have a significant impact in the quality of the results. We also decided to remove the results corresponding to the Urban2 and Urban3 scenes due to the fact that our current implementation can handle a maximum of 255 candidates, but the RGRID-R bases have more than 255 candidates for the Urban scenes. This limitation will be avoided in future implementations. The parameters used for all tests were $\lambda = 100$, $\mu = 1$, $\gamma = 20$, and 50 Gauss-Seidel iterations; these values were obtained empirically and might not be the optimal parameters for every scene.

The average results are presented in Table 3. The POC-derived bases show a slight improvement with respect to the reduced grid bases, both in accuracy (AEE and AAE), and a considerable improvement in efficiency. The increased accuracy may be explained by the fact that the reduced grid bases contain a large number of spurious candidates which increase the uncertainty in the QMMF

Table 3. Evaluation of the different bases under study with respect to the EC-QMMF optical flow estimation that can be obtained with each basis. The columns show the mean and standard deviation (SD) of the average end-point error (AEE, in pixels), average angular error (AAE, in degrees) and Efficiency percentage, measured over six test scenes. The B. Time column indicates the average time required for the basis estimation (including the block-matching reduction stage), whereas E. Time represents the average time required for the optical flow estimation. Total computation time is the sum of B. Time and E. Time. Values shown in bold face correspond to the best case.

	Mean AEE	SD AEE	Mean AAE	SD AAE	Mean Eff	SD Eff	B. Time	E. Time
$\mathcal{D}_{\text{POC5-R}}$	0.493	0.223	7.529	2.967	**89.136**	**14.376**	**0.266**	**1.233**
$\mathcal{D}_{\text{POC8-R}}$	**0.480**	**0.212**	7.412	2.931	75.320	24.523	0.368	1.520
$\mathcal{D}_{\text{RGRID-R}}$	0.495	0.225	**7.478**	**2.433**	48.318	34.092	3.532	3.305
$\mathcal{D}_{\text{PGRID-R}}$	0.588	0.310	8.198	2.445	46.760	29.102	2.087	3.164

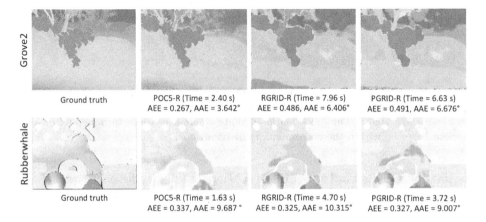

Fig. 2. Optical flow estimation results for the Grove2 scene (upper row) and the Rubberwhale scene (lower row) using the POC5-R, RGRID-R, and PGRID-R bases. The AAE, AEE, and total computation time are shown for each case. The parameters used for the EC-QMMF model were: $\lambda = 1000$, $\mu = 1$, $\gamma = 20$, and 50 Gauss-Seidel iterations.

optimization algorithm. Note also that the computation times are considerably smaller for the POC bases, in particular the basis reduction time which includes the block-matching stage. This is because, in this stage, all candidates must be tested for every pixel, and the initial grid bases are highly inefficient. Finally, Figure 2 presents the results for the Grove2 and Rubberwhale scenes.

4 Conclusions

A methodology for the estimation of efficient vector bases for the combinatorial estimation of optical flow was presented. These bases are obtained as the locations of the maxima of the phase-correlation function estimated for overlapping regions of the images, and can be further reduced by a candidate pre-selection stage based on a block-matching optical flow estimation with low computational cost. Our tests show that the resulting bases, when used in a global optical flow estimation, perform better than bases obtained from regular grids, in terms of both computational complexity and estimation accuracy. This is likely due to the fact that the POC-derived bases contain a higher percentage of vectors which are similar to the true motions, and a lower number of spurious vectors which may confound the optimization algorithms.

References

1. Barron, J., Fleet, D., Beauchemin, S.: Performance of optical flow techniques. International Journal of Computer Vision 12, 43–77 (1994)
2. Wedel, A., Brox, T., Vaudrey, T., Rabe, C., Franke, U., Cremers, D.: Stereoscopic scene flow computation for 3d motion understanding. International Journal of Computer Vision 95, 29–51 (2011)
3. Baker, S., Scharstein, D., Lewis, J., Roth, S., Black, M., Szeliski, R.: A database and evaluation methodology for optical flow. International Journal of Computer Vision 92, 1–31 (2011)
4. Horn, B.K.P., Schunck, B.G.: Determining Optical Flow. Artificial Intelligence 17, 185–203 (1981)
5. Viola, P., Jones, M.: Robust Real-time Object Detection. International Journal of Computer Vision 57, 137–154 (2002)
6. Boykov, Y., Veksler, O., Zabih, R.: Fast approximate energy minimization via graph cuts. IEEE Transactions on Pattern Analysis and Machine Intelligence 23, 1222–1239 (2001)
7. Sun, J., Zheng, N.N., Shum, H.Y.: Stereo matching using belief propagation. IEEE Transactions on Pattern Analysis and Machine Intelligence 25, 787–800 (2003)
8. Ramirez-Manzanares, A., Rivera, M., Kornprobst, P., Lauze, F.: Variational multivalued velocity field estimation for transparent sequences. Journal of Mathematical Imaging and Vision 40, 285–304 (2011)
9. Veksler, O.: Reducing search space for stereo correspondence with graph cuts. In: British Machine Vision Conference, vol. 2, pp. 709–719 (2006)
10. Alba, A., Arce-Santana, E., Aguilar Ponce, R.M., Campos-Delgado, D.U.: Phase-correlation guided area matching for realtime vision and video encoding. Journal of Real-Time Image Processing (2012) (in press)
11. Rivera, M., Ocegueda, O., Marroquin, J.: Entropy-controlled quadratic markov measure field models for efficient image segmentation. IEEE Transactions on Image Processing 16, 3047–3057 (2007)
12. Reyes, A., Alba, A., Arce-Santana, E.R.: Optical flow estimation using phase only-correlation. Procedia Technology 7, 103–110 (2013)
13. Silverman, B.W.: Density Estimation for Statistics and Data Analysis. Chapman and Hall, London (1986)

Stereo and Motion Based 3D High Density Object Tracking

Junli Tao, Benjamin Risse, and Xiaoyi Jiang

University of Auckland, Computer Science
University of Münster, Computer Science, Neurobiology
jtao076@aucklanduni.ac.nz,
b.risse@wwu.de,
xjiang@uni-muenster.de

Abstract. In order to understand the behavior of adult *Drosophila melanogaster* (fruit flies), vision-based 3D trajectory reconstruction methods are adopted. To improve the statistical strength of subsequent analysis, high-throughput measurements are necessary. However, ambiguities in both stereo matching and temporal tracking appear more frequently in high density situations, aggravating the complexity of the 3D tracking situation. In this paper we propose a high density object tracking algorithm. Instead of approximating trajectories for all frames in a direct manner, in ambiguous situations, tracking is terminated to generate robust tracklets based on the modified tracking-by-matching method. The terminated tracklets are linked to ongoing (unterminated) tracklets with minimum linking cost in an on-line fashion. Furthermore, we introduce a set of new evaluation metrics to analyze the tracking results. These metrics are used to analyse the effect of detection noise and compare our tracking algorithm with two state-of-the-art 3D tracking methods based on simulated data with hundreds of flies. The results indicate that our proposed algorithm outperforms both, the tracking-by-matching algorithm and a global correspondence selection approach.

Keywords: Drosophila melanogaster, fruit flies, 3D tracking, tracklets, stereo matching, Kalman filter, evaluation metrics.

1 Introduction

For almost all animals, the ability to move is pivotal for finding food, mating partners or escaping from dangerous situations. During evolution, an increasingly complex nervous system allowed sophisticated locomotion control. Therefore, vision based locomotion analysis of various organisms is an important subject in neurobiological research [13].

Drosophila melanogaster (i.e. fruit fly) is one of the most popular model organisms to study the nervous system. It is a holometabolous insect. In the larval stage, movement is restricted to two dimensions and behavioral experiments are well established using 2D tracking [12,15]. In the adult stage several 2D behavioral experiments are done by cutting the wings [3] or using an arena with flat

R. Klette, M. Rivera, and S. Satoh (Eds.): PSIVT 2013, LNCS 8333, pp. 136–148, 2014.
© Springer-Verlag Berlin Heidelberg 2014

ceiling [17] to restrict the locomotion to two dimensions. However these manipulations lead to unnatural behavior [5].

Reconstructing 3D trajectories of hundreds of objects with similar appearance is challenging. On the one hand, more than one camera is necessary to determine the 3D positions with cross view correspondences. On the other hand, those 3D positions are associated over time to generate trajectories. Thus, two subprocesses are involved to obtain 3D trajectories: stereo matching between different views and temporal tracking over time. Both leading to the so-called general multi-index assignment problem, which is non-deterministically polynomial-time hard ($\mathcal{NP}$-hard) [2].

For a small number of simultaneously tracked objects (about 10 objects), epipolar constraint is sufficient for stereo matching [16]. However, in high density scenes (e.g. hundreds of objects) the ambiguity of both tasks increased significantly: If there are multiple objects close to an epipolar line in view 2 corresponding to a single object in view 1, stereo matching is ambiguous (Figure 1 (left,mid)). Temporal tracking is more ambiguous if there are more than one possible successors within the search region of a tracked object (Figure 1 (right)). Furthermore, the number of occlusion increases in high density scenes which affects both, cross views and temporal associations.

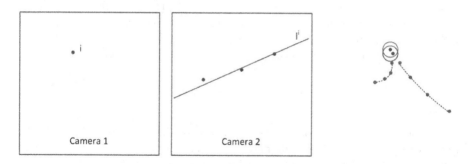

Fig. 1. Stereo and temporal ambiguities. The projection i of a object in Camera 1 (left) may have multiple candidates, as multiple projections are located on or close to its epipolar line l^i in Camera 2 (mid). Right: Blue and purple empty circles denote the search region for two tracklets shown with blue and purple solid circles respectively. Projections in current frame are represented by red solid circles.

1.1   Related Work

Methods for estimating 3D trajectories are typically based on stereo matching and temporal tracking; consequently they require two or more cameras. In [4,18], 2D trajectories are calculated in the image plane, and then matched between cameras to reconstruct 3D trajectories. Alternatively, in [11,6,14], stereo matching is used to reconstruct 3D coordinates, then followed by tracking 3D points to obtain 3D trajectories. However, these methods are vulnerable to either stereo or tracking ambiguities. In [9], several more frames are considered together to deal with stereo matching ambiguities. A modified Hungarian method is proposed to handle stereo matching for sequences containing up to seven objects [1]. Beside utilizing several cameras, a single-camera setup in combination with two mirrors is used in [7] to track up to 10 flies in a comparatively small test tube. In [6,14], more than two cameras are used for the 3D tracking task. [6] adopts three cameras for reconstructing a 3-dimensional hull for a fly, and then tracks the hull using the extended Kalman filter (EKF). In a similar approach [14] employs up to eleven cameras for realtime trajectory estimation.

[20] handles stereo matching and tracking simultaneously by minimizing a cost function related to the epipolar constraint, kinetic coherency, and observation matches. However the domain of the cost function increases exponentially for both, the number of objects and the number of frames. In [16], a third camera is employed to verify stereo pairs in the other two views. Stereo matching and temporal tracking are conducted alternatively to further reduce the ambiguities, but generating fragmented or incorrectly merged trajectories.

Multiple pedestrian tracking is a different task but shares certain similarities with fruit fly tracking. Both aim to reconstruct trajectories of multiple objects. In high density scenes, occlusions happen more frequently, which increases the difficulty to obtain good results. Pedestrian tracking adopts appearance, motion and temporal cues to deal with occlusions [19,8]. Appearance is considered as the most important cue to avoid identity switch [8]. However, fruit flies share similar appearance so that appearance is not a useful cue for reducing identity switches in temporal tracking. As the size of the object is small, occlusion time is relatively short. Thus, motion and temporal cues are reasonable selections for fruit fly temporal tracking.

1.2 Our Approach

In this paper, we propose a robust 3D tracking algorithm for high density object trajectory reconstruction. Trinocular stereovision is adopted to reduce stereo ambiguity in binocular stereovision by utilizing the projection consistency [16]. The tracking algorithm is an extended version of the Tracking-by-Matching (TbM) algorithm, which uses the epipolar constraint for stereo matching and the Kalman filter for temporal tracking [16]. In the conventional TbM approach trajectories were extended as long as there are valid successors available. If no valid successors are found, tracks are terminated and reinitialized if the ambiguity is solved in at least two of the three views [16]. Unfortunately this leads to fragmented or incorrectly merged trajectories and prevents the preservation of fly identities.

In the proposed approach only unambiguous situations are used to generate robust *tracklets* (i.e. trajectory segments). Tracklets which can not be associated to a unique successor are terminated and subsequently linked to appropriate temporally and spatially ongoing tracklets in an on-line fashion. We use both, motion and location context for tracklet association. The 3D trajectories are reconstructed with paired 2D trajectories.

A set of new evaluation metrics is proposed to quantify the tracking performance. The effect of detection noise is analyzed with these new metrics.

The proposed algorithm outperforms the state-of-the-art algorithms [16,20] in sequences with up to 200 simulated objects so that ground truth is available.

2   Notation

Given three time-synchronized sequences recorded from calibrated cameras Camera 1, Camera 2 and Camera 3. Then $\mathbf{I}_t^i$ represents an image obtained from Camera i ($i = 1, 2, 3$), at time t. In each $\mathbf{I}_t^i$, the detected fruit flies (i.e. detections) in each view at each frame are denoted by $D_t^i = \{d_{n^i,t}^i\} = \{(u_{n^i,t}^i, v_{n^i,t}^i)\}$ for $n^i = 1, \ldots, N_t^i$, where $(u_{n^i,t}^i, v_{n^i,t}^i)$ is the centroid of a blob (i.e. projection of a fly) in view i.

Stereo pairs are generated by matching blobs $d_{n^i,t}^i$ from D_t^1, D_t^2 and D_t^3 between the views. These matches can be associated over time to generate trajectories $S = \{s_{t_s:t_e}^k\}, k = 1, \ldots, K$, where K denotes the number of trajectories and t_s, t_e denote the start and end time of a trajectory. A trajectory $s_{t_s:t_e}^k = \{s_{t_s}^k, \ldots, s_{t_e}^k\}$ consists of a set of states s_t. A state is defined by

$$s_t = ((d_{n^1,t}^1, d_{n^2,t}^2, d_{n^3,t}^3), (\mathbf{v}_{n^1,t}^1, \mathbf{v}_{n^2,t}^2, \mathbf{v}_{n^2,t}^3)) \tag{1}$$

containing the projection term $(d_{n^1,t}^1, d_{n^2,t}^2, d_{n^3,t}^3)$ and the corresponding velocity term $(\mathbf{v}_{n^1,t}^1, \mathbf{v}_{n^2,t}^2, \mathbf{v}_{n^2,t}^3)$ belonging to a object in three views, where $(\mathbf{v}_{n^i,t}^i = (\nu_{u,n^i,t}^i, \nu_{v,n^i,t}^i))$. The 3D trajectories $\mathbf{T} = \{T_{t_s:t_e}^k\}$, where $T_t^k = (x, y, z)$ is the 3D location, are obtained from S by triangulating stereo pairs from triplets.

3   Proposed Algorithm

The proposed causal approach aims to handle 3D trajectory reconstruction in high density scene, see Figure 2. Because of the high occlusion rate, trajectories are frequently fragmented (missing valid triplet) or merged (multiple trajectories sharing one triplet). Thus, our approach proposes to generate robust tracklets by modifying the TbM method [16], and then associate tracklets using 2D motion and location context information.

3.1   Robust Tracklet Generation

The TbM method proposed in [16] is adopted to generate robust tracklets with more tracklet termination constraints. All candidate stereo pairs are verified based on epipolar line between any two views. Thus, the resultant triplets all satisfy the projection consistency. For the first three time-synchronized frames, triplets are found by exhausted search cross the three views, see Figure 2. Then, valid triplets are employed to initialize a triplet Kalman filter tracker. One Kalman filter is applied to one element of a triplet respectively. With the estimated velocities $(\mathbf{v}_{n^1,t}^1, \mathbf{v}_{n^2,t}^2, \mathbf{v}_{n^2,t}^3)$ from the filters, predicted locations in the image planes are optained for frames $\mathbf{I}_{t+1}^i$ by utilizing a constant velocity model.

Subsequently, search regions around the predicted locations are used to compare the detections with the predictions. Ambiguities (e.g. more than one detection is located in the search region) are addressed by verification, correction and fetching as described in [16].

In order to obtain robust tracklets, triplet tracking is terminated if one of the following termination conditions is satisfied:

- no valid triplet found within the search region;
- missing detections in more than one view;
- more than one tracklets associated with one valid triplet.

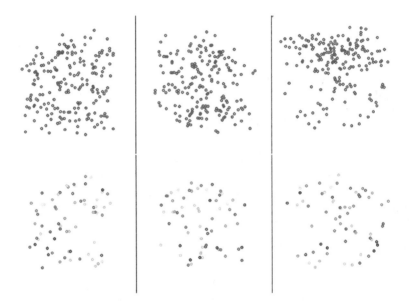

Fig. 2. Detections (up) and valid triplets (down) in three time-synchronized frames with 200 objects. Up: one red circle denotes a detection (object). Down: corresponding triplets are given by the same color across the views. Comparing detections and valid triplets indicates that invalid triplets are discarded.

3.2 Causal Tracklet Association

At time t, the terminated traklets are denoted by $S^- = \{s^l_{t_s:t_e}\}$ and the unterminated tracklets, namely ongoing tracklets, are denoted by $S^+ = \{s^k_{t_s:t}\}$. In a first step, unambiguous detections are associated to the ongoing tracklets S^+. The tracklets satisfying at least one of the termination conditions are terminated and assigned to the terminated tracklets S^-. Afterwards, terminated tracklets S^- are linked with ongoing tracklets S^+ *online* using the current frame instead of the whole seauence as proposed in [18,19]. As mentioned above, only motion and temporal cues can be used for linkage because of the similar appearance of fruit flies. $s^l_{t_s:t_e}$ and $s^k_{t_s:t}$ is linkable if the number of missing frames is within the range:

$$0 < t - t_e < \tau \tag{2}$$

where τ is the maximum gap between the linkable tracklet pairs and is set according to the frame rate and the occlusion time.

In order to calculate the association cost between a ongoing tracklet s^k and a terminated tracklet s^l, the tail triplet locations of the terminated tracklet $(d^{1,l}_{n_1,t_e}, d^{2,l}_{n_2,t_e}, d^{3,l}_{n_3,t_e})$ are extended to $p^{i,l}_{fwd}$, defined by:

$$p^{i,l}_{fwd} = (u^{i,l}_{n_i,t_e} + \nu^{i,l}_{u,n_i,t_e} \times \Delta t, \quad v^{i,l}_{n_i,t_e} + \nu^{i,l}_{v,n_i,t_e} \times \Delta t) \tag{3}$$

$$\Delta t = t^k_s - t^l_e \tag{4}$$

where Δt is the time difference between s^l and s^k. The head triplet locations of the ongoing tracklet $(d^{1,k}_{n_i,t_s}, d^{2,k}_{n_2,t_s}, d^{3,k}_{n_3,t_s})$ are extended to $p^{i,k}_{bwd}$, defined by:

$$p^{i,k}_{bwd} = (u^{i,k}_{n_i,t_s} - \nu^{i,k}_{u,n_i,t_s} \times \Delta t, \quad v^{i,k}_{n_i,t_s} - \nu^{i,k}_{v,n_i,t_s} \times \Delta t) \tag{5}$$

The linear motion extended head and tail locations are compared to the real head and tail locations to produce the motion based linking cost L_m:

$$L_m = \frac{1}{3} \sum_{i=1}^{3} (w_1 \mathrm{dist}(d^{i,k}_{n^i,t_s}, p^{i,l}_{fwd}) + w_2 \mathrm{dist}(d^{i,l}_{n^i,t_e}, p^{i,k}_{bwd})) \tag{6}$$

$$w_1 + w_2 = 1 \tag{7}$$

where w_1, w_2 are the weight value for considering the forward and backward triplet location differences respectively.

This motion based linking costs L_m are used to identify candidates within the terminated tracklets S^- to be linked to ongoing tracklets in S^+. If there is only one close terminated tracklet $s^{l_1} \in S^-$ satisfying

$$L^*_m = \min_{s^* \in S^+} \frac{1}{3} \sum_{i=1}^{3} (w_1 \mathrm{dist}(d^{i,*}_{n^i,t_s}, p^{i,l_1}_{fwd}) + w_2 \mathrm{dist}(d^{i,l_1}_{n^i,t_e}, p^{i,*}_{bwd})) < \tau_1 \tag{8}$$

s^{l_1} is matched to the ongoing tracklet s^* and s^* is removed from S^+ for this time step (Figure 3 left). τ_1 is selected based on the frame rate and the maximal flight speed.

If two terminated tracklets $s^{l_1}, s^{l_2} \in S^-$ are temporally and spatially close, equation 9 and 10 are satisfied:

$$|t^{l_1}_e - t^{l_2}_e| < \tau_2 \tag{9}$$

$$\frac{1}{3} \sum_{i=1}^{3} \mathrm{dist}(d^{i,l_1}_{n^i,t_e}, d^{i,l_2}_{n^i,t_e}) < \tau_3 \tag{10}$$

Again, τ_2 and τ_3 are constant thresholds based on the frame rate and the maximal flight speed. The respective other tracklet, e.g. s^{l_2}, is considered as context when

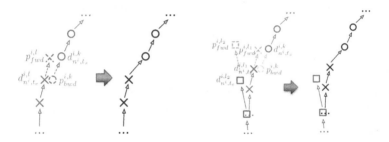

Fig. 3. Illustration of the motion cost based (left) and the context cost based (right) associations. The terminated tracklets are highlighted in blue and red and the ongoing tracklets are highlighted in green.

linking s^{l_1}. The context term for the linking costs L_c of s^{l_1} is defined similar to the motion based linking costs by:

$$L_c = \frac{1}{3}\sum_{i=1}^{3}(w_1\text{dist}(d_{n^i,t_s}^{i,k}, p_{fwd}^{i,l_2}) + w_2\text{dist}(d_{n^i,t_e}^{i,l_2}, p_{bwd}^{i,k})) \tag{11}$$

The ongoing tracklet s^* is matched to s^{l_1}, if equation (12) is satisfied:

$$L_c^* = \min_{s^* \in S^+}\frac{1}{3}\sum_{i=1}^{3}(w_1\text{dist}(d_{n^i,t_s}^{i,*}, p_{fwd}^{i,l_2}) + w_2\text{dist}(d_{n^i,t_e}^{i,l_2}, p_{bwd}^{i,*})) > L_m^* \tag{12}$$

given the motion based linking costs L_m^* (equation (8); see Figure 3 right).

Fig. 4. Frame triplet generated by the simulator

4   Simulator and Evaluation Metrics

4.1   Ground Truth

Quantitative evaluation of fruit fly trajectories is very difficult in real-world high-density scenes. In order to measure the performance of the proposed method, a simulator used in [16] is adopted to generate test sequence. It generates both, synthetic images from three cameras including all camera matrices and 2D/3D ground truth. Detections are generated by adopting background subtraction to extract the blobs from the synthetic sequences. The center of mass of each segmented blob is used as $d_{n^i,t}^i$. As a result, occlusions and image noise is within the 2D detections D_t^i similar to real world conditions (Figure 4).

4.2 Evaluation Metrics

In [16] and [20] E_{ca} and RAE are used to measure the tracking algorithms performance. The number of inaccurate 3D locations and wrong associations are divided by the number of frames (E_{ca}) or by the number of all objects in all frames (RAE). Both offer a general measure for performance. We propose several metrics to evaluate the tracked trajectories in more details. MT, Acc, and IDS are proposed to measure the stereo accuracy:

- MT specifies the number of missed triplets, i.e. the ground truth triplets which are not matched to any valid detected triplets.
- Acc specifies the number of inaccurate 3D locations. If the Euclidean distance between the reconstructed 3D locations from detected triplets and 3D ground truth locations is between 5 and 10cm, Acc is incremented.
- IDS specifies the number of identity switches. If the Euclidean distance between the reconstructed 3D locations from detected triplets and 3D ground truth locations is lager than 10cm, it is counted as a wrong match.

In addition, Occ is used to measure detected occlusions:

- Occ specifies the number of detected occlusions. If one detection is matched to multiple triplets, Occ is incremented.

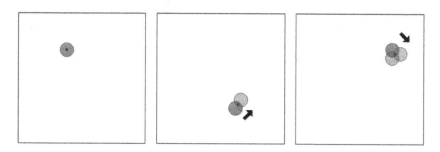

Fig. 5. Occlusions lead to shifted centers. The detected centers (small red circles) of an object (big green circles) in Camera 2 and Camera 3 are shifted due to occlusions. Arrows denote the shifting directions.

To evaluate the quality of the trajectories, $Frag$ is proposed to measure the fragmentation of the trajectories, and *Complete Tracks*, *Partial Tracks*, and *Lost Tracks* are employed to measure the completeness of the tracked paths:

- *Frag* specifies the number of fragments. It counts the number of fragments for all trajectories in a sequence.
- *Complete Tracks* specifies the number of completed trajectories. If both, 95% of the trajectory is tracked and 95% 3D locations are accurate, this trajectory is counted as a complete track.
- *Lost Tracks* specifies the number of lost trajectories. If more then 50% of the trajectory is lost it is counted as a lost track.
- *Partial Tracks* specifies the number of partially tracked trajectories, which are neither *Complete Tracks*, nor *Lost Tracks*.

5   Experiments

Sequences with 10 to 200 objects are used to test the algorithm. All cameras cover the whole tracking chamber and are located with a distance of 80cm to the chambers center. Rotations around the y-axis are 0°, 120° and -120° for camera 1, 2 and 3 respectively. The scene is captured with a resolution of 800×800 pixels and a frame rate of 150fps. The chamber is set to be $20 \times 20 \times 20 cm^3$. The flies are represented with a radius of $2mm$. The maximum speed is set to $0.8m/s$ [10]. A screen shot from the resultant synthetic images is given in Figure 4. Based on the maximum speed and experiment experience, the linking parameters are set to be $\tau = 7, \tau_1 = 10, \tau_2 = 3, \tau_3 = 20$.

5.1   Detection-Based Ground Truth

Due to occlusions, nearby targets and noise, detections in the images do not match to the 2D ground truth. As a consequence, triangulated pairs of detections do not match to the 3D ground truth. Therefore, detection-based 3D ground truth is generated: For all detections for time t (i.e. D_t^1, D_t^2, D_t^3), triplets are determined by employing stereo matching and projection consistency [16]. These triplets are compared to the 2D ground truth, selecting only detections with an average Euclidean distance below a certain threshold. The detection-based ground truth was then calculated by triangulating the remaining detections.

The aberration between the detection-based ground truth and the 3D ground truth from the simulator is given in Table 1 (*MT*, *Acc*, *IDS* and *Occ* are given in % by dividing the measures by the number of frames). Obviously, the more objects need to be tracked, the more missed triplets, inaccurate locations, identity switches and detected occlusions can be measured, which decreases the overall tracking performance. In fact, *MT*, *Acc* and *IDS* increase with the number of occlusions, since the blob centers are shifted in case of overlapping silhouettes (Figure 5): Shifted blob centers lead to inaccurate stereo pairs which can not be corrected by projection consistency [16], some triplets are missed in the detection-based ground truth (compare to *MT*). If matching the shifted centers is still successful (Section 3), triangulation leads to wrong 3D locations (compare to *Acc*). Other shifted blob centers are, however, erroneously assigned to the real 3D ground truth locations because they are located in a certain range of tolerance, leading to identity switches (compare to *IDS*).

Table 1. Detection-based ground truth measure results

# objects		General(1000 frames)					High-Density (150 frames)		
		10	20	30	40	50	100	150	200
MT	Abs.	128	521	681	1106	1436	147	489	921
	%	0.13	0.52	0.68	1.11	1.44	0.98	3.26	6.14
Acc	Abs.	0	5	11	48	40	6	15	25
	%	0.0	0.01	0.01	0.05	0.04	0.04	0.1	0.17
IDS	Abs.	129	522	682	1107	1437	148	490	922
	%	0.13	0.52	0.68	1.11	1.44	0.99	3.27	6.15
Occ	Abs.	21	119	289	846	1248	889	1850	3423
	%	0.02	0.12	0.29	0.85	1.25	5.93	12.33	22.82

5.2 Comparison

The results of proposed algorithm are compared with detection-based ground truth (see Table 2 and 3). The numbers shown in brackets are the corresponding results from Table 1. Obviously, our proposed algorithm outperforms detection-based ground truth measurements by reducing *IDS* and *MT* while slightly increasing *Acc*. *IDS* is reduced significantly due to temporal tracking information. Similar to the detection-based ground truth *MT* and *Acc* increase with the number of objects. Trajectories are more fragmented in high density scenes (e.g. 53 fragmentations occur for 200 objects, whereas no fragmentations are measured for 10 objects). Almost all objects are tracked for all frames (compare to *Complete Tracks*). Only for very high object densities this measure is decreased (Table 3).

Furthermore, the proposed algorithm is compared to the algorithms proposed in [20] and [16], namely Global-Correspondence Selection (GCS) and Tracking-by-Matching (TbM). The results measured with E_{ca} are shown in Table 4. Based on E_{ca} both, the TbM method and the proposed method outperform the GCS approach. Most accurate trajectories are generated by the tracklet-based method.

Table 2. Comparison between the our algorithm and the detection-based ground truth using the proposed metrics for 10-50 objects

(# objects, # frames)	(10,1000)	(20,1000)	(30,1000)	(40,1000)	(50,1000)
MT	0(128)	16(521)	23(681)	54(1106)	67(1436)
Acc	0(0)	12(5)	32(11)	111(48)	107(40)
IDS	0(129)	0(522)	0(682)	0(1107)	0(1437)
Frag	0	1	3	7	16
Complete Tracks	10	20	30	40	49
Partial Tracks	0	0	0	0	1
Lost Tracks	0	0	0	0	0

Table 3. Comparison between the our algorithm and the detection-based ground truth using the proposed metrics for 100-200 objects

(# objects, # frames)	(100,150)	(150,150)	(200,150)
MT	29 (147)	473 (489)	745 (921)
Acc	21 (6)	76 (15)	132 (25)
IDS	0 (148)	0 (490)	36 (922)
Frag	4	26	53
Complete Tracks	99	135	172
Partial Tracks	1	13	26
Lost Tracks	0	2	2

Table 4. Comparison between the our algorithm and the TbM and GCS approach using the E_{ca} quality measure

# objects	10	20	30	40	50	100	150	200
TbM	0.009	0.052	0.33	0.326	0.544	1.16	3.353	6.727
GCS	0.085	1.657	0.791	0.317	2.517	n/a	n/a	n/a
Proposed	0.00	0.034	0.064	0.163	0.206	0.38	1.98	4.63

A further comparison between the TbM and proposed method is given for very high-density scenes (Table 5). The results of proposed algorithm is shown in brackets. The proposed method reduces fragmentation with the proposed

Table 5. Comparison between our algorithm and the TbM approach in very high-density situations using the proposed metrics. The numbers shown in brackets are the corresponding results from Table 3.

(# objects, # frames)	(100,150)	(150,150)	(200,150)
MT	394 (29)	1093 (473)	1880 (745)
Acc	17 (21)	68 (76)	108 (132)
IDS	73 (0)	248 (0)	382 (36)
Frag	14 (4)	42 (26)	75 (53)
Complete Tracks	87 (99)	122 (135)	138 (172)
Partial Tracks	13 (1)	24 (13)	58 (26)
Lost Tracks	0 (0)	4 (2)	4 (2)

linking strategy. More complete trajectories are obtained as the termination and association process terminates ambiguous tracklet tracking and retrieves the corresponding tracklets later on. With the termination and association, less identity switches occur. As the corrected tracklets from *IDS* might contain inaccurate 3D locations as a result of shifted centers, *Acc* is slightly increased.

6   Conclusions

In this paper, we proposed a tracklet-based probabilistic 3D tracking algorithm for high-density situations. This algorithm is compared to two state-of-the-art algorithms, by utilizing a set of new evaluation metrics to analyze the tracking results in details. It has been shown that tracklet-based probabilistic tracking outperforms both, a Global Correspondence Selection algorithm and a conventional probabilistic tracking algorithm.

Furthermore, the proposed metrics offer information to perceive more about the tracking results by evaluating detection-based ground truth. These metrics in combination with synthetic data offer help to set up real-world experimental settings because of the possibility to quantify trade-offs between the number of fruit flies to be observed, the frame rate used for recording, the image resolution or other crucial parameters.

Thus, our future work will mainly focus on two mutually influencing challenges: On the one hand, we will design and improve our real-world setups by quantifying above mentioned trade-offs using simulated data. On the other hand, we will adjust our tracking algorithm to facilitate high-throughput behavioral experiments for freely flying fruit flies. For example, a more precise velocity model could be used for an overall better prediction performance.

References

1. Ardekani, R., Biyani, A., Dalton, J.E., Saltz, J.B., Arbeitman, M.N., Tower, J., Nuzhdin, S., Tavaré, S.: Three-dimensional Tracking and Behaviour Monitoring of Multiple Fruit Flies. J. Royal Society Interface 10, 1–13 (2013)
2. Burkard, R.E., Dell'Amico, M., Martello, S.: Assignment Problems, 1st edn. Society of Industrial Mathematics (2009)
3. Colomb, J., Reiter, L., Blaszkiewicz, J., Wessnitzer, J.: Open Source Tracking and Analysis of Adult Drosophila Locomotion in Buridan's Paradigm with and without Visual Targets. PloS One 7(8), e41642 (2012)
4. Du, H., Zou, D., Chen, Y.Q.: Relative Epipolar Motion of Tracked Features for Correspondence in Binocular Stereo. In: 11th Internitional Conference Computer Vision, pp. 1–8. IEEE Press, Rio de Janeiro (2007)
5. Fry, S.N., Bichsel, M., Müller, P., Robert, D.: Tracking of Flying Insects Using Pan-tilt Cameras. J. Neurosci Methods 101(1), 59–67 (2000)
6. Grover, D., Tower, J., Tavaré, S.: O fly, Where Art Thou? J. Royal Society 5, 1181–1191 (2008)
7. Kohlhoff, K.J., Jahn, T.R., Lomas, D.A., Dobson, C.M., Crowther, D.C., Vendruscolo, C.M.: The iFly tracking system for an automated locomotor and behavioural analysis of Drosophila melanogaster. Integrative Biology (2011)
8. Kuo, C., Nevatia, R.: How Does Person Identity Recognition Help Multi-person Tracking? In: Computer Vision and Pattern Recognition, pp. 1217–1224. IEEE Press, Colorado Springs (2011)
9. Liu, Y., Li, H., Chen, Y.Q.: Automatic Tracking of a Large Number of Moving Targets in 3D. In: Fitzgibbon, A., Lazebnik, S., Perona, P., Sato, Y., Schmid, C. (eds.) ECCV 2012, Part IV. LNCS, vol. 7575, pp. 730–742. Springer, Heidelberg (2012)

10. Marden, J.H., Wolf, K.E.: Areal performance of Drosophila melanogaster from populations selected for upwind flight ability. Journal of Experimental Biology 200, 2747–2755 (1997)
11. Pereira, F., Stuer, H., Graff, E.C., Gharib, M.: Two-frame 3d Particle Tracking. J. Measurement Science Technology 17, 1–8 (2006)
12. Risse, B., Thomas, S., Otto, N., Löpmeier, T., Valkov, D., Jiang, X., Klämbt, C.: FIM, a Novel FTIR-Based Imaging Method for High Throughput Locomotion Analysis. PloS One 8(1), e53963 (2013)
13. Sokolowski, M.A.: Drosophila: Genetics Meets Behavior. J. Nature Reviews Genetics 2(11), 879–890 (2001)
14. Straw, A.D., Branson, K., Neumann, T.R., Dickinson, M.H.: Multi-camera Real-time Three-dimensional Tracking of Multiple Flying Aanimals. J. Royal Society 8, 395–409 (2011)
15. Tao, J., Klette, R.: Tracking of 2D or 3D Irregular Movement by a Family of Unscented Kalman Filters. J. Information Communication Convergence Engineering 1, 307–314 (2012)
16. Tao, J., Risse, B., Jiang, X., Klette, R.: 3D Trajectory Estimation of Simulated Fruit Flies. In: 27th Image Vision Computing New Zealand, pp. 31–36. ACM, Dunedin (2012)
17. Valente, D., Golani, I., Mitra, P.P.: Analysis of the Trajectory of Drosophila Melanogaster in a Circular Open Field Arena. PloS One 2(10), e1083 (2007)
18. Wu, H.S., Zhao, Q., Zou, D., Chen, Y.Q.: Acquiring 3d Motion Trajectories of Large Numbers of Swarming Animals. In: 12th Internitional Conference Computer Vision Workshop, pp. 593–600. IEEE Press, Kyoto (2009)
19. Yang, B., Nevatia, R.: An Online Learned CRF Model for Multi-target Tracking. In: Computer Vision and Pattern Recognition, pp. 2034–2041. IEEE Press, Oregon (2012)
20. Zou, D., Zhao, Q., Wu, H.S., Chen, Y.Q.: Reconstructing 3d Motion Trajectories of Particle Swarms by Global Correspondence Selection. In: 12th Internitional Conference Computer Vision, pp. 1578–1585. IEEE Press, Kyoto (2009)

TV-L$_1$-Based 3D Medical Image Registration with the Census Cost Function

Simon Hermann[1,2] and René Werner[3]

[1] Department of Computer Science, The University of Auckland, New Zealand
[2] Department of Computer Science, Humboldt University of Berlin, Germany
[3] Department of Computational Neuroscience, University Medical Center
Hamburg-Eppendorf, Germany

Abstract. A recent trend in computer vision is to combine the census cost function with a TV-L$_1$ energy minimization scheme. Although this combination is known for its robust performance in computer vision applications, it has not been introduced to 3D medical image registration yet. Addressing pulmonary motion estimation in 4D (3D+t) CT images, we propose incorporating the census cost function into a 3D implementation of the 'duality-based approach for realtime TV-L$_1$ optical flow' for the task of lung CT registration. The performance of the proposed algorithm is evaluated on the DIR-lab benchmark and compared to state-of-the-art approaches in this field. Results highlight the potential of the census cost function for accurate pulmonary motion estimation in particular, and 3D medical image registration in general.

Keywords: Medical image registration, census transform, pulmonary motion estimation, 4D CT.

1 Introduction

This paper is motivated by the clinical need for fast and accurate registration of 3D computed tomography (CT) images. Recent advances in computer vision resulted in strong performing 2D optical flow estimation algorithms, which include the census cost function into a TV-L$_1$ energy minimization scheme. This paper demonstrates their potential for the task of pulmonary motion analysis. Figure 1 illustrates the application context.

The applied registration method is a 3D variant of the 'duality-based approach for realtime TV-L$_1$ optical flow', which was published in 2007 by Zach et al. [27]. They introduced a coupled convex approximation of a TV-L$_1$ energy functional, defined by an L$_1$ data term and a total variation (TV) regularization term. Both terms are alternately minimized within an iterative scheme. The decoupling of data and smoothness term, combined with a point-wise gradient-descent step to minimize the data term residual, makes this algorithm very applicable to be implemented on parallel hardware architectures. For the sake of simplicity, we refer to this particular minimization scheme as TV-L$_1$. However, there are other concepts to minimize the same energy; see for example Brox et al. [2].

R. Klette, M. Rivera, and S. Satoh (Eds.): PSIVT 2013, LNCS 8333, pp. 149–161, 2014.
© Springer-Verlag Berlin Heidelberg 2014

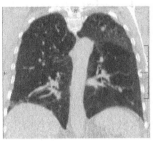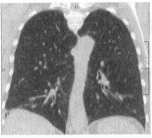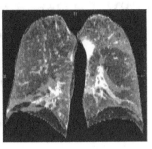

Fig. 1. Illustration of the task of 3D lung CT registration for pulmonary motion analysis. Left and middle: Coronal views of lung CT images at end-expiration (EE) and end-inspiration (EI). Right: Overlay of the EE (blue) and EI (orange) lung structures. These structures are to be aligned by a physiologically plausible, non-linear transformation; the corresponding displacements are interpreted as the motion field between EE and EI.

The census cost function is based on the census transform, which was introduced in 1994 by Zabih and Woodfill [26]. The census transform is a binary representation of all intensity differences at a pixel in relation to its immediate pixel neighborhood. It is based on ordering statistics and encodes in addition the spatial relationship between the considered pixels. The census cost function, which is the Hamming distance of two binary representations, is often applied for correspondence analysis in discrete methods. Those methods usually combine a data cost accumulation scheme with a cost limitation function to provide piecewise smooth and consistent solutions. An established example of such a combination is semi-global matching (SGM), as introduced by Hirschmüller [11] for stereo analysis.

In 2011, Müller et al. [14] discussed the formulation of an L_1 data term for arbitrary non-linear residuals in coupled energy minimization schemes such as TV-L_1. They highlighted the performance gain for dense 2D optical flow estimation that results when intensity-based data terms are replaced by the census cost function. For the performance of correspondence detection methods using census data terms we refer to the KITTI Vision Benchmark Suite.[1]

The work presented in this paper may be considered as an extension of the method proposed by Pock et al. [16], who applied the intensity-based TV-L_1 scheme [27] to lung CT registration. The introduction of the census cost function, following Müller et al. [14], represents a novel contribution to 3D medical image registration in general, and to pulmonary motion estimation in 4D CT image data in particular.

The paper is structured as follows: Section 2 presents the clinical background and informs about the state-of-the-art in 3D pulmonary medical image registration. Section 3 outlines TV-L_1 optical flow estimation, the applied numerical scheme, and the incorporation of the census data term. Experiments and results are presented in Section 4. Section 5 concludes.

---

[1] http://www.cvlibs.net/datasets/kitti/

2   Image Registration for Pulmonary Motion Estimation

Since the adaption of cardic imaging protocols for time-resolved thoracic and abdominal CT in the last decade, 4D CT scanners and images are making their way into an increasing number of medical facilities [21]. Here, the 3D CT images of a 4D CT data set are assumed to sample the patient's breathing cycle. A typical application scenario of 4D CT data is the estimation of breathing-induced effects on a planned dose distribution (dose accumulation) during radiotherapy treatment planning of thoracic and abdominal tumors [7]. Dose accumulation aims at understanding the interaction between organ and tumor motion and the process of dose delivery for a specific treatment modality.

It is usually performed on a pixel-by-pixel basis and requires non-linear 3D registration to estimate the displacement fields between different frames of the 3D CT image sequence [13,24].

The reliability of the extracted information, which is applied, for example, to dose accumulation, is directly linked to the accuracy of the registration [15]. This motivation led to great interest in 3D medical image registration of lung CT data over the past years. Although there is a great diversity of registration approaches in this field (see, for example, [1,7,15]), from a methodological perspective it is noticeable that the majority of these approaches realizes a minimization of common intensity-based distance measures or data terms, which are usually formulated as squared L$_2$ norms. Here, we refer to the EMPIRE10[2] study (EMPIRE = Evaluation of Methods for Pulmonary Image REgistration 2010) as a recent and large comparison benchmark. Considering the top-ranked algorithms as current state-of-the-art in this field, it is interesting to see that six of the top-ten approaches used variants of SSD (sum of squared intensity distances) as data terms during the initial study phase [15].

Thus, in contrast to computer vision applications, the use of an L$_1$ data term is not common for pulmonary motion estimation in 4D CT data. The same is true for the application of TV-based regularization. Nevertheless, some work exists in this direction: For example, three of the EMPIRE10 participants proposed using SAD (sum of absolute intensity differences) as distance measure, with some recent publications on lung registration also following this idea (e.g. [8]). As mentioned before, Pock et al. and, in addition, Urschler et al. proposed applying the 'duality-based approach for realtime TV-L$_1$ optical flow' of Zach et al. [27] for 3D lung CT registration [22,16]. However, the published registration errors are considerably larger when compared to state-of-the-art algorithms for lung registration.

To our best knowledge, the integration of a census cost function as penalty term for TV-L$_1$ has not yet been evaluated in the given context.

---

[2] http://empire10.isi.uu.nl

3   Formulation of Duality-Based TV-L$_1$ Optical Flow

This section provides a formulation of the duality-based TV-L$_1$ optical flow energy optimization. It follows the notation of Zach et al. and Pock et al. [27,16]. The integration of an arbitrary data term is taken from Müller et al. [14].

3.1   Basic Notations

The input of the algorithm are two single channel images I_0 and I_1, defined on an n-dimensional image domain $\Omega \subset \mathbb{R}^n$ with $I : \Omega \longrightarrow \mathbb{R}$. A point $\mathbf{x} \in \Omega$ describes a position within the image domain and $I(\mathbf{x})$ refers to the intensity of an image I at $\mathbf{x}$.

The output is an n-dimensional vector field $\mathbf{u} : \Omega \longrightarrow \mathbb{R}^{m\mid n}$, with $\mathbf{u} = (u_1, ..., u_m, 0_{m+1}, ..., 0_n)$, that describes the displacement from the base or reference image I_0 to the match or target image I_1. Here, m refers to the degrees of freedom of the elements of the vector field. A typical example for $m < n$ is the case of stereo estimation for rectified image pairs, where $n = 2$ but $m = 1$. For the task of 3D medical image registration we have $n = m = 3$.

3.2   The Energy Functional

The approach for recovering the displacement field $\mathbf{u}$ is based on minimizing the energy functional

$$E(\mathbf{u}) = \int_\Omega \sum_{b=1}^m |\nabla u_b(\mathbf{x})| + \lambda |\rho(\mathbf{x}, \mathbf{u}(\mathbf{x}))| \, d\mathbf{x} \tag{1}$$

where $\rho(\mathbf{x}, \mathbf{u})$ refers to a generic residual with $\rho := \rho_{I_0,I_1} : \Omega \times \mathbb{R}^{m\mid n} \longrightarrow \mathbb{R}$, which is evaluated between I_0 and I_1 at position $\mathbf{x}$ under consideration of $\mathbf{u}(\mathbf{x})$. To minimize this energy, the following convex approximation of Eq. (1) was introduced by Zach et al [27]:

$$E(\mathbf{u}, \mathbf{v}) = \int_\Omega \sum_{b=1}^m \left[|\nabla u_b(\mathbf{x})| + \frac{1}{2\theta}(u_b(\mathbf{x}) - v_b(\mathbf{x}))^2 \right] + \lambda |\rho(\mathbf{x}, \mathbf{v}(\mathbf{x}))| \, d\mathbf{x} \tag{2}$$

with $\mathbf{v} : \Omega \longrightarrow \mathbb{R}^{m\mid n}$. This can be efficiently solved by applying the following iterative scheme:

(1) For every b and fixed v_b, minimize over u_b:

$$\underset{u_b}{\arg\min} \left\{ \int_\Omega |\nabla u_b(\mathbf{x})| + \frac{1}{2\theta}(u_b(\mathbf{x}) - v_b(\mathbf{x}))^2 \, d\mathbf{x} \right\} \tag{3}$$

(2) For fixed $\mathbf{u}$, minimize over $\mathbf{v}$:

$$\underset{\mathbf{v}}{\arg\min} \left\{ \int_\Omega \sum_{b=1}^m \frac{1}{2\theta}(u_b(\mathbf{x}) - v_b(\mathbf{x}))^2 + \lambda |\tilde{\rho}(\mathbf{x}, \mathbf{v})| \, d\mathbf{x} \right\} \tag{4}$$

where the residual ρ is linearized around the fixed value $\mathbf{u}$ using the Taylor expansion [14]:

$$\rho(\mathbf{x}, \mathbf{v}(\mathbf{x})) \approx \tilde{\rho}(\mathbf{x}, \mathbf{v}(\mathbf{x})) = \rho(\mathbf{x}, \mathbf{u}(\mathbf{x})) - (\mathbf{u} - \mathbf{v})\nabla\rho(\mathbf{x}, \mathbf{u}) \tag{5}$$

3.3 The Numerical Scheme

The minimization problem defined by Eq. (3) is the TV energy functional as introduced by Rudin et al. [17]. It is solved by the efficient numerical scheme proposed by Chambolle [6]. With $\mathbf{p} \in \mathbb{R}^n$, and omitting the dependency on $\mathbf{x}$ for better readability, the solution of Eq. (3) is for $b = 1, .., m$:

$$u_b = v_b - \theta \operatorname{div} \mathbf{p}_b \tag{6}$$

with

$$\nabla(\theta \operatorname{div} \mathbf{p}_b - v_b) = |\nabla(\theta \operatorname{div} \mathbf{p}_b - v_b)|\mathbf{p}_b \tag{7}$$

To solve this equation, the following iterative fixed point scheme is applied:

$$\mathbf{p}_b^{k+1} = \frac{\mathbf{p}_b^k + \tau\nabla(\operatorname{div} \mathbf{p}_b^k - \frac{1}{\theta}v_b)}{1 + \tau|\nabla(\operatorname{div} \mathbf{p}_b^k - \frac{1}{\theta}v_b)|} \tag{8}$$

with $\mathbf{p}_b^0 = \mathbf{0}$ and τ as a time step.

The minimization problem of Eq. (4) can be solved by applying the thresholding scheme described in [27]:

$$\mathbf{v} = \mathbf{u} + \begin{cases} \lambda\theta\nabla\tilde{\rho} & \text{if } \tilde{\rho} < -\lambda\theta|\nabla\tilde{\rho}|^2 \\ -\lambda\theta\nabla\tilde{\rho} & \text{if } \tilde{\rho} > \lambda\theta|\nabla\tilde{\rho}|^2 \\ -\frac{\tilde{\rho}\nabla\tilde{\rho}}{|\nabla\tilde{\rho}|^2} & \text{if } |\tilde{\rho}| \leq \lambda\theta|\nabla\tilde{\rho}|^2 \end{cases} \tag{9}$$

3.4 The Census Cost Function as Data Residual

The census transform, as introduced by Zabih and Woodfill [26], assigns a binary signature vector to an image position $\mathbf{x}$. The signature is calculated based on the ordinal characteristic of $I(\mathbf{x})$ in relation to intensities within a defined neighborhood $\mathcal{N}_\mathbf{x}$ of $\mathbf{x}$. The binary signature vector $C[\mathbf{x}]$ at $\mathbf{x}$ is generated as follows:

$$C[\mathbf{x}] = \left\{ \Upsilon[I(\mathbf{x}) \geq I(\mathbf{y})] \right\}_{\mathbf{y} \in \mathcal{N}_\mathbf{x}} \tag{10}$$

where $\Upsilon[\cdot]$ returns 1 if true, and 0 otherwise. The residual $\rho(\mathbf{x}, \mathbf{u})$ is the Hamming distance of two signature vectors. Formally, we write

$$\rho(\mathbf{x}, \mathbf{u}) = \Gamma\{C_0[\mathbf{x}] \oplus C_1[\mathbf{x} + \mathbf{u}]\} \tag{11}$$

where C_0 and C_1 refer to census signatures of the images I_0 and I_1. $\Gamma\{\cdot\}$ is an operator that counts the 1's of the binary string in the argument. For efficiently counting 1's in bit strings, we refer to Warren's 'Hackers Delight' [23].

3.5   Implementation Details

Before the input images are given to the algorithm, their dynamic is reduced to an intensity domain of $[0, 1]$, with a scale factor that is based on the maximum intensity of both images. In order to restrict the focus during the registration process on a specific region of interest, the algorithm takes binary lung segmentation masks $S_0, S_1 : \Omega \rightarrow \{0, 1\}$ as optional input data. In case that segmentation masks are provided, the input images are cropped accordingly and the evaluation of the data term is omitted where $S_0(\mathbf{x}) = 0$. This provides a way of coping with motion discontinuities near the lung borders, which are the consequence of the lungs sliding along the inner part of the chest wall, and additionally speeds up the run-time of the algorithm.

The numerical scheme from section 3.3 is embedded into a coarse-to-fine approach, a common technique to overcome local minima. We employ Gauss pyramids with L levels, where $\ell = 1$ refers to the finest and $\ell = L$ refers to the coarsest level. If the input images exhibit an anisotropic spatial resolution (CT data usually offer high in-plane resolution when compared to the slice thickness; cf. Section 4.1), we follow a common strategy, see for example [18,12]: In a first step, we scale down only along the image axes with a high resolution until the pixel spacing is almost identical for all image dimensions. The following downscaling steps are then performed along all image axes and are subsequently referred to as 'isotropic levels'.

At the coarsest level, the displacement field is initialized with zero and the result of each level is propagated to the next finer level. At the beginning of each level, the dual variables $\mathbf{p}_b$ with $b = \{1, 2, 3\}$ are initialized with zero. Each level consists of a fixed number of image warps η and a fixed number v of iterations, in which the alternating numerical scheme is applied. After each iteration on isotropic levels, the intermediate solution is first filtered by a median filter to remove potential outliers (see [25]), followed by a Gauss filter with a fixed window size ω and a fixed σ. The scheme is summarized in Algorithm 1.

Our TV-L$_1$ implementation is C++ based, and the algorithm is executed on an Intel®Core™ i7 Quad-Core Processor with 2.4 GHz. We use OpenMP to utilize hyper-threading. No calculation was, however, outsourced to a GPU. This should be noted because one of the main features of the applied algorithm is that it is especially well suited to be implemented on GPUs, which could result in an additional run-time improvement over our CPU-based implementation.

4   Experiments

The performance of the algorithm was evaluated on ten thoracic 4D CT data sets, provided by the DIR-lab[3] of the University of Texas M.D. Anderson Cancer Center (Houston, USA) [3,4].

---

[3] http://www.dir-lab.com

---

input : images I_0 and I_1
ouput: displacement field **u**

initialization of image pyramids
set $\mathbf{u}^L = \mathbf{0}$

for $\ell \leftarrow L$ **to** 1 **do**

   for $b \leftarrow 1$ **to** 3 **do**
     | set $\mathbf{p}_b^\ell = \mathbf{0}$
   end

   for $w \leftarrow 1$ **to** η **do**

      warp $I_1^\ell \xrightarrow{\mathbf{u}_w^\ell} I_0^\ell$, by means of trilinear interpolation

      for $i \leftarrow 1$ **to** v **do**
         solve Eq. (9)
         for $b \leftarrow 1$ **to** 3 **do**
           | solve Eq. (8)
         end
         if ℓ *is isotropic level* **then**
           | filter $\mathbf{u}_w^\ell$ with a $3 \times 3 \times 3$ median filter
         end
         smooth $\mathbf{u}_w^\ell$ with a Gauss filter (ω, σ)
      end

   end

   if $\ell > 1$ **then**
     | initialize $\mathbf{u}^{\ell-1}$ with $\mathbf{u}^\ell$
   else
     | return current solution $\mathbf{u}^1$
   end

end

Algorithm 1. Census-based TV-L₁ algorithm

4.1   Image Data and Evaluation

Each 4D CT image sequence of the DIR-lab data pool consists of 3D CT images for ten different breathing phases. The dimension of the sequences varies between 256×256×94 and 512×512×136 pixel, the spatial resolution between $0.97 \times 0.97 \times 2.5$ mm³ and $1.16 \times 1.16 \times 2.5$ mm³. To be in line with most of the related publications, we focussed on the registration of the end-inspiration (EI, base image) and end-expiration (EE, target image) scans for evaluation purposes. These are the scan pairs with the largest motion amplitudes. The corresponding lung segmentations are generated using basic image processing operations with manual correction, followed by a level set-based refinement; cf. [20] for details.

For each EI and EE scan pair, 300 anatomical landmark pairs within the lungs (prominent bifurcations of the bronchial or vessel trees) have been annotated and are provided by the DIR-lab. The landmark pairs serve as ground truth information for quantitative evaluation of the registration accuracy, for which the Euclidean distances between the landmark positions in the target image and the positions of the transformed reference landmarks are computed.

The resulting landmark-based registration errors are compared with corresponding numbers that can be found in current literature and on the DIR-lab website. These numbers can, however, be computed in two different ways. Let $\hat{\mathbf{x}}_{I_0}$ be a landmark position in the reference image, $\hat{\mathbf{x}}_{I_0} + \mathbf{u}(\hat{\mathbf{x}}_{I_0})$ its transformed position, and $\hat{\mathbf{x}}_{I_1}$ the true landmark position in the target image. One way is to directly compute $\|\hat{\mathbf{x}}_{I_0} + \mathbf{u}(\hat{\mathbf{x}}_{I_0}) - \hat{\mathbf{x}}_{I_1}\|_2$. Instead, the DIR-lab proposes moving the transformed reference landmark towards the next pixel center before calculating its distance to $\hat{\mathbf{x}}_{I_1}$. This 'snap-to-pixel evaluation' is justified by arguing that human observers only select integer pixel locations in image pairs when identifying landmark sets. Working on the same integer grid would therefore increase consistency when comparing registration results with landmark positions as defined by the human observers. In this paper, we follow the DIR-lab argumentation and evaluation strategy. We also list the intra-observer errors as given on the DIR-lab website. For a landmark $\hat{\mathbf{x}}_{I_0}$, this value describes the mean distance between 'true' positions $\hat{\mathbf{x}}_{I_1}$ if they are detected by a human observer in several runs. In other words: The final goal is to end up with registration errors in the order of and below these observer errors.

Furthermore, we applied the common intensity-based registration approach of Schmidt-Richberg et al. [19] to the DIR-lab data, which is one of the top-ten-ranked approaches of the EMPIRE10 benchmark. This allows us to present some qualitative comparison of the estimated motion fields in addition to the quantitative landmark-based evaluation.

4.2   Algorithm Configuration

In this paper, we used the following registration parameters:

Census-Based TV-L₁ Registration: Census evaluated in a $5 \times 5 \times 5$ neighborhood on isotropic and $5 \times 5 \times 3$ neighborhood on anisotropic levels; image pyramids with 5 levels; $\eta = 32$ and $v = 2$ for each level, Gauss smoothing of the flow with $(\omega, \sigma) = (5 \text{ pixel}, 1.0 \text{ pixel})$; $\lambda = 30$, $\tau = 0.25$, $\theta = 0.1$.

Intensity-Based TV-L₁ Registration: Same parameters as for the census-based registration, except for the number of warps per level (now: $\eta = 128$) and the relative influence of the residual (now: $\lambda = 150$).

Registration Approach of Schmidt-Richberg et al.: default parameter setting as reported in the paper [19].

4.3   Results

Intensity (SAD)- vs. Census-Based TV-L₁ Registration. The registration results and estimated motion fields of data set 08 (maximal landmark displacement from all data sets) are illustrated in Fig. 2. The figure demonstrates that both the TV-L₁-based registration with common intensity-based data term

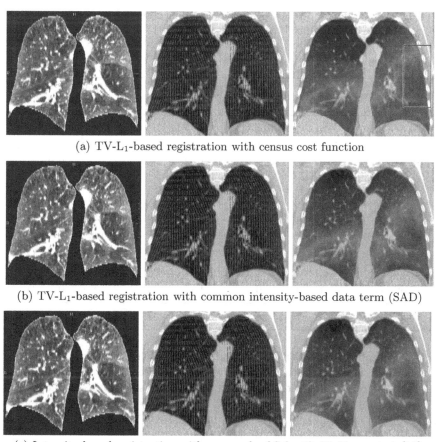

(a) TV-L$_1$-based registration with census cost function

(b) TV-L$_1$-based registration with common intensity-based data term (SAD)

(c) Intensity-based registration with approach of Schmidt-Richberg et al. [19]

Fig. 2. Illustration of registration results (here: DIR-lab case 08, registration masked by lung segmentation data). From left to right: Overlay of lung structures of the reference (orange) and the warped target image (blue), estimated motion vectors between EI and EE, and color-coded visualization of the motion field magnitude inside the lungs (blue: <2 mm motion; red: >25 mm). Rows from top to bottom: (a) census-based TV-L$_1$ registration, (b) standard intensity-based TV-L$_1$ registration, and (c) the registration approach following [19].

(i.e. SAD) and the proposed variant that minimizes the census cost function yield a visually good alignment of inner lung structures (see Fig. 1 for the displacement prior registration). The estimated motion fields also look similar for the two variants, with small differences being visible, e.g., near the outer left lung border (see highlighted area), and the field calculated by means of the census data term exhibits in general slightly larger motion amplitudes.

However, these small differences lead for the particular data set and the given algorithm configuration to a reduction of the landmark-based registration error from 1.51 mm to 1.11 mm when applying the census cost function instead of

Table 1. Mean landmark distances and corresponding standard deviations before and after registration (snap-to-pixel evaluation) and the intra-observer error for repeated landmark identification for the individual data sets values as specified by the DIR-lab. All values in mm.

#	No reg.	Obs. error	w/o lung masks Intensities	Census	with lung masks Intensities	Census
01	3.89 (2.78)	0.85 (1.24)	1.57 (1.29)	0.79 (0.93)	1.29 (1.11)	**0.78** (0.92)
02	4.34 (3.90)	0.70 (0.99)	0.76 (0.98)	0.80 (0.96)	**0.73** (0.92)	0.78 (0.92)
03	6.94 (4.05)	0.77 (1.01)	2.37 (2.33)	1.02 (1.18)	1.24 (1.19)	**0.93** (1.09)
04	9.83 (4.86)	1.13 (1.27)	1.73 (1.95)	1.23 (1.27)	1.31 (1.29)	**1.24** (1.30)
05	7.48 (5.51)	0.92 (1.16)	1.99 (2.30)	1.27 (1.52)	1.44 (1.61)	**1.22** (1.43)
06	10.89 (6.97)	0.97 (1.38)	1.79 (1.61)	1.09 (1.35)	1.38 (1.20)	**0.94** (0.99)
07	11.03 (7.43)	0.81 (1.32)	3.67 (4.59)	1.87 (3.06)	1.36 (1.22)	**1.01** (0.96)
08	14.99 (9.01)	1.03 (2.19)	7.09 (8.56)	3.01 (5.16)	1.51 (1.71)	**1.11** (1.28)
09	7.92 (3.98)	0.75 (1.09)	2.06 (1.70)	1.11 (1.24)	1.16 (1.03)	**0.98** (1.00)
10	7.30 (6.35)	0.86 (1.45)	2.01 (2.66)	1.17 (1.87)	1.32 (1.51)	**0.94** (1.03)
$\varnothing_{err}$	8.46 (6.58)	0.88 (1.31)	2.50 (2.80)	1.34 (1.85)	1.27 (1.28)	**0.99** (1.09)

intensity differences (registration with lung masks). This trend can be observed for most of the other data sets as well; corresponding results can be found in Table 1. The table also illustrates the advantage of lung segmentation information for the registration process, with especially high differences for the intensity-based registration (mean error without lung masks: 2.50 mm; with lung masks: 1.27 mm).

Comparison to State-of-the-Art Approaches. Corresponding error values for the approach of Schmidt-Richberg et al. [19] and related numbers of other state-of-the-art algorithms for pulmonary motion estimation are summarized in Table 2. Minimum values are highlighted by a gray background and with bold letters. In case of two identical mean values, the standard deviation (found in brackets behind each error value) determines the minimum.

In contrast to published data on TV-L_1-based image registration [16,22], we achieved registration errors in the order of the state-of-the-art approaches already for our implemented SAD-based TV-L_1 variant. However, these values are only obtained if lung segmentation masks are used during the registration process. This common pre-processing step has not been described in [16,22] and may be the reason for the comparably weak performance reported in these papers.

Replacing the intensity-based data term with the census cost function significantly reduces registration errors. The resulting values of our census-based TV-L_1 algorithm are competitive to the lowest registration errors that are currently published on the DIR-lab benchmark. This holds for both registration with (cf. Table 2) and without employing lung segmentation data (see, e.g., [8] with a reported average registration error of 1.43 mm). It should be mentioned

Table 2. Landmark-based registration errors for the approach following [19] and corresponding published numbers after registration of the end-inspiration and -expiration images of the DIR-lab 4D CT data sets; values given in mm (snap-to-pixel evaluation). 'Our approach' refers to the masked census-based TV-L$_1$ registration.

	Our approach	CCW+ [5][1]	HSS+ [10][2]	HW [9]	RHK+ [18]	SEW+ [19]
01	0.78 (0.92)	0.85 (1.00)	0.98 (1.00)	0.80 (0.92)	**0.78 (0.91)**	0.87 (0.93)
02	0.78 (0.92)	0.74 (0.99)	0.83 (1.02)	0.77 (0.92)	**0.74 (0.87)**	0.84 (0.95)
03	0.93 (1.09)	0.93 (1.07)	1.08 (1.15)	**0.92 (1.10)**	0.94 (1.07)	1.02 (1.13)
04	1.24 (1.30)	1.33 (1.51)	1.45 (1.53)	**1.22 (1.24)**	1.26 (1.26)	1.35 (1.27)
05	1.22 (1.43)	**1.14 (1.25)**	1.55 (1.75)	1.21 (1.47)	1.22 (1.48)	1.39 (1.47)
06	0.94 (0.99)	1.04 (1.05)	1.52 (1.28)	**0.90 (1.00)**	0.97 (1.03)	1.25 (1.14)
07	1.01 (0.96)	1.03 (1.01)	1.29 (1.22)	0.98 (1.01)	**0.91 (1.00)**	1.19 (1.12)
08	1.11 (1.28)	1.11 (1.18)	1.75 (2.40)	1.16 (1.45)	**1.07 (1.24)**	2.55 (3.70)
09	**0.98 (1.00)**	1.04 (1.00)	1.22 (1.07)	1.00 (0.97)	1.03 (1.01)	1.23 (1.16)
10	**0.94 (1.03)**	1.05 (1.10)	1.47 (1.68)	0.99 (1.28)	0.98 (1.10)	1.15 (1.25)
$\varnothing_{err}$	**0.99 (1.09)**	1.03 (1.12)	1.31 (1.41)	0.99 (1.13)	0.99 (1.10)	1.29 (1.41)
$\varnothing_{time}$	110 s	192 s[4]	55/73 min[3]	**46 s**	104 s	64 min

[1] Ranked 1st on DIR-lab homepage; please note that the 300 freely available landmark correspondences, which are used throughout our paper, are only a subset of the landmarks used for evaluation by the DIR-lab.
[2] Ranked 2nd on DIR-lab homepage; see above note on the used landmark sets.
[3] Times for balanced flow; format: cases 01-05 / 06-10 (after additional preprocessing).
[4] Sum of mean times of grid search and filtering as given in table 5 of [5].

that employing lung masks in the registration process leads to invalid motion fields outside the specified region of interest. This is not acceptable for several applications, such as dose accumulation for abdominal structures during radiotherapy planning for lung tumors. Therefore, error values for registration without segmentation masks are as well of interest in the given application context.

The reported gain in performance due to the introduction of the census data term into TV-L$_1$-based medical image registration is also reflected by the values listed in Table 2 for the approach [9]. In [9], we describe an extension of the 'high accuracy optical flow' formulation of Brox et al. [2] for 3D medical image registration in combination with the census cost function; we refer to the corresponding paper for methodical details.

5 Conclusions

This paper reports about a 3D implementation of the 'duality-based approach for realtime TV-L $_1$ optical flow' in combination with the census cost function. This combination constitutes a novel contribution to 3D medical image registration in general and pulmonary motion estimation in 4D CT images in particular. The algorithm was evaluated on the DIR-lab benchmark for lung CT registration and results demonstrate competitive performance compared to current state-of-the-art methods. Registration accuracy, computation times, as well as the robustness regarding registration without segmentation masks highlight the potential of the census cost function for medical image registration tasks.

Acknowledgments. The authors thank Dr. Clemens Rabe for a helpful discussion on the linearization of the census data residual, Prof. Dr. Reinhard Klette for helpful comments on early drafts and Dr. Gisela Klette for thoroughly proof reading this paper.

References

1. Brock, K.K.: On behalf of the Deformable Registration Accuracy Consortium: Results of a multi-institution deformable registration accuracy study (MIDRAS). Int. J. Radiat. Oncol. Biol. Phys. 76, 583–596 (2010)
2. Brox, T., Bruhn, A., Papenberg, N., Weickert, J.: High Accuracy Optical Flow Estimation Based on a Theory for Warping. In: Pajdla, T., Matas, J(G.) (eds.) ECCV 2004. LNCS, vol. 3024, pp. 25–36. Springer, Heidelberg (2004)
3. Castillo, R., Castillo, E., Guerra, R., Johnson, V.E., McPhail, T., et al.: A framework for evaluation of deformable image registration spatial accuracy using large landmark point sets. Phys. Med. Biol. 54, 1849–1870 (2009)
4. Castillo, R., Castillo, E., Martinez, J., Guerrero, T.: Ventilation from four-dimensional computed tomography: density versus Jacobian methods. Phys. Med. Biol. 55, 4661–4685 (2010)
5. Castillo, E., Castillo, R., White, B., Rojo, J., Guerrero, T.: Least median of squares filtering of locally optimal point matches for compressible flow image registration. Phys. Med. Biol. 57, 4827–4833 (2012)
6. Chambolle, A.: An Algorithm for Total Variation Minimization and Applications. J. Mathematical Imaging Vision 20, 89–97 (2004)
7. Ehrhardt, J., Lorenz, C.: 4D Modeling and Estimation of Respiratory Motion for Radiation Therapy. Springer, Berlin (2013)
8. Heinrich, M.P., Jenkinson, M., Brady, M., Schnabel, J.A.: MRF-based deformable registration and ventilation estimation of lung CT. IEEE Trans. Medical Imaging 32, 1239–1248 (2013)
9. Hermann, S., Werner, R.: High Accuracy Optical Flow for 3D Medical Image Registration using the Census Cost Function. In: Klette, R., Rivera, M., Satoh, S. (eds.) PSIVT 2013. LNCS, vol. 8333, pp. 23–35. Springer, Heidelberg (2013)
10. Hoog, A.C.B., Singh, T., Singla, P., Podgorsak, M.: Evaluation of advanced Lukas-Kanade optical flow on thoracic 4D-CT. J. Clin. Monit. Comput. 27, 433–441 (2013)
11. Hirschmüller, H.: Accurate and Efficient Stereo Processing by Semi-Global Matching and Mutual Information. In: IEEE Conf. Computer Vision Pattern Recognition, pp. 807–814 (2005)
12. Kabus, S., Lorenz, C.: Fast Elastic Image Registration. Medical Image Analysis for the Clinic: A Grand Challenge, 81–89 (2010)
13. Li, H., Li, Y., Zhang, X., Li, X., Liu, W., et al.: Dynamically accumulated dose and 4D accumulated dose for moving tumors. Med. Phys. 39, 7359–7367 (2012)

14. Müller, T., Rabe, C., Rannacher, J., Franke, U., Mester, R.: Illumination-Robust Dense Optical Flow Using Census Signatures. In: Mester, R., Felsberg, M. (eds.) DAGM 2011. LNCS, vol. 6835, pp. 236–245. Springer, Heidelberg (2011)

15. Murphy, K., van Ginneken, B., Reinhardt, J., Kabus, S., Ding, K., et al.: Evaluation of registration methods on thoracic CT: The EMPIRE10 Challenge. IEEE Trans. Medical Imaging 30, 1901–1920 (2011)

16. Pock, T., Urschler, M., Zach, C., Beichel, R.R., Bischof, H.: A Duality Based Algorithm for TV-L1-Optical-Flow Image Registration. In: Ayache, N., Ourselin, S., Maeder, A. (eds.) MICCAI 2007, Part II. LNCS, vol. 4792, pp. 511–518. Springer, Heidelberg (2007)

17. Rudin, L.I., Osher, S., Fatemi, E.: Nonlinear total variation based noise removal algorithms. Physica D 60, 259–268 (1992)

18. Rühaak, J., Heldmann, S., Kipshagen, T., Fischer, B.: Highly Accurate Fast lung CT Registration. In: SPIE Medical Imaging: Image Processing. SPIE, vol. 8669, p. 86690Y (2013)

19. Schmidt-Richberg, A., Ehrhardt, J., Werner, R., Handels, H.: Diffeomorphic Diffusion Registration of Lung CT Images Medical Image Analysis for the Clinic: A Grand Challenge, pp. 55–62 (2010)

20. Schmidt-Richberg, A., Werner, R., Handels, H., Ehrhardt, J.: Estimation of slipping organ motion by registration with direction-dependent regularization. Med. Image Anal. 16, 150–159 (2012)

21. Simpson, D.R., Lawson, J.D., Nath, S.K., Rose, B.S., Mundt, A.J., Mell, L.K.: Utilization of advanced imaging technologies for target delineation in radiation oncology. J. Am. Coll. Radiol. 6, 876–883 (2009)

22. Urschler, M., Werlberger, M., Scheurer, E., Bischof, H.: Robust Optical Flow Based Deformable Registration of Thoracic CT Images. In: Medical Image Analysis for the Clinic: A Grand Challenge, pp. 195–204 (2010)

23. Warren, H.S.: Hacker's Delight, pp. 65–72. Addison-Wesley Longman, New York (2002)

24. Werner, R., Ehrhardt, J., Schmidt-Richberg, A., Albers, D., Frenzel, T., et al.: Towards accurate dose accumulation for Step-&-Shoot IMRT: Impact of weighting schemes and temporal image resolution on the estimation of dosimetric motion Eeffects. Z. Med. Phys. 22, 109–122 (2012)

25. Wedel, A., Pock, T., Zach, C., Bischof, H., Cremers, D.: An Improved Algorithm for TV-L1 Optical Flow. In: Cremers, D., Rosenhahn, B., Yuille, A.L., Schmidt, F.R. (eds.) Statistical and Geometrical Approaches to Visual Motion Analysis. LNCS, vol. 5604, pp. 23–45. Springer, Heidelberg (2009)

26. Zabih, R., Woodfill, J.: Non-parametric Local Transforms for Computing Visual Correspondence. In: Eklundh, J.-O. (ed.) ECCV 1994. LNCS, vol. 801, pp. 151–158. Springer, Heidelberg (1994)

27. Zach, C., Pock, T., Bischof, H.: A Duality Based Approach for Realtime TV-L1 Optical Flow. In: Hamprecht, F.A., Schnörr, C., Jähne, B. (eds.) DAGM 2007. LNCS, vol. 4713, pp. 214–223. Springer, Heidelberg (2007)

An Automatic Timestamp Replanting Algorithm for Panorama Video Surveillance[*]

Xinguo Yu, Wu Song, Jun Cheng, Bo Qiu, and Bin He

National Engineering Research Center for E-Learning, Central China Normal University,
Wuhan, China 430079
xgyu@mail.ccnu.edu.cn

Abstract. Timestamp replanting is required when we want to remove timestamps in individual videos and to plant a timestamp into their merged panorama video. This paper presents a preliminary automatic timestamp replanting
algorithm for producing panorama surveillance video. Timestamp replanting is
a challenge problem because localization, removal, and recognition of timestamp are three difficulty tasks. This paper develops methods to attack the difficulties to finish the tasks. First, it presents a novel localization procedure which
first localizes second-digit by using a pixel secondly-periodicity method. And
then it localizes timestamp via extracting all digits of timestamp. Second, it
adopts a homography-based method to conduct timestamp removal. Third, it
presents a digit-sequence recognition method to recognize second-digit and on-
line template matching to recognize the other digits. Experimental results show
that the algorithm can accurately localize timestamp in a very low computing
cost and that the performances of replanting are visually acceptable.

Keywords: Video Surveillance, Timestamp Localization, Timestamp Replanting, Secondly-Periodicity, Second-Digit Localization.

1 Introduction

A timestamp is a sequence of characters or/and encoded information indicating when
a certain event occurred, usually giving date and time of day, sometimes accurate to a
small fraction of a second [11]. The information of video and image timestamp can be
stored in the text channel and video/image players can choose whether the timestamp
is overlaid on each frame/image according users' option. Alternatively, a timestamp is
superimposed into each image [2,9,11]. In analog videos timestamps have to be superimposed into videos; in digital videos timestamps may purposely be superimposed
into videos so that they cannot be easily changed, of course, videos may have both
encoded the information and the superimposed timestamp. In the panorama video

---

[*] Partially supported by National Natural Science Foundation of China (No.61272206),
National Key Technology R&D Program of China during "12th Five-Year Plan"
(No.2011BAK14B01), and Collaboration Innovation Base on Educational Digital Media
and Visualization.

R. Klette, M. Rivera, and S. Satoh (Eds.): PSIVT 2013, LNCS 8333, pp. 162–171, 2013.

surveillance scenario we need to replant superimposed timestamps in some types of applications.   A panorama surveillance video is merged from multiple videos taken by individual cameras. Each individual video may have a superimposed timestamp. To produce a good quality of panorama surveillance video we need to remove the timestamp of each individual video. The timestamp replanting problem for panorama surveillance is a superposed timestamp replanting problem and it is a challenge problem because localization, removal, and recognition of timestamp are three challenging tasks.

The timestamp replanting also is a very interesting and its localization, removal and recognition are three special character (or text) processing problems in video analysis. The first thought of localizing timestamp is to adopt one of the text localization methods in the literature. However, the existing text localization algorithms cannot get the satisfactory results [3-5]. Two papers specifically addressed the timestamp localization. Yin et al [9] used a rule-based text localization method. This method mainly takes an image processing approach but it proposed a spatial–temporal suppression technique to enhance the timestamp localization performance. This algorithm probably cannot properly localize second-digit because it uses temporal suppression. Covavisaruch et al [2] also mainly takes an image processing approach but it proposed a non-timestamp edge elimination technique to enhance the timestamp localization performance. These two papers reported that they can achieve 96.1% and 85.6% of accuracies respectively for home videos. This level accuracy is not enough for the industrial standard algorithm.   Li et al [6-7] first proposed another new algorithm to localize the digits of digital video clock (digital video clock can be considered as a type of timestamp).   They adopted the image processing methods to get character candidates and they identified second-digit by finding the character candidate that secondly changes its colors. One of its demerits is that its image processing portion is error-prone and time consuming. A procedure was presented in [10] for localizing the four digits of digital video clock, using a pixel secondly-periodicity method to localize second-digit. This procedure was designed based on the fact that second-digit pixels secondly change their grey values in a certain degree.

This paper develops a novel algorithm for replanting timestamp for panorama surveillance video, which comprises localization, removal, and recognition three main procedures. First we propose a procedure to localize the timestamp by revising the procedure that localizes the clock digits presented in [10]. Then we develop a homography-based procedure to remove timestamp. This procedure mainly adopts the techniques presented in [1]. Third, we form a procedure to recognize the digits on timestamp. This procedure first uses the digit-sequence method to recognize s-digit. And then it creates online templates of digits and it uses the online template matching method to recognize the digits on a timestamp. Based on the results of these three main steps we can plant a timestamp on the merged panorama video. Notice that this paper assumes that the procedure for forming panorama video is available already.

The rest of the paper is organized as follows. Section 2 takes an overview of the timestamp replanting algorithm proposed in this paper.   Section 3 presents the procedure of timestamp localization. Section 4 presents the procedure to recognize timestamp. Section 5 presents the procedure of timestamp removal and Replanting. Section 6 gives the experimental results. We draw the conclusion of the paper in Section7.

2   Overview of Timestamp Replanting Algorithm

This section first gives the pseudocode of the timestamp replanting algorithm proposed in this paper and then briefly explains the main steps of the algorithm. Normally a timestamp contains a digital video clock and a date as the sample timestamps in Fig 4-6 show.   The digital video clock has the four clock-digits representing second, ten second, minute, and ten minute, denoted as s-digit, ts-digit, m-digit, and tm-digit in the rest of the paper, respectively.

Algorithm I: Timestamp Replanting

Input: multiple videos with superimposed timestamps.

Output: a merged panorama video with a planted timestamp.

Step 1: timestamp localization for each individual video

  1.1   s-digit localization

  1.2 acquisition of the digit color of timestamp

  1.3 timestamp bounding box determination

Step 2: timestamp recognition for each individual video

  2.1 recognize s-digit in digit-sequence match method;

  2.2 prepare online digit templates from s-digit instances;

  2.3 recognize digits of timestamp;

Step 3: timestamp removal for each individual video and timestamp replanting for panorama video

  3.1 identify a neighbor frame of the considering frame that has a proper camera motion.

  3.2 find the homography between the considering frame and the identified neighbor frame.

  3.3 remove the timestamp of the considering frame according to the obtained homography.

  3.4 insert a timestamp into the merged panorama video.

Fig. 1. The pseudocode of the timestamp replanting algorithm proposed in this paper

As Fig 1 depicts our algorithm comprises three main components: localization, removal, and recognition of timestamp. Our localization is a novel one and significantly improves the existing technique for timestamp localization. Timestamp localization can be solved by the static region detection method for some kinds of videos such as sports video, home video, and news videos. But in the panorama video surveillance scenario, cameras may be static or have non-continuous camera motion. Thus most of objects in the videos are static. Hence static region detection method has difficulty in detecting timestamp. We propose a novel way to localize the timestamp, in which it first localizes s-digit. Then it learns the digit color of timestamp after it localizes s-digit region.   It extracts the timestamp digits by using the learnt color and then obtains the bounding box of the timestamp. We conduct timestamp recognition in several steps. We first recognize the s-digit in digit-sequence method and we recognize other digits using online template matching. Timestamp removal component first identifies a neighbor frame of the considering frame that has a proper camera motion with respect to the considering frame. Then it finds their homography matrix. It finishes the timestamp removal by replacing the pixels inside the timestamp in the considering frame by the corresponding pixels under the obtained homography.

3   Timestamp Localization

This section aims to find the bounding boxes of the timestamp. We first localize s-digit and localize other digits by using the learnt color from s-digit instances. Finally, we form the bounding box of timestamp based on the digit segmentation results.

3.1   S-Digit Localization

Here we first present a method to get the bounding box of s-digit by using pixel second-periodicity method. This method bases on a piece of knowledge: the pixels in the s-digit region of a working video clock approximately change its value every second [10]. Let W and H be the width and the height of frame. Let F_i be the considered frame of a R frame-rate video. Then $F_{i-R}, F_{i-R+1}, ..., F_{i-1}$ and $F_i, F_{i+1}, ..., F_{i+R-1}$ are the R frames in the preceding and the succeeding second, respectively. Let $c(k, p)$ be the grey value of pixel p in frame F_k. With these notations we define the following two conditions D_1 and D_2.

$$D_1 : \begin{cases} \mid c(k,p) - C_1 \mid < \beta_1 & \text{for } k = i - R + 1 \text{ to } i - 1, \text{ where } C_1 = \frac{1}{R} \sum_{k=i-R}^{i-1} c(k,p), \\ \mid c(k,p) - C_1 \mid > \beta_2 & \text{for } k = i + 1 \text{ to } R - 1. \end{cases}$$

$$D_2 : \begin{cases} \mid c(k,p) - C_2 \mid < \beta_1 & \text{for } k = i + 1 \text{ to } i + R - 1, \text{ where } C_2 = \frac{1}{R} \sum_{k=i}^{i+R-1} c(k,p), \\ \mid c(k,p) - C_2 \mid > \beta_2 & \text{for } k = i - R + 1 \text{ to } i - 1. \end{cases}$$

β_1 is the threshold of the variance of digit colors within one second of no digit change and β_2 is the threshold for the difference between font color and font-background color. These two thresholds link to the human sight ability to percept the digits from video so they have relatively constant values. Currently we set their values based on our observation for several hundreds of videos. In our future work we will learn their values from a big volume of videos.

For pixel p in frame Fi we define a function $T(i, p)$.

$$T(i, p) = \begin{cases} 1 & \text{if } D_1 \text{ or } D_2 \text{ holds,} \\ 0 & \text{otherwise.} \end{cases} \tag{1}$$

Pixel p has a second-change at F_i if $T(i, p) = 1$. And we define the accumulator $S(i)$ below.

$$S(i) = \sum_{p \in B} T(i, p). \tag{2}$$

By summing $S(i)$ for 10 seconds we have $\Omega(k)$ being defined on the domain $[0, R)$.

$$\Omega(k) = \sum_{i=0}^{9} S(k + i * R) \qquad k \in [0, R) \tag{3}$$

Thus we can know the transit frame of digit second is F_t such that $\Omega(t) = \arg \max_k \Omega(k)$ and $\Omega(t)$ is larger than a threshold.

We define the pixel second-periodicity function $\phi(i, p)$ below. Here $\phi(i, p) = 1$ means that p has a second-periodicity value change referring to F_t.

$$\phi(i, p) = \begin{cases} 1 & \text{if } T(i, p) = 1 \ \& \ | i\%R - F_t \ |< 2, \\ 0 & \text{otherwise.} \end{cases} \tag{4}$$

A pixel second-periodicity measure function is defined as.

$$A(i, p) = \sum_{j=0}^{9*R} \phi(i + j \times R, p) \tag{5}$$

We claim that p is in the second area if $\aleph(p) = 1$ and the function $\aleph(\bullet)$ is defined as follows.

$$\aleph(p) = \begin{cases} 1 & \text{if } A(i, p) > \beta_3, \\ 0 & \text{otherwise.} \end{cases} \tag{6}$$

β_3 is the threshold for the second-periodicity measure function $A(i,p)$ and $A(i,p) \leq \beta_3$ indicates that p is not enough second-periodicity index. β_4 is the threshold for the number of the found second-region pixels. Hence, $N = \sum_{p=0}^{W*H} \aleph(p)$ is the number of the pixels that have a high pixel second-periodicity indexes. We claim there is no working clock when $N < \beta_4$; otherwise the bounding box of $\aleph(p)$ is the approximate place of s-digit. Then a local analysis can get the bounding box of s-digit.

3.2   Acquisition of the Digit Color of Timestamp

Since all timestamp digits have the same color so that we can learn the digit color of timestamp from the instance of s-digits. Here we describe the method for acquiring the digit color of timestamp. We collect all the instances of the digits on s-digit from a 10-second long clip as Fig 2(a) shows. Fig 2(b) is the histogram of these s-digit instances, called the instance histogram. From $\aleph(\bullet)$ in section 3.1 we can know some colors of timestamp digits. Hence we can know that a portion of the histogram belongs to the histogram of the digit color. Then we can identify the digit color histogram by searching the separate point between the background histogram and digit color histogram.

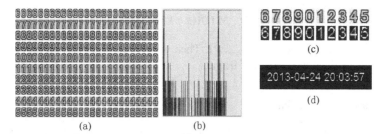

Fig. 2. The illustration for digit color acquisition and digit extraction as well as digit color conversion. The cropped 10-second s-digit instances are in (a); the histogram of the instances in (a) is given in (b); 10 s-digits and their converted version are given in (c); a converted timestamp is given in (d).

3.3   Timestamp Bounding Box Determination

After we acquired the Gaussian of the digit color of timestamp we can segment the digits of timestamp by color as Fig 2(d) shows. Then extended rectangle of the bounding box of these digits is considered as the bounding box of timestamp. To be safe our box is a little larger than the real bounding box of timestamp. And this is not harm to solve our problem.

4   Timestamp Recognition

4.1   S-Digit Recognition

Let Π_1 and Π_2 be two regions of image with the same dimension. Then we use M (Π_1, Π_2) to denote the matching result between them, defined as follows.

$$M(\Pi_1, \ \Pi_2) = \frac{<\Pi_1, \Pi_2>}{|\Pi_1| \times |\Pi_2|}. \tag{7}$$

where $<\bullet, \bullet>$ is the dot product of two vectors and $|\Pi|$ is the dimension of vector, i.e. the area of Π.

Since we have known s-digit location and s-digit transit frames in Section 3, now we can collect all image instances of "0" to "9" in 10 seconds at the s-digit place without knowing what digit is on each instance yet. But we know that the s-digits in the frames from t+k*R+1 to t+(k+1)*R are the same if frame t is s-digit transition frame. Thus, the s-digit in the frames t+k*R+1 to t+ (k+1)*R is number k if we assume that the s-digit in the frames from t to t+R is "0". In other words, we know that the s-digits in the frames from t to t+10*R form a digit periodic increasing sequence according to the clock knowledge. But we do not know that the starting digit of this sequence yet. We select frame t+ (k+0.5)*R to represent the frames from t+k*R+1 to t+ (k+1)*R and denote this frame as F^k and the s-digit instance of F^k as S^k. Let D(j) be the standard template of digit "j", j=0, 1,2,…,9 in s-digit dimension. Then U(x), the measurement of the sequence starting with x, is defined as follows.

$$U(x) = \sum_{k=0}^{9} M\left(D((x+k)\%10), S^k\right) \tag{8}$$

Thus U (x) is defined on $\{0, 1, 2, 3,\ldots, 9\}$. Then we identify the maximum point of U(x), which tells us the s-digits on any frame.

4.2   Timestamp Recognition

After we recognize the seconds of digital video clock we prepare the digit online templates from the instances of s-digit. We use the usual color segmentation to extract digits of timestamp due to we have obtained the digit color in section 3.2 as Fig 2 shows. Based on this good digit binarilized map we can localize all the timestamp digits by using a routine procedure. Now we can use the online template matching method to recognize all timestamp digits.

5   Timestamp Removal and Replanting

In the proposed algorithm, we assume that the cameras never change their intrinsic parameters and that the camera only do slight tilt motion. The proposed algorithm comprises a procedure to acquire the homography matrixes between the considering frame and one of its neighbor frames. This procedure first obtains homographies between the considering frame and its neighbor frames using the method presented in [1] and then it chooses one of neighbor frames according to their homographies. Thus, we can remove the timestamp by recovering the pixels covered by timestamp with the corresponding pixels in the chosen neighbor image. We use the procedure presented in [1] to produce the panorama surveillance video. Once we obtain the panorama surveillance video we replant a superimposed digital timestamp into it according to the recognized time.

6   Experimental Results

We implemented our timestamp replanting algorithm in Visual C++ and tested the algorithm on 300 mepg2 video clips. We first experiment accuracy and computing time of s-digit localization because it is the main step of timestamp localization. Then we conduct the timestamp recognition, timestamp removal, and timestamp replanting experiments on a set of frames.

6.1   Experiments on S-Digit Localization

This paper adopts the novel s-digit localization method presented in our previous paper [10]. This method uses the pixel secondly-periodicity of s-digits. Thus this method can accurately localize s-digit in a very low cost of computing. We conduct experiments to evaluate the accuracy and computing time of s-digit localization and the results are given in Table 1. In Table 1, #yes and % indicate the numbers and the percent that our methods correctly localize the s-digit; μ and σ are the means and the variances of the computing times of localizing s-digit for a batch of videos; 1st-100, 2nd-100, and 3rd-100 means the first to the third 100 videos of the total 300 videos. From Table 1, we can conclude that our method can achieve an accuracy of   99% for localizing s-digits for mpeg2 video in 2.5 seconds.

Table 1. Accuracy and computing time in second of s-digit localization for 300 mpeg2 videos

Localization accuracy		computing time of s-digit localization					
		1st-100		2rd-100		3rd-100	
#yes	%	μ	σ	μ	σ	μ	σ
297	99.0%	2.445	0.0274	2.406	0.0273	2.440	0.0237

6.2   Experiments on Timestamp Replanting

Before replanting timestamp in panorama video we need to remove timestamp from each of individual videos and to recognize timestamp. So we do experiments on time-stamp ´recognition, timestamp removal, and replanting. For timestamp recognition separately recognize s-digit, ts-digit, minute digits, and date digits for 300 mpeg2 (we first convert the surveillance videos into mpeg2). Table 2 shows that our algorithm can achieve a very high accuracy of timestamp recognition.

Table 2. Accuracy of timestamp recognition

name	s-digit		ts-digit		minutes		date	
method	digit-seq		online temp.		online temp.		online temp.	
#total	#yes	%	#yes	%	#yes	%	#yes	%
300	300	100%	299	99.7%	300	100%	299	99.7%

Fig. 3. The digit extracted images of four timestamps

Fig. 4. The four samples of various timestamps and their result images after timestamps are removed

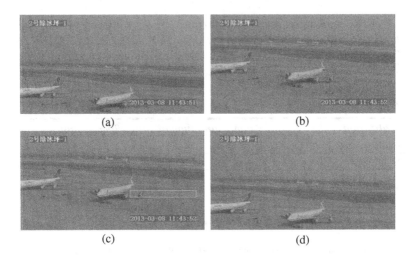

Fig. 5. A frame and its timestamp removal performance. The frame in (a) is the frame we want to remove its timestamp; the frame in (b) is one of the neighbor frames (a); The corresponding area in the frame in (b) of the timestamp in the frame in (b) is shown in (c); The frame in (a) changes into the frame in (d) after its timestamp is removed.

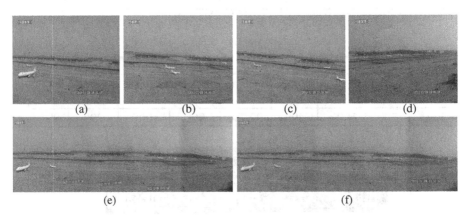

Fig. 6. Four concurrent frames from four different cameras and their panorama frame with replanting timestamp. The frames in (a) to (d) are from four different cameras. The frame in (e) is the panorama frame of four frames in (a) to (d) without timestamp replanting; the frame in (f) is the panorama frame of four frames in (a) to (d) with timestamp replanting.

Fig 3 gives the digit extraction results of four different timestamps. Fig 3 shows that noise points of digit extraction are near digits so we can get the proper timestamp bounding box even with some noise. Fig 4 gives five timestamps and their appearances after we conduct timestamp replanting step. Fig 5 shows a sample frame and its removing effect. From these two figures, we conclude that our algorithm has good performance in removing timestamp. Thus we can say that our timestamp replanting algorithm is promising to be developed into a tool for real application. Fig 6 shows the effect of timestamp replanting. When we do not do timestamp replant the three skew timestamps appear in the merged panorama frame; after we do the timestamp replanting a single timestamp is in the proper place of the panorama frame.

7   Conclusions and Future Work

We have presented an algorithm for replanting timestamp for panorama surveillance videos. This algorithm can accurately localize timestamp in a very low computing cost because it uses a very efficient timestamp localization procedure that first localizes s-digit and then segments all the digits of timestamp by using digit color. For timestamp removal, we use the corresponding pixels in one of neighbor frames of considering frame to replace the pixels covered by the timestamp. The experimental results show that the results of timestamp removal are very good.

In the near future we plan to develop an algorithm that can replant timestamp in real time robustly so that it can be used in real applications. Especially we need to improve our homography acquisition procedure in computing time. We will also need to improve our algorithm to cope with different types of timestamps.

References

1. Brown, M., Lowe, D.G.: Recognising panoramas. In: IEEE International Conference on Computer Vision (ICCV 2003), October 13-16, vol. 2, pp. 1218–1225 (2003)
2. Covavisaruch, N., Saengpanit, C.: Timestamp detection and recognition in video frames. In: Int'l Conference on Imaging Science, Algorithms and Technology (CISST 2004), Las Vegas, Nevada, USA, June 21-24, pp. 173–178 (2004)
3. Chugh, S., Jain, Y.K.: Character localization from natural images using nearest neighbours approach. Int'l Journal of Scientific & Engineering Research 2(12), 1–6 (2011)
4. Epshtein, B., Ofek, E., Wexler, Y.: Detecting text in natural scenes with stroke width transform. In: IEEE Int'l Conference on Computer Vision and Pattern Recognition (2010)
5. Jung, K., Kim, K.I., Jain, A.K.: Text information extraction in images and video: a survey. Pattern Recognition 37(5), 977–997 (2004)
6. Li, Y., Wan, K., Yan, X., Yu, X., Xu, C.: Video clock time recognition based on temporal periodic pattern. In: ICASSP 2006, vol. II, pp. 653–656 (2006)
7. Li, Y., Xu, C., Wan, K., Yan, X., Yu, X.: Reliable video clock time recognition. In: ICPR 2006, vol. 4, pp. 128–131 (2006)
8. Xu, C., Wang, J., Wan, K., Li, Y., Duan, L.: Live sports event detection based on broadcast video and web-casting text. ACM Multimedia, 226–730 (2006)
9. Yin, P., Hua, X.-S., Zhang, H.-J.: Automatic timestamp extraction algorithm for home videos. In: IEEE Int' l Symposium on Circuits and Algorithms (ISCAS 2002), vol. 2, pp. 73–76 (2002)
10. Yu, X.: Localization and extraction of the four clock-digits using the knowledge of the digital video clock. In: Int'l Conf. on Pattern Recognition (ICPR 2012), November 11-15, pp. 1217–1220 (2012)
11. http://www.2mcctv.com/blog/2012_08_09-time-stamping-on-security-cameras/

Virtual View Synthesis
Based on DIBR and Image Inpainting

Yuhan Gao[1], Hui Chen[1], Weisong Gao[2], and Tobi Vaudrey[3]

[1] School of Information Science and Engineering,
Shandong University, Jinan, Shandong, China
`huichen@sdu.edu.cn`
[2] Multimedia R & D Center, Hisense, Qingdao, China
`gaoweisong@hisense.com`
[3] Department of Computer Science
The University of Auckland, Auckland, New Zealand
`t.vaudrey@auckland.ac.nz`

Abstract. In 3DTV research, virtual view synthesis is a key component to the technology. Depth-image-based-rendering (DIBR) is an important method to realize virtual view synthesis. However, DIBR always results in hole problems where the depth and colour values are not known. Hole-filling methods often cause other problems, such as edge-ghosting and cracks. This paper proposes an algorithm that uses the depth and colour images to address the holes. It exploits the assumption of a virtual view between two laterally aligned reference cameras. The hole-filling method is performed on the blended depth image by morphological operations, and inpainting of the holes is obtained with the position information provided by the filtered depth maps. A new interpolation method to eliminate edge-ghosting is also presented, which additionally uses a post-processing technique to improve image quality. The main novelty of this paper is the unique image blending, which is more efficient than pre-processing depth maps. It is also the first method that is using morphological closing in the depth map de-noising process. The method proposed in this paper can effectively remove holes and edge-ghosting. Experimental quantitative and qualitative results show the proposed algorithm improves quality dramatically on traditional methods.

Keywords: Virtual View Synthesis, Depth-Image-Based-Rendering (DIBR), Image Inpainting, Interpolation.

1 Introduction

Recently, 3DTV has attracted considerable attention because of its wide application. Virtual view synthesis is one of the key steps to realize a full 3DTV system. The most widely used technique is depth-image-based rending(DIBR), which combines a reference image with its corresponding depth information to synthesize the virtual viewpoint in the scene. DIBR could not only render high quality images fast, but also new views of any position. However, DIBR would

R. Klette, M. Rivera, and S. Satoh (Eds.): PSIVT 2013, LNCS 8333, pp. 172–183, 2014.

cause holes due to the occlusion between the foreground/background, and also background that is only visible from the new view but not from the reference. Additionally, there is a problem that some false edges from the foreground object are projected to the new viewpoint. This is called edge-ghosting.

To deal with the hole and edge-ghosting problems, various algorithms have been proposed. Vazquez *et al.* [1] filled the holes based on the neighbouring pixels from the colour image only; it could not effectively address the issue of large holes. Domanski *et al.* [2] adopted a mapping method to generate a virtual view from each reference image independently and then blended them into one virtual view, but did not consider location of the holes. Narayanan *et al.* [3] proposed a depth and texture method to render complex scenes, while they did not propose an effective solution to the edge-ghosting problems.

The contributions of this paper are:

- a novel blending algorithm that is more efficient than preprocessing depth maps, but obtains similar quality
- a hole filling scheme that adopts a morphological closing operation along with a novel image inpainting method based on blended depth images
- an edge-ghosting eliminating method is proposed by interpolating pixels in the inpainting image
- the entire process addresses hole filling and edge-ghosting in an effective manor.

The remaining sections of this paper are organized as follows. Section 2 describes principles of DIBR. Section 3 explains the proposed algorithm. The experimental results are in Section 4. The paper is concluded in Section 5.

2   Depth-Image-Based-Rendering (DIBR)

Fehn [4] proposed that when using a pinhole camera model, if the camera coordinate system coincided with the world coordinate system of the reference view, it is possible to render the virtual view with DIBR technology. In order to realize virtual viewpoint rendering using DIBR, the following is required: a colour map, depth map, and camera parameters of the reference point, as well as the virtual viewpoint camera parameters.

2.1   3D Warping

3D Warping, which was proposed by McMilian [5] first, is the core of DIBR. It could mainly be divided into two steps: all the pixels in the reference image are projected to their corresponding three-dimensional space using the depth information, then the points of the three-dimensional space are projected to the virtual viewpoint image plane.

Fehn gave a transformation equation that is applicable to realistic settings:

$$\mathbf{m} = \mathbf{A} \mathbf{P}_n \mathbf{C} \mathbf{M} \tag{1}$$

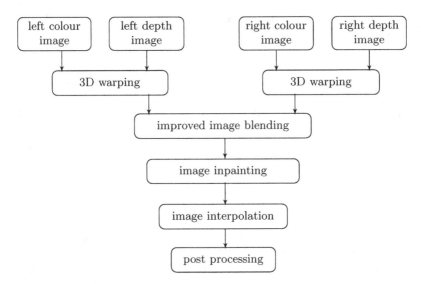

Fig. 1. The proposed view synthesis scheme

M is a world point (in world space coordinates) and $\mathbf{m} = (\mathbf{u}, \mathbf{v})$ is the respective projection in camera pixel coordinates. The matrix **A** denotes the intrinsic parameters that represent the inner structure of the camera (focal length, pixel size, skew, distortion, and principal point). The matrix **C** denotes the extrinsic parameters, which indicate the relationship between the world coordinates and the camera coordinates. $\mathbf{P_n}$ is the normalized perspective projection matrix from view n.

2.2 Problems of DIBR

When generating a new view image with 3D warping, there is a problem that several pixels may be projected to the same pixel on the virtual image, this is called a visibility issue. Moreover, some regions that are occluded in the reference image may become visible in the new virtual image. These new exposed regions become blank holes areas. Another issue is edge-ghosting, which is caused by the inaccurate edge matching of the colour and/or depth image. Therefore, the key problem is to cope with these regions correctly. This paper proposes a new method to fill holes and remove edge-ghosting.

3   Proposed Algorithm

The processing pipeline of the proposed algorithm consists of four steps: improved blending method, image inpainting based on depth image, image interpolation and post filtering. Fig. 1 shows the process of the proposed algorithm.

In the 3D warping step, the standard steps of DIBR are applied, i.e., the left and right colour images are warped to the virtual viewpoint using their corresponding depth images. Next, the traditional method is improved by blending warped colour images. In the image inpainting step, an image inpainting method based on filling holes via the depth image is proposed. A new interpolation algorithm is also presented to remove edge-ghosting during the image interpolation step. Finally, post processing is applied to improve image quality. Details are discussed in the following subsections.

3.1   3D Warping and Image Projection

In the first step, all 3D points $\mathbf{M}$ from the reference image are calculated by Eq. (1) using image points $\mathbf{m}$, the reference projection matrix $\mathbf{P}_{REF}$. The depth image $Z(u, v)$ is obtained from $\mathbf{M}$. In the second step, 3D point $\mathbf{M}$ is projected to warped virtual view with $\mathbf{P}_W$.

When obtaining the depth image in the warped projected virtual view $Z_W(u, v)$ conflicts can occur when two or more world points occupy the same pixel coordinate. One way to deal with this is to use the nearest point to the virtual camera, as used in Mori et $al.$ [6]. The equation is shown below.

$$Z_W(u, v) = \underset{m_W}{\operatorname{argmin}} \left(Z_W(u, v) \in (0, \infty) \right) \tag{2}$$

in other words, the lowest depth value above zero (in front of camera) at warped pixel point $m_W(u, v)$ is used.

The warped colour image $I_W(u, v)$ is constructed using the colour value from the original reference image. For conflicts, the colour value of the original reference point selected by Eq. (2) is used. In other words, the colour of the closest point in front of the virtual camera is selected.

3.2   Image Blending

The starting point for image blending is one or more images reprojected to a virtual view. Once the reprojected views are obtained, there can be pixel conflicts from from the multiple reference images. The subsections below show how the proposed algorithm deals with these conflicts in a stereo camera environment when warping to a virtual view between the two reference cameras.

Traditional Blending. The virtual view image is rendered by blending the warped left and right image, which have been translated from the reference viewpoints to the virtual viewpoint using Eq. (1) (see Fig. 1). The traditional image blending approach from Li et $al.$ [7] is illustrated by:

$$I(u, v) = (1 - \alpha)I_L(u, v) + \alpha I_R(u, v) \tag{3}$$

$$\alpha = \frac{|t - t_L|}{|t - t_L| + |t - t_R|} \tag{4}$$

$I(u, v)$ is the blended virtual view image at pixel (u, v). $I_L(u, v)$ and $I_R(u, v)$ are the warped virtual images from the left and right reference viewpoints, respectively . The blending factor α is calculated by Eq. (4) t is the translation vector from the extrinsic matrix of the virtual view. t_L and t_R are the left and right translation vectors, respectively. This blending factor has more weight if the virtual viewpoint is closer to a particular reference image (in world coordinates).

Improved Image Blending. One problem of the traditional method is that some pixels may have conflicting overlaps from the reference images. Additionally, there are usually so many holes in the blended image. Several methods [8,6] pre-filter depth images before warping in an attempt to reduce noise. In practise this does not have any obvious improvements. For example, Mori *et al.* adopted median and bilateral filtering, and it provided a minor improvement (the result is shown in Table 1). Additionally, it caused some inaccurate pixels and lump holes when blending depth images. Therefore, pre-filtering the depth images is not used in the presented algorithm. Instead, the improved blending method from Eq. (5) is used. An example result is shown in Figure 3a. This heuristic blending is based on the assumption of a stereo camera configuration, where the project virtual image lies between the two cameras (in the height-depth plane). The blended image I_B is calculated as follows:

$$
I_B(u, v) = \begin{cases} I_L(u, v) & \text{if } c_1 \\ I_R(u, v) & \text{else if } c_2 \\ 0 & \text{else if } c_3 \\ (1 - \alpha)I_L(u, v) + \alpha I_R(u, v) & \text{otherwise} \end{cases} \tag{5}
$$

where

$$
\begin{aligned}
c_1 &= \Big(Z_L(u, v) \neq 0 \ \wedge \ Z_R(u, v) \neq 0 \ \wedge \ Z_R(u + 1, v) = 0 \Big) \\
&\qquad \vee \ \Big(Z_L(u, v) \neq 0 \ \wedge \ Z_R(u, v) = 0 \Big) \\
c_2 &= \Big(Z_L(u, v) \neq 0 \ \wedge \ Z_R(u, v) \neq 0 \ \wedge \ Z_L(u - 1, v) = 0 \Big) \\
&\qquad \vee \ \Big(Z_L(u, v) = 0 \ \wedge \ Z_R(u, v) \neq 0 \Big) \\
c_3 &= \Big(Z_L(u, v) = 0 \ \wedge \ Z_R(u, v) = 0 \Big)
\end{aligned} \tag{6}
$$

$Z_L(u, v)$ and $Z_R(u, v)$ are the values of depth images projected from the original left and right depth maps to the virtual view. A value of $Z_*(u, v) = 0$ represents a hole (unknown) at (u, v). The left image colour value is used in the blended image if a point in the left depth image is not a hole, while it is in the right image (second part of c_1). The left image value is also assumed if a point in both depth images is valid but the right neighbouring pixel in the right depth image is a hole, since holes in right depth image are often on the right side of real scene (first part of c_1). The exact opposite is assumed for the right hand image (see c_2). If both the left and right depth image points contain a hole, the corresponding pixel value in the blended image would also be a hole. Otherwise, the pixel value in blended image would be summed with the traditional weighting coefficient α, see Eq. (4). This blending method reduces holes with marginal computational difference.

The depth image is blended Z_B in a similar fashion to the colour images above. An example result is shown in Fig.2a:

$$Z_B(u,v) = \begin{cases} Z_L(u,v) & \text{if } c_1 \\ Z_R(u,v) & \text{else if } c_2 \\ 0 & \text{else if } c_3 \\ (1-\alpha)Z_L(u,v) + \alpha Z_R(u,v) & \text{otherwise} \end{cases} \qquad (7)$$

3.3   Image Inpainting

After creating the blended image, some holes still exist. This blended colour image does not remove all holes. There have been many research efforts to further fill the holes. Criminisi *et al.* [9] used exemplar-based inpainting to inpaint the image, this is computationally expensive and may result in edge-ghosting. Oh *et al.* [10] filled the holes with background pixels, this can result in foreground pixels mistakenly being assumed as background. Zhang *et al.* [8] improved the image, but with some holes still existing. Li *et al.* [7]adopted a blending image that still had some holes not yet removed. The following explains a new image inpainting method that utilizes the depth values to fill holes.

Depth Image Filtering. The depth image is a grey-scale image, and grey value represents the depth of the points in a world coordinate. Both the colour images and depth images are warped and blended, then the colour image is inpainted based on the blended depth image. Since the hole region has no depth values, the depth image requires filtering and interpolation. Mori *et al.* used median and bilateral filtering but could not remove the lump holes, Jung and Ho [11] copied neighbouring background depth values to hole regions. This process may change some background pixels to foreground, or vice-versa.

The method proposed in this paper adopts morphological operations on the depth images. A closing operation (dilation then erosion) that uses a diamond structured window is chosen to fill the holes in the depth image [12]. This closing operation fills any hole smaller than the chosen window, it also fills any cracks that are thinner than the window. The filtering results are shown in Fig. 2. The red regions represent holes. Fig. 2a is the original blended depth image. Fig. 2b is using the Mori *et al.* method with median and bilateral filtering. Fig. 2c is the result of this papers filtering. By comparing Fig. 2b with 2c, it is clear that small cracks and spot noise are removed with the median plus bilateral filtering, however the large lump holes are still present. Comparing those results with the presented method in Fig. 2c; all lump holes, cracks and spot noise are removed and the filtering result is as good if not better than the results in Fig. 2b.

Depth-Based Image Inpainting. The image blending above can remove most holes. However, larger holes still exist which are often located in areas where

(a) original depth image (b) Mori *et al.* [6] method   (c) presented filtering

Fig. 2. Preprocessing result of depth image

occlusion occurs. Therefore, this paper proposes a new image inpainting method to fill holes. It uses the blended and filtered depth image to distinguish background and foreground. The pixel is blended with coloured pixels at the same depth within a specified region. When the background pixels are inpainted, it removes the effects from foreground pixels, and holes of background are weighted by points in background at the same depth, and vice versa. Each pixel is handled as Eq. (9). The depth value of the points around a pixel are compared, if the depth value is smaller than a threshold, it is determined that they are at the same depth as Eq. (10). The resulting inpainted colour image I_J is calculated from the blended image I_B from Eq. (5).

$$I_J(u,v) = \begin{cases} I_B(u,v) & \text{if } Z_B(u,v) = 0 \\ J(u,v) & (otherwise) \end{cases} \tag{8}$$

$$J(u,v) = \frac{\sum\limits_{(i,j)\in R} D(i,j)\,W(i,j)\,I_B(i,j)}{\sum\limits_{(i,j)\in R} D(i,j)\,W(i,j)} \tag{9}$$

$$D(i,j) = \begin{cases} 1 & \text{if } |Z_B(i,j) - Z_B(u,v)| < T_Z \\ 0 & \text{otherwise} \end{cases} \tag{10}$$

$$W(i,j) = \frac{1}{(i-u)^2 + (j-v)^2} \tag{11}$$

where $J(u,v)$ is the hole inpainting function. The pixel (i,j) is within the region R about pixel (u,v). $D(i,j)$ is depth weighting factor at pixel (i,j), with T_Z being the inpainting depth threshold. $W(i,j)$ is a weighting coefficient that reduces the weight given by quadratic distance from the original pixel. In other words, Eq. (8) will only fill in holes from the original blended image if there is a hole. From there, Eq. (9) is used to inpaint the image based on a local depth threshold and neighbourhood weighting factor.

Fig. 3 demonstrates the process with an example. Fig. 3a shows a sample blended image I_B where the pink regions are holes and the green frame is highlighting the hole regions. Fig.3d is the inpainting result I_J. From analysing this figure, it is noticeable that the lump holes in green frame region are restored.

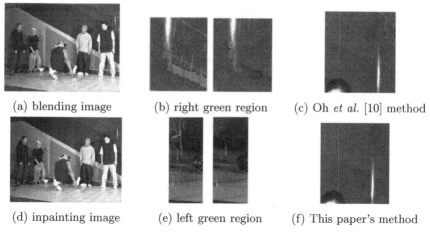

(a) blending image   (b) right green region   (c) Oh *et al.* [10] method

(d) inpainting image   (e) left green region   (f) This paper's method

Fig. 3. Result of inpainting

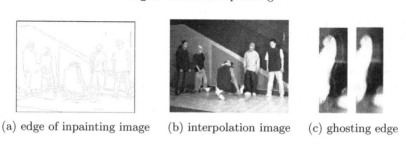

(a) edge of inpainting image   (b) interpolation image   (c) ghosting edge

Fig. 4. Result of interpolation process deployed in this paper

Fig. 3b and 3e are zoomed views of the green frame regions in Fig.3a and Fig.3d, respectively. The left hand image in each of these figures is the blended image, while the right is the inpainted image. The method proposed in Oh *et al.* is compared with this paper's inpainting method in Fig. 3c and 3f. From the figure, one could see the Oh *et al.* method has some speckles as the example pink region shows, while this paper's method could obtain a less noisy image.

3.4   Image Interpolation

In the process of view synthesis, some false edges of the foreground object are projected to new viewpoint. It is termed edge-ghosting. Mori *et al.* solved this problem by expanding the border of the occlusion, however, this would cause background points to become foreground points. The proposed method solves the problem of edge-ghosting by exploiting the edge analysis of the colour image in addition to using the depth image. A pixel is considered inaccurate if: the grey-value difference between its adjacent pixel is larger than a threshold, it does not belong to an edge, and if the depth of its adjacent pixel is below a threshold. An inaccurate pixel's colour is then averaged using a neighbourhood of pixels at a similar depth. The inpainted image I_J is converted to a grey-scale image I_G for the purposes of threshold calculations. To determine the edge, the Canny edge detector [13] is used on the grey-scale image I_G to calculate the edge image E_G (where 0 is not an edge and any positive value is an edge). Fig. 3d shows a sample of the Canny edge detection results. The resulting interpolation image I_P is calculated from Eq. (12).

$$I_P(u, v) = \begin{cases} P(u, v) & \text{if } c_4 \\ I_J(u, v) & \text{otherwise} \end{cases} \tag{12}$$

$$c_4 = \Big(E_G(u, v) = 0 \Big) \wedge \Big(|I_G(u, v) - I_G(u, v - 1)| > T_G \\ \wedge \Big(|Z_B(u, v) - Z_B(u, v - 1)| < T_Z \Big) \tag{13}$$

$$P(u, v) = \frac{1}{4} \sum_{(i,j) \in N_4} I_J(i, j) \tag{14}$$

where T_G and T_Z represent the grey and depth thresholds, respectively. P is the neighbourhood interpolation function with N_4 representing the four-neighbours of pixel (u, v), excluding itself.

Fig. 4b is an example interpolation result. Fig. 4c show magnified areas showing the removal of edge-ghosting. The left shoe image (inpainted image) shows a very prominent ghost edge, while this is clearly removed in the right hand shoe image (interpolated image).

3.5 Post Processing

For clearing up the tiny spots to obtain a new view image with better quality, speckle reducing anisotropic diffusion (SRAD) [14] is used to post process the image. This method is widely used in processing radar imaging, and could erase speckles, at the same time, preserve edge parts. This method is applied here to eliminate tiny spots in the new view. Fig. 5c shows the results.

4   Experimental Results and Discussion

For testing the algorithm, a set of sequences named 'breakdancers' was used which are generated and distributed by Interactive Visual Group at Microsoft Research [15]. The sequences contains 8 viewpoints, the depth of the image is consistent with the resolution of the colour image 1024×768. Eight distinct video sequences from eight distinct viewpoints are provided. This includes the: colour images, corresponding depth images, and camera parameters for each view. For the experimental results below, the camera 2 and camera 4 are selected as the reference points of view. These views are used to recreate virtual camera viewpoint 3, where the raw data from the camera 3 sequence is used as the ground truth. The parameters used for these test sequences were: depth image closing operation used a diamond window with parameter of 7, depth based

Table 1. Experimental results for presented blending method

measure	blending with depth preprocessing	presented method
PSNR	30.4775	30.4047
SSIM	0.9080	0.9086

Table 2. Results for proposed inpainting, interpolation and post filtering

measure	inpainting	interpolation	post filtering
PSNR	32.5193	33.2696	33.7350
SSIM	0.9271	0.9334	0.9345

inpainting region $R = 10 \times 10$, depth threshold $T_Z = 5$, colour (grey) threshold $T_G = 5$, and Canny edge parameter $\sigma = 5$.

In order to measure the effectiveness of the proposed method, the following measures are used: peak signal-to-noise ratio (PSNR) and structural similarity (SSIM) [16]. PSNR is an evaluation function measuring the quality of the reconstructed image, a higher value is better than a lower one. SSIM is used to evaluate the similarity between two images, a value of 0 means no similarity, while a value of 1 means exact similarity.

Firstly, blending using preprocessed depth maps is compared with this paper's blending method. We can see in Table 1 that using preprocessed depth maps has only marginal improvement over this paper's blending method, while adding a large computational cost. Therefore, it is not necessary to use preprocessing on the depth maps before blending the colour images.

Secondly, PSNR and SSIM are calculated in every step of this experiment. The results are given in Table 2. From this table we can see quantitatively that the presented inpainting method, interpolation method and post filtering method all improved quality of the synthesized virtual image. The inpainting alone provides an increase of 2.1 to PSNR and 0.02 for SSIM. Interpolation adds another 0.7 to the PSNR, and a further 0.01 to the SSIM. The post filtering process adds only marginal improvements (0.4 to PSNR and nearly nothing on the SSIM). The post filtering SRAD is not the novel part of this paper, but shows that it does provide some improvement in the post-process. The improvements are also obvious in qualitatively in the experimental figures. Fig. 3d highlights how well the image inpainting can fill holes, especially lump holes as the green frame region highlights. From the comparison in Fig. 4c, it is clear that this paper's interpolation method could remove edge-ghosting.

The proposed method is compared with the traditional synthesis method and Oh *et al.* in Table 3. The results quantitatively indicate that this paper's method improves image quality dramatically compared to the other methods. Fig. 5 shows the qualitative results of the different methods. Fig. 5d to 5f are amplifications of the green framed regions of the respective figures. From those figures,

Table 3. Comparative results for proposed method

measure	proposed method	traditional synthesis	Oh *et al.* [8]
PSNR	33.7350	30.4286	31.8150
SSIM	0.9345	0.8071	0.8365

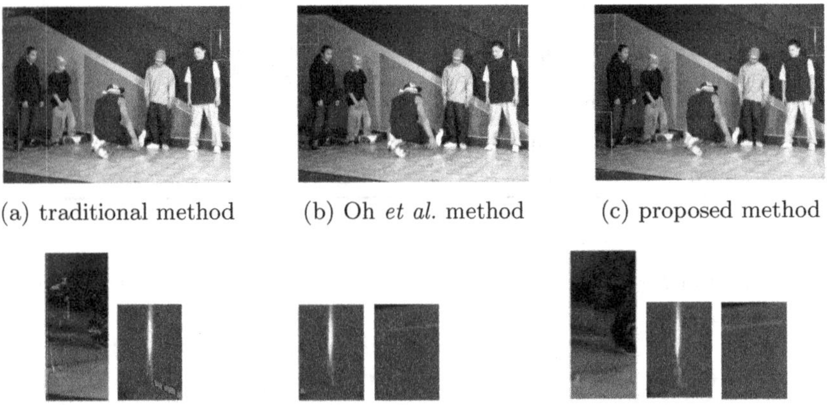

(a) traditional method   (b) Oh *et al.* method   (c) proposed method

(d) green region of (b)   (e) green region of (c)   (f) green region of (d)

Fig. 5. Qualitative results highlighting lump holes

one can see that the traditional method could not remove lump holes, Oh *et al.* clears up big holes with some cracks still existing (the comparison is in Fig. 3c and 3f). The proposed method removes not only holes but also edge-ghosting and has a higher similarity to the original image.

5   Conclusion

In this paper, a new algorithm was described for realizing virtual view synthesis. The holes are filled by morphological image inpainting based on a depth image that is blended in a novel way without pre-processing. Meanwhile, the ghosting edges are eliminated with image interpolation. The experimental results clearly showed quantitatively and qualitatively that the presented method provides high quality results, and better than some other selected methods.

The test data that was selected (generating a virtual view between two cameras) is what the algorithm was designed to be used on. Further work and considerations need to be taken if wanting to synthesise views outside the assumptions of the algorithm. Making these blending assumptions more geometrically flexible is the aim of future work.

Acknowledgments. This work is supported by the Natural Science Found of Shandong NSFSD under No.2009ZRB01675 and No.ZR2013FM032 and Multimedia R & D Center of Hisense.

References

1. Vazquez, C., Tam, W.J., Speranza, F.: Sterescopic Imaging: Filling Disoccluded Areas in Depth Image-Based Rendering. In: Proceedings of SPIE, Orlando, FL, USA, vol. 6392 (2006)
2. Domaski, M., Gotfryd, M., Wegner, K.: View Synthesis For Multiview Video Transmission. In: International Conference on Computer Vision and Pattern Recognition, Florida, USA, pp. 433–439 (2009)
3. Narayanan, P., Kumar, P., Reddy, K.: Depth+Texture Representation For Image Based Rendering. In: Proceedings of Fourth Indian Conference on Computer Vision, Graphics and Image Processing, Kolkata, Indian, pp. 113–118 (2004)
4. Fehn, C.: Depth-image-based rendering(DIBR), Compression, and Transmission For a New Approach on 3DTV. In: Proceedings of the SPIE, San Jose, CA, USA, vol. 5291, pp. 93–104 (2004)
5. McMillan, L.: An Image-Based Approach to Three-Dimensional Computer Graphics. Technical Report. University of North Carolina at Chapel Hill, Chapel Hill, NC, USA (1997)
6. Mori, Y., Fukushima, N., Yendo, T., Fujii, T., Tanimoto, M.: View Generation With 3D Warping Using Depth Information for FTV. Signal Processing: Image Communication 24(1), 65–72 (2009)
7. Li, M., Chen, H., Li, R., Chang, X.: An Improved Virtual View Rendering Method Based on Depth Image. In: International Conference on Computer Communication, Jinan, China, pp. 381–384 (2011)
8. Zhang, L., Tam, J., Wang, D.: Stereoscopic Image Generation Based on Depth Images For 3DTV. IEEE Transactions on Broadcasting 51(2), 191–199 (2005)
9. Criminisi, A., Perez, P., Toyama, K.: Region Filling and Object Removal by Exemplar-Based Image Inpainting. IEEE Transactions on Image Processing 13(9), 1200–1212 (2004)
10. Oh, K., Yea, S., Vetro, A., Ho, Y.: Virtual View Synthesis Method and Self Evaluation Metrics for Free Viewpoint Television and 3D Video. International Journal of Imaging Systems and Technology 20(4), 378–390 (2010)
11. Jung, J., Ho, Y.: Virtual View Synthesis Using Temporal Hole Filling with Bilateral Coefficients. In: IEEE International Conference on Research, Innovation and Vision for the Future, pp. 1–4 (2012)
12. Herk, M.V.: A Fast Algorithm for Local Minimum and Maximum Filters on Rectangular and Octagonal Kernels. Patt. Recog. Letters 13, 517–521 (1992)
13. Canny, J.: A Computational Approach To Edge Detection. IEEE Transactions on Pattern Analysis and Machine Intelligence 8(6), 679–698 (1986)
14. Yu, Y., Acton, S.: Speckle Reducing Anisotropic Diffusion. IEEE Transactions on Image Processing 11, 1260–1270 (2002)
15. Microsoft Research, Image-Based Realities-3D Video Download, http://research.microsoft.com/en-us/um/people/sbkang/3dvideodownload/.
16. Wang, Z., Bovik, A.C., Sheikh, H.R., Simoncelli, E.P.: Image quality assessment: From error visibility to structural similarity. IEEE Transactions on Image Processing 13(4), 600–612 (2004)

Implementation Strategy of NDVI Algorithm with Nvidia Thrust

Jesús Alvarez-Cedillo, Juan Herrera-Lozada, and Israel Rivera-Zarate

Instituto Politecnico Nacional
Parallel Processing Department
Up. Adolfo López Mateos Edif. CIDETEC, 07700 Mexico City
{jaalvarez,jlozada,irivera}@ipn.mx

Abstract. The calculation of Normalized Difference Vegetation Index (NDVI) has been studied in literature by multiple authors inside the remote sensing field and image processing field, however its application in large image files as satellite images restricts its use or need preprocessed phases to compensate for the large amount of resources needed or the processing time. This paper shown the implementation strategy to calculates NDVI for satellite images in RAW format, using the benefits of economic Supercomputing that were obtained by the video cards or Graphics Processing Units (GPU). Our algorithm outperforms other works developed in NVIDIA CUDA, the images used were provided by NASA and taken by Landsat 71 located on the Mexican coast, Ciudad del Carmen, Campeche.

1 Introduction

It is recognized that the degree of greenness, either during periods of drought or heavy rain can be an indicator of its strength and resilience to climate change conditions (Potter et al.). 1999, Cao et al. 2004; Stow et al. 2003, Peters et al. 2003). However, information on the tolerance threshold of the ecosystems of this region in years of extreme weather events does not exist. This paper calculates NDVI images for large images captured by satellite using the supercomputing as a tool and by using GPU video cards.

1.1 Normalized Difference Vegetation Index

It is well known in remote sensing that the relationship between bands near Infrared and red allow a verification test of the abundance or scarcity of vegetation in a region. The NDVI is used to identify the presence of green vegetation on the surface and characterize their spatial distribution and the state of evolution over time. This is determined primarily by weather conditions.

The interpretation of the index must also consider the phenomenological cycles and annual development to distinguish natural oscillations, vegetation changes in the temporal and spatial distribution caused by other factors. Water has reflectance $R > IRC$ [15][16] therefore NDVI negative values. Clouds have similar

R. Klette, M. Rivera, and S. Satoh (Eds.): PSIVT 2013, LNCS 8333, pp. 184–193, 2014.

values of R and CRF [16], so that its NDVI is close to 0. Bare soil with sparse vegetation has positive values although not very high. Dense vegetation that is moist and well developed presents the highest values of NDVI.

The NDVI has great value in ecological terms, as it is a good estimate of the fraction of photo synthetically active radiation intercepted by vegetation (FPAR) [1], primary productivity [2][3]. NDVI calculation exploits the properties of the high absorption bands in the visible and strong near infrared reflectance, with these values to find the relationship between the near infrared band (700-1300 nm) and red band (650 nm) which corresponds, in the TM, the relationship between bands 4 and 3 and SPOT, between strips 3 and 2. (TM4/TM3 or SPOT3/SPOT2).

The first use of vegetation index [4] was simply using the radiation of Infrared and red properties although this procedure is not named as vegetation index. The procedure shown was reported by Jordan et al, and still is useful, but has a big problem in that the range of values obtained can vary from 0 to infinity.

For this reason it is common to calculate NDVI (Normalized Difference Vegetation Index). NDVI was reported by Rouse et al. In 1973 [5], having the advantage that their values from -1 to +1. 1.2. EASY GPU PROGRAMMING

To design a small optimal program in the GPU, it is important to determine which options could be used for the programming.

Available options are:

1. CUDA: A set of native applications NVIDIA based on C language, is a powerful programming environment which requires experience to manage resources.
2. OpenCL: A set of native NVIDIA graphics applications based on OPENGL language.
3. THRUST: A set of optimized applications and simple based on C++ language: THRUST was selected because the optimized code is simple, having a small learning curve and works perfectly in any generation GPUs

THRUST is a template library for C++ and NVIDIA CUDA language, and based on the Standard Template Library (STL) [6]. THRUST can implement high-performance applications in parallel with a minimal programming effort through a high-level interface that is fully compatible with CUDA ,C and C++.

THRUST provides a collection of primitive parallel data, scanning data, sort information, and reduces operating expressions and formulas, which together can implement complex algorithms with simple and readable source code. To describe the calculations in terms of these high-level abstractions, this tool provides an option to develop efficient and optimal automatic applications. As a result, THRUST can be used to develop prototypes and CUDA applications, in terms of productivity, programming is very simple and concise, making it ideal where robustness and absolute return are very important. [7]

2   Previous Work

A wide range of NDVI changes having dispensed with these different models and apply large images knowing that its vegetation is abundant. This concept has been applied to SAVI (Soil Adjusted Vegetation Index) introduced by Huete (1988) [8]. The NDVI formula was used by Tucker & Sellers [9]. We also tested ARVI (Atmospherically Resistant Vegetation Index) reported by Kaufman and Tanre (1992) [10] for the EOS-MODIS. The ARVI changes NDVI equation behavior and its calculation is as follows:

Where, as before, NIR and RED (or VIS) is the response in the near-infrared and red (or visible) bands respectively.

Bearing in mind these principles, models have been applied to several areas of southern Mexico for a variety of crops, and natural vegetation. Three RGB bands, overall TM bands and 432 of the 321 Spot were used.

The blue band, is marked in the image areas as an vegetation index. Being a normalized index corrected the strong variations that exist in TM4/TM3 simple relationship between pixels of bands 4 and 3, which here is reduced to the limits of -1 to 1.

After applying the formula derived NDVI and once reaching the limits of negative and positive values, it is possible to indicate them in the image and, within their variants. The final phase is the map generation.

3   Implementation Strategy

3.1   Programming Model

THRUST operates two container types of vectors, host_vector & device_vector. As the name suggests, host_vector is stored in the memory of the CPU, while the device vector is processed in the GPU memory.

THRUST vector containers are defined as a typical output vector of C++, std :: vector. Similarly std :: vector, device_vector and host_vector are generic containers (capable of storing any type of data) that can be resized dynamically. Figure 1 shows the programing model of NVIDIA THRUST.

The equality operator can also be used to copy a host_vector to a vector or a host_vector to device_vector or device_vector to vector.

It is important to note that individual elements of a device_vector can be accessed using the standard bracket notation. However, for each of these accesses its necessary to call the function "cudaMemcpy" and this should be used sparingly.

3.2   Algorithm Development

Designing a parallel algorithm is complicated because there are no optimal tools to generate programs of this type. The development of such programs are scaled and there is a solution for every case which is more or less optimal.

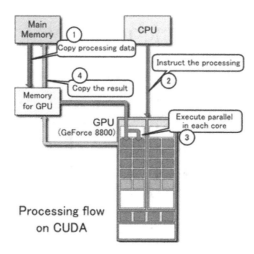

Fig. 1. Processing flow on NVIDIA CUDA and NVIDIA THRUST

To design the algorithm it was decided to generate a sequential process, as a base code and this source code was transformed to parallel code. Development requires the following concept formalization:

pixel where i=1,2,3,....n

As can be seen in contrast to the traditional method that takes a tour of the matrix in rows and columns, the suggested procedure only takes a tour of rows.

This feature is special, and indicates where to deploy and develop the device. This device manages memory vectors which consume raw or, simple memory, and this kind of memory is called linear.

The optimization model NVIDIA THRUST is an interface application to implement this style of programming without problems.

Trusth programming model has important differences to CUDA, to optimize the process, but using a lot of memory resources on the GPU. The low cost of the Nvidia card, allows run procedures directly, without having to partition the data problem. When the GPU memory is assigned, we create a transformation operator; this operator is a vector that executes in parallel the code inside, directly to architecture in a single step.

Thrust Nvidia handles transformation operators and direct operations in shared memory of the GPU; the operations it performs are called processing operations, and is typically found in the library file funcional.h as well as the basic operations. See Figure 2.

Our code is trying to solve NDVI, with a more simple,optimal code compared to the works reported by several authors in Literature with CUDA.

We defined our transformation operator source code as shown in Algorithm 1.

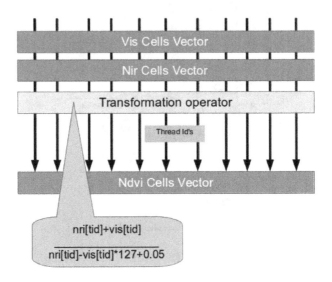

Fig. 2. Nvidia Thrust programming strategy

Algorithm 1. NDVI Cuda core source code

```
struct NDVI: THRUST::binary_function < char, char, char >
{
__device__float operator() (const char &A, const char &B )
{
return ( (( B + A ) / ( B - A ) ) +1 )* 127+0.05;
}
};
```

As can be seen, the transform operator is of a binary type, very similar in characteristic to CUDA, where the operator can acquire ownership of the device being executed at _device_, the CPU _host_ or both.

The typical computational complexity of this algorithm is $O(n_2)$, and after going through the incredibly convert operator in $O(k)$, where k is a constant number of instructions programmed into the transformation operator. (In our case a multiplication, division and a sum).Furthermore the manipulation of the image (read and write) is constant over time and can not be parallelized.Following the method and respecting the Thrust programming model:

Our proposed algorithm is shown in the algorithm 2.As we can see the programming style is simple and because it is a vector operation, this was designed in a simple style

The code #1 shows how the vector operation was defined and the final operation.

Algorithm 2. NDVI Paralell Algorithm

Input: Given a set of images I={I vis , I nir } R2 of n x n size quantified in the range of an image [0,255] .

Output: one Indvi image ,2D , n x n size

1: load I vis to host_vis
2: load I nir to host_nir
3: Copy host_vis to device_vis
4: Copy host_nir to device_nir
5: Apply transformation operator to i item of NDVI in device_nir
6: Copy device_NDVI to I nir

4   Results and Analysis

4.1   Algorithm Validation

Among the great variety of urban spaces we only present an example of an image of positive values that indicates the method of analysis. But in each case study, small index variations result in new images of similar vegetation. To validate the algorithm, we compare our results with those generated with the tool ImageJ.

ImageJ is a Java image processing program inspired by NIH Image for Macintosh. It runs, either as an on-line applet or as a down loadable application.

Figure 3 and 4 show two gray-scale images, both images were obtained by Mex-sat, VIS and NIR respectively. Both images have a RAW format of 8547 rows x7585 columns at 8 bits.

typical behaviors.

Figure 5 shows the resulting NDVI image in (red-1.0) * (red-blue) at RAW format of 8547 rows x7585 columns at 8 bits and the corresponding histogram

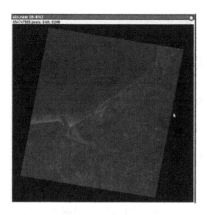 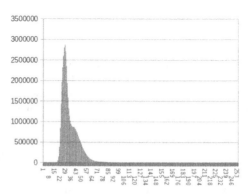

Fig. 3. Left:VIS image histogram right:Ciudad del Carmen, Campeche. Vis image in (red-1.0) * (red-blue) at RAW format of 8547 rows x7585 columns at 8 bits.

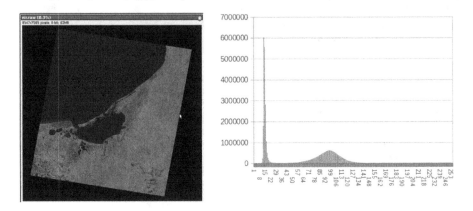

Fig. 4. left:NIR image, right:NIR image histogram

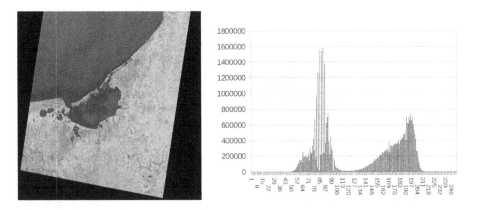

Fig. 5. Left:resulting NDVI image, right:Histogram resulting NDVI image

4.2   Stream Data

When analyzing data from the calculation of NDVI (Figure 6) it was observed that when the data is less than ten thousand, the sequential implementation is faster than any of the parallel implementations, but when the data is greater than ten million data, THRUST is faster than CUDA.

It can also be seen that in the parallel versions using linear vectors gives better speeds below ten thousand data, but when the data is greater than ten million times the best data was obtained using the floating type (primitive data).

This behavior is repeated with the use of images of a large amount of data (Figure 7- Top). When the data are greater than ten million times the best data was obtained when handling a floating rate. It is observed that the behavior of the execution times of the programs implemented with CUDA and THRUST have some degree of parallelism, THRUST being faster. This means that CUDA

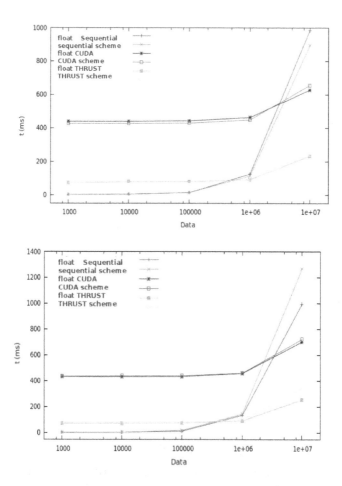

Fig. 6. Top:Comparison of different implementations with different types of NDVI, Bottom:Comparison of different implementations, with different types of large amounts of data

implementations used in this work are likely to be optimized while algorithms that use the interface of application (API) are optimized algorithms THRUST

In analyzing the performance of CUDA and THRUST versions regarding its sequential version, these are the best values of acceleration (speedup). Figure 7-Bottom was obtained using data from the floating rate rather than structures, and because algorithms are used THRUST optimized implementations, with THRUST running better than CUDA.

Similar behavior, where THRUST implementations require less time than those achieved with CUDA have been reported in other studies [11] [12][13][14].

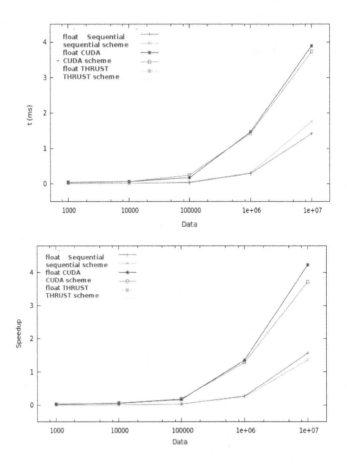

Fig. 7. Top:Comparison of speedups for CUDA and THRUST with different types of data when processed using NDVI , Bottom:Comparison of different implementations THRUST-CUDA

5   Conclusions

The parallelization of NDVI for a GPU can be implemented in CUDA or THRUST, however, as mentioned before, the use of CUDA means having knowledge of architecture at the hardware level. Such work must be distributed among the GPU processors through the allocation of threads, blocks, grids. On the other hand when using THRUST programming this does not require knowledge; in addition this programming is more efficient, but this does not imply that it is possible to achieve these levels of efficiency with CUDA and finally THRUST is a library based on CUDA.

Note that the resulting code using THRUST is less than is obtained when using CUDA, as well as its interface is similar to that of the STL (Standard

Template Library) which makes implementation simple, and can be combined in a single CUDA program.

Regarding the type of data, the best implementations were achieved when using float type data structures instead of generalizing on the basis of this work.

A better implementation of this algorithm is based on primitive data instead of complex data.

References

1. Zhang, Y., Tian, Y., Knyazikhin, Y., Martonchik, J.V., Diner, D.J., Leroy, M., Myneni, R.B.: Prototyping of MISR LAI and FPAR Algorithm with POLDER Data over Africa. IEEE Transactions on Geoscience and Remote Sensing 38(5) (2005)
2. Paruelo, J.M., Epstein, H.E., Lauenroth, W.K., Burke, I.C.: ANPP estimates from NDVI for the central grasslands region of the U.S. Ecology, 953–958 (1997)
3. Tucker, C.J.: Red and photographic infrared linear combinations for monitoring vegetation. Rem. Sens. of Environ. 8, 127–150 (1979)
4. Jordan, C.F.: Derivation of leaf area index from quality of light on the forest floor. Ecology 50, 663–666 (1969)
5. Rouse, J.W., Haas, R.H., Schell, J.A., Deering, D.W.: Monitoring vegetation system in the great plains with ERTS. In: Ecology Third ERST Symposium, NASA SP-351, vol. 1, pp. 309–317 (1973)
6. NVIDIA Co., CUDA Toolkit 4.0, THRUST Quick Start Guide, PG-05688-040_v01 (2011)
7. Ruestch, G., Micikevicius, P.: Optimizing Matrix Transpose in CUDA. Tech report, NVIDIA (2009)
8. Huete, A.R.: A Soil-Adjusted Vegetation Index (SAVI). Remote Sensing of Environment 25, 295–309 (1988)
9. Tucker, C.J., Sellers, P.J.: Satellite remote-sensing of primary production. International Journal of Remote Sensing, 1395–1416 (1986)
10. Kaufman, Y.J., Tanre, D.: Atmosoherically resistant vegetation index (ARVI) for EOS-MODIS. In: Proc. IEEE Int. Geosci. And Remote Sensing Symp. 1992, pp. 261–270. IEEE, New York (1992)
11. Faber, R.: Cuda Application Design and Development. Elsevier (2011)
12. Xiu, D.: Numerical Methods for Stochastic Computations: A Spectral Method Approach. Princeton University Press (2010)
13. Rubinstein, R.Y.: Simulation and the Monte Carlo Method. John Willey and Sons (1981)
14. Rosenthal, J.S.: Parallel computing and Monte Carlo algorithms. Far East Journal of Theoretical Statistics 4, 207–236 (2000)
15. A.S Hope, Estimation of wheat canopy resistance using combined remotely sensed spectral reflectance and thermal observations. In: Department of Geography, San Diego State University, San Diego, California 92182 USA (2010), http://dx.doi.org/10.1016/0034-4257(88)90035-1\
16. King, M.D., Kaufman, Y.J., Menzel, W.P., Tanre, D.: Remote sensing of cloud, aerosol, and water vapor properties from the moderate resolution imaging spectrometer (MODIS), Geoscience and Remote Sensing. IEEE Transactions Geoscience and Remote Sensing 30(1), 2–27 (1992)

Generation of a Super-Resolved Stereo Video Using Two Synchronized Videos with Different Magnifications

Yusuke Hayashi[1], Norihiko Kawai[1], Tomokazu Sato[1],
Miyuki Okumoto[2], and Naokazu Yokoya[1]

[1] Graduate School of Information Science, Nara Institute of Science and Technology
8916-5 Takayama, Ikoma, Nara 630-0192, Japan
{hayashi.yusuke.hq7,norihi-k,tomoka-s,yokoya}@is.naist.jp
http://yokoya.naist.jp
[2] Tokuyama College of Technology, Gakuendai, Shunan, Yamaguchi 745-8585, Japan
okumoto@tokuyama.ac.jp

Abstract. In this paper, we address the problem of changing the optical zoom magnification of stereo video that uses a stereo camera system with 4K or 8K digital cameras. We proposes a solution for generating a zoomed stereo video from a pair of zoomed and non-zoomed videos. To achieve this, part of the non-zoomed video image is isolated and super-resolved, so that the resolution of the image becomes the same as that of the optically-zoomed image. The non-zoomed video is super-resolved by energy minimization using the optically-zoomed image as an example. The effectiveness of this method is validated through experiments.

Keywords: Stereo video, Super-resolution, Energy minimization.

1 Introduction

The increasing popularity of 3D TV is leading to an increase in 3D video generation. Two methods are typically used to generate stereo videos of real scenes: one uses two identical video cameras that are arranged in parallel, and the other converts 2D video (captured using a single video camera) to 3D [1]. In this paper, we address the problem of changing the optical zoom magnification of stereo video. When using two cameras, the stereo camera system that synchronizes the optical zoom magnifications of the two cameras is mechanically complex and costly. This is especially true for a 3D digital cinema camera system using 4K (4096×2160) or 8K (8192×4320) cameras. However, 2D/3D conversion often gives unnatural stereoscopic images [2]. This paper proposes a solution by generating a zoomed stereo video from a pair of optically-zoomed and non-zoomed videos in the stereo camera system.

Most conventional methods for super-resolution can be broadly classified into two categories. One uses multiple low-resolution images and the other uses high-resolution images as examples. In the former method, input images are super-resolved by aligning multiple low-resolution images with sub-pixel accuracy

R. Klette, M. Rivera, and S. Satoh (Eds.): PSIVT 2013, LNCS 8333, pp. 194–205, 2014.

[3, 4, 5, 6]. This method requires the capture of many images of the same scene without moving objects. Therefore, this approach is not suitable for our solution. In the latter example-based method, correspondences between a target low-resolution image and example high-resolution images are determined, which are used to super-resolve the target image [7, 8]. In this category, several attempts have been made at efficiently obtaining good results. Hashimoto et al. [9] proposed a method of efficiently searching for correspondences using a binary tree dictionary. Baker et al. [10] restricted the category of examples in the database by considering that the quality of the resultant image largely depends on the examples.

In this paper, we use the example-based super-resolution approach. We propose a new system to generate a zoomed stereo video from two synchronized cameras with different magnifications, which has not previously been attempted. In our method, any camera unit can be used for generating stereo video images unlike the mechanical approach where a new system is required every time a new camera unit is released. In the proposed method, we isolate part of a non-zoomed video image that corresponds to the other optically-zoomed image. This is then super-resolved using the example optically-zoomed image, so that it has the same zoomed resolution. This is effective because there is a high correlation between the target low-resolution image and the high-resolution image captured by the two cameras arranged in parallel.

2   Generation of Super-Resolved Stereo Video

Figure 1 illustrates the flow of the proposed method. In this study, we shoot a target scene using two cameras that are set so that their optical axes are parallel, and horizontal lines are parallel. To simplify our explanation, let the optically zoomed left-eye image be L, and the non-zoomed right-eye image be R. First, the section corresponding to L is cut out from R, and the cutout right-eye image is called R_d (Process I). Next, R_d is enlarged to the size of L using initial values for the generated image, R_s (Process II). Then, an energy function is defined based on the pattern similarity between L and R_s, and the difference in intensity between R_d and R_s. We then minimize the energy to super-resolve the image, by repeating two processes: search L for a similar texture (Process III-1) and update all the pixel values in R_s (Process III-2). In the following sections, we describe the cutout and energy minimization methods.

2.1   Cutout of Non-zoomed Image

To isolate R_d so that it corresponds to the shooting range of L, we estimate the transform matrix $\mathbf{M}$ that projects the four corners of L onto four points in R for every frame, as shown in Fig. 2. The transform matrix, $\mathbf{M}$, defined as

$$\mathbf{M} = \begin{pmatrix} s & 0 & t_x \\ 0 & s & t_y \\ 0 & 0 & 1 \end{pmatrix}. \tag{1}$$

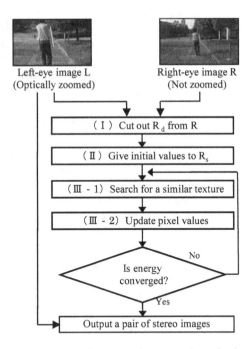

Left-eye image L   Right-eye image R
(Optically zoomed)   (Not zoomed)

(I) Cut out R$_d$ from R

(II) Give initial values to R$_s$

(III - 1) Search for a similar texture

(III - 2) Update pixel values

Is energy
converged?   No

Yes

Output a pair of stereo images

Fig. 1. Flow diagram of proposed method

The translation parameters, t_x and t_y, are determined in advance by calibrating the camera. The scaling parameter, s (where the zoom magnification is $1/s$), is determined so that a similarity measure between R_d and L is maximized.

The similarity measure is based on the normalized cross-correlation between two graphs generated using the average intensities of the scanlines in images L and R. To successfully generate stereo images that can be fused by human eyes, it is important to align the horizontal lines. Thus, to determine the magnification parameter s, it is more effective to use the average intensity for each horizontal line

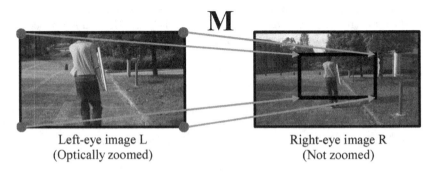

Left-eye image L   Right-eye image R
(Optically zoomed)   (Not zoomed)

Fig. 2. Projection of four corners using transform matrix **M**

Average of intensities

Fig. 3. Example of graph for average intensities of scan lines

than the vertical line. As shown in Fig. 3, graph $h_L(y)$ of L is generated so that
the vertical axis is the y coordinate of L, and the horizontal axis is the average
pixel value on one horizontal line. For the graph $h_R(y)$, R_d is first cut out from
R using the tentative matrix $\mathbf{M}$ and then enlarged to the size of L. The tentative
graph $h_R(y)$ is then generated from the enlarged R_d in the same way as for L.
The graphs for the R, G and B components are generated, and the sum of the
normalized cross-correlations for R, G and B are used as a similarity measure.

After determining $\mathbf{M}$, we need to compensate for the color tone of R_d. The R,
G and B values of the image R_d are linearly transformed so that graphs $h_R(y)$
for RGB fit the graphs $h_L(y)$ for RGB in a least-squares manner.

2.2 Definition of Energy Function

The energy function, E, is defined using two different kinds of energy terms.
E_{ssd} represents the pattern similarity between R_s and L, and E_{dif} represents
the intensity difference between R_s and R_d.

$$E = \sum_{\mathbf{x}_i \in R_s} \{\lambda E_{ssd}(\mathbf{x}_i, \mathbf{x}_j) + (1 - \lambda)E_{dif}(\mathbf{x}_i, g(\mathbf{x}_i))\}, \tag{2}$$

$$E_{ssd}(\mathbf{x}_i, \mathbf{x}_j) = \sum_{\mathbf{p} \in W} \{R_s(\mathbf{x}_i + \mathbf{p}) - L(\mathbf{x}_j + \mathbf{p})\}^2, \tag{3}$$

$$E_{dif}(\mathbf{x}_i, g(\mathbf{x}_i)) = \{R_s(\mathbf{x}_i) - R_d(g(\mathbf{x}_i))\}^2. \tag{4}$$

Here, W is a square window, and λ is a weight for balancing the two terms.
$\mathbf{x}_i$ denotes a pixel in R_s, and $\mathbf{x}_j$ is a pixel from L. $R_s(\mathbf{x}_i)$, $R_d(\mathbf{x}_i)$ and $L(\mathbf{x}_i)$
represent the intensities of the pixel $\mathbf{x}_i$ in the images R_s, R_d and L. $g(\mathbf{x}_i)$ denotes
a pixel position in R_d that corresponds to the pixel $\mathbf{x}_i$ in R_s. The relationship is

$$g(\mathbf{x}_i) = \mathbf{M}'\mathbf{x}_i, \tag{5}$$

where the matrix $\mathbf{M}'$ is the same as matrix $\mathbf{M}$ except that the translation parameters are 0. E_{ssd} represents the effect of increasing the resolution of the generated image, and E_{dif} represents the preservation of the texture of the original
right-eye image.

2.3   Iterative Energy Minimization

The energy function, E, is minimized using the framework of a greedy algorithm. In the proposed method, the energy function is minimized by iterating the following two processes: search for similar patterns in L (III-1) and update pixel values in R_s (III-2).

Process (III-1). The whole pixel values in R_s are fixed, and the position $\mathbf{x}_k$ of the most similar texture pattern to $\mathbf{x}_i$ is updated so as to satisfy the following equation:

$$\mathbf{x}_k = f(\mathbf{x}_i) = \operatorname*{argmin}_{\mathbf{x}_j \in \phi(\mathbf{x}_i)} E_{ssd}(\mathbf{x}_i, \mathbf{x}_j), \tag{6}$$

where $\phi(\mathbf{x}_i)$ is the search region of L that corresponds to the pixel $\mathbf{x}_i$ in the generated image. Here, $\phi(\mathbf{x}_i)$ includes a set of pixels on the epipolar line and several pixels above and below the epipolar line.

Process (III-2). The pixel values $R_s(\mathbf{x}_i)$ in the generated image are updated in parallel so as to minimize the energy function E defined in Eq.(2) while keeping all the similar pairs fixed. The energy function E is resolved into the element energy $E(\mathbf{x}_i)$ for each pixel $\mathbf{x}_i$ in R_s.

$$E(\mathbf{x}_i) = \lambda \sum_{\mathbf{p} \in W} \{R_s(\mathbf{x}_i) - L(f(\mathbf{x}_i + \mathbf{p}) - \mathbf{p})\}^2 + (1 - \lambda)\{R_s(\mathbf{x}_i) - R_d(g(\mathbf{x}_i))\}^2. \tag{7}$$

Each element energy includes only one parameter and the total energy, E, consists of the sum of all element energies. Therefore, E can be minimized by minimizing each element energy. $R_s(\mathbf{x}_i)$ that minimizes $E(\mathbf{x}_i)$ can be calculated by differentiating $E(\mathbf{x}_i)$ with respect to $R_s(\mathbf{x}_i)$, and is

$$R_s(\mathbf{x}_i) = \frac{\lambda \sum_{\mathbf{p} \in W} L(f(\mathbf{x}_i + \mathbf{p}) - \mathbf{p}) + (1 - \lambda)R_d(g(\mathbf{x}_i))}{\lambda N_W + (1 - \lambda)}, \tag{8}$$

were N_W denotes the number of pixels in the window.

Additionally, in order to reduce the computational cost and avoid local minima, we use a coarse-to-fine approach for energy minimization. We first generate an image pyramid. In the coarsest level, the above processes (III-1) and (III-2) are iterated until the energy converges. The pixel correspondences between images L and R_s in the last iteration are committed memory. In subsequent levels, the generated texture in the previous level is used for the initial pixel values. The processes (III-1) and (III-2) are iterated until convergence where the search area for each pixel in R_s in the process (III-1) is limited to a range around the memorized corresponding position in the previous level. In addition, in the finest level, we repeat the energy minimization while reducing the size of the window. This enables more detailed textures to be reproduced.

Table 1. Estimated zoom magnifications

Ground truth	1.0	1.1	1.2	1.3	1.4	1.5	1.6	1.7	1.8	1.9	2.0
Estimated result	1.001	1.106	1.204	1.300	1.396	1.497	1.613	1.721	1.831	1.908	1.996

3   Experiments

In order to demonstrate the effectiveness of the proposed method, we have performed experiments using a stereo image dataset [11, 12] and real stereo video captured by two parallel digital video cameras (Red Digital Cinema Camera Company: Red One).

We first confirmed the validity of the estimation of the zoom scale by process (I). Then, we calculated the super-resolved results, and compared them to the results of conventional methods.

3.1   Confirmation of Validity of the Zoom Scale Estimation

In this section, we confirm the validity of the scale estimation method described in Section 2.1. In this experiment, we used a stereo image (right and left images with 4096×2160 pixels) of a real stereo video in which the zoom magnifications of the two cameras were the same. To simulate a stereo pair with different zoom magnifications, the right-eye image was resized as a non-zoomed image and the left-eye image was cut out and resized as an optically-zoomed image so that the resolutions of the two images became the same. We resized the right-eye image to 2048×1080 pixels as a non-zoomed image. We cut out the left-eye image to simulate a zoom, changing the magnification from 1.0 to 2.0 with a 0.1 skip and resizing the respective cutout images to 2048×1080 pixels. Figure 4 shows the examples of input stereo pairs with different zoom magnifications.

Table 1 shows the estimated zoom magnifications using the proposed method. The estimated magnifications were almost the same as the ground truth in many cases. However, when the zoom magnification was 1.8, the error ratio was 1.7%. Other cases had worse results. This is attributed to the fact that the graph $h_L(y)$ is relatively flat when the magnification is 1.8, because the board with a regular pattern occupies a large area of the image.

3.2   Experiments Using a Stereo Image Dataset

In this experiment, we used two images (Aloe with 640×554 pixels, and Tsukuba with 384×288 pixels) selected from the stereo image dataset [11, 12]. We reduced the size of each right image to simulate a pair of input images with different zoom magnifications. In this experiment, we did not use an image pyramid for the coarse-to-fine approach because the input image size was small enough. In the original scale, we first set the window size W to be 7×7 pixels, and reduced it to 5×5 and 3×3 pixels as the energy converges.

(a) Simulated a non-zoomed right-eye image

(b) Simulated optically-zoomed left-eye images with different magnifications (From left to right, top to bottom: 1.0, 1.2, 1.4, 1.6, 1.8, 2.0)

Fig. 4. Examples of input stereo pairs with different zoom magnifications

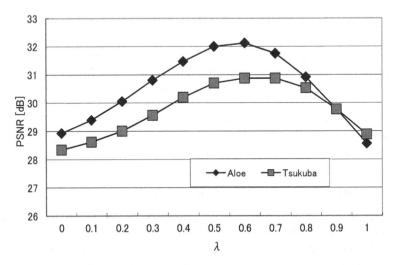

Fig. 5. PSNR with different λ

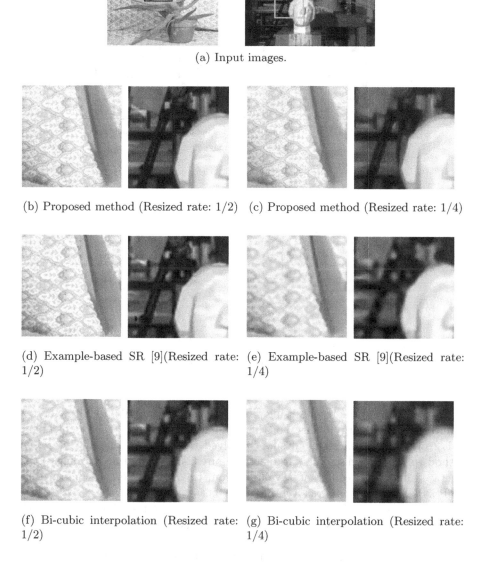

(a) Input images.

(b) Proposed method (Resized rate: 1/2) (c) Proposed method (Resized rate: 1/4)

(d) Example-based SR [9](Resized rate: (e) Example-based SR [9](Resized rate:
1/2)   1/4)

(f) Bi-cubic interpolation (Resized rate: (g) Bi-cubic interpolation (Resized rate:
1/2)   1/4)

Fig. 6. Super-resolved results by three methods

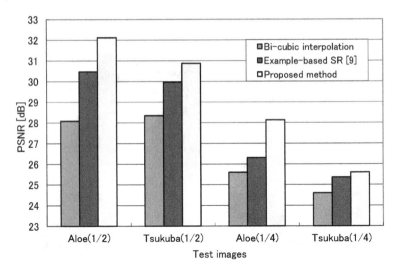

Fig. 7. PSNR of all test images

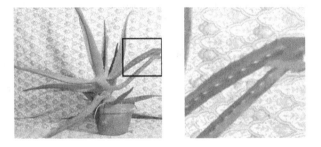

Fig. 8. Example of unnatural generated texture

First, we verified the results using different λ values (from 0.0 to 1.0), where λ balances the two energy terms. For this simulation, we resized each right image to 1/2 of the original size and super-resolved the images using the proposed method with a known scaling parameter. Figure 5 shows the PSNR values of the generated images for different λ values. From this result, we can confirm that the PSNR becomes higher as λ approaches 0.6.

Next, we compared the results of three methods: the proposed method with $\lambda = 0.6$, an example-based super-resolution method [9], and bi-cubic interpolation. We resized each right image to 1/2 and 1/4 of the original size. Figure 6 shows the results that correspond to the two resized rates using the three methods. By comparing these images, we can confirm that the proposed method successfully generated the high-frequency component. When the resized rate was

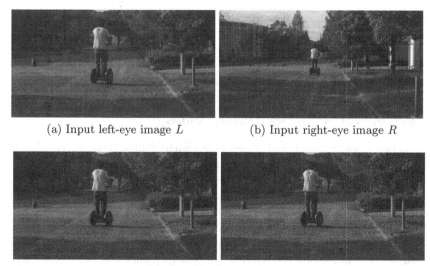

(a) Input left-eye image L (b) Input right-eye image R

(c) Generated stereo image

Fig. 9. Input images and generated result

(a) Proposed method

(b) Bi-cubic interpolation

Fig. 10. Comparison of results

1/4, the difference was especially noticeable. Figure 7 shows the PSNR values of the results of each method. The PSNR values of the proposed method are the highest for both images, when compared with the other methods. However, as shown in Fig. 8, the image generated using our method with $\lambda = 1.0$ includes some incorrect texture patterns. This is because similar patterns do not exist in the optically zoomed high-resolution image due to occlusions.

3.3   Experiments Using Real Stereo Video

In this experiment, we captured stereo video with 4096×2160 pixels using two digital video cameras. We changed the magnification of the left camera and kept the right magnification fixed. In the proposed method, $\lambda = 0.6$, as was suggested by our preliminary experiments (see Fig. 5). For the coarse-to-fine approach, we resized the input image to 1/8, 1/4 and 1/2 of the original size. We set the window size, W, to be 13×13 pixels. At the finest level, the window size was reduced to 9×9 and 5×5 pixels as the energy converged. In this experiment, approximately 5 minutes were required to generate each pair of stereo images using a PC (Intel Core i7 3.40GHz of CPU and 8.00 GB of memory).

Figure 9 shows the input images of the target frame and a pair of stereo images generated using the proposed method. The generated stereo images can be viewed stereoscopically. We have also confirmed that our method compensated for the color tone of the generated right-eye image. Figure 10 shows the magnified images generated by the proposed method and by using bi-cubic interpolation. Using Fig. 10, we can confirm that the texture generated by the proposed method is clearer than that by bi-cubic interpolation. The experimental results demonstrate the effectiveness of this method for improving the quality of the real stereo video.

4   Conclusion

We have proposed a new system for generating high-resolution stereo video from two synchronized videos with different magnifications. In the proposed method, a non-zoomed video is super-resolved by energy minimization, using the optically-zoomed image as an example. In experiments using a stereo dataset and real video, we have demonstrated the effectiveness of the proposed method by comparing our results to conventional methods. In the future, we will focus on improving the quality of the generated image by considering occlusions.

Acknowledgments. This research was partially supported by Grant-in-Aid for Scientific Research (A), No. 23240024 and Challenging Exploratory Research, No. 25540086.

References

1. Mendiburu, B.: 3D Movie Making - Stereoscopic Digital Cinema from Script to Screen. Focal Press (2009)
2. Mita, T.: 2D to 3D image upconversion technology. Journal of Institute of Image Information and Television Engineers 67(2), 116–121 (2013) (in Japanese)
3. Park, S.C., Park, M.K., Kang, M.G.: Super-resolution image reconstruction: A technical overview. IEEE Signal Processing Magazine 20(3), 21–36 (2003)
4. Iketani, A., Sato, T., Ikeda, S., Kanbara, M., Nakajima, A., Yokoya, N.: Super-resolved video mosaicing for documents by extrinsic camera parameter estimation. In: Proc. Int. Conf. on Computer Vision and Graphics, pp. 327–336 (2004)
5. Irani, M., Peleg, S.: Improving resolution by image registration. Graphical Models and Image Processing 53(3), 231–239 (1991)
6. Farsiu, S., Robinson, M., Elad, M., Milanfar, P.: Fast and robust multiframe super resolution. IEEE Trans. Image Processing 13(10), 1327–1344 (2004)
7. Freeman, W.T., Jones, T.R., Pasztor, E.C.: Example-based super-resolution. IEEE Computer Graphics and Applications 22, 56–65 (2002)
8. Begin, I., Ferrie, F.P.: Blind super-resolution using a learning-based approach. In: Proc. Int. Conf. on Pattern Recognition, vol. 2, pp. 85–89 (2004)
9. Hashimoto, A., Nakaya, T., Kuroki, N., Hirose, T., Numa, M.: Binary tree dictionary for learning-based super-resolution. IEICE Trans. D J96-D(2), 357–361 (2013) (in Japanese)
10. Baker, S., Kanade, T.: Hallucinating faces. In: Proc. IEEE Int. Conf. on Automatic Face and Gesture Recognition, pp. 83–88 (2000)
11. Scharstein, D., Szeliski, R.: A taxonomy and evaluation of dense two-frame stereo correspondence algorithms. Int. Journal of Computer Vision 47(1-3), 7–42 (2002)
12. Hirschmuller, H., Scharstein, D.: Evaluation of cost functions for stereo matching. In: Proc. IEEE Conf. on Computer Vision and Pattern Recognition, pp. 1–8 (2007)

Video Saliency Modulation in the HSI Color Space for Drawing Gaze

Tao Shi and Akihiro Sugimoto

National Institute of Informatics,
2-1-2 Hitotsubashi, Chiyoda-ku, Tokyo 101-8430, Japan
shitao.2011@my.bristol.ac.uk,
sugimoto@nii.ac.jp

Abstract. We propose a method for drawing gaze to a given target in videos, by modulating the value of pixels based on the saliency map. The change of pixel values is described by enhancement maps, which are weighted combination of center-surround difference maps of intensity channel and two color opponency channels. Enhancement maps are applied to each video frame in the HSI color space to increase saliency in the target region, and to decrease that in the background. The TLD tracker is employed for tracking the target over frames. Saliency map is used to control the strength of modulation. Moreover, a *pre-enhancement* step is introduced for accelerating computation, and a post-processing module helps to eliminate flicker. Experimental results show that this method is effective in drawing attention of subjects, but the problem of flicker may rise in minor cases.

Keywords: visual focus of attention, saliency, video modulation, gaze navigation.

1 Introduction

To understand the behavior of human visual attention is an important task in the study of neuroscience. Human gaze can be directed by the ability of learning, recall, or recognition. More frequently, the direction of gaze is controlled by our born ability to discriminate object appearances. To understand the principle of human vision, creating a computational model for visual attention is a primary task in the cross subject of neuroscience and computer science.

One promising way to estimate the visual focus of attention is to use a saliency map, which identifies image regions that draw more human attention. Koch and Ullman [9] firstly proposed a prototype of saliency map model. Itti et al. [6] summarized the previous work and proposed the basic bottom-up saliency map model. Afterwards, Itti et al. [7] extended the saliency map to deal with videos by addinsg flicker and motion detection. In later years, more models of saliency computation were proposed. The graph-based visual saliency [4] added an 'activation' step after the extraction of original features. The ability of feature selection was improved in this work, but the proposed algorithm is more complex.

R. Klette, M. Rivera, and S. Satoh (Eds.): PSIVT 2013, LNCS 8333, pp. 206–219, 2014.

Huang et al. [5] proposed a saliency model in HSV color space, for extracting regions of interest. Although their proposed saliency map is defined in a more human-perception oriented color space, key functions of map components are similar to those of Itti et al. 's bottom-up model.

One of the potential applications of saliency maps is the gaze-based interface where we need to draw user's visual attention. With the help of saliency map, it is possible to navigate the visual focus of attention by modulating features in the image. By this way, we can encourage the audience to watch the information we stress, without any aid of texts or overlapped graphics. In broadcasting of sports games, on the other hand, following the motion of a single player by image modulation will lead to a comfortable visual experience. Additionally, if we apply such image modulation to rear-view images displayed inside a car, the driver need not to read texts anymore while driving.

An early trial on gaze navigation by image modulation was to shift the hue and luminance to raise attraction, and then remove the modulation immediately when the subject's gaze has moved to the target [1]. A pixel-wise modulation for still images was, on the other hand, proposed by Hagiwara et al. [3]. In this method the gaze was drawn to a given target in the modulated image, but unnatural color was observed in the modulated image. Another algorithm to modulate an image and video was proposed [11,13]. In this work the saliency map was generated in L*a*b* space, and the map was applied to images for modulation. Although this approach produced a fine and neutral result, a threshold map for each image needed to be manually preset, which made the method impractical in the real situation. In their work, each frame was independently adjusted and coherence between video frames was not taken into account.

Similar to the works above, translating the visual attention to a specified region using video modulation is our primary task. Namely, the goal of this work is to draw the gaze to a given target in a video by modulating the frames of the video. During the process, a target region is manually specified in the first frame, and the corresponding regions in subsequent frames of a video are automatically tracked by the TLD tracker [8], which is known to work robustly and accurately. Saliency in the region is estimated by a saliency map [7], with which we create a mask. Then we generate several centre-surround difference maps from the image and multiply them with the mask. After this, the maps are added back to the image as the modulation. The key idea of this operation is to enlarge the local contrast on the target. Considering the visual satisfaction for the viewer, we modulate both intensity and color simultaneously in the HSI space. Since we aim to draw the viewer's focus effectively and to make the modulation as less noticeable as possible, the strength of modulation is determined to raise of target's saliency as well as to maintain the similarity to the original image. Moreover, we introduce a *pre-enhancement* step to accelerate computation required for the modulation. Due to inconsistency of modulation across the video, the appearance of objects may fluctuate between frames, which is commonly known as flicker. To reduce this effect, all frames are rendered by a post-processing operation, which results in smoothing the modulations over frames. Experiments

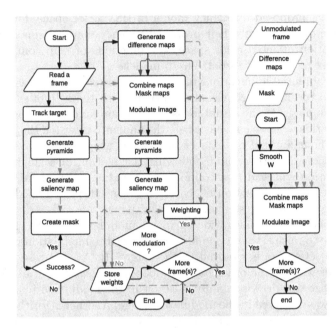

Fig. 1. Flowchart of process. Our method consists of two main parts: the processing loop part (on the left) and the output loop part (on the right).

using subjects demonstrate that our method can increase the time of fixation on the target, and that the flicker is more suppressed for intensity modulation than color modulation.

2   System Overview

A video is decomposed into frames and processed sequentially in our method. Firstly, pyramids are generated in a frame, which participate in constructing a saliency map. Meanwhile, the TLD tracker gives a bounding box of the tracked object, and then we create an binary image highlighting the bounding box area. By multiplying this image with the saliency map, we create the grayscale mask for modulation. To simplify the system, we only focus on pixel-wise modulation, in which each pixel has no movement in space. Therefore, orientation and motion are not modulated in our method. To prevent unnatural flickers, enhancement of flicker is also excluded from our method. Therefore difference maps only for intensity, red-green opponency and blue-yellow opponency, are generated from pyramids.

A flowchart of the entire algorithm is illustrated in Fig. 1. The procedures on the left constitute the processing loop, which generates the values of modulation to be applied on each frame. The procedures on the right constitute the output loop, which smooths the values over the time and applies them on frames.

In the processing loop part, the difference maps are weighted, combined, and masked, resulting in 3 enhancement maps. To make a better use of the co-herence between frames, and for fast computation, the initial difference map weights of each frame are passed from the previous frame. This step is called *pre-enhancement* in our method. The enhancement maps are converted to en-hancement maps of hue, saturation, intensity and the image is also decomposed into the H, S, I channels. The modulation is executed through vector combi-nation of each channel and its corresponding enhancement map. Then, after the conversion of the image back to RGB space, the current status is evaluated through the saliency map to have a decision: if the target region achieves the maximum of saliency in the image, the process terminates (illustrated by green arrow in Fig. 1); otherwise weights increments are calculated to promote boost-ing of this frame (illustrated by red arrow). Finally weights are saved before the next frame processing starts.

The output loop part is to established to solve the flickers due to unpredictable change of weights. The key idea here is the smoothing of weights over the time. To accelerate the speed of modulation, we use the cached pyramids and masks obtained from the processing loop parts. The output loop part executes after the processing loop part completes for a frame, but a delay of a few frames exists for the smoothing of weights over the time. Since the processing is currently not real time, the output loop part can also run independently when the processing loop part terminates.

3   Saliency Map Creation

Visual attention is human's ability of selecting a region in the visual field to reduce scene analysis. In order to quantify the human visual attention, we need a saliency map for each frame. Our saliency map is generated based on the bottom-up model proposed by Itti et al. [6] [7]. An input RGB frame is firstly split into 3 channels: r, g, b. Then 5 images are generated from the channels: $I = (r+g+b)/3, R = r-(g+b)/2, G = g-(r+b)/2, B = b-(r+g)/2$, and $Y = r+g-2(|r-g|+b)$. All of the mono-color images are normalized by I and small values (< 0.1 for example) in them are set to zero. Next, Gaussian pyramids of each image are created: $I(\sigma), R(\sigma), G(\sigma), B(\sigma), Y(\sigma)$, where $\sigma \in [0,8]$ represents the scale. For orientation detection, 4 Gabor pyramids $O(\sigma, \theta)$ are also created from I [2]. For detecting time-varied features, 4 motion pyramids $R(\sigma, \theta)$ are created from $O(\sigma, \theta)$ and its shifts according to the Reichardt model [12].

Next, feature maps are created through absolute across-scale difference of scales in each pyramid. Among them, the color opponent feature maps come from difference between mono-color pyramids. In order to highlight the most discriminative feature within each map, we have a normalization step upon each feature map. Here we employ the simple max-local normalization [6] to compute fast and preserve more features. The reason for this is that our modulation mask generation needs the detail of small-salient features in the map, which the iterative normalization cannot provide. After normalization, feature maps are added in the across-scale manner, resulting in conspicuity maps. Finally the normalized conspicuity maps are combined into a master saliency map $\mathcal{S}$. In our implementation saliency maps are linearly normalized to the fixed range [0,1], which guarantees that the pixel with value 1 is the maxima of saliency.

Differently from the model by Itti et al. [7], the feature maps of flicker and conspicuity map of flicker are removed in our implementation. Our intensive experiments suggested that the flicker detection module always makes modulated videos flickering, which plays a negative role in keeping the modulated video smooth. To make the video visually comfortable, we decided to remove the flicker module.

4 Generating Enhancement Maps

In order to quantify the modulation, we create a grayscale image, called *enhancement map* in this paper, holding the adjustment on pixels in every particular channel. In creating the enhancement maps, we start from creating a mask, which discriminates the area to raise saliency from the area to decrease saliency.

4.1 Target Filtering

By employing the TLD tracker [8], we can fetch a bounding box of a target. In processing each frame, we firstly create a raw binary image B, in which pixels inside the bounding box are set to 1, while those outside are 0. In order to exclude the background from raising saliency, the area of the target object should be refined. Since the saliency map always highlights moving objects, we make use of it to accurately extract the target. The final mask is generated by:

$$M = \mathcal{S} \times (B * H),$$

where $\times$ denotes the pixel-wise product, $*$ denotes convolution, and H is a Gaussian kernel. Convolving B with H smooths the border of the bounding box, making the border less noticeable. Then, by means of the pixel-wise product, we highlight only highly salient pixels in the resulting mask. After these, the range of mask M is normalized to [0,1] to guarantee a constant maximum value for each frame across the video.

4.2 Extracting Center-Surround Difference

Raw features are extracted through center-surround differences between different scales in a pyramid. This procedure is similar to generating feature maps in the saliency model [7]. Here we name an image holding raw features as a *difference map*. To modulate intensity and color modules, their corresponding difference maps are generated through subtracting surrounding scales from centre scales:

$$D_I(c, s) = I(c) \ominus I(s),$$

$$D_{RG}(c, s) = (R(c) - G(c)) \ominus (G(s) - R(s)),$$

$$D_{BY}(c, s) = (B(c) - Y(c)) \ominus (Y(s) - B(s)),$$

where c, s denote scales, $c \in \{0, 1, 2\}, s = c + \delta, \delta \in \{3, 4\}$. They are not same as feature maps: firstly, in order to keep the peak/valley property of features, difference maps are signed; secondly, scales enrolled (starting from 0) here are lower than those in feature maps (starting from 2). This is beacuse we found that lower scales work in more detail, producing more visually comfortable results.

4.3 Weighting the Difference Maps

To effectively navigate the gaze in any circumstances, saliency on the target should be enhanced and, at the same time, saliency outside the target (in the background) needs decreasing. To decrease saliency, we can subtract difference maps from the background to suppress the discriminative features. For each difference map D (including $D_I(c, s), D_{RG}(c, s), D_{BY}(c, s)$), we denote the maps in charge of increasing and decreasing saliency respectively as D_1 and D_2:

$$D_1 = D \times M, \ D_2 = D \times (1 - M).$$

In a channel, each difference map contains features on its own center-surround scales. In some scales the features are homogenous between the target and the background, while in the other scales they are discriminative. To modulate saliency as effectively as possible, we let the discriminative scales contribute more to our work. This is achieved through assigning weights to maps. We denote the mean and the standard deviation for peak values in the absolute map $|D_1|$ by $\hat{\mu}_1$ and $\hat{\sigma}_1$, and those in $|D_2|$ by $\hat{\mu}_2, \hat{\sigma}_2$. Then the weights for D_1 and D_2 are designed respectively as:

$$w_1 = \hat{\sigma}_1 e^{(\hat{\mu}_1 - \hat{\mu}_2)}, \ w_2 = \hat{\sigma}_2 e^{(\hat{\mu}_2 - \hat{\mu}_1)}.$$

We take only the absolute peaks in calculation because centre-surround features only exist in a local peak or valley. A weight is large only when the mean value of features in its corresponding region (target/background) is larger than that in another region, and when there is a large discrimination in its region.

4.4 Enhancement Maps

An enhancement map is the across-scale combination of weighted difference maps. The difference maps are enlarged to the size of original image before combination. In a channel, let E_1 be an enhancement map in charge of increasing saliency, and E_2 be that in charge of decreasing saliency:

$$E_1 = \bigoplus_{c=0}^{2} \bigoplus_{s=c+3}^{c+4} w_1(c, s) n(D_1(c, s)),$$

$$E_2 = \bigoplus_{c=0}^{2} \bigoplus_{s=c+3}^{c+4} w_2(c,s)n(D_2(c,s)),$$

where $n(\cdot)$ is a rescaling operation to fit the map to [-1, 1]: $n(A) = \frac{A}{\max |A|}$.

Then a master enhancement map can be created from E_1 and E_2:

$$E = \alpha[n(E_1) - \beta_d n(E_2)],$$

where α is a rate controlling the strength of each time of modulation, and β_d is a ratio constraining the modulation on the background. To maintain the same visual perception even after the modulation, pixels in the background (which have a large population) are modulated as slightly as possible. Since the size of the tracked target is almost fixed throughout the video, the value of β_d is initialized only by the portion of the target area to the background area. In most cases β_d becomes a small value between [0,1] due to the area of the background being much larger than that of the target. We remark that when areas of the target and the background are equal with each other, β_d becomes 1 to guarantee the same speed in modulating two parts.

To make the target getting close to the saliency maxima, α is proportional to the difference between the peak saliency in the target area and 1:

$$\alpha = \begin{cases} k[1 - \max(\mathcal{S} \times B)] & \text{for intensity,} \\ k\beta_c[1 - \max(\mathcal{S} \times B)] & \text{for RG and BY,} \end{cases}$$

where the coefficient k constrains the modulation speed, and β_c is the ratio constraining the color modulation. β_c is also initialized during processing at the first frame: it becomes a large value only when the target area is both brighter and more saturated than the background. The reason for this is that we only execute strong color modulation on vivid objects to prevent unnatural appearances of other objects.

4.5   Weight Management

To save the computational cost, we take over the modulation at a frame t to that at its next frame $t + 1$. Since features in even nearby frames have differences, directly applying enhancement maps of frame t to $t + 1$ will cause blurring. Therefore, we take only the weights at t and apply them to difference maps at $t + 1$. The step of constructing the enhancement map in this way is named *pre-enhancement*.

We provide each difference map D^t with a pre-enhancement weight W^t (where t denotes a frame index). For the first frame, we set all $W_1^1(c,s) \leftarrow 0$ and $W_2^1(c,s) \leftarrow 0$. We define increments ΔW by the products of all multipliers on difference maps in the construction of enhancement maps:

$$\Delta W_1^t(c,s) = \alpha^t \frac{1}{\max |D_1^t(c,s)|} \frac{1}{\max |E_1^t|} w_1^t(c,s),$$

$$\Delta W_2^t(c,s) = \alpha^t \beta_d \frac{1}{\max |D_1^t(c,s)|} \frac{1}{\max |E_1^t|} w_1^t(c,s).$$

Then all W^t are adjusted by adding the increments (subscripts 1, 2 and parameters c, s are eliminated):

$$W^t \leftarrow W^t + \Delta W^t.$$

Except for the first frame, we firstly construct pre-enhancement maps before calculating new weights:

$$E_0^t = \bigoplus_{c=c_1}^{c_3} \bigoplus_{s=c+\delta_1}^{c+\delta_2} [W_1^t(c,s)D_1^t(c,s) - W_2^t D_2^t(c,s)].$$

Then we apply the pre-enhancement maps to the image and evaluate the saliency. New weights are calculated only when the peak saliency of target is less than 1. It saves the computation when the predicted weights meet the required modulation of this frame. In most cases, the weights $W_1^1(c,s)$ and $W_2^1(c,s)$ increase frame after frame to raise the saliency of the target to the maximum. However, when the stimuli in the background is weakened, the required modulation for target decreases. In order to make W^t convergent, we multiply the weights with a coefficient γ^t between $[0, 1]$ before applying the pre-enhancement of the next frame (subscripts 1, 2 and parameters c, s are omitted):

$$W^{t+1} = \gamma^t W^t.$$

γ^t has a small value when the image differs significantly from the original image, while it returns to 1 when no modulation is applied. Therefore γ^t and α^t always promote the modulation in two directions: γ^t aims to make the modulated image similar to the original image, while α^t encourages the image to have more modulation. They cooperate to get W^t fixed when the target region in the original image has already the saliency maxima. In all other cases, they cooperate to make the modulation as effective and un-noticeable as possible.

In the output loop part of our method, all frames can be rendered according to the weights generated in the processing loop part. To reduce the flicker resulted from the inconsistency of frame modulation, before the rendering, each weight is averaged with its neighboring values in the temporal domain:

$$\overline{W}^t = \frac{1}{2T+1} \sum_{\tau=t-T}^{t+T} W^\tau,$$

where $(2T+1)$ is the number of participating frames in an operation. After this operation, modulations on contiguous frames become familiar, thus flickering from the modulation are greatly reduced. More frames participating in an averaging operation can produce more visually comfortable result, but also increase the delay of output. In our experiments the choice of $(2T+1) = 9$ produced good results.

5   Saliency Modulation in the HSI Space

To achieve a natural appearance of the modulated image, enhancement maps are applied to the image in the HSI color space. In this space, a color value consists of hue θ, saturation ρ, and intensity i. Every RGB pixel of the original image needs to be converted to the HSI space for modulation [10].

5.1   Intensity Modulation

Since the intensity enhancement map E_I is created from the intensity channel of each pixel, we are able to modulate the intensity individually. We simply combine every value in the map E_I (denoted by e_I) to its corresponding intensity value of the pixel:

$$i \leftarrow i + e_I.$$

5.2   Color Opponency Modulation

After intensity modulation, the intensity of each pixel is fixed. The color opponency modulation of each pixel works on the pixel's chromatic plane (which is a rounded horizontal profile with a constant intensity in the HSI space). We denote an individual value in E_{RG} by e_{RG}, and that in E_{BY} by e_{BY}. For each pixel, we project values of both e_{RG} and e_{BY} as the magnitude of vectors in the unit circle of a chromatic plane (Fig. 2a). The directions of vectors follow the directions of colors that win in the opponency. We obtain a vector e_C for each pixel by combining e_{RG} and e_{BY}:

$$e_C = \frac{\sqrt{3}}{2} e_{RG} \, u_0 + (\frac{1}{2}|e_{RG}| - e_{BY}) \, v_0,$$

where u_0 is the unit vector with hue $\theta_u = -\frac{\pi}{6}$ (along the R-G opponent axis), and v_0 is the unit vector with hue $\theta_v = \frac{\pi}{3}$ (along the B-Y opponent axis).

e_C can then be converted to the polar coordinate system: $e_C = (e_\theta, e_\rho)$, where the magnitude of e_θ is the modulation for saturation and angle e_ρ is that for hue. Now for each pixel, the color modulation is carried out through the vector addition:

$$\theta \leftarrow \theta + e_\theta, \; \rho \leftarrow \rho + e_\rho.$$

The modulated image is then converted back to RGB space.

5.3   Data Correction

Because the HSI space is an irregular double-cone space, raising the saturation or intensity of a pixel may result in an out-of-range value (as it shown in Fig. 2b). Simply constraining θ, ρ, i value within [0,1] may shift the hue value after the conversion to the RGB space. Due to the irregular surface of the space, formulating the surface with H, S, I values is hard and thus using a convex linear combination is not appropriate. Our solution to this problem is to fix

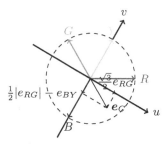

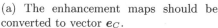

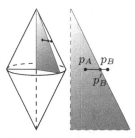

(a) The enhancement maps should be converted to vector e_C.

(b) A section with constant hue in the HSI space. In the section, p_A is enhanced to p_B, but should be corrected to p'_B.

Fig. 2. Conversion of enhancement maps and illustration of the 'out of range' problem

the maximum out-of-range channel (either r, g, or b) to 1, while keeping h and i unchanged, and then to find the maximum admissible ρ inversely. In this subsection only, we denote the individual pixel values of r, g, b by non-italic r, g, b to differentiate the notation of the entire image. When r is out-of-range and also the largest in r, g, b, we set r to 1. The corrected g and b values are:

$$g = \frac{\sqrt{3}}{2}(1 - i)\tan\theta + \frac{3}{2}i - \frac{1}{2}, \quad b = -\frac{\sqrt{3}}{2}(1 - i)\tan\theta + \frac{3}{2}i - \frac{1}{2}.$$

Similarly, we can apply this strategy to other cases where g or b is out-of-range. When g gets out of range, g is set to 1, and

$$r = i - 2(1 - i)\frac{\cos\theta}{\cos\theta - \sqrt{3}\sin\theta}, \quad b = 2i + 2(1 - i)\frac{\cos\theta}{\cos\theta - \sqrt{3}\sin\theta} - 1;$$

when b is out-of-range, we set b to 1, and

$$r = i - 2(1 - i)\frac{\cos\theta}{\cos\theta + \sqrt{3}\sin\theta}, \quad g = 2i + 2(1 - i)\frac{\cos\theta}{\cos\theta + \sqrt{3}\sin\theta} - 1.$$

6   Experiments

6.1   Experiment Design and Preparation

We implemented our method in MATLAB, and prepared 2 original video clips (with names given as A0[1], B0[2]) for processing. Both of them were single shots with 30fps. For each clip we defined 2 completely different bounding boxes for the TLD tracker, to obtain 2 versions of modulated video (one version is named A1, B1, and the other version is A2, B2). Some snapshots of each video clip are shown in Fig. 3 The specifications of each video and bounding boxes are illustrated in Table 1. The relative area of the target is computed by the proportion of the target area to the image area.

---

[1] Source: <ftp://ftp.tnt.uni-hannover.de/pub/svc/testsequences/>
[2] Source: <http://www.youtube.com/watch?v=aU5Hq_Kz7n0>

(a) Original frame in A0   (b) Modulated version A1   (c) Modulated version A2

(d) Original frame in B0   (e) Modulated version B1   (f) Modulated version B2

Fig. 3. Snapshots of original and modulated videos. The white bounding boxes indicate the target regions to be modulated in A1/B1, while the black boxes corresponds to those in A2/B2.

Table 1. Specification of clips and targets

Resource	Resolution	Length (frames)	Proportion of area 1	2
A	352×288	300	0.0056	0.0576
B	852×480	300	0.0263	0.0021

In total, 6 videos (including original and modulated versions) were used for each subject. Each video was equally treated and played once for each subject. 15 subjects participated in our experiments. We divided 15 subjects into 3 groups. For different groups, videos were shown in a different order, and videos of the same content were displayed alternatively. These were designed to reduce the impact of human high-level vision (gaze movements directed by thoughts for example). We also forced the subjects to reset their fixation points between videos to eliminate the effect of the previous content to the next one. After watching videos, each subject reported whether or not each video he/she watched was modulated, and whether he/she observed flicker in each video.

Table 2. Rates of successfully directed samples before and after modulation

Video	A1	A2	B1	B2
Original	0.0188	0.0350	0.0989	0.0076
Modulated	0.0813	0.1020	0.1497	0.0594

During the experiments, a Tobii TX300[3] eye tracker was employed to track the fixation point of the subjects. We used only the first sample in the duration of each frame as the fixation position in this frame.

6.2   Experimental Results

Over an entire video, by taking the rate of the number of fixation points falling into the bounding box of each frame to the number of valid frames, we computed the rate of successfully directed fixations. The rates of fixations before and after modulation for each modulated version are shown in Table 2.

Here we can see for all the modulation on different contents, the rates of fixations on the targets in modulated videos all greatly increased compared to those in the original videos. This indicates that our method successfully drew the gaze to given targets. However, the rate for modulated videos itself did not achieve a large value. This is because human gaze is always wandering over the image and it is hard to force someone always to look at the target over the entire video. Moreover, the area of the target affects the success of modulation. We can see in the same content, a larger area has a high probability of fixation falling into it, while a small area is hard to attract gaze.

To analyze the tracked fixations in more detail, we calculated the relative distances from fixations to the bounding box in each frame. Then we created a grid of 2-D containers and binned all the distances into the grid, resulting in a target-centered 3-D histogram. Among all the containers, the one at (0,0) bins all the data of in-bounding-box fixation, while the other containers bin the fixation in their particular positions to the target. We then plotted 2-D heat-maps where the color of each grid represents the height of each container. Fig. 4 shows the heat-map for modulation version B1, which had the lowest growth (51.41%) of the falling-in rate. We can observe that the target (the black van) was originally salient in a large bunch of gaze attractions. After modulation, the accumulation on container (1,0) was diluted and some energy was transferred to (0,0).

Statistics of questionnaire are shown in Fig. 5. For each video, the blue bar illustrates the ratio of subjects who felt the video was modulated, and the red bar shows the ratio of subjects who observed flicker. For all contents, the feeling of modulation on modulated versions was higher than that on the original version. This means that our modulation was easy to be noticed. For content B, we can see that the observation of flicker was almost proportional to the growth of falling-in rates in Table 2. Although the feeling of flicker should be eliminated, we have to admit that flicker does attract gaze. However, for the feeling of flicker, A0 received a higher mark than its modulated versions. No subject observed flicker in A1 although in this video both color opponency modules were greatly modulated. This may come from the quality of video and the moving characteristic of the target.

To investigate the relationship between the perceived flicker and the strength of modulation, we computed the mean and the standard deviation of difference

---

[3] Product information: http://www.tobii.com/en/eye-tracking-research/global/products/hardware/tobii-tx300-eye-tracker/

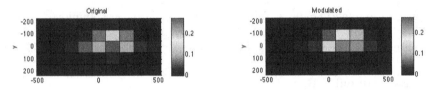

Fig. 4. Heat-map of containers of video B0 vs. B1

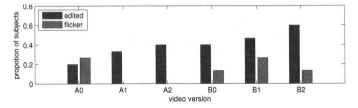

Fig. 5. Subjective judgements of modulation and flicker

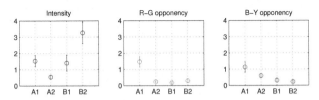

Fig. 6. Mean and standard deviation of weights of modules

map weights for each module (shown in Figure 6).In this figure, a larger mean indicates that the clip is more strongly modulated, while a larger standard deviation indicates greater fluctuation of modulation is caused across frames. We observe that a strong modulation in one of the color opponency modules might be the cause of perceived flicker. Especially for video B2, although the modulation on intensity was great, the colors were adjusted very slightly, which made it less likely to be marked as 'flickering'. Reason for this may be human vision is more sensitive to color opponent contrast than intensity contrast.

7   Conclusion

We have successfully navigated human gaze to our given targets in videos, by modulating saliency of videos under the HSI space. For every frame the modulation was simultaneously carried out for intensity, red-green opponency, and blue-yellow opponency. Given the target tracked by the TLD tracker, saliency in the target region becomes boosted, while saliency in the background becomes reduced. This is evaluated with the help of a saliency map. Moreover, our proposed method employs the *pre-enhancement* step for computation efficiency, as well as a post-processing module for the prevention of flickers. Experimental results showed that this method can effectively draw attention of subjects to the predefined targets. We discovered that subjects were more likely to notice the cue of modulation when exposed to greatly modulated videos. The observation of flicker was likely to be stronger when color opponency channels are greatly modulated. To reduce the flicker effect is left for future work on this topic. In our experiments, the size of bounding box was always maintained, and the tracker might sometimes lose the target. Therefore, to find a more robust way of target tracking, with an ability of zooming the bounding box with the target, is another piece of future work. Additionally, a real-time modulation is also promising development for the need of on-line processing.

References

1. Bailey, R., McNamara, A., Sudarsanam, N., Grimm, C.: Subtle gaze direction. ACM Trans. on Graphics 28(4), 1–14 (2009)
2. Greenspan, H., Belongie, S., Goodman, R., Perona, P., Rakshit, S., Anderson, C.: Overcomplete steerable pyramid filters and rotation invariance. In: Proc. of IEEE Conf. on CVPR, pp. 222–228 (1994)
3. Hagiwara, A., Sugimoto, A., Kawamoto, K.: Saliency-based image editing for guiding visual attention. In: Proc. of the 1st Int. Workshop on Pervasive Eye Tracking & Mobile Eye-Based Interaction, pp. 43–48 (2011)
4. Harel, J., Koch, C., Perona, P.: Graph-based visual saliency. Advances in Neural Information Processing Systems 19, 545–552 (2007)
5. Huang, C., Liu, Q., Yu, S.: Regions of interest extraction from color image based on visual saliency. The Journal of Supercomputing 58(1), 20–33 (2010)
6. Itti, L., Koch, C., Niebur, E.: A Model of saliency-based visual attention for rapid scene analysis. IEEE Trans. on PAMI 20(11), 1254–1259 (1998)
7. Itti, L., Dhavale, N., Pighin, F.: Realistic avatar eye and head animation using a neurobiological model of visual attention. In: Proc. of SPIE. Applications and Science of Neural Networks, Fuzzy Systems, and Evolutionary Computation VI, vol. 5200, pp. 64–78 (2004)
8. Kalal, Z., Mikolajczyk, K., Matas, J.: Tracking-Learning-Detection. IEEE Trans. on PAMI 6(1), 1–14 (2011)
9. Koch, C., Ullman, S.: Shifts in selective visual attention: towards the underlying neural circuitry. Matters of Intelligence 188, 115–141 (1987)
10. Ledley, R., Buas, M., Golab, T.: Fundamentals of true-color image processing. In: Proc. of the 10th ICPR, pp. 791–795 (1990)
11. Mendez, E., Feiner, S., Schmalstieg, D.: Focus and context in mixed reality by modulating first order salient features. In: Proc. of the 10th Int. Symposium on Smart Graphics, pp. 232–243 (2010)
12. Reichardt, W.: Evaluation of optical motion information by movement detectors. Journal of comparative physiology. A, Sensory, Neural, and Behavioral Physiology 161(4), 533–547 (1987)
13. Veas, E., Mendez, E., Feiner, S., Schmalstieg, D.: Directing attention and influencing memory with visual saliency modulation. In: Proc. of the SIGCHI Conf. on Human Factors in Computing Systems, pp. 1471–1480 (2011)

Posture Based Detection of Attention in Human Computer Interaction

Patrick Heyer *, Javier Herrera-Vega, Dan-El N. Vila Rosado,
Luis Enrique Sucar, and Felipe Orihuela-Espina

National Institute for Astrophysics, Optics and Electronics,
Sta. Maria Tonantzintla, Puebla, Mexico
{patrickhey,vega,dnvr301080,esucar,f.orihuela-espina}@ccc.inaoep.mx
http://ccc.inaoep.mx/

Abstract. Unacted posture conveys cues about people's attentional disposition. We aim to identify robust markers of attention from posture while people carry out their duties seated in front of their computers at work. Body postures were randomly captured from 6 subjects while at work using a Kinect, and self-assessed as attentive or not attentive. Robust postural features exhibiting higher discriminative power across classification exercises with 4 well-known classifiers were identified. Average classification of attention from posture reached 76.47%±4.58% (F-measure). A total of 40 postural features were tested and those proxy of head tilt were found to be the most stable markers of attention in seated conditions based upon 3 class separability criteria. Unobtrusively monitoring posture of users while working in front of a computer can reliably be used to infer attentional disposition from the user. Human-computer interaction systems can benefit from this knowledge to customize the experience to the user changing attentional state.

Keywords: attention, human-computer interaction, posture.

1 Introduction

Human-computer interfaces can benefit from effectively interrogating the user cognitive state.

Static body postures can be mined for regulators communicating the attentional and affective state of subjects during normal human communication process [1]. In this sense, posture analysis is a plausible transparent communication channel to enhance human-computer interaction (HCI) [2–4].

In this work, we hypothesized that unacted postural features, can provide important clues regarding the user's attentional state. In other words, classification of attention is possible from postural features with reasonably high accuracy reliably across analysis methods. Moreover, we further hypothesized, that in non acted situations, some postural features can permeate through different analysis strategies consistently affording high discriminative power. Providing evidence

---

* Corresponding author.

R. Klette, M. Rivera, and S. Satoh (Eds.): PSIVT 2013, LNCS 8333, pp. 220–229, 2014.

regarding this latter, we perceive it as the strongest contribution of this paper. Importantly, we are not so much interested in finding the optimal classifying strategy, only a collateral goal, for which we might have then applied model selection techniques e.g. [5], but in identifying markers of attention that consistently deliver solid repeatable results regardless of the analysis approach. Indeed, intentionally, all classifiers and feature selection strategies are well known to facilitate reproduction of results as well as ensuring that we can focus our efforts on the assessment of the postural markers of attention rather than on the subtleties and implications of the analysis approach.

In order to test our hypotheses, we set up an experiment in which participants were intermittently (randomly) monitored unobtrusively, and immediately following, interrogated about their attention a few times during a normal working day. During monitoring events, skeletal features were captured employing a Kinect, to which we add a few more derived features. Extensive classification exercises using different classifiers, features selection algorithms, and parameterization allow us to explore the feature set overall classification and discriminative power of the features both individually and in association to other features. Our results suggests that both of our hypotheses are correct.

Average classification rates are above 75% despite absence of optimization attempts whilst regarding the second hypothesis we found a critical subset of 4 postural features affording sustained discriminative power regardless of the classifying analysis.

2 Related Work

Feasibility of postural analysis in HCI has been demonstrated from a range of technologies. Pressure sensing chairs are a popular choice. Using them, D'Mello and Graesser [6] investigated detection of emotions including boredom, confusion, delight, engagement and frustration. Despite the low explained variance by their logistic regression model (16%), their study had important implications for distinguishing between emotions, whether they are recognised as cognitive or affective states. Similarly Mota [7] used also a pressure sensing chair to infer three levels of attention. Their Hidden Markov Models (HMMs) achieved an overall accuracy of 87% when the user was part of the training set but only 76% in new users, questioning generalizability.

Different sensing technologies had also been explored. For instance, video analysis identified Body Lean Angle (BLA) as a successful cue in the classification of emotion [8]. This video analysis depends on color tracking, and thus needs to be calibrated to the users clothes, and would vary depending on light conditions. Grafsgaard [9] shows that seated posture can be measured in a non intrusive setting using a Kinect. Moreover, this sensing approach facilitates acquisition of a preset of metrics that can be used for postural analysis.

Irrespective of the sensing technology, it is perhaps more exciting the range of cognitive and affective states that might be somehow encoded in the posture. Besides machine learning literature, research from psychology can point us towards cues that can be expected to capture the unconscious regulators present at normal communication processes [1].

3   Methods

An experiment has been conducted at the National Institute for Astrophysics, Optics and Electronics (INAOE) aiming at unveiling attentional markers encoded in the seated posture of people at work during office hours. Six volunteers, including 4 males and 2 females, were recruited from INAOE's academic staff and students (age range: 24-31 years; height mean±std=1670±94mm).

3.1   Experimental Setup

Following pilot tests, the Kinect sensor was mounted on a tripod behind, above and centered around the screen and at 120cm and with a tilt downward of -20°for optimal detection of upper body as illustrated in Figure 1a.

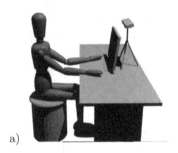

a)   b)

Fig. 1. a) Schematic representation of the setup of the posture capturing environment. Optimal position of the sensor was chosen following pilot over 18 different tested configurations. b) An exemplary postural sample with the feature sets represented by circles and lines. White dots corresponds to raw skeletal features (3D $< x, y, z >$ location). The connecting lines among the raw features are only illustrative as no topological relations are implied. Coloured lines represent extracted features.

For maximal ecological validity, experimental sessions were carried out at each participant regular desk. After volunteering, a suitable date would be agreed between the researcher and the subject for data collection. Data collection would proceed throughout the working day (8 hours). Instructions to the volunteer were kept to a minimum, reinforcing two critical elements: to behave as naturally as possible during the day, and to answer as honestly as possible when asked about their recent attentional state. The participants were aware of the objective of the experiment, but were blind to the times and frequency posture capture events were to occur.

3.2   Data Acquisition Protocol

To prevent anticipation as well as acted or biased postures the software was designed so that posture captures would occur at random intervals. For each posture capture event, the Kinect will take a 2 seconds video (sampled at 30 Hz) and dormant intervals lasted randomly between 40 and 60 minutes. An average of 11 posture capture events per session were acquired. The user would at all times remain unaware of the next posture capture event. Following a posture capture event, a pop up dialog in the computer screen asks the user to evaluate his preceding attitude as *ATTENTIVE* or *NOT ATTENTIVE*. The answers act as class labels conforming a self-reported ground truth.

The Kinect sensor was controlled by means of the OpenNI library [10]. Skeletal landmarks for the head, torso, shoulders and elbow joints were tracked and recorded. Wrists were ignored based on subjective appreciation. The Kinect output were saved into .oni files for off-line analysis.

3.3   Data Processing and Postural Feature Set Construction

To avoid Kinect output repetition as well as increase intra-subject subtle variability, the 60 frames long videos of each posture capture event were split into 6 equal-length chunks of 10 frames. Each chunk brought forth 1 attention observation sample. All 6 samples originating from the same posture capture event were labeled with the same attentional class. For each sample, skeletal landmarks were derived by averaging the 3D recording at each video frame. In total, 377 labeled samples were obtained. For each sample, an initial set of raw 24 postural features were retrieved directly from the skeleton expressing the average 3D $< x, y, z >$ position of 8 key locations of the upper body; *Head, Torso, Right (R)-Elbow, Left (L)-Elbow, R-Hip, L-Hip, R-Shoulder, L-Shoulder* as illustrated in Figure 1. In addition, this raw feature set was enriched by set of 16 derived or extracted features whether implemented from literature [9] or developed by ourselves described in Table 1. A postural feature set was therefore built for each sample incorporating a total of 40 features.

3.4   Classification Analysis

The 377 labeled feature vectors conform our dataset for classification. A total of 5940 ($= 3 \times 22 \times 3 \times 30\times$) classification exercises were carried out in Weka [11] arising for the use of 3 different feature selection strategies, 4 different classifiers (with 22 different parameterizations summarized in Table 2), 3 different dataset partitions for training-test purposes and 30 fold repetitions.

Three feature selection strategies were employed:

No Attribute Selection. Feature selection is absent. The full set of features is used for classification.

Correlation-based Feature Selection (CFS). A subset of features with high correlation with the class but uncorrelated with each other avoiding attribute redundancy is selected [12].

Table 1. Description of derived postural feature subset. Raw skeletal features can be appreciated in Figure 1.

Feature	Description
Elbow distance	Euclidean distance between elbows
Shoulder distance	Euclidean distance between shoulders
Collar	Midpoint R-Shoulder/L-Shoulder
Torso-Collar	Vector formed by Torso-Collar
Collar-Head	Vector formed by Collar-Head
PPunto	Cross product of Torso-Collar Collar-Head vectors
Angle	Angle on the YZ axis between Torso-Collar and Collar-Head
Quartile head	Quartile occupied by the head position of the observation with respect to the head position throughout the subject's session
Quartile torso	Quartile occupied by the torso position of the observation with respect to the torso position throughout the subject's session
Quartile collar	Quartile occupied by the collar position of the observation with respect to the collar position throughout the subject's session

Consistency-based Feature Selection. A feature set is chosen such that it is minimal on number of features and complies with a consistency criterion[13].

In addition, four well-known classifiers were tested:

Naive Bayes. A probabilistic classifier where features are assumed to be conditionally independent given the class. A two level graph (class-features) is built and class is predicted by evidence propagation of feature values [14].

Tree Augmented Naive Bayes (TAN). An extension of a Naive Bayes (NB) classifiers where the structure is augmented allowing edges among attributes, thus dispensing with its strong assumptions about independence [15].

Decision Tree. The classifier is given by a tree where attributes are tested along the tree in successive nodes and when a leaf is reached the instances is classified with the class assigned to the leaf [16].

Support Vector Machines (SVM). A classifier is obtained by constructing the hyperplane in the n-dimensional space that split optimally instances in its respective class, where the optimal criteria is defined in terms of the widest possible margin between the hyperplane and the instances (support vectors) closer to it [17].

Finally, 3 random dataset partitions were explored (train/test); 70/30%, 75/25% and 80/20%. Each classification exercise is a combination of selecting one combination of feature selection strategy, classifier and parameterization, and dataset partition at a time.

Table 2. Parameterizations for the 4 classifiers. BS: Binary Splits; CF: Confidence Factor; mNO: minimum number of objects; nF: Internal number of folds; REP: Reduce error pruning; STR: Subtree raising; UP: Unpruned; UL: Use Laplace; UKE: Use Kernel Estimator; USD: Use Supervised Discretization; RBF: Radial Basis Functions.

Classifier	Parameterization
Decision Tree (DT)	• BS=False; CF=0.25; mNO=2; nF=3; REP=False; STR=T; UP=False; UL=False • BS=True; CF=0.25; mNO=2; nF=3; REP=False; STR=T; UP=False; UL=False • BS=False; CF=0.25; mNO=2; nF=3; REP=True; STR=T; UP=False; UL=False • BS=True; CF=0.25; mNO=2; nF=3; REP=True; STR=T; UP=False; UL=False • BS=True; CF=0.25; mNO=2; nF=3; REP=False; STR=T; UP=True; UL=False • BS=False; CF=0.25; mNO=2; nF=3; REP=False; STR=T; UP=True; UL=False • BS=False; CF=0.25; mNO=2; nF=3; REP=False; STR=T; UP=True; UL=True • BS=False; CF=0.25; mNO=2; nF=3; REP=False; STR=False; UP=False; UL=True • BS=False; CF=0.25; mNO=2; nF=3; REP=False; STR=False; UP=False; UL=False
Naive Bayes (NB)	• UKE =False; USD=False • UKE =True; USD=False • UKE =False; USD=True
Support Vector Machine (SVM)	• Polynomial Kernel (p=1) • Polynomial Kernel (p=2) • Polynomial Kernel (p=3) • Polynomial Kernel (p=4) • Polynomial Kernel (p=5) • RBF Kernel (G=0.01) • RBF Kernel (G=0.05)
Tree Augmented Naive Bayes	• Estimator = simple; α=0.25 • Estimator = simple; α=0.5 • Estimator = simple; α=0.75

3.5   Evaluation

We have evaluated the performance of every pair *feature selection algorithm-classifier* based on standard metrics:

- Sensitivity=TP/(TP+FN)
- Specificity=TN/(TN+FP)
- Precision=TP/(TP+FP)
- Recall=TP/(TP+FN)
- F-Measure=2(Precision × Recall)/(Precision+ Recall)

where TP represents true positives, TN are true negatives, FP are false positives and FN are false negatives. Output of the classification exercises were stored in a database for further statistical processing.

Statistical analysis was carried out in package R [18]. Effect of the classifier and feature selection on the overall classification accuracy as measured by Precision, Recall and F-measure was assessed using an ANOVA model (significance threshold 5%). Tukey post-hoc analysis was used to conduct pairwise comparison when the ANOVA model was found significant. The point biserial correlation coefficient between measured features and categorical independent attentional class was calculated in MATLAB (Mathworks, UK).

Table 3. Summary of classification results by classifier and feature selection strategy expressed in percentage. Results indicate mean±std grand averaged across the 3 different dataset partitions and 30 fold.

Precision		
Classifier \Selection	**NoAttSelection**	**CfsSubsetEval**	**ConsistencySubsetEval**
Decision Tree	77.58±6.37	77.93±7.52	78.04±7.15
Naive Bayes	78.35±6.62	78.58±5.69	78.90±6.50
Tree augmented NB	75.55±6.05	76.43±6.57	76.43±6.52
SVM	70.46±5.94	69.01±4.94	69.42±5.27
Recall		
Classifier \Selection	**NoAttSelection**	**CfsSubsetEval**	**ConsistencySubsetEval**
Decision Tree	75.90±7.23	77.77±0.50	78.51±9.24
Naive Bayes	69.09±6.77	72.40±6.43	72.14±6.59
Tree augmented NB	75.93±6.66	77.35±6.49	78.40±7.02
SVM	84.32±5.93	86.36±5.30	86.91±5.22
F-Measure		
Classifier \Selection	**NoAttSelection**	**CfsSubsetEval**	**ConsistencySubsetEval**
Decision Tree	76.39±4.60	77.02±5.32	77.63±4.72
Naive Bayes	73.09±4.68	75.10±4.29	75.04±4.37
Tree augmented NB	75.43±4.11	76.63±4.79	77.07±4.59
SVM	76.49±3.84	76.55±3.69	77.02±4.01

4   Results

4.1   Classification of Attention

Following visual inspection all 377 samples were accepted for further analysis. Sensitivity reached $79.22 \pm 9.02\%$ (max. 98.52%) and specificity reached $66.62 \pm 13.26\%$ (max. 97.22%). Average classification reached an F-Measure of 76.47% and the best classification achieved 88.55%. Classification rates by classifier and feature selection strategy are presented in Table 3.

There was a statistically significant difference between classifiers as determined by one-way ANOVA ($F(3,5936) = 69.91$, $p < .000$). Tukey post-hoc test revealed that the F-Measure was statistically significantly different for Naive Bayes. There was a statistically significant difference between feature selection strategies as determined by one-way ANOVA ($F(2,5937) = 3.17$, $p < .000$). Tukey post-hoc test revealed that there was significant differences between not carrying out feature selection and other strategies, as well as between feature selection strategies.

4.2   Markers of Attention

In order to identify stable markers of attention different criteria might be considered; (a) those features that are more consistently selected[1], (b) the correlation

---

[1] This obviously excludes the no feature selection strategy.

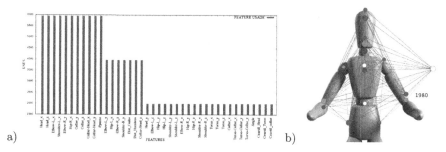

Fig. 2. a) Histogram of feature usage across feature selection strategies. The consequence of the 3 selection strategies can be easily appreciated; b) Feature co-occurrence for the consistency based feature selection. Coloured circles correspond to raw features; x - red, y - green, z - blue. White circles correspond to derived features. The one rightmost is the *PPunto*. Size of the circle is proportional to the point biserial correlation coefficient between the feature and the class descriptor. The number to the right indicates the number of cases or simulations represented. Features not selected under this scheme have been ghosted for presentation purposes. An analogous graph can be constructed for the CFS.

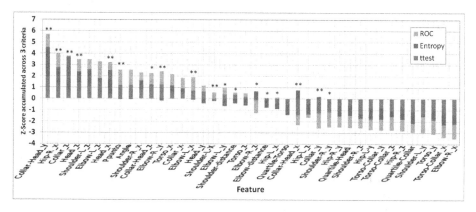

Fig. 3. Ranking of features by class separability criteria, proxy of individual discriminative power. The stacked bars corresponds to the three different criteria used, namely; t-test, entropy and receiver operating characteristic (ROC) curve. For each criterion, the absolute value of the criterion used were normalised to a z-score (within criterion output distribution). The higher the bar, the more individual discriminative power by the feature. Combined discriminative power of feature sets is the result of the feature selection strategies. The asterisks above each bar indicates when the feature has been filtered by the feature selection strategies; one asterisk indicate that it has been selected only by one strategy, and the double asterisk indicate that the feature has been selected by both feature selection strategies.

coefficient between the feature and the class, (c) degree of co-occurrence of features, and (d) feature discriminative power.

Frequency of feature usage across classification exercises is presented in Figure 2a. Degree of co-occurrence among features as well as the point biserial correlation coefficient between the features and the attentive state is presented in Figure 2b. Finally, feature discriminative power as estimated from average classification across simulations filtering out the individual feature is illustrated in Figure 3.

5 Discussion and Conclusions

Previous work [9, 6] had already demonstrated the feasibility of estimating attention by unobtrusively monitoring the user's posture. This study further elaborates on this topic by aiming to identify robust postural features that can maintain discriminative power across different classification approaches. Our results suggest that unacted posture is a reasonable proxy of attention with average classification accuracy despite no attempt of optimizing the classification approach.

Our results suggest that persons paying attention to the computer have a tendency to tilt their heads. Specifically, we have identified the set of features conformed by Collar-Head-y, R-Hip-x, Collar-z and Head-z to maintain high discriminative power across different analysis but also being consistently selected and exhibiting high correlation with attentional state. The take home message is that the given adequate postural descriptors, classification of attention can be resilient to changes in the classification approach. However, since both the classifiers and feature selection attributes are possible confounders we cannot claim that the salient set of features found here will remain so under different configurations. Consequently, we believe it is key to focus research, not so much in the analysis but in identifying those postural markers of attention.

The major limitation of this feasibility study is the assumption that attention must be directed to the computer system. Other situations during work may obviously require the user to be attentive but not facing the screen. Currently, we lack expert evaluation of the video streams, thus there is the implicit assumption that the self-assessed attentional class labels are correct. This prevented comparison with D'Mello et al's [4]. Comparison against [9] is also difficult since they used Pearson coefficient which is inappropriate for categorical variables.

We continue to collect more data to enlarge our dataset to eliminate limitations associated to small cohort size, and plan to keep developing more aggressive features. A leave-one-out validation will explore generalization to subjects outside the cohort. This research may impact office-based HCI systems which might tailor the experience to the user changing attentional state.

Acknowledgments. This project has been funded by Microsoft Latin American and Caribbean Research (LACCIR) Federation (R1211LAC001).

References

1. Ekman, P., Friesen, W.V.: The repertoire of nonverbal behavior: Categories, origins, usage, and coding. Semiotica 1, 49–98 (1969)
2. Castellano, G., Villalba, S.D., Camurri, A.: Recognising Human Emotions from Body Movement and Gesture Dynamics. In: Paiva, A.C.R., Prada, R., Picard, R.W. (eds.) ACII 2007. LNCS, vol. 4738, pp. 71–82. Springer, Heidelberg (2007)

3. Kapoor, A., Mota, S., Picard, R.W.: Towards a learning companion that recognizes affect. In: AAAI Fall Symposium (2001)
4. D'Mello, S., Jackson, T., Craig, S., Morgan, B., Chipman, P., White, H., Person, N., Kort, B., El-Kaliouby, R., Picard, R., Graesser, A.: AutoTutor Detects and Responds to Learners Affective and Cognitive States. In: Proceedings of the Workshop on Emotional and Cognitive Issues in ITS in Conjunction with the 9th International Conference on Intelligent Tutoring Systems, p. 13 (2008)
5. Escalante, H.J., Montes, M., Sucar, L.E.: Journal of Machine Learning Research 10, 405–440 (2009)
6. D'Mello, S.K., Graesser, A.C.: Mining Bodily Patterns of Affective Experience during Learning. In: de Baker, R.S.J., Merceron, A., Pavlik, P.I. (eds.) The 3rd International Conference on Educational Data Mining (EDM), Pittsburgh, PA, USA, June 11-13 (2010)
7. Mota, S., Picard, R.W.: Automated Posture Analysis for Detecting Learner's Interest Level. In: Computer Vision and Pattern Recognition Workshop (2003)
8. Sanghvi, J., Castellano, G., Leite, I., Pereira, A., McOwan, P.W., Paiva, A.: Automatic analysis of affective postures and body motion to detect engagement with a game companion. In: Billard, A., Jr., P. H. K., Adams, J. A., Trafton, J. G (Eds.) Proceedings of the 6th International Conference on Human Robot Interaction (HRI) Lausanne, Switzerland, March 6-9, pp. 305–312 (2011)
9. Grafsgaard, J.F., Boyer, K.E., Wiebe, E.N., Lester, J.C.: Analyzing Posture and Affect in Task-Oriented Tutoring. In: Youngblood, G.M., McCarthy, P.M. (eds.) Proceedings of the Twenty-Fifth International Florida Artificial Intelligence Research Society Conference (FLAIRS), Marco Island, Florida, May 23-25. AAAI Press (2012)
10. OpenNI, http://www.openni.org/
11. Weka Machine Learning Project Weka University of Waikato, http://www.cs.waikato.ac.nz/~ml/weka
12. Hall, M.A.: Correlation-based Feature Subset Selection for Machine Learning. Hamilton, New Zealand (1998)
13. Liu, H., Setiono, R.: A probabilistic approach to feature selection - A filter solution. In: 13th International Conference on Machine Learning, pp. 319–327 (1996)
14. John, G.H., Langley, P.: Estimating Continuous Distributions in Bayesian Classifiers. In: Eleventh Conference on Uncertainty in Artificial Intelligence, San Mateo, pp. 338–345 (1995)
15. Friedman, N., Geiger, D., Goldszmidt, M.: Bayesian network classifiers. Machine Learning 29(2-3), 131–163 (1997)
16. Witten, I.H., Frank, E., Hall, M.A.: Data Mining: Practical Machine Learning Tools and Techniques, 3rd edn. Morgan Kaufmann, Burlington (2011)
17. Cortes, C., Vapnik, V.N.: Support-Vector Networks. Machine Learning 20 (1995)
18. R statistical package, http://www.r-project.org/

Evaluation of AFIS-Ranked Latent Fingerprint Matched Templates

Ram P. Krish[1], Julian Fierrez[1], Daniel Ramos[1],
Raymond Veldhuis[2], and Ruifang Wang[1]

[1] Biometric Recognition Group - ATVS, EPS - Univ. Autonoma de Madrid
C/ Francisco Tomas y Valiente, 11 - Campus de Cantoblanco - 28049 Madrid, Spain
{ram.krish,julian.fierrez,daniel.ramos,ruifang.wang}@uam.es
[2] Chair of Biometric Pattern Recognition, Faculty EEMS,University of Twente,
P.O. Box 217, 7500 AE Enschede, The Netherlands
r.n.j.veldhuis@utwente.nl

Abstract. The methodology currently practiced in latent print examination (known as ACE-V) yields only a decision as result, namely individualization, exclusion or inconclusive. From such a decision, it is not
possible to express the strength of opinion of a forensic examiner quantitatively with a scientific basis to the criminal justice system. In this
paper, we propose a framework to generate a score from the matched
template generated by the forensic examiner. Such a score can be viewed
as a measure of confidence of a forensic examiner quantitatively, which
in turn can be used in statistics-based evidence evaluation framework,
for e.g, likelihood ratio. Together with the description and evaluation of
new realistic forensic case driven score computation, we also exploit the
developed experimental framework to understand more about matched
templates in forensic fingerprint databases.

Keywords: ACE-V methodology, criminology, forensics, latent fingerprint, likelihood ratio, quantification of evidence.

1 Introduction

Latent fingerprints (or partial fingermarks) lifted from the crime scenes have
been used for identification for more than a century. The use of fingerprints in
criminology was popularized by Sir Francis Galton in late 19th century. The
philosophy surrounding its use in criminology is the fact that fingerprint of
an individual is unique, and the friction ridge pattern being persistent over
time [1]. Starting from early 20th century, several methods were proposed to
formalize a standard friction ridge analysis for forensic examination. Eventually
the forensic examination methodology matured to a standard procedure called
ACE-V (analysis, comparison, evaluation and verification) which is currently
followed in the forensic community. But recently this kind of procedure has
been criticized, arguing for a robust quantitative evaluation of the weight of
evidence [4] [2].

R. Klette, M. Rivera, and S. Satoh (Eds.): PSIVT 2013, LNCS 8333, pp. 230–241, 2014.
© Springer-Verlag Berlin Heidelberg 2014

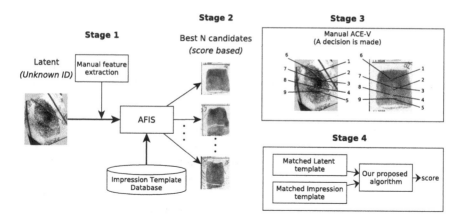

Fig. 1. Stage 1 to Stage 3 captures the Latent fingerprint examination methodology currently practiced. In Stage 4, we propose our framework to generate a score from matched template obtained from Stage 3.

The various stages involved in current forensic examination methodology are summarized in Stage 1, Stage 2 and Stage 3 in Fig.1. In Stage 1, a forensic examiner manually extracts the minutiae features from a latent fingerprint, and these feature are then converted into a digital template format used by an Automated Fingerprint Identification System (AFIS). In Stage 2, the AFIS compares the manually extracted latent template with all the templates in the forensic database and shortlists a set of possible suspects ranked based on a similarity score. In Stage 3, the forensic examiner manually follows the ACE-V methodology for the given latent print against all the templates shorlisted by the AFIS, and yields a decision whether the prints match, do not match or the comparison is inconclusive.

ACE-V methodology comprises of the following four phases [6] [12]:

1. *Analysis :* The examiner looks for sufficiency of the details present in the given latent print. This comprises of checking for ridge clarity, quantity of Level 1, Level 2 and Level 3 details, and determining the anatomical sources - whether the print came from finger, palm, toe or foot.
2. *Comparison :* Once the latent print passes the analysis phase, many useful friction ridge details together with the minutiae feature are extracted manually and are compared against one or more exemplar/reference fingerprints shorlisted by an AFIS to determine whether they are in agreement.
3. *Evaluation :* Based on the conclusions derived from the analysis and comparison phases, the forensic examiner yields a decision as *individualization (identification or match), exclusion (non-match) or inconclusive.*
4. *Verification :* In this phase, another qualified forensic examiner reexamines the previous decision by following the above three phases.

The latent fingerprints which are the unintentional traces left behind by the perpetrator or by the victim are of poor quality in nature [9] [7] [3]. So, a reliable manual feature extraction is mainly influenced by the perception and decision making ability of a forensic examiner, which eventually affects the final decision. One of the more popularly cited examples where an erroneous individualization was made is the Brandon Mayfield case. Other similar cases of erroneous individualization have been reported in [8].

There is no established protocol to characterize any uncertainty involved in the ACE-V procedure. Also, there is no scientific framework currently in use at the criminal justice system to express the strength of opinion of a forensic examiner quantitatively. The new paradigm coming forward in this regard [10] avoids hard identification decisions by considering evidence reporting methods that incorporate uncertainty and statistics. Amongst all the methods of evidence evaluation, the likelihood ratio is receiving greater attention [5] [12]. To use likelihood ratio incorporating the ACE-V level, scores are required in place of decisions. This was the motivation for the current work, where we developed a framework, Stage 4 in Fig.1 to take the matched templates from the ACE-V stage and generate a score as a measure of confidence for forensic examiner. This score can be used in statistics-based evidence evaluation framework to derive quantitative weight to express the strength of opinion of the examiner with adequate scientific basis.

The remainder of the paper is organized as follows. We first explain in detail about the real forensic casework databases used in this study, then the method developed to generate a score as a measure of confidence for a forensic examiner. We then present the experimental protocol and results, followed by a discussion on the usefulness of the technique developed in quantifying the evidence of fingerprints.

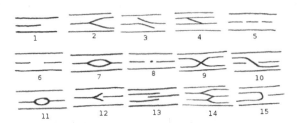

Fig. 2. Minutiae types used in Guardia Civil Database. Names corresponding to individual type numbers can be found in Table 1.

2   Database

The forensic fingerprint database largely used in academic domain is the NIST Special Database (SD) 27, which was made publicly available by NIST. This database is used by researchers working in forensic domain to understand about the challenges, as well as to have a transparent and benchmark database to

Table 1. List of typical and rare minutiae in Guardia Civil Database. Numbering with respect to Fig.2.

No	TypeName	No	TypeName	No	TypeName
1	Ridge Ending	6	Interruption	11	Circle
2	Bifurcation	7	Enclosure	12	Delta
3	Deviation	8	Point	13	Assemble
4	Bridge	9	Ridge Crossing	14	M-structure
5	Fragment	10	Transversal	15	Return

evaluate the approaches developed by the researchers. This database has both images as well as minutiae validated by forensic examiners.

NIST SD27 minutiae template database is broadly classified into two: 1) *ideal*, and 2) *matched* minutiae database. The *ideal* minutiae set for latents was manually extracted by a forensic examiner without any prior knowledge of its corresponding impression image. The *ideal* minutiae for impressions was initially extracted using an AFIS, and then these minutiae were manually validated by at least two forensic examiners. The *matched* minutiae templates contains those minutiae which are in common between the latent and its mated impression image. There is a one-to-one correspondence in the minutiae between the latent and its mate in the matched template. This ground truth was established by a forensic examiner looking at the images and the *ideal* minutiae following an ACE-V procedure. For NIST SD27 database, only the ideal-latent templates had type information for each minutiae in addition to location and orientation attributes. The other three datasets (ideal-impression, matched-latent and matched-impression) do not have type information but only location and orientation attributes.

In this study, we also acquired the forensic fingerprint database from Guardia Civil, the law enforcement agency of the Government of Spain. The Guardia Civil database (GCDB) is similar to the NIST SD27 database except that all the templates in ideal and matched sets in GCDB have type information. Apart from having typical minutiae types (*ridge-endings, bifurcations*), GCDB also comprises rare minutiae types like *fragments, enclosures, points/dots, interruptions, etc.* Please refer to Fig.2 and Table 1 for a comprehensive list of all minutiae feature types present in GCDB. Table 2 shows the statistics of various types of minutiae features present in the 258 template pairs available in GCDB. Rest of the minutiae types were not observed so far in this collection of GCDB.

We will follow the notation GCDB-M and NIST-SD27-M to denote the matched template database of GCDB and NIST SD27 respectively. In Fig.3, we show a latent fingerprint and its corresponding impression with typical features and some of the rare features annotated with their correspondences.

Table 2. Statistics of typical and rare minutiae present in Guardia Civil Database. Numbering with respect to Fig.2.

No	Contribution	No	Contribution	No	Contribution
1	56%	4	0.265%	7	2.058%
2	36.38%	5	4.515%	8	0.332%
3	0.166%	6	0.232%	10	0.0332%

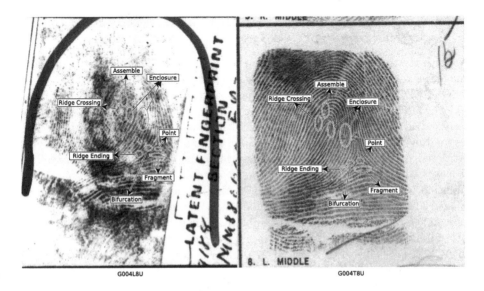

Fig. 3. Typical and some rare minutiae features on a latent and its mated impression fingerprint. The latent image G004L8U and the impression image G004T8U were taken from NIST SD27 database.

The latent and impression images used here were taken from NIST SD27 database, and the typical and rare minutiae features were manually annotated on them.

3   Algorithm

We propose an algorithm to generate a score for the templates in GCDB-M. This algorithm can be adapted to templates from NIST-SD27-M by discarding the weights for type information when calculating *typeError* explained in the algorithm. The various stages involved in the computation of the score are as follows:

3.1   Alignment and Correspondence

Since the framework is developed to deal with matched databases, we expect that for genuine matches, superimposing the centroids of both latent and impression minutiae points with appropriate rotation alignment would lead to an approximate fitting of point patterns based on mated pairs with minimum overall fitting error, and for impostors it would lead to a high fitting error.

As typical minutiae features are the majority with 92% (see Table 2), we only use typical features to estimate the rotation parameters. By rotating the latent template over the impression template w.r.t centroid in a range of $[-45°, +45°]$, we find the closest matching minutiae pairs, and add their distance. The rotation for which the average sum of closest pairs is the minimum is considered to be the best rotation alignment for their approximate pattern fitting.

After the alignment, all those minutiae pairs which are within a threshold distance are considered to be mated pairs, and their correspondences are established.

3.2   Fitting and Orientation Errors

Once the correspondences are established for all the typical minutiae features, the scores are computed hierarchically looking at each of minutiae attributes, namely *location, orientation* and *type* information. Scores based on *type* information are discussed in the next subsection.

For all the typical minutiae which established correspondences based on optimal rotation, we find a fitting error using an affine transformation for the mated minutiae patterns by least square fitting. This score is denoted as *fittingError*, which is averaged w.r.t total number of mated minutiae pairs.

Again for all the mated minutiae pairs, we sum up all the orientation differences of corresponding minutiae and average this sum of degrees w.r.t total number of mated pairs. When averaging the orientations, the circularity of degrees are taken care of. This score is denoted as *orientationError*.

3.3   Type Errors

If the mated pairs disagree w.r.t *type* information, which otherwise are mated based on only location and orientation attributes, we associate a penalty for such type of mismatches. The penalty for each typical minutiae type is a constant factor estimated from Table 2. This score is denoted as *typeError*. This is possible because the *type* information for both latent and impression are estimated manually by a forensic examiner, and we assume type information is available here.

Based on the alignment estimated using *typical* minutiae, we also look for the presence of *rare* minutiae correspondences. If they are within a location and orientation threshold, then they constitute mated pairs, and thus correspondence is established. As the percentage of occurrence of rare minutiae is very small, around 8%, we only estimate *typeError* for rare minutiae. The penalty for each rare minutiae type is a constant factor estimated from Table 2.

3.4   Final Score

Since all the individual scores we have generated are of different nature, namely *fittingError* in distance, *orientationError* in degrees, *typeError* in probability based cost, these scores are combined using logistic regression to generate the final score [11]:

$$\begin{aligned} finalScore = &(\alpha \times fittingError) \\ &+ (\beta \times orientationError) \\ &+ (\gamma \times typeError) \end{aligned} \qquad (1)$$

where α, β, γ are the logistic regression coefficients for each classifier respectively.

This final score can be viewed as a measure of confidence of the forensic examiner numerically, otherwise the forensic examiner only have a logical decision at the stage of ACE-V. Note that the $finalScore$ is a dissimilarity score, so the higher the score the higher the distance between a match and non-match.

4   Experiments

4.1   Experimental Protocol

The total number of latent fingerprint templates in GCDB-M is 258, with their corresponding matched impression fingerprint templates. This size of GCDB-M is equivalent to the publicly available NIST-SD27-M. This way, we could do some performance comparisons between databases, unbiased in terms of partitioning for train and test dataset sizes. For training the logistic regression coefficients, we used 129 template pairs and 129 for testing.

4.2   Results

We performed a 2-fold cross validation to study the performance of the developed approach by comparing the degree of overlap between matching and non-matching scores in the matched databases. Various parameters like the distance and orientation thresholds were finetuned to minimize this degree of the overlap.

We also tested the performance of a commercial SDK from Neurotechnology Verifinger 4.3which is a general purpose matcher, on both GCDB-M and NIST-SD27-M. When using Verifinger for the analysis, all 258 template pairs of GCDB-M and NIST-SD27-M were used for testing.

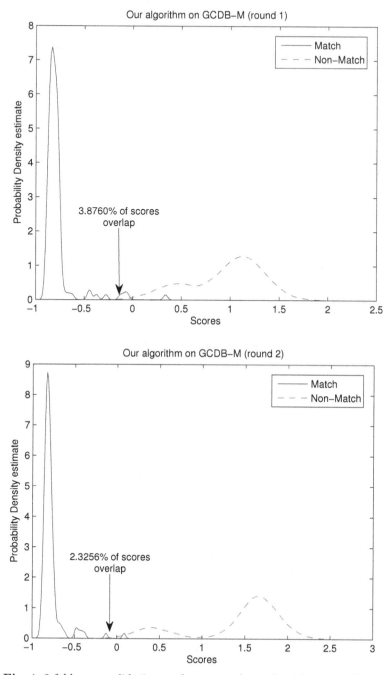

Fig. 4. 2-fold cross validation performance of our algorithm on GCDB-M

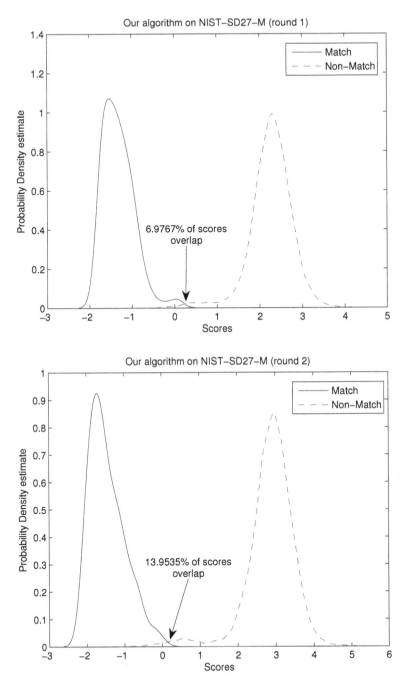

Fig. 5. 2-fold cross validation performance of our algorithm on NIST-SD27-M

Table 3. Degree of overlap of scores generated by our algorithm and Verifinger. Verifinger on GCDB-M is not reported here because the results were too inconsistent.

	GCDB-M	NIST-SD27-M
Our algorithm	3.1008%	10.4651%
Verifinger	-	7.7519%

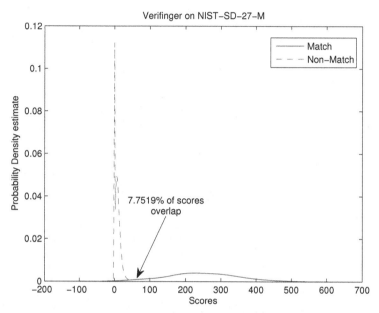

Fig. 6. Performance of Verifinger on NIST-SD27-M

Fig.4 and Fig.5 shows the degree of overlap of scores on both GCDB-M and NIST-SD27-M using our proposed algorithm respectively. In Table 3, we summarize the degree of overlap of scores in percentage. Since we performed a 2-fold cross validation, the average degree of overlap is shown in the table for our algorithm on both GCDB-M and NIST-SD27-M, but in the figures, the individual overlaps are shown.

Using our algorithm, the average degree of score overlap was 3.10% for GCDB-M, and for each round of cross validation, the degree of score overlaps were 3.87% and 2.32% respectively. Similarly, for NIST-SD27-M, the average degree of score overlap was 10.46%, and for each round, the degree of score overlaps were 6.97% and 13.95% respectively. Fig.6 shows the performance of Verifinger on NIST-SD27-M with a score overlap of 7.75%.

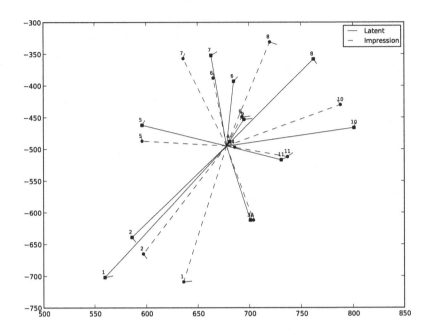

Fig. 7. An example from GCDB-M where a genuine match having high dissimilarity score. The solid lines represent the latent minutia pattern with respect to its centroid, and dashed lines represent the impression minutia pattern with respect to its centroid.

Fig.7 shows a latent (*solid lines*) and its mated impression (*dashed lines*) minutiae (*location* and *orientation*) from GCDB-M superimposed over their centroids before estimating alignment parameter (*rotation*) which leads to high dissimilarity score. Ideally, the mated templates are supposed to show less dissimilarity, but in this case, nonlinear deformations leads to wrong orientation parameter estimation. For e.g, the pairs (1,1), (8,8), (3,3), (11,11) show high nonlinear deformations compared against the pairs (2,2), (5,5), and (6,6). Such disparities makes it difficult to optimally estimate the best alignment parameter, and as a consequence leads to high fitting error among the mated minutiae pairs. This shows the limitation of the Affine transformation model used in the algorithm for estimating fitting error to capture the nonlinear deformations of the pattern globally.

5   Discussions

We developed a framework to generate a score from matched templates generated by the forensic examiner as a result of ACE-V. This score can be viewed as a measure of confidence of the forensic examiner numerically in place of a logical decision. Such a score can be exploited by any statistics based evidence evaluation framework to include the ACE-V stage. We tested the algorithm on GCDB-M as well as on the publicly available NIST-SD27-M database. We also exploited this framework to understand more about the nature of matched template forensic fingerprint databases.

A deeper analysis about the importance of rare minutiae features, as well as an implementation of the likelihood ratio approach based on these scores to express the strength of opinion of forensic examiners quantitatively is in order.

Acknowledgment. R.K. and R.W. are supported by Marie Curie Fellowships under project BBfor2 (FP7-ITN-238803). This work has also been partially supported by Spanish Guardia Civil, Cátedra UAM-Telefónica, and projects Bio-Shield (TEC2012-34881) and Contexts (S2009/TIC-1485).

References

1. Barnes, J.G.: Chapter 1, History, The Fingerprint Sourcebook, U.S Department of Justice (2011)
2. Nagar, A., Choi, H.-S., Jain, A.K.: Evidential Value of Automated Latent Fingerprint Comparison: An Empirical Approach, IEEE Transactions on Information Forensics and Security (2012)
3. Jain, A.K., Feng, J.: Latent Fingerprint Matching. IEEE Transactions on Pattern Analysis and Machine Intelligence, 88–100 (2011)
4. Neumann, C., Evett, I.: James Skerrett, Quantifying the weight of evidence assigned to a forensic fingerprint comparison: a new paradigm. J. R. Statist. Soc. A 175, 371–415 (2012)
5. Evett, I., et al.: Expressing evaluative opinions: A position statement. Science and Justice (2011)
6. Expert Working Group on Human Factors in Latent Print Analysis. Latent Print Examination and Human Factors: Improving the Practice through a Systems Approach, NIST (2012)
7. Champod, C., Lennard, C.J., Margot, P., Stoilovic, M.: Fingerprints and other ridge skin impressions. CRC (2004)
8. Cole, S.: More than zero: Accounting for error in latent fingerprint identification. Journal of Criminal Law and Criminology, 985–1078 (2005)
9. Alonso-Fernandez, F., Fierrez, J., Ortega-Garcia, J.: Quality Measures in Biometric Systems. IEEE Security Privacy (2012)
10. Saks, M.J., Koehler, J.J.: The Coming Paradigm Shift in Forensic Identification Science. Science, 892–895 (2005)
11. Alonso-Fernandez, F., Fierrez, J., Ramos, D., Gonzalez-Rodriguez, J.: Quality-Based Conditional Processing in Multi-Biometrics: application to Sensor Interoperability. IEEE Transactions on Systems, Man and Cybernetics Part A (2010)
12. Srihari, S.N.: Quantitative Measures in Support of Latent Print Comparison: Final Technical Report: NIJ Award Number: 2009-DN-BX-K208, University at Buffalo, SUNY (2013)

Exemplar-Based Hole-Filling Technique
for Multiple Dynamic Objects

Matteo Pagliardini[1,2], Yasuhiro Akagi[1], Marcos Slomp[1,3], Ryo Furukawa[3],
Ryusuke Sagawa[4], and Hiroshi Kawasaki[1]

[1] Kagoshima University, 1-21-24 Korimoto Kagoshima, Japan
[2] CPE Lyon, 43 Boulevard du 11 Novembre 1918 69616 Villeurbanne, France
[3] Hiroshima City University, 3-4-1 OzukaHigashi AsaMinami-Ku Hiroshima, Japan
[4] AIST, 1-1-1 Higashi Tsukuba Ibaraki, Japan

Abstract. Entire shape reconstruction of dynamic objects is an important research subject with applications on film production, virtual reality, modeling and engineering. Typically, entire shape reconstruction of real objects is achieved by combining the outcome of objects scanned from multiple directions. However, due to limitations on the number of 3D sensors enclosing the scene, occlusions inevitably occur, causing holes to appear on the reconstructed surfaces. These issues are intensified if dynamic, moving objects are considered. Volumetric and polygonal approaches exist to address these problems. Most notably, exemplar-based polygonal methods have gained momentum due to their overall improved visual quality. In this paper we propose an extension to the plain exemplar-based technique that allows for multiple dynamic objects. With our method, adequate hole-filling candidates are sampled from spatial and temporal domains and then used to synthesize likely plausible surfaces with smooth boundaries for the hole regions.

Keywords: 3D scan, hole filling, exemplar based technique.

1 Introduction

Surface reconstruction is one of the most relevant topics in computer vision, with extended applicability to computer graphics, engineering and medical imaging, to cite a few. Typically, 3D reconstruction of real scenes is achieved through either pattern-based or range-finder-based scanning techniques, both of which rely on cameras. These camera-based systems are, however, sensitive to occlusion and noise and thus prone to introducing holes on the reconstructed surface. If dynamic scenes are considered, such as a moving actor, the severity and frequency of these holes are further aggravated.

Computer vision researchers have been addressing this problem since long. Common solutions can be categorized in two groups: image-space preprocessing or surface-domain post-processing approaches. Image-based methods are more likely to mitigate the occurrence of holes due to noise, but face difficulties regarding occlusions. Surface-based techniques, on the other hand, employ exemplar-based schemes that refer to other regions of the object. Holes are then filled by

R. Klette, M. Rivera, and S. Satoh (Eds.): PSIVT 2013, LNCS 8333, pp. 242–253, 2014.

replacing them with some other region of the surface that may closely resemble the fractured region.

These surface-domain filters are more sophisticated than their image-based counterparts. One factor that contributes to their complexity is the need for extracting and evaluating features of the partially reconstructed object. In fact, it is very likely that no suitable region exists on the surface to replace a hole. All of these factors combined impose a great challenge to robust hole reconstruction algorithms.

In this paper we propose a technique that is capable of detecting potential holes in a reconstructed object and infer substitute regions for the missing parts based on an animated sequence of the object. The central idea of our method is to scan for eligible hole-filling candidate areas in different poses (frames) of the reconstructed object in case the current pose alone proves insufficient. We are, by no means, suggesting that our technique is universal and robust enough to encompass all sorts of datasets. Instead, our primary goal with this research is to establish an initial investigation on the feasibility of using temporal information contained in dynamic datasets for surface hole inference/reconstruction. We hope that more researchers will get interested in the subject and further improve on the state-of-the-art based on the foundation developed here. Meanwhile, as mentioned in the future work, we seek to continue further validating the algorithm as we manage to obtain more interesting real datasets.

2   Related Work

Range data from multiple sources can be coalesced into a single shape through polygon-based or volume-based techniques. Polygon-based efforts include synthesizing a mesh from unorganized points [1], employing deformable models encoded as a level-sets [2], and mesh tessellation/stitching from overlapped surfaces (zippering) [3]. Once the geometry of a hole is established, a better shape can be refined through a postprocessing stage.

On the other side, volume-based methods attempt to discretize unstructured points into voxels which are later used to extract a more suitable surface description. For the initial voxelization stage, signed distance fields are typically used [4–8]. Euclidean signed distance is preferable [5, 6], but the high computational cost associated to it makes it less attractive than other simplified models such as line-of-sight distance[1] [4, 7, 8]. Once voxels are obtained, the shape of the underlying object can be regularized through level-set or Graph-cut related algorithms. Finally, the resulting polygonal mesh can be extracted through one of the many variants of the marching cubes algorithm [9].

Volume-based approaches, however, are incapable of accounting for voxels that were not observed. According to the seminal space-carving method of Curless et al. [4], first all voxels are initialized as unseen, and those in between each viewpoint and the object are marked as empty; as the method carves the

---

[1] The distance between the center of a voxel and the first intersection point on the surface along the line from the viewpoint to the voxel.

volume immediately in front of the observed objects – with any unobserved voxel remaining as unseen – an excess mesh is produced along boundaries of unseen and empty volume regions. For a sufficiently large number of captured images, this excess will likely not be connected to the mesh of the target object and can thus be pruned away. However, on a more realistic scenario, untangling the excess mesh from the real mesh becomes difficult and laborious. Furukawa *et al.* refined the discrimination of unseen voxels near the object based on a Bayesian approach, producing plausible results even for very small input sets [7, 8].

Within the scope of surface-driven hole-filling algorithms, Poisson distribution and exemplar-based schemes are commonplace [10–15]. Poisson distribution is particularly useful for smooth interpolation of geometrical data along the boundaries of the hole-damaged region. Either voxel and polygon-based schemes can benefit from this interpolation: Kazhdan and Hoppe [11] rely on Poisson distribution to establish a characteristic function to assist during isosurface extraction, while Zhao et al. [15] refine the position of a linearly-interpolated points along the missing region through a Poisson distribution. These methods, however, fail to propagate high-frequency features into the hole region. Exemplar-based techniques, in contrast, can reproduce more faithfully the overall features of the object into the missing areas. Although exemplar methods are more widely adopted for 2D inpainting problems, Kawai *et al.* have shown that they can be successfully modified for 3D inpaintings as well [12–14]. A key component of Kawai *et al.* algorithm is the concept of coherency, evaluated by comparing the similarity of hole-filled shape with that of the rest of the mesh. The algorithm attempts to maximize this coherency in order to patch the holes in a more object-encompassing fashion. Compared to Poisson-based methods, exemplar-driven reconstructions tend to appear more realistic at the expense of requiring more sophisticated mechanisms for feature extraction and evaluation.

In this paper, we investigate a temporal extension to the exemplar-based technique of Kawai *et al.* [12–14]. We have refrained from investigating volume-based hole-filling approaches in the temporal domain due to the relatively scarce literature on the subject. The technique hereby described is thus completely polygon-oriented. As is usually the case, polygonal techniques tend to have lower computational costs than their volume-based counterparts.

3   Overview

The proposed method builds upon the research of Kawai *et al.* [12–14]. Missing regions are inferred through an iterative process that attempts to minimize an energy function which models the level of coherency of the inferred surface. Coherency is evaluated by comparing patches of the inferred region against other thoroughly chosen patches around the mesh. The algorithm does not promptly address strict feature recovery, but rather concentrate on propagating frequencies into the hole region. Our technique also enables partial control over the frequencies recovered by meddling with the patch size p_S.

As proposed, the technique has been extended to animated sequences of the object. This way, coherent hole filling shape can be inferred from information contained in different time frames as well. Since the location of holes is likely to differ among distinct frames, missing regions are retrieved by looking at neighboring frames. In addition, assuming a frame rate compatible to the movement characteristics of the captured sequence, our technique can fill holes in dynamic scenes without resorting to any sort of tracking. For the extreme case where coherent shapes can not be inferred from any frame, a classic exemplar-based hole filling is performed instead.

The process begins by delimiting three regions for each individual pose of the time-varying sequence:

1. the hole region, which is initialized with a coarse shape that roughly fills the hole and will evolves at each iteration.
2. the extended region, consisting of all points for which a sphere of radius p_S extruded from them encloses at least one point of the missing region.
3. the remaining region – or data region – on which shape information is consulted during the hole filling process.

For brevity in the explanations below, we will adhere to the following notation: we note P^n as being a 3D point belonging to time frame n; $Patch(P^n)$ refers to the enclosing patch region centered at point P^n with radius p_S; we use Ω^n as the union of the points of the extended and missing regions of frame n; the superscript c demotes the index of the current frame being processed; and finally, Φ corresponds to the union of the data region of all frames currently investigated.

The rationale of the algorithm is that detailed shape information is gradually propagated from the extended region toward the hole region, while sustaining a higher degree of mesh coherency. To that end, each iteration of the proposed method performs two tasks: a matching step such that each point P_k^c of Ω^c is associated with a surface patch $Patch(\hat{P}_k^c)$, $\hat{P}_k^c \in \Phi$; and an alteration step in which points of the missing region are modified in an attempt to minimize the energy function (i.e., maximize mesh coherency).

During the first stage, a data patch $Patch(\hat{P}_k^c)$ is appointed as the best match for each hole/extended point P_k^c of Ω^c based on neighborhood similarities. This locality constraint can be elegantly modeled through the sum of squared differences (SSD) between data patches $Patch(P_{data \in \Phi}^m)$ and the hole/extended region patch $Patch(P_k^c)$. A patch $Patch(P_{data \in \Phi}^m)$ is a best match for a patch $Patch(P_k^c)$, i.e. $P_{data \in \Phi}^m = \hat{P}_k^c$, if $argmin_{i \in \Phi}(SSD(P_k^c, P_i^m))$ is solved for $P_{data \in \Phi}^m$. After the matching step all the shape pairs $(P_k^c, \hat{P}_k^c)$ are established.

In such terms, coherency can be thought of as the extent in which it is possible to find good matching surface candidates that fit the missing region. Mathematically, this can be expressed as a normalized weighted average of the sum of squared differences between the matching shape pairs:

$$E = \frac{\sum_{P_k^c \in \Omega^c} \omega_{P_k^c} SSD(P_k^c, \hat{P}_k^c)}{\sum_{P_k^c \in \Omega^c} \omega_{P_k^c}} \tag{1}$$

where $\omega_{P_k^c}$ denotes the weight associated to P_k^c. The weight of a point is determined based on its integrity: points in either data or extended region receive a weight of 1 because their position is set and will not be further modified by the algorithm, while points in the hole region are assigned normalized weights proportional to their distance to the boundary of the hole. This acknowledges that points in the middle of the hole will be less correlated to the mesh than those close to the extended region.

In the subsequent stage, the position of the points in the hole region are modified in order to minimize the energy function. Kawai *et al.* has demonstrated that for fixed shape pairs $(P_k^c, \hat{P}_k^c)$, the energy representing their coherency can be minimized by analyzing parallel orthographic projections of all points of the missing region.

After each iteration, remeshing is performed to ascertain that the point density in the hole region remains uniform. The computational time imposed by the algorithm is directly related to the amount of SSD computations required during the matching step. Kawai *et al.* have proposed the use of curvature filtering to narrow the computations only to patches with similar curvature characteristics. In practice, however, we found that this improvement does not significantly reduce the computational time. With the assistance of the graphics hardware and some algorithmic optimizations we were able to devise a fast and efficient SSD computation routine. An overview of the algorithm is depicted in Figure 1.

4   Exemplar-Based Spatio-temporal Hole-Filling

Throughout this section we detail the proposed algorithm, including implementation-specific optimizations that allow for efficient searches of hole filling candidates over multiple frames.

4.1   Stepped Reconstruction

We have adopted the same approach as Kawai *et al.* for tessellating the initial shape of the hole region [12–14]. A coarse to fine filling scheme is employed, allowing for stepped frequency reconstruction. In short, at the very beginning, large patch sizes are used, yielding in a low density of points in the hole region; as the algorithm iterates, the patch size is gradually reduced, causing the point density in the hole region to increase. This iterative behavior implicitly induces coherent and progressive frequency propagation into the missing region. At the end of each iteration, remeshing is performed on the hole region in order to maintain the uniformity of the points for the next iteration.

4.2   Refinement Scheme for Potential Candidates

The goal of this matching step is to locate fitting surface regions that can fill the hole. More formally, this step is about finding the shape pairs $(P_k^c, \hat{P}_k^c)$ for each point $P_k^c \in \Omega^c$. In case of single frame hole-filling, the candidates are searched through the whole of the mesh. If multiple frames are considered, we can restrain the search by assuming slow movement variation compared to the

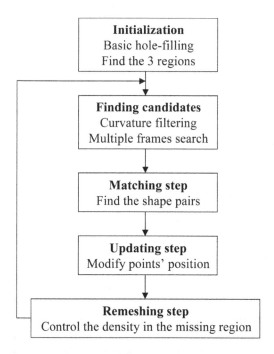

Fig. 1. Overview of the hole-filling method

overall frame-rate. For each point $P_k^c \in \Omega^c$ to be matched in the current frame c, we search within a certain number of neighboring frames. In addition, the entire mesh of each frame is not considered; instead we orient the search only to patches intersected by some sphere centered at P_k^c. We estimate the radius R of this sphere by analyzing the size of the mesh and the ratio between the rate of change in movement and the frame-rate of the sequence.

The radius of the sphere is expected to increase based on the distance of the current frame c and the queried frame m, that is, according to $|m - c|$. The time-space constraint narrows candidates from $\bigcup_{m \in TS} (D^m)$ to the restricted set $\bigcup_{m \in TS} (D_{|S_c^m(P_k^c)}^m)$, where D^m corresponds to the data region of frame m, TS is the set of frames being considered, and $S_c^m(P_k^c)$ is the sphere defined previously. The set is further narrowed down during the curvature filtering step. Figure 2 summarizes the candidate refinement scheme.

4.3   Accelerating SSD Computations Using the GPU

Kawai *et al.* evaluates $SSD(P_1, P_2)$ in two steps. First, the involved patches $Patch(P_1)$ and $Patch(P_2)$ need to be overlapped. This alignment is done based on the principal directions of their respective curvatures. Once the patches

Fig. 2. Flow of the candidates refinement method

overlap, all points in $Patch(P_1)$ are orthographically projected onto the surface of $Patch(P_2)$. The SSD function is thus expressed as a normalized sum of distances:

$$SSD(P_1, P_2) = \frac{\sum_{p_k \in Patch(P_1)} \|P_k - Proj(P_k)\|^2}{N(Patch(P_1))} \qquad (2)$$

where $Proj(P_k)$ corresponds to the parallel orthographic projection of P_k onto the surface of $Patch(P_2)$ along its normal direction, and $N(Patch(P_1))$ is the number of points in $Patch(P_1)$.

During each matching step, a large amount of SSD computations must be performed in order to establish the appropriate shape pairs. The computational overhead associated with patch alignment and projections is the the main performance bottleneck of the technique. In an attempt to minimize the number of SSD computations, Kawai *et al.* proposed a curvature-driven filtering step. However, we have observed that this improvement alone is not sufficient for reducing the computational time substantially.

Instead we tackle the performance issue by minimizing redundant computations. The curvature of a patch can be estimated based on its principal directions and extreme curvature values. This information can be obtained through a combination of principal component analysis and bi-quadratic fitting. Patches can then be stored and referenced directly in a curvature-oriented canonical coordinate system. This eliminates the need for the overlapping phase of the SSD since all patches naturally overlap in this space.

In addition, we propose the use of GPU rasterization capabilities for approximating ray-triangle intersections of the SSD formulation above. To that end, we render each patch (in the canonical curvature space above) to a small off-screen depth buffer. Note that we are not interested in any other pixel attribute except for depth. Conveniently, since patch rendering is subject to orthographic projection, the rasterized depth values vary linearly. As these depth buffer are rendered, we cache them in system memory and perform SSD computations on the CPU by simple image-space pixel-wise differences. The squared differences of each depth pixel are then accumulated and normalized by the size of the depth map, producing the final SSD value. The impact on performance greatly overcomes the additional memory requirements: we were able to move from about one hour in Kawai *et al.* reference implementation to just under 5 minutes.

4.4   Maximizing Mesh Coherency

After matching is performed, the energy representing the coherency of the reconstructed surface is minimized for the fixed shape-pairs found during the initial matching step. Considering all shape pairs $(P_k^c, \hat{P}_k^c)$ at once, we first translate each $Patch(\hat{P}_k^c)$ onto their respective local space in P_k^c. The overlapping is achieved using the principal directions of the curvature of $Patch(\hat{P}_k^c)$ and $Patch(P_k^c)$. Once again we use the patches stored during the curvature computation to eliminate redundant matrix calculations. When all patches overlap, all the P_k^c are orthographically projected onto these patches along their normal directions. The new position of P_k^c is obtained through the weighted average of all the resulting intersections:

$$P_k^c = \frac{\sum_{P_i^c \in Patch(P_k^c)} \omega_{P_i^c} Proj_{P_i^c}(P_k^c)}{\sum_{P_i^c \in Patch(P_k^c)} \omega_{P_i^c}} \tag{3}$$

where $Proj_{P_i^c}(P_k^c)$ is the projection of P_k^c on the surface $Patch(\hat{P}_i^c)$ translated and reoriented to overlap $Patch(P_i^c)$ on P_i^c.

Because the correlation of the missing region with the rest of the mesh increase along the iterations, we chose to modify the parameters defining the weights $\omega_{P_k^c}$ associated with the points of the missing region as the correlation changes. For the first iterations the weights of the points inside the hole region are set really small because there is no correlation between the mesh and the missing region. The weights increase gradually with each iterations, hence driving the incremental propagation of the shape inside the missing region.

5   Results and Discussions

We have evaluated our method according to three criteria: subjective visual quality, root mean square error (RMSE) and computational time. We tested our algorithm on both synthetic and real data sets. For the next results, all the meshes have been re-sized to fit a bounding cube of side 1.

5.1   Evaluation with Static Synthetic Data

To demonstrate the advantages of our temporal exemplar-based hole-filling algorithm over the pure exemplar-based method, we begin with a simple synthetic setup based upon the Armadillo model. We built a short sequence consisting of only two frames, with no apparent movement, except that the first frame contains an artificially carved hole (the second frame can thus be though of as the ground truth result). This is illustrated in Figure 3.

The result achieved by our hole reconstruction algorithm is depicted in Figure 4. There is some noticeable improvement between the standard exemplar-based method and our temporal extension. This improvement can be quantitatively confirmed based on the RMSE values in Table 1.

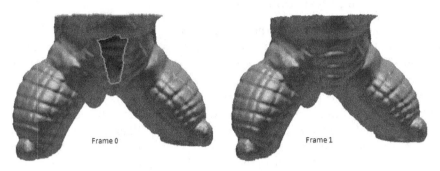

Fig. 3. Simple static data set

Fig. 4. a : Pure exemplar-based reconstruction i.e. only the first frame was used / b : Time-space exemplar-based reconstruction

Table 1. Evaluation of accuracy

Method	a	b
RMSE	0.00377271	0.00128592

5.2   Evaluation with Synthetic Dynamic Data

This experiment is built upon the Stanford bunny model. This time, instead of just replicating the mesh and carving a hole in one of the frames, we now alter the position and orientation of the bunny in each frame. Two kinds of hole are carved, such as at different positions over frames and the same position through the frames; meaning that there is no ground truth reference frame anymore for the latter case. Refer to Figure 5 for a depiction of this synthetic data-set.

Results of our technique on this data-set are shown in Figure 6. As can be observed, all holes were filled in a plausible, naturally consistent fashion. Table 2 lists small RSME values for this experiment, confirming the capabilities of our algorithm.

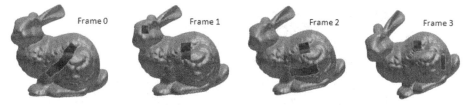

Fig. 5. Between each frames, the mesh is translated following the x axis and rotated of a small angle

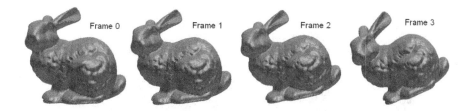

Fig. 6. Reconstructed meshes

Table 2. Evaluation of accuracy

Object:	frame 0	frame 1	frame 2	frame 3
RMSE:	0.00248812	0.00154282	0.00261936	0.000971361

5.3 Evaluation with Real Dynamic Data

Finally, we subject our algorithm to a densely reconstructed animated face. The face was captured through a scanning system built upon projected coherent light patterns. The data-set is shown in Figure 7, and results of our hole-filling technique on this data-set are available in Figure 8.

It can be observed that the majority of holes due to occlusions have been filled with appropriately coherent surfaces. Although the overall result is attractive, the technique is prone to fail if the boundaries do not give enough clues about the missing region. As a future work, we plan on driving the feature recovery using a more restrictive spatio-temporal search procedure.

5.4 Discussion on Computational Cost

The GPU-assisted evaluation of SSD substantially accelerates the algorithm. The bulk of the computational time is thus related to establishing the patches. This is further aggravated due to the fact that we rely on a dynamic, coarse to fine mesh refinement, which forces patches to be reestablished multiple times. Performance is therefore mostly constrained by the amount of density steps performed. When handling several frames, the reconstruction at each iteration is done for all frames simultaneously. This allows for significant savings on patch

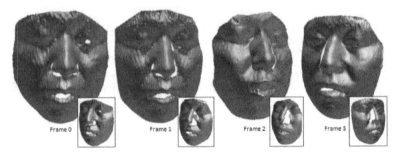

Fig. 7. The positions of the occluded parts change along the face orientation

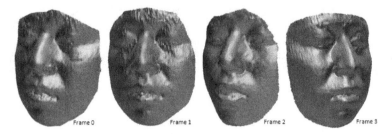

Fig. 8. Reconstructed meshes

recomputations. In other words, the overall computational time for N frames is inferior than N times the computational time of reconstructing one frame. The 4-frames reconstruction mentioned previously (figure 6) took around 7 minutes.

6   Conclusion

This paper introduced a novel approach for filling holes in dynamic scenes. The isotropic characteristic of our weighting function enables our technique to search for potential candidates in both spatial and temporal spaces. This detaches our method from object tracking, thus adding to the robustness and speed of our algorithm. In addition, even if a persistent hole exists at the same location throughout all frames, we can still fill the hole in a coherent fashion. Accuracy, performance and visual quality of the method were validated based on the experiments on static and dynamic scenes of multiple moving objects. As future research we would like to leverage the ability of the algorithm to recover features by introducing additional spatial constrains over the position of the selected patches.

References

1. Hoppe, H., DeRose, T., Duchamp, T., McDonald, J., Stuetzle, W.: Surface reconstruction from unorganized points. In: ACM SIGGRAPH, pp. 71–78. ACM Press (1992)

2. Whitaker, R.T.: A level-set approach to 3d reconstruction from range data. IJCV 29(3), 203–231 (1998)
3. Turk, G., Levoy, M.: Zippered polygon meshes from range images. In: SIGGRAPH 1994, pp. 311–318. ACM Press (1994)
4. Curless, B., Levoy, M.: A volumetric method for building complex models from range images. Computer Graphics 30(Annual Conference Series), 303–312 (1996)
5. Masuda, T.: Registration and integration of multiple range images by matching signed distance fields for object shape modeling. CVIU 87(1-3), 51–65 (2002)
6. Sagawa, R., Nishino, K., Ikeuchi, K.: Adaptively merging large-scale range data with reflectance properties. IEEE Trans. on PAMI 27(3), 392–405 (2005)
7. Furukawa, R., Itano, T., Morisaka, A., Kawasaki, H.: Shape-merging and interpolation using class estimation for unseen voxels with a gpu-based efficient implementation. In: IEEE The 6th International Conference on 3-D Digital Imaging and Modeling, pp. 289–296 (2007)
8. Furukawa, R., Itano, T., Morisaka, A., Kawasaki, H.: Improved space carving method for merging and interpolating multiple range images using information of light sources of active stereo. In: Yagi, Y., Kang, S.B., Kweon, I.S., Zha, H. (eds.) ACCV 2007, Part II. LNCS, vol. 4844, pp. 206–216. Springer, Heidelberg (2007)
9. Lorensen, W.E., Cline, H.E.: Marching cubes: A high resolution 3d surface construction algorithm. In: SIGGRAPH 1987, pp. 163–169. ACM Press, New York (1987)
10. Bolitho, M., Kazhdan, M., Burns, R., Hoppe, H.: Parallel poisson surface reconstruction. In: Bebis, G., Boyle, R., Parvin, B., Koracin, D., Kuno, Y., Wang, J., Wang, J.-X., Wang, J., Pajarola, R., Lindstrom, P., Hinkenjann, A., Encarnação, M.L., Silva, C.T., Coming, D. (eds.) ISVC 2009, Part I. LNCS, vol. 5875, pp. 678–689. Springer, Heidelberg (2009)
11. Kazhdan, M., Bolitho, M., Hoppe, H.: Poisson surface reconstruction. In: Proceedings of the Fourth Eurographics Symposium on Geometry Processing, SGP 2006, pp. 61–70. Eurographics Association, Aire-la-Ville (2006)
12. Kawai, N., Sato, T., Yokoya, N.: Efficient surface completion using principal curvature and its evaluation. In: ICIP, pp. 521–524 (2009)
13. Kawai, N., Sato, T., Yokoya, N.: Surface completion by minimizing energy based on similarity of shape. In: ICIP, pp. 1532–1535 (2008)
14. Kawai, N., Zakhor, A., Sato, T., Yokoya, N.: Surface completion of shape and texture based on energy minimization. In: ICIP, pp. 897–900 (2011)
15. Zhao, K.H., Osher, S., Fedkiw, R.: Fast surface reconstruction using the level set method. In: First IEEE Workshop on Variational and Level Set Methods, pp. 194–202 (2001)

Line Segment Detection with Hough Transform Based on Minimum Entropy

Zezhong Xu[1,2] and Bok-Suk Shin[1]

[1] Department of Computer Science, The University of Auckland
Auckland, New Zealand
[2] College of Computer Information Engineering, Changzhou Institute of Technology
Changzhou, Jiangsu, China
{zxu531@aucklanduni.ac.nz,b.shin@auckland.ac.nz}

Abstract. The Hough transform is a popular technique used in the field of image processing. In this paper, fitting and interpolation techniques are employed to compute high-accuracy peak parameters by considering peak spreading. The entropy is selected to measure the scatter-degree of voting. The voting in each column is considered as a random variable and voting values are considered as a probabilistic distribution. The corresponding entropies are computed and used to estimate the peak parameters. Endpoint coordinates of a line segment are computed by fitting a sine curve with more cells. It is more accurate and robust compared to solving directly two equations. The proposed method is tested on simulated and real images.

Keywords: Hough transform, peak detection, entropy, endpoints.

1   Introduction

The *Hough transform* (HT) [1,2,3] is a common technique for line segment extracting. However, image noise and parameter quantization [4,5,6] cause peak spreading problems in Hough space.

In order to deal with peak spreading and to achieve accurate peaks, researchers have proposed variations and extensions to the HT.

Some papers are focused on peak enhancement [7] in accumulator space by modifying the HT voting scheme. By assigning different weights [8] or utilizing a voting kernel [9,10], peaks in Hough space become more distinct and peak finding becomes easier. Other papers aim at obtaining high accuracy peak parameters, given an existing peak. Two accurate peak detection methods are presented in [11,12]; a smoothing window and interpolation are employed to achieve accurate peak parameters. Another high accuracy HT [13] is based on the theoretical symmetry of the butterfly.

The information-theoretic measure of entropy [14,15,16] is often applied in image analysis, such as for clustering or pattern recognition [17], distortion correction [18], image alignment [19], or image thresholding [20,21]. The peak localization method presented here is motivated by information entropy. The peak is located at θ where voting is clustered and entropy is minimal.

R. Klette, M. Rivera, and S. Satoh (Eds.): PSIVT 2013, LNCS 8333, pp. 254–264, 2014.
© Springer-Verlag Berlin Heidelberg 2014

The HT can also be used for extracting complete parameters of a line segment in an image although the HT provides only distance ρ and the angle θ.

Some methods provide a complete line-segment description using the HT. One kind of methods is based on image space [22,23,24]. After applying the standard HT, the line is broken into disjoint segments in image space. The endpoints of a line segment are determined by taking the projection of the feature points on either the x- or y-axis. Two thresholds are needed for the length of line segment and gaps between line segments. Another kind of methods is based on the Hough space. By analysing the butterfly distribution [25,26] around a peak in the accumulator array, butterfly features are used to discover parameters of a line segment. The first and last non-zero values are obtained and used to compute the endpoints of the line segment by solving two sets of simultaneous equations [27,28,29,30]. However, how to find the first and the last non-zero voting value is a difficult problem.

This paper focuses on improving accuracy and robustness of peak detection. By considering various uncertainties, the voting in each column is considered as a random variable and voting values are considered as a probabilistic distribution. Corresponding entropies are computed and used to estimate the peak parameter. Endpoint coordinates of a line are computed by fitting a sine curve with upside and downside cells in columns around a peak rather than solving two equations generated from just two cells.

The rest of the paper is organized as follows. Section 2 describes our peak detection method based on minimum entropy. Section 3 outlines endpoint detection by fitting sine curves. Section 4 compares methods by providing experimental results. Section 5 concludes.

2   Peak Detection

After voting all pixels in an image for all possible cells into Hough space, the next step is peak detection. Considering the peak spreading, we locate the peak where the voting is the most clustered.

2.1   Voting Distribution around a Peak

Under an ideal situation, voting distribution around a peak is symmetrical and convergent into a focal cell in the middle column. In each column around a peak, the sum of voting values is a constant; see Fig. 1. A peak can be found and computed easily in this case.

However, due to various uncertainties, like image noise, quantization noise, or line thickness, cells around an actual peak are usually not symmetrical and there is not a focal cell. In each column around a peak, the sum of voting values is constant only approximately; see Fig. 2. Voting is scattered in ρ direction in some θ columns. The degree of voting scattered or clustered is different in the columns. The final peak is located where the voting is the 'most clustered'.

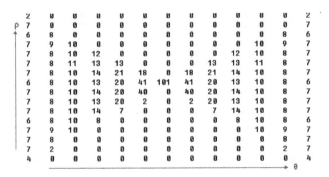

Fig. 1. An ideal peak region

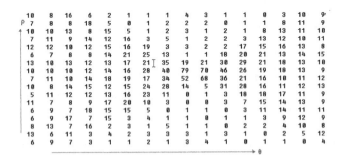

Fig. 2. An actual peak region

2.2 Entropy of Voting

In information theory [14], if X is a discrete random variable with distribution $P(X = x_k) = p_k$ $k = 1, 2, \cdots$ then the entropy of X is defined as follows:

$$E(X) = -\sum p_k \log p_k \tag{1}$$

The entropy is used to measure the uncertainty of the probability distribution. The smaller the entropy E is, the larger the cluster-degree is. Voting in each column is considered to be a random variable; entropy can be used to measure the voting scattering. In θ_i column in the peak region, the probability of voting for a cell $H_{ij}(\theta, \rho)$ is computed as $p_{ij} = H_{ij}(\theta, \rho)/\Sigma H_{ij}(\theta, \rho)$ where j belongs to a peak region. The entropy of the θ_i column is then

$$E_i = -\sum p_{ij} \log p_{ij} \tag{2}$$

Because voting distributions differ in different column, the E_i-values for columns also differ. The more clustered a voting is, the smaller the entropy. The more scattered a voting is, the bigger the entropy. A lower entropy distribution means that voting is clustered and can be considered as a peak. By minimizing information entropy of voting, an optimal θ peak is detected.

2.3 Peak θ Computation

Around a peak region, we perform the following operations: (1) Compute the entropy E_i of each θ_i column according to Equ. (2). Fig. 3 shows the entropy E of each θ column. (2) Fitting a curved function f.

$$f : E = f(\theta)$$

(3) Compute θ_{peak} where the fitted function has a minimum $\theta_{peak} = \theta | f'(\theta) = 0$.

2.4 Peak ρ Computation

Around a peak region, we also do: (1) Compute means

$$m_i = \sum [H_{ij}(\rho, \theta) \cdot \rho_j] / \sum H_{ij}(\rho, \theta) \qquad (3)$$

of each θ column. (2) A sinusoidal curve fitting. Sine curve is a nonlinear function. Fitting directly a sine curve is difficult, so we fit it by taking advantage of a linear function. In the equation of standard HT $\rho = x \cdot \cos \theta + y \cdot \sin \theta$, the relation between ρ and θ is not linear. It can be linear by using the following transform:

$$\rho / \cos \theta = y \cdot \tan \theta + x$$

$\rho / \cos \theta$ and $\tan \theta$ are in linear relation. With all these $(m_i / \cos \theta_i, \tan \theta_i)$, a linear function is fitted. The RANSAC technique is employed by considering various uncertainties:

$$g : \rho / \cos \theta = g(\tan \theta) \triangleq b_1 \tan \theta + b_0$$

(3) Interpolation to compute ρ_{peak} corresponding to ρ_{peak}:

$$\rho_{peak} = b_0 \cos(\theta_{peak}) + b_1 \sin(\theta_{peak}) \qquad (4)$$

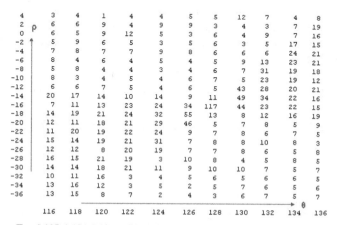

Fig. 3. Entropy of each column around a peak

2.5 Multiple Line Detection

The existence of multiple lines in the given image leads to overlays of multiple peaks in Hough space. If two peaks are far away, peak detection is only a little influenced because the final peak parameters are fitted and interpolated. If a peak region overlaps partly with other peak regions, the voting values and entropies in the overlapped columns become bigger. These columns are neglected for fitting and interpolation.

After a peak $(\rho_{peak}, \theta_{peak})$ is detected, the voting values corresponding to this peak are removed in order not to preclude the detection of another peak. First, with $(\rho_{peak}, \theta_{peak})$, those pixels contributing to this peak are selected in the image space. Second, the votes of those pixels are inverted by decreasing value of corresponding cells by 1.

3 Endpoint Detection

We find the endpoint coordinates of a line segment, called left endpoint $p(x_l, y_l)$ and right endpoint $p(x_r, y_r)$. Left and right is defined by the origin (i.e. the perpendicular point). See Fig. 4. According to the equation of the HT, if we have two cells (θ_1, ρ_1) and (θ_2, ρ_2) where a left endpoint votes for, the coordinates of the left endpoint can be computed directly by solving two simultaneous equations

$$\rho_1 = x \cdot \cos\theta_1 + y \cdot \sin\theta_1$$
$$\rho_2 = x \cdot \cos\theta_2 + y \cdot \sin\theta_2$$

By considering various uncertainties, rather than solving directing two equations, we compute the coordinates of endpoints by fitting more cells.

3.1 Valid Cell Identification

Due to parameter quantization and image noise, a peak region is not distinct in Hough space. It is usually as in Fig. 5. Cells corresponding to endpoints can not be determined simply by identifying zero and non-zero voting values, which is used in many methods for extracting endpoints.

The collinear pixels and image noise all vote for the cells in a peak region. The voting values from collinear pixels are considered as foreground, while the voting

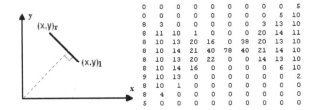

Fig. 4. Left endpoint and right endpoint

ρ	144	146	148	150	152	154	156	158	160	162	164
24	3	8	6	6	5	3	5	2	4	3	7
22	6	8	6	9	10	8	2	5	4	2	12
20	6	3	6	5	3	3	5	1	2	12	16
18	9	7	4	6	2	1	3	4	1	18	15
16	7	4	3	2	4	3	0	3	20	18	18
14	19	12	8	5	6	5	6	6	20	18	19
12	11	17	5	5	6	5	5	24	23	18	12
10	22	22	20	4	1	6	12	31	22	15	12
8	15	14	27	24	3	5	48	27	23	18	14
6	15	18	15	33	47	61	45	32	17	17	20
4	15	17	28	36	73	99	43	27	21	20	18
2	16	16	22	30	48	5	29	27	24	20	10
0	15	20	18	37	8	7	5	19	21	16	16
-2	17	18	27	21	4	6	6	5	17	15	13
-4	14	22	27	5	6	7	11	9	4	16	15
-6	18	18	13	6	4	4	4	8	7	4	15
-8	13	18	7	7	8	5	5	4	5	2	2
-10	15	11	4	5	5	6	4	2	5	5	2
-12	19	6	7	10	9	8	5	6	5	6	6
-14	6	6	9	6	7	8	8	7	2	4	9
-16	6	6	2	5	5	5	9	5	8	8	5

Fig. 5. Peak region before background separation

values from noise or other pixels are considered as background. A threshold is determined to divide cells in a peak region into background and foreground cells. In each column, a threshold is determined by a maximum inter-class variance method. Thus, background cells are separated. A peak region after background separation is shown in Fig. 6.

3.2 Endpoint Coordinate Computation

Consider foreground cells in the left column of the peak; upside cells are selected to compute the right endpoint and downside cells are selected to compute the

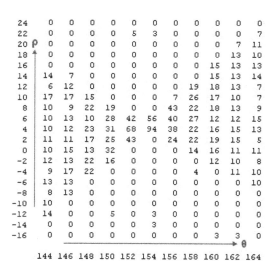

ρ	144	146	148	150	152	154	156	158	160	162	164
24	0	0	0	0	0	0	0	0	0	0	0
22	0	0	0	0	5	3	0	0	0	0	7
20	0	0	0	0	0	0	0	0	0	7	11
18	0	0	0	0	0	0	0	0	0	13	10
16	0	0	0	0	0	0	0	0	15	13	13
14	14	7	0	0	0	0	0	0	15	13	14
12	6	12	0	0	0	0	0	19	18	13	7
10	17	17	15	0	0	0	7	26	17	10	7
8	10	9	22	19	0	0	43	22	18	13	9
6	10	13	10	28	42	56	40	27	12	12	15
4	10	12	23	31	68	94	38	22	16	15	13
2	11	11	17	25	43	0	24	22	19	15	5
0	10	15	13	32	0	0	0	14	16	11	11
-2	12	13	22	16	0	0	0	0	12	10	8
-4	9	17	22	0	0	0	0	4	0	11	10
-6	13	13	0	0	0	0	0	0	0	0	10
-8	8	13	0	0	0	0	0	0	0	0	0
-10	10	0	0	0	0	0	0	0	0	0	0
-12	14	0	0	5	0	3	0	0	0	0	0
-14	0	0	0	0	0	3	0	0	0	0	0
-16	0	0	0	0	0	0	0	0	3	3	0

Fig. 6. Peak region after background separation

left endpoint. While in the right column of a peak, upside cells and downside cells are respectively used to compute right and left endpoint. Using all cell parameters (θ_i, ρ_i) for which the left endpoint votes, a sine curve is fitted.

As discussed above, $\rho/\cos\theta$ and $\tan\theta$ are in a linear relationship. With all these $(\rho_i/\cos\theta_i, \tan\theta_i)$, a linear function is fitted:

$$g : \rho/\cos\theta = g(\tan\theta) \triangleq b_1 \tan\theta + b_0 \tag{5}$$

Endpoint coordinates are then as follows: $x_l = b_0$ and $y_l = b_1$. Similarly, the right endpoint can be computed by fitting cell parameters (ρ_i, θ_i) for which the right votes.

4   Experimental Results

In this section, the proposed peak detection and endpoint extracting methods are applied to a set of simulated data to test the accuracy of line detection, and applied to real world image to verify the performance of line-segment detection.

4.1   Tests with Simulated Images

We generate $M \times N = 200 \times 200$ binary images that contain randomly generated noisy pixels. Endpoint coordinates of one line segment are also produced randomly, and line parameters (θ, ρ) are computed and recorded as ground truth.

We test the methods in term of different counts of noisy pixels, different quantization, or different line thickness. Fig. 7 shows the detection error under ideal conditions. Fig. 8 shows the detection error when parameter quantization, line thickness and image noise are comprehensively considered.

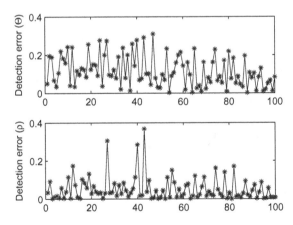

Fig. 7. Test under ideal conditions. Count of noise: 0, parameter quantization: 1, line thickness: 0.

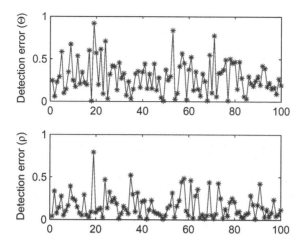

Fig. 8. Comprehensive test. Count of noise: 500, parameter quantization: 2, line thickness: 2.

The detection results from the proposed peak detection method based on minimum entropy (*ME*) are compared with results of a method using smoothing and interpolating (*S&I*) [12], and with results of least-squares fitting (*LSF*). 100 random line segments are tested in terms of the absolute error with respect to the ground truth. Detection results are shown in Fig. 9, where the count of noise is 500, parameter space is quantized as (2,2), and line thickness is 2.

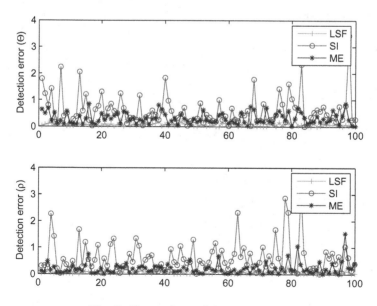

Fig. 9. Comparison of detection errors

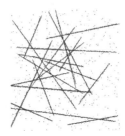

Fig. 10. Line segment detection in simulated images

With the proposed method based on minimum entropy, sub-cell accuracy is achieved. Detection results with the proposed method are close to the results of least-square fitting, even under coarse parameter quantization and image noise.

4.2   Endpoint Tests

A simulated image, which contain 500 random noise pixels and 20 random line segments, is used to test the proposed method. The parameter space is quantized with $(\Delta\theta, \Delta\rho) = (2, 2)$ and thickness of line segment is 2. Detection results are shown in Fig. 10. All line segments are detected in spit of image noise, coarse parameter quantization and line thickness.

4.3   Real World Tests

We use crystalline graphite fibre images [31] to test the proposed method for extracting line segments. A detection result is shown in Fig. 11; in this image only the 50 longest line segments are extracted. Although these fibre images are very complicated, many line segments are detected by identifying valid cells and fitting a sine curve with more cells parameters.

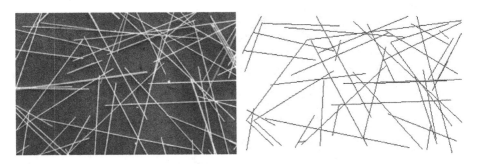

Fig. 11. Line segment detection for fibre image. *Left*: Original image. *Right*: Detected line segments.

5   Conclusions

A line segment detection method with Hough transform is proposed. The method for the distance and angle detection is based on minimum entropy and has been compared with other methods. Using fitting and interpolating techniques based the minimum entropy, the Hough transform can yield very accurate peak parameters that are close to results from least-squares fitting for simulated images. The method for endpoints extraction applies fitting a sine curve. It is more accurate and robust compared with methods that solve simultaneous equations.

Acknowledgments. The authors would like to thank Reinhard Klette for his comments and kind support. The first author thanks Jiangsu Overseas Research & Training Program for University Prominent Young & Middle-aged Teachers and Preside for granting a scholarship to visit and undertake research at The University of Auckland.

References

1. Hough, P.V.C.: Methods and means for recognizing complex patterns, U.S. Patent 3.069.654 (1962)
2. Duda, R.O., Hart, P.E.: Use of the Hough transformation to detect lines and curves in pictures. Comm. ACM. 15(1), 11–15 (1972)
3. Ballard, D.H.: Generalizing the Hough transform to detect arbitrary shapes. Pattern Recognition 13(2), 111–122 (1981)
4. Zhang, M.: On the discretization of parameter domain in Hough transform. In: Proc. IEEE ICPR 1996, pp. 527–531 (1996)
5. Lam, W.C.Y., Lam, L.T.S., Yuen, S.Y., Leung, D.N.K.: An analysis on quantizing the hough space. Pattern Recognition Letters 15(10), 1127–1135 (1994)
6. Van Veen, T.M., Groen, F.C.A.: Discretization errors in the Hough transform. Pattern Recognition 14, 137–145 (1981)
7. Ji, J., Chen, G., Sun, L.: A novel Hough transform method for line detection by enhancing accumulator array. Pattern Recognition Letters 32(11), 1503–1510 (2011)
8. Guo, S., Pridmore, T., Kong, Y., Zhang, X.: An improved Hough transform voting scheme utilizing surround suppression. Pattern Recognition Letters 30, 1241–1252 (2009)
9. Fernandes, L.A.F., Oliveira, M.: Real-time line detection through an improved Hough transform voting scheme. Pattern Recognition 41(1), 299–314 (2008)
10. Palmer, P.L., Kittler, J., Petrou, M.: An optimizing line finder using a Hough transform algorithm. Computer Vision Image Understanding 67(1), 1–23 (1997)
11. Niblack, W., Petkovic, D.: On improving the accuracy of the Hough transform: Theory, simulation, and experiments. In: IEEE Conf. Computer Vision Pattern Recognition, pp. 574–579 (1988)
12. Niblack, W., Petkovic, D.: On improving the accuracy of the Hough transform. Machine Vision Applications 3, 87–106 (1990)
13. Du, S., Tu, C., Sun, M.: High accuracy Hough transform based on butterfly symmetry. Electron Letters 48(4), 199–201 (2012)

14. Shannon, C.E.: The mathematical theory of communication. The Bell System Tech. J. 27, 379–423 (1948)
15. Titterington, D.M.: The maximum entropy method for data analysis. Nature 312(38), 1–382 (1984)
16. Yuan, L., Kesavan, H.K.: Minimum entropy and information measure. IEEE Trans. Syst., Man, Cybern. 28(3), 488–491 (1998)
17. Watanabe, S.: Pattern recognition as a quest for minimum entropy. Pattern Recognition 13(5), 381–387 (1981)
18. Rosten, E., Loveland, R.: Camera distortion self-calibration using the plumb-line constraint and minimal hough entropy. Machine Vision Applications 22(1), 77–85 (2011)
19. Zhu, D., Wang, L., Yu, Y., Tao, Q., Zhu, Z.: Robust ISAR Range Alignment via Minimizing the Entropy of the Average Range Profile. IEEE Geoscience Remote Sens. Lett. 6(2), 204–208 (2009)
20. Brink, A.: Using spatial information as an aid to maximum entropy image threshold selection. Pattern Recognition Letters 17(1), 29–36 (1996)
21. Abutaleb, A.S.: Automatic thresholding of gray-level pictures using two dimensional entropy. Computer Vision Graphics and Image Processing 47, 22–32 (1989)
22. Yamato, J., Ishii, I., Makino, H.: Highly accurate segment detection using Hough transformation. Systems and Computers in Japan 21(1), 68–77 (1990)
23. von Gioi, R.G., Jakubowicz, J., Morel, J.M., Randall, G.: On Straight Line Segment Detection. Journal of Mathematical Imaging and Vision 32(3), 313–347 (2008)
24. Nguyen, T.T., Pham, X.D., Jeon, J.: An improvement of the standard Hough transform to detect line segments. In: Proc. IEEE Int. Conf. Ind. Technology, pp. 1–6 (2008)
25. Furukawa, Y., Shinagawa, Y.: Accurate and robust line segment extraction by analyzing distribution around peaks in Hough space. Computer Vision Image Understanding 92(1), 1–25 (2003)
26. Du, S., Tu, C., van Wyk, B.J., Ochola, E.O., Chen, Z.: Measuring straight line segments using HT butterflies. PLoS One 7(3), e33790 (2012)
27. Atiquzzaman, M., Akhtar, M.W.: Complete line segment description using the hough transform. Image Vision Comp 12(5), 267–273 (1994)
28. Atiquzzaman, M., Akhtar, M.W.: A robust Hough transform technique for complete line segment description. Real-Time Imaging 1(6), 419–426 (1995)
29. Kamat, V., Ganesan, S.: A Robust Hough Transform Technique for Description of Multiple Line Segments in an Image. In: Proceedings of 1998 International Conference on Image Processing (ICIP 1998), vol. 1, pp. 216–220 (1998)
30. Kamat-Sadekar, V., Ganesan, S.: Complete description of multiple line segments using the Hough transform. Image and Vision Computing 16(9-10), 597–613 (1998)
31. http://www.ilo.orgoshencimagesstoriesenlargedPart01RES_imgsRES200F2

Easy-to-Use and Accurate Calibration of RGB-D Cameras from Spheres

Aaron Staranowicz[1], Garrett R. Brown[1], Fabio Morbidi[2], and
Gian-Luca Mariottini[1]

[1] Univ. of Texas at Arlington, CSE Dept.
500 UTA Boulevard, Arlington, TX 76019, USA
[2] Inria Grenoble Rhône-Alpes
655 Avenue de l'Europe, Montbonno t, France

Abstract. RGB-Depth (or RGB-D) cameras are increasingly being
adopted for real-world applications, especially in areas of healthcare and
at-home monitoring. As for any other sensor, and since the manufacturer's parameters (e.g., focal length) might change between models,
calibration is necessary to increase the camera's sensing accuracy. In this
paper, we present a novel RGB-D camera-calibration algorithm that is
easy-to-use even for non-expert users at their home; our method can
be used for any arrangement of RGB and depth sensors, and only requires that a spherical object (e.g., a basketball) is moved in front of
the camera for a few seconds. A robust image-processing pipeline automatically detects the moving sphere and rejects noise and outliers in
the image data. A novel closed-form solution is presented to accurately
compute an initial set of calibration parameters which are then utilized
in a nonlinear minimization stage over all the camera parameters including lens distortion. Extensive simulation and experimental results show
the accuracy and robustness to outliers of our algorithm with respect to
existing checkerboard-based methods. Furthermore, an *RGB-D Calibration Toolbox* for MATLAB is made freely available for the entire research
community.

Keywords: RGB-Depth Cameras, Camera Calibration, Kinect, Computer Vision.

1 Introduction

RGB-Depth (or RGB-D) cameras consist of an *RGB* and a *depth* sensor that
capture color images along with per-pixel depth information (depth map) [1,2].
These features have promoted the wide adoption of low-cost RGB-D cameras
(e.g., the Microsoft *Kinect* [1]) in numerous at-home applications, such as body
tracking [3,4], gait monitoring for tele-rehabilitation [5,6], tracking of facial
expressions [7], object and gesture recognition [8,9,10].

All the aforementioned applications require the precise knowledge of the *RGB-
D camera-calibration parameters*, i.e., the relative position and orientation of its
on-board RGB and depth sensors, as well as of their parameters (focal lengths,

R. Klette, M. Rivera, and S. Satoh (Eds.): PSIVT 2013, LNCS 8333, pp. 265–278, 2014.
© Springer-Verlag Berlin Heidelberg 2014

Manufacturer Calibration   Our Calibration

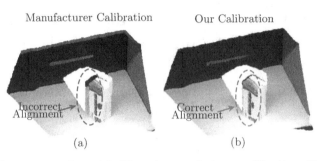

(a)   (b)

Fig. 1. *(a)* Scene perception with Kinect's manufacturer calibration. The texture is not correctly aligned with the 3-D point cloud; *(b)* Improved scene perception after our RGB-D camera calibration.

principal points, and lens-distortion [11]). As shown in Fig 1, calibrating RGB-D cameras is indeed essential to improve the sensing accuracy of these cameras since the calibration parameters can differ in each model from the manufacturer's settings.

Calibrating RGB-D cameras still represents an open challenge, especially for what concerns accuracy and ease of use for non-expert users at their home. Some approaches [12, 13] require the impractical use of an external source of infrared light (e.g., a halogen lamp). Jung et al. [14] use a custom-made large wood panel with tens of circular holes, which requires the user to perform an initial time-consuming manual correspondence association of the holes' centers between each RGB and depth image pair. Other methods [15, 16, 17, 18] have simply extended standard corner-based calibration methods to RGB-D cameras; however, these methods are not robust to outliers, and are not accurate as they make use of only a small number of corners detected in the depth image. Furthermore, they require the user to provide an initial estimate of the calibration parameters which might not be available for other RGB and depth-sensor arrangements other than the Kinect. The existing ROS Kinect-calibration toolbox [13, 19] can only be used with the Microsoft sensor, and it cannot be used to calibrate sensors (e.g., Time of Flight (ToF) cameras) that do not provide an infrared (IR) image. Furthermore, the toolbox is not user-friendly and the calibration must be performed offline since RGB and IR images cannot be simultaneously captured by the Kinect.

In this paper, we present a novel method for the calibration of RGB-D cameras that is accurate and easy-to-use even for non-expert users. Our method is *practical* since the user is only required to move a spherical object (e.g., a basketball) in front of the camera. No geometrical knowledge about the size of the basketball is required and an image-processing pipeline has been designed that automatically detects the spherical object in both the RGB image (as an ellipse) and the depth map (as a sphere), while discarding spurious data (outliers).

Our calibration algorithm is *accurate* since it relies on a novel least-squares (LS) method that is used to precisely initialize a nonlinear minimization stage over all the camera parameters including lens distortion and to remove outliers

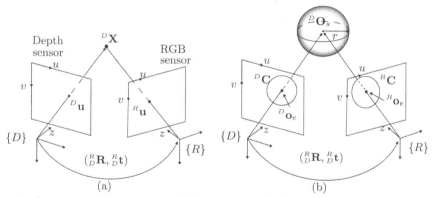

Fig. 2. *(a) Imaging model of an RGB-D camera: (left)*, depth sensor $\{D\}$; *(right)*, RGB sensor, $\{R\}$; $({}_{D}^{R}\mathbf{R}, {}_{D}^{R}\mathbf{t})$ is the 3-D rigid-body motion between the two sensors. *(b)* A *sphere* with radius r and center ${}^{D}\mathbf{O}_s$ (in $\{D\}$) is projected onto the RGB-camera image plane at an image conic, ${}^{R}\mathbf{C}$, (in general, an ellipse). The *centers of each ellipse*, i.e., ${}^{R}\mathbf{o}_e$ and ${}^{D}\mathbf{o}_e$ are the inputs of our calibration method.

by means of RANSAC [20]. This represents a significant improvement over existing algorithms (such as [15,18]) that require initial values for these calibration parameters to be provided by the user. It is also worth emphasizing here that the overall accuracy of our method is due to the adoption of spheres as calibration objects. In fact, the sensor noise in the RGB and depth images is minimized by the adoption of sphere- and ellipse-fitting algorithms in the image processing pipeline.

Our approach is *widely applicable*, and it can be potentially used to calibrate depth- and RGB-sensor pairs in *any* 3-D relative configuration (i.e., not necessarily pointing in the same direction as in the Microsoft Kinect). A new calibration toolbox for MATLAB, called *RGB-D Calibration Toolbox*, has been developed and made available on the Internet[1] for the entire research community.

The rest of this paper is organized as follows: Sect. 2 reviews some basic facts on pinhole camera modeling and image projection of spheres. Sect. 3 describes our calibration algorithm, and in Sect. 4 numerical and real-world experimental results are presented and discussed. Finally, in Sect. 5, conclusions are drawn and some promising subjects of future research are outlined.

2 Basics

2.1 RGB-D Camera Model

Figure 2(a) shows the general RGB-D imaging model considered in this paper. Under the pinhole camera model [11], a generic 3-D point in the *depth-sensor*

---

[1] http://ranger.uta.edu/%7Egianluca/dcct/

*frame, $\{D\}$, $^D\mathbf{X} \triangleq [X^D, Y^D, Z^D]^T$, is projected at a pixel point $^R\mathbf{u} \triangleq [u^R, v^R]^T$
on the image plane of the RGB-sensor frame $\{R\}$*, according to:

$$^R\lambda\, ^R\widetilde{\mathbf{u}} = \,^R\mathbf{K}\, [^R_D\mathbf{R} \mid\, ^R_D\mathbf{t}]\, ^D\widetilde{\mathbf{X}}, \tag{1}$$

where the tilde indicates the extension to homogeneous coordinates of a vector,
and $^R\lambda$ is a scale factor, chosen so that the last coordinate of the term on the
right-hand side of (1) is equal to 1. The intrinsic calibration matrices, $^R\mathbf{K}$ and
$^D\mathbf{K}$, of the RGB and of the depth sensors are defined as:

$$^R\mathbf{K} \triangleq \begin{bmatrix} f_u^R & s^R & u_0^R \\ 0 & f_v^R & v_0^R \\ 0 & 0 & 1 \end{bmatrix}, \quad ^D\mathbf{K} \triangleq \begin{bmatrix} f_u^D & s^D & u_0^D \\ 0 & f_v^D & v_0^D \\ 0 & 0 & 1 \end{bmatrix}, \tag{2}$$

where f_u and f_v represent the focal lengths (in pixels) in both image-axes directions; $[u_0, v_0]^T$ is the principal point in pixels, and s is the skew factor [11]. Note
that the superscripts D and R have been dropped since the previous expressions
equally apply to both reference frames.

The depth sensor typically outputs a so-called *depth map*, i.e., a set of image
points along with their corresponding depth value (in meters) on the z-axis. Each
depth-map feature is thus defined as $^D\mathbf{u} \triangleq [u^D, v^D, Z^D]^T$. Differently from an
RGB camera, $^D\mathbf{u}$ can be used to uniquely compute the corresponding point in
3-D coordinates, $^D\mathbf{X}$, as:

$$^D\widetilde{\mathbf{X}} = \begin{bmatrix} ^D\mathbf{K}^{-1} & \mathbf{0}_{3\times 1} \\ \mathbf{0}_{1\times 3} & 1 \end{bmatrix} ^D\bar{\mathbf{u}}, \tag{3}$$

where $\mathbf{0}_{3\times 1}$ denotes a 3×1 matrix of zeros and the upper bar in $^D\bar{\mathbf{u}}$ indicates a
vector obtained from $^D\mathbf{u}$ as follows:

$$^D\bar{\mathbf{u}} \triangleq \left[u^D Z^D, v^D Z^D, Z^D, 1 \right]^T. \tag{4}$$

2.2   Image Projection of a Sphere

A sphere with 3-D center, $^D\mathbf{O}_s$, and radius r, (see Fig. 2(b)) can be algebraically
represented by [11]:

$$^D\mathbf{Q} = \begin{bmatrix} \mathbf{I}_3 & -^D\mathbf{O}_s \\ -^D\mathbf{O}_s^T & ^D\mathbf{O}_s^T\, ^D\mathbf{O}_s - r^2 \end{bmatrix}, \tag{5}$$

where $\mathbf{I}_3$ denotes the 3×3 identity matrix. In general, a sphere $^D\mathbf{Q}$ projects in
the image plane at an ellipse, and its projection in the RGB image at the ellipse
$^R\mathbf{C}$ is given by [21]:

$$^R\mathbf{C}^* = \,^R_D\mathbf{P}\, ^D\mathbf{Q}^*\, ^R_D\mathbf{P}^T \quad \text{where} \quad ^R_D\mathbf{P} \triangleq \,^R\mathbf{K}[^R_D\mathbf{R}|^R_D\mathbf{t}], \tag{6}$$

being $^R\mathbf{C}^* = \text{adj}(^R\mathbf{C})$ (the adjugate of $^R\mathbf{C}$) the dual conic of $^R\mathbf{C}$, and $^D\mathbf{Q}^* =
\text{adj}(^D\mathbf{Q})$, (note that the adjugate is equal to the inverse if the matrix is in-
vertible). The conics $^R\mathbf{C}$ and $^D\mathbf{C}$ will play a key role in the RGB-D camera-
calibration algorithm described in the next section.

3   Joint RGB-Depth Camera Calibration

3.1   Overview

During calibration we assume that the user moves the spherical calibration object in front of the RGB-D camera. *Feature-Extraction* pipeline detects and tracks in real time the two ellipses $^R C$ and $^D C$ corresponding to the projection of the sphere in both the RGB and depth sensor, respectively.

Given a set of ellipses acquired over a certain time frame, our goal is to compute an estimate of the intrinsic parameters $^D K$ and $^R K$ (plus the radial lens-distortion parameters, k_c^D and k_c^R), as well as of the extrinsic parameters $_D^R R$ and $_D^R t$. We do this in two steps: first, an initial and accurate least-squares solution is obtained with a novel formulation that leverages all the detected (image) centers $^R o_e$ and $^D o_e$ of the two ellipses. Second, the parameters and inliers estimated in the previous phase are used to provide a refined (and final) estimate of all the camera-calibration parameters.

It is worth pointing out here the novelty and importance of the least-square approach to get an initial and accurate estimate of the camera parameters, while almost all of the state-of-the-art calibration methods require a separate (thus sub-optimal) estimate. Sometimes, the manufacturer's calibration parameters are used as initial values (e.g., the Kinect). However, these are not available for general RGB- and depth-sensor arrangements (e.g., Time-of-flight camera and webcam). In addition, the calibration parameters can vary significantly among different models (cf. Fig. 1(a)).

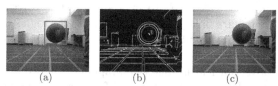

Fig. 3. *RGB Feature-Detection Pipeline: (a)* A background subtraction is used to limit the search image space. *(b)* Canny-edge detector is used to find image edges; upper and lower bounds are used in Hough voting to find the edges of the ellipse. *(c)* RANSAC-based ellipse fitting finally detects the ellipse.

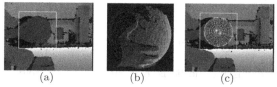

Fig. 4. *Depth Feature Detection Pipeline: (a)* The depth image presents irregular sphere edges: the white box shows the search area obtained with background subtraction. *(b)* RANSAC on point cloud to detect inliers (green) and outliers (red) and to fit the sphere (blue). *(c)* The fitted-sphere center is reprojected on the image (red dot).

3.2   Feature Detection Pipeline

In this phase, the RGB and the depth images are processed to automatically detect and track the two ellipses, $^R\mathbf{C}$ and $^D\mathbf{C}$, which correspond to the projection of the sphere on the image planes of the two sensors. In our implementation, the user is simply required to move the sphere in front of the RGB-D camera. We have observed that tracking one ellipse in each image is more robust than tracking single corner features (e.g., in the case of a checkerboard calibration rig), since our method leverages ellipse and sphere-fitting algorithms that make use of *all* the observed points on an ellipse to minimize the image noise while removing potential outliers.

For the detection of the ellipse $^R\mathbf{C}$ in the RGB image, a background subtraction algorithm is first used to determine a search area for the moving sphere (see Fig. 3(a)). Then a Canny-edge detector [22] is applied to that image portion, and a circular Hough transform [23] is used to automatically obtain the pixel coordinates of those points lying on the ellipse (as in Fig. 3(b)). Finally, a RANSAC-based ellipse-fitting algorithm [24, 25] is used to estimate the parameters of the ellipse $^R\mathbf{C}$, such as its center $^R\mathbf{o}_e$ (see Fig. 3(c)).

For the detection of the ellipse $^D\mathbf{C}$ in the depth image, adopting the same strategy for the RGB image would not work, as the edges of the sphere in the depth image are highly irregular (see Fig. 4(a)). Our approach consists of first using a random $^D\mathbf{K}$ to reproject in 3-D with (3) those depth-image points $^D\mathbf{u}$ within a search area around the sphere detected with background subtraction. Note that the random $^D\mathbf{K}$ does not distort, but only scales the resulting 3-D point cloud. We then use a Hough voting scheme to detect which 3-D points belong to the sphere, and RANSAC to fit a sphere. The corresponding image points in the depth map are finally deemed as inliers (cf., Fig. 4(b)). Finally, the center of the sphere is reprojected on the depth image thus obtaining the center of the ellipse (red dot in Fig. 4(c)).

As mentioned above, our feature-detection pipeline has two major advantages when compared to the detection and tracking of corner features in checkerboard-based methods [16,17,14,13]. First, because of the Hough voting and the RANSAC fitting, our feature-extraction phase reduces noise in the images and is robust to outliers (such as user's hand or fingers while holding the spherical object). Second, the feature-detection procedure is *completely automatic* and *robust* to severe occlusions that can often occur in a non-lab setting.

3.3   Initial Least-Squares Solution

Differently from the existing methods, our calibration strategy does not require the intervention of an expert user to initialize the RGB-D calibration parameters. We obtain an initial estimate of $^R\mathbf{K}$ by using the state-of-the-art method described in [26] which uses the same RGB images obtained from Sect. 3.2. Our novel least-squares method accurately estimates the camera parameters $^D\mathbf{K}$, $^R_D\mathbf{R}$, and $^R_D\mathbf{t}$, by using the extracted ellipse centers.

By substituting (3) in (1), and by using the ellipse center positions $^D\mathbf{o}_e$ and $^R\mathbf{o}_e$ (pixels), it is straightforward to obtain the following expression[2]:

$$\left[^R\mathbf{K}^{-1}\,{}^R\widetilde{\mathbf{o}}_e\right]_\times \underbrace{\left[^R_D\mathbf{R}\,{}^D\mathbf{K}^{-1} \mid {}^R_D\mathbf{t}\right]}_{^R_D\mathbf{M}} {}^D\bar{\mathbf{o}}_e = \mathbf{0}_{3\times1}, \tag{7}$$

where $^D\bar{\mathbf{o}}_e \in I\!\!R^4$ is obtained from $^D\mathbf{o}_e \in I\!\!R^3$ as the $^D\bar{\mathbf{u}}$ in (4). We have empirically observed that the sample mean of the z-coordinates of the visible points on a sphere, can be successfully used as Z^D in $^D\bar{\mathbf{o}}_e$.

The interesting fact about (7) is that this expression can be solved as a standard direct-linear-transformation (DLT) method [11]. A closed-form estimate of $^R_D\mathbf{M}$ is then obtained from (7) from at least six RGB-depth image pairs of a single sphere. Once the $^R_D\mathbf{M}$ matrix has been estimated and normalized (so that $^R_D\mathbf{M}_{3,3} = 1$), its fourth column coincides with $^R_D\mathbf{t}$, while $^D\mathbf{K}$ and $^R_D\mathbf{R}$ are easily obtained from a QR factorization of its left-upper 3×3 submatrix.

Our DLT solution uses RANSAC to remove outliers (e.g., blurred images). Degenerate cases in solving the DLT problem [11] occur when all the spheres' centers lie on a common plane or line. While this case is quite rare in practice, we address this possible problem by checking the rank of the homogeneous system used by DLT to discard those ellipses sampled at each RANSAC iteration.

3.4   Nonlinear Minimization Step

In this phase, we use the initial estimates as inputs to a nonlinear-minimization procedure to obtain refined Maximum-Likelihood (ML) estimates of *all* the calibration parameters (intrinsic, extrinsic, and lens distortion).

Consider the pinhole camera model in (1); by assuming that each point in $\{R\}$ follows a Gaussian distribution with the ground-truth position as its mean and measurement-noise covariance $\mathbf{\Phi}$, the log-likelihood function can be written as:

$$\mathcal{L}_1 = -\frac{1}{2N}\sum_{i=1}^{N}\boldsymbol{\epsilon}_i^T\mathbf{\Phi}^{-1}\boldsymbol{\epsilon}_i, \tag{8}$$

where

$$\boldsymbol{\epsilon}_i = {}^R\widetilde{\mathbf{o}}_e^i - \frac{1}{{}^R\lambda_i}L(\mathbf{k}_c^R){}^R\mathbf{K}\left[^R_D\mathbf{R}\mid{}^R_D\mathbf{t}\right]{}^D\widetilde{\mathbf{O}}_s^i, \tag{9}$$

where $^R\lambda_i$ is an unknown scale factor. Note that $^D\widetilde{\mathbf{O}}_s^i$ is the center of the i−th sphere obtained from both the depth-map points and the current estimate of $^D\mathbf{K}$, by using our sphere-fitting RANSAC algorithm described in Sect. 3.2, and that the radial-distortion function $L(\mathbf{k}_c^R)$ is as described in [11].

Another source of useful information comes from the conic reprojection constraint in (6). As such, and similarly to the previous derivations, its log-likelihood can be written as:

$$\mathcal{L}_2 = -\frac{1}{2N}\sum_{i=1}^{N}\frac{1}{\left(\sigma_q^i\right)^2}\|{}^R\mathbf{C}_i^* - {}^R_D\mathbf{P}^D\mathbf{Q}_i^*{}^R_D\mathbf{P}\|_F^2, \tag{10}$$

---

[2] $[\mathbf{x}]_\times$ denotes the skew-symmetric matrix associated to a vector $\mathbf{x} \in I\!\!R^3$.

where $\|\cdot\|_F$ denotes the Frobenius norm and the dual quadric $^D\mathbf{Q}_i^*$ is calculated with (5) by using the estimated 3-D center, $^D\widetilde{\mathbf{O}}_s^i$, and radius, r_i, of the i-th sphere determined as described in Sect. 3.2. As found in [18], the variance $\left(\sigma_q^i\right)^2$ has been chosen to be a quadratic function of the distance to each sphere Z^D, which in our experiments revealed effective. The radial distortion function $L(\mathbf{k}_c^D)$ is used here for the reprojection error of the ellipse center.

Combining (8) and (10) together, we maximize the overall log-likelihood as:

$$\underset{^D\mathbf{K},\mathbf{k}_c^D,^R\mathbf{K},\mathbf{k}_c^R,_D^R\mathbf{R},_D^R\mathbf{t}}{\operatorname{argmin}} \rho_1\mathcal{L}_1 + \rho_2\mathcal{L}_2, \tag{11}$$

where ρ_1 and ρ_2 are positive weighting parameters.

4   Simulation and Experimental Results

4.1   Simulation Results

We realized an simulation scenario to assess the accuracy of our method against the ground-truth over a large set of realizations. In this scenario, a set of spheres are positioned in front of the camera, and are evenly spaced of 25 cm within a cubical volume. This arrangement was only selected to make our validation procedure repeatable and systematic: comparable results could be obtained with spheres randomly placed within the same cubical volume.

In the first test, we examined the performance of our method in the case of increasing image noise (over 100 iterations for each noise level), while observing 90 spheres. A zero-mean white Gaussian noise with increasing power was added to the RGB and to the depth images. In particular, the pixel standard deviations in both images, σ_p^R and σ_p^D, were chosen in the range from 0 to 1 pixels. A noise on the depth measurements was also simulated; in order to match our empirical observations of Kinect's accuracy, this standard deviation σ_m^D [m] has been chosen as a quadratic function of the distance of each sphere from the camera. In this first test, we also compared the performance of our calibration method against Zhang's method [16]. For testing Zhang's algorithm, we created twelve 9×9 calibration checkerboard patterns observed from 21 different viewpoints. Note that an initial comparison for different Kinect calibration methods was performed in an earlier work [27].

Figs. 5(a)-5(f) report the comparison between our method and Zhang's method for an increasing noise power. In particular, Figs. 5(a)-5(b) show the standard deviation for each of the translation error-vector components, $\mathbf{e} = [e_x, \ e_y, \ e_z]^T = _D^R\hat{\mathbf{t}} - _D^R\mathbf{t}$, for both our and Zhang's algorithms, respectively. We omitted the plots of the mean errors which were all around zero, thus indicating unbiased estimates. As the figures show, our method results in an error lower than 1 mm on each axis, whereas the error for Zhang's method is about 7 cm for the image noise equal to 1.5 pixels. Similarly, Figs. 5(c)-5(d) report the standard deviation of the estimated rotation between the RGB and depth cameras (roll-pitch-yaw angle errors in degrees) for our method and Zhang's, respectively. In this case our estimates are almost three orders of magnitude lower than Zhang's. These results clearly

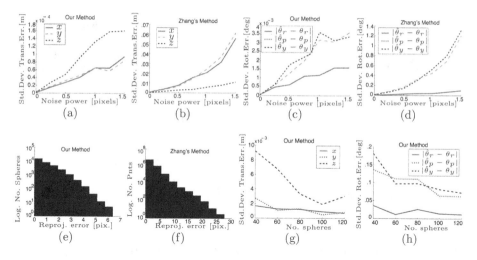

Fig. 5. *Simulation results*: *(a)-(d)* Translation and rotation estimation errors (standard deviation) with increasing noise power for our method (*(a)* and *(c)*) and Zhang's (*(b)* and *(d)*). *(e)-(f)* Distribution of the reprojection errors obtained using our method and Zhang's method (note the different scale on the vertical axis). *(g)-(h)* Translation and rotation errors for an increasing number of spheres.

indicate the power of our method: as expected, the conic fitting and the robust estimators of our method have the capacity to decrease the overall sensitivity to noise in the data, and allow a final accurate estimate. Figs. 5(e)-5(f) report the distribution of the pixel reprojection error when $\sigma_p^R = \sigma_p^D = 1$ pixel for 100 realizations. Our calibration method has a reprojection error always lower than 6 pixels while Zhang's method achieves a higher reprojection error (27 pixels).

In the second test, we studied the influence of an increasing number of spheres (from 40 to 120) on the estimated RGB-D calibration parameters. The standard deviation of the Gaussian image noises was fixed to $\sigma_p^R = \sigma_p^D = 1$ pixel. For each given number of spheres, we considered 100 realizations. Figs. 5(g)-5(h) illustrate the results as standard deviation of the translation and angular error, and show that 40 image-pairs of a sphere are generally sufficient to get a very accurate estimate (e.g., std. deviation lower than 1 mm for translation) of the calibration parameters.

4.2   Experimental Results

We used the Microsoft Kinect to compare the accuracy of our calibration method against Zhang's method [16], Herrera's method [17], and the Robot Operating System (ROS) Kinect calibration toolbox [19]. As detailed below, a ground truth set of calibration parameters was obtained by means of the Stereo Camera MATLAB Calibration Toolbox (CalTechTbx) [28]. We will first give a brief overview of the aforementioned calibration methods and describe their pros and cons. Then, we will present the calibration results.

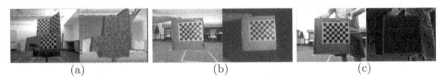

(a)   (b)   (c)

Fig. 6. Feature extraction for: *(a)* Zhang's Method (RGB + Depth); *(b)* ROS Calib Tbx. (RGB + IR); *(c)* Herrera's Method (RGB + Disparity).

Our Calibration: For our method, we subsampled 130 RGB-D image pairs of a basketball (from 1 to 4 meters) from a video of approximately 30 seconds by running the feature-extraction procedure described in Sect. 3.2. We randomly subsampled every 7th video frame. Any spurious frames would be discarded in Sect. 3.3.

Overview of the Other Calibration Methods: The aforementioned methods differ from our calibration method since they rely on checkerboard calibration panels that must be simultaneously observed by both the RGB and depth sensor.

Each method uses a set of RGB images of the checkerboard to estimate $^R\mathbf{K}$. The estimation process is very similar among all these methods and rely on an accurate and automatic corner-extraction algorithm. However, note that Zhang's method cannot take advantage of this automatic algorithm and it required manual user intervention since 3 checkerboards must be simultaneously observed as a calibration scene. Also, these methods require the user to accurately specify the geometric properties of the checkerboard (e.g., size of the squares, the number of squares, etc.).

The major difference among these methods is in the acquisition and treatment of data from the depth sensor. Zhang's method requires the user to select a certain number of points on each checkerboard plane in the depth-map. These points are then converted to 3-D and used to extract the normal to each plane. Herrera's method is similar to Zhang's method, however, Herrera's method relies on the disparity image which is used to estimate a depth-map. Both the ROS toolbox and CalTechTbx require the infrared (IR) image from the Kinect, and then detect corner features in them as done for the RGB. Note that, in order to ensure the checkerboard is clearly visible in the IR image, an external (halogen) light must be used to enhance the contrast of the image and the Kinect's IR projector must be covered. Also note that these methods are mostly designed around the Kinect, since the IR image might not be available from other depth sensors (e.g., ToF cameras). Furthermore, Kinect does not allow simultaneous acquisition of IR and RGB; as a result, their calibration phase is not real time, and it requires slow asynchronous data collection. All these drawbacks make these methods clearly not usable by non-expert users.

Discussion: For Zhang's method in [16], we considered a set of 14 RGB-D image pairs of 3 rigidly-attached checkerboard panels (see Fig. 6(a)). The method requires an initial guess for $^D\mathbf{K}$; for that, we used the preset values in [16]. For Herrera's method in [17], we captured a set of 60 RGB-Disparity image pairs

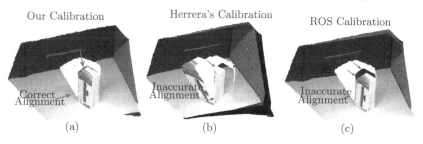

Our Calibration   Herrera's Calibration   ROS Calibration

Correct Alignment   Inaccurate Alignment   Inaccurate Alignment

(a)   (b)   (c)

Fig. 7. *Experiment Results*: Each image is a colorized 3-D point cloud based on each algorithm's estimated calibration parameters. *(a)* Our Calibration. *(b)* Herrera's Calibration. *(c)* ROS Calibration.

of a single checkerboard (see Fig. 6(b)). For both the CalTechTbx in [28] and ROS's method [19], we captured a set of 60 RGB-IR image pairs (see Fig. 6(c)). Note that while the number of images used by each method are different (e.g., our method uses 130 image pairs while Zhang's method uses 14 image pairs), the actual *number of measurements* is lower in our case. In fact, our method considers each image of a sphere as 1 measurement for a total of 130 measurements. Meanwhile Zhang's method considers 3 checkerboard panels per view with a total number of measurements to be ~ 2000 over the whole set of images.

In the first experiment, we qualitatively compared the calibration parameters obtained by our method with those estimated by other approaches. We do this by visualizing a textured point cloud corresponding to the observation of a box on top of a desk. This visualization nicely encompasses the accuracy over *all* the parameters since, the depth image is first mapped to 3-D using $^D\hat{\mathbf{K}}$, and then each 3-D point is expressed in the RGB frame by means of $^R_D\hat{\mathbf{R}}$ and $^R_D\hat{\mathbf{t}}$. Finally, a color is assigned by projecting this map onto the RGB image with $^R\hat{\mathbf{K}}$. Fig. 7 illustrates the results of this process: the accuracy of our calibration method (cf. Fig. 7(a)) is indeed much higher than Herrera's and ROS (cf. Figs. 7(b)-7(c). Zhang's results have not been reported because its large errors in the estimates (e.g., over 1 m. along the y direction) result in a meaningless reprojected map. Note that, this qualitative experiment focuses on the effect of the calibration algorithms; this is why we exclude the manufacturer's calibration (cf. Fig. 1(a)).

A quantitative assessment of the performance of our method is reported in Table 1, which shows the $^R_D\hat{\mathbf{R}}$, $^R_D\hat{\mathbf{t}}$, and $^D\hat{\mathbf{K}}$ produced by each method. The first three columns represent the $^R_D\hat{\mathbf{R}}$ expressed as roll ($\hat{\theta}_r$), pitch ($\hat{\theta}_p$), and yaw ($\hat{\theta}_y$) angles in degrees. The angles calculated from our method and Zhang's method are comparable with those of the CalTechTbx. Herrera's method and the ROS method seem to have a 2 degree bias along the yaw angle with respect to Cal-TechTbx. The fourth through the sixth columns report the three coordinates of $^R_D\hat{\mathbf{t}}$ expressed in meters. Our method and Herrera's method are similar to the CalTechTbx. Zhang's method, as aforementioned, produces a wrong estimate of $^R_D\hat{\mathbf{t}}$ with 1 meter along the y axis. The ROS method is biased along the y direction with 2.8 cm since only 1 RGB-IR image pair can be used by this toolbox to estimate the extrinsic parameters. The last four columns of Table 1 report $^D\hat{\mathbf{K}}$ expressed as $\hat{f}_u$ and $\hat{f}_v$ for the focal length and $\hat{u}_0$ and $\hat{v}_0$ for the principal point.

Table 1. *Experimental Results:* ${}^R_D\hat{\mathbf{R}}$, ${}^R_D\hat{\mathbf{t}}$, and ${}^D\hat{\mathbf{K}}$ for each method

	$\hat{\theta}_r$ [deg.]	$\hat{\theta}_p$ [deg.]	$\hat{\theta}_y$ [deg.]	$\hat{t}_x$ [m.]	$\hat{t}_y$ [m.]	$\hat{t}_z$ [m.]	$\hat{f}_u^D$ [pix.]	$\hat{f}_u^D$ [pix.]	$\hat{u}_0^D$ [pix.]	$\hat{v}_0^D$ [pix.]
CalTechTbx	-0.68	-0.69	0.25	-0.023	-0.000	0.001	585.9	587.0	314.0	253.0
Our	-0.04	-0.12	0.11	-0.025	-0.000	-0.000	555.4	559.0	312.0	250.0
Zhang	-0.11	0.11	0.01	-0.549	1.013	0.010	575.0	575.0	320.0	240.0
Herrera	0.56	0.82	2.13	-0.019	-0.006	0.004	577.4	523.0	317.0	222.8
ROS	0.09	0.00	2.72	-0.029	0.028	0.001	574.6	574.7	329.5	240.2

Zhang's method used a fixed preset ${}^D\hat{\mathbf{K}}$, which is not optimized during the iterations. Also observe that $\hat{f}_u^D$ and $\hat{f}_u^D$ are within 10 pixels for Herrera's method and 30 pixels for our method with respect to the CalTechTbx. The estimate for the distance between the RGB and depth sensors obtained by our method is the closest one to the ground truth, as well as to the ~ 2.5 cm that can be measured on the Kinect.

5   Conclusions

In this work, we have presented a novel and easy-to-use calibration method for RGB-D cameras, which utilizes the image projection of a sphere (observed from multiple viewpoints) as the only calibration object. Our method relies on a novel closed-form solution for the calibration of the depth sensor, which is used to accurately initialize a nonlinear minimization strategy providing a refined estimate of *all* the calibration parameters of the RGB-D camera (including lens distortion). The proposed algorithm is *practical*, since it needs no user intervention in extracting the image features when compared to existing calibration methods, and is *robust* to outliers. Extensive simulation and real-world experiments validate our algorithm. A MATLAB toolbox implementing our method has been developed, and it has been made freely available for the research community.

References

1. Microsoft® Kinect Camera (2011) (Web): http://www.xbox.com/en-US/KINECT.
2. Konolige, K.: Projected texture stereo. In: Proc. IEEE Int. Conf. Robot. Automat. In: Proc. IEEE Int. Conf. Robot. Automat, Anchorage, Alaska, U.S, pp. 148–155 (May 2010)
3. Shotton, J., Fitzgibbon, A., Cook, M., Sharp, T., Finocchio, M., Moore, R., Kipman, A., Blake, A.: Real-time human pose recognition in parts from single depth images. In: Int. Conf. Vis. Pattern Rec. (2011)
4. Newcombe, R., Izadi, S., Hilliges, O., Molyneaux, D., Kim, D., Davison, A., Kohli, P., Shotton, J., Hodges, S., Fitzgibbon, A.: KinectFusion: Real-time dense surface mapping and tracking. In: 10th IEEE Intl. Sym. on Mixed and Aug. Real., pp. 127–136 (2011)

5. Morbidi, F., Ray, C., Mariottini, G.L.: Cooperative active target tracking for heterogeneous robots with application to gait monitoring. In: Proc. IEEE Int. Conf. Intell. Rob. Sys., pp. 3608–3613 (September 2011)

6. Gabel, M., Gilad-Bachrach, R., Renshaw, E., Schuster, A.: Full body gait analysis with kinect. In: Intl. Conf. of the IEEE Eng. in Med. and Bio. Soc. (August 2012)

7. Cai, Q., Gallup, D., Zhang, C., Zhang, Z.: 3D Deformable Face Tracking with a Commodity Depth Camera. In: Daniilidis, K., Maragos, P., Paragios, N. (eds.) ECCV 2010, Part III. LNCS, vol. 6313, pp. 229–242. Springer, Heidelberg (2010)

8. Frank, B., Schmedding, R., Stachniss, C., Teschner, M., Burgard, W.: Learning Deformable Object Models for Mobile Robot Navigation using Depth Cameras and a Manipulation Robot. In: Proc. Robotics: Science and Systems VI's Workshop on RGB-D: Advanced Reasoning with Depth Cameras (June 2010)

9. Lai, K., Bo, L., Ren, X., Fox, D.: A Large-Scale Hierarchical Multi-View RGB-D Object Dataset. In: Proc. IEEE Int. Conf. Robot. Automat, pp. 1817–1824 (May 2011)

10. Ramey, A., Gonzalez-Pacheco, V., Salichs, M.A.: Integration of a low-cost RGB-D sensor in a social robot for gesture recognition. In: Proc. 6th Int. Conf. Human-robot Inter., Lausanne, Switzerland, pp. 229–230 (March 2011)

11. Hartley, R., Zisserman, A.: Multiple View Geometry in Computer Vision, 2nd edn. Cambridge Univ. Press (2003)

12. Burrus, N.: Kinect calibration (Web): http://nicolas.burrus.name/index.php/Research/KinectCalibration

13. Mihelich, P., Konolige, K.: Technical description of kinect calibration (Web): http://www.ros.org/wiki/kinect_calibration/technical

14. Jung, J., Jeong, Y., Park, J., Ha, H., Kim, D.J., Kweon, I.: A Novel 2.5D Pattern for Extrinsic Calibration of ToF and Camera Fusion System. In: Proc. IEEE/RSJ Intl. Conf. on Intel. Rob. Syst., pp. 3290–3296 (September 2011)

15. Smisek, J., Jancosek, M., Pajdla, T.: 3D with kinect. In: IEEE Intl. Conf. on Computer Vision Workshops, pp. 1154–1160 (November 2011)

16. Zhang, C., Zhang, Z.: Calibration between Depth and Color Sensors for Commodity Depth Cameras. In: Intl. Workshop on Hot Topics in 3D, in Conjunction with ICME (July 2011)

17. Herrera, C., Kannala, J., Heikkilä, J.: Joint depth and color camera calibration with distortion correction. IEEE Trans. Pattern Anal. 34(10), 2058–2064 (2012)

18. Khoshelham, K., Elberink, S.O.: Accuracy and Resolution of Kinect Depth Data for Indoor Mapping Applications. Sensors 12(2), 1437–1454 (2012)

19. Mihelich, P.: ROS openni-launch package for Intrin. and Extrin. Kinect Calib (2013), (Web): http://www.ros.org/wiki/openni_launch/Tutorials/

20. Fischler, M.A., Bolles, R.C.: Random Sample Consensus: A Paradigm for Model Fitting with Applications to Image Analysis and Automated Cartography. Commun. ACM 24, 381–395 (1981)

21. Cipolla, R., Giblin, P.: Visual motion of curves and surfaces. Cambridge University Press, New York (2000)

22. Canny, J.: A Computational Approach to Edge Detection. IEEE Trans. Pattern Anal. 8(6), 679–698 (1986)

23. Ballard, D.H.: Generalizing the Hough Transform to Detect Arbitrary Shapes. Pattern Recog. 13(2), 111–122 (1981)

24. Fitzgibbon, A., Pilu, M., Fisher, R.B.: Direct least square fitting of ellipses. IEEE Trans. Pattern Anal. 21(5), 476–480 (1999)

25. Halíř, R., Flusser, J.: Numerically stable direct least squares fitting of ellipses. In: Proc. 6th Int. Conf. Cen. Eur. on Com. Graph. Vis., vol. 21(5), pp. 125–132 (Febraury 1998)
26. Wong, K., Zhang, G., Chen, Z.: A Stratified Approach for Camera Calibration Using Spheres. IEEE Trans. on Img. Proc. 20(2), 305–316 (2011)
27. Staranowicz, A., Mariottini, G.L.: A comparative study of calibration methods for kinect-style cameras. In: Proc. 5th Intl. Conf on PETRAE, pp. 49:1–49:4 (2012)
28. Camera Calibration Toolbox for Matlab (2010) (Web):
http://www.vision.caltech.edu/bouguetj/calib_doc/

Tree Species Classification Based on 3D Bark Texture Analysis

Ahlem Othmani[1,2], Alexandre Piboule[2], Oscar Dalmau[3], Nicolas Lomenie[4],
Said Mokrani[1], and Lew Fock Chong Lew Yan Voon[1]

[1] Laboratory LE2I - UMR CNRS 6306
12 rue de la fonderie, 71200 Le Creusot, France
{ahlem.othmani,lew.lew-yan-voon}@u-bourgogne.fr, mokranicampus@yahoo.fr
[2] Office National des Forêts, Pôle R&D de Nancy
11 rue de l'Ile de Corse, 54000 Nancy, France
alexandre.piboule@onf.fr
[3] Centro de Investigacion en Matematicas A.C
Guanajuato GTO 36000, Mexico
dalmau@cimat.mx
[4] Laboratory LIPADE - EA 2517, Université Paris Descartes
45 rue des Saints-Pères, 75006 Paris, France
nicolas.lomenie@mi.parisdescartes.fr

Abstract. Terrestrial Laser Scanning (TLS) technique is today widely used in ground plots to acquire 3D point clouds from which forest inventory attributes are calculated. In the case of mixed plantings where the 3D point clouds contain data from several different tree species, it is important to be able to automatically recognize the tree species in order to analyze the data of each of the species separately. Although automatic tree species recognition from TLS data is an important problem, it has received very little attention from the scientific community. In this paper we propose a method for classifying five different tree species using TLS data. Our method is based on the analysis of the 3D geometric texture of the bark in order to compute roughness measures and shape characteristics that are fed as input to a Random Forest classifier to classify the tree species. The method has been evaluated on a test set composed of 265 samples (53 samples of each of the 5 species) and the results obtained are very encouraging.

Keywords: Tree species classification, 3D pattern recognition, 3D bark texture analysis, forest inventory.

1 Introduction

TLS is today a well established technique for the acquisition of precise and reliable 3D point clouds from which forest inventory attributes can be calculated at the single tree level [1] [2]. Numerous work on the calculation of the Diameter at Breast Height (DBH), the height of the tree, the volume of wood and so on can be found in the literature. However, to the best of our knowledge not much

R. Klette, M. Rivera, and S. Satoh (Eds.): PSIVT 2013, LNCS 8333, pp. 279–289, 2014.

has been done in the field of tree species recognition at the single tree level although it is a very important issue if one would like to analyze the 3D data of each of the species of a mixed planting separately. One can only find some work concerning tree species recognition using a combination of TLS data and hyperspectral [3] or panoramic images [4][5]. The aim of our work is to recognize tree species based on TLS data only for two major reasons. The first one is to save acquisition time and/or to avoid the use of multiple acquisition systems for capturing different types of datasets. The second reason is to avoid the need for data coregistration and/or fusion techniques in order to simplify data processing.

Using TLS data only, we can only analyze 3D geometrical shape features such as the shape of the leaves, the general shape of the crown and the variations in geometry across the surface of the bark known as the 3D geometric texture of the bark in order to recognize the tree species. In our case, we have to exclude leaf shape analysis because our forest inventory data are mostly acquired during winter when the trees are leafless. The reason is to reduce occlusions due to leaves for more accurate wood volume calculation and also to do the measurement outside the growing period of the trees. The general shape of the canopy is a good characteristic feature of the species of a tree for isolated trees. However, in a forest planting, the management type and the density have a big impact on the canopy. They render it polymorphic so that it is difficult to use the shape of the canopy as a discriminating criterion for tree species recognition. Finally, the bark is probably the most discriminating feature of the species even if it is subject to changes during the tree's life because of age, injuries and modified growth pattern due to environmental disturbances.

Fig. 1 illustrates the 3D geometric texture characteristics of the bark of the five most important tree species that we have to recognize. One can notice that each of the five tree species has a distinguishable 3D geometric bark texture characteristic. The beech has a relatively smooth surface, the spruce is less smooth compared to the beech and it has circular scars, the pine and the oak are rough with vertical strips but the growth pattern is different, and the hornbeam is smooth with an undulating texture.

hornbeam   oak   spruce   beech   pine

Fig. 1. 3D point clouds of the five tree species

We thus propose a method that analyzes the 3D geometric texture of the bark in order to classify and recognize the tree species. For the analysis a 30 cm long segment of the tree trunk at about 1.3 m from the ground (breast height) called a patch is considered. 30 cm is a good trade-off between a small patch for rapid processing times and a long enough segment that contains sufficient texture patterns for recognition.

Our method consists of several steps. Firstly, a 3D deviation map is computed from the 3D point cloud of the 30cm long segment of the tree trunk at breast height. The first step is described in details in section 2. Secondly, the 3D deviation map is transformed into a 2D deviation map or height map that is next segmented in order to reveal characteristic shape features of the tree species. The second step is presented in section 3. Finally, classification features are computed from both the 2D deviation map and the segmented 2D deviation map and fed as input to a Random Forest classifier for tree species classification. The classification features and the selection of the most pertinent features are presented in section 4. In section 5, we describe the test set used to evaluate our method and discuss about the classification results obtained before concluding in section 6.

2   3D Deviation Map of the Tree Bark

We define the 3D geometric texture of a 3D surface as the local variations of the original meshed surface denoted by M_o with respect to a smoothed version of the same meshed surface denoted by M_s as illustrated in Fig. 2 for some tree trunk segments.

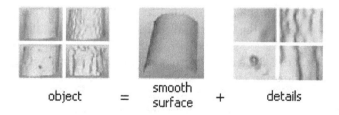

object   =   smooth surface   +   details

Fig. 2. 3D geometric texture model

To extract the 3D geometric texture of a patch, we first apply a denoising filter, implemented in the RapidForm software, to the 3D point cloud in order to remove ghost points. Next, the 3D point cloud is meshed and smoothed. Finally, the deviation between the original mesh and the smoothed mesh is computed. This yields a 3D deviation map representation of the geometric texture that can be modeled by a dataset $DM3 = \{(x, y, z, d) : x, y, z, d \in \mathbb{R}\}$ where (x, y, z) are the coordinates of the 3D points or vertices of the smoothed mesh and d, the Euclidean distance between a point of the smoothed mesh M_s of coordinates (x, y, z), denoted by $\mathbf{v}(x, y, z)$, and its nearest neighbor in the original mesh M_o, denoted by $\tilde{\mathbf{v}}(x', y', z')$. d is computed according to equation 1.

$$d(\mathbf{v}, \tilde{\mathbf{v}}) = \sqrt{(x - x')^2 + (y - y')^2 + (z - z')^2} \tag{1}$$

$\tilde{\mathbf{v}}(x', y', z')$ is determined using the efficient Aligned Axis Bounding Box (AABB) tree structure [6]. It is equal to

$$\tilde{\mathbf{v}} = argmin_{\mathbf{p}_i \in M_o} \|\mathbf{p}_i - \mathbf{v}\| \tag{2}$$

The smoothed mesh is computed using Taubin's λ/μ smoothing algorithm [7]. It consists in basically performing the Laplacian smoothing two consecutive times with different scaling factors denoted by λ and μ. A first step with $\lambda > 0$ (shrinking step) and a second step with a negative scaling factor $\mu < -\lambda < 0$ (unshrinking step). Laplacian smoothing consists in iteratively moving each of the vertices of the mesh to a new position that corresponds to the weighted average position of the neighboring vertices. The new position $\mathbf{v'}_i$ of a vertex i is given by Eq. 3:

$$\mathbf{v'}_i = \mathbf{v}_i + \lambda \, \Delta \mathbf{v}_i \tag{3}$$

where $\mathbf{v}_i$ is the current position, λ a scalar that controls the diffusion speed and $\Delta \mathbf{v}_i$ the Laplacian operator given by Eq. 4. It is a weighted sum of the difference between the current vertex $\mathbf{v}_i$ and all its neighbors $\mathbf{v}_j$.

$$\Delta \mathbf{v}_i = \sum_{j:\mathbf{v}_j \in i^*} w_{i,j}(\mathbf{v}_j - \mathbf{v}_i) \tag{4}$$

where i^* is the set of all the neighbors of the vertex $\mathbf{v}_i$. Taubin's λ/μ smoothing algorithm is run with equal weights $w_{i,j}$ for each of the neighbors such that $\sum_{j:\mathbf{v}_j \in i^*} w_{i,j} = 1$ and with λ and μ equal to 0.6307 and $-$ 0.6732, respectively (values suggested by Taubin). It is run iteratively until the mesh is sufficiently smoothed.

The smoothness of a 3D surface is usually quantified by the minimum, maximum, mean and Gaussian curvatures of each of the points of the mesh. Consequently, we have studied the evolution of the median of these curvature values as a function of the number of iterations of Taubin's algorithm for several samples of the five species to classify. Our study showed that there is no significant difference in the curvature against number of iterations curve for the four types of curvature values. We have thus decided to consider only the median of the maximum curvatures curve, as shown in Fig. 3, to determine the smoothing stopping criterion.

We have chosen to stop the smoothing process when the slope of the tangent to the curve is less than or equal to -0.01. For this value of the slope we have noticed that the mesh is sufficiently smoothed while preserving the main structures of the trunk.

3   2D Deviation Map

The next step of our method is the transformation of the 3D deviation map, a dataset $DM3 = \{(x, y, z, d) : x, y, z, d \in \mathbb{R}\}$, into a 2D deviation map, a dataset $DM2 = \{(X, Y, d) : X, Y, d \in \mathbb{R}\}$. It is a dimensionality reduction problem

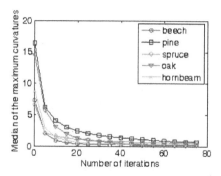

Fig. 3. The median of the maximum curvatures against the number of iterations for each of the five tree species

that should preserve the intrinsic geometry of the data. The two classical techniques for dimensionality reduction is Principal Component Analysis (PCA) and Multidimensional Scaling (MDS). However, they are not appropriate for our 3D deviation map because they are linear techniques and our 3D deviation map is a non linear structure.

One can find in the literature several non linear techniques that are more appropriate for our 3D deviation map. Among all these techniques we have chosen the Maximum Variance Unfolding (MVU) dimensionality reduction algorithm proposed by Weinberger et al. [8] because it is fast and it gives good results. An example of the 2D deviation map obtained using MVU is illustrated in Fig. 4.

hornbeam   beech   pine   oak   spruce

Fig. 4. Example of 2D deviation map for each of the five species

The 2D deviation map is a set of points in a 3D space. It is different from the point cloud in the sens that the third dimension represents a distance from a plane surface defined by the other two dimensions. It is like a height map or relief map defined by a set of points. The idea now is to cluster the points that are above a certain distance or "height" from the plane in order to define clusters or regions whose shape will allow us to classify the different species. The result of the clustering is a segmented 2D deviation map. To acheive this, a first thresholding step is done in order to keep the most salient features, e.g. the points with the highest deviation values. The threshold value is empirically defined as the median value of the deviation values. In this way only all the points in the 2D deviation map that have a height value greater than the median value are kept.

Secondly, DBSCAN a density based algorithm for discovering clusters proposed by Ester et al. [9] is used to cluster the points in order to build regions. DBSCAN is chosen because it is a fast and efficient algorithm even for large spatial set of points which is our case. DBSCAN is based on the notion of density of points in an ϵ-neighborhood. It has two required parameters: the neighborhood size (ϵ) and the minimum number of points in the ϵ-neighborhood ($minPts$). For our application $\epsilon = 0.6$ and $minPts = 8$.

An example of the segmented 2D deviation map for each of the five species is illustrated in Fig. 5.

| hornbeam | beech | pine | oak | spruce |

Fig. 5. An example of segmented 2D deviation map for each of the five species

4   Classification Features

From the 2D deviation map and the segmented 2D deviation map, we can compute about 128 features for classification. These features are, for example :

- The number of clusters per segmented 2D deviation map.
- The roughness features described in section 4.1.
- The principal component analysis features described in section 4.2.
- The shape and intensity features presented in section 4.3. Each cluster is defined by a set of shape and intensity features. We calculate the median, the mean, the standard deviation, the minimum and the maximum of the intensity and the shape features of all the clusters and use them as classification features.

4.1   Roughness Features

The 2D deviation map represents the geometric details of the surface of the bark from which roughness measures can be computed. Many types of measures can be found in the literature. The most common ones are statistical values such as the root mean square value, the arithmetical mean and the standard deviation respectively given by Eqs. (5)-(7).

$$s_q = \sqrt{\frac{1}{n} \sum_{i=1}^{n} d(\mathbf{v}_i, \tilde{\mathbf{v}}_i)^2} \tag{5}$$

$$s_a = \frac{1}{n} \sum_{i=1}^{n} |d(\mathbf{v}_i, \tilde{\mathbf{v}}_i)| \tag{6}$$

$$s_D = \sqrt{\left(\frac{1}{n}\sum_{i=1}^{n} d(\mathbf{v}_i, \tilde{\mathbf{v}}_i)^2\right) - \left(\frac{1}{n}\sum_{i=1}^{n} d(\mathbf{v}_i, \tilde{\mathbf{v}}_i)\right)^2} \qquad (7)$$

4.2   Principal Component Analysis Features

Principal Component Analysis (PCA) is a technique for dimension reduction and feature extraction. It uses linear transformations to map data from a high dimensional space to a low dimensional space. The new variables in the low dimensional space are called principal components. Some of the features that can be calculated for each of the clusters of points of the segmented deviation map using PCA are listed below.

- The percentage of the total variance explained by each principal component.
- The maximum and the median distances between the observations and the center of the data set as well as the ratio between the maximum and the median distances.
- The longest and shortest diameter (length of the major and the minor axis).
- The aspect ratio defined as the major axis length divided by the minor axis length.
- The orientation or the direction of the first and the second principal component.

The minimum, maximum, mean, median and standard deviation values of these PCA features for all the clusters of the segmented 2D deviation map are used as features for classification.

4.3   Shape and Intensity Features from Segmented 2D Deviation Map

To characterize the clusters of points in the segmented deviation map, shape and intensity features are calculated for each cluster. The intensity features are the maximum and the median intensity of the points of the cluster. To calculate the shape features, the alpha shape (α-shape) algorithm proposed by Edelsbrunner et al. [10] is used to compute the ∞-shape that corresponds to the convex hulls of the clusters of points. The 0.6-shape that best represents the real shape has also been computed. From the ∞-shape and the 0.6-shape, shape features such as perimeter, area, solidity, roundness, compactness, RFactor, shape, convexity and concavity are computed and used as classification features. The mathematical expressions of some of these features are given by Eqs. (8)-(12). To discriminate between the strips of the pine that are close and narrow and those of the oak that are touching each other, the ratio between the area of the convex hull and the area of the 0.6-shape is used as feature.

$$Solidity = \frac{Area}{ConvexArea} \qquad (8)$$

$$Roundness = \frac{4 \times Area}{\pi \times MajorAxisLength^2} \qquad (9)$$

$$Compactness = \frac{\sqrt{\frac{4}{\pi} \times Area}}{MajorAxisLength} \qquad (10)$$

$$RFactor = \frac{PerimeterOfConvexHull}{MajorAxisLength \times \pi} \qquad (11)$$

$$Shape = \frac{Perimeter^2}{Area} \qquad (12)$$

5   Experiments and Results

The 3D TLS data used to evaluate our method were captured using either a
FARO Photon 120 or a FARO Focus3D scanner with a resolution of about 6mm
at 10m. All trees at a distance of about 6m and with a Diameter at Breast Height
(DBH) of about 30cm are manually located in the scans. Next, non occluded
tree trunk segments of about 30cm long and at a height of about 1.30m from the
ground are extracted using a software that we have developed, the "Computree"
software [2], in order to constitute the evaluation database.

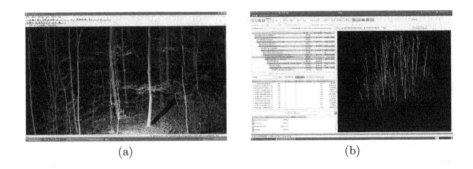

(a)   (b)

Fig. 6. (a) 3D point cloud captured by FARO Photon 120 scanner   (b) Computree
Software screenshot

We used two different datasets D1 and D2 to validate our approach experimentally. The test site of D1 is a state mixed forest in Montiers-sur-Saulx,
France. The second test site of D2 is a mixed forest stands of grove and coppice-
under-grove forests in Lorraine, France. Both datasets contain the five different
species of trees represented in Fig. 1. D1 and D2 are composed of 20 patches per
species and 33 patches per species, respectively. Classification is done using the
R Language implementation of the Random Forest (RF) classifier proposed by
Breiman [11]. The RF classifier is built with recommended values for the number

of decision trees (1000) and the number of features used to split the node in the decision tree growing process denoted by $Mtry$ ($Mtry = \sqrt{D}$ where D is the feature vector size). We have tested 128 features and used RF to select the 30 most pertinent ones to evaluate our method. So, the value of D is 30.

Three tests are done using datasets D1, D2 and a combination of D1 and D2, respectively. For each test, stratified 10-fold cross-validation is performed multiple times with the dataset reshuffled and re-stratified before each round. Also, for each round, a new classifier build with the recommended values of the number of trees and of the $Mtry$ parameter is used. The confusion matrices with average results are reported in Tables (1)-(3) and the accuracy rates for the three tests are summarized in Table 4.

Table 1. Confusion matrix for D1 cross-validation (1: hornbeam, 2: oak, 3: spruce, 4: beech, 5: pine)

	1	2	3	4	5	Accuracy
1	20	0	0	0	0	100 %
2	0	20	0	0	0	100 %
3	0	0.8	19.2	0	0	96 %
4	1.8	0	0.2	18	0	90 %
5	2.2	0	1	0.2	16.6	83 %

Table 2. Confusion matrix for D2 cross-validation (1: hornbeam, 2: oak, 3: spruce, 4: beech, 5: pine)

	1	2	3	4	5	Accuracy
1	33	0	0	0	0	100 %
2	0.6	31.8	0	0	0.6	96.3 %
3	0	0	31.6	0.6	0.8	95.7 %
4	1.8	0	0.6	32.4	0	98.1 %
5	0.8	1	0	0	31.2	94.5 %

For both datasets, each with a different terrain and architecture character-istics, we obtained good classification results. One can note from the confusion table that the accuracy ranges from 83% to 100%. The worst accuracy of 83% is for the pine that is misclassified as any one of the other four species in the three tests. Pine is mainly confused with hornbeam: the two species have strips. We can differentiate two families of tree species from the five tested species: species that have straps or cracks such as the hornbeam, the oak and the pine, and smooth surface species such as the beech and the spruce. We note that our algo-rithm mixes mainly intra-family species (spruce and beech) but also inter-family species. Future work will focus on finding more pertinent features to discriminate inter and intra family species.

Table 3. Confusion matrix for D1 and D2 cross-validation (1: hornbeam, 2: oak, 3: spruce, 4: beech, 5: pine)

	1	2	3	4	5	Accuracy
1	53	0	0	0	0	100 %
2	0	52.6	0	0	0.4	99.3 %
3	0	0	51.6	0.4	1	97.4 %
4	0.4	0	0.4	52.2	0	98.5 %
5	1.4	0.4	0.4	0.4	50.4	95.1 %

Table 4. Accuracy rates for the three tests

	Min	Average	Max	σ
Test 1	83%	93.8%	100%	6.5%
Test 2	94.5%	96.92%	100%	1.9%
Test 3	95.1%	98.06%	100%	1.7%

We can note that training and testing with dataset D3 (test 3) gives overall better accuracy rate than the other tests. This may be due to the fact that D3 contains more samples. Nevertheless, the result is relatively good enough and we can consider that the classifier performs reasonably well since the datasets D1 and D2 are composed of patches extracted from 3D data acquired from two different forest sites.

6 Conclusions

We have proposed a method for classifying five different tree species using TLS data only. The method is based on the analysis of the 3D geometric texture of the bark in order to identify the species class to which pertains the tree under analysis. In our method, the 3D geometric texture is transformed into a 2D deviation map on which roughness measures and shape features are computed and used as features for classification using the Random Forest classifier. Results obtained on a dataset composed of 265 samples with equal number of samples of each species are quite good (83% to 100%). In future work we plan to do more tests with other datasets in order to verify this observation. Moreover, we would also like to study the influence of the distance to scanner and of the DBH on the results. Indeed, in the current dataset the samples are all extracted from trees located at about 6m from the scanner and with a DBH of about 30cm.

Acknowlegments. This work is financially supported by the "Conseil Régional de Bourgogne" under contract N⁰ 2010 9201AAO048S06469 and N⁰ 2010 9201CPERO007S06470, and the 'Office National des Fôrets".

References

1. Dassot, M., Constant, T., Fournier, M.: The Use of Terrestrial LiDAR Technology in Forest Science: Application fields, Benefits and Challenges. Annals of Forest Science 6, 959–974 (2011)
2. Othmani, A., Piboule, A., Krebs, M., Stolz, C., Lew Yan Voon, L.F.C.: Towards Automated and Operational Forest Inventories with T-LiDAR. In: SilviLaser - 11th International Conference on LiDAR Applications for Assessing Forest Ecosystems, Hobart, Australia, October 16-19 (2011)
3. Puttonen, E., Suomalainen, J., Hakala, T., Rikknen, E., Kaartinen, H., Kaasalainen, S., Litkey, P.: Tree species classification from fused active hyperspectral reflectance and LIDAR measurements. Forest Ecology and Management 260, 1843–1852 (2010)
4. Haala, N., Reulke, R., Thies, M., Aschoff, T.: Combination of terrestrial Laser Scanning with high resolution panoramic Images for Investigations in Forest Applications and tree species recognition. In: Proceedings of the ISPRS Working Group V/1, IAPRS - XXXIV (PART 5/W16), Dresden, Deutschland, February 19-22. Panoramic Photogrammetry Workshop (2004)
5. Reulke, R., Haala, N.: Tree species recognition with fuzzy texture parameters. In: Klette, R., Žunić, J. (eds.) IWCIA 2004. LNCS, vol. 3322, pp. 607–620. Springer, Heidelberg (2004)
6. Alliez, P., Tayeb, S., Wormser, C.: AABB Tree, CGAL 3.5 edn. (2009)
7. Taubin, G.: Geometric Signal Processing on Polygonal Meshes. State of the Art Report, Eurographics (2000)
8. Weinberger, K.Q., Packer, B.D., Saul, L.K.: Nonlinear dimensionality reduction by semidefinite programming and kernel matrix factorization. In: Proceedings of the Tenth International Workshop on AI and Statistics (AISTATS 2005), Barbados, WI (2005)
9. Ester, M., Kriegel, H.P., Sander, J., Xu, X.: A density-based algorithm for discovering clusters in large spatial databases with noise. In: Proceedings of 2nd International Conference on Knowledge Discovery and Data Mining (KDD 1996), Portland, OR, USA, pp. 226–231 (1996)
10. Edelsbrunner, H., Kirkpatrick, D.G., Seidel, R.: On the Shape of a Set of Points in the Plane. IEEE Transactions on Information Theory IT-29(4) (July 1983)
11. Breiman, L.: Random Forests. Machine Learning, 5–32 (October 2001)

Singular Vector Methods for Fundamental Matrix Computation

Ferran Espuny[1] and Pascal Monasse[2]

[1] School of Environmental Sciences, University of Liverpool
Ferran.Espuny-Pujol@liverpool.ac.uk
[2] Université Paris-Est, LIGM (UMR CNRS 8049),
Center for Visual Computing, ENPC, F-77455 Marne-la-Vallée
pascal.monasse@enpc.fr

Abstract. The normalized eight-point algorithm is broadly used for the computation of the fundamental matrix between two images given a set of correspondences. However, it performs poorly for low-size datasets due to the way in which the rank-two constraint is imposed on the fundamental matrix. We propose two new algorithms to enforce the rank-two constraint on the fundamental matrix in closed form. The first one restricts the projection on the manifold of fundamental matrices along the most favorable direction with respect to algebraic error. Its complexity is akin to the classical seven point algorithm. The second algorithm relaxes the search to the best plane with respect to the algebraic error. The minimization of this error amounts to finding the intersection of two bivariate cubic polynomial curves. These methods are based on the minimization of the algebraic error and perform equally well for large datasets. However, we show through synthetic and real experiments that the proposed algorithms compare favorably with the normalized eight-point algorithm for low-size datasets.

Keywords: 3D Reconstruction, Fundamental Matrix, Closed Form.

1   Introduction

1.1   Overview

The *fundamental matrix* is a two-view tensor which encodes the relative geometry between two images, named *epipolar geometry* [4,7]. Concisely, for each point in one image the fundamental matrix determines a line of possible corresponding points on the other image, called the *epipolar line* associated to the point. Since all epipolar lines in one image pass through the projection of the other camera center (the *epipole*), the fundamental matrix is constrained to have rank two.

The fundamental matrix plays a central role in the theory of 3D reconstruction from stereo images. It is used at initial stages to achieve a sparse projective reconstruction of a scene, and to extract the camera motion either from intrinsically calibrated cameras or by a self-calibration approach. It is also used to

R. Klette, M. Rivera, and S. Satoh (Eds.): PSIVT 2013, LNCS 8333, pp. 290–301, 2014.

rectify the images as a preliminary step in order to achieve a dense reconstruction of a scene. The rank-two constraint is crucial for motion estimation and for image rectification algorithms requiring the existence of epipoles [8,6].

For its robust computation in presence of outlier point correspondences, the fundamental matrix needs to be estimated from minimal subsets of data in random sampling methods. This is a requirement of the RANSAC [5] algorithm and variants. It can also be estimated using non-minimal but relatively small sets of data in the local random sampling method of Chum *et al.* [3]. Finally, it is estimated using all the available inlier correspondences, yielding an initial solution for an overall error optimization, known as *bundle adjustment* [15]; even in this context, the size of the available dataset can be low due to typical problems in feature detection and matching. In this paper we will focus on the closed-form and fast computation of the fundamental matrix given noisy inlier data; our final goal is to improve the accuracy of the existing approaches in this context.

The normalized eight-point algorithm introduced by Hartley [9] allows computing in closed form an estimate of the fundamental matrix given at least eight correspondences between two images. A closed-form variant using seven correspondences exists which benefits from the rank-two constraint (see e.g. Zhang [16]). This broadly used method is an improvement over previous ones achieved through a prior data normalization step.

The *rank-two constraint* on the fundamental matrix is imposed by the normalized eight-point algorithm in an *a posteriori* step which does not take into account the error to minimize. Iterative strategies have been proposed to overcome this drawback [10], and modern optimization approaches exist that take into account the rank-two constraint at some computational expense [2,11,17]. In contrast, we propose two closed-form solutions for the direct computation of a fundamental matrix satisfying the rank-two constraint.

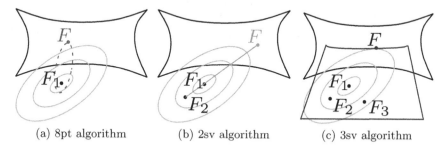

(a) 8pt algorithm   (b) 2sv algorithm   (c) 3sv algorithm

Fig. 1. Geometric Interpretation of the Singular Vector Methods. We represent in black the hypersurface of $\mathbb{P}^8$ with equation $\det(F) = 0$ and, in front of it, the three matrices F_1, F_2, F_3 corresponding to the singular values $s_1 \leq s_2 \leq s_3$ of A in (4); in cyan, the level sets of the algebraic error function. The solution given by the 8-point algorithm (red) is obtained as the closest matrix in Froebenius norm to F_1 on the hypersurface. Our first proposed solution (green) lies on the intersection of the line F_1, F_2 with the hypersurface. Our second proposal (blue) lies on the intersection of the plane spanned by F_1, F_2, F_3 with the hypersurface.

1.2   The Rank-Two Constraint

The fundamental 3×3 matrix F between two images can be expressed as

$$F = K^{-T} \, [t]_\times \, R \, K'^{-1} \,, \tag{1}$$

with R the relative rotation matrix and t the translation vector between the images, K and K' being the camera intrinsic calibration matrices. $[t]_\times$ denotes the 3×3 matrix corresponding to the linear operator mapping a vector to its vector product with t on the left: $[t]_\times \, x = t \times x$.

Due to the factor $[t]_\times$ in (1), the matrix F has rank 2 (unless $t = 0$, meaning no parallax). Conversely, any rank-two matrix accepts such a decomposition. The epipoles are then $e = K \, t$ and $e' = K' \, R^T \, t$, respectively left and right null vectors of F: $e^T \, F = 0$ and $F \, e' = 0$. For several applications, it is mandatory to get a rank-two solution F.

For a point correspondence $x_i \leftrightarrow x'_i$ between the two images (expressed in homogeneous coordinates), the *epipolar constraint* is written

$$x_i^T \, F \, x'_i = 0 \,. \tag{2}$$

The *geometric error* of F at a point correspondence $x_i \leftrightarrow x'_i$ is the point to line distance $\mathrm{dist}(x_i, Fx'_i)$. We take as geometric error of F the root mean square error (RMSE) of the geometric error of F over all the available correspondences:

$$GeomErr(F) = \sqrt{\frac{1}{n} \sum_{i=1}^{n} \mathrm{dist}(x_i, Fx'_i)^2} \,. \tag{3}$$

The simplest existing method for the computation of the fundamental matrix proceeds as follows. For $n \geq 8$ point correspondences between two images, the data coordinates are normalized linearly (we use the *isotropic scaling* normalization described e.g. in [7]), and then the epipolar constraint (2) on the transformed coordinates is expressed as a linear system of the type

$$A \, f = 0 \,, \tag{4}$$

f being a 9×1 vector representing the coefficients of F. The system is homogeneous due to a scale ambiguity in the fundamental matrix.

We denote by f_i the i-th eigenvector of $A^T A$ with associated eigenvalue s_i^2, $s_i \geq 0$ being the singular values of A sorted by *increasing value*, $s_1 \leq s_2 \leq \cdots \leq s_9$, and we denote by F_i the 3×3 matrix associated to f_i (the right singular vectors of A). The homogeneous least-squares problem associated to (4) is the minimization of the so-called *algebraic error*:

$$\arg\min \|A \, f\| \ \text{s.t.} \ \|f\| = 1 \,. \tag{5}$$

Its solution is given by f_1, the eigenvector of $A^T A$ corresponding to the smallest singular value of A. The solution provided by the *Direct Linear Transform (DLT)* is the de-normalization of the matrix F_1, which does not satisfy the rank-two constraint. Setting to zero the smallest singular value of the SVD decomposition of F_1, we obtain the rank-two matrix closest in Frobenius norm to the minimum of the algebraic error. This corresponds to an orthogonal projection of F_1 on the manifold of rank-two matrices, see Figure 1. The de-normalization of that matrix is the final solution given by the *normalized eight-point algorithm*.

In general, one is more interested in the minimization of the geometric error (3), the Gold standard error or its approximation, the Sampson error [7]. However, there is no known closed-form solution for the minimization of such errors. Therefore, there is still interest in simple closed-form methods with low computational cost, even if based on minimizing the algebraic error.

This paper proposes two alternative algorithms to enforce the rank-two constraint (see Figure 1). The solutions we propose intersect a line or a plane with the manifold of rank-two matrices. These are constructed by taking into account F_2 and F_3, the next right-singular vectors of A, in order to have a better control of the increasing error when computing F. We show that this has a low computational burden, being closed-form, and generally provides a precision gain, especially with few correspondences or in near-degenerate cases, such as low b/h (ratio baseline/distance to scene).

In next section, we show through simulation the effect of the classical projection, its poor performance for low-size datasets and the relation with the singular vectors of A. Then, we present our alternative proposals based on two and three right-singular vectors of A instead of just one for the standard eight-point algorithm. We report the results on synthetic and real data before concluding.

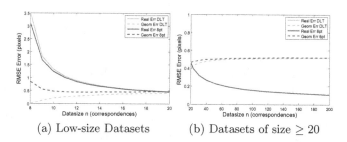

(a) Low-size Datasets   (b) Datasets of size ≥ 20

Fig. 2. Performance of the DLT (cyan) and normalized eight-point (red) algorithms for variable size datasets and noisy data. Median over 5000 runs of the obtained geometric (3) and real (6) errors in dashed and continuous lines, respectively.

2   Performance of the Normalized Eight-Point Algorithm for Low-Size Datasets

We carried out the following simulation with the initial purpose of showing the performance of the normalized eight-point algorithm for low-size datasets, and later to compare this algorithm with our proposed improvements. We simulated a camera with calibration matrix $K = \begin{pmatrix} 900 & 0 & 320 \\ 0 & 900 & 240 \\ 0 & 0 & 1 \end{pmatrix}$ with a 640×480 image, corresponding to an horizontal angular field of view of approximately 40 degrees. A variable number n of 3D points was generated at a minimum distance $h = 1$ in the direction of the principal axis inside a cuboid of depth ΔZ; the width and height of the cuboid were chosen so that its image was inside the domain $[0, 640] \times [0, 480]$. A second camera position was generated at a distance b of the first one. The obtained image points were perturbed with uniform noise with standard deviation $\sigma = 1$ pixel. The experiment was repeated 5000 times for each value of n, and the geometric errors (3) of the obtained fundamental matrices were computed using the data correspondences.

In order to have an unbiased error measure of each fundamental matrix, we randomly generated a dense cloud of 1000 points inside the simulation cuboid and computed at each iteration as *real error* the geometric error of the exact correspondences $y_i \leftrightarrow y_i'$ obtained by projecting that cloud:

$$RealErr(F) = \sqrt{\frac{1}{1000} \sum_{i=1}^{1000} \text{dist}(y_i, F y_i')^2} . \qquad (6)$$

Given that we are not considering outlier data, the geometric errror (3) gives us a measure of the goodness of the fundamental matrix for reconstructing the given matches; in constrast, the real error (6) serves us to validate the goodness of the fundamental matrix for reconstructing new correspondences or for motion estimation (e.g. in self-calibration). This error is expected to be worse for low-size datasets, for which many points in the dense cloud used for evaluation are far from the few given data points used for model fitting. Notice that in absence of ground truth correspondences $y_i \leftrightarrow y_i'$, the real error is not computable.

We show in Figure 2 the results of a simulation attempting to cover a broad range of realistic scenes and camera motions: for each iteration, the scene depth variation ΔZ was randomly chosen between $10^{-4} h$ (satellite images) and h (close scenes), and the baseline size b was randomly chosen between $0.01h$ and h.

Observing the real error, a first remark is that for low-size datasets the enforcement of the rank-two constraint (eight-point algorithm) improves the solution given by F_1, the minimum of the algebraic error. However, the geometric error (as well as the algebraic error, and the Sampson error [7]) increases with that enforcement. Observe that for low-size datasets the geometric errors corresponding to the noisy data are not necessarily correlated with the real errors of the models (which we estimate using a dense cloud of exact points). This does not hold for bigger size datasets, which in our simulation tend to be dense inside the cuboid. When dealing with real images, the errors can only be computed using the available data, which can be low-size due to typical problems in feature detection and matching.

A second remark is that the normalized eight-point algorithm behaves quite poorly for very low-size datasets, in comparison with its performance with general datasets. In our simulation, the real error (6) is divided by a factor of 3 when considering datasets of $n = 12$ correspondences instead of $n = 8$. This behaviour was reported before in [3], where the normalized eight-point algorithm was compared to its variant for 7 correspondences, which takes as solution $F = F_1 + \alpha F_2$, for α such that $\det(F_1 + \alpha F_2) = 0$ [7].

It can be observed in Figure 3 that the groundtruth fundamental matrix, when decomposed into the orthonormal basis $\{F_i\}_{i=1,\dots,9}$, has significant coefficients not only in the right-singular vector F_1, but also in the right-singular vector F_2 and, in minor measure, F_3. This is because the matrices F_i are computed using noisy data. Based on this observation, we propose two solutions for a better closed-form computation of the fundamental matrix for low-size datasets.

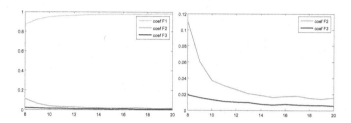

Fig. 3. Significance of Singular Vectors. For low-size datasets, we show the average squared coefficients of the groundtruth fundamental matrix with respect to the three right-singular vectors F_1, F_2, F_3 (top), and only for F_2, F_3 (bottom).

3   The Two Singular Vector Algorithm

The normalized eight-point algorithm imposes the rank-two constraint on the fundamental matrix ignoring the fact that the algebraic error may increase drastically for certain directions. We propose a first alternative to this strategy which consists in selecting the rank-two matrix close to the algebraic minimum moving in the best direction for minimizing the algebraic error.

Whereas the solution of the normalized eight-point algorithm is given by a modification of F_1, our first proposal, the *two singular vector algorithm*, is to compute the fundamental matrix as (see Figure 1):

$$\tilde{F} = F_1 + \alpha F_2 \ , \ \text{for } \alpha \text{ s.t. } \det(F_1 + \alpha F_2) = 0 \ . \tag{7}$$

This proposal is commonly used for computing three possible fundamental matrices given 7 correspondences, and has been previously used in a non-minimal context without further validation [14]. The computation of α in (7) can be done in closed form as in those cases, consisting in the resolution of the univariate cubic equation in α given by (7). In case that we obtain three possible real values α when solving (7), we choose the one that has minimum geometric error (other error choices gave similar performance).

The algebraic error associated to a solution of (7) can be obtained straightforwardly using the singular values of A:

$$\|A \tilde{f}\|^2 = s_1^2 + \alpha^2 s_2^2 \ . \tag{8}$$

Although the value of this error is clearly bigger than $\|A\,\tilde{f_1}\|^2 = s_1^2$, it may be smaller than the algebraic error of the normalized eight-point algorithm.

Using the general simulation proposed in Section 2, we show in Figure 4 the median (over 5000 runs) of the real and geometric errors associated to the two singular vector algorithm for noisy data ($\sigma = 1$ pixel). In Section 6 we will show using both simulation and real images that the performance of this method is superior to what could be concluded from the results hereby.

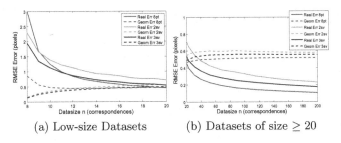

(a) Low-size Datasets   (b) Datasets of size ≥ 20

Fig. 4. Performance of the normalized eight-point algorithm (8pt, in red), the two singular vector algorithm (2sv, in green), and the three singular vector algorithm (3sv, in blue). We show the median over 5000 runs of the geometric (3) and real (6) errors.

4   The Three Singular Vector Algorithm

A plausible criticism to the previous algorithm is that, even if it imposes the rank constraint on the fundamental matrix, the increase in algebraic error is known but remains uncontrolled. Our second proposal addresses this issue by imposing the rank-two constraint while minimizing the algebraic error. Concisely, we compute the fundamental matrix as

$$\hat{F} = F_1 + \alpha F_2 + \beta F_3 \;, \tag{9}$$

with

$$(\alpha, \beta) = \arg\min s_1^2 + \alpha^2 s_2^2 + \beta^2 s_3^2 \\ \text{s.t.} \quad G(\alpha, \beta) = 0 \tag{10}$$

where $G(\alpha, \beta) = \det(F_1 + \alpha F_2 + \beta F_3)$.

Using Lagrange multipliers, the solution to the problem (10) can be searched inside the set of real values α, β, μ that satisfy:

$$2s_2^2\,\alpha + \mu\,\partial_\alpha G(\alpha, \beta) = 0 \;, \tag{11}$$

$$2s_3^2\,\beta + \mu\,\partial_\beta G(\alpha, \beta) = 0 \;, \tag{12}$$

$$G(\alpha, \beta) = 0 \;. \tag{13}$$

Assuming for the moment that $\partial_\beta G(\alpha, \beta) \neq 0$, the equations (11) and (12) have a compatible solution μ if the following cubic equation in α, β holds

$$s_2^2 \, \alpha \, \partial_\beta G(\alpha, \beta) = s_3^2 \, \beta \, \partial_\alpha G(\alpha, \beta) \,. \tag{14}$$

Otherwise, if $\partial_\beta G(\alpha, \beta) = 0$, by (12) it holds $\beta = 0$, which can be obtained too by imposing equation (14).

Therefore, the solution(s) of (10) will lie in the intersection of two plane cubics, given by equations (13) and (14). In conclusion, theoretically there are at most 9 solutions of (10). In general, the minimum of (10) is reached at a unique value (α, β).

The exact intersection of the two cubics (13) and (14) can be obtained by solving their resultant with respect to β, which is a univariate polynomial in α of degree 9. In practice, for each real root α of this polynomial, we compute the corresponding β using (13), and finally select as solution the (α, β) with minimum geometric error (the Sampson error gave similar performance). We obtained experimentally better results using the geometric error than using the algebraic error, which however we need to generate the set of candidate solutions in closed form.

Using again the general simulation proposed in Section 2, Figure 4 shows the median real and geometric errors associated to the three singular vector algorithm for noisy data ($\sigma = 1$ pixel). From the observed results we conclude that for general computations of the fundamental matrix (general camera motions and scenarios), the closed-form three singular vector algorithm outperforms the normalized eight-point algorithm for datasets of sizes between 8 and 12. Other applications are discussed in next section.

5   Applicability to General-Size Datasets

We have already shown, using the general scenario described in Section 2, that the use of more than one right-singular vector can be useful for low-size datasets (Figure 4). The reason is that the smallest singular values of the matrix A in (4) are close to each other for those datasets.

We can imagine two degenerate scenarios where this is also the case: small baseline motions and distant scenes. In fact, these problems can be solved by computing a planar homography instead of the fundamental matrix; the configurations close to them, however, cannot be modelled using a homography.

An example is given in satellite imagery, where the distance from the camera to the scene is much bigger than both the baseline size and the scene depth. We show in Figure 5 the simulation results (median over 5000 runs) corresponding to the *Pleiades* system (http://smsc.cnes.fr/PLEIADES/), where, using the notation introduced in Section 2, we approximately have $b/h = 0.2$, $\Delta Z/h = 0.00014$. For any data size, the two singular vector algorithm outperforms the other closed-form methods.

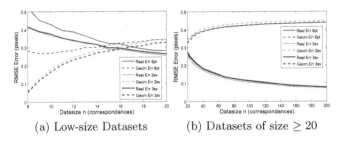

| (a) Low-size Datasets | (b) Datasets of size ≥ 20 |

Fig. 5. Performance with simulated satellite data. Geometric (3) and real (6) errors.

6   Experimental Results

6.1   Numerical Stability Evaluation

We plot in Figure 6 the errors as a function of noise standard deviation by the different methods, at various datasizes, for general camera motions and scenarios simulated as in Section 2; see also Figure 4 for a clear picture when $\sigma = 1$. A first remark is that all methods exhibit a linear dependence on noise level, showing that the proposed methods have correct numerical stability. In all cases, the 3sv method outperforms the 2sv method, which is to be expected concerning the algebraic error, since solutions of (7) are inside the minimization space of (9).

It can be also observed that for high noise levels the geometric error increases as the dataset size increases, the behaviour of the normalized eight-point algorithm for datasets of size $n = 8$ and close values being particularly critical. For the low dataset sizes, the 3sv outperforms the 8pt algorithm, whereas for the 2sv this seems only true for dataset sizes $n = 8, 9$. For bigger datasets, there is a very slight advantage for the normalized eight-point algorithm over 3sv.

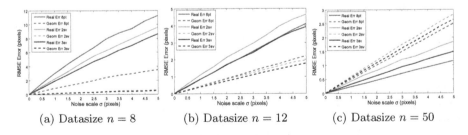

| (a) Datasize $n = 8$ | (b) Datasize $n = 12$ | (c) Datasize $n = 50$ |

Fig. 6. Errors against noise for different datasizes

6.2   Real Data

We first test the algorithms on stereo pairs from the SyntIm INRIA database (http://perso.lcpc.fr/tarel.jean-philippe/syntim/paires.html)   (see Figure 7), whih are small size images (mostly 512×512) with a moderate number of SIFT matches [12] obtained by using demanding parameters in

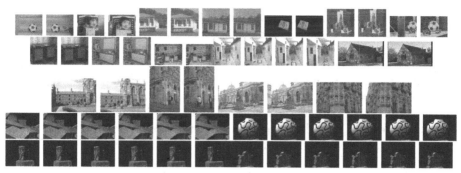

Fig. 7. Image pairs used for the validation with real images. From top to bottom and from left to right: Baballe, BalMouss, BatInria, BatSynt, Billet, Color, GrRub, Sabine, Serfaty, Sport; next, images from Hartley-Zisserman's book [7], and then images from Strecha's website; the last two row images are from Aanæs *et al.* [1].

Table 1. Results on 10 SyntIm stereo pairs, 5 pairs from Hartley-Zisserman's book [7] and 3 pairs from Strecha's site. The first column is the pair name, n the number of inlier correspondences after RANSAC. In each cell are indicated the root mean/max square geometric error over the data correspondences. In each test, the least error over the three constraint-enforcing methods (8pt, 2sv, and 3sv) is in **bold**.

Pair	n	8pt	2sv	3sv
Baballe	9	0.65/1.79	0.21/0.48	**0.20/0.43**
BalMouss	24	0.49/1.41	0.92/3.20	**0.41/0.93**
BatInria	46	0.59/**1.87**	0.82/2.52	**0.58**/1.92
BatSynt	26	0.52/1.84	**0.46**/1.74	0.59/**1.31**
Billet	11	0.39/0.72	0.16/0.38	**0.15/0.28**
Color	15	0.61/1.49	0.31/0.76	**0.30/0.66**
GrRub	24	0.66/1.54	0.66/1.45	**0.65/1.52**
Sabine	16	**0.38**/1.01	0.60/1.39	0.51/**0.97**
Serfaty	39	0.75/1.97	0.59/**1.72**	**0.59**/1.83
Sport	115	**0.37/1.24**	1.16/3.65	0.39/1.52
bt.000, bt.002	62	**0.50**/1.45	0.50/1.44	0.50/**1.44**
bt.000, bt.004	41	**0.72/1.82**	0.72/1.86	0.73/1.86
bt.000, bt.006	28	0.86/**2.79**	0.84/2.87	**0.83**/2.87
chapel	31	0.69/**1.69**	**0.68**/1.73	0.68/1.72
keble	50	0.33/1.01	0.33/**0.95**	**0.32**/1.02
Brussels	671	0.35/1.34	0.35/1.34	**0.35/1.34**
Dresden	1615	**0.22/0.79**	0.23/1.03	0.23/1.01
Leuven	904	**0.48/1.69**	0.55/1.89	0.54/2.13

order to avoid outliers. The SIFT matches are filtered by a non-parametric variant of RANSAC [13], and the remaining outliers are manually discarded to obtain a real noisy inlier dataset for our algorithms. We report in Table 1 the results. In all but two datasets, one of our proposed algorithms outperforms the 8-point algorithm, usually the three singular vector algorithm. We also tested on image pairs from Hartley-Zisserman's book [7] (http://www.robots.ox.ac.uk/~vgg/hzbook/code/) and from Strecha's website (http://cvlab.epfl.ch/data/strechamvs/). Results are reported in Table 1. Even though the number n of inliers is higher, we can see that 2sv and 3sv yield comparable precision.

Aanæs *et al.* [1] propose a large dataset of calibrated image sequences (http://roboimagedata.imm.dtu.dk/index.html). We take some $1/4$ size sequences (300×400) and consider as stereo pair the first image of a sequence and successive images in that sequence. Statistics are reported in Table 2. As we compare image 1 with further images in the sequence, the number n of inlier correspondences tends to decrease as the b/h ratio increases. Images 1 and 2 have $b/h \sim 0.03$, and images 1 and 6 have $b/h = 0.17$. In all sequences, the most accurate method is either 2sv or 3sv. Many times, one of both outperforms the eight-point algorithm, especially for small b/h. Notice for example the dramatic failure of the latter for pairs $(1, 5)$ and $(1, 6)$ of SET037. Even for relatively high n a significant improvement can be obtained with 3sv.

Table 2. Results with DTU data sets (see Table 1 caption). The data error (mean/max) is measured using available groundtruth calibration and depicted in column 'data error'.

Set	pair	n	data error	8pt	2sv	3sv
037	1,2	15	0.48/1.06	0.51/1.41	0.44/**0.92**	**0.44**/0.94
037	1,3	13	0.67/1.83	0.51/**0.41**	**0.50**/1.01	0.50/0.99
037	1,4	8	0.60/1.39	0.07/0.14	0.02/0.03	**0.01/0.03**
037	1,5	8	0.97/2.41	6.50/12.7	**0.15/0.25**	0.19/0.38
037	1,6	8	0.37/0.75	9.00/23.5	0.21/0.54	**0.12/0.26**
040	1,2	16	0.43/1.19	0.41/1.11	**0.18/0.43**	0.19/**0.35**
040	1,3	17	0.63/1.34	0.32/0.86	**0.30**/0.86	0.30/**0.82**
040	1,4	18	0.68/1.65	0.40/0.84	0.37/0.84	**0.37/0.78**
040	1,5	16	0.75/1.39	0.53/1.08	0.50/**1.04**	**0.50**/1.06
040	1,6	15	1.04/2.59	1.67/4.41	0.54/**0.90**	**0.54**/0.97
041	1,2	31	0.17/0.39	0.26/1.07	**0.16**/0.38	0.16/**0.36**
041	1,3	27	0.32/1.21	0.77/2.06	0.29/**0.88**	**0.25**/1.02
041	1,4	25	0.30/0.98	0.39/1.05	0.18/0.46	**0.14/0.42**
041	1,5	25	0.34/1.09	0.37/0.90	**0.21/0.47**	0.21/0.48
041	1,6	21	0.24/0.63	**0.20**/0.50	0.61/1.82	0.20/**0.49**
042	1,2	21	0.46/1.87	0.50/1.46	0.23/**0.42**	**0.23**/0.42
042	1,3	15	0.19/0.45	0.27/0.63	0.18/0.34	**0.16/0.33**
042	1,4	17	0.77/2.55	0.62/1.22	1.08/2.09	**0.48/0.87**
042	1,5	15	0.96/3.15	1.40/3.54	0.93/1.90	**0.69/1.70**
042	1,6	14	0.66/2.00	1.14/2.71	1.04/1.97	**0.52/1.03**

7 Conclusion

We have shown that a small modification of the eight-point algorithm provides in several cases a better precision. The two singular vector algorithm is quite similar to the seven-point algorithm. The three singular vector algorithm is slightly more complex to implement, but it is more likely to improve the precision. Whatever the case, our recommendation is to compute the errors resulting from the three considered rank-two enforcement algorithms and keep the least of them.

Acknowledgments. Part of this work was funded by the Agence Nationale de la Recherche, Callisto project (ANR-09-CORD-003).

References

1. Aanæs, H., Dahl, A.L., Pedersen, K.S.: Interesting interest points. Int. J. Comput. Vis. 97, 18–35 (2012)
2. Chesi, G., Garulli, A., Vicino, A., Cipolla, R.: Estimating the fundamental matrix via constrained least-squares: a convex approach. IEEE Trans. Pattern Anal. Mach. Intell. 24(3), 397–401 (2002)
3. Chum, O., Matas, J., Kittler, J.: Locally optimized RANSAC. In: Michaelis, B., Krell, G. (eds.) DAGM 2003. LNCS, vol. 2781, pp. 236–243. Springer, Heidelberg (2003)
4. Faugeras, O., Luong, Q.-T., Papadopoulou, T.: The Geometry of Multiple Images: The Laws That Govern the Formation of Images of A Scene and Some of Their Applications. MIT Press, Cambridge (2001) ISBN 0262062208
5. Fischler, M.A., Bolles, R.C.: Random sample consensus: A paradigm for model fitting with applications to image analysis and automated cartography. Comm. ACM 24(6), 381–395 (1981)
6. Gluckman, J., Nayar, S.K.: Rectifying transformations that minimize resampling effects. In: Proc. CVPR (2001)
7. Hartley, R., Zisserman, A.: Multiple View Geometry in Computer Vision, 2nd edn. Cambridge University Press (2004) ISBN 0521540518
8. Hartley, R.I.: Theory and practice of projective rectification. Int. J. Comput. Vis. 35, 115–127 (1999)
9. Hartley, R.I.: In defence of the 8-point algorithm. In: Proc. ICCV (1995)
10. Hartley, R.I.: Minimizing algebraic error in geometric estimation problems. In: Proc. ICCV (1998)
11. Kahl, F., Henrion, D.: Globally optimal estimates for geometric reconstruction problems. In: Proc. ICCV (2005)
12. Lowe, D.: Distinctive image features from scale-invariant keypoints. Int. J. Comput. Vis. 60, 91–110 (2004)
13. Moisan, L., Stival, B.: A probabilistic criterion to detect rigid point matches between two images and estimate the fundamental matrix. Int. J. Comput. Vis. 57(3), 201–218 (2004)
14. Schaffalitzky, F., Zisserman, A., Hartley, R.I., Torr, P.: A six point solution for structure and motion. In: Vernon, D. (ed.) ECCV 2000. LNCS, vol. 1842, pp. 632–648. Springer, Heidelberg (2000)
15. Triggs, B., Mclauchlan, P., Hartley, R., Fitzgibbon, A.: Bundle adjustment – a modern synthesis. In: Proc. VA Workshop (1999)
16. Zhang, Z.: Determining the epipolar geometry and its uncertainty: a review. Int. J. Comput. Vis. 27(2), 161–195 (1998)
17. Zheng, Y., Sugimoto, S., Okumoti, M.: A branch and contract algorithm for globally optimal fundamental matrix estimation. In: Proc. CVPR (2011)

Global Haar-Like Features: A New Extension of Classic Haar Features for Efficient Face Detection in Noisy Images

Mahdi Rezaei[1], Hossein Ziaei Nafchi[2], and Sandino Morales[3]

[1] The University of Auckland, New Zealand
m.rezaei@auckland.ac.nz
[2] Synchromedia Laboratory, École de Technologie Supérieure, Canada
hossein.zi@synchromedia.ca
[3] The University of Auckland, New Zealand
sandinomorales@gmail.com

Abstract. This paper addresses the problem of detecting human faces in noisy images. We propose a method that includes a denoising preprocessing step, and a new face detection approach based on a novel extension of Haar-like features. Preprocessing of the input images is focused on the removal of different types of noise while preserving the phase data. For the face detection process, we introduce the concept of *global* and *dynamic global* Haar-like features, which are complementary to the well known classical Haar-like features. Matching dynamic global Haar-like features is faster than that of the traditional approach. Also, it does not increase the computational burden in the learning process. Experimental results obtained using images from the MIT-CMU dataset are promising in terms of detection rate and the false alarm rate in comparison with other competing algorithms.

Keywords: Face detection, Global Haar-like features, Phase-preserving denoising, AdaBoost.

1 Introduction

Face detection is the key step in many face analysis systems [21,23]. Current research is aiming at increasing the robustness of the detectors [22,16,9]. Among the proposed face detection algorithms, boosting-based detection with efficient use of integral image, Haar-like features and a cascade of weak classifiers, have defined high-performance systems [22,16,10].

Following the well-known Viola-Jones face detector [19], many researches have achieved further improvements in the performance of this detector. Currently, research in the field can be categorized into four subject areas:

1. Speeding up the learning process.
2. Speeding up the face detection.

R. Klette, M. Rivera, and S. Satoh (Eds.): PSIVT 2013, LNCS 8333, pp. 302–313, 2014.
© Springer-Verlag Berlin Heidelberg 2014

Fig. 1. Detection results using the standard Haar-like detector. *Left*: Detection results on a "noisy" input image. *Right*: Detection results on the denoised image.

3. Defining a better trade-off between detection rate and false-positive rate.
4. Combining the three mentioned criteria.

For example, heuristic methods trying to improve the detection speed [13], or different version of AdaBoost like. Float boost [5], ChainBoost [20], cost-sensitive boosting [9,1], KLBoost [7], FCBoost [16], or RCECBoost [15] that aim at speeding up the AdaBoost convergence, or at improving the final performance of the detector.

Some variations of the Haar-like features have been proposed to improve the performance of boosting-based detectors [6,11,12]. These types of Haar-like features algorithms were introduced to deal with rotated faces and to improve the detection/false-positive rate. Any of these face detectors uses similar variations of the image preprocessing step suggested by Viola and Jones [19]. In that paper the authors utilized a fast variance-normalization preprocessing for face/non-face windows for dealing with illumination artifacts (as defined in [18] and [17]).

In this paper, we propose an image preprocessing step different to variance-normalization, to overcome the problem of noisy images and that of images contaminated with illumination artifacts. We use the image denoising method suggested by Kovesi in [2]. This method is able to preserve the important *phase information* of the images, based on the non-orthogonal and complex-valued log-Gabor wavelets. Figure 1 shows an example of the results obtained with a standard Haar-like detector for a "noisy" input image (left), and on the denoised version of the same image (right).

We apply this technique of denoising in conjunction with a novel version of the Haar-like features method which together lead to an outperforming result. As the main contribution of the paper, we propose *global* Haar-like features which complement the commonly used standard Haar-like features. With global Haar-like features we introduce a new point of view to take benefit from the intensity information of the whole sliding query window. This is in contrast to the standard Haar-like features that only looks through dark-bright adjacent regions. We also propose *dynamic global* Haar-like features aiming to update global feature values based on intensity variations over the query image.

Since adding new features can increase the computational burden, only selected classical Haar-like features (during the learning process) are candidates for becoming global features. We designed a face detector system through boosting denoised features with an efficient use of *standard* and *global* Haar-like features. Outstanding experimental results, in terms of the detection rate and the false-positive rate, show the robustness of the proposed method when using ideal, noisy, and illumination artifacts affected images.

The rest of the paper is organized as follows. Section 2 provides a discussion of the image denoising method based on a phase-preserving algorithm. Global and dynamic global Haar-like features are detailed in Section 3. Section 4 focuses on training a cascade of classifiers based on global and dynamic global features. Section 5 deals with experimental results, and Section 6 concludes.

2   Phase-Preserving Denoising of Images

A phase-preserving denoising method was proposed by Kovesi in [2]. It assumes that phase information of images is the most important feature and tries to preserve this information, of course by trying to keep the magnitude information, as well.

Let M_ρ^e and M_ρ^o denote the even-symmetric and odd-symmetric wavelets at a scale ρ which are known as quadratic pairs. Considering the responses from each quadrature pair of the filters, a resultant response vector is defined as follows:

$$[e_\rho(x), o_\rho(x)] = [f(x) * M_\rho^e, f(x) * M_\rho^o] \tag{1}$$

where $*$ denotes convolution, and values $e_\rho(x)$ and $o_\rho(x)$ are the real and imaginary parts in the complex-valued frequency domain. The amplitude of the transform at a given wavelet scale is given by:

$$A_\rho(x) = \sqrt{e_\rho(x)^2 + o_\rho(x)^2} \tag{2}$$

and the local phase is given by:

$$\varphi_\rho(x) = \tan^{-1}\left[\frac{o_\rho(x)}{e_\rho(x)}\right] \tag{3}$$

Having one response vector for each filter scale, there will be an array of such vectors for each pixel x in a signal. The denoising process includes defining an appropriate noise threshold for each scale as well as reducing the magnitudes of the response vectors, while maintaining the phase without any changes. The most important step of the denoising process is determining the thresholds. For this end, Kovesi [2] used the expected response of the filters to a pure noise signal.

If the signal is purely Gaussian white noise, then the position of the resulting response vectors from a wavelet quadratic pair of filters at some scale will form a 2D Gaussian distribution in the complex plane. Kovesi [2] showed that the distribution of the magnitude responses can be modelled by the Rayleigh distribution

$$R(x) = \frac{x}{\sigma_g^2} \exp^{\frac{-x^2}{2\sigma_g^2}} . \tag{4}$$

$$F_{haar} = F_{white} - F_{black} = 15573 - 14733 = 840$$

$$F_{haar} = F_{white} - F_{black} = 23429 - 19326 = 4103$$

Haar feature applied in eye region

Fig. 2. Improved result for F_{haar} (integral image) after phase-preserving denoising. *Top*: Original image. *Middle*: Denoised image. *Bottom*: Sample of an applied Haar-like feature.

Also, the amplitude response from the smallest scale of the filter pair across the whole image will be the noise with Rayleigh distribution.

Finally by estimating the mean value μ_r and standard deviation σ_r of the Rayleigh distribution, the shrinkage threshold can be estimated. The thresholds are automatically determined and applied for each filter scale.

A number of parameters impacts the quality of the denoised output image. The threshold of noise standard deviations to be rejected (k), the number of filter scales to be used (N_ρ) and the number of orientations (N_r) are the key parameters.

We set the parameters $k = 3$, $N_\rho = 4$ and $N_r = 4$ in our experiments. These parameters result in an acceptable representation of small and middle-size faces. However, for large faces, it can lead to erroneous results. One approach is using a set of different parameters to obtain different images. Another approach is scaling the original images and then using the same parameters for conversions.

We used the second approach for a better speed-up. After a conversion to the denoised form, adaptive histogram equalization is used for both training and test images.

Figure 2 shows the discriminate advantage of using denoised images. The sample Haar-like feature applied on the eye region shows increased feature values (F_{haar}) which leads to a faster convergence of the classifier.

3   Global Haar-Like Features

Viola and Jones used five types of Haar-like features, which, from now on, we identify as *local features*. The value of a local feature f_i is computed by subtraction of white and black regions, $w_i - b_i$, using integral image [19].

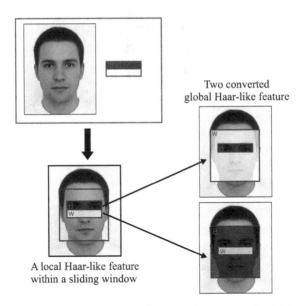

Two converted
global Haar-like feature

A local Haar-like feature
within a sliding window

Fig. 3. Extraction of Global Haar-features from a standard Haar-feature

3.1   Global Features

For every given local feature, we introduce two global Haar-like features (in short, global features) as $F_b = F - b_i$ and $F_w = F - w_i$ where F is the integral value of the whole reference model (window). Global features will be used in conjunction with the local ones (Figure 3). We call them global features, as these feature values provides global information in addition to a standard (local) one.

If a local feature is being selected by a boosting algorithm for the formation of a cascade, then it would be a candidate to be a global feature as well. Global features are faster than local features, since the required values for calculating them are already computed at earlier stages. Figure 3 illustrates conversion steps from a local feature to global ones.

A problem with weak classifiers is that in the last stages, many of them are needed to reject 50% of non-face samples. The inclusion of these weak classifiers highly increases the computational cost. Therefore, global features are an efficient alternative, as they are faster to calculate and also because they provide a better classification, due to adding a new level of information by extracting different patterns than the local features.

In short, the term *global* in this paper refers to a comparison between the whole window and a portion of that window, while the common local features refer to *adjacent* rectangles of *equal* size.

3.2   Dynamic Global Features

Let b_i and w_i denote the integral values for the black and white regions of the ith local feature, respectively, defining the local feature value as $w_i - b_i$. Let F

be the integral value of the reference model (sliding window). The current local feature is now accompanied by two global feature values, to be used in a weak classifier of the cascade for a given sliding window. In the dynamic version of global features, we update F by

$$F = F + \sum_{i=1}^{j \leq n} (w_i - b_i) \tag{5}$$

where, n is the total number of local features in the current cascade and j is current index over the global feature being assessed.

By using this equation, as the input windows progress through the cascade, the value of F is updated using the global features. We call this type of features *dynamic global* Haar-like features (in short, dynamic global features). Experimental results show that the dynamic global features can obtain a higher detection rate and less false positive rate in comparison with the non-dynamic version of the global features.

4 Boosting Cascades with Local and Global Features

In this section, a cascade of weak classifiers is designed by considering the global features. It is common that each stage of a cascade should reject 50% of negative samples while the true detection rate remains close to optimal.

When global features are considered, it is important to decide which of the local features should be considered as being global. One approach is to temporarily keep a current global feature and continue searching for the next local feature, without considering the effect of the current global feature. If global features show a better rejection rate, then it is efficient to choose the reserved global feature as the desired feature and then searching for next local features again. Also, even if their rejection rate becomes equal or near to equal, the global features are preferred.

Pseudocode for the learning cascades is provided as Algorithm 1. Applying the learning process, the following weak classifiers are obtained, where the optional pairs (ϕ_b^k, ϕ_w^k) denote global features:

$$(\theta_l^k, (\phi_b^k, \phi_w^k)), \ldots, (\theta_l^n, (\phi_b^n, \phi_w^n)). \tag{6}$$

We observed that when not using dynamic global features, the number of global features selected during the cascade design is insignificant. Also, the effect of only using global features is not noticeable.

However, by using the dynamic global features, the number of global features selected was noticeable. The use of dynamic global features increases the performance of Haar-like feature based face detectors, in terms of detection rate, false alarm rate, and average number of features met in a window, and consequently results in a speed-up. Therefore, we preferred to use dynamic global features in conjunction with the local features.

Algorithm 1. Learning weak classifiers by using local and dynamic global features

---

Input: N_p positive samples; N_n negative samples.

Initialisation: Let $F_w = F_b = F$, where F is the sum of intensities in the whole window. Let $k = 1$.

Output: $(\theta_l^k, (\phi_b^k, \phi_w^k)), \ldots, (\theta_l^n, (\phi_b^n, \phi_w^n))$.

1. Find k^{th} local weak classifier θ_l^k with threshold $T_l^k = \sum_{i=1}^{m_k}(w_i - b_i)$; where m_k is the total number of local features in the kth classifier.

2. Find next $(k + 1^{th})$ weak classifier θ_l^{k+1};

3. Find k^{th} pair of global weak classifiers ϕ_b^k and ϕ_w^k, corresponding to the black and white parts of the local feature, respectively; set $T_b^k = \sum_{i=1}^{m_k}(F_b - b_i)$, and $T_w^k = \sum_{i=1}^{m_k}(F_w - w_i)$;

4. Decide to choose best classifier(s) among (ϕ_b^k), (ϕ_w^k), and θ_l^{k+1};

5. **if** A global classifiers is selected **then**

6.   Update the values of F_w and F_b as: $F_w = F_w + w_i$, $F_b = F_b - b_i$;

7.   Set $k = k + 1$, find the next local weak classifier θ_l^k;

8.   Go to Step 3;

9. **else**

10. $k = k + 1$;

11.   Add θ_l^k to the cascade and search for next local weak classifier θ_l^{k+1};

12.   Go to Step 3;

13. **end if**

---

5   Experimental Results

While a standard Haar-like classifier performs well in face detection under ideal lighting conditions [22], it seriously has difficulties when detecting faces under challenging illumination conditions, even for straight forward looking faces. However, we observed that after a phase-preserving denoising, and using the suggested global and dynamic global features, considerable improvements can be achieved in the true detection rate in comparison to that obtained using a standard Haar-like classifier. Choosing proper denoising parameters (k, N_ρ and N_r) can lead to further improvements.

In order to validate the methods proposed in this paper, we designed four classifiers using two preprocessing methods and different combinations of the local, global and dynamic global features.

The first detector was trained based on a variance-normalized samples using only the standard local Haar-like features (VN+Standard Local Haar).

The second classifier (VN+DyGlobal) was also learned from variance-normalized preprocessed samples, but this time using both local and dynamic global features.

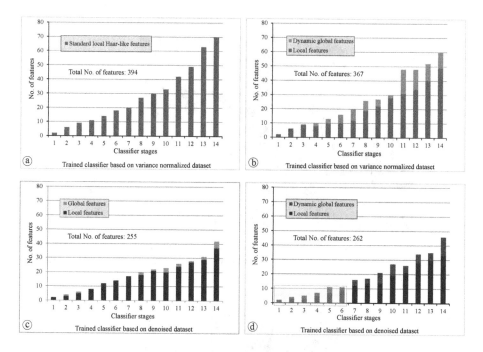

Fig. 4. Distribution of features for different learned cascades, each consists of 14 stages

The third detector is learned by local and global features, and the training dataset is enhanced by phase-preserving denoising technique (PPD+Global).

And the last detector (PPD+DyGlobal) uses local and dynamic global features, also based on the denoised training dataset.

For training all four classifiers, we used a large dataset of 10,000 face samples from different ages, genders, races and nationalities, mainly from AR [8] and Yale [4] datasets.

In addition, 50,000 non-face samples were considered as negative samples to train each stage of the cascade. Non-face samples were selected randomly from a dataset of scene categories [3]. This dataset consists of fifteen natural scene categories, including buildings, offices, roads, and landscapes.

We evaluated the performance of the four classifiers in terms of number of features involved in each stage, speed, and precision rate.

Figure 4 depicts the distribution graphs of local and global features for each of the four mentioned classifiers. Graph (a) is related to the first classifier (VN+ Standard Local Haar) and it shows a total number of 394 features in a cascade of 14 weak classifiers. The graph shows that classifier (a) involves highest number of features, compared to other three classifiers. This means higher computational cost to confirm or reject a face candidate.

Graph (b) represents a faster classifier with a considerably smaller number of local features and also a total number of 367 features including both local and Dynamic global features, trained based on variance normalized dataset.

Fig. 5. Sample detection results for the first two classifiers trained based on standard Haar features (blue circles) or dynamic global features (green squares), using a variance-normalized dataset

Fig. 6. Sample detection results for the last two classifiers trained based on global features (blue circles) or dynamic global features (red squares), using the proposed denoised dataset

Graphs (c) and (d) show feature distributions when we trained the classifiers with a phase-based denoised dataset. While the total number of features in graph (c) and (d) are very close to each other (255, and 262 respectively), the Classifier PPD+DyGlobal outperforms the other three classifiers as follows: Considering 50% rejection rate for each stage, 97% of non-face images will be rejected within the first six stages (weak classifiers), so having the minimum number of features in the first six stages plays a very crucial rule (i.e. the smaller the number of features, the faster the classifier). Classifier (d) contains only 40 features in its first six stages, while classifiers (a), (b), and (c) involve 60, 56, and 46 features in

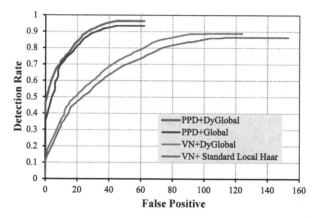

Fig. 7. ROC curve of the proposed detectors on MIT-CMU dataset. PPD+DyGlobal denotes the classifier trained based on denoised samples using the local and dynamic global features. PPD+Global denotes the classifier trained based on denoised samples using local and global features. Similarly, the two other detectors, are learned from variance normalized samples.

the six early stages which means 50%, 40%, and 15% slower operation compared to the PPD+DyGlobal classifier.

In addition to computational cost, we also need to consider effectiveness and accuracy of the four classifiers in terms of recall rate and false alarm.

Figures 5 and 6 show detection results for some sample images that were not used in the training phase in none of the four classifiers. The figures illustrate that the classifier we trained based on dynamic global classifier and phase-based denoising provides more accurate results. Figure 7 illustrates the *receiver operating characteristic* (ROC) curves for the four mentioned detectors evaluated on the MIT-CMU [24] dataset. The figure shows that the best results were obtained using the PPD+DyGlobal detector. Observe that PPD+Global also performed better than the considered local methods.

As further evaluation, Table 1 provides a comparison between the proposed PPD+DyGlobal classifier, standard Viola-Jones, as well as four other state-of-the-art face detection techniques [16,11,15,20]. The overall results confirm that the proposed method not only incorporates a smaller number of features (as discussed in the first part of the experimental section) but also outperforms the others in terms of a higher detection rate and a smaller number of false-positives due to global information provided by the proposed dynamic global features.

Table 1. Comparison between PPD+DyGlobal and state-of-the-art face detection techniques

Method	Proposed	VJ[19]	RCBoost[16]	Pham[11]	Opt[15]	Chain[20]
Detection rate (%)	96.4	86.3	94.00	91.00	95.00	93.00
# False-positives	62	153	96	170	900	130

6 Conclusions

In this research, we studied the effect of a preprocessing technique on input images for boosting-based face detectors. Phase-preserving denoising of images is used to preprocess the input images. The paper also proposed a new type of Haar-like features, called global Haar features, for the first time. This type of features supports faster calculations than local Haar features and provides a new level of global information from the query patches. We also proposed to use a dynamic version of the global features that updates its value dynamically as the classifier assess next local features.

Four distinct cascades are learned with and without using the denoised images and global Haar features. Finally, resulting detection rates and false-alarm rates shown a significant advantage for the proposed technique against state-of-the-art face detection systems, especially for challenging lighting conditions and noisy input images.

The proposed technique is expected to be effective on various object detection fields, as we also applied the proposed technique as part of a vehicle detection system [14] with superior results. We highly recommend to use, and to do further study on the proposed *global Haar-like features* for different kinds of boosting or Haar-based object detectors, not limited to face detection.

Acknowledgment. The authors thank professor Reinhard Klette for discussions and comments on the paper.

References

1. Hou, X., Liu, C.L., Tan, T.: Learning boosted asymmetric classifiers for object detection. In: Computer Vision and Pattern Recognition, pp. 330–338 (2006)
2. Kovesi, P.: Phase Preserving Denoising of Images. Digital Image Computing, Techniques and Applications (1999)
3. Lazebnik, S., Schmid, C., Ponce, J.: Beyond Bags of Features: Spatial Pyramid Matching for Recognizing Natural Scene Categories. In: Computer Vision and Pattern Recognition, pp. 2169–2178 (2006)
4. Lee, K.C., Ho, J., Kreigman, D.: Acquiring linear subspaces for face recognition under variable lighting. IEEE Trans. Pattern Analysis Machine Intelligence 27, 684–698 (2005)
5. Li, S.Z., Zhang, Z.: Floatboost learning and statistical face detection. IEEE Trans. PAMI 26, 1112–1123 (2004)
6. Lienthart, R., Maydt, J.: An Extended Set of Haar-like Features for Rapid Object Detection. In: International Conference on Image Processing, pp. 900–903 (2002)
7. Liu, C., Shum, H.Y.: Kullback-leibler boosting. In: Computer Vision and Pattern Recognition, pp. 587–594 (2003)
8. Martinez, A.M., Benavente, R.: The A.R. face dataset. CVC Technical Report (1998)
9. Masnadi Shirazi, H., Vasconcelos, N.: Cost-Sensitive Boosting. IEEE Trans. PAMI 33, 294–309 (2011)
10. Masnadi Shirazi, H., Vasconcelos, N.: High Detection-rate Cascades for Real-Time Object Detection. In: ICCV, pp. 1–6 (2007)

11. Pham, M.T., Cham, T.J.: Fast Training and Selection of Haar features using Statistics in Boosting-based Face Detection. In: International Conference on Computer Vision, pp. 1–7 (2007)
12. Pham, M.T., Gao, Y., Houng, V.T.D., Cham, T.J.: Fast Polygonal Integration and Its Application in Extending Haar-like Features to Improve Object Detection. In: Computer Vision and Pattern Recognition, pp. 942–949 (2010)
13. Rezaei, M., Klette, R.: Novel Adaptive Eye Detection and Tracking for Challenging Lighting Conditions. In: Park, J.-I., Kim, J. (eds.) ACCV Workshops 2012, Part II. LNCS, vol. 7729, pp. 427–440. Springer, Heidelberg (2013)
14. Rezaei, M., Terauchi, M.: Vehicle Detection Based on Multi-feature Clues and Dempster-Shafer Fusion Theory. In: 6th Pacific-Rim Symposium on Image and Video Technology (2013)
15. Saberian, M.J., Vasconcelos, N.: Learning Optimal Embedded Cascades. IEEE Trans. PAMI 34, 2005–2018 (2012)
16. Saberian, M.J., Vasconcelos, N.: Boosting Classifier Cascades. In: Neural Information Processing Systems (2010)
17. Struc, V., Vesnicer, B., Mihelic, F., Pavesic, N.: Removing illumination artifacts from face images using the nuisance attribute projection. In: IEEE International Conference on Acoustics Speech and Signal Processing, pp. 846–849 (2011)
18. Vaudrey, T., Morales, S., Wedel, A., Klette, R.: Generalized Residual Images Effect on Illumination Artifact Removal for Correspondence Algorithms. Pattern Recognition 44, 2034–2046 (2011)
19. Viola, P., Jones, M.: Robust Real-Time Face Detection. International Journal of Computer Vision 57, 137–154 (2004)
20. Xiao, R., Zhu, L., Zhang, H.J.: Boosting chain learning for object detection. In: Computer Vision and Pattern Recognition, pp. 709–715 (2003)
21. Yang, M.H., Kriegman, D., Ahuja, N.: Detecting faces in images: A survey. IEEE Trans. PAMI 24, 34–58 (2002)
22. Zhang. C., Zhang, Z.: Boosting-Based Face Detection and Adaptation. Morgan & Claypool (2010)
23. Zhang, C., Zhang, Z.: A Survey of Recent Advances in Face Detection. Microsoft Research. Technical Report, MSR-TR-2010-66 (2010)
24. Carnegie Mellon University image dataset,
    http://www.vasc.ri.cmu.edu/idb/html/face/frontal_images

High Accuracy Ellipse-Specific Fitting

Tomonari Masuzaki[1,*], Yasuyuki Sugaya[1], and Kenichi Kanatani[2]

[1] Toyohashi University of Technology
{masuzaki,sugaya}@iim.cs.tut.ac.jp
[2] Okayama University
kanatani2013@yahoo.co.jp

Abstract. We propose a new method that always fits an ellipse to a point sequence extracted from images. The currently known best ellipse fitting method is hyper-renormalization of Kanatani et al., but it may return a hyperbola when the noise in the data is very large. Our proposed method returns an ellipse close to the point sequence by random sampling of data points. Doing simulation, we show that our method has higher accuracy than the method of Fitzgibbon et al. and the method of Szpak et al., the two methods so far proposed to always return an ellipse.

Keywords: ellipse-specific fitting, random sampling, hyperaccuracy correction.

1 Introduction

Detecting circles and ellipses in images is the first step of many computer vision applications including industrial robotic operations and autonomous navigation [4,6,8]. To this end, point sequences constituting elliptic arcs are detected by image processing operations [5,11,20,21,22], and then an ellipse equation is fitted to them. The simplest technique for the latter is to minimize the *algebraic distance*, i.e., the sum of squares of the ellipse equation. The solution is obtained analytically. Since the algebraic distance is 0 if all coefficients are 0, we need to impose some constraint on them, and the solution depends on it. Methods of this type are called *algebraic*. The oldest and best known algebraic method is *least squares (LS)*, which constrains the sum of squares of the coefficients to 1. A more accurate algebraic method was proposed by Taubin [24]. The most accurate algebraic method known is HyperLS [13,14].

Although algebraic methods do not require iterations, we can achieve higher accuracy by incorporating iterations. The standard procedure is *maximum likelihood (ML)*, which minimizes the *reprojection error*, i.e., the sum of the distances from data points to the fitted ellipse [4]. The reprojection error is well approximated by what is known as the *Sampson error* [4], which can be minimized by various means including the *FNS (Fundamental Numerical Scheme)* of Chojnatcki et al. [2], the *HEIV (Heteroscedastic Errors-in-Variable)* of Leedan and

---

* Corresponding author.

R. Klette, M. Rivera, and S. Satoh (Eds.): PSIVT 2013, LNCS 8333, pp. 314–324, 2014.

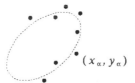

Fig. 1. Fit an ellipse to given points

Meer [18] and Matei and Leedan [19], and the *projective Gauss-Newton itera-tions* of Kanatani and Sugaya [15]. The exact ML solution can be obtained by iterating Sampson error minimization [16].

Rather than minimizing some cost function, we may directly derive equations to solve so that the resulting solution has high accuracy. The oldest method of this type is *iterative reweight*, which was improved by Kanatani [7,8] to a high accuracy scheme called *renormalization*. It was further improved by Al-Sharadqah and Chernov [1] and Kanatani et al. [12] to *hyper-renormalization*. On the other hand, one can apply what is called *hyperaccurate correction* to the ML solution so as to further improve the accuracy [9,17]. Hyper-renormalization and hyperaccurate correction both achieve the theoretical accuracy limit called the *KCR lower bound* [8,10] up to a high degree and are regarded as the most accurate of all currently known methods.

However, all these are methods to fit a quadratic equation in x and y, or a *conic*, to a point sequence. Usually, an ellipse results if the sequence is extracted from an elliptic arc, but a hyperbola or a parabola could result when the se-quence is very short and the noise is very large. It is Fitzgibbon et al. [3] who first proposed a method that only fits an ellipse. It is an algebraic method, and the computation is very easy, but the accuracy is low. Recently, Szpak et al. [23] introduced a high accuracy ellipse-specific method based on Sampson error min-imization. In this paper, we incorporate to hyper-renormalization a procedure for avoiding non-ellipses and demonstrate by experiments that our technique outperforms the method of Szpak et al. [23].

2   Ellipse Fitting

Curves represented by a quadratic equations in x and y in the form

$$Ax^2 + 2Bxy + Cy^2 + 2f_0(Dx + Ey) + f_0^2 F = 0, \tag{1}$$

are called *conics*, which include ellipses, parabolas, hyperbolas, and their degen-eracies such as two lines [6]. The condition that Eq. (1) represents an ellipse is

$$AC - B^2 > 0. \tag{2}$$

Our task is to compute the coefficients $A, ..., F$ so that the ellipse of Eq. (1) passes through given points $(x_\alpha, y_\alpha), \alpha = 1, ..., N$, as closely possible (Fig. 1). In

Eq. (1), f_0 is a constant that has the order of the image size for stabilizing finite length numerical computation (we set $f_0 = 600$ in our experiments). For a point sequence (x_α, y_α), $\alpha = 1, ..., N$, we define 6-D vectors

$$\xi_\alpha = (x_\alpha^2,\ 2x_\alpha y_\alpha,\ y_\alpha^2,\ 2f_0 x_\alpha,\ 2f_0 y_\alpha,\ f_0^2)^\top,$$
$$\theta = (A,\ B,\ C,\ D,\ E,\ F)^\top. \tag{3}$$

The condition that (x_α, y_α) satisfies Eq. (1) is written as

$$(\xi_\alpha, \theta) = 0, \tag{4}$$

where (a, b) denotes the inner product of vectors a and b. Since vector θ has scale indeterminacy, we normalize it to unit norm: $\|\theta\| = 1$.

Since Eq. (4) is not exactly satisfied in the presence of noise, we compute a θ such that $(\xi_\alpha, \theta) \approx 0$, $\alpha = 1, ..., N$. For computing a θ that is close to its true value, we need to consider the statistical properties of noise. The standard model is to regard the noise in (x_α, y_α) as independent Gaussian random variable of mean 0 and standard deviation σ. Then, the covariance matrix of the vector ξ_α has the form $\sigma^2 V_0[\xi_\alpha]$, where

$$V_0[\xi_\alpha] = 4 \begin{pmatrix} x_\alpha^2 & x_\alpha y_\alpha & 0 & f_0 x_\alpha & 0 & 0 \\ x_\alpha y_\alpha & x_\alpha^2 + y_\alpha^2 & x_\alpha y_\alpha & f_0 y_\alpha & f_0 x_\alpha & 0 \\ 0 & x_\alpha y_\alpha & y_\alpha^2 & 0 & f_0 y_\alpha & 0 \\ f_0 x_\alpha & f_0 y_\alpha & 0 & f_0^2 & 0 & 0 \\ 0 & f_0 x_\alpha & f_0 y_\alpha & 0 & f_0^2 & 0 \\ 0 & 0 & 0 & 0 & 0 & 0 \end{pmatrix}, \tag{5}$$

which we call the *normalized covariance matrix* [8,10,15].

3   Hyper-renormalization

The hyper-renormalization of Kanatani et al. [12] can be described as follows:

1. Let $W_\alpha = 1$, $\alpha = 1, ..., N$, and $\theta_0 = 0$.
2. Compute the following matrices M and N:

$$M = \frac{1}{N} \sum_{\alpha=1}^{N} W_\alpha \xi_\alpha \xi_\alpha^\top,$$

$$N = \frac{1}{N} \sum_{\alpha=1}^{N} W_\alpha \left(V_0[\xi_\alpha] + 2\mathcal{S}[\xi_\alpha e^\top] \right)$$

$$- \frac{1}{N^2} \sum_{\alpha=1}^{N} W_\alpha^2 \left((\xi_\alpha, M_5^- \xi_\alpha) V_0[\xi_\alpha] + 2\mathcal{S}[V_0[\xi_\alpha] M_5^- \xi_\alpha \xi_\alpha^\top] \right), \tag{6}$$

where $\mathcal{S}[\cdot]$ denotes symmetrization $(\mathcal{S}[A] = (A + A^\top)/2)$ and the vector e is defined to be

$$e = (1, 0, 1, 0, 0, 0)^\top. \tag{7}$$

The symbol M_5^- denotes the pseudoinverse of M with truncated rank 5, i.e., with the smallest eigenvalue replaced by 0 in the spectral decomposition.

3. Solve the generalized eigenvalue problem

$$N\theta = \mu M\theta, \tag{8}$$

and compute the unit eigenvector θ for the largest eigenvalue μ.

4. If $\theta \approx \theta_0$ up to sign, return θ and stop. Else, let

$$W_\alpha \leftarrow \frac{1}{(\theta, V_0[\xi_\alpha]\theta)}, \qquad \theta_0 \leftarrow \theta, \tag{9}$$

and go back to Step 2.

Hyper-renormalization is regarded as achieving practically the highest accuracy among existing methods, but it returns a non-ellipse, typically a hyperbola [12], when the sequence is very short and the noise is very large, as our experiments later show.

4   Ellipse Specific Methods

For fitting only an ellipse, Fitzgibbon et al. [3] proposed to minimize the *algebraic distance*

$$J_{\mathrm{LS}} = \sum_{\alpha=1}^{N}(\xi_\alpha, \theta)^2, \tag{10}$$

subject to $AC - B^2 = 1$. This constraint is written as

$$(\theta, N_{\mathrm{F}}\theta) = 1, \qquad N_{\mathrm{F}} \equiv \begin{pmatrix} 0 & 0 & 1 & 0 & 0 & 0 \\ 0 & -2 & 0 & 0 & 0 & 0 \\ 1 & 0 & 0 & 0 & 0 & 0 \\ 0 & 0 & 0 & 0 & 0 & 0 \\ 0 & 0 & 0 & 0 & 0 & 0 \\ 0 & 0 & 0 & 0 & 0 & 0 \end{pmatrix}. \tag{11}$$

The solution that minimizes Eq. (10) subject to this constraint is obtained by solving a generalized eigenvalue problem

$$N_{\mathrm{F}}\theta = \mu M_{\mathrm{LS}}\theta, \tag{12}$$

and computing the unit eigenvector θ for the largest eigenvalue μ, where the matrix M_{LS} is defined by

$$M_{\mathrm{LS}} = \frac{1}{N}\sum_{\alpha=1}^{N}\xi_\alpha\xi_\alpha^\top. \tag{13}$$

It has been widely observed, however, that the resulting ellipse is heavily biased. This is because the algebraic distance does not take into account the statistical properties of ξ_α expressed by its covariance matrix.

Recently, Szpak et al. [23] proposed a new ellipse specific method. They minimized

$$J = \frac{1}{N} \sum_{\alpha=1}^{N} \frac{(\boldsymbol{\xi}_\alpha, \boldsymbol{\theta})^2}{(\boldsymbol{\theta}, V_0[\boldsymbol{\xi}_\alpha]\boldsymbol{\theta})} + \frac{\lambda \|\boldsymbol{\theta}\|^4}{(\boldsymbol{\theta}, N\boldsymbol{\theta})^2}, \tag{14}$$

where λ is a small constant. The first term on the right is called the *Sampson error*, which approximates the reprojection error up to high order noise terms. The second term on the right diverges if $(\boldsymbol{\theta}, N_F\boldsymbol{\theta}) = 0$, i.e., if $\boldsymbol{\theta}$ represents a parabola. Since the domain of $\boldsymbol{\theta}$ is separated into the region $(\boldsymbol{\theta}, N_F\boldsymbol{\theta}) > 0$ of ellipses and the region $(\boldsymbol{\theta}, N_F\boldsymbol{\theta}) < 0$ of hyperbolas, minimization search starting from the ellipse domain does not cross the boundary $(\boldsymbol{\theta}, N_F\boldsymbol{\theta}) = 0$, on which J is ∞. Szpak et al. [23] used the Levenberg-Marquardt method for minimizing Eq. (14), choosing λ as small as possible as long as an ellipse results.

5   Proposed Method

It has been observed that the accuracy of hyper-renormalization is higher than Sampson error minimization [12,17]. Hence, it is reasonable to retain the solution of hyper-renormalization as long as it is an ellipse. If the hyper-renormalization iterations do not converge within a fixed limit, or if the resulting solution is not an ellipse, we switch to random sampling: we randomly choose from the point sequence five different points and compute the conic that passes through them. If a non-ellipse results, we discard the five points and choose new five points. If an ellipse results, we compute its Sampson error (the first term on the right of Eq. (14)) and choose the solution for which the Sampson error is the smallest. The procedure is summarized as follows:

1. Fit an ellipse to a point sequence (x_α, y_α), $\alpha = 1, ..., N$, by hyper-renormalization, and compute its parameter vector $\boldsymbol{\theta}$. If

$$(\boldsymbol{\theta}, N_F\boldsymbol{\theta}) > 0, \tag{15}$$

   return $\boldsymbol{\theta}$ and stop.
2. If the hyper-renormalization iterations do not converge within a fixed limit (we set it to 100 times in our experiment), or if the resulting solution is not satisfy Eq. (15), we randomly choose five different points and compute the conic that passes through them.
3. If $\boldsymbol{\theta}$ does not satisfy Eq. (15), we discard the five points and choose new five points.
4. If the computed $\boldsymbol{\theta}$ satisfies Eq. (15), compute its Sampson error.
5. Repeat the above step many times (1000 times in our experiment) and choose the solution for which the Sampson error is the smallest.

6   Experiment

We generated four point sequences shown in Fig. 2. The points have equal arc length separations on each ellipse. Random Gaussian noise of mean 0 and standard deviation σ is added independently to the x and y coordinates of each

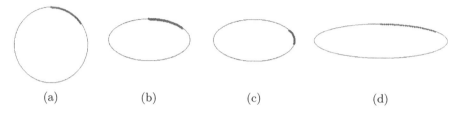

Fig. 2. Point sequences for our experiment. The number of points is 30, 30, 15, and 30 and the average distance between neighboring points is 2.96, 3.31, 2.72, and 5.72 for (a), (b), (c), and (d), respectively.

Fig. 3. The true value $\bar{\boldsymbol{\theta}}$, the computed value $\boldsymbol{\theta}$, and its orthogonal component $\Delta^{\perp}\boldsymbol{\theta}$ to $\bar{\boldsymbol{\theta}}$

point, and an ellipse is fitted. Since the computed value $\boldsymbol{\theta}$ and its true value $\bar{\boldsymbol{\theta}}$ are both unit vectors, we measure the error $\Delta\boldsymbol{\theta}$ by the orthogonal component [15]

$$\Delta^{\perp}\boldsymbol{\theta} = \boldsymbol{P}_{\bar{\theta}}\boldsymbol{\theta}, \tag{16}$$

where $\boldsymbol{P}_{\bar{\theta}}(\equiv \boldsymbol{I} - \bar{\boldsymbol{\theta}}\bar{\boldsymbol{\theta}}^{\top})$ is the orthogonal projection matrix along $\bar{\boldsymbol{\theta}}$ (Fig. 3). We evaluate the RMS error

$$D = \sqrt{\frac{1}{10000}\sum_{a=1}^{10000}\|\Delta^{\perp}\boldsymbol{\theta}^{(a)}\|^2}, \tag{17}$$

over 10000 trials using different noise each time (the superscript (a) indicates the value for the ath trial).

Figure 4 shows the ratio of non-ellipse occurrences by hyper-renormalization and the RMS error for the data in Fig. 2(a)~(d). The horizontal axis indicates the noise level σ divided by the average distance between neighboring points, which we call the *relative noise level*. Interrupted plots indicate that beyond that noise level convergence was not always reached after a specified number of iterations. The dotted lines indicate the KCR lower bound [8,10] given by

$$D_{\text{KCR}} = \frac{\sigma}{\sqrt{N}}\sqrt{\text{tr}\bar{\boldsymbol{M}}_5^-}. \tag{18}$$

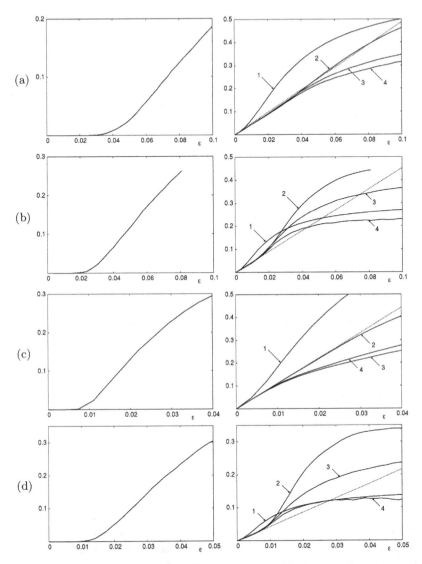

Fig. 4. Left column: The ratio of non-ellipse occurrences by hyper-renormalization for the data in Fig. 2(a) – (d). The horizontal axis is for the relative noise level ϵ. Right column: The corresponding RMS fitting error: 1. The method of Fitzgibbon et al. [3]. 2. hyper-renormalization. 3. The method of Szpak et al. [23]. 4. Proposed method. The dotted lines indicate the KCR lower bound. Interrupted plots indicate that convergence is not reached after a specified number of iterations above that noise level.

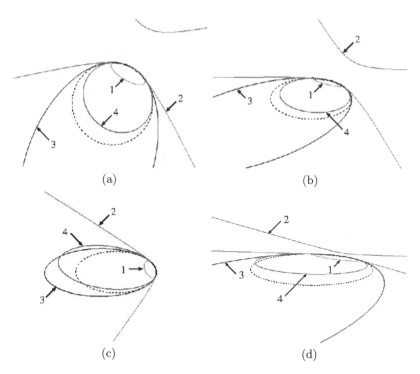

Fig. 5. Fitting examples for a particular noise when hyper-renormalization returns a hyperbola. 1. The method of Fitzgibbon et al. [3]. 2. hyper-renormalization. 3. The method of Szpak et al. [23]. 4. Proposed method. The dotted lines indicate the true shapes. The relative noise level ϵ is 0.169, 0.151, 0.092, and 0.087 for (a), (b), (c), and (d), respectively.

As we can see, the accuracy of the method Fitzgibbon et al. [3] is generally very low, while hyper-renormalization[1] and the method of Szpak et al.[2] [23] are very accurate; they almost achieve the KCR lower bound when the noise is very small. However, the method Fitzgibbon et al. [3] can outperform hyper-renormalization and the method of Szpak et al. [23] when the points are chosen from a low-curvature part as in Fig. 2(d) and the noise is very large. Since the method of Szpak et al. [23] and the proposed method both restrict the solution to be an ellipse, their RMS error is smaller than hyper-renormalization in all cases, and in most cases our method is superior to that of Szpak et al. [23].

The reason that a hyperbola is fitted to an elliptic arc is, according to our interpretation, that a few heavily deviated points "pull" the curve to be a hyperbola. Such "bad points" are automatically ignored in the course of our random sampling, but all the points play the same role for the method of Szpak et al. [23]. This may be the cause of higher performance of our method. However, we

---

[1] We used the code at: http://www.iim.cs.tut.ac.jp/~sugaya/
[2] We used the code at: https://sites.google.com/site/szpakz/

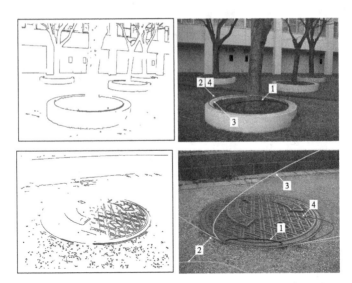

Fig. 6. Left: Edges extracted from real images. Red edge pixels (200 points above and 140 points below) are used for ellipse fitting. Right: Fitted ellipses superimposed on the original image. 1. The method of Fitzgibbon et al. [3]. 2. hyper-renormalization. 3. The method of Szpak et al. [23]. 4. Proposed method.

observe that the difference between the method of Szpak et al. [23] and ours is very small for high-curvature arc as in Fig. 2(c).

Figure 5 shows fitting examples for a particular noise when hyper-renormalization returns a hyperbola. The dotted lines indicate the true shapes. We can observe a clear contrast: the method of Fitzgibbon et al. [3] fits a small and flat ellipse, while the method of Szpak et al. [23] fits a large ellipse close to the fitted hyperbola. Our method is in between, fitting an ellipse closer to the true shape.

The left of Fig. 6 shows edge images of real scenes. We fitted an ellipse to the edge points indicated in red (200 points above and 140 points below) by different methods. In the right, fitted ellipses superimposed on the original images are shown. The method of Fitzgibbon et al. [3] fits a small and flat ellipse in both cases. In the above example, hyper-renormalization returns an ellipse (hence our method) which is fairly accurate; the method of Szpak et al. [23] also fits an ellipse close to it. However, hyper-renormalization returns a hyperbola in the example below, and the method of Szpak et al. [23] fits a very large ellipse close to that hyperbola. We can see that our ellipse is somewhat between the small and flat ellipse of Fitzgibbon et al. [3] and the large ellipse of Szpak et al. [23].

7 Concluding Remarks

We have proposed a new method that always fits an ellipse to a point sequence extracted from images. The currently known best method is hyper-renormalization of Kanatani et al. [12], but it may return a hyperbola when the noise in the data is very large. Our proposed method incorporates random sampling so that an ellipse always results. Doing simulation, we showed that our method has higher accuracy than the method of Fitzgibbon et al. [3] and the method of Szpak et al. [23], the two currently known ellipse-specific methods. We also observed that when hyper-renormalization returns a hyperbola, the method of Szpak et al. [23] tends to fit a large ellipse close to that hyperbola while the method of Fitzgibbon et al. [3] tends to fit a small and flat ellipse. Our method fits an ellipse somewhat in between.

According to our experiences, we have never observed hyperbolas fitted to edge points of elliptic arcs in real applications unless artificial noise is added or edges are artificially limited to very short segments. If a hyperbola results from an elliptic arc, we should regard this as an indication of insufficient information in the data so that ellipse fitting no longer has meaning. Yet, even in such an extreme circumstance, our method can fit a tolerable ellipse.

Acknowledgements. The authors thank Wojciech Chojnacki of the University of Adelaide, Australia, and Ali Al-Shadraqah of the East Carolina University, USA for helpful discussions on ellipse fitting. This work was supported in part by JSPS Grant-in-Aid for Young Scientists (B 23700202) and for Challenging Exploratory Research (24650086).

References

1. Al-Sharadqah, A., Chernov, N.: A doubly optimal ellipse fit. Computational Statistics and Data Analysis 56(9), 2771–2781 (2012)
2. Chojnacki, W., Brooks, M.J., van den Hengel, A., Gawley, D.: On the fitting of surfaces to data with covariances. IEEE Trans. Patt. Anal. Mach. Intell. 22(11), 1294–1303 (2000)
3. Fitzgibbon, A., Pilu, M., Fisher, R.B.: Direct least squares fitting of ellipses. Patt. Anal. Mach. Intell. 21(5), 476–480 (1999)
4. Hartley, R., Zisserman, A.: Multiple View Geometry in Computer Vision, 2nd edn. Cambridge University Press, Cambridge (2004)
5. Ioannou, D., Huda, W., Laine, A.F.: Circle recognition through a 2D Hough transform and radius histogramming. Image Vis. Comput. 17(1), 15–26 (1999)
6. Kanatani, K.: Geometric Computation for Machine Vision. Oxford University Press, Oxford (1993)
7. Kanatani, K.: Renormalization for unbiased estimation. In: Pro. 4th Int. Conf. Comput. Vis (ICCV 1993), Berlin, Germany, pp. 599–606 (May 1993)
8. Kanatani, K.: Statistical Optimization for Geometric Computation: Theory and Practice. Elsevier, Amsterdam (1996); reprinted, Dover, York, NY, U.S.A. (2005)
9. Kanatani, K.: Ellipse fitting with hyperaccuracy. IEICE Trans. Inf. & Syst. E89-D(10), 2653–2660 (2006)
10. Kanatani, K.: Statistical optimization for geometric fitting: Theoretical accuracy analysis and high order error analysis. Int. J. Comput. Vis. 80(2), 167–188 (2008)
11. Kanatani, K., Ohta, N.: Automatic detection of circular objects by ellipse growing. Int. J. Image Graphics 4(1), 35–50 (2004)

12. Kanatani, K., Al-Sharadqah, A., Chernov, N., Sugaya, Y.: Renormalization Returns: Hyper-renormalization and Its Applications. In: Fitzgibbon, A., Lazebnik, S., Perona, P., Sato, Y., Schmid, C. (eds.) ECCV 2012, Part III. LNCS, vol. 7574, pp. 384–397. Springer, Heidelberg (2012)
13. Kanatani, K., Rangarajan, P.: Hyper least squares fitting of circles and ellipses. Comput. Stat. Data Anal. 55(6), 2197–2208 (2011)
14. Kanatani, K., Rangarajan, P., Sugaya, Y., Niitsuma, H.: HyperLS and its applications. IPSJ Trans. Comput. Vis. Appl. 3, 80–94 (2011)
15. Kanatani, K., Sugaya, Y.: Performance evaluation of iterative geometric fitting algorithms. Comput. Stat. Data Anal. 52(2), 1208–1222 (2007)
16. Kanatani, K., Sugaya, Y.: Unified computation of strict maximum likelihood for geometric fitting. J. Math. Imaging Vis. 38(1), 1–13 (2010)
17. Kanatani, K., Sugaya, Y.: Hyperaccurate correction of maximum likelihood for geometric estimation. IPSJ Trans. Comput. Vis. Appl. 5, 19–29 (2013)
18. Leedan, Y., Meer, P.: Heteroscedastic regression in computer vision: Problems with bilinear constraint. Int. J. Comput. Vis. 37(2), 127–150 (2000)
19. Matei, J., Meer, P.: Estimation of nonlinear errors-in-variables models for computer vision applications. IEEE Trans. Patt. Anal. Mach. Intell. 28(10), 1537–1552 (2006)
20. Roth, G., Levine, M.D.: Extracting geometric primitives. CVGIP: Image Understand 58(1), 1–22 (1993)
21. Roth, G., Levine, M.D.: Geometric primitive extraction using a genetic algorithm. IEEE Trans. Pattern Anal. Mach. Intell. 16(9), 901–905 (1994)
22. Rosin, P.L., West, G.A.W.: Nonparametric segmentation of curves into various representations. IEEE Trans. Pattern Anal. Mach. Intell. 17(12), 1140–1153 (1995)
23. Szpak, Z.L., Chojnacki, W., van den Hengel, A.: Guaranteed ellipse fitting with Sampson distance. In: Fitzgibbon, A., Lazebnik, S., Perona, P., Sato, Y., Schmid, C. (eds.) ECCV 2012, Part V. LNCS, vol. 7576, pp. 87–100. Springer, Heidelberg (2012)
24. Taubin, G.: Estimation of planar curves, surfaces, and non-planar space curves defined by implicit equations with applications to edge and range image segmentation. IEEE Trans. Patt. Anal. Mach. Intell. 13(11), 1115–1138 (1991)

A Trajectory Estimation Method for Badminton Shuttlecock Utilizing Motion Blur

Hidehiko Shishido, Itaru Kitahara, Yoshinari Kameda, and Yuichi Ohta

University of Tsukuba
Tennoudai 1-1-1, Tsukuba, Ibaraki 305-8573, Japan
shishido@image.iit.tsukuba.ac.jp,
{kitahara,kameda,ohta}@iit.tsukuba.ac.jp

Abstract. To build a robust visual tracking method it is important to consider issues such as low observation resolution and variation in the target object's shape. When we capture an object moving fast in a video camera motion blur is observed. This paper introduces a visual trajectory estimation method using blur characteristics in the 3D space. We acquire a movement speed vector based on the shape of a motion blur region. This method can extract both the position and speed of the moving object from an image frame, and apply them to a visual tracking process using Kalman filter. We estimated the 3D position of the object based on the information obtained from two different viewpoints as shown in figure 1. We evaluated our proposed method by the trajectory estimation of a badminton shuttlecock from video sequences of a badminton game.

Keywords: Visual Object Tracking, Motion Blur, Kalman Filter, Statistically Estimation, Badminton Shuttlecock.

1 Introduction

The research on visual object tracking for sports-events is conducted as application cases of computer vision and contributes to developing the tactics of games[1-7]. Because players and balls are the tracking target of the visual tracking processes, a visual tracking method that can handle multiple objects with fast and complicated movement is needed. Moreover, because a shuttlecock is a small (approximately 7cm) item, objects inside the video frame are observed in low resolution. For example, when we capture the game with a general-use video camera, the observation size in a frame might be just about a few pixels.

In this paper, we focus on a badminton shuttlecock as the tracking target since it has the cited problems conspicuously. A shuttlecock is composed of feathers of birds such as waterfowls, attached to the hemispheric cork with adhesive. Since it is much more lightweight than balls used for other games, attaching a transmitter or a marker for position sensing might be difficult. Such attachment would represent extra weight in the object causing trajectory changes. Thus, the tracking method using visual information is expected to be a promising solution to extract the trajectories.

R. Klette, M. Rivera, and S. Satoh (Eds.): PSIVT 2013, LNCS 8333, pp. 325–336, 2014.
© Springer-Verlag Berlin Heidelberg 2014

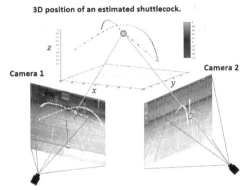

Fig. 1. The estimate result of the proposed method using a video sequence of a badminton game. (2 trajectories)

However, there is an additional problem to track the shuttlecock. Due to its structure, during the badminton game (rally) the moving velocity changes inconsistently and drastically during each rally due to the air resistance [8]. In order to solve the problem, we develop a tracking method that can get extractable information of the object motion depending on the motion speed. When an object moves with low velocity for the shutter-speed of a video camera, there is little motion blur in each frame and it is possible to estimate its accurate position. On the other hand, it is difficult to estimate the accurate position, when the shuttlecock moves fast because the motion blur occurs on one frame. In this case, however, we can estimate the velocity information by analyzing the shape of the motion blur region.

We utilize information provided by motion blur, and we propose a visual tracking method for an object that has variously and drastically changes its moving velocity. A summary of this method is shown in figure 2. Our method defines the shuttle's state by referring the velocity, for not only specifying the color class, but also switching the input information to Kalman filter. When the velocity is low, we observe only the position and estimate the velocity as the difference. At high velocity, we observe the only velocity, and estimate the position by integrating the velocity values. When the velocity is middle, we observe both of the position and velocity.

2   Related Work

Recently, several visual object tracking methods are actively developed using physical or probabilistic movement model. For example, Yang et. al.proposes a visual tracking method applying color and gradient orientation histogram features using a particle filter [17]. Another strategy applying Haar-like features and gradual adaboost through particle filter is proposed by Li et. al [18]. Vasileios et. al. improved the visual tracking precision by updating two observation points

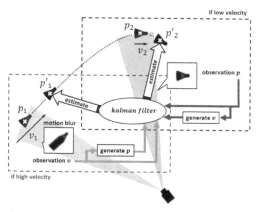

Fig. 2. A visual tracking method of an object that has variously and drastically changes its moving velocity by utilizing the motion blur. Because the observation precision of the position is high when the velocity is slow, we input to a Kalman filter "position (*Observation position*)" and "distance between the observed positions in the former and present frame (*Observation velocity*)". When the velocity is fast, we input to the Kalman filter "observed velocity (*Observation velocity*)" and "estimated position (*Observation position*)".

dynamically (1. An observation point calculated using only the Mean Shift in the observation point of the Kalman filter; 2. An observation point calculated from Mean Shift and the estimate point of the Kalman filter) [12]. Chang et al. separate into three the tracking level depending on the target sequence and proposes a visual tracking method inputting to the Kalman filter an observation value calculated per level [13]. Furthermore, recently, a visual tracking method that used a particle filter together with Kalman filter was studied. Satoh et. al. reduce the number of the particles in comparison with previous studies by using Kalman filter together in simple tracking method based on the information of the color, and succeed in the object tracking [14]. Xu et. al. use Kalman filter analytically and update the particles [15]. This way, the effectiveness of using a particle filter based on the probabilistic model together with the Kalman filter based on the physical motion model is appropriately shown. We follow this approach to improve the tracking accuracy. The motion of a shuttlecock can be expressed with a simple dynamics model and irregular motions due to turns or air resistance can be included using a probabilistic model.

If we insist on tracking the object just in the 2D image space, it becomes difficult when the target object is not observed in an image frame by occlusion. An effective solution is using images from multiple viewpoints [11, 16]. In our approach, we also capture the target object by using at least two video cameras, and reconstruct the motion model in 3D space.

Usually, motion blur is regarded as a source of the observation error that reduces the accuracy of tracking process. On the other hand, there are studies that improve the accuracy by estimating motion blur from observing every frame

Camera	front				side			
Background court	inside		outside		inside		outside	
shuttle speed	high	low	high	low	high	low	high	low
image	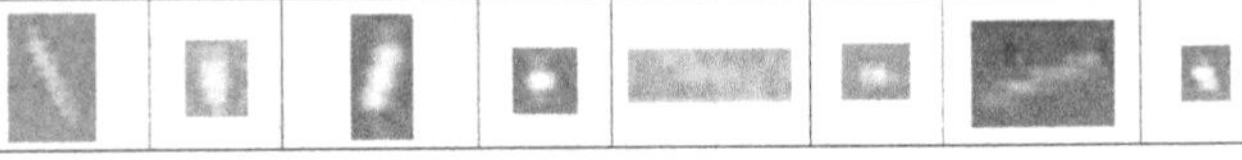							

Fig. 3. Examples of the appearance of a badminton shuttlecock with motion blur (4pixels – 35pixels)

[9, 10, 19]. However, they do not directly use the motion blur as a source of object tracking, but restore the blurred image before the tracking process. Figure 3 shows how a fast moving object's position estimation accuracy will generally decrease because of the motion blur. However we understood that the velocity of the object could be directly estimated from the shape of the motion blur region.

3 Badminton Shuttlecock Tracking Method Using Motion Blur

In this paper, we tackle some issues of visual object tracking. First of all, the target object (shuttlecock) moves very fast. Second, the observed size of the shuttlecock is small. And third, the moving velocity changes inconsistently and drastically during each rally.

For the first issue, we propose a tracking method to estimate the moving velocity from the shape of the motion blur region. For the second issue, we renounce to calculate the likelihood from texture information such as gradient, and instead use the color information. Color information is affected by the environmental conditions such as lighting change and background color. So we generate a probability model of the observed shuttlecock's color to absorb the fluctuation. In the case of the third issue, we develop a tracking method that switches the estimating method depending on the velocity. When the velocity is slow, we input into Kalman filter the current *observed position* and as *observed velocity*, we input the distance between the positions observed in the former and present frames. When the velocity is fast, we input into Kalman filter the *observed position* and the *observed velocity* estimated by the shape of the motion blur.

3.1 The Detection of a Moving Object Region

At the beginning of the object tracking or after having lost sight of the shuttlecock, we detect the shuttlecock by the following processes. At first, moving object candidate regions are extracted by background subtraction processing. In this process player regions are excluded by referring to the player region size. In addition, we mask out the region such as a court-line and the net in where it is difficult to accurately perform the segmentation processing due to the high

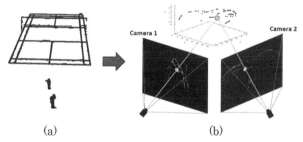

Fig. 4. (a) Masked out region for shuttlecock candidate. (b) Shuttlecock detection by using background subtraction method and the estimation of the 3D position.

brightness level. As shown in figure 4, we execute these processes in the frames captured from two viewpoints, and calculate the 3D position of the shuttlecock by stereo-vision. The 3D position of the shuttlecock is the observed position for Kalman filter.

3.2 Construction of the Kalman Filter

A 3D position, velocity, and acceleration are used for the state of the shuttlecock in the frame k.

$$X_k = \{x_k, \dot{x}_k, \ddot{x}_k, y_k, \dot{y}_k, \ddot{y}_k, z_k, \dot{z}_k, \ddot{z}_k\} \tag{1}$$

The state model of the Kalman filter is denoted by the Equation (2).

$$X_k = AX_{k-1} + Bu_k + \omega_k \tag{2}$$

Here, A is a state transition matrix, and the movement of the shuttlecock forms a parabola with the air resistance,

$$A = \begin{bmatrix} 1 & \delta_t & 0 & 0 & 0 & 0 & 0 & 0 & 0 \\ 0 & 1 & \delta_t & 0 & 0 & 0 & 0 & 0 & 0 \\ 0 & \frac{-c}{m}\delta_t & 0 & 0 & 0 & 0 & 0 & 0 & 0 \\ 0 & 0 & 0 & 1 & \delta_t & 0 & 0 & 0 & 0 \\ 0 & 0 & 0 & 0 & 1 & \delta_t & 0 & 0 & 0 \\ 0 & 0 & 0 & 0 & \frac{-c}{m}\delta_t & 0 & 0 & 0 & 0 \\ 0 & 0 & 0 & 0 & 0 & 1 & \delta_t & 0 \\ 0 & 0 & 0 & 0 & 0 & 0 & 1 & \delta_t \\ 0 & 0 & 0 & 0 & 0 & 0 & \frac{-c}{m}\delta_t & 0 \end{bmatrix}, B = \begin{bmatrix} 0 & \cdots & 0 & 0 \\ \vdots & \ddots & \vdots & \vdots \\ 0 & \cdots & 0 & 0 \\ 0 & \cdots & 0 & -g \end{bmatrix} \tag{3}$$

δ_t is the time lag between two frames. Bu_k is a control input concerning a state transition. m is mass and c expresses the amount of air resistance. Since the acceleration due to gravity g applied in the direction of z is not included in the state transition matrix of A, The matrix B is defined including this consideration. On the other hand, in the frame k, when the estimated 3D position of the shuttlecock is made into z_k, an observation model is expressed by the Equation (4),(5).

$$z_k = \hat{H}_k X_k + \varepsilon_k \tag{4}$$

$$\hat{H}_k = \begin{bmatrix} p_x & 0 & 0 & 0 & 0 & 0 & 0 & 0 & 0 \\ 0 & v_x & 0 & 0 & 0 & 0 & 0 & 0 & 0 \\ 0 & 0 & 0 & 0 & 0 & 0 & 0 & 0 & 0 \\ 0 & 0 & 0 & p_y & 0 & 0 & 0 & 0 & 0 \\ 0 & 0 & 0 & 0 & v_y & 0 & 0 & 0 & 0 \\ 0 & 0 & 0 & 0 & 0 & 0 & 0 & 0 & 0 \\ 0 & 0 & 0 & 0 & 0 & 0 & p_z & 0 & 0 \\ 0 & 0 & 0 & 0 & 0 & 0 & 0 & v_z & 0 \\ 0 & 0 & 0 & 0 & 0 & 0 & 0 & 0 & 0 \end{bmatrix} \tag{5}$$

$$\hat{H}_k = \begin{cases} p_{background-diff}, v_{interframe} & (if\ LowSpeed) \\ p_{particle-center}, v_{blur} & (if\ HighSpeed) \end{cases}$$

$$p : position, v : velocity$$

An *observation model* defines a position and velocity. ε_k is the random noise which occurs at the time of observation. The observation noise is a variance matrix computed from the observation error of the observation trajectory acquired manually and a trajectory without observation noise. According to the velocity gained by a process explained later ahead in this paper, the *observation model* $\hat{H}_k$ according to the object's velocity is obtained by choosing the *observation information* given to a Kalman filter.

3.3   Likelihood Calculation Using the Information of the Color

We calculate the likelihood of the tracked object using the information of the color. Figure 5(a) shows the distribution of the illuminance value in the observed badminton shuttlecock regions. The illuminance level of the shuttlecock is affected by the movement blur. Furthermore, the color of the shuttlecock looks mixed with the color of the background. Therefore, we divide the scenery of the badminton frame in two regions: the background and the court itself.

The influence of the movement blurring has a linear relation with velocity. Therefore, we classify the distribution into three classes ("fast" "middle velocity" "slow"), and we decide a likelihood model corresponding to each velocity. As clustering method, we employee k-means algorithm. As shown in Figure 5(a), the illuminance value of the shuttlecock observed in the court region and outside the court region are well segmented into two clusters. Figure 5(b) and (c) show the clustered results of the shuttlecock illuminance observed in the court region and outside the court region, respectively. In the figures, when the shuttlecock's speed is fast, it receives high influence from the motion blur, thus, the shuttlecock's color is seemingly mixed with the background color. In the figure's RGB space it is represented in the cyan-colored class. Similarly, when the shuttlecock is slow, as there is little influence of the motion blur, thus, the shuttlecock's color is observed as its original color. In the figure, it is represented in the pink-colored class. Finally, the middle velocity case is represented in the figure by the purple-colored class.

We assume the distance from the center of gravity of each colored-class and the actual shuttlecock's color as a likelihood function, and we decide to use six kinds of likelihood functions by the predictive position and velocity of the shuttlecock selectively. In addition, the predictive position of the shuttlecock judges whether the shuttlecock is observed in the court or the outside. The output formula of likelihood function $L(d)$ is presented in equation (6).

$$L(d_{a,b}) = \frac{1}{\sqrt{2\pi}\sigma} exp\left(-\frac{(d_{a,b})^2}{2\sigma^2}\right) \tag{6}$$

Likelihood function $L(d)$ is a function of Euclid distance d from the center of gravity of each class. We assume that a normal distribution function becomes variance σ^2. The variance σ^2 sets it in reference to sample frame group. The likelihood function chooses $L(d_a)$, if the predictive position of the shuttlecock is the inside of the court. The outside likelihood function of the court considers is $L(d_b)$.

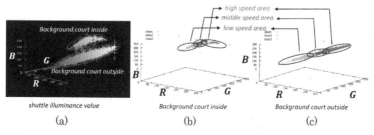

Fig. 5. (a)Distribution of the illuminance value of the observed badminton shuttlecock regions. (b) Clustering of the illuminance value of the shuttlecock observed in the court region. (c) Clustering of the illuminance value of the shuttlecock observed in the outside court region.

3.4   Acquisition of the 3D Position and Velocity of the Object Using Particles

Our method can statistically estimate the 3D position and velocity information of the object by using particles as shown in figure 6. The particles are scattered around a 3D position predicted by Kalman filter. The initial variance is a range (spherical) of process noise ω_k. The spherical variance range is transformed into an ellipsoid form figure 6(a) by using a velocity vector predicted by Kalman filter. It is possible to place a particle in the range where the motion blur has an effect by using a predictive velocity vector.

Then, the method repositions the particle as weighted by the output of the likelihood function figure 6(b). At this point, the particles in 3D space express the shape of the motion-blurred shuttlecock as shown in figure 6(c). The center of gravity of all particles is the 3D position of the shuttlecocks. We can acquire a velocity vector by analyzing the distribution of the relocation particle figure 6(d) as equation (7). The movement velocity v of the shuttlecock in the 3D position g is calculated dividing the length of the major axis l and the shutter-speed (opening time) t. Here, the length l of the major axis of an ellipsoid formed by particles is the distance that the shuttlecock moves during the shutter opening time t of the capturing camera.

$$v = l/t \qquad (7)$$

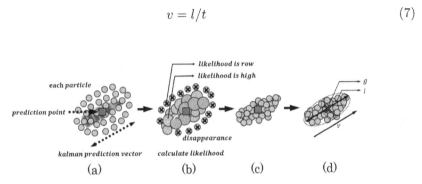

Fig. 6. (a) Transform a spherical distribution into an ellipsoid form. (b) Likelihood calculation, (c) Particle relocation, (d) Acquisition of a position and the velocity

3.5 Likelihood Calculation of the Position of the Former Frame

As the detection of the shuttlecock and construction of Kalman filter is impossible in the early frames after the shuttlecock has been hit, due to its fast movement, the visual tracking process mentioned above does not work. We solve this problem by rewinding the time-line, going from the initial observation frame (i.e., the first frame that the Kalman filter works) to former frame by using only the likelihood calculation (without Kalman filter prediction step). As shown in figure 7, the position in time $(-t)$ can be tentatively predicted by the motion model of the shuttlecock described in section 3.1, and the position and velocity can be statistically estimated by using our method described in section 3.4.

In the frames just after the shuttlecock was hit, the motion blur is too strong to observe the position of the shuttlecock. As the result, the shuttlecock is not found by using particle scatters as shown in figure 8(a). In this case, we set

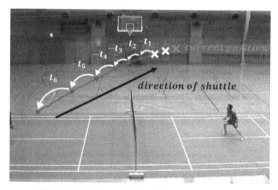

Fig. 7. Estimated Position in Time $-t_k$

a straight line between the last observed position (the shuttlecock was hit in the previous rally) and the most former position estimated by the time-rewind approach. Next the large particle scatter region along the extracted line is created (see Figure 8(b)). Because a lot of objects that have similar color exist in this region, the reliability of estimated position might be low. However the estimated position is useful for construction of the Kalman filter.

By using this approach it is possible to estimate the position of the object with variations in sizes of the blur region.

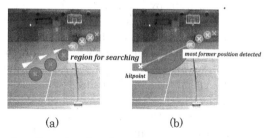

(a)   (b)

Fig. 8. (a) Illustration then the shuttlecock is not found by the particle scatters. (b) The large particle scatters region along the line between hit point and firstly detected position of the shuttlecock.

4 Experiment

We evaluate the effectiveness of the proposed method by using the video sequences synchronously captured using two video cameras. We capture the videos by using SONY BRC-300 cameras with 640×480 resolution, 30fps, and $1/60$ sec shutter speed. The test video sequence includes a rally of the badminton game.

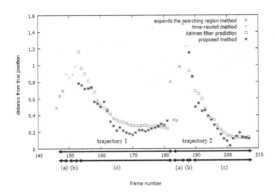

Fig. 9. The error of the position estimation across the frame

Table 1. The error reduction rate by our proposed method

	□ prediction error average [m]	*proposal method error average [m]	reduction rate
Trajectory1	0.44	0.37	18%
Trajectory2	0.35	0.32	10%
Trajectory1,2average	0.40	0.34	14%

Figure 9 shows the estimation error calculated during 2 strokes. The estimation error of the predicted position by Kalman filter is plotted as "□", and the estimated error by the proposed method is "*". The Error reduction rate by our method is shown in the table 1. We can see that our method, with the motion blur, improves the estimation results compare with the Kalman filter. However, when the number of the observations is not sufficient the Kalman filter cannot construct. For example the visual tracking by using Kalman filter does not work at the frame 146-152, and 182-187.

The "×" expresses the error of the estimated position by the time-rewind approach. As the result, we can confirm that our method described in section 3.5 well estimates the shuttlecock position at the frame 149-152, 187. The range of the error is approximately less than 1m. However, a visual tracking is still difficult when the shuttlecock is not observed in the large particle scatters region as shown at frames 146-148,182-186. Therefore, we expand the search region as described in section 3.5, it at frames 146-148, 182-186. The "■" expresses the error of the estimated position by the method that expands the searching region. By using rewinding the time-line method (denoted by "×") we lower the error. The error range is approximately less than 1.5m.

5   Conclusion

In this paper, we proposed a visual object tracking and trajectory estimation method that is robust to low observing resolution, and wide range of the variation of the target object velocity. The key-idea behind our method is the use of the motion blur region characteristic for observing the moving velocity of the target object. Furthermore, our method is capable to estimate the position of the shuttlecock during very fast motion by rewinding the time sequence.

We conducted on experiments to confirm the effectiveness of the proposed visual tracking and trajectory estimation method. We confirmed that the observation using the particle could improve the estimation error by about 14% compared with the ordinary tracking method by Kalman filter (see Table 1).

References

1. Gandhi, H., Collins, M., Chuang, M., Narasimhan, P.: Real–Time Tracking of Game Assets in American Football for Automated Camera Selection and Motion Capture. Procedia Engineering 2(2), 2667–2673 (2010)
2. Lu, W.-L., Okuma, K., Little, J.J.: Tracking and recognizing actions of multiple hockey players using the boosted particle filter. Image and Vision Computing 27(1-2), 189–205 (2009)
3. Chen, H.-T., Tien, M.-C., Chen, Y.-W., Tsai, W.-J., Lee, S.-Y.: Physics-based ball tracking and 3D trajectory reconstruction with applications to shooting location estimation in basketball video. J. Vis. Commun. Image R 20(3), 204–216 (2009)
4. Chen, H.-T., Chen, H.-S., Hsiao, M.-H., Chen, Y.-W., Lee, S.-Y.: A Trajectory-Based Ball Tracking Framework with Enrichment for Broadcast Baseball Videos. In: International Computer Symposium (ICS 2006), Taiwan, vol. III, pp. 1145–1150 (December 2006)
5. Yan, F., Christmas, W., Kittler, J.: Layered Data Association Using Graph-Theoretic Formulation with Application to Tennis Ball Tracking in Monocular Sequences. IEEE Transactions on Pattern Analysis and Machine Intelligence 30(10), 1814–1830 (2008)
6. Ren, J., Orwell, J., Jones, G.A., Xu, M.: Tracking the soccer ball using multiple fixed cameras. Computer Vision and Image Understanding 113(5), 633–642 (2009)
7. Chen, H.-T., Tsai, W.-J., Lee, S.-Y.: Ball tracking and 3D trajectory approximation with applications to tactics analysis from single-camera volleyball sequences. Multimedia Tools and Applications 60(3), 641–667 (2012)
8. Alam, F., Chowdhury, H., Theppadungporn, C., Subic, A.: Measurements of Aerodynamic Properties of Badminton Shuttlecocks. Procedia Engineering 2(2), 2487–2492 (2010)
9. Jin, H., Favaro, P., Cipolla, R.: Visual Tracking in the Presence of Motion Blur. In: Computer Vision and Pattern Recognition (CVPR 2005), vol. 2, pp. 18–25 (June 2005)
10. Park, Y., Lepetit, V., Woo, W.: Handling Motion-Blur in 3D Tracking and Rendering for Augmented Reality. IEEE Transactions on Visualization and Computer Graphics (TVCG) 18(9), 1449–1459 (2012)
11. Wu, Z., Hristov, N.I., Hedrick, T.L., Kunz, T.H., Betke, M.: Tracking a Large Number of Objects from Multiple Views. In: IEEE 12th International Conference on Computer Vision (ICCV 2009), pp. 1546–1553 (September-October 2009)
12. Karavasilis, V., Nikou, C., Likas, A.: Visual Tracking by Adaptive Kalman Filtering and Mean Shift. In: Konstantopoulos, S., Perantonis, S., Karkaletsis, V., Spyropoulos, C.D., Vouros, G. (eds.) SETN 2010. LNCS, vol. 6040, pp. 153–162. Springer, Heidelberg (2010)

13. Huang, C., Wu, B., Nevatia, R.: Robust Object Tracking by Hierarchical Association of Detection Responses. In: Forsyth, D., Torr, P., Zisserman, A. (eds.) ECCV 2008, Part II. LNCS, vol. 5303, pp. 788–801. Springer, Heidelberg (2008)
14. Satoh, Y., Okatani, T., Deguchi, K.: A Color-based Tracking by Kalman Particle Filter. In: International Conference on Pattern Recognition (ICPR 2004), vol. 3, pp. 502–505 (August 2004)
15. Xu, X., Li, B.: Adaptive Rao-Blackwellized Particle Filter and Its Evaluation for Tracking in Surveillance. IEEE Transactions on Image Processing 16(3), 838–849 (2007)
16. Reilly, V., Idrees, H., Shah, M.: Detection and Tracking of Large Number of Targets in Wide Area Surveillance. In: Daniilidis, K., Maragos, P., Paragios, N. (eds.) ECCV 2010, Part III. LNCS, vol. 6313, pp. 186–199. Springer, Heidelberg (2010)
17. Yang, C., Duraiswami, R., Davis, L.: Fast Multiple Object Tracking via a Hierarchical Particle Filter. In: IEEE International Conference on Computer Vision (ICCV 2005), vol. 1, pp. 212–219 (October 2005)
18. Li, Y., Ai, H., Yamashita, T., Lao, S., Kawade, M.: Tracking in Low Frame Rate Video: A Cascade Particle Filter with Discriminative Observers of Different Lifespans. IEEE Transactions on Pattern Analysis and Machine Intelligence 30(10), 1728–1740 (2008)
19. Wu, Y., Ling, H., Yu, J., Li, F., Mei, X., Cheng, E.: Blurred Target Tracking by Blur-driven Tracker. In: IEEE International Conference on Computer Vision (ICCV), pp. 1100–1107 (2011)

Fast Human Detection in RGB-D Images with Progressive SVM-Classification

Domingo Iván Rodríguez González and Jean-Bernard Hayet

Centro de Investigación en Matemáticas (CIMAT)
Guanajuato, GTO., México
{drodriguez,jbhayet}@cimat.mx

Abstract. In this article, we propose a new, fast approach to detect human beings from RGB-D data, named Progressive Classification. The idea of this method is quite simple: As in several state-of-the-art algorithms, the classification is based on the evaluation of HOG-like descriptors within image test windows, which are divided into a set of blocks. In our method, the evaluation of the set of blocks is done progressively in a particular order, in such a way that the blocks that most contribute to the separability between the human and non-human classes are evaluated first. This permits to make an early decision about the human detection without necessarily reaching the evaluation of all the blocks, and therefore accelerating the detection process. We evaluate our method with different HOG-like descriptors and on a challenging dataset.

1 Introduction

The last decade has produced tremendous advances in the field of pedestrian detection. As an illustration of this evolution and of its impact on other computer vision areas, the availability of powerful detectors has modified radically the main paradigms in use for pedestrian target tracking. Traditional stochastic filtering approaches (Kalman filters, particle filters) coexist now with the so-called "detection-based" approaches that do not formulate anymore the tracking problem as an inference problem within Markov models, but instead as a problem of optimization, namely by association of positive detections given by reliable pedestrian detectors along sequences of frames [1]. Such progress has been made possible mainly by the appearance of a few robust, reliable human detectors such as the one proposed by Dalal and Triggs [2], based on an exhaustive classification of all possible test windows contained in the image as belonging to the pedestrian or non-pedestrian class. Now, one of the main bottlenecks with detection-based methods is specifically the computational times involved in the exhaustive testing of all possible windows, at several scales. These computational times can be dramatically reduced e.g. if the scene geometry is known, but it is not always possible to have this kind of prior knowledge. In this paper, we focus on the reduction of the computational times involved in the use of the acclaimed HOG-based detector [2], by taking advantage of the spatial and semantic structure contained in the HOG descriptor. This way, in most classification cases, we

R. Klette, M. Rivera, and S. Satoh (Eds.): PSIVT 2013, LNCS 8333, pp. 337–348, 2014.
© Springer-Verlag Berlin Heidelberg 2014

can make an earlier decision, and produce a significant saving of computational resources. The main contributions of this work are (1) a progressive classification technique based on the HOG-SVM strategy allowing a much faster processing of images and (2) the proposal for a new depth/texture descriptor for RGB-D images. We compare our strategy for pedestrian detection on RGB-D images with several other HOG-like detectors from the literature on a challenging dataset.

This article is organized as follows: In Section 2, we review related works; In Section 3, we recall the principle of HOG descriptors, describe similar descriptors for RGB-D images, including a new one, and pinpoint the HOG-SVM score structure. In Section 4, we describe progressive classification, based on the exploitation of this score structure and on the disparities among the test window blocks in terms of class separability. In Section 5, we give results validating our approach on several pedestrian databases and in Section 6, we draw conclusions.

2   Related Work

One of the first pedestrian detection schemes that successfully combined visual features and classification techniques has been the one of Papageorgiou et al. [3], that used Haar-wavelets with Support Vector Machines (SVM). The next milestone has been the work of Viola and Jones [4], where Haar wavelets were used in combination with a cascade AdaBoost. This resulted in impressive results for face detection. In Sabzmeydani [5], the aforementioned cascade classifier was used with Shapelets as features. Dalal and Triggs [2] use Histograms of Oriented Gradients (HOG), together with Support Vector Machines. Their approach has been successful for pedestrian detection, as HOGs robustly encode the objects shape, and not only differences of contrast. Comparative studies on possible features and classifiers have shown that the combination HOG-SVM was the best one for pedestrian detection [6]. As the HOG-SVM process is quite heavy, proposals have been made to use integral histograms [7] or to replace trilinear interpolation in the histogram construction by spatial convolution [8].

Based on the aforementioned schemes, several combined, part-based classifiers have been proposed. In [9], the HOG-based detector is used to detect the whole body and its upper part. Both are combined with a face detector, a skin detector and a motion detector into a robust classifier. In [10], the pedestrian detection is made in stereo-vision, by using HOG-SVM classifiers for intensity, optical flow and depth images. In the work of [11], several features (HOG, Haar wavelets...) are concatenated into a large description vector used for classification (either with SVM or Adaboost). In [12], a pedestrian detector is obtained by combining several HOG-SVM classifiers trained for each part of the person, which allows robustness for highly deformed bodies.

In this paper, we focus on pedestrian detection methods in RGB-D images. Among the few works in which detectors specific to RGB-D images, [13] propose two descriptors, one (HOD) using only depth information, and a second one (Combo-HOD) combining the output of two different classifiers, one for the depth data, one for the texture. In [14], a descriptor is proposed that is based on the 3D orientations of the surface normals.

3   HOG-Based Descriptors in Multiple Channel Images

Since the pioneer work of Dalal and Triggs [2], HOG-based classification has been very popular for detecting instances of a particular class, such as pedestrians. We first quickly recall how HOG features are extracted and how they are used in classification problems, then we expose a few existing extensions of these features to RGB-D images, and we present a new descriptor, called HOGD.

3.1   HOG-Based Classifiers for Pedestrian Detection

Histograms of Gradient (HOGs) have been originally defined as a dense representation of the local shape and appearance of the image. They capture the local texture information on a cell basis, by generating a discrete distribution (histogram) of the gradient orientations inside this cell, similarly to what SIFT does for sparse interest points, i.e. for wide baseline image matching.

The original HOG features and their corresponding HOG descriptor are described in Section 3.2, together with its variants on RGB-D images. In the following, and in a generic way, we will refer to the extracted descriptor vector (from any of the mentioned methods) as $\mathbf{D}$. The SVM linear classifier response for detecting instances of a given class has the well-known linear form:

$$f_{\alpha,b}(\mathbf{D}) = \alpha \cdot \mathbf{D} + b, \tag{1}$$

where $\alpha \in \mathbb{R}^K$ (K being the dimension of $\mathbf{D}$) and $b \in \mathbb{R}$ are the linear SVM learning parameters and $\cdot$ is the usual dot product in $\mathbb{R}^K$. What is remarkable is that $\mathbf{D}$ has a clear spatial structure, resulting from the per-block concatenation. We intend to use this underlying structure to accelerate the decision process.

3.2   HOG Descriptors for RGB and RGB-D Images

In order to extend the approach of [2] to RGB-D images, some proposals have been done to provide image descriptors $\mathbf{D}$ that, in addition to the texture information (as in HOG), also include depth information. We describe briefly four of those descriptors that we use for evaluation purposes.

Histogram of Oriented Gradients (HOG): We implemented the original HOG version proposed by Dalal and Triggs for RGB images [2]. The image gradient is computed over a 64×128 detection window. The detection window is subdivided into a grid of cells of 4×4 pixels, and a 1D orientation histogram of 9 bins is associated to each cell to capture the local distribution of gradient orientations. Each pixel contributes, according to the gradient magnitude, to the histograms of the 4-connected cells by trilinear interpolation in x, y and orientation. Adjacent cells are grouped into blocks of 2×2 cells with an overlap of one cell in each direction, so that there are 105 blocks in the whole detection window. The histograms of the four cells within a block are locally normalized for contrast variations and then concatenated to form a vector of dimension 36.

The final HOG descriptor is a vector of dimension 3780 used to train a linear SVM classifier. Finally, a detection window is scrolled over an image at multiple scales, so that at each position and scale the HOG descriptor is computed and a classification decision is made by the linear SVM classifier.

Histogram of Oriented Depths (HOD): Designed for RGB-D images, it was first introduced by Spinello and Arras [13] based on HOG. It captures the local shape and appearance of a depth image through the local distribution of depth gradient orientations. The HOD implementation used for this paper follows the same procedure described above to compute HOG descriptors using depth images instead of RGB images. The resulting HOD descriptor is also a 3780 dimension vector. The detection process can be accelerated by taking advantage of depth properties: for each pixel, compatible scales are determined according to its depth information. A HOD descriptor is computed at a given position and scale only if there are enough pixels within the detection window that have a depth compatible with the current scale. This technique produces a significant improvement of the computational time to evaluate the descriptor and to perform the overall detection process. For more details, see [13].

Combo-HOD: It was also proposed by Spinello and Arras [13] to use both texture and depth information in RGB-D images, by combining the classification response of two classifiers based on HOG and HOD descriptors. Both descriptors are independently computed at each position and scale over the texture and depth images, and two linear SVM classifiers are also independently trained. In order to combine the classification responses, a posterior probability is calculated for each type of information as the probability of being a person ($y = 1$) given that the SVM response f is known $p(y = 1|f)$. A sigmoid function is fitted to map SVM responses to probabilities (See Platt et al. [15]). The final combined probability is the weighted average of both probabilities, so that each type of information contributes to the final decision depending on its detection confidence. Spinello and Arras [13] select the weights according to the false positive rate for each type of information at the equal error rate point of a validation set (i.e., at the point of the ROC curve specified by its precision value). Here, we modified a bit this policy by selecting the weights inversely proportional to the intersection of the distributions $p(f|y = 1)$ and $p(f|y = -1)$ estimated by Gaussian kernels on a validation set. This is equivalent to measuring the separability generated by each classifier. It is reported in [13] that the combination of texture and depth information results in a significant improvement of the detection rate.

HOGD: We propose a different descriptor that combines texture and depth information in a single descriptor. We concatenate the HOG and HOD descriptors into a single vector of dimension 7560. A single linear SVM classifier is trained with the HOGD descriptors from the training set. In spite of the increase in dimensionality, training time, and memory, this descriptor has the advantage of determining the contribution balance of texture and depth information by

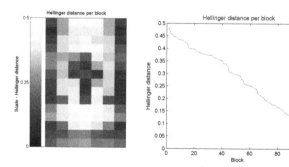

Fig. 1. Distribution of individual Hellinger distances (Eq. 5), for the HOG-SVM classifier, on a block basis. On the left, all blocks are depicted at their respective place in the test window (the brightest is the color, the highest is the distance). It is remarkable that blocks corresponding to the pedestrian silhouette can discriminate more. On the right, the same blocks distances distribution is depicted with decreasing values.

learning, so that this balance does not have to be determined by selecting an error rate point or evaluating a validation set as in [13]. It is also less expensive in time to classify this descriptor, since no posterior probability is required.

3.3   Block-Based Structure in the Descriptor Vector

In all HOG-related approaches, the descriptor vector $\mathbf{D}$ has a block structure, as it results from the concatenation of histograms evaluated inside the set of cells corresponding to the blocks. Hence, the classifier output can be rewritten as a sum of responses β_i by the N different blocks composing the test window,

$$
\begin{aligned}
f_{\alpha,b}(\mathbf{D}) &= \sum_{i=0}^{N} \beta_i + b, \\
\beta_i &= \sum_{k=0}^{M} \alpha_{iM+k} \mathbf{D}_{iM+k},
\end{aligned}
\tag{2}
$$

where M is the number of elements in the descriptors arising from each block. In HOG-like classification methods, the detection process does not consider a specific order for blocks i, as they are all evaluated and summed up in the classifier response. Here, we specify an order to the blocks, so as to evaluate the classifier at different stages of the incorporation of the blocks, and eventually to make an early decision on the binary output, to accelerate the detection process.

As an example, one could expect that in pedestrian detection, blocks corresponding to a pedestrian silhouette are more discriminative, whereas those holding background information or clothes are less discriminative. Hence, by evaluating the first ones as soon as possible, it may be possible to make an early decision about the presence or absence of a pedestrian inside a test window.

4   Progressive Classification

In the following, we define progressive classification as the classification process resulting from adding gradually (in a specific order!) to the global classifier score the individual contribution β_i of each block $\mathbf{D}_i$. We also refer to the partial classifier output after evaluating i blocks as $f_{0:i}$, defined recursively as

$$
\begin{cases}
f_{0:0} = & b, \\
f_{0:i} = f_{0:i-1} + \beta_i \text{ for } i > 0.
\end{cases}
\tag{3}
$$

4.1   Block Ordering

To evaluate the importance of any block in the classifier output, we use a criterion reflecting the class separability caused by each individual block i. For that purpose, let us define as f_i (with only one index) the output of the SVM classifier resulting from using only one block (block i):

$$
f_i = \beta_i + b.
\tag{4}
$$

Once the learning has been done, we use our verification dataset to evaluate the discriminability of each atomic, block-based classifier i. With all the ground truth data compared to the application of the classifiers, we use Gaussian kernels to estimate the discrete distributions $P_i^+ = P(f_i|y = 1)$ and $P_i^- = P(f_i|y = -1)$, for each block. The more these distributions overlap, the less discriminative the block will be for the detection process. To evaluate this overlapping, we use the Hellinger distance (based on the Bhattacharyya coefficient) between P_i^+ and P_i^-:

$$
d(P_i^+, P_i^-) = \sqrt{1 - \sum_{f^k} P_i^+(f^k) P_i^-(f^k)},
\tag{5}
$$

where f^k covers all the discretized values of the score value f_i. This distance takes values between 0 and 1, where 1 occurs when the distributions are the same, and 0 when they have no common support. Hence, the closer to zero is $d(P_i^+, P_i^-)$, the more separated are the pedestrians/non-pedestrians classes. In Fig. 1, we depict these computed values for each block in the detection window.

The selected order of evaluation of the blocks is then the one corresponding to decreasing values of $d(P_i^+, P_i^-)$, in such a way that the blocks with the positive and negative classes most separated will be evaluated first.

4.2   Early Decision

Let us define $p_i = P(y = 1|f_{0:i})$ as the probability that a tested sample is positive, given that the partial output of the classifier (up to block i) is $f_{0:i}$

$$
p_i = P(y = 1|f_{0:i}) = \frac{1}{1 + \exp(A_i f_{0:i} + B_i)},
\tag{6}
$$

where A_i and B_i are the parameters of a sigmoid, adjusting the distributions $P_{0:i}^+ = P(f_{0:i}|y = 1)$ and $P_{0:i}^- = P(f_{0:i}|y = -1)$, obtained by evaluating the partial, block-ordered classifier from block 1 to i, as explained in [15].

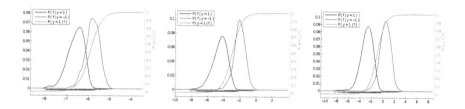

Fig. 2. Evolution of the $P_{0:i}^+$ (blue) and $P_{0:i}^-$ (red) distributions while incorporating (from left to right) 10, 50 and 105 ordered blocks. In green, we depict the corresponding p_i probability to be an instance of the class, given $f_{0:i}$.

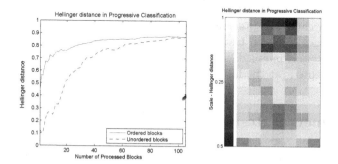

Fig. 3. Evolution of the Hellinger distance with the partial scores f_i (from Eq. 2). Left: The dashed curve is the evolution of the Hellinger distance when the number of blocks is increased, without ordering the blocks; the solid curve is the same with ordered blocks. Right: We display the separability of the partial classifier ending with each block. It can be noticed that the most discriminative blocks are evaluated first.

We depict (in blue and red, respectively) different partial distributions $P_{0:i}^+$, $P_{0:i}^-$ distributions in Fig. 2, for $i = 10, 50, 105$. Observe that the separability goes increasing with i. Moreover, we depict (in green) the p_i sigmoid curves for all these cases. Then, in Fig. 3, we show the evolution of the Hellinger distances $d(P_{0:i}^+, P_{0:i}^-)$ with and without ordering of the blocks.

To make an early decision, we associate, to each ordered level i, a rejection threshold U_i, in such a way that if p_i (deduced from the evaluated $f_{0:i}$) is inferior to this threshold, the decision is made of an early rejection of the test window, without having to evaluate the rest of the blocks, expecting that the evaluation of the following blocks will not bring a large enough contribution. The decision at the step $i < N$ is made according to the following rule:

$$\begin{cases} y = -1 \text{ if } p_i < U_i \\ \text{No decision is made otherwise and } i = i + 1. \end{cases} \qquad (7)$$

where p_i is the probability of a positive classification, derived from the partial output $f_{0:i}$ in Eq. 6. For the progressive classification to be effective, we heuristically define U_i as an increasing function of i. The idea is that at the final stage of the evaluation $(i = N)$, then we apply the threshold for the originally designed SVM, namely U_f; however, in the intermediary stages, we apply lower thresholds, since partial scores may be abnormally low because of some local phenomenon (illumination, occlusion...). Hence, the threshold at stage i is defined as

$$U_i = \frac{i}{N} U_f. \tag{8}$$

The defined threshold is a rejection threshold, and one could design a similar approach for an early acceptation threshold. However, in the case of object detection in a given image, the number of negative tests is by order of magnitudes superior to the number of positive tests. This suggests that an early rejection threshold will have much higher effect on the global computational time performance than an early acceptation threshold. Hence, if there is enough evidence in the first stages that the test window corresponds to a pedestrian, then the evaluating process is pursued, up to a point where the test window is definitely rejected or accepted (at the last stage $i = N$).

5   Experimental Results

We tested our method on our own dataset of RGB-D images captured with a Kinect sensor. The dataset was generated in a challenging environment with hard illumination conditions. It contains more than 2000 images, with an important variability of pedestrian appearances and poses, and the objects are located within a wide depth range (1 to 10 meters). We divided it into a learning set (1834 positive examples and 516 negative images), and a testing set (523 test images). We trained our linear SVM classifiers using the bootstrapping technique to improve the classification results as most works in this domain do. A few examples from this dataset are given in Fig 4. All the results in the following have been determined on these 523 test images. Close multiple detections from the classifier are merged by a simple criterion of overlapping. Detections are furthermore validated as positive when the detected window relative overlapping with the ground truth window reaches a threshold value.

Handling the Sensor Depth Resolution Variations with Range. It is important to note that the Kinect sensor has a limited depth range and that its resolution decreases as the distance to the sensor increases. The technical specification recommends to use it in a range between 0.8 to 4 meters, because depth information is significantly lost farther than this limit. Therefore, we can not perform detection with the same confidence for near and far depth ranges.

We observed that global results (on the whole range of depths) are degraded mainly because the relevant features are not the same at different depth ranges. Hence, we propose to train different classifiers for three different depth intervals.

We divided the set of training images into three subsets according to the distance of the sample to the sensor: 0 to 4 meters, 4 to 8 meters and farther than 8 meters. During detection, the correct linear SVM classifier is selected for

Fig. 4. A few examples of the dataset we used for evaluation purposes in this paper

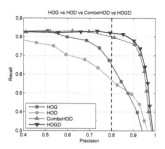

Fig. 5. Global performance comparison between the four HOG-based descriptors

the current image scale. This training procedure generates different contribution balances between texture and depth information for each depth range. For near samples, depth information has a greater contribution than texture, and for far samples, texture information is more discriminative. For ComboHOD, different weights are determined for each interval, and for HOGD, the independent learning processes generates three different detectors.

Since progressive classification orders the blocks according to the separability of each block alone, a different order is determined for each depth range. In the cases of HOGD and ComboHOD, a greater proportion of depth blocks are evaluated within the first blocks for the nearest depth range, whereas more texture blocks are computed first for the farthest range. Thus we can probabilistically determine which information is more discriminative at different depths.

Performance Comparison among HOG-Based Descriptors. Figure 5 shows a performance comparison between the four HOG-based descriptors on the same test set of RGB-D images. We observe that Combo-HOD and HOGD outperform HOG and HOD. This demonstrates that the combination of texture and depth information behaves better than a single type of information. Furthermore, we note that our new descriptor HOGD performs slightly better than ComboHOD on most of the operation domain.

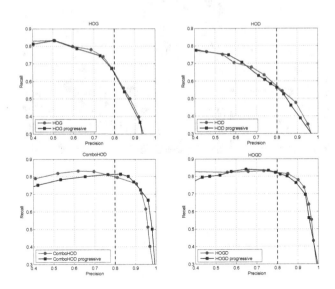

Fig. 6. ROC curves for detection performance with (blue) and without (red) progressive classification, for each HOG-based detector

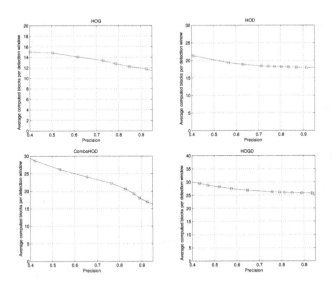

Fig. 7. Average computed blocks per image for each HOG-based descriptor using progressive classification. It must be remembered that HOG and HOD descriptors have a total of 105 blocks, whereas Combo-HOD and HOGD descriptors have 210 blocks.

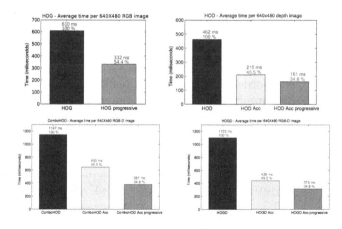

Fig. 8. Average time per image using progressive classification. Blue bars correspond to the original detection process. Yellow bars correspond to the detection process with acceleration using scale/depth information (when depth is available). Green bars show the average time with both acceleration using scale and progressive classification.

Computational Time Gains from Progressive Classification. In Fig. 6, we show the detection performance for each HOG-based detector with progressive classification. Even if this method does not compute the classification score on the whole testing window, it can be seen that the overall detection performance is not affected by making early decisions in progressive classification.

Fig. 7 shows the average number of computed blocks per detection window with progressive classification, as a function of the required precision rate (obtained for different values of the final U_f along ROC curves). Only a small percentage of the 105 blocks are finally computed, resulting in a significant reduction of computational processing. When the desired precision increases, then U_f also increases, and so does the number of early decisions. This is accentuated for the basic HOG-SVM classifier: The average number of evaluated blocks is around 15, to be compared with the 105 blocks included in the original version.

Finally, Fig. 8 depicts the average time reduction for each HOG-based descriptor. We can see, for example, that the average detection time is 45% smaller when using progressive classification for the original HOG (this time reduction is not linear with the number of processed blocks reduction, because of overheads in the algorithm). It must be remembered that for descriptors that rely on depth information, an additional acceleration technique is implemented, based on scale-depths correspondences. The average times are presented (1) without this scale-based acceleration method; (2) using this scale-technique alone (when possible, i.e. when depth is used) and (3) along with the progressive classification.

6 Conclusion

We have presented two promising contributions in the area of pedestrian detection from RGB-D images: The first one is a new descriptor combining texture and depth elements in the form of a HOG-like descriptor, and for which we show that it exhibits better detection performances than other descriptors in the literature; the second one is a new strategy to accelerate the detection process by making early decision about the presence of a pedestrian in a test window, based on determining a specific order of evaluation of the blocks forming the HOG-like descriptors. For the descriptors we evaluated, this improvement allows significant gains in computational times, without significant losses in the performance.

References

1. Ben Shitrit, H., Berclaz, J., Fleuret, F., Fua, P.: Tracking multiple people under global appearance constraints. In: Proc. of IEEE Int. Conf. on Computer Vision, ICCV (2011)
2. Dalal, N., Triggs, B.: Histograms of oriented gradients for human detection. In: Proc. of IEEE Int. Conf. on Computer Vision and Pattern Recognition (CVPR), pp. 886–893 (2005)
3. Papageorgiou, C., Oren, M., Poggio, T.: A general framework for object detection. In: Proc. of IEEE Int. Conf. on Computer Vision (ICCV), pp. 555–562 (1998)
4. Viola, P.A., Jones, M.J.: Rapid object detection using a boosted cascade of simple features. In: Proc. of IEEE Conf. on Computer Vision and Pattern Recognition (CVPR), pp. 511–518 (2001)
5. Sabzmeydani, P., Mori, G.: Detecting pedestrians by learning shapelet features. In: Proc. of IEEE Conf. on Computer Vision and Pattern Recognition, CVPR (2007)
6. Enzweiler, M., Gavrila, D.M.: Monocular pedestrian detection: Survey and experiments. IEEE Trans. Pattern Anal. Mach. Intell. 31, 2179–2195 (2009)
7. Dollar, P., Belongie, S., Perona, P.: The Fastest Pedestrian Detector in the West. In: Proc. of British Machine Vision Conf., BMVC (2010)
8. Wang, X., Han, T.X., Yan, S.: An HOG-LBP Human Detector with Partial Occlusion Handling. In: Proc. of IEEE Int. Conf. on Computer Vision, ICCV (2009)
9. Choi, W., Savarese, S.: Multiple Target Tracking in World Coordinate with Single, Minimally Calibrated Camera. In: Daniilidis, K., Maragos, P., Paragios, N. (eds.) ECCV 2010, Part IV. LNCS, vol. 6314, pp. 553–567. Springer, Heidelberg (2010)
10. Enzweiler, M., Eigenstetter, A., Schiele, B., Gavrila, D.M.: Multi-cue pedestrian classification with partial occlusion handling. In: Proc. of IEEE Conf. on Computer Vision and Pattern Recognition (CVPR), pp. 990–997 (2010)
11. Wojek, C., Schiele, B.: A performance evaluation of single and multi-feature people detection. In: Rigoll, G. (ed.) DAGM 2008. LNCS, vol. 5096, pp. 82–91. Springer, Heidelberg (2008)
12. Felzenszwalb, P.F., Girshick, R.B., McAllester, D., Ramanan, D.: Object Detection with Discriminatively Trained Part Based Models. IEEE Trans. on Pattern Analysis and Machine Intelligence 32 (2010)
13. Spinello, L., Arras, K.O.: People detection in rgb-d data. In: Proc. of IEEE/RSJ Int. Conf. on Intelligent Robots and Systems, IROS (2011)
14. Tang, S., Wang, X., Lv, X., Han, T.X., Keller, J., He, Z., Skubic, M., Lao, S.: Histogram of oriented normal vectors for object recognition with a depth sensor. In: Lee, K.M., Matsushita, Y., Rehg, J.M., Hu, Z. (eds.) ACCV 2012, Part II. LNCS, vol. 7725, pp. 525–538. Springer, Heidelberg (2013)
15. Platt, J.C.: Probabilistic outputs for support vector machines and comparisons to regularized likelihood methods. In: Advances in Large Margin Classifiers, pp. 61–74. MIT Press (1999)

An Object Recognition Model Based on Visual Grammars and Bayesian Networks

Elias Ruiz and Luis Enrique Sucar

Instituto Nacional de Astrofísica, Óptica y Electrónica
Departamento de Ciencias Computacionales
Luis Enrique Erro 1, Tonantzintla, Puebla, México
{elias_ruiz,esucar}@inaoep.mx
http://www.inaoep.mx

Abstract. A novel proposal for a general model for object recognition is presented. The proposed method is based on symbol-relational grammars and Bayesian networks. An object is modeled as a hierarchy of features and spatial relationships using a symbol-relational grammar. This grammar is learned automatically from examples, incorporating a simple segmentation algorithm in order to generate the lexicon. The grammar is created with the elements of the lexicon as terminal elements. This representation is automatically transformed into a Bayesian network structure which parameters are learned from examples. Thus, recognition is based on probabilistic inference in the Bayesian network representation. Preliminary results in modeling natural objects are presented. The main contribution of this work is a general methodology for building object recognition systems which combines the expressivity of a grammar with the robustness of probabilistic inference.

Keywords: Visual Grammars, Bayesian Networks, Object Recognition

1 Introduction

Most current object recognition systems are centered in recognizing certain type of objects, and do not consider their structure. This implies several limitations: (i) the systems are difficult to generalize to any type of object, (ii) they are not robust to noise and occlusions, (iii) the model is difficult to interpret.

This paper proposes a model that achieves a hierarchical representation of a visual object in order to perform object recognition tasks, based on a visual grammar [3] and Bayesian networks (BNs) [8]. Thus, we propose the incorporation of a visual grammar in order to develop an understandable hierarchical model so that from basic elements (obtained by a simple image segmentation algorithm) it will construct more complex forms by certain rules of composition defined in the grammar, in order to achieve object recognition in a limited context (e.g. images of natural objects).

The importance of addressing this issue from a hierarchical approach is that it can build a more robust model which can represent variability in a class of

R. Klette, M. Rivera, and S. Satoh (Eds.): PSIVT 2013, LNCS 8333, pp. 349–359, 2014.

objects and can handle occlusions and partial information. This is combined with the advantages of a BNs for dealing with uncertainty, such as incomplete information and noise. Additionally, a model expressed as a symbolic grammar provides a transparent and understandable representation.

We propose a method for learning the grammar from examples and then transforming this representation to Bayesian network for object recognition using probabilistic inference. The terminal elements are also learned from examples, based on simple and general visual features (edges and uniform regions), which provide the lexicon for the grammar. The grammar is a symbol-relation grammar which incorporates spatial relationships.

A symbol-relation grammar is learned for each class of object, and then transformed automatically to a Bayesian network which incorporates the symbols and relations as nodes, and the arcs represent the structure derived from the grammar rules. Intermediate nodes in this BN structure are hidden, so we learn the parameters of the model using Expectation-Maximization algorithm (EM). Once the structure and parameters of the BN are obtained, it can be used for recognizing a class of object using probabilistic inference.

The proposed method has been evaluated experimentally with several classes of natural objects with promising results. The main contribution of this work is a general methodology for building object recognition systems which combines the expressivity of a grammar with the robustness of probabilistic inference.

Next we present a brief review of alternative hierarchical approaches for object recognition and contrast them with our approach. Then we describe in detail the proposed model, including the model building and recognition methods. We present experimental results in learning visual grammars for several object classes, and then using these for recognition. We conclude with a summary and directions for future work.

2   Related Work

There are several works using a hierarchical approach for object recognition based on visual grammars [1,2,6,7,9]. In these studies, there is a clear consensus in the usage of a certain kind of grammar to represent hierarchically the terminal elements (Lexicon). However, they differ in what terminal elements to use and how to handle the uncertainty in order to perform object recognition. In addition, they are usually designed for specific types of objects (e.g., car plate recognition, pedestrian or face recognition) so that the models developed are difficult to generalize. In these works the grammar is described manually. Similarly, the model which handles the uncertainty is restricted to a fixed structure.

The proposed model differs in several aspects from previous work:

- It is based on a symbol-relation grammar which incorporates spatial relationships.
- The grammar is learned from example images of a class of objects.
- The terminal elements are simple and general so they can be used for different types of objects, and the lexicon is also learned from examples.

- The grammar is automatically transformed to a BN which provides a robust and efficient techniques for object recognition.

We consider the use of Symbol-Relation grammars because of the convenience of putting the relationships in predicate logic, which is natural in this kind of grammar. Also, it is desirable that the grammar is automatically learned from examples, for greater generality; the grammar is independent of the lexicon definition used. Finally, the transformation to a model that considers uncertainty must also be automatic and analogous (but independent) to the hierarchy described in the grammar.

We use Bayesian networks to represent the information given by the grammar incorporating uncertainty. Other studies use different schemas or even probabilistic grammars. Bayesian networks have several advantages, such a preserving the structure given by the grammar and providing efficient algorithms for parameter learning and probabilistic inference.

3   Object Recognition Model

The proposed method compromises two phases: (i) model construction and transformation to a BN (Fig. 1); and (ii) image pre-processing and object recognition using probabilistic inference, (Fig. 2). Next we describe each phase in detail.

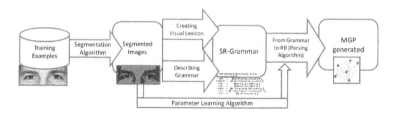

Fig. 1. Model construction. Starting from training images, these are segmented and a lexicon and a visual grammar are induced, obtaining a description of the objects in terms of the lexicon and a SR grammar. Then the model is transferred to a BN, whose parameters are also learned from examples.

3.1   Model Construction

Segmentation and Lexicon. Segmentation is performed with simple RGB quantization (32 levels) and edge extraction using Gabor Filters [4]. Small regions are deleted by fusion with other regions. The idea is to use simple and general features as basic elements so they can be applied for different classes of objects. These regions define a visual dictionary. Every region is described with

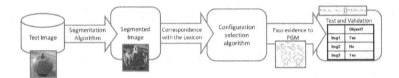

Fig. 2. Object recognition. The test image is segmented with the visual dictionary and we obtain correspondences of regions with the visual lexicon. After that, the algorithm evaluates subsets of those regions with their spatial relationships that are candidates to be evaluated in the previously trained BN in order to do inference. At the end, we obtain a result by probabilistic inference in the BN obtaining the probability of the presence of an object in the image.

Fig. 3. In the picture, the color segments are examples of terminal elements found. Each segment is attached with an element of the Lexicon. The Lexicon is composed of edge type elements and homogeneous regions, given by a segmentation algorithm based on quantization of the RGB channels. In this example two orientations of edge elements were used. (Best seen in color.)

its color histogram and shape features. From a segmented dataset with negative and positive images, we use a *k-means* algorithm in order to select the clusters which appear more often in the positive images (two times in positive images against negative images). The centroids of these clusters are considered as terminal elements in our grammar. All the terminal elements constitute the *Visual Lexicon*. An example of terminal elements obtained by this method are illustrated in the Fig. 3. According to our model, the Lexicon can be improved by incorporating local features or a better segmentation algorithm. These changes may provide better results in recognition tasks. This will not affect other layers of our model like grammar learning or its transformation into a Bayesian Network.

Spatial Relationships and Candidate Rules. Although there are different types of spatial relationships, in our model we use topological and order relationships. The relationships used in our model were: $Inside\_of(A, B)$ (A region is within B region), $Contains(A, B)$ (A region covers completely B region), $Ady(A, B)$ (A is touched by B and A is located left from B), $Above(A, B)$ (A is touched by B and A is located above from B), $Invading(A, B)$ (A is covering partially B more than $Above$ and $Left$ but less than $Contains$). In each relationship we also consider that the two regions are also adjacent. We use these relationships because they preserve the coherence when we subsume two regions in another new one. The new non-terminal elements generated preserve all the relationships from its children with other elements, and loose its internal relationships.

Learning the Grammar. A visual grammar describes objects hierarchically. It can represent a diagram, flowchart, or a geometric drawing. For example, the description of a flowchart is made by decomposition: complex elements are decomposed in simple elements (from the complete image to arrows or simple boxes). For our model, we need a grammar that allows us to model the decomposition of a visual object into its parts and how they relate with another parts. Symbol-Relation grammars *(SR-grammars)*, which are described in [3], provide this type of description and incorporate the possibility of adding rewriting rules (R) to specify relationships between terminals and non-terminals symbols after decompositions from all the non-terminals. A Symbol Relation-Grammar is defined as:

$G = (V_N, V_T, V_R, S, P, R)$ where:

- V_N is a finite set of non terminal symbols.
- V_T is a finite set of terminal symbols.
- V_R is a finite set of relational symbols between $V_N \cup V_T$.
- $S \in V_N$ is the starting symbol.
- P is a finite set of labelled rewriting rules, called s-item productions of the form:

$$l : Y^0 \rightarrow \langle \mathbf{M}, \mathbf{R} \rangle$$

where:
  - l is a integer labelling the s-production.
  - $\langle \mathbf{M}, \mathbf{R} \rangle$ is a sentence on V_R and $V_N \cup V_T$
    * $\mathbf{M}$ is a set of s-items (v, i) with $v \in V_N \cup V_T$ and i is a natural number used to distinguish different ocurrences of the same symbol.
    * $\mathbf{R}$ is a set of r-items of the form $r(X^i, Y^j)$, with $X^i, Y^j \in \mathbf{M}$ and $r \in V_R$
  - $Y \in V_N$, $Y^0 \notin \mathbf{M}$

As a convention, the index "0" will only be used to denote the symbol on the left-hand side of every s-production.

The next step is to generate the rules that make up the grammar. Using the training images, we search the most common relationships between the clusters obtained. Such relationships become candidate rules to build the grammar. This is an iterative process where the rules are subsumed and converted to a new non-terminal elements of the grammar. This new non-terminal element can be seen as a product of the composition process: two terminal regions in the image are merged into a new one. This new region is the new non-terminal element in the grammar. If we repeat this process, the starting symbol of the grammar represents the object that we want to recognize.

The stop criterion (to learn each rule) is a frequency threshold for the rule (the rule needs to be found in at least n images of the training set). This criterion also avoids generating a higly complex grammar. As an example, the relationship $Inside\_of(C_1, C_2)$ is subsumed into a new non-terminal element named NT_1. The rule obtained is: $1 : NT_1^0 \rightarrow < \{C_1^2, C_2^2\}, \{Inside\_of(C_1^2, C_2^2)\} >$. As a convention, the superscript zero will only be used to denote the symbol on the left-hand side of every s-production, the superscript 2 is used on the right side. Superscript 3 or higher are used when there are two or more instances of one terminal or non-terminal element in the same rule. Superscript 1 is not used.

We incorporate a restriction in SR-grammars in order to avoid circular productions (the PGM generated would have infinite structure). For example, these two rules are not allowed: $A^0 \rightarrow \langle B^2 \rangle$ and $B^0 \rightarrow \langle A^2 \rangle$, where A produces B and B produces A. In a formal sense, the restriction is as follows: for every rule of the form $Y^0 \rightarrow \langle \mathbf{M}, \mathbf{R} \rangle$, where $\mathbf{M}$ is a set of terminal and non terminal elements, and $\mathbf{R}$ is a set of relationships between elements of $\mathbf{M}$, we have that, $\forall x \in \mathbf{M}$ is not a daughter of Y^0. Thus, the learned grammar will not have cycles.

Transformation of the Grammar. We transform the grammar into a BN, using the following procedure. For every production rule, $Y^0 \rightarrow \langle \mathbf{M}, \mathbf{R} \rangle$, we produce the node Y^0 in the grammar and connect this node with all $x \in \mathbf{M}$. For every relationship $r(a, b) \in \mathbf{R}$ we produce the node r connected with its parents $a, b \in \mathbf{M}$.

The transformation procedure is illustrated with the following example. If we consider the next grammar (we have deleted the superscripts for simplicity):
$G = (VN, VT, VR, S, P, R)$;
$VN = \{NT\_R2\_C24\_C12, NT\_R1\_C9\_C25, NT\_R1\_C9\_C26, NT\_R7\_C9\_C31,$
$NT\_R1\_C42\_C9, NT\_R1\_C49\_C19, NT\_R1\_C9\_C69, NT\_R3\_C11\_C96\}$;
$VT = \{Term\_C24, Term\_C12, Term\_C9, Term\_C19, Term\_C11\}$;
$VR = \{Above, Ady, Invading, Inside\_of\}$;
$S = NT\_R3\_C11\_C96$

where the rule productions are defined by P :

1. $NT\_R3\_C11\_C96 \rightarrow < \{Term\_C11, NT\_R1\_C9\_C69\}, \{Inside\_of(Term\_C11, NT\_R1\_C9\_C69)\} >$;
2. $NT\_R1\_C9\_C69 \rightarrow < \{Term\_C9, NT\_R1\_C49\_C19\}, \{Ady(Term\_C9, NT\_R1\_C49\_C19)\} >$;
3. $NT\_R1\_C49\_C19 \rightarrow < \{NT\_R1\_C42\_C9, Term\_C19\}, \{Ady(NT\_R1\_C42\_C9, Term\_C19)\} >$;
4. $NT\_R1\_C42\_C9 \rightarrow < \{NT\_R7\_C9\_C31, Term\_C9\}, \{Ady(NT\_R7\_C9\_C31, Term\_C9)\} >$;
5. $NT\_R7\_C9\_C31 \rightarrow < \{Term\_C9, NT\_R1\_C9\_C26\}, \{Invading(Term\_C9, NT\_R1\_C9\_C26)\} >$;
6. $NT\_R1\_C9\_C26 \rightarrow < \{Term\_C9, NT\_R1\_C9\_C25\}, \{Ady(Term\_C9, NT\_R1\_C9\_C25)\} >$;
7. $NT\_R1\_C9\_C25 \rightarrow < \{Term\_C9, NT\_R2\_C24\_C12\}, \{Ady(Term\_C9, NT\_R2\_C24\_C12)\} >$;
8. $NT\_R2\_C24\_C12 \rightarrow < \{Term\_C24, Term\_C12\}, \{Above(Term\_C24, Term\_C12)\} >$;

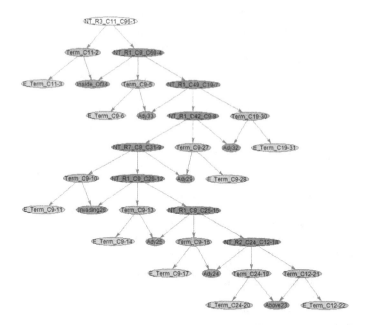

Fig. 4. Bayesian Network generated by the example grammar. Evidence is given only to leaf nodes. Nodes with two parents (in red) represent relationship nodes. Leaf nodes with only one parent (in green) represent terminal elements. Other nodes (in dark blue and light blue) represent non-terminal and terminal elements (but evidence is not given to these ones).

The algorithm generates the structure of a Bayesian network illustrated in Fig. 4.

Parameter Learning. Once the BN is obtained, its parameters are learned from examples, using positive and negative validation sets. The intermediate elements in the BN (nodes which are related to non-terminal elements in the SR-grammar) are considered as hidden nodes, so we use Expectation-Maximization (EM) to learn the parameters of the network. In each experiment we iterated the EM algorithm ten times at most. We use a subjective initialization for the probabilities of the hidden nodes, and the parameters of the evidence (terminal) nodes are initialized from the training image features.

3.2 Object Recognition

For object recognition, an image is initially segmented and converted to regions which are mapped to the terminal elements of the lexicon. Finding a valid configuration means to discover a relationship that has a match with the grammar rule as represented in the BN. This match is converted to evidence in the BN. The relationship is subsumed in the image and the process is repeated until the grammar is completed or the image has no configuration applicable to the BN. If the complete grammar is found, there is a high probability that the object learned with the grammar appears in the image. The method is briefly described in Alg. 1. An example of some configurations obtained in a sample image are illustrated in the Fig. 5.

Algorithm 1: Grammar Search. BN is the built Bayesian Network from de Grammar.

Data: BN, Image ;   /* Segmented Image */
Result: Candidate-Grammar ;   /* corresponding with the image */

foreach *Relationship of V_T's in* **BN** do
    foreach *Relationship applicable in* **Image** do
        Call to **Expand** with **BN** and **Image**
        Check Evidence in Relationships and nodes
        Seek relationships in **Image** that match with
        neighbor relationships in **BN**
        // side, below and upward
        if *No relationships in* **Image** *or* **BN** *has no more nodes* then
            Accept **Candidate-Grammar** and finish
        if *there are n relationships in* **Image** then
            Call to **Expand** for every relationship (Recursion)

---

4   Results

To evaluate experimentally the proposed model, we consider different object classes from the Caltech database [5]: bikes, sailboats, faces, airplanes, compact-disc, soccer-ball, boombox. A grammar is learned for each object class using a training set (45 images), and the parameters for the corresponding BN are estimated from a validation set (other 45 images). Then the obtained model is tested using a different set of test images (the number varies between 90 and 668). Recognition is evaluated based on the posterior probability given by probability propagation in the BN (according to a predefined threshold that provides a compromise between precision and recall)

Examples of detected objects are illustrated in Fig. 5, 6 and 7; as in previous images, different colors in these images are used for a better differentiation only. As we can see, the method discovered certain regions (terminal elements) that are category specific. Also, the grammar and corresponding BN are particular for each class of object.

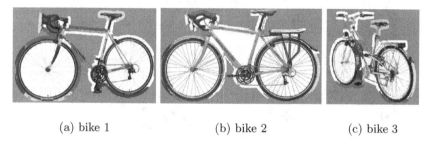

(a) bike 1   (b) bike 2   (c) bike 3

Fig. 5. Regions detected for a bike example. The colored regions are the terminal elements detected and provided as evidence to the BN. Different colors are used for a better differentiation only. In spite of the simple segmentation algorithm, the grammar helps to detect parts of the object. The grammar has detected the background and edges of the bike, because these were the most invariant elements along the images of the training set.

(a) sailboat 1   (b) sailboat 2   (c) sailboat 3

Fig. 6. Example of sailboat images. The sails (white regions) and its edges are detected. Although the model detects only part of the object (the sail), this part is more invariant than the rest of the object and provides a good clue for sailboat recognition; this was discovered automatically by the method.

Recognition results are evaluated in terms of accuracy, precision and recall:

$$Accuracy = \frac{TP + TN}{TP + FP + TN + FN}$$
$$Precision = \frac{TP}{TP + FP}$$
$$Recall = \frac{TP}{TP + FN},$$

where TP is the true positive, TN the true negative, FP the false positive and FN the false negative rate in each experiment. The model obtained for each

Fig. 7. Example of face images. The detected terminal elements are depicted, which correspond to different parts of the face that the system discovered were appropriate for recognizing faces.

Table 1. Recognition results of the model in Caltech 256 database. Positive examples are obtained from the specified class and negative examples are obtained from the background class (257-clutter).

Class	Accuracy	Precision	Recall	Time	Num Examples
Faces101	84.88	88.44	80.23	50 min.	668
Airplanes	75.6	69.2	92.22	12 min.	180
compact-disc	75.5	83.82	63.33	14 min.	180
Soccer Ball	74.4	84.33	60.00	13 min.	180
Boombox	72.7	73.56	71.11	12 min.	180

class of object was evaluated with a set of test images, that include positive and negative examples. The negative examples were obtained from the background dataset images, provided in the 256-Caltech Database. The results for several classes of objects are summarized in the Table 1; with an average of nearly 80% precision with similar average recall. Although these results are in general not superior to other methods in the state of the art, we consider that they are promising as the proposed method provides a general framework that still needs to be optimized. For example, the definition of the terminal elements can be improved by extending the types of uniform and edge regions. Also, currently the grammar is restricted to binary relations and does not incorporate alternatives ("OR" rules). Lastly, the learned relations are currently hard and can be extended to consider partial relations.

5   Conclusions and Future Work

A novel and general model for object recognition based on visual grammars and Bayesian Networks was described. This approach combines Symbol-Relation grammars and Bayesian networks to describe an object in an image. The Bayesian Network is generated automatically from the grammar, and the grammar is learned automatically from examples. The terminal elements (lexicon) and parameters are also learned from examples. Object recognition is done via probabilistic inference in the BN model. We have performed preliminary experiments with several natural object classes with promising results.

The main contribution of this work is proposing a general methodology for developing object recognition systems, that combines the richness and expressivity of formal grammars and the robustness and efficiency of Bayesian networks. We consider that this work contributes to the final goal of developing more general vision systems, analogous to those developed for voice and language.

There are several avenues for future research:

1. Improve and extend the visual dictionary by enriching the types of terminal elements.
2. Extend the grammar to incorporate rules with more than two elements as well as OR rules.
3. Consider partial relations when learning the grammar.
4. Evaluate the model with other classes of objects.

References

1. Chang, L., Jin, Y., Zhang, W., Borenstein, E.: Context, Computation, and Optimal ROC Performance in Hierarchical Models. International Journal of Computer Vision 93(2), 117–140 (2011)
2. Felzenszwalb, P.F.: Object Detection Grammars. In: ICCV Workshops, p. 691. IEEE, Barcelona (2011)
3. Ferrucci, F., Pacini, G., Satta, G., Sessa, M.I., Tortora, G., Tucci, M., Vitiello, G.: Symbol-relation grammars: a formalism for graphical languages. Inf. Comput. 131(1), 1–46 (1996)
4. Gabor, D.: Theory of Communication. JIEE 93(3), 429–459 (1946)
5. Griffin, G., Holub, A., Perona, P.: Caltech-256 Object Category Dataset. Technical Report 7694, California Institute of Technology (2007)
6. Meléndez, A., Sucar, L.E., Morales, E.F.: A Visual Grammar for Face Detection. In: Kuri-Morales, A., Simari, G.R. (eds.) IBERAMIA 2010. LNCS, vol. 6433, pp. 493–502. Springer, Heidelberg (2010)
7. Ommer, B., Buhmann, J.M.: Learning Compositional Categorization Models. In: Leonardis, A., Bischof, H., Pinz, A. (eds.) ECCV 2006. LNCS, vol. 3953, pp. 316–329. Springer, Heidelberg (2006)
8. Pearl, J.: Probabilistic Reasoning in Intelligent Systems: Networks of Plausible Inference. Morgan Kaufmann, San Francisco (1988)
9. Zhu, S.C., Mumford, D.: A Stochastic Grammar of Images. Foundations and Trends in Computer Graphics and Vision 2(4), 259–362 (2006)

Color Image Segmentation with a Hyper-Conic Multilayer Perceptron

Juan Pablo Serrano, Arturo Hernández, and Rafael Herrera

Center for Research in Mathematics
Computer Science Department
Guanajuato, Guanajuato, Mexico
{jpsr,artha,rherrera}@cimat.mx
http://www.cimat.mx

Abstract. We apply the Hyper-Conic Artificial Multilayer Perceptron (HC-MLP) to color image segmentation, where we consider image segmentation as a classification problem distinguishing between foreground and background pixels. The HC-MLP was designed by using the conic space and conformal geometric algebra. The neurons in the hidden layer contain a transfer function that defines a quadratic surface (spheres, ellipsoids, paraboloids and hyperboloids) by means of inner and outer products, and the neurons in the output layer contain a transfer function that decides whether a point is inside or outside a sphere. The Particle Swarm Optimization algorithm (PSO) is used to train the HC-MLP. A benchmark of fifty images is used to evaluate the performance of the algorithm and compare our proposal against statistical methods which use copula gaussian functions.

Keywords: Color Image Segmentation, Artificial Neural Networks, Geometric Algebra.

1 Introduction

Image segmentation continues to be an important research area in computer vision applications. A great variety of segmentation algorithms and its applications have been proposed in the literature [1,2,3,4,5]. In this paper we use the Hyper-Conic Multilayer Perceptron (HC-MLP) [6] for color image segmentation, since the color image segmentation problem can be considered as a supervised pixel classification problem. We compare the performance of the HC-MLP with two classifiers: the copula-based probabilistic algorithm and the independent probabilistic model. The input data space consists of the RGB color space vectors of each pixel in the image without any preprocessing.

There exist several proposals in the literature [7,8,9] for color image segmentation using artificial neural networks. Our proposal is to use the higher order hyper-conic neuron of the HC-MLP instead of the hyperplane neuron of the classical MLP. The neurons in the hidden layer (the hyper-conic neurons) and output layer (spherical neurons) of the HC-MLP have transfer functions that define quadratic surfaces and spherical surfaces [10] respectively. The hyper-conic

R. Klette, M. Rivera, and S. Satoh (Eds.): PSIVT 2013, LNCS 8333, pp. 360–371, 2014.

and spherical neurons allow us to simplify the topology of the multilayer perceptron and, at the same time, produce more complex and flexible non-linear decision regions to classify the points in the input data space. The design of the neurons is based on geometrical ideas of (conformal) geometric algebra by using the inner and outer products.

The rest of this paper is organized as follows: In Section 2, we provide an overview of conformal geometric algebra and the conic space. In Section 3, we review the PSO algorithm. In Section 4, we give a detailed implementation of the HC-MLP. In Section 5 we describe the experiments and compare our results with the supervised probabilistic classifiers. Finally, conclusions and future work are discussed in Section 6.

2   Geometric Preliminaries

2.1   Conformal Geometric Algebra

The conformal model provides a way of dealing with Euclidean Geometry within a higher dimensional space. Let $e_0, e_1, ..., e_n, e_\infty$ be a basis of $\mathbb{R}^{n+2}$. We will consider the Euclidean points $x = x_1e_1 + x_2e_2 +, ..., x_ne_n \in \mathbb{R}^n$ to be mapped to points in $\mathbb{R}^{n+1,1}$ according to the following conformal transformation:

$$\mathbb{P}(x) = (x_1e_1 + x_2e_2 + ... + x_ne_n) + \frac{1}{2}x^2e_\infty + e_0, \qquad (1)$$

where $\mathbb{R}^{n+1,1}$ is a $(n + 2)$-dimensional real vector space that includes the Euclidean space $\mathbb{R}^n$ and has two more independent directions generated by two basic vectors e_0 and e_∞ [11]. Furthermore, it is endowed with a scalar product of vectors satisfying: $e_i \bullet e_i = 1$, $e_i \bullet e_j = 0$, $e_i \bullet e_\infty = 0$, $e_i \bullet e_0 = 0$, $e_\infty \bullet e_0 = -1$, $e_\infty \bullet e_\infty = 0$, $e_0 \bullet e_0 = 0$, where $1 \leq i, j \leq n$. Note that the Euclidean points $x \in \mathbb{R}^n$ are now mapped into points of the null cone in $\mathbb{R}^{n+1,1}$. The vectors e_0 and e_∞ represent the origin and a point at infinity respectively. The number x^2 is:

$$x^2 = x \bullet x = \sum_{i=1}^{n} x_i^2. \qquad (2)$$

A hyper-sphere in $\mathbb{R}^n$ is determined by its center $c \in \mathbb{R}^n$ and its radius $\rho \in \mathbb{R}$. Its conformal model representation is the point:

$$\mathbb{S}(c, \rho) = \mathbb{P}(c) - \frac{1}{2}\rho^2e_\infty. \qquad (3)$$

The representation of the sphere s in *Outer Product Null Space* notation (OPNS) in $\mathbb{R}^n$, can be written with the help of $n + 1$ conformal points that lie on it, i.e.

$$s^* = \bigwedge_{i=1}^{n+1} \mathbb{P}(x_i). \qquad (4)$$

A hyper-plane Θ in $\mathbb{R}^n$ is represented by:

$$\Theta(n, \delta) = n + \delta e_\infty, \tag{5}$$

where n is the normal vector to the hyper-plane in $\mathbb{R}^n$ and $\delta > 0$ is its oriented distance (with respect to n) to the origin. A hyper-plane in $\mathbb{R}^n$ can be defined by n points belonging to it. Thus, in the conformal model, it is represented by the outer product of the n image conformal points plus the vector e_∞, i.e.

$$\Theta^* = \left(\bigwedge_{i=1}^n P_i \right) + e_\infty. \tag{6}$$

Distance between points

The inner product between the points $\mathbb{P}(x)$ and $\mathbb{P}(y)$ is directly proportional to the square of the Euclidean distance of the points $\{x, y\}$ multiplied by -2,

$$\mathbb{P}(x) \bullet \mathbb{P}(y) = x \cdot y - \frac{1}{2}y^2 - \frac{1}{2}x^2 = -\frac{1}{2}(x - y)^2 \tag{7}$$

$$(x - y)^2 = -2(\mathbb{P}(x) \bullet \mathbb{P}(y)) \tag{8}$$

The conformal points $\mathbb{P}(x)$ and $\mathbb{P}(y)$ are null and as a consequence, $\mathbb{P}(x) \bullet \mathbb{P}(y) = 0$ if and only if $x = y$.

Distance between a point and a hyper-plane

Similarly, it is possible to calculate the signed distance between a point and a hyper-plane. For a point $\mathbb{P}(x)$ and hyper-plane $\Theta(n, \delta)$, the signed distance of the point to the hyper-plane is given by:

$$\mathbb{P}(x) \bullet \Theta(n, \delta) = x \cdot n - \delta. \tag{9}$$

The distance is zero if the point x lies on the hyper-plane. The distance is positive if the point x is on the same side of the plane as the normal vector n and negative if it is on the opposite side [11].

Point inside or outside a hyper-sphere

The inner product between a point $\mathbb{P}(x)$ and a hyper-sphere $\mathbb{S}(c, \rho)$

$$\mathbb{P}(x) \bullet \mathbb{S}(c, \rho) = \frac{1}{2}\rho^2 - \frac{1}{2}(c - x)^2 \tag{10}$$

can be used to decide whether a point is inside or outside of the hyper-sphere [11]:

- $\text{Sign}(\mathbb{P}(x) \bullet \mathbb{S}(c, \rho)) > 0 : x$ is inside the hyper-sphere.
- $\text{Sign}(\mathbb{P}(x) \bullet \mathbb{S}(c, \rho)) < 0 : x$ is outside the hyper-sphere.
- $\mathbb{P}(x) \bullet \mathbb{S}(c, \rho) = 0 : x$ is on the hyper-sphere.

2.2   Conic Space Model

By identifying points $\bar{x} = (x_1, x_2) \in \mathbb{R}^2$ with points $\vec{x} = (x_1, x_2, 1)$, it is well known that for a given symmetric 3×3 matrix A, the set of points $(x_1, x_2) \in \mathbb{R}^2$ such that

$$\begin{bmatrix} x_1 & x_2 & 1 \end{bmatrix} \begin{bmatrix} a_{1,1} & a_{1,2} & a_{1,3} \\ a_{1,2} & a_{2,2} & a_{2,3} \\ a_{1,3} & a_{2,3} & a_{3,3} \end{bmatrix} \begin{bmatrix} x_1 \\ x_2 \\ 1 \end{bmatrix} = 0, \tag{11}$$

lie on a conic. Equation (11) can be written as the scalar product between two vectors of $\mathbb{R}^6$:

$$\mathbb{D}(x_1, x_2) \cdot \mathcal{T}(A) = 0 \iff a_{1,1}x_1^2 + 2a_{1,2}x_1x_2 + 2a_{1,3}x_1 + a_{2,2}x_2^2 + 2a_{2,3}x_2 + a_{3,3} = 0 \tag{12}$$

where

$$\mathbb{D} : (x_1, x_2) \in \mathbb{R}^2 \mapsto \begin{bmatrix} x_1^2 & x_1x_2 & x_1 & x_2^2 & x_2 & 1 \end{bmatrix} \in \mathbb{R}^6 \tag{13}$$

and $\mathbb{D}(\mathbb{R}^2) = \mathbb{D}^2$,

$$\mathcal{T} : A \in \mathbb{R}^{3 \times 3} \mapsto \begin{bmatrix} a_{1,1} & 2a_{1,2} & 2a_{1,3} & a_{2,2} & 2a_{2,3} & a_{3,3} \end{bmatrix}^T \tag{14}$$

The Inner Product Null Space (IPNS) of $a = \mathcal{T}(A) \in \mathbb{R}^6$ is the set of all the points $X = \mathbb{D}(x_1, x_2) \in \mathbb{D}^2 \subset \mathbb{R}^6$ satisfying $X \cdot a = 0$, i.e. the points belonging to the conic represented by A. Given $a = \mathcal{T}(A), b = \mathcal{T}(B) \in \mathbb{R}^6$, the bivector $a \wedge b$ represents the intersection of the conics defined by A and B. The vectors a and b are linearly independent if they represent different conics. More precisely, the IPNS of $a \wedge b$ is the set of points X such that $0 = X \rfloor (a \wedge b) = (X \cdot a)b - (X \cdot b)a$, i.e. X belongs to both conics. The symbol $\rfloor$ denotes contraction of multivectors.

The Outer Product Null Space (OPNS) of a multivector $C \in Cl_6$ is the set of points X satisfying $X \wedge C = 0$. A conic through $(\bar{x}_1, \bar{x}_2, \bar{x}_3, \bar{x}_4, \bar{x}_5)$ is represented by $C = X_1 \wedge X_2 \wedge X_3 \wedge X_4 \wedge X_5$, where $X_i = \mathbb{D}(\bar{x}_i)$ for $i = 1, .., 5$. For instance, the distance from a point $X_0 = \mathbb{D}(x_{1,0}, x_{2,0}) \in \mathbb{D}^2$ and a multivector $C_{<5>} \in Cl(\mathbb{R}^6)$ can be obtained as follows:

$$dist(X, C_{<5>}) = (X \wedge C_{<5>})^* = (X \wedge C_{<5>})I_{<6>}^{-1}. \tag{15}$$

If $C = X_1 \wedge X_2 \wedge X_3 \wedge X_4 \wedge X_5$ then

$$dist(X_0, C_{<5>}) = (X_0 \wedge X_1 \wedge X_2 \wedge X_3 \wedge X_4 \wedge X_5)^*$$

$$= \det \begin{vmatrix} x_{1,0}^2 & x_{1,0}x_{2,0} & x_{1,0} & x_{2,0}^2 & x_{2,0} & 1 \\ x_{1,1}^2 & x_{1,1}x_{2,1} & x_{1,1} & x_{2,1}^2 & x_{2,1} & 1 \\ x_{1,2}^2 & x_{1,2}x_{2,2} & x_{1,2} & x_{2,2}^2 & x_{2,2} & 1 \\ x_{1,3}^2 & x_{1,3}x_{2,3} & x_{1,3} & x_{2,3}^2 & x_{2,3} & 1 \\ x_{1,4}^2 & x_{1,4}x_{2,4} & x_{1,4} & x_{2,4}^2 & x_{2,4} & 1 \\ x_{1,5}^2 & x_{1,5}x_{2,5} & x_{1,5} & x_{2,5}^2 & x_{2,5} & 1 \end{vmatrix} \tag{16}$$

$$= a_{1,1}x_{1,0}^2 + 2a_{1,2}x_{1,0}x_{2,0} + 2a_{1,3}x_{1,0}$$
$$+ a_{2,2}x_{2,0}^2 + 2a_{2,3}x_{2,0} + a_{3,3}$$
$$= \mathcal{T}(\vec{x}^T \vec{x}) \cdot \bar{a},$$

3   Particle Swarm Optimization (PSO)

A PSO algorithm consists of a swarm of particles, each of which is a potential solution to the optimization problem, which are dispersed in a multidimensional search space as follows: the position of each particle is adjusted according to its own experience and those of its neighbors [12]. The social component of the particle velocity update reflects information obtained from all the particles in the swarm. In this sense, the social information of the particle i is the best position found by the swarm, referred to by $\bar{g}_i$. A cognitive component represents the personal search of each particle, referred to by the vector $\bar{l}_i$. The velocity $v_{ij}(t+1)$ of particle i in the j-th canonical direction, $j = 1, ..., n$, at time step $t+1$, is calculated as follows:

$$v_{ij}(t+1) = w v_{ij}(t) + c_1 r_{1j}(t)[l_{ij}(t) - x_{ij}(t)] + c_2 r_{2j}(t)[g_{ij}(t) - x_{ij}(t)] \quad (17)$$

where w is the inertia weight, $x_{i,j}(t)$ is the position of particle i in the j-th direction at time step t, c_1 and c_2 are positive acceleration constants used to scale the contribution of the cognitive and social components respectively. Finally, $r_{1j}(t), r_{2j}(t) \sim U(0,1)$ are random values in the range $[0,1]$, sampled from a uniform distribution. The pseudo-code of the PSO algorithm is illustrated in Figure 1.

4   Hyper-Conic Neural Network

The hyper-conic neuron contains a transfer function that defines decision boundaries such as spheres, ellipsoids, paraboloids and hyperboloids. Figure 2 shows the architecture of the HC-MLP whose hyper-conic neurons in the hidden layer use the outer product in conic space. The input signals $x = [x_1, x_2, ..., x_n]$ are propagated through the network from left to right. The symbols $o_1, ...o_k, ..o_p$ denote the output vector $\bar{o}$ from the hidden layer to the output layer. The output vector of the output layer are described by the vector $\bar{y} = [y_1, y_2, ..., y_k, ..., y_q]$. Therefore, the output of the neuron o_i in the hidden layer can be written as a function composition of a non-linear associator and the sigmoid function G as follows:

$$o_i = \frac{1}{1 + exp(-(X \wedge C^i)I^{-1})}, \quad (18)$$

where

$$\beta = \frac{n^2 + 3n + 2}{2} \quad (19)$$

is the dimension of the conic space $\mathbb{R}^\beta$, $C^i = \mathbb{D}(\bar{x}_1) \wedge \mathbb{D}(\bar{x}_2) \wedge \cdots \wedge \mathbb{D}(\bar{x}_{\beta-1})$ is a $(\beta - 1)$-blade, the points $\bar{x}_j \in \mathbb{R}^2$ are the points to be estimated, and I denotes the pseudoscalar of the conic space $\mathbb{R}^\beta$. The distance computed in the non-linear associator in (18) can, in general, be positive or negative, depending on the position of the point with respect to the conic. As we have seen, the distance is zero if the point is on the conic surface.

Algorithm 1. PSO Algorithm

for all particle i **do**
   //Create and initialize an $n - dimensional$ swarm, S
   //position $\bar{x} = x_1, .., x_n$ and velocity $\bar{v} = v_1, .., v_n$.
end for
while stop criteria not met **do**
   for all particle i **do**
      if $f(S_i.\bar{x}) < f(S_i.\bar{lb})$ **then**
         $S_i.\bar{l} = S_i.\bar{x}$ //set personal best $\bar{l} = \{l_1, ..., l_n\}$ as best position found so far by the particle.
      end if
      if $f(S_i.\bar{x}) < f(S_i.\bar{gb})$ **then**
         $S_i.\bar{g} = S_i.\bar{x}$ //set global best $\bar{g} = \{g_1, ..., g_n\}$ as best position found so far by the whole swarm.
      end if
   end for
   for all particle i **do**
      for each canonical direction indexed by j **do**
         $S_i.v_j(t+1) = w \bullet S_i.v_j(t) + c_1 \bullet r_{1j}(t) \bullet [S_i.l_j(t) - S_i.x_j(t)]$
            $+ c_2 \bullet r_{2j}(t) \bullet [S_i.g_j(t) - S_i.x_j(t)]$ //update the velocity.
         $S_i.x_j(t+1) = S_i.x_j(t) + S_i.v_j(t+1)$ //update position
      end for
   end for
end while

Fig. 1. Particle Swarm Optimization Algorithm

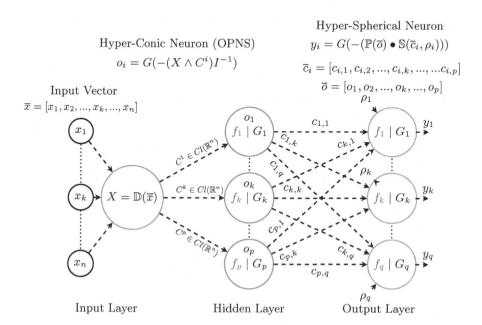

Fig. 2. HC-MLP Model where the HCN is implemented by using the outer product null space

The output y_i for the neuron i in the output layer is written as a function composition as follows:

$$y_i = \frac{1}{1 + exp(-(\mathbb{P}(\bar{o}) \bullet \mathbb{S}(\bar{c}_i, \rho_i)))} \tag{20}$$

where $\mathbb{P}(\bar{o})$ is the conformal point of the output vector of the neurons in the hidden layer, $\mathbb{S}(\bar{c}_i, \rho_i)$ is the hyper-sphere (represented in conformal space) whose center is the point $\bar{c}_i$ given by the weight vector of the neuron i in the output layer and its radius is ρ_i. A particle swarm algorithm is used for training the HC-MLP. The training stage of the HC-MLP finds the vector of parameters that determines the quadratic surfaces of the neurons in the hidden layer, as well as, the centers and radii of the spheres in the output layer. The parameters are enconded in a vector that represents a particle for the PSO algorithm.

5   Experimental Setup and Results

Since color image segmentation can be interpreted as a supervised classification problem, we use the HC-MLP to classify the pixels of 50 test images. The experimental setup is as follows:

- The patterns which are used during the training and testing stages belong to 3-dimensional space.
- The components of the input vector of each pattern are given by the values of the RGB color model.
- We work with the images from the databases used in [14,2] and available online at [15]. Three images of the database are presented in Figure 4.
- The training patterns are taken from labelling-lasso images which are divided into two sets referenced as a training set and a testing set.
- Pixels of each image were normalized by the min-max normalization method in the interval $[-1, +1]$.
- The outputs are encoded as -1 for foreground and +1 for background.
- The objective function is based on the mean square error function (MSE).
- The stop criteria is given by the number of epochs in the interval [1,100] or whether the MSE on the validation data set presents an increment during the training.
- The population size for the PSO algorithm is set to 20 particles initialized in the interval (-100,+100).
- The parameters used in the PSO algorithm are given as follows [13]:
  - inertia weight value is set to 0.7;
  - social component value is set to 1.49618;
  - cognitive component value is set to 1.49618.
- For comparison purposes, the tree evaluation measures which are used in this work are (see Figure 3):
  - accuracy;
  - sensitivity;
  - specificity.

The sensitivity and specificity measures explain the percentage of well classified pixels for each class, foreground and background, In the last column of the figure 4, we present two examples of classifications done with the HC-MLP. For

$$accuracy = \frac{tp+tn}{tp+fp+fn+tn}$$

	Truth	
	Positive	Negative
Model Positive	tp	fp
Model Negative	fn	tn

$$sensitivity = \frac{tp}{tp+fn}$$

$$specificity = \frac{tn}{tn+fp}$$

(a)   (b)

Fig. 3. (a) A confusion matrix for binary classification. (b) Definitions of accuracy, sensitivity and specificity

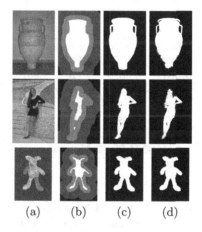

(a)   (b)   (c)   (d)

Fig. 4. (column a) The color image. (column b) The labelling-lasso image with training data for background (dark gray), for foreground (white) and the validation data (gray). (column c) The correct classification with foreground (white) and background (black). (column d) Classification with the HC-MLP.

comparison purposes, Table 1 shows the minimum, median, mean, maximum and standard deviation values of the specificity, sensitivity and accuracy values obtained by using the I-M and the GC-M models [2]. We present the results obtained by the HC-MLP when using 1, 2 and 3 neurons in the hidden layer.

According to Table 1, the HC-MLP presents a better performance than the I-M model for all evaluation measures, except for the minimum values. The mean accuracy of the HC-MLP when using 1, 2 or 3 neurons in the hidden layer is better than the mean accuracy of the I-M model (79.5%). For instance, the I-M model presents 8.12% more errors than the HC-MLP with 2 neurons in the hidden layer.

We found that the best architecture for the HC-MLP for this classification problem is the one using 2 neurons in the hidden layer. The mean value for the specificity measure given by the HC-MLP is better than the average of the specificity produced by the GC-M model. The average of the accuracy value using the HC-MLP is slightly better (approximately 0.5%) than the average accuracy produced by the GC-M. The maximum values for all evaluations using HC-MLP are better than those produced by the GC-M. However, the average of the sensitivity by using the GC-M is better than that produced by the HC-MLP, and so are minimum values. On the other hand, there are cases in which

Table 1. Descriptive results for all evaluation measures. BG stands for the background class and FG stands for the foreground class. (The best values are typed in boldface.)

Measure	Minimum	Median	Mean	Maximum	Std. deviation
I-M					
Specificity - BG	0.4040	0.8570	0.8170	0.9930	0.1330
Sensitivity - FG	0.3950	0.7630	0.7680	1.0000	0.1720
Accuracy	0.5710	0.7920	0.7950	0.9760	0.1070
GC-M					
Specificity - BG	**0.5510**	0.9240	0.8850	0.9940	0.1080
Sensitivity - FG	**0.4840**	0.8750	**0.8540**	0.9980	0.1270
Accuracy	**0.5870**	0.8890	0.8710	0.9870	0.0830
HC-MLP - 1 Neuron					
Specificity - BG	0.1487	0.9565	0.9130	**1.000**	0.1376
Sensitivity - FG	0.0344	**0.8813**	0.7995	**1.000**	0.2227
Accuracy	0.5244	0.8814	0.8648	**1.000**	0.1070
HC-MLP - 2 Neurons					
Specificity - BG	0.0993	0.9684	0.9269	**1.000**	0.1363
Sensitivity - FG	0.0000	0.8686	0.8085	**1.000**	0.2157
Accuracy	0.5196	**0.8899**	**0.8762**	**1.000**	0.1054
HC-MLP - 3 Neurons					
Specificity - BG	0.2069	**0.9762**	**0.9358**	**1.000**	0.1196
Sensitivity - FG	0.0409	0.8336	0.7712	**1.000**	0.2464
Accuracy	0.5206	0.8884	0.8648	**1.000**	0.1144
HC-MLP - from 1 to 3 Neurons					
Specificity - BG	0.1487	0.9597	0.9298	1.000	0.1265
Sensitivity - FG	0.1585	0.8962	0.8421	1.000	0.1752
Accuracy	0.5244	0.9183	0.8919	1.000	0.0942

either the classification problem is linearly separable or the decision regions can be efficiently designed using only one conic surface. For instance, Figure 5 shows two images of different complexity according to their data distributions, which are shown in the cubes of the third column. It is possible to see that for the first image, it is enough to use only one conic surface, while for the second one it is necessary to have a higher number of conics to produce the correct decision boundary separating background and foreground. In this sense, we selected the best values obtained by using 1,2 and 3 neurons in the hidden

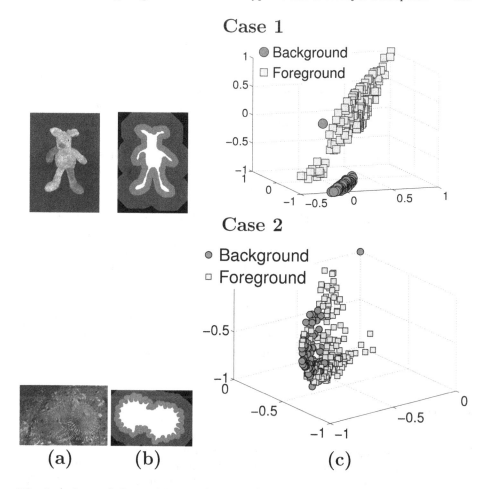

Fig. 5. (column a) Original Image. (column b) The labelling-lasso image with training data for background (dark gray), for foreground (white) and the validation data (gray). (column c) Space structure of the training set and validation set.

layer for each image. The results obtained are presented at the end of Table 1. The HC-MLP presents a better performance than those of the I-M and the GC-M for all evaluation measures, except for the minimum values produced by the I-M and GC-M models.

6 Conclusions

In this paper, we use the Hyper-Conic Multilayer Perceptron for color image segmentation, since the color image segmentation problem can be considered as a supervised pixel classification problem. We found that the best architecture for the HC-MLP for this classification problem is the one using 2 neurons in the hidden layer. HC-MLP presents a better performance than the I-M model. The average of the accuracy value using HC-MLP is slightly better then the average accuracy produced by the GC-M. According to Table 1, HC-MLP obtains the best value to classify the foreground and background with respect to the I-M and GC-M models on most images. However, there are images for which the number of neurons (1 to 3) used in the hidden layer is not sufficient.

On the other hand, we have also selected the best values produced by the different architectures composed by 1, 2 and 3 neurons in the hidden layer of the HC-MLP. The aim is to show that it is neccesary to apply different architectures depending on the pixel distribution of the images in order to achieve the segmentation. In this paper, we have chosen 1, 2 and 3 neurons to simplify the topology of the HC-MLP for this image database. The immediate future work is to use a HC-MLP endowed with a higher number of neurons in order to deal with those images which require a more complex architecture. Furthermore, we will also investigate the design of an algorithm to adapt the number of neurons in the hidden layer according to the pixel distribution of each image.

Acknowledgments. The authors gratefully acknowledge the financial support from the National Council for Science and Technology of Mexico (CONACyT) and from the Center for Research in Mathematics (CIMAT). The third author would like to thank the International Centre for Theoretical Physics for its hospitality and support.

References

1. Cheng, H.-D., Jiang, X.H., Sun, Y., Wang, J.: Color image segmentation: advances and prospects. Pattern Recognition 34(12), 2259–2281 (2001)
2. Salinas-Gutiérrez, R., Hernández-Aguirre, A., Rivera-Meraz, M.J.J., Villa-Diharce, E.R.: Supervised Probabilistic Classification Based on Gaussian Copulas. In: Sidorov, G., Hernández Aguirre, A., Reyes García, C.A. (eds.) MICAI 2010, Part II. LNCS, vol. 6438, pp. 104–115. Springer, Heidelberg (2010)
3. Szeliski, R.: Computer vision: algorithms and applications, pp. 235–269. Springer (2011)
4. Hernandez-Lopez, F.J., Rivera, M.: Binary segmentation of video sequences in real time. In: MICAI, pp. 163–168. IEEE Proceedings (2010)
5. Hernandez-Lopez, F.J., Rivera, M.: Change detection by probabilistic segmentation from monocular view. In: Machine Vision and Applications (2012) (to appear)
6. Serrano Rubio, J.P., Hernández Aguirre, A., Herrera Guzmán, R.: A Conic Higher Order Neuron Based on Geometric Algebra and Its Implementation. In: Batyrshin, I., Mendoza, M.G. (eds.) MICAI 2012, Part II. LNCS, vol. 7630, pp. 223–235. Springer, Heidelberg (2013)
7. Lescure, P., Meas-Yedid, V., Dupoisot, H., Stamon, G.: Color segmentation on biological microscope images. In: Proceeding of SPIE, Application of Artificial Neural Networks in Image Processing IV, San Jose, California, January 28-29, pp. 182–193 (1999)
8. Rae, R., Ritter, H.J.: Recognition of human head orientation based on artificial neural networks. IEEE Trans. Neural Network 9(2), 257–265 (1998)

9. Fang, Y., Pan, C., Liu, L.: On-line training of neural network for color image segmentation. In: Wang, L., Chen, K., S. Ong, Y. (eds.) ICNC 2005. LNCS, vol. 3611, pp. 135–138. Springer, Heidelberg (2005)

10. Perwass, C., Banarer, V., Sommer, G.: Spherical decision surfaces using conformal modelling. In: Michaelis, B., Krell, G. (eds.) DAGM 2003. LNCS, vol. 2781, pp. 9–16. Springer, Heidelberg (2003)

11. Dorst, L., Fontijne, D., Mann, S.: Geometric Algebra for Computer Science: An Object-Oriented Approach to Geometry. The Morgan Kaufmann Series in Computer Graphics, pp. 23–57, 355–389. Morgan Kaufmann Publishers Inc., San Francisco (2007)

12. Engelbrecht Andries, P.: Fundamental of Computational Swarm Intelligence. Wiley (2005)

13. Van den Bergh, F., Engelbrecht, A.P.: A study of particle swarm optimization particle trajectories. Information Sciences 176(8), 937–971 (2006)

14. Blake, A., Rother, C., Brown, M., Perez, P., Torr, P.: Interactive image segmentation using an adaptive GMMRF model. In: Pajdla, T., Matas, J(G.) (eds.) ECCV 2004. LNCS, vol. 3021, pp. 428–441. Springer, Heidelberg (2004)

15. Rother, C., Kolmogorov, V., Blake, A., Brown, M.: Image and video editing, http://research.microsoft.com/en-us/um/cambridge/projects/visionimagevideoediting/segmentation/grabcut.htm

TimeViewer, a Tool for Visualizing the Problems of the Background Subtraction

Alejandro Sánchez Rodríguez[1], Juan Carlos González Castolo[1], and
Óscar Déniz Suárez[2]

[1] Centro Universitario de Ciencias Económico Administrativas, Universidad de
Guadalajara, México
[2] Grupo VISILAB, Universidad de Castilla La-Mancha, España

Abstract. This paper is about the TimeViewer tool that facilitates understanding of the most common problems in Background Subtraction. The tool displays patterns of each frame, and through the historical values of the pixels allows for visual identification of changes in a sequence of pixels. The paper demonstrates the usefulness of TimeViewer by showing how it visually presents the most common Background Subtraction problems.

Keywords: TimeViewer, Background Subtraction, Change Detection, Motion Detection.

Introduction

A human being generates most of his knowledge through his eyes. It is something so natural and instinctive that, at the beginning of Computer Vision, it was underestimated and considered a trivial operation. Computer vision consists of extracting information from a huge amount of data.

Background Subtraction (BS) consists of minimizing this amount of information, by distinguishing between foreground movement and static background. BS eliminates background data which is not significant in the scene where a movement is of interest. The extracted data is thus prepared and then passed to some other visual process. BS thus helps accelerate the treatment of the relevant information, as well as assign this information the necessary resources in an optimal manner.

Movement is represented by a series of static images which, when played one after another, generate the *illusion* of movement. Hence, the amount of data flow to be analyzed is considerable and lacks the initial significance. BS aims to find patterns of movement from series of frames by determining which pixels should and which should not be considered for further analysis.

This paper considers the most common problems in the Background Subtraction and shows how the *TimeViewer* tool helps in visualizing the patterns unique to a scene corresponding to each problem. The tool uses the historic values of the pixels, from the past frames, and allows to visually differentiate what is happening with

R. Klette, M. Rivera, and S. Satoh (Eds.): PSIVT 2013, LNCS 8333, pp. 372–384, 2014.

a pixel sequence. After all, the best way to identify possible patterns is by directly observing the images produced by the tool, according to [1].

TimeViewer can also be used as a teaching tool. Researchers can visualize and more easily comprehend a particular BS problem by observing the patterns generated by changes in pixel values trough time. Thus, it is easier to analyze the problem represented by a particular scenario.

Section 1 of this paper, provides an overview of the BS. In the section 2 the architecture, as well as performance, of the *TimeViewer* tool is presented. Section 3 presents examples of the implementation of the tool in different problems in BS. Finally. the section 4, provides a brief discussion of the utility of the tool.

1   Background Subtraction Problems

Background Subtraction (BS) is a method for simplification or reduction of data [2]. It is used on videos where the flow of information is abundant and repetitive. BS processes a sequence of images in order to leave a binary mask that represents the objects of interest or *Foreground* as active, and the rest of the scene considered as *Background* is discarded [3]. This is accomplished by comparing the values of color and brightness of each pixel, from image to image.

BS starts out from the fact that there is some *movement* in the scene. It is important to emphasize this supposition, because the humans do not need movement for identification of foreground. Even in a unique image humans identify what is the background and which is the objects of interest. In the field of computational sciences, this is called **Object Recognition**. [4].

BS starts out from the illusion of movement created by a sequence of images with differences between them [5]. Because of this, the method is only applicable to image sequences or video.

According to [6] , BS is a primary process in tasks such as **Surveillance**, **Traffic Monitoring**, **Tracking and Detection People** and **Gesture Recognition**, because it reduces the amount of information for further treatments.

The *Background* is composed of everything that is uninteresting, like static elements of the scene (walls, floor, furniture, etc) or objects with cyclic or insignificant movements (trees, flags water fountains, ventilators, etc). BS has two main stages: the *initialization* and the *maintenance* of the background model [7].

The **Background** concept used in this paper is taken from [8] and it is defined as: **Everything that remains static or cyclic in a video or image sequence during a predetermined amount of time.**

According to [2], there are four possible types of movement in an image sequence or video:

1. Fixed camera, moving object and **static background**.
2. Fixed camera, several moving objects and **static background**.
3. Mobile camera, relatively still scene.
4. Mobile camera, scene with several moving objects.

This study analyzes the cases one and two, where the background remains *constant* and the camera is fixed.

Currently, the evaluation of the different BS algorithms is performed by using *Datasets* manufactured for this purpose. These datasets consist of three elements: a) a group of training images b) images for the algorithm's execution and c) images used to check the results. See [7], [9], [10], [6].

In BS many unique and varied situations appear. This makes it necessary to test each BS algorithm in the various scenarios for which it is intended. In some of the scenarios errors in the background models may appear. According to [7] the main difficulties are these:

- Moved Objects. Objects that are considered part of the Background model and for some reason they change their location in the scene. This movement integrates such objects to the foreground, while they should still be considered part of the background.
- Time of Day. The global illumination of the scene changes gradually throughout the day in open environments, which causes different background models having to be considered.
- Light Switch. Global and sudden changes of illumination provoke that the Background model has to be discarded and a new one applied. Unlike the previous problem, the global sudden change of all Background can be regarded as a trigger for the change of Background model.
- Waving Trees. This refers to periodic and sporadic movements that are brought about by objects that should belong to the Background. The common example is the waving of the leaves in the trees (hence the name). Such movement should be ignored though it is frequently detected as Foreground.
- Camouflage. It is a problem that occurs when the pixels pertaining to Foreground objects have similar values to the pixels belonging to the Background model. This causes that even when there is a movement in the Foreground, changes are not perceived, because they are considered as part of the Background model.
- Bootstrapping. Some scenes present situations where it is not possible to obtain a full Background model, because of the constant appearance or movement of objects.
- Foreground Aperture. When an object of a specific homogeneous color in the foreground spans a large part of the vision field and stays there long enough, even though it is moving, some parts of its interior will be considered as part of the background model due to its movement being undetectable.
- Sleeping Person. This problem occurs when an object is initially identified as part of the Foreground and goes into a state of repose for a period of time long enough for the algorithm to include it in the Background model.
- Walking Person. When an object initially considered part of the Background moves, the region becomes Foreground. Here, the problem lies in that the newly discovered region of the Background should be considered as part of the Background immediately and not considered as another Foreground object.

- Shadows. Refers to the change in tonality or brightness of Background regions (shadows) that cause a changes in pixel values, but should not be considered as part of the Foreground.

The authors in [11] propose two more scenarios:

- Local Light Switch. Situation which arises when only some regions of Background have a sudden change of illumination and should continue to belong to the Background model.
- Reflections. If an object and its reflection are assumed as part of the Foreground, the size and shape of the object in question are different than the expected one. For example, a person and his reflection come to be regarded as a single object, which may hinder its location due to oversize.

2   Architecture

In Background Subtraction, one of the most efficient ways of checking the results of an algorithm, is **visually**, just as recommended by the authors in [1]. Even the images utilized for checking the results in [7] y [9], were manually segmented. In [1], the authors mention that *quantitative* forms of evaluation, are inferior and cannot be compared to the *qualitative* ones that are done visually by the investigators themselves.

Certainly, humans naturally and unconsciously keep the history of what we see. For the analysis of the behavior of patterns it was necessary to develop the TimeViewer tool, that allows observation of patterns of behavior of the pixels through time. The tool allows to see (not only register) the values of the pixels, and that way bring more *natural* view that allows understanding of what is *seen*. The algorithm is inspired by the work of [12] and [5].

2.1   Features

The TimeViewer tool was designed and coded to allow a view of the history of changes in a sequence of images, under the next features:

1. Read the images from a video or directory
2. Transform the data to make pixel history observable
3. Visualize the original sequence and the results of the data transformation
4. Allow the user to stop the sequence at any time
5. Restart the reproduction after being stopped
6. Save the images shown in the windows at any time
7. The lecture, transformation process and visualization must be done in real time, without delays
8. Optional: Obtain the images from a video-camera, live
9. Optional: Save the sequence of results images either one by one or in video format

The TimeViewer architecture is divided into three layers as shown in Figure 1:

- User Interface. Allows the user to stop viewing, display resume and save images from the screen to the working directory.
- TimeViewer Functions. Here the functions of image reading, image accumulation, transforming matrices of accumulated data and displaying the processed information for qualitative analysis are performed.
- TimeViewer Interface. The reading of video or images is done directly from a video camera or a from directory. Also, the resulting images can be stored in the working directory.

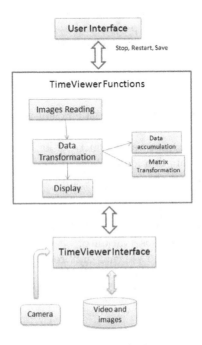

Fig. 1. TimeViewer Architecture

2.2   Implementation

TimeViewer was developed with the OpenCV library, which contains functions that allow the reading of image archives and videos. This library temporarily stores the images or frames in dynamic arrangements. Those arrangements can be manipulated by performing operations directly in the video RAM memory. Besides, the library possesses functions necessary for visualization and interactive control, that allow manipulation and the reproduction in real time. It also features storage functions for the images and video in different formats.

The main functions of TimeViewer are:

Image reading: The reading of the images was done in RAW uncompressed format.

Data Transformation: The transformation of data is done in two steps:
1. Reading and accumulation.
2. Matrix Transformation, as it can be seen in the Figure 2, and according to the equation:

$$Origin[x, y, z] = Destination[x, z, y]$$

Fig. 2. Image accumulation and transformation

Visualize: The algorithm presents a screen with the original images and the image of the resulting transformation in another one.

Currently, the tool has diverse variations depending on the type of history that is desired. The first variation works with videos in grey scale, generating a window of pixel history at the time. Other variations split images in channels (depending in the color model) generating a reproduction and pixel history window for each channel.

3   Results

The *TimeViewer* tool allows the user to play a video and, at the same time, check the pixel history of certain line of the original image, to stop the reproduction and to save images. It works in real time and it can show the pixel history of any line of the original image.

3.1   Moved Object

Objects that are considered part of the background and that for some reason change their location in the scene, are integrated into the foreground, while they should be kept as part of the background. Figure 3(a) shows initial pattern, in Figure 3(b), person moved an object, then Figure 3(c) shows the final pattern.

Scene in Figure 4(a) shows the initial position of objects, then in Figure 4(b) a person moved the chair, and left it in different location, Figure 4(c).

(a) Initial scene   (b) Irregularities   (c) Final scene

Fig. 3. Moved Object, historic

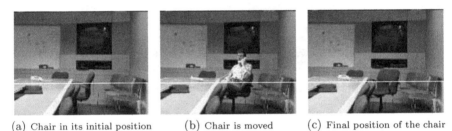

(a) Chair in its initial position   (b) Chair is moved   (c) Final position of the chair

Fig. 4. Moved Object, scene

3.2   Time of Day

The global lightning of the scene changes gradually during the day in outdoor environments, which causes the necessity to consider different background models.

Patterns showed in Figures 5(a),5(b) and 5(c) belong to the same scene, only the illumination changes. Figures 6(a), 6(b) and 6(c) show the scene.

(a) Initial pattern   (b) Gradual change of illumi-   (c) Motion presence
                              nation

Fig. 5. Time of Day, historic

(a) Low illumination   (b) Gradual increase of illumi- (c) Presence of a person in the
nation, highlighting new objects scene

Fig. 6. Time of Day, scene

3.3   Light Switch

Global and sudden changes in lightning cause the background model to be discarded and a new one to be generated. Unlike the last problem, the global and sudden change of all the background model can be considered as a trigger for the change of background model.

Initial pattern (Fig. 7(a)). When the light is turn on the background pattern changes (Fig. 7(b)), Here, a global change can be appreciated. Figure 7(c) shows when the light is turned off and the pattern switches back to its initial model.

Figure 8(a) shows the initial scene. In Figure 8(b), the light is turned off 8(c).

(a) Initial pattern   (b) Sudden change of back- (c) Return to the original pat-
ground pattern   tern

Fig. 7. Light Switch, historic

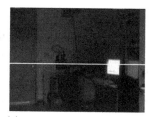

(a) Initial scene   (b) A person enters the scene (c) Scene with low illumination

Fig. 8. Light Switch, scene

3.4 Waving Trees

Waving trees refers to movements that do not cease during a period of time, but which are provoked by object that must belong to the background. The common example is the undulation of the leafs in the trees, a movement which must be discarded but is noticeable.

In Figure 9(a), pattern is constantly undulating, yet a foreground region is perfectly noticeable (Figs. 9(b) and 9(c)).

Scene with a tree in constant undulation (Fig. 10(a)), then, a person appears (Fig. 10(b)); back to initial scenario (Fig. 10(c))

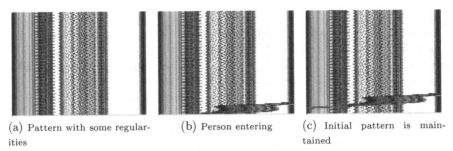

(a) Pattern with some regularities   (b) Person entering   (c) Initial pattern is maintained

Fig. 9. Waving Trees, historic

(a) Initial scene, the tree is moved   (b) Presence of a person   (c) Back to initial scene

Fig. 10. Waving Trees, scene

3.5 Bootstrapping

Some scenes are situations where a full background model is not obtained due to an object that periodically appears and disappears.

In this problem, an ideal background model can not be constructed, due to constant appearance-disappearance of objects. Figures 11(a), 11(b) and 11(c) shows this situation. Figures 12(a), 12(b) and 12(c) display the same scene at different time.

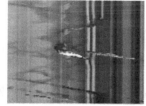

(a) Some sections have regular patterns (b) New sections with regular patterns (c) New sections with regular patterns

Fig. 11. Bootstrapping, historic

(a) Initial scene   (b) Scene after some time   (c) Final scene

Fig. 12. Bootstrapping, scene

3.6   Light Switch (local)

This situation only occurs when only some regions of the background suddenly change their illumination but must be kept as part of the background model. Figures 13(a), 13(b) and 13(c) display patterns in which such changes can be appreciated. Scenes in Figures 14(a), 14(b) and 14(c) show different local light changes.

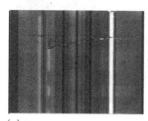
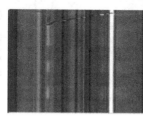

(a) Pattern with local changes   (b) Object presence   (c) Local ligth changes

Fig. 13. Local Light Switch, historic

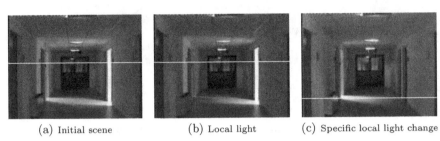

(a) Initial scene   (b) Local light   (c) Specific local light change

Fig. 14. Local Light Switch, scene

3.7 Sleeping Person

This problem occurs when and object is initially identified as part of the foreground and it then changes to a rest state for a long enough period of time for the algorithm to integrate it to the background model. Figure 15 shows a pattern with some local objects. The entire scene is shown in Figure 16.

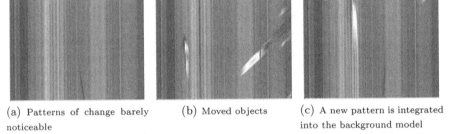

(a) Patterns of change barely   (b) Moved objects   (c) A new pattern is integrated
noticeable   into the background model

Fig. 15. Sleeping Person, historic

(a) Initial scene   (b) Scene with some new ob-   (c) Some objects stopped
                           jects

Fig. 16. Sleeping Person, scene

3.8 Shadows

Due to the lightning conditions on the scene, the foreground objects often cast shadows (Fig. 17), which due to the contrast with the background are considered as part of the foreground object. Some algorithms [8] try to resolve this issue through considering variations of color shades.

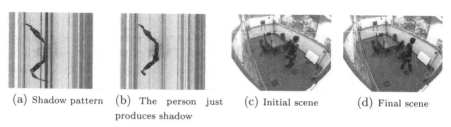

(a) Shadow pattern   (b) The person just   (c) Initial scene   (d) Final scene
                         produces shadow

Fig. 17. Shadows: historic and scene

3.9 Reflections

Another phenomenon are the reflections on the object's surfaces. Usually, this effect is considered an special case of shadows, however, one of the main characteristics that makes reflections different from the shadows, is that reflections have well defined borders and can be identical to the foreground object. In Figures 18) the apparent lack of differences between the foreground object and the background can be observed.

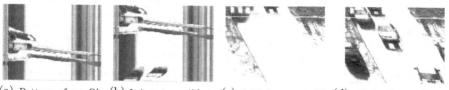

(a) Pattern of an Ob-   (b) It is not possible to   (c) Initial scene with   (d) Reflections main-
ject and its reflection   differentiate the reflec-   objects and their reflec-   tained the same prop-
                          tion from the object   tions   erties that the original
                                                                              objects

Fig. 18. Reflections, historic and scene

4 Conclusions

As already mentioned, various authors state that there is no better analysis in BS that the qualitative one, which is done visually. TimeViewer is a tool to support such analysis.

TimeViewer has also proved to be an excellent learning tool for those starting their studies and research in the area of **background subtraction, motion detection, change detection,** etc., because it eases the comprehension of different problems through the visualization of the pixel history in a sequence of images, as well as the storage of said snapshots from said historic for a detailed analysis.

Future work is aimed at using the pixel history for analysis of the movement of objects in a video, detecting patterns and trajectories. There is also potential as a video editing tool that needs to be explored.

Acknowledgements This work has been supported by Consejo Nacional de Ciencia y Tecnología (CONACyT), México, Centro Universitario de Ciencias Económico-Administrativas (CUCEA) of the Universidad de Guadalajara, México, and Project TIN2011-24367 from the Spanish Ministry of Economy and Competitiveness, España.

References

1. Radke, R.J., Andra, S., Al-Kofahi, O., Roysam, B.: Image change detection algorithms: a systematic survey. IEEE Transactions on Image Processing 14(3), 294–307 (2005)
2. Shapiro, L.G., Stockman, G.C.: Computer Vision. Prentice Hall (2001)
3. Benezeth, Y., Jodoin, P.M., Emile, B., Laurent, H., Rosenberger, C.: Comparative study of background subtraction algorithms. Journal of Electronic Imaging 19(3), 033003 (2010)
4. Pinto, N., Cox, D.D., Dicarlo, J.J.: Why is real-world visual object recognition hard? PLoS Computational Biology 4(1), e27 (2008)
5. Adelson, E.: Mechanisms for motion perception. Optics & Photonics News, 24–30 (August 1991)
6. Cheung, S.C.S.: Robust techniques for background subtraction in urban traffic video. In: Proceedings of SPIE, vol. 5308(1), pp. 881–892 (2004)
7. Toyama, K., Krumm, J., Brumitt, B., Meyers, B.: Wallflower: principles and practice of background maintenance. In: Proceedings of the Seventh IEEE International Conference on Computer Vision 1(c), vol. 1, pp. 255–261 (1999)
8. Bradski, G., Kaehler, A.: Learning OpenCV: Computer vision with the OpenCV library. O'Reilly Media (2008)
9. Tiburzi, F., Escudero, M., Bescos, J., Martinez, J.M.: A ground truth for motion based video-object segmentation. In: 2008 IEEE International Conference on Image Processing, Proceedings of ICIP 2008. Workshop on Multimedia Information Retrieval: New Trends and Challenges, vol. 1, pp. 17–20. IEEE, San Diego (2008)
10. Datasets for the Eleventh IEEE International Workshop on Performance Evaluation of Tracking and Surveillance (2009)
11. Cristani, M., Farenzena, M., Bloisi, D., Murino, V.: Background Subtraction for Automated Multisensor Surveillance: A Comprehensive Review. EURASIP Journal on Advances in Signal Processing 2010, 1–24 (2010)
12. Adelson, E., Bergan, J.R.: Spatiotemporal energy models for the perception of motion. Journal of the Optical Society of America A Optics and Image Science 2(2), 284–299 (1985)

Block-Based Search Space Reduction Technique for Face Detection Using Shoulder and Head Curves

Supriya Sathyanarayana, Ravi Kumar Satzoda,
Suchitra Sathyanarayana, and Srikanthan Thambipillai

Nanyang Technological University, Singapore

Abstract. Conventional face detection techniques usually employ sliding window based approaches involving series of classifiers to accurately determine the position of the face in an input image resulting in high computational redundancy. Pre-processing techniques are being investigated to reduce the search space for face detection. In this paper, we propose a systematic approach to reduce the search space for face detection using head and shoulder curves. The proposed method includes Gradient Angle Histograms (GAH) that are applied in a block-based manner to detect these curves, which are further associated to determine the search space for face detection. A performance evaluation of the proposed method on the datasets (CASIA and Buffy) shows that an average search space reduction upto 80% is achieved with detection rates of over 90% for specific parameters of the dataset.

Keywords: search space reduction, face detection, visual search, face localization, computational efficiency, head and shoulder curve.

1 Introduction

In the recent past, appearance based methods have been most widely adopted for face detection [1]. In such methods [2], a sliding window is used to scan the entire image to find faces of all possible sizes. However, computing the classifiers in every sub-window demands high computational power [3]. In [3], methods are proposed to reduce the search space where the sliding window method is applied for face detection.

Skin color is one of the commonly used attribute for reducing the possible search space for face detection [4]. However, this requires sensitive skin color models to accurately segment required regions of interest (ROIs). Upper body detection is explored in [5], to reduce the ROIs for face detection. Oriented Integration of Gradients (OIG) is proposed in [5] as a feature to describe the sub-parts of human head-shoulder curves, which are then detected using a classifier followed by Hough voting scheme to localize their position.

[2] propose a method based on an active testing framework, in which the image space is decomposed in a quad-tree fashion, and in each iteration of the

R. Klette, M. Rivera, and S. Satoh (Eds.): PSIVT 2013, LNCS 8333, pp. 385–396, 2014.

algorithm, regions of the image space with a higher probability of presence of face are refined, while pruning the other regions.

Head and shoulder profile as a feature unique to humans has been used in face localization [6] and human detection [5]. In this paper, we propose a computationally efficient technique to reduce search space for detecting faces by extracting head and shoulder curves. The proposed technique is aimed at short-listing sub-windows that give a higher probability of presence of face. Gradient angle histograms [7] are used in the proposed method to effectively determine the ROIs for face detection. Our method processes the edge information of the image and being a block based approach, the method is scalable to a range of scales for a given image size. The scope of this paper is limited to front facing humans.

2   Proposed Method

In this section, we describe the proposed method in detail. As shown in Fig. 1(a), the proposed method detects the head and shoulder curves of the human being of a given scale. The scale is defined by the ratio $P_X : P_Y$, where P_X is the distance between the top of the head to the shoulders, and P_Y is the distance between the two shoulders in pixels. Given this scale, the proposed method detects possible right and left, head and shoulder curves as shown in Fig. 1, that satisfy the given scale.

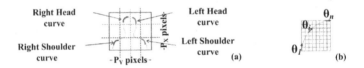

Fig. 1. (a) Head and shoulder curves of a human of scale defined by P_X and P_Y pixels. (b) Illustration showing the linear approximation of the curve [8].

2.1   Gradient Angle Histograms for Curve Detection

As shown in [9], a curve can be divided into smaller segments such that each segment can be approximated by the tangent passing through the mid-point of that segment. This is illustrated in Fig. 1(b). A curve C has a gradual change in tangential orientation from θ_1 to θ_n.

We propose to use gradient angle histograms (GAH) to identify curves of specific curvatures that can be associated with head and shoulder curves of a human, as shown in Fig. 1(a). GAH was shown to be an effective way in [7] to detect linear edges in a block-based approach. Given the edge map E_B of an image block I_B, GAH (represented by $\mathbf{h}$) is the histogram of gradient angles, where $h_i \in \mathbf{h}$ represents the count of edge pixels having the gradient angles in

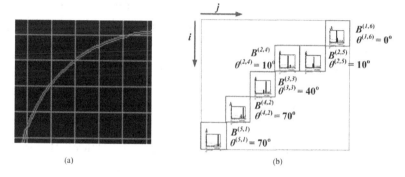

(a)   (b)

Fig. 2. A convex curve is divided into blocks $B^{(i_1,j_1)}$, $B^{(i_2,j_2)}$, ..., $B^{(i_N,j_N)}$. The curve appears as linear segments and GAHs show peaks corresponding to the gradient angles of these linear edges in each block.

the i-th bin. Given the edge block E_B and the gradient angles $\theta(x,y)$ of every edge pixel in E_B, GAH can be used iteratively in the following way to extract possible linear edges in E_B. In each iteration j, we get bin k with the maximum height in $\mathbf{h}$, which represents a possible linear edge in E_B [7]. Edge pixels with gradient angles in the range of $\theta_k - \epsilon \leq \theta \leq \theta_k + \epsilon$, centered around the k-th bin in GAH will result in $E_j \subset E_B$ with possible linear edges. This can be summarized as the following:

$$k = \arg\max_i \mathbf{h} \tag{1}$$

$$E_j = \{e(x,y) \in E_B | \theta_k - \epsilon \leq \theta(x,y) \leq \theta_k + \epsilon\} \tag{2}$$

The above equations are repeated after removing the k-th entry in the GAH $\mathbf{h}$, to get the next peak in $\mathbf{h}$. This is repeated until a termination condition T is reached. We denote this operation as

$$\{\mathbf{\Theta}^B, \mathbf{E}^B\} = \mathbf{\Phi}(\mathbf{h}^B, E^B, T) \tag{3}$$

where $\mathbf{\Theta}^B$ denotes the set of angles θ_ks in the GAH h^B for block B, and the boldfaced $\mathbf{E}^B$ denotes the set of edge maps that are obtained using θ_ks using equations (1). The termination condition depends on the application in which GAH is applied and we will define it later in this section. It is to be noted that GAH differs from HoG (Histogram of Oriented Gradients) in terms of how they are computed and used [1]).

The above GAH formulation can be used to detect a curve as follows. We divide a curved edge, with a known curvature, i.e. given it is a convex or concave curve, using a set of blocks $B^{(i_1,j_1)}$, $B^{(i_2,j_2)}$, ..., $B^{(i_N,j_N)}$, such that they are along the curve as shown in Fig. 2. It can be seen that the segments of the curve appear as linear edge segments in each block. GAHs are computed in each block as shown in Fig. 2. These GAHs are represented by the set $\mathbf{H}$, given by:

$$\mathbf{H} = \{\mathbf{h}^{(i_1,j_1)}, \mathbf{h}^{(i_2,j_2)}, \cdots, \mathbf{h}^{(i_N,j_N)}\} \tag{4}$$

Applying $\boldsymbol{\Phi}(\cdot)$ on each block of $\mathbf{H}$, we get $\boldsymbol{\Theta}^{(i,j)}$. If we consider that highest peaks in each GAH, $\boldsymbol{\Phi}(\cdot)$ on $\mathbf{H}$ will give peaks at $\boldsymbol{\Theta} = \{\theta_k^{(i_1,j_1)}, \cdots, \theta_k^{(i_N,j_N)}\}$. As indicated in Fig. 2, these gradient angles correspond to the edge pixels of the line segments that form the curve. If these linear segments are approximated as the tangents of the curved segments in the blocks, then they should satisfy (5), i.e.,

$$\theta_k^{(i_1,j_1)} > \theta_k^{(i_2,j_2)} > \cdots > \theta_k^{(i_N,j_N)} \qquad (5)$$

2.2 Detecting Shoulder and Head Curves Using Block-Based Gradient Angle Histograms

Given an $X \times Y$ sized image I, it is envisaged to detect shoulder-head region that can be captured within a window of size $P_X \times P_Y$ pixels, where X and Y denote the vertical and horizontal axes respectively. We first divide I into $b_s \times b_s$ sized blocks, such that a curve is decomposed into smaller linear segments in each block. In every block $B^{(i,j)}$, we apply Sobel filters [10] and compute the edge map denoted by $E^{(i,j)}$. For every edge pixel $E_{(x,y)}^{(i,j)}$ in the (i,j)-th block, its gradient angle $\theta_{(x,y)}^{(i,j)}$ is computed using the same Sobel kernels. In every block $B^{(i,j)}$, GAHs are computed for the constituent edge pixels. Therefore, for the $X \times Y$ image we have $\mathbf{H}$ which is set of $\frac{X}{b_s} \times \frac{Y}{b_s}$ GAHs corresponding to all blocks, i.e.,

$$\mathbf{H} = \begin{bmatrix} \mathbf{h}^{(0,0)} & \mathbf{h}^{(0,1)} & \cdots & \mathbf{h}^{(0,\frac{Y}{b_s}-1)} \\ \vdots & \vdots & \ddots & \vdots \\ \mathbf{h}^{(\frac{X}{b_s}-1,0)} & \mathbf{h}^{(\frac{X}{b_s}-1,1)} & \cdots & \mathbf{h}^{(\frac{X}{b_s}-1,\frac{Y}{b_s}-1)} \end{bmatrix} \qquad (6)$$

Applying $\Phi(\cdot)$ on $\mathbf{H}$, we get the following:

$$\boldsymbol{\Theta} = \boldsymbol{\Phi}(\mathbf{H}, E, T) = \begin{bmatrix} \boldsymbol{\Theta}^{(0,0)} & \boldsymbol{\Theta}^{(0,1)} & \cdots & \boldsymbol{\Theta}^{(0,\frac{Y}{b_s}-1)} \\ \vdots & \vdots & \ddots & \vdots \\ \boldsymbol{\Theta}^{(\frac{X}{b_s}-1,0)} & \boldsymbol{\Theta}^{(\frac{X}{b_s}-1,1)} & \cdots & \boldsymbol{\Theta}^{(\frac{X}{b_s}-1,\frac{Y}{b_s}-1)} \end{bmatrix}$$

The termination condition T is defined as a simple threshold $b_s/4$. In other words, $\boldsymbol{\Theta}^{(i,j)}$ will have θ_ks corresponding to all bins in the GAH $\mathbf{h}^{(i,j)}$ which are higher than $b_s/4$. The selected gradient angles in each $\boldsymbol{\Theta}^{(i,j)}$ are further constrained in different ways to detect the shoulder and head curves. This will be explained next.

Referring to Fig. 1(a), we identify four curves which are curves of interest, i.e. right and left head curves, and right and left shoulder curves. In terms of the direction of convexity, we consider the right head and shoulder curves as right curves. Similarly, the left head and shoulder curves will hence forth be also called as left curves, unless otherwise stated explicitly.

In order to detect the left and right curves, we divided the GAH $\mathbf{h}$ into two ranges called the right and left angle ranges denoted by Δ_R and Δ_L respectively. Referring to Fig. 3, a peak in Δ_R represents a linear edge that slants diagonally

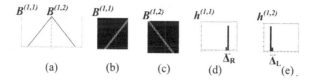

Fig. 3. GAH is divided into right and left ranges Δ_L and Δ_R that will be used to find the right and left shoulder and head curves

upwards, i.e. ∕, whereas a peak in Δ_L of the GAH indicates a linear edge slanting diagonally downwards, i.e. ∖. It can be seen in Fig. 3 that the right and left slant edges, shown in Fig. 3(b) & (c), result in distinct peaks in different regions of their respective GAHs shown in Fig. 3(d) & (e).

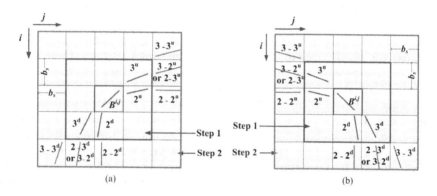

Fig. 4. Ranking of blocks for right and left curve detection

We will now explain the right curve detection process. The same can be applied for detecting the left curve by changing the different parameters like angle ranges etc. Referring to Fig. 4 (a), let us consider a block $B^{(i,j)}$, which is part of the right curve. The $\Theta^{(i,j)}$ for this block is checked to find $\theta_k \in \Delta_R$, i.e. if there are any edge pixels that are forming a right slant linear edge. This step is the first and critical step because we consider that the right curve must necessarily have a segment that has a gradient angle in Δ_R. If no such θ exists, the next block is processed. If θ_ks exist in Δ_R, then we consider the block for further processing. The $\theta_k \in \Delta_R$ with maximum h_k is considered as a the anchor angle $\theta_a^{(i,j)}$ and block $B^{(i,j)}$ is considered as the anchor block. This anchor block will be used to check further if there are left and right shoulder curves.

With $B^{(i,j)}$ as the center, we first consider a 3×3 neighborhood of blocks (as shown in Fig. 4 (a)), which shows the possible linear edges that can form the right curve with the center being $B^{(i,j)}$ block. We rank these blocks as p^u or p^d where $p = 2, 3$, and u and d indicate up and down (with respect to $B^{(i,j)}$). p indicates the rank of the block, i.e. the order in which it will be processed when going up or down to form the right curve. These ranks were decided based on the manual inspection of human images in datasets like Buffy dataset [11], CASIA dataset [12]. It was seen that the right shoulder tends to be flat (or horizontal) in block $B^{(i,j+1)}$ as compared to slanting further up in block $B^{(i-1,j+1)}$. Therefore, $B^{(i,j+1)}$ is given as higher rank, i.e. 2^u, as compared to $B^{(i-1,j+1)}$ (ranked 3^u). Similar observations can be made about the blocks below $B^{(i,j)}$ to rank them as shown in Fig. 4 (a).

Therefore, given $B^{(i,j)}$ and the anchor angle $\theta_a^{(i,j)}$, we first go to 2^u ranked block ($B^{(i,j+1)}$) and check for θ_ks in $\Theta^{(i,j+1)}$ such that the following condition is satisfied: $\theta_k^{(i,j+1)} \leq \theta_a^{(i,j)} - \delta_2$ where δ_2 is the expected change in the gradient angle that should occur if the linear edge segment in the anchor block curves as we go towards the outer blocks, i.e. $B^{(i,j+1)}$. If there are multiple $\theta_k^{(i,j+1)}$ that satisfy the above condition, we consider the θ_k which has the highest count in the GAH $h^{(i,j+1)}$. These conditions will ensure the curvature condition defined in (5) is satisfied. If $B^{(i,j+1)}$ does not satisfy any of these conditions, then we consider the next ranked block, i.e. $B^{(i-1,j+1)}$ which is ranked 3^u. This must also satisfy the same condition for θ_k but has a smaller δ_3 such that $\delta_3 < \delta_2$. This is because the linear edge in $B^{i-1,j+1}$ is slanting upwards more than $B^{(i,j+1)}$ and hence, it is expected to have a lesser gradient angle variation than $B^{(i,j+1)}$ (based on observation from datasets that was described above).

The same is repeated for blocks $B^{(i+1,j)}$ and $B^{(i+1,j-1)}$ that are below the anchor block, which are ranked 2^d and 3^d respectively. The angles must meet similar conditions as above but with a positive δ_2 and δ_3 because the gradient angles in blocks lower than the anchor block are higher than the anchor block (according to (5)). If any of these conditions are not met in the 3×3 neighborhood of $B^{(i,j)}$, no further processing for $B^{(i,j)}$ is done and the next block is processed for identifying the anchor block.

After identifying the block in the 3×3 neighborhood of the anchor block, we perform another check with the blocks that surround this neighborhood. This is the second stage of processing. This is an optional step depending on user requirement in terms of the curvature constraint one wants to ensure. In our experiments, we found that going for one more layer of blocks helped to reduce the false positives. Therefore, we cover a 5×5 neighborhood around the anchor block to ensure that we have captured a curve in it.

The ranks of the blocks in the outer ring of blocks in the 5×5 neighborhood of the anchor blocks are marked as $p - q^u$ or $p - q^d$, where $p = 2, 3$ indicates the rank of the origin block in 3×3 neighborhood, $q = 2, 3$ indicates the rank of the current block. This is shown in Fig. 4 (a). For example, $B^{(i,j+2)}$ has the rank $2 - 2^u$, which implies that it could have a edge from block $B^{(i,j+1)}$ which was previously ranked as 2. Block $B^{(i-1,j+2)}$ has two ranks: $2 - 3^u$ and $3 - 2^u$. If the right curve is detected in $B^{(i,j+1)}$ in the first stage of processing, then we process $B^{(i-1,j+2)}$ after processing $B^{(i,j+2)}$. If the right curve is detected in $B^{(i-1,j+1)}$ in the first stage of processing, then we process $B^{(i-1,j+2)}$ first and then we look into $B^{(i-2,j+2)}$. A similar approach is taken to rank the blocks in the lower half of the neighborhood as shown in Fig. 4.

Now, given the blocks identified in the 3×3 neighborhood of the anchor block $B^{(i,j)}$, which could potentially be having the right curve, we consider these blocks in the 3×3 neighborhood as the new anchor blocks. Therefore, we will have two new anchor blocks B_a^u and B_a^d corresponding to the blocks above and below the main anchor block $B^{(i,j)}$. We now repeat the above process of checking the GAHs with B_a^u and B_a^d, using the ranks for the blocks in 5×5 neighborhood (discussed above). The δ_a parameter is increased or decreased depending on the block that is being processed in a similar approach as described earlier for the first stage so as to satisfy (5).

If we are able to trace a curve within the $k \times k$ window ($k = 5$ in our case), then a right curve is considered to be detected, which is anchored at block $B^{(i,j)}$. If there was any discontinuity while traversing from $B^{(i,j)}$ to its $k \times k$ neighborhood, further analysis of $B^{(i,j)}$ is terminated and the next edge block is considered for the entire analysis described above. This is repeated for all blocks in Θ to detect anchor blocks that have either the right or the left curve. We generate maps $\mathbf{R}$ and $\mathbf{L}$, such that: $\mathbf{R} \in \mathbb{R}^{\frac{X}{b_s} \times \frac{Y}{b_s}}$ & $\mathbf{L} \in \mathbb{R}^{\frac{X}{b_s} \times \frac{Y}{b_s}}$ where an element in $\mathbf{R}$ say $\mathbf{R}(i,j)$ is set to 1 if we find an anchor block for a right curve at index (i,j). Similarly $\mathbf{L}$ is defined.

2.3   Associating Left and Right Curves for Face Localization

Once all the valid left and right curves are recorded in $\mathbf{L}$ and $\mathbf{R}$, the next level of association is performed to identify regions in the image that could possibly have a front facing human. Recalling that our aim is to detect shoulder-head region which is defined within a $P_X \times P_Y$ pixels sized window, we construct an association window by grouping $u \times v$ blocks, where $u = P_X/b_s$ and $v = P_Y/b_s$. This is illustrated in Fig. 5 (a).

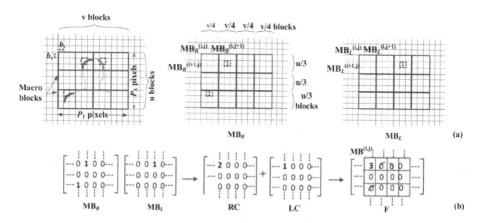

Fig. 5. (a)Association of Right and Left Curves to detect possible shoulder-head regions. (b)Kernels $\mathbb{K}_R$ and $\mathbb{K}_L$ applied on the Macroblocks $\mathbf{MB}_R(i,j)$ and $\mathbf{MB}_L(i,j)$ resulting in Matrices $\mathbf{RC}$ and $\mathbf{LC}$ respectively, and eventually matrix $\mathbf{F}$

Having determined the number of blocks, i.e. $u \times v$, that fit the $P_X \times P_Y$ pixels window, we generate what we call as macroblock left and right arrays, denoted as $\mathbf{MB}_L$ and $\mathbf{MB}_R$ respectively. In order to compute every element in $\mathbf{MB}_R$ and $\mathbf{MB}_L$, denoted by $\mathbf{MB}_R(i,j)$ and $\mathbf{MB}_L(i,j)$, we consider a group of $u/3 \times v/4$ elements in $\mathbf{R}$ and $\mathbf{L}$, in a rastor scan method, as shown in Fig. 5 (a). Therefore, the dimensions of these macroblock arrays are given by: $\mathbf{MB}_R \in \mathbb{R}^{\frac{X}{\frac{u}{3} \times b_s} \times \frac{Y}{\frac{v}{4} \times b_s}}$ and $\mathbf{MB}_L \in \mathbb{R}^{\frac{X}{\frac{u}{3} \times b_s} \times \frac{Y}{\frac{v}{4} \times b_s}}$. Each element $\mathbf{MB}_R(i,j)$ and $\mathbf{MB}_L(i,j)$ is assigned the value 0 or 1 using the following equations:

$$
\mathbf{MB}_R^{(i,j)} = \begin{cases} 0 \text{ if } \sum_{r=i\frac{u}{3}}^{(i+1)\frac{u}{3}} \sum_{s=j\frac{v}{4}}^{(j+1)\frac{v}{4}} \mathbf{R}^{(r,s)} = 0 \\ 1 \text{ otherwise} \end{cases} \qquad \mathbf{MB}_L^{(i,j)} = \begin{cases} 0 \text{ if } \sum_{r=i\frac{u}{3}}^{(i+1)\frac{u}{3}} \sum_{s=i\frac{v}{4}}^{(j+1)\frac{v}{4}} \mathbf{L}^{(r,s)} = 0 \\ 1 \text{ otherwise} \end{cases}
$$

(7)

In other words, if any block in the group of $u/3 \times v/4$ blocks (which is one macroblock array element) has an anchor block (either left or right slant edge), we assign 1 to that group (macroblock array element). Fig. 5 (a) & (b) shows an example of macroblock array assignment. It can be seen from Fig. 5 (a) & (b) that if a group of $u/3 \times v/4$ blocks has an anchor block, we assign its corresponding position in macroblock array to 1.

We now define 3×4 kernels $\mathbb{K}_L$ and $\mathbb{K}_R$ in the following way:

$$
\mathbb{K}_L = \begin{bmatrix} 0 & 1 & 0 & 0 \\ 0 & 0 & 0 & 0 \\ 1 & 0 & 0 & 0 \end{bmatrix} ; \mathbb{K}_R = \begin{bmatrix} 0 & 0 & 1 & 0 \\ 0 & 0 & 0 & 0 \\ 0 & 0 & 0 & 1 \end{bmatrix}
$$

(8)

which are convolved with $\mathbf{MB}_R$ and $\mathbf{MB}_L$ respectively as shown in Fig. 5 (d). Considering the $\mathbb{K}$s are not square-odd matrix, which can be centered at the center of the kernel, the top left element of $\mathbb{K}$s, i.e. $\mathbb{K}(0,0)$s are aligned with every element of $\mathbf{MB}_L$ and $\mathbf{MB}_R$. The convolution output is placed on the top left corner element over which the convolution kernels are moved as shown in Fig. 5(b). The convolution operation results in $\mathbf{RC}$ and $\mathbf{LC}$ matrices given by:

$$
\mathbf{RC}(i,j) = \sum_{k=1}^{k=3} \sum_{l=1}^{l=4} \mathbf{MB}_R(i+k-1, j+l-1)\mathbb{K}_R(k,l)
$$

(9)

$$
\mathbf{LC}(i,j) = \sum_{k=1}^{k=3} \sum_{l=1}^{l=4} \mathbf{MB}_L(i+k-1, j+l-1)\mathbb{K}_L(k,l)
$$

(10)

where $1 \leq i \leq \frac{X}{\frac{u}{3}b_s}$ and $1 \leq j \leq \frac{Y}{\frac{v}{4}b_s}$. The matrices $\mathbf{RC}$ and $\mathbf{LC}$ capture the number of right and left curves in the left and right halves of the $u \times v$ window respectively, as shown in Fig. 5 (b). We then get the position of face localization window by generating $\mathbf{F}$ matrix given by: $\mathbf{F} = \mathbf{RC} + \mathbf{LC}$. If $\mathbf{F}(i,j) \geq 3$, then we consider a window with its top left corner positioned at (i,j)-th position to have a face. This condition allows us to check for the presence of at least 3 of the 4 curves that form the head and shoulder curves. This is shown in Fig. 5 (b).

3   Results and Discussion

In this section, we present the evaluation of the proposed algorithm for reducing the search area of face detection. We will first evaluate the detection rate of the proposed algorithm on two different datasets. The first dataset is the Biometric Database (CASIA Face Image Database - CASIA-FaceV5 300-399) with 500 images of 100 subjects [12]. This dataset contains five different images of each subject; the subject being a front facing human in a constrained background set up. The variations among the images include angular movements of the person with respect to the camera, changes in illumination, and imaging distance. Considering that we are demonstrating the algorithm for one particular scale, we have taken 480 images from this dataset, which are of similar scale by manual inspection. The second dataset is a subset of the Buffy Dataset [11]. This contains images with unconstrained backgrounds. 108 images of front facing humans from this dataset were considered for the evaluation. The second performance metric we will evaluate is the amount of search space reduced using the proposed algorithm.

3.1   Accuracy Analysis

As discussed in Section 2, the proposed algorithm being a block based approach, parameters that can influence the detection accuracy for a given scale are block size (b_s), number of bins in the GAH, block-wise GAH threshold setting (T), maximum gradient angle change allowed between blocks while detecting the curves (δ_2 and δ_3 in Section 2). It was found that the block size (b_s) is the most critical parameter that impacts the detection rate, and other parameters were tuned based on observations with respect to the scale. For example, T is set to a value proportional to b_s, $|\delta_2|$ and $|\delta_3|$ are set to 50° and 20° with respect to the scale of the human we have considered for detection. However, these parameters can also be varied and their impact on detection rate can be studied. In the scope of this paper, we will evaluate and discuss the effect of change in block size b_s on the detection rate.

We first generated the ground truth which includes marking a bounding box around the face in each image of the two datasets. During evaluation phase, if the association window resulting from the proposed algorithm has detected a true shoulder-head region and the window encloses the ground truth window, then it is considered as a True Positive (TP) window. In addition to TP windows, there can be false positive (FP) windows. If the proposed algorithm gives at least one TP window for an input image, then we consider that the head-shoulder curve is correctly detected. Therefore, if we have n_{TP} images with at least one TP window, then the detection rate is given by n_{TP}/n_{total}, where the dataset contains n_{total} number of images.

Table 1 gives the detection rates for each dataset and different block setting. It can be seen that the detection rate is 99.5% for CASIA dataset at a block size of 6 and it is 94% for Buffy dataset at a block size of 8. The detection rates reduce for both datasets as the block sizes are increased. This shows that for a

Table 1. Accuracy analysis results

	CASIA				Buffy		
	$P_X \times P_Y = 150 \times 200$ $X \times Y = 240 \times 320$				$P_X \times P_Y = 150 \times 150$ $X \times Y = 405 \times 720$		
Block Size	6	8	12	16	8	12	16
Detection Rate	99.5	85.1	79.9	70.7	94.4	74.0	79.6
False Positives per frame	1.78	0.44	0.27	0.08	6.37	2.71	2.36
Number of windows per frame	3.32	1.44	1.30	0.71	8.15	3.74	3.66

given scale of the humans in a dataset, a particular block size gives the highest detection rates.

CASIA, b_s = 6   CASIA, b_s = 8   CASIA, b_s = 12   CASIA, b_s = 16   Buffy, b_s = 8   Buffy, b_s = 12   Buffy, b_s = 16

(a)   (b)

Fig. 6. Detection windows resulting from the proposed algorithm as the block size increases for a specific image in CASIA dataset (a) and Buffy dataset (b)

In Table 1, we list the average false positives per frame (FPPF) for each dataset under varying block sizes. It can be seen from Table 1 that the FPPF is less than 2 and 6.5 for CASIA and Buffy datasets respectively. In other words, an average of 2 false positive windows are detected per frame in the case of CASIA dataset. This number is about 6 in the case of Buffy dataset. The number of false positive windows increases in Buffy because of the unconstrained backgrounds which have more variations as compared to CASIA dataset. In both cases, the FPPF is highest for the smallest block size. This is because, at smaller block sizes, there is a higher probability for curves to be detected from the edge pixels, which are further combined to form curves. In case of higher block size setting, this probability is lesser.

CASIA, b_s = 12 CASIA, b_s = 16   Buffy, b_s = 16   Buffy, b_s = 12   Buffy, b_s = 8   Buffy, b_s = 8   Buffy, b_s = 12

CASIA, b_s = 8   CASIA, b_s = 16   Buffy, b_s = 12   Buffy, b_s = 16   Buffy, b_s = 16   Buffy, b_s = 8   Buffy, b_s = 12

Fig. 7. Detection results under varying background conditions and complexities

In Table 1, we include average total number of windows per frame for each dataset. For each input image, we count the total number of windows, i.e. all

TP windows and FP windows. Table 1 gives the average number of windows over the entire dataset. This metric is particularly important to determine the amount of image area that needs to be searched by the face detection algorithm. Fig. 6 (a) & (b) show that there are more number of windows detected when the block sizes are smaller as compared to higher block sizes and that the FP windows reduce as the block sizes increase. Fig. 7 shows more examples of correct detection windows by the proposed algorithm under varying backgrounds and complexities of the input images.

3.2 Amount of Search Space Reduction

We determine the percentage savings in search area for face detection. If an image has at least one TP window, we take the total search area for face detection as the union of all the detection windows, which include both TP and FP windows. The ratio between the total image size ($X \times Y$) and the total number of pixels in the search area enclosed by this union of detection windows is used to determine the percentage savings for each image. This percentage savings in search area directly corresponds to a proportional decrease in sliding window based face detection techniques such as [2].

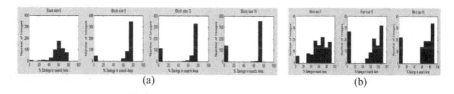

Fig. 8. Distribution of search space savings: (a) CASIA (b_s = 6, 8, 12 and 16 (from L to R)) (b) Buffy (b_s = 8, 12, 16 (From L to R)). x-axis: % savings in search area, y-axis: Number of images.

We show the distribution of percentage savings for each dataset under different block size settings in Fig. 8 (a) & (b). There is a cluster of distribution around 0%, corresponding to the missed detections, i.e. no TP windows. The second cluster is seen at a higher percentage for images that have at least one TP window.

Referring to Fig. 8 (a) which shows the distributions for CASIA dataset, we observe that the percentage savings in search area is spread across bins ranging from 40% to 80% for a block size setting b_s = 6. This shows that with this block setting, there are false positives along with the true positive windows, but overall detection rate is high since there are very few missed-detections (the cluster around zeroth bin the histogram is less than 10). Block sizes of 8, 12, 16 show a high concentration of the count in the histogram at 80% savings, which means that they result in very low false positive rates and high precision. But, the bin at 0% is also populated for the three block sizes, which accounts for the cases that are missed-detections under these block size settings. Similar observations can be drawn from the histograms for the Buffy dataset also as shown in Fig. 8 (b) for different block size settings.

4   Conclusions

We have proposed an effective strategy for search space reduction for face detection. The block-based nature of the approach allows for performance gains through parallelism. Evaluation of our algorithm on two standard datasets, CASIA frontal face and Buffy Stickmen was shown to yield a reduction of search space by upto 80% of the image area. It was established that optimal block settings can be derived for a given scale of humans in the image, depending on the required accuracy and savings in search areas. It was shown that the method can cater to varying scales of human faces by deploying it iteratively or by combining GAH information in a hierarchical manner. The method was shown to perform well for profile view of persons on the datasets considered.

References

1. Zhang, C., Zhang, Z.: A survey of recent advances in face detection. Technical Report Microsoft Research (2010)
2. Viola, P., Jones, M.: Robust real-time face detection. In: IEEE ICCV, vol. 2, pp. 747–747 (2001)
3. Sznitman, R., Jedynak, B.: Active testing for face detection and localization. IEEE Trans. PAMI 32(10), 1914–1920 (2010)
4. Xu, D., Chen, Y.L., Wu, X., Ou, Y., Xu, Y.: Integrated approach of skin-color detection and depth information for hand and face localization. In: 2011 IEEE Intl. Conf. on Robotics and Biomimetics (ROBIO), pp. 952–956 (2011)
5. He, F., Li, Y., Wang, S., Ding, X.: A novel hierarchical framework for human head-shoulder detection. In: 4th Intl. Cong. on Img. & Sig. Proc., vol. 3, pp. 1485–1489. IEEE (2011)
6. Sun, Y., Wang, Y., He, Y., Hua, Y.: Head-and-shoulder detection in varying pose. In: Wang, L., Chen, K., S. Ong, Y. (eds.) ICNC 2005. LNCS, vol. 3611, pp. 12–20. Springer, Heidelberg (2005)
7. Satzoda, R.K., Suchitra, S., Srikanthan, T.: Gradient angle histograms for efficient linear hough transform. In: 16th IEEE Intl. Conf. on Img. Proc. (ICIP), pp. 3273–3276 (2009)
8. Kolesnikov, A.: Constrained piecewise linear approximation of digital curves. In: 19th Intl. Conf. Pat. Rec (ICPR), pp. 1–4. IEEE (2008)
9. Zucker, S.W., David, C., Dobbins, A., Iverson, L.: The organization of curve detection: Coarse tangent fields and fine spline coverings. In: 2nd Intl. Conf. on Comp. Vis., pp. 568–577 (1988)
10. Gonzalez, R.C., Woods, R.E.: Digital image processing, vol. 2 (2009)
11. Ferrari, V., Eichner, M., Marin-Jimenez, M., Zisserman, A.: Buffy stickmen v 3.01 dataset
12. Chinese Academy of Sciences Institute of Automation, C.A.: CASIA-FaceV5 dataset

A Thermal Facial Emotion Database
and Its Analysis

Hung Nguyen[1], Kazunori Kotani[1], Fan Chen[1], and Bac Le[2]

[1] Japan Advanced Institute of Science and Technology,
1-1 Asahidai, Nomi, Ishikawa, Japan
{nvhung,ikko,chen-fan}@jaist.ac.jp
[2] University of Science, Ho Chi Minh city,
227 Nguyen Van Cu, Ho Chi Minh city, Vietnam
lhbac@hcmuns.edu.vn

Abstract. In recent years, thermal image has extensively been used in many fields such as military (e.g., target acquisition, surveillance, night vision, homing and tracking) and civilian purposes (e.g., medical diagnosis, thermal efficiency analysis, environmental monitoring). It may be a promising alternative for investigation of facial expression and emotion. Currently there are very few database to support the research in facial expression and emotion, however most of them either only include posed thermal expression images or lack thermal information. For these reasons, we propose and establish a natural visible and thermal facial emotion database. The database contains seven spontaneous emotions of 26 subjects. We also analyze a visible database, a thermal database to recognize expression and thermal information to recognize emotion.

Keywords: Facial expression analysis, thermal image, visible image, spontaneous database, facial emotion, KTFE database.

1   Introduction

Although we have spent many years in doing research on facial expression analysis since the work of Darwin in 1872 [1], we have still not understood clearly how the human brain works to analyze the facial expression and how computer could reach the accuracy rate of automatic facial expression analysis as human. Facial expression analysis continues to be an active research topic for behavioral scientists. There is such a huge research on facial expression analysis, already described and surveyed in detail in [2],[3],[4]. Currently most research work uses visible images or videos and has achieved good result. However, under the lack of illumination, even darkness or exceeding of source of light, the result of visible expression analysis is not good. On the other hand, thermal images are not sensitive to light conditions. Consequently, using thermal images helps us to complete the gaps of visible images. Besides, the skin temperature changes are useful to classify the emotions [5] and facial expression is a good emotion-related behavior [6]. We can infer emotions from skin temperature and expressions from

R. Klette, M. Rivera, and S. Satoh (Eds.): PSIVT 2013, LNCS 8333, pp. 397–408, 2014.
© Springer-Verlag Berlin Heidelberg 2014

several special emotions. Moreover, most of the current databases used for research are visible and posed. The expressions, from those databases, are usually obtained from unreal emotion and overplay features. Secondly, there are a few thermal facial image databases but they are posed thermal expression images. Even though a database is built in posed and spontaneous expressions, it still meets some mistakes such as when they designed data acquisition, they forgot about time lag phenomenon or expressions are elicited by asking participants to imitate sample expressions, exaggerated expressions. With these reasons, we propose and establish a thermal facial expression and emotion database to allow the research in facial expression analysis to be more realistic. In this paper, we describe in detail the materials and methods to design and collect the thermal facial emotion database - KTFE (Kotani Thermal Facial Emotion) database. To verify the effectiveness of our spontaneous database, we use PCA (Principal Component Analysis), EMC (Eigenspace Method based on Class features) and PCA-EMC to classify facial expressions of a visible and thermal facial image database. We have also used PCA and PCA-EMC to classify emotions of thermal facial emotion database leading to very attractive results.

2 Review of Existent Natural and Infrared Databases

Innumerable natural databases for facial expression analysis have been built since many years, such as Cohn-Kanade (CK) [7], UA-UIUC [8], MMI [9], UT-Dallas [10], Belfast [11], AAI [12] and so on. A comprehensive survey of these databases is given in [3].

Compared to the number of existing visible databases, only very few thermal face databases are available in the literature. Furthermore, these databases only include some posed thermal data and one spontaneous thermal data. In this

Table 1. Current thermal facial database

Ref	Size	Wave band	Education	Lightning	Exp Des
NIST Equinox [13]	600 subjects 1919 infrared images	8-12μm 3-5μm	Posed	Above, left and right	Smiling, frowning, surprise
IRIS [14]	30 subjects, 4228 pairs of thermal and visible images	7-14μm	Posed	Left, right, both lights, dark	Surprise, laughing, anger
USTC-UVIE [15]	215 subjects	8-14 μm	Posed and spontaneous	Left, right and front	Happy, angry, neutral, disgusted, fearful, sad, and surprised

document, we listed and compared several databases of infrared facial expression, along with the information related to the name, the number of subjects, wave band of thermal camera, lighting, illumination and expression description as table 1. Firstly, NIST Equinox [13] has been used in many researches of thermal image, which is not available anymore. Secondly, IRIS Thermal/Visible Face Database [14] is very useful only for face recognition because posed expressions are elicited by asking subjects to perform a series of emotional expressions in front of a camera. Thirdly, USTC-NVIE database [15] is a very good database and adaptable for a good posed and spontaneous thermal database. However, their procedure for data acquisition to induce emotions has a mistake. In their video clips to evoke emotion, the gaps between each emotion clip are 1-2 min long which is too short for participants to establish a neutral emotion status. They do not mention about the recording time before ending of each emotion clip. The changing of human temperate is later than the changing of emotion. Therefore, the time before ending of each emotion clips is very important. In a short, there is only one facial expression database using visible and thermal image, although many expression databases use visible or thermal only. Furthermore, there exist several unclear and non-suitable procedures in these databases. These reasons motivated us to propose and build up another natural visible and infrared facial emotion database.

Table 2. Information of participants in building the KTFE database

Number	Age	Sex	Education	Glasses	Nationality
2	32	2 M	Post Doc	2No	Vi
1	31	1M	Post Doc	1No	Vi
2	30	1M,1F	PhD	1Yes, 1No	Vi
1	29	1M	Master	1Yes	Vi
6	28	3M,3F	3Master, 3PhD	5Y,1No	Vi, Thai
1	27	1F	Master	1No	Vi
5	26	3M,2F	4Master, 1PhD	3Yes, 2No	Vi
5	25	4M,1F	2Master,3PhD	2Yes, 3No	Vi
2	24	2F	2Bachelor	2Y	Vi, Thai
1	12	1M	Pupil	1No	Jap

3   Materials and Method

3.1   Participants

The database contains 26 subjects from 11 year-old to 32 year-old as depicted in table 2. To ensure accuracy in results of the experiments, all of the participants were asked to take rest, maintain in good mood for 2 hours prior to the measurements and to avoid the presence of cosmetic substances on their face at the time of experiment. Before taking the experiment, each participant consented to join the test and also signed the test agreement.

3.2   Measurement Devices and Environment

Room Setup. The room for conducting the experiment is L shaped with 8m∗12m ∗3.5m and the omitted area is about 6m². The experiment room was always kept quiet to ensure no effect to induce the participants emotions. During the data acquisition, the internal temperature of the room that is used for conducting experiments is maintained between 24°C and 26°C because of the sensitivity of the facial surface to the environmental temperature. To control the humidity and temperature of the room, we used the building air conditioning system, and the flow of air condition was not directed to the testing area. To keep the constant illumination between day and night, kept both the door and the curtains closed during the experiment. The experiment area had infrared camera, equipped with laptop, desk, chair, LCD screen, mass storage disk, head phone, and two special curtains. Two curtains separated the participant from the experimenter as a result of which the participants felt more comfortable and not shy, making it easier to induce their emotions. The view of the room and experiment area is depicted in Fig.1.

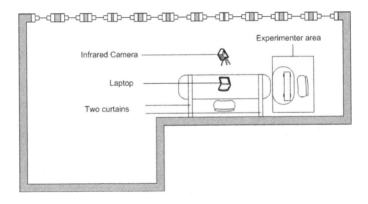

Fig. 1. Overview of experiment room

Camera Setup. We used an Infrared Camera NEC R300 to obtain the visible and thermal videos. The infrared camera has 3.1mega pixels visible camera capturing 5 frames per second and a long wavelength infrared (LWIR) camera opening from 8μm to 14 μm. The thermal sensitivity is 0.03⁰C at 30⁰C. Thermal infrared imaging data were captured at 5ft/s. The camera was placed at a height of 1.5m above the floor and 0.85m in front of the participants. To obtain the correct temperature of participants, the calibration was set up before each experiment and updated automatically per minute. We used NS9500 PRO, supporting real-time monitor, to capture both visible and thermal data and NS9500 STD to view, enhance, analyze, and extract the thermal data.

3.3   Procedures

Stimuli. In this experiment, we use selected emotional video clips to evoke the emotion of the participant. The video clips were gained by four persons from the internet and judged by the authors. There are four angry clips, four disgust clips, four fearful clips and one fearful game, six happy clips, seven sad clips, three surprised clips and two neutral clips. We further classified each emotion class into four sub-classes according to their intensive levels.

Data Acquisition. The experiment room had only one participant and experimenter during data collection. The participant was seated comfortably in an armchair in front of a laptop screen as shown in Fig.1. Fig.2 shows the data acquisition procedure, which fixes the former database mistake. Depending on the participants, we did not ask them to not wear on or take off their glasses. We also did not require them to keep their head fixed in one position because we wanted to obtain the spontaneous emotions. The participants were given an introduction of the purpose and procedure of the experiment prior to taking data and then they were asked to wear headphone. Before and after each session, the instrumental music turned on to help the participant return to the neutral feeling. In each session, we tested only one emotion and specially paid attention to the time lag phenomenon. When participants did not to take some fearful or angry clips, we stopped this session to protect the human right. After experiment of each person, we asked them to give the report contributed their feeling to each emotion video clips. These self-reported data were helped us to label the recorded videos.

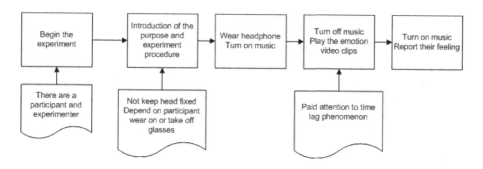

Fig. 2. Data acquisition procedure

3.4   KTFE Database Design

The first version of KTFE database, which contains seven spontaneous emotions of 26 subjects, includes 126 gigabyte of visible and thermal facial emotion videos, visible facial expression image database and thermal facial expression image database. To obtain the thermal expression image database, we manually

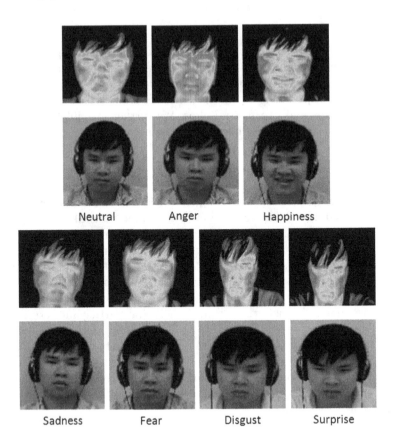

Fig. 3. Sample thermal and visible images of seven expressions

choose the expressions using NS9500STD software. There are three persons to select manually the suitable frames for every emotion of each person and extract into thermal images. The visible image database is also manually extracted and chosen by two persons.

4   Data Analysis

In this section, we bring a fundamental evaluation of usability of the visible facial database, thermal facial database and conduct the thermal data to analyze emotions. Before evaluating of these databases, to avoid any undesired noise in the thermal images, visible images, we use median smoothing filter to reduce noises and blurring. The preprocessing for visible image is to normalize image to facial space containing only face. To analyze the facial expression using thermal infrared data of expressions, after reducing the effect of noise, we use three convention methods PCA, EMC, PCA-EMC. With PCA, the aim is to build a face space, including the basis vectors called principal components, which better describe the face images [16]. To estimate emotions using PCA, we divide the training set into five classes and compute the eigen-space as following:

Step 1: Concatenating each row of a thermal data of each frame by row, the thermal data can be transformed to a column vector. Given M frames of thermal data as training data, we convert these datum to corresponding column vectors

Step 2: The mean of training data has to be calculated and then subtracted from each original thermal data in the datum.

Step 3: Calculate the eigenvectors and eigen-values of the covariant matrix. For each test thermal data, we project it to the eigen-space of each class and derive the reconstruction thermal data from each eigen-space. Using mean square error, measuring the similarity, between input thermal data and reconstruction thermal data, we can choose a suitable class for input thermal data which is a minimum of mean square errors [16].

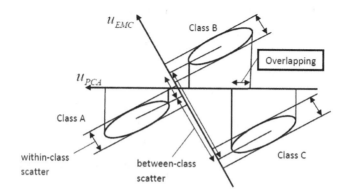

Fig. 4. Examples of a eigenvector of PCA and EMC [18]

In reference [17], the authors proposed eigen-space method based on class-features (EMC) to analyze the facial expressions. The difference between PCA and EMC is that PCA finds the eigenvector to maximize the total variance of the projection to line, while EMC is obtained eigenvector to maximize the difference between the within-class and between-class variance. The Fig.4 shows the advantage of EMC over PCA. The difference between the within-class and between-class covariance is calculated as following:

$$S = S_B - S_W. \tag{1}$$

$$S_B = \frac{1}{M} \sum_{f \in F} M_f (\overline{x}_f - \overline{x})(\overline{x}_f - \overline{x})^\tau. \tag{2}$$

$$S_W = \frac{1}{M} \sum_{f \in F} \sum_{f \in F}^{M_f} M_f (\overline{x}_{fm} - \overline{x}_f)(\overline{x}_{fm} - \overline{x}_f)^\tau. \tag{3}$$

$$\overline{x}_f = \frac{1}{M} \sum_{m=1}^{M_f} x_{fm}; \overline{x} = \frac{1}{M} \sum_{f \in F} \sum_{m=1}^{M_f} x_{fm}. \tag{4}$$

where F is a set of expression classes, M_f facial-patterns are given for each class $f \in F$ and x_{fm} is an N-dimension vector of the $m - th$ facial patterns,$m = \overline{1, M_f}$

To estimate emotion using EMC, we divide the training set into five classes then calculate the eigenvectors and eigen-values of the matrix S and compute the eigen-space. For each test thermal data, we project it into the eigen-space of each class and an emotion is chosen if it gets maximum of cosine of angle between obtained vector after projection and eigenvector of each class. With PCA-EMC, we use PCA to reduce the dimension and then apply EMC to the obtain data.

Table 3. Confusion matrices of expression analysis of visible images with PCA

	Ag	Ha	Fe	Ne	Sa
Ag	78.23	6.06	7.51	8.20	-
Ha	2.30	46.62	8.35	40.08	2.65
Fe	5.46	5.39	82.80	6.35	-
Ne	5.96	34.79	5.92	36.31	17.02
Sa	-	12.68	3.65	14.09	69.58
Avg	62.71				

Table 4. Confusion matrices of expression analysis of visible images with PCA-EMC

	Ag	Ha	Fe	Ne	Sa
Ag	84.42	5.00	9.33	1.25	-
Ha	6.73	51.80	2.67	36.26	2.54
Fe	3.30	2.69	86.23	5.83	1.95
Ne	6.78	32.73	7.05	42.62	10.82
Sa	-	3.83	0.67	5.71	89.79
Avg	70.97				

4.1   Evaluation of the Visible Image Database

The preprocessing for visible image is to normalize image to facial space containing only face. The three well-know algorithms are used to classify images to emotions. There are PCA [16], EMC[8] and PCA-EMC methods. We extracted the visible image database from KTFE database. It includes 330 images of 22 subjects for 5 expressions. The rate of testing and training is 40 percent and 60 percent of total images, respectively. Table 3, 4, 5, including confusion matrices and average recognitions, shows the performance of these algorithms with respect to our visible image database. According to confusion matrices, anger

Table 5. Confusion matrices of expression analysis of visible images with EMC

	Ag	Ha	Fe	Ne	Sa
Ag	71.88	6.05	8.84	13.23	-
Ha	5.04	42.36	7.76	41.03	3.81
Fe	0.98	9.22	74.51	12.35	2.94
Ne	9.08	39.44	8.58	28.13	14.77
Sa	-	7.08	1.76	13.7	77.46
Avg	58.87				

Table 6. Confusion matrices of emotion classification of thermal data with PCA

	Ag	Ha	Fe	Ne	Sa
Ag	59.17	0.00	22.50	0.00	18.33
Ha	0.00	61.86	17.61	6.80	13.73
Fe	9.92	13.58	57.34	1.54	17.62
Ne	10.19	9.51	3.08	69.82	7.40
Sa	5.96	22.21	2.35	4.35	65.12
Avg	62.66				

Table 7. Confusion matrices of emotion classification of thermal data with PCA-EMC

	Ag	Ha	Fe	Ne	Sa
Ag	81.33	0.00	18.67	0.00	0.00
Ha	0.00	65.98	10.49	10.76	12.77
Fe	9.60	11.46	54.35	7.83	16.76
Ne	17.01	16.05	5.17	56.95	4.82
Sa	8.31	14.07	2.23	7.79	67.60
Avg	65.24				

expression do not recognize by sadness and vice versa. There are some confusion between happiness and neutral because some persons do not reveal their smiling.

4.2 Evaluation of the Thermal Data

To classify emissions using thermal data, we used PCA, PCA-EMC. The thermal data was extracted from KTFE. It includes 3.5GB thermal data for five emotions. The training and testing data are 40 percent and 60 percent of the total thermal data. From table 6, 7, 8, no instance of anger is incorrectly recognized as happiness. Neutral emotion and anger emotion are the most recognized by PCA and PCA-EMC, respectively. Based on the results, we confirm that thermal data are important addition information to support for expressions and emotions analysis.

Table 8. Confusion matrices of emotion classification of thermal data with EMC

	Ag	Ha	Fe	Ne	Sa
Ag	81.33	0.00	14.67	4.00	0.00
Ha	2.71	64.64	12.03	4.12	16.50
Fe	5.88	12.28	55.60	1.18	25.06
Ne	5.17	10.67	9.97	58.29	15.90
Sa	1.36	11.26	12.83	10.26	64.29
Avg	64.83				

Table 9. Confusion matrices of expression analysis of thermal images with PCA

	Ag	Ha	Fe	Ne	Sa
Ag	64.14	3	8.57	3	21.29
Ha	2.73	74.79	3.97	12.44	6.07
Fe	3.01	3.72	78.37	11.49	3.41
Ne	1.25	7.20	5.08	86.47	-
Sa	5.84	-	-	4.82	89.34
Avg	78.62				

Table 10. Confusion matrices of expression analysis of thermal images with PCA-EMC

	Ag	Ha	Fe	Ne	Sa
Ag	92.28	-	4.29	-	3.43
Ha	-	83.82	3.03	9.26	3.89
Fe	-	3.86	90.58	5.56	-
Ne	-	9.90	1.36	88.74	-
Sa	3.76	6.29	-	7.80	82.15
Avg	87.51				

Table 11. Confusion matrices of expression analysis of thermal images with EMC

	Ag	Ha	Fe	Ne	Sa
Ag	83.08	-	-	-	16.92
Ha	-	99.36	0.06	0.5	0.08
Fe	-	-	100	-	-
Ne	-	-	-	100	-
Sa	6.54	-	-	0.07	93.39
Avg	95.17				

4.3 Evaluation of the Thermal Image Database

Before classifying images to emotions, the preprocessing is similar to the preprocessing for the visible images. The PCA, EMC, PCA-EMC also used to classify
the emotions. In this experiment, we use 330 images of 22 subjects for 5 expressions. We used 40 percent images and 60 percent images in total images to test

and train, respectively. From table 9, 10, 11, EMC method, suitable for thermal images, gave very high classify rate.

5   Conclusions

We proposed a KTFE database in this research for expression and emotion recognition, which has several advantages: Firstly, this is one of the first natural spontaneous visible and thermal videos. These databases will allow researchers on facial expressions and emotions to have more approaches more realistic; Secondly, this database already fixed some mistakes which the former database met when they did experiment settings such as the time lag phenomenon; Thirdly, we also had several researches in our data and obtained some results to support researchers using our database. The results on thermal data give us a promising future on facial research. In future, we will continue developing our data and working on thermal data to contribute better results.

References

1. Darwin, C.: The expression of the emotions in man and animals. Oxford University, New York (1872)
2. Tian, Y., Kanade, T., Cohn, J.: Facial Expression Analysis, Handbook of Face Recognition, pp. 247–275. Springer, New York (2005)
3. Zeng, Z., Pantic, M., Roisman, G.T., Huang, T.S.: A survey of affect recognition methods: Audio, visual, and spontaneous expressions. IEEE Trans. Pattern Anal. Mach. Intell. 31(1), 39–58 (2009)
4. Fasel, B., Luettin, J.: Automatic facial expression analysis: a survey. Pattern Recognition 36, 259–275 (2003)
5. Khan, M.M., Ward, R.D., Ingleby, M.: Classifying pretended and evoked facial expression of positive and negative affective states using infrared measurement of skin temperature. Trans. Appl. Percept. 6(1), 1–22 (2009)
6. Nakanishi, R., Matsumura, K.I.: Facial skin temperature decreases in infants with joyful expression. Infant Behavior and Development 31, 137–144 (2008)
7. Kanade, T., Cohn, J., Tian, Y.: Comprehensive database for facial expression analysis. In: Proc. IEEE Intl. Conf. Face and Gesture Recognition, pp. 46–53 (2000)
8. Sebe, N., Lew, M.S., Cohen, I., Sun, Y., Gevers, T., Huang, T.S.: Authentic Facial Expression Analysis. In: Proc. IEEE Intl. Conf. Automatic Face and Gesture Recognition, AFGR (2004)
9. Pantic, M., Bartlett, M.S.: Machine Analysis of Facial Expressions, Face Recognition, pp. 377–416. I-Tech Education and Publishing, Vienna (2007)
10. O'Toole, A.J., Harms, J., Snow, S.L., Hurst, D.R., Pappas, M.R., Ayyad, J.H., Abdi, H.: A video database of moving faces and people. IEEE Trans. Pattern Anal. Mach. Intell. 27(5), 812–816 (2005)
11. Douglas-Cowie, E., Cowie, R., Schroeder, M.: The description of naturally occurring emotional speech. In: Proc. 15th Int. Conf. Phonetic Sciences, Barcelona, Spain, pp. 2877–2880 (2003)
12. Roisman, G.I., Tsai, J.L., Chiang, K.S.: The emotional integration of childhood experience: Physiological, facial expressive, and self-reported emotional response during the adult attachment interview. Development Psychol. 40(5), 776–789 (2004)

13. NIST Equinox database, http://www.equinoxsensors.com/products/HID.html
14. IRIS database,
    http://www.cse.ohio-state.edu/otcbvs-bench/Data/02/download.html
15. Wang, S., Liu, Z., Lv, S., Lv, Y., Wu, G., Peng, P., Chen, F., Wang, X.: A Natural Visible and Infrared Facial Expression Database for Expression Recognition and Emotion Inference. IEEE Transactions on Multimedia 12(7), 682–691 (2010)
16. Lin, D.T.: Facial Expression Classification Using PCA and Hierarchical Radial Basis Function Network. Journal of Information Science and Engineering 22, 1033–1046 (2006)
17. Kurozumi, T., Shinza, Y., Kenmochi, Y., Kotani, K.: Facial Individuality and Expression Analysis by Eigenspace Method Based on Class Features or Multiple Discriminant Analysis. In: ICIP (1999)
18. Yabui, T., Kenmochi, Y., Kotani, K.: Facial expression analysis from 3D range images; comparison with the analysis from 2D images and their integration. In: ICIP (2003)

Comparative Analysis of the Variability of Facial Landmarks for Forensics Using CCTV Images

Ruben Vera-Rodriguez, Pedro Tome, Julian Fierrez, and Javier Ortega-Garcia

Biometric Recognition Group - ATVS, Escuela Politecnica Superior
Universidad Autonoma de Madrid, Avda. Francisco Tomas y Valiente, 11
Campus de Cantoblanco - 28049 Madrid, Spain
{ruben.vera,pedro.tome,julian.fierrez,javier.ortega}@uam.es

Abstract. This paper reports a study of the variability of facial landmarks in a forensic scenario using images acquired from CCTV images. This type of images presents a very low quality and a large range of variability factors such as differences in pose, expressions, occlusions, etc. Apart from this, the variability of facial landmarks is affected by the precision in which the landmarks are tagged. This process can be done manually or automatically depending on the application (e.g., forensics or automatic face recognition, respectively). This study is carried out comparing both manual and automatic procedures, and also 3 distances between the camera and the subjects. Results show that landmarks located in the outer part of the face (highest end of the head, ears and chin) present a higher level of variability compared to the landmarks located the inner face (eye region, and nose). This study shows that the landmark variability increases with the distance between subject and camera, and also the results of the manual and automatic approaches are similar for the inner facial landmarks.

Keywords: Forensics, face recognition, video surveillance, data analysis.

1 Introduction

Automatic face recognition over forensic caseworks is still a challenge for the research community. Large amounts of research are being carried out trying to compensate variability sources (such as illumination, pose, facial expressions, occlusions, etc.) that affect significantly reducing the performance of the face recognition systems. In a forensic scenario, these variability factors are crucial, because forensic examiners have to frequently deal with face images extracted from CCTV cameras and other low quality sources, which make the task really difficult.

Many different techniques have been developed to automatically tag facial landmarks on a face [1–5]. These techniques achieve good results over good quality and frontal faces, but are still not that good for the cases of having high variability and low quality images. On the other hand, humans are subjective

R. Klette, M. Rivera, and S. Satoh (Eds.): PSIVT 2013, LNCS 8333, pp. 409–418, 2014.
© Springer-Verlag Berlin Heidelberg 2014

and do not work as systematically as computers. For this reason, in practice forensic examiners make use of semiautomatic systems, which can help in the suspects identification tasks [6].

Among the tasks carried out by forensic examiners, they analyse the intra-variability of two face images, a set of gallery images (with known identity) and the probe image. In an anthropometric analysis they extract manually a set of facial landmarks, then compute some distances between them, which can be used as features in their analysis. Figure 1 shows a diagram of this procedure.

This paper focuses on analysing the variability of facial landmarks in a forensic scenario over a database of face images acquired from CCTV images. This landmarking variability is affected by two factors, on the one hand the accuracy of the process of landmark tagging, which can be done manually or automatically and can vary significantly due to the quality of the images, and on the other hand it is also affected by the intrinsic variation of the landmarks, due to changes in pose, expression or occlusions among others.

In this paper, we carry out the study using SCface database, which is comprised of CCTV images at three different distances (1, 2.6 and 4.20 meters) between the camera and the persons. We analyse both the effect of the distance between the subject and the camera in the landmark variability, and we also compare the variability of an automatic system compared to a manual landmark tagging imitating the work of a forensic examiner. Some of the findings of this study are that in general facial landmarks located in the outer part of the face (highest point on the head, ears and chin) have a high level of variability, due possibly to hair occlusions. Regarding the distances between the camera and the persons, the variability increases gradually with the distance. Surprisingly, very similar results are achieved for both manual and automatic approaches, although not all the landmark points were able to be tagged by the automatic system. The findings of this paper could be included in the work carried out by a forensic examiner within a anthropometrical facial analysis.

The remainder of the paper is organized as follows. Section 2 describes the data used in the experimental work of this paper, comprised of 130 persons and 3 distances between camera and subjects. Section 3 describes the task of landmark tagging and the image processing. Section 4 describes the experimental results achieved and finally Section 5 draws the final conclusions and future work.

2   SCface Database

This section describes the subset of the SCface database [7] used in our experiments. SCface is a database of static images of human faces with 4.160 images (in visible and infra-red spectrum) of 130 subjects.

The dataset used in this paper is divided into 6 different subsets: i) mugshot images, which are high resolution frontal images, and ii) five visible video surveillance cameras. Each of these subsets contains 130 images, one per subject. The images were acquired in an uncontrolled indoor environment with the persons walking towards several video surveillance cameras having different qualities.

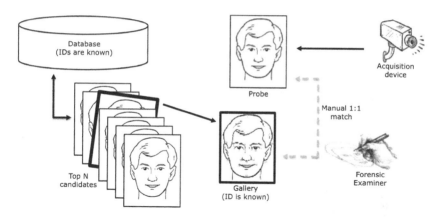

Fig. 1. General procedure followed by a forensic examiner to compare two face images

Additionally the images were acquired at three different distances: 1.00 meters (Close), 2.60m (Medium) and 4.20m (Far) respectively while the subject walked towards the cameras. Fig. 2 shows an example of a mugshot image, and the images acquired by one of the surveillance cameras. As can be seen there is a considerable scenario variation in terms of quality, pose and illumination. The effect of the pose is specially important due to the different angles between the person and the cameras.

This database is of particular interest from a forensic point of view because images were acquired using commercially available surveillance equipment, under realistic conditions. One of its drawbacks is that it is just comprised of one mugshot session, so it is not possible to study the landmark variability for the mugshot images, as several pictures per person are needed. For this study, we use the 5 available images per person and per distance to analyse the variability of the facial landmarks (1950 images in total, 3 distances × 5 cameras × 130 persons). Also, we carry out this study both in a manual way imitating the work that a forensic examiner would perform, and using an automatic system to detect the facial landmarks.

3   Facial Landmark Tagging and Image Processing

This section describes the process of facial landmark tagging and image processing in order to analyse the variability of facial landmarks.

The first step after database collection was to define a set of facial landmarks to include in this study. A set of 21 facial landmarks was defined following recommendations from the Spanish Guardia Civil [8], Netherland Forensic Institute [9] and ENFSI [10], including the irises (2 landmarks) , inner and outer eye corners (4), eyebrow ends (4), mouth corners (2), nose corners (2), center of the nose (1), chin (1), upper and lower ears ends (4) and highest point on the head (1). Figure 3 shows the 21 facial landmarks considered in this study.

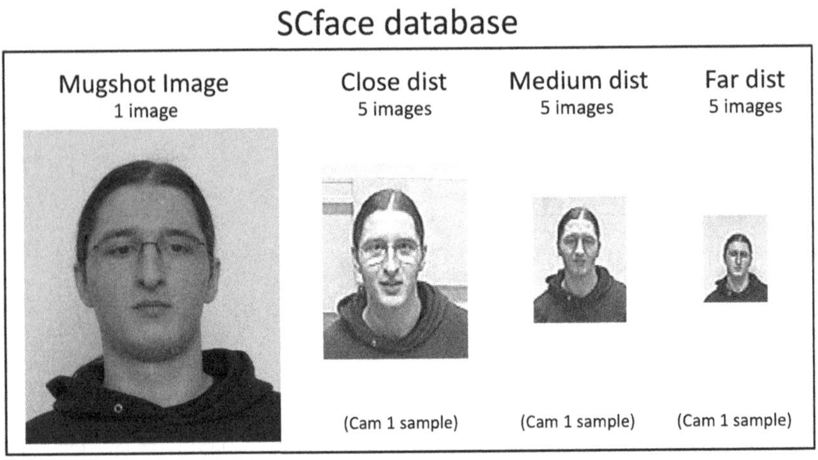

Fig. 2. Example of images of SCface database. High quality mugshot image, and 3 CCTV images acquired at three distances: close, medium and far, for one of the five CCTV cameras.

The process of facial landmark tagging was carried out both manually and automatically. The manual landmark tagging was carried out by the same person, imitating the work of a forensic examiner. In this case the set of 21 landmarks was tagged for the whole database. On the other hand, it is interesting to compare this experimental work with an automatic system. For this case, Luxand FaceSDK [5] was used, which is a high performance face recognition comercial software based on facial landmarks features. In this case, a set of 13 facial landmarks (in red in Fig. 3) were considered, as the automatic system was not able to locate most of the other 8 remaining landmarks.

A second stage of image processing was carried out in order to normalise the facial images to the same size and position. Thus, the midpoint between the eye corners (midpoint between points 6 and 8, and midpoint between 9 and 11) was computed and used instead of the irises positions to align the faces, because the position of the irises can vary if the person does not look at the camera directly. The positions of these two points were fixed having 75 horizontal pixel between them following the recommendation from the ISO standard [11]. Therefore, translation, rotation and scaling of the original images was carried out to normalize the database. This was done in the same way for images collected at different distances between the camera and person. Figure 4 shows an example of the three CCTV face images shown in Figure 2 but size normalised, and showing the positions of the 21 facial landmarks in red and the positions of the center of the eyes in green. As can be seen, this is a challenging scenario for both manual and automatic landmark tagging due to the low quality of the images to analyze.

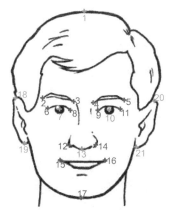

Fig. 3. Set of 21 facial landmarks defined. In red are the landmarks considered for automatic tagging. The manual process considers the whole set of 21 landmarks.

4   Experimental Results

This section describes the experimental work carried out to analyse the variability of facial landmarks considering a forensic scenario using images from CCTV cameras. Three different experiments were designed and are described here.

4.1   Person Specific Landmarking Variability

In this experiment a person specific landmarking variability (LV) was studied. Thus, the 5 available facial images per person and per distance were considered. The mean and standard deviation for each facial landmark were computed for the two (x,y) spatial dimensions ($\sigma_{x,i}$, $\sigma_{y,i}$, with $i=1,...,13$ or 21 depending on the automatic or manual landmark tagging process), assuming following a gaussian distribution. Figure 5 shows two example face images superimposing for each facial landmark the result of tagging the 5 available images. An elipse around each facial landmark is computed using as the radios $2\sigma_{x,i}$, $2\sigma_{y,i}$. Throughout this paper the variability of the different facial landmarks was computed as $\pm\,2\times$mean$(\sigma_{x,i},\sigma_{y,i})$, covering this way a 95.44% of the hypothesized gaussian distribution. For example, in the image shown in Figure 5(a) the landmark for the highest point on the head shows a variability of $\pm$ 25.4 pixels considering a normalization of the face images with 75 horizontal pixels between the eye positions.

This procedure was followed for the 130 persons comprising the database, and it was found that the variability of the facial landmarks, specially for the outer ones varies significantly from person to person. The variability of these landmarks on the outer part of the face (highest point on the head, chin and ears) is very dependent on hair occlusions, more frequent in women than men for the population considered.

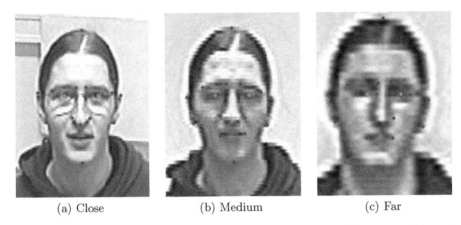

(a) Close   (b) Medium   (c) Far

Fig. 4. Same example as in Fig. 2 (only for the CCTV images) but normalizing the faces with 75 pixels between the center of the eyes. Also, the 21 manual facial landmarks are shown (red), plus the center of the eyes (green).

4.2 Distance Specific Landmarking Variability

This section reports the experimental results achieved for the global landmarking variability (i.e., an average of the individual results) considering the effect of the 3 distances between the camera and the persons. In order to compute a global landmarking variability (LV), the mean of the different individual values of the variability of each facial landmark is computed, following the equation:

$$LV_i = \frac{1}{N} \sum_{j=1}^{N} (\sigma_{x,i,j} + \sigma_{y,i,j}) \tag{1}$$

where $i=1,...,13$ or 21 (for automatic or manual tagging respectively) are the landmarks and $j=1,...,N$, being N the maxima number of persons in the database, 130 in this case. This procedure is followed for each of the three distances considered.

Figures 6(a,c,e) show the results achieved for the case of manual landmark tagging, and Figures 6(b,d,f) show the same but for the case of automatic landmark tagging. Here we focus on the analysis of the distance for the manual case, as next section compares the case of manual vs. automatic landmark tagging.

As can be seen, there is a clear increment of the landmark variability regarding the acquisition distance between the subject and the camera for all the facial landmarks considered (except for the ears). The outer facial landmarks (highest point on the head, ears and chin) present the highest variability, then the mouth and nose areas, and the parts with the least variability are the eyes and eyebrows. It is worth noting that the normalisation of the faces was done using the center of the eyes, so it is also natural that these parts present less variability than the rest. It is also worth noting that as the landmark tagging is carried out over the original size images, close images have a bigger size compared to face images, as

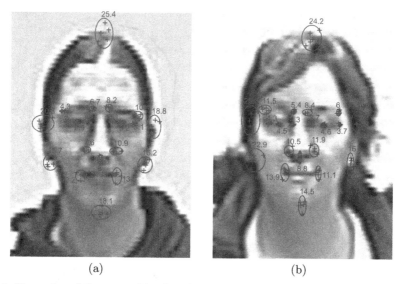

(a)   (b)

Fig. 5. Examples of the manual landmarking variability for two persons present in the SCface database for images taken at 2.60 meters distance between the person and the camera.

can be seen in Figure 2. Therefore, the process of landmark tagging can be done with more precision for the close images and therefore reducing the landmark variability.

4.3   Manual vs. Automatic Landmarking Variability

Figure 6 show the landmark variability for both manual (a, c, e) and automatic (b, d, f) procedures. The number of facial landmarks tagged is different in both cases, 21 for manual and 13 for automatic tagging, as described above. The results show that the landmark variability is very similar for the set of common landmarks. Specifically, for the close images, the landmarks located in the ocular region present lower variability for the automatic system compared to the manual case, while the landmarks located in the mouth region present a higher variability for the automatic system.

For the medium distance, both ocular and mouth region present in general a lower variability for the automatic system, but in the far distance where the quality of the images is very low the manual procedure achieves a lower landmark variability. It is also worth noting that the automatic system only considers 13 facial landmarks as it was not able to locate correctly most of the remaining 8 landmarks (mainly the outer ones), but in general it achieves better results than expected a priori.

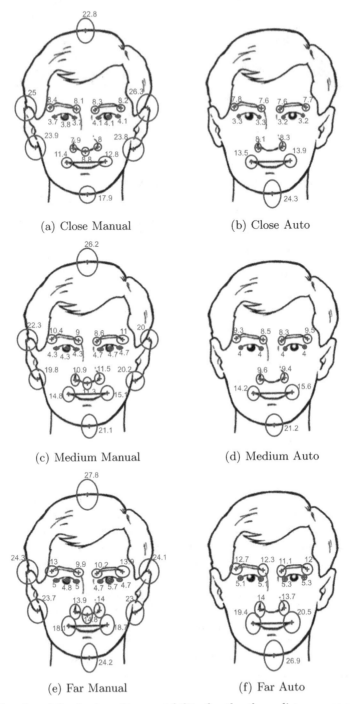

(a) Close Manual   (b) Close Auto

(c) Medium Manual   (d) Medium Auto

(e) Far Manual   (f) Far Auto

Fig. 6. Results of the landmarking variability for the three distances considered between the persons and the camera: far (3 meters), medium (2 meters) and close (1 meter).

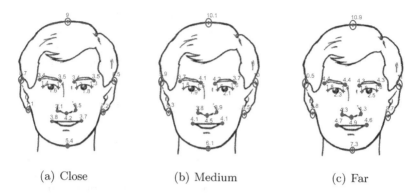

(a) Close   (b) Medium   (c) Far

Fig. 7. Results of the landmarking variability for the three distances considered between the persons and the camera: close (1 meter), medium (2 meters) and far (3 meters), for a high quality database of mugshot images [12].

4.4   CCTV Images vs. Mugshot Images Landmarking Variability

For completeness, results achieved in this analysis can be compared with a previous similar work [12], using in this case a database of mugshot images acquired in a controlled scenario. In this case, the images were of a much higher quality as the images from SCface database considered here. Also, three distances between the subject and the camera were analysed (1, 2 and 3 meters). In this case, there were 8 images per distance and per person, for a total of 50 persons (1200 images in total).

Results achieved for this study using a manual landmark approach are shown in Figure 7. As can be seen, the landmark variability is much lower in all three distances compared to the results achieved in this paper. In this case, also landmarks from the inner parts of the face are more consistent than those from the outer parts. This significant difference of the variability is mainly due to the quality of the images considered, in this case of high quality and therefore achieving lower landmark variability. It is also worth mentioning that SCface database was acquired in uncontrolled conditions while the other database was acquired in a controlled scenario.

5   Conclusions

This paper reports a study of the variability of facial landmarks over a CCTV database with low quality images and large range of variability factors. Face images are taken with three distances between the persons and the 5 CCTV cameras (1, 2.60 and 4.20 meters). 21 facial landmarks were defined and the database was manually tagged imitating the procedure followed by a forensic examiner. Also, an automatic system was used to tag 13 out of the 21 landmarks defined. The main conclusions are that the landmarks located in the outer part of the face have a much higher variability compared to the landmarks placed near the eyes. A reason for this is mainly that these are the areas which can have hair occlusions more frequently like the highest point on the head and the ears.

Regarding the distances between the camera and the person, the landmarking variability increases with the distance. Comparing the two manual and automatic tagging approaches, the results show that the landmark variability is very similar for the set of common landmarks, having in some cases lower variability for the automatic system.

A final comparison of these results with a previous study over a controlled database of mugshot images, shows that the CCTV images present a significantly higher landmark variability, which is mainly due to lower quality of the images making very difficult to tag the facial landmarks with high precision.

Acknowledgments. R. Vera is supported by a Juan de la Cierva Fellowship from the Spanish MINECO. This work has been partially supported by a contract with Spanish Guardia Civil and projects BBfor2 (FP7-ITN-238803), Bio-Shield (TEC2012-34881), Contexts (S2009/TIC-1485), TeraSense (CSD2008-00068) and "Catedra UAM-Telefonica".

References

1. Gupta, S., Markey, M.K., Bovik, A.C.: Anthropometric 3D Face Recognition. Int. Journal of Computer Vision 90(3), 331–349 (2010)
2. Arca, S., Campadelli, P., Lanzarotti, R.: An Efficient Method to Detect Facial Fiducial Points for Face Recognition. In: Proc. of International Conference on Pattern Recognition (ICPR 2004), vol. 1, pp. 532–535 (2004)
3. Arca, S., Campadelli, P., Lanzarotti, R.: A Face Recognition System based on Automatically determined Facial Fiducial Points. Pattern Recognition 39(3), 432–443 (2006)
4. Beumer, G.M., Tao, Q., Bazen, A.M., Veldhuis, R.N.J.: A Landmark Paper in Face Recognition. In: Proc. of Int. Conference on Automatic Face and Gesture Recognition (FG 2006), USA, pp. 73–78 (2006)
5. Luxand FaceSDK, http://www.luxand.com/facesdk/
6. Jain, A.K., Klare, B., Park, U.: Face Matching and Retrieval in Forensics Applications. IEEE Multimedia 19(1), 20 (2012)
7. Grgic, M., Delac, K., Grgic, S.: Scface - surveillance cameras face database. Multimedia Tools Appl. 51(3), 863–879 (2011)
8. Spanish Guardia Civil, http://www.guardiacivil.es/
9. Netherlands Forensic Institute (NFI), http://www.forensicinstitute.nl
10. European Network of Forensic Science Institutes, http://enfsi.eu/
11. ISO/IEC JTC 1/SC 37 N 504, Biometric Data Interchange Formats Part 5: Face Image (2004)
12. Vera-Rodriguez, R., Tome, P., Fierrez, J., Exposito, N., Vega, F.J.: Analysis of the Variability of Facial Landmarks in a Forensic Scenario. In: Proc. of International Workshop on Biometrics and Forensics (IWBF 2013), pp. 1–4 (2013)

Human Action Recognition from Inter-temporal Dictionaries of Key-Sequences

Analí Alfaro, Domingo Mery, and Alvaro Soto

Department of Computer Science
Pontificia Universidad Católica de Chile
ajalfaro@uc.cl,
{dmery,asoto}@ing.puc.cl

Abstract. This paper addresses the human action recognition in video by proposing a method based on three main processing steps. First, we tackle problems related to intraclass variations and differences in video lengths. We achieve this by reducing an input video to a set of key-sequences that represent atomic meaningful acts of each action class. Second, we use sparse coding techniques to learn a representation for each key-sequence. We then join these representations still preserving information about temporal relationships. We believe that this is a key step of our approach because it provides not only a suitable shared representation to characterize atomic acts, but it also encodes global temporal consistency among these acts. Accordingly, we call this representation inter-temporal acts descriptor. Third, we use this representation and sparse coding techniques to classify new videos. Finally, we show that, our approach outperforms several state-of-the-art methods when is tested using common benchmarks.

Keywords: human action recognition, key-sequences, sparse coding, inter-temporal acts descriptor.

1 Introduction

Human action recognition is relevant to the development of potential applications such as surveillance systems, human-computer interaction and video annotation. However, there are many challenges that deserve careful attention. These include *i)* the fact that features should be reliable so that researchers can develop programs that achieve adequate representation of human actions; *ii)* the existence of high inner-class variations such as human poses, occlusions, viewpoints and dynamic backgrounds, which stand as obstacles to the task of classification; and *iii)* variations in the duration of an action, which can prevent quick recognition. Many studies have tried to address these problems over the past few years. Approaches to action representation use both global and local representations. Global representations consider holistic features such as silhouettes, motion and volumes. Bobick and Davis [3] and Efros et al. [6] proposed to describe the motion inside of a volume (stack of person-centered frames). Another methods

R. Klette, M. Rivera, and S. Satoh (Eds.): PSIVT 2013, LNCS 8333, pp. 419–430, 2014.
© Springer-Verlag Berlin Heidelberg 2014

represent silhouettes as three-dimensional shapes in order to extract features [9]. Fathi and Mori [7] argue that low-level features are uninformative and propose the use of mid-level ones. In general, global features fail to fully address the noise introduced by clothes, lighting and body deformations. A local representation may be more robust than a global one in situations of high variation. The emergence of methods that can be useful for finding spatio-temporal interest points [5,14] have allowed researchers to address the aforementioned problems. Many researchers have used dictionaries based on local features to develop robust action recognition systems. Several approaches can be used to produce a dictionary, including Bag-of-Words [16,8,15], Random Forest [25,26], and more recently Sparse Dictionary Learning [10,11,23]. The sparse analysis establishes that a natural signal (eg. images) can be broken down into a linear combination of atoms which form a dictionary. Sparse coding techniques can be used to model an action based on the combination of training samples. The dictionary is adapted in order to capture the inherent structure of the data. For example, Guo et al. [11] built a class-specific dictionary from silhouette-based descriptors. The reconstruction error of each class is used for classification. Tanaya and Ward [10] proposed local motion pattern descriptors and evaluated several classification methods using sparse coding. Tran et al. [23] used a body-part descriptor to develop a dictionary for each part and class, and classified them based on the reconstruction error. These approaches have a common aspect: they use low-level features to find dictionaries. However, this information may be similar between different actions and it may incur into misclassification.

On the other hand, there are methods that use a single frame to achieve recognition [4]. Still others use a set of frames [8,10,11,18,21]. These approaches tend to manually select short sequences containing the atomic information of the action in order to address the time variation problem. Unlike of these methods we argue that the key-sequences selected to represent a video should be carefully selected. This is an important aspect to ensure an appropriate video representation. Additionally, we claim that it is necessary to rescue the inter-temporal relationship among which key-sequences.

The main focus of our work is to break down an action into acts such that the interaction among these parts summarizes the whole. The video of an action can thus be represented as a set of *key-sequences* containing the acts and their temporal relationships. By articulating both aspects, we can arrive at a complete description of the action. We propose breaking a video down into key-sequences using a non-supervised procedure. The key-sequences are then described using a descriptor obtained from Sparse Dictionary Learning. Our findings prove that our approach is effective and that it outperforms the state of the art on several datasets.

The main intuitions and contributions of this paper can be summarized as follows:

- We demonstrate the relevance of exploring the subsequence feature space in order to identify key atomic acts, or key-sequences, that can be unique or shared among action classes. In particular, we propose a method where each video is represented by a set of meaningful acts or key-sequences.

– We noted that human action classes can be characterized as a composition of unique and shared atomic acts. Furthermore, the temporal ordering of these atomic acts provides highly discriminative information to recognize different human actions. We then propose a new representation, called an *inter-temporal acts descriptor*, that is able to encode local information to characterize atomic acts and also to preserve a global temporal ordering among them.

The rest of the paper is organized as follows. Section 2 describes the proposed method for describing a video using the called an *inter-temporal acts descriptor* and the classification strategy. Section 3 presents the experiments and the discussion of our results. Finally, Section 4 contains concluding remarks.

2 Method

In this section, we describe the proposed method following Fig. 1. The method consists of three main steps: *i)* Video decomposition in key-sequences, *ii)* Learning of spatio-temporal dictionaries of key-sequences, and *iii)* The classification strategy.

2.1 Video Decomposition in Key-Sequences

In order to reduce the dimensionality of the recognition problem, we propose summarizing a video sequence using a few representative *key-sequences*. A key-sequence is a small number of consecutive frames composed of acts (or atomic motions) of an action that can be used to recognize it. For instance, the action 'diving' can be split into three acts: 'jump', 'twist' and 'entry'. These acts should contain enough information to address a successful classification of the action. The key-sequences should satisfy the following *consistency criteria: i)* They should strongly characterize the class of an action, which means that an action can be visually recognized by observing its key-sequences. *ii)* The key-sequences should be temporally sorted, thus, the k-th key-sequence of a video of an action should be similar to the k-th key-sequence of another video of the same action. Note that each person has his or her own way for doing an action, which means that the acts may appear to be different. Nevertheless, the acts should be consistent for all videos belonging to the same class.

The procedure for obtaining the key-sequences of a class is repeated for each class c, for $c = 1 \ldots N$. Let $\mathbf{B}^c = \{\mathbf{v}_i\}_{i=1}^p$ be a set of p training videos of class c, where $\mathbf{v}_i = \{\mathbf{f}_{i,j}\}_{j=1}^{r_i}$ is a set of r_i frames. For each video $\mathbf{v}_i$, we built a set $\mathbf{S}_i$ with all of the possible subsequences $\mathbf{s}_{i,j} = \{\mathbf{f}_{i,k}\}_{k=j}^{j+t-1}$ of t consecutive frames: $\mathbf{S}_i = \{\mathbf{s}_{i,j}\}_{j=1}^{r_i-t+1}$. Thus, the set of subsequences of the class is $\mathbf{S}^c = \{\mathbf{S}_i\}_{i=1}^p$.

Each subsequence in $\mathbf{S}^c$ is described in appearance and motion using the well-known HOG3D descriptor [13]. It generates a feature space $\mathbf{H}^c = f_{\mathrm{HOG3D}}(\mathbf{S}^c)$ with a large collection of high-dimensional spatio-temporal descriptors. Our goal is to find groups of descriptors with high levels of similarity that summarize the

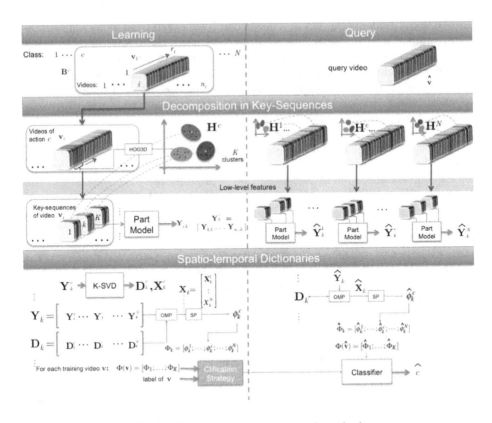

Fig. 1. Block diagram of proposed method

overall behavior from the class. We find these groups by applying a K-means clustering algorithm over $\mathbf{H}^c$, and define $\mathbf{Z}^c = \{\mathbf{z}_k\}_{k=1}^K$ as the set of the K estimated centroids for class c. We expect each centroid to represent an act which should be present in every video. Thus, we define the K key-sequences of video $\mathbf{v}_i$ as those K subsequences $\{\hat{\mathbf{s}}_{i,k}\}_{k=1}^K \in \mathbf{S}_i$, where $\hat{\mathbf{s}}_{i,k} = \mathbf{s}_{i,q(i,k)}$ is a subsequence, and where description $\mathbf{h}_{i,q} = f_{\mathrm{HOG3D}}(\mathbf{s}_{i,q})$ is the most similar one to each centroid of $\mathbf{Z}^c$ and $q(i,1) < q(i,2) \ldots < q(i,K)$ in order to ensure the temporally sorted subsequences. The key-sequences are estimated as follows: First, we compute the indices of the most similar subsequences as $w_k = argmin_{q'} \|\mathbf{z}_k - \mathbf{h}_{i,q'}\|$. Second, we sort the indices w as $\{q(i,k)\}_{k=1}^K = \mathrm{sort}(\{w_k\}_{k=1}^K)$ (see Fig. 2).

Low-Level Feature Extraction: A sequence of the video $\mathbf{v}_i$ could contain not only the actor, but also some noise from dynamic backgrounds, the objects intervening in the scene, clothes, etc. In order to overcome this problem, the actor is detected using a model of body part detection applied to the key-sequences of the video [2]. The goal is to extract relevant information from limbs where motions are performed. Thus, given a key-sequence of a video $\hat{\mathbf{s}}_{i,k}$ with t frames, we apply the body part model only to the central frame $(t-1)/2$, for an odd t, because it is enough to produce an estimate of the location of the parts and to

Fig. 2. Central frame from key-sequences of lifting and diving actions(UCF-Sports)

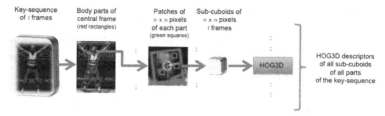

Fig. 3. Part model: low-level features of a key-sequence

avoid the cost of making this in each frame. The model delivers the bounding box of ten parts of the body: torso, forearms, arms, thighs, legs and head (see Fig. 3).

We then extract local spatio-temporal features from spatio-temporal *cuboids* defined by the bounding box of the body parts propagated across the frames of the key-sequence. For each cuboid, we randomly generate spatial patches of $n \times n$ pixels and extract *sub-cuboids*. A sub-cuboid is formed by lining up the 2D patches from each frame of the key-sequence. The size of each spatio-temporal sub-cuboid is $n \times n \times t$. These sub-cuboids are described using HOG3D, which yields a collection of descriptors $\mathbf{Y}_{i,k}$, for video $\mathbf{v}_i$ and key-sequence k. We call this function $\mathbf{Y}_{i,k} = f_{\text{low-level}}(\mathbf{v}_i, k, c)$. Hereafter, the descriptors of the sub-cuboids will be denominated *low-level features*. The description of the k-th key-sequence of all n_c videos of class c are arranged in $\mathbf{Y}_k^c = [\mathbf{Y}_{1,k} \ldots \mathbf{Y}_{ik} \ldots \mathbf{Y}_{n_c,k}]$, and it will be called the low-level features from class c and temporal order k.

2.2 Learning of Spatio-temporal Dictionaries of Key-Sequences

The actions can be similar to each other or they can share features. This is true for the actions 'run' and 'long jump,' for example. When these actions are broken down into their key-sequences we note the presence of the act of running in both actions. The local information extracted from this act is clearly similar in both actions. Therefore, we believe that it is possible to represent a video as a combination of characteristics from different actions. A high value of this combination in a given class indicates a high probability that a video belongs to that class.

It follows that each key-sequence from a video can be encoded at a high level so that the temporal relationship between these descriptors can be identified. The temporal relationship is important for articulating the relationship between sequences. Our method computes a *inter-temporal acts descriptor* from temporal dictionaries. These features provide information about the contribution of all classes to the performance of an act in a key-sequence.

We use two levels of *sparse dictionaries* [1] to calculate the temporal dictionaries. At the lower level, we identify one dictionary for each class from low-level features. At the high level, we identify temporal dictionaries and their sparse representations. These sparse representations are used to build a feature that describes a video as a combination of the contributions of each class that considers the temporal relationship between their key-sequences.

Class-Based Temporal Sparse Dictionary: In this level, a sparse dictionary of each class is created using the low-level features obtained in Section 2.1. The descriptors are organized into groups according to the ordering imposed by the key-sequences. Hence, we calculate a dictionary $\mathbf{D}_k^c$ for each class and each temporal order $\mathbf{Y}_k^c$ using K-SVD [1]:

$$\min_{\mathbf{D}_k^c, \mathbf{X}_k^c} ||\mathbf{Y}_k^c - \mathbf{D}_k^c \mathbf{X}_k^c||_F^2 \text{ subject to } ||x_l||_0 \leq \lambda_1, \tag{1}$$

where the last term indicates that the number of nonzero entries of each column of $\mathbf{X}_k^c$ must not exceed λ_1.

Concatenated Temporal Sparse Dictionary: In this level, all sparse dictionaries $\mathbf{D}_k^c$ ($c = 1 \ldots N$) with the same k-th order are concatenated to form a temporal dictionary . Let $\mathbf{Y}_k = [\mathbf{Y}_k^1 \| \ldots \| \mathbf{Y}_k^c \| \ldots \| \mathbf{Y}_k^N]$ be the matrix of the k-th order containing the concatenated low-level features from the N classes with the same temporal order position k. Let $\mathbf{D}_k = [\mathbf{D}_k^1 \| \ldots \| \mathbf{D}_k^c \| \ldots \| \mathbf{D}_k^N]$ be the concatenated temporal dictionary. The goal is to find $\mathbf{X}_k$, the sparse representation of $\mathbf{Y}_k$ by solving:

$$\min_{\mathbf{X}_k} ||\mathbf{Y}_k - \mathbf{D}_k \mathbf{X}_k||_F^2 \text{ subject to } ||x_l||_0 \leq \lambda_2, \tag{2}$$

using, for example, a matching pursuit algorithm like OMP [19]. This sparse representation is useful because it provides information about the contribution of the classes for each sample. Thus, $\mathbf{X}_k$ can be seen as $[\mathbf{X}_k^1 ; \ldots \mathbf{X}_k^c ; \ldots \mathbf{X}_k^N]$, where $\mathbf{X}_k^c$ represents the sparse matrix of class c in temporal order k. Therefore, we can take advantage of this information for computing the contribution of a certain class for a video.

Describing inter-temporal acts: Our purpose is to learn how to produce a representation which characterizes the videos as a combination of the classes and their temporal relationships. Let a video $\mathbf{v}$ represent a set of low-level features $\{\mathbf{Y}_k^c\}_{c=1}^N$ for all classes for temporal order k, where $\mathbf{Y}_k^c = f_{\text{low-level}}(\mathbf{v}, k, c)$. The contribution of a given class and a given order to the video $\mathbf{v}$ is computed by applying a sum pooling (SP) in the atoms from its class. We define the sum pooling operator SP as:

$$\phi_k^c = \sum_{l=1}^{P} x_k^c(l), \tag{3}$$

where the $\mathbf{X}_k^c = [x_k^c(1); \ldots; x_k^c(P)]$ indicates the P atoms of the sparse representation of $\mathbf{Y}_k^c$ according to dictionary $\mathbf{D}_k$. Each low-level feature belongs to a given video $\mathbf{v}$ of class c and temporal order k. The $\sum(\cdot)$ term is the sum pooling (SP) generated by projecting on the P-atoms of the class. Finally, the sum pooling application produces a value ϕ_k^c that is interpreted as the contribution that is delivered by the class c to the video $\mathbf{v}$ in the temporal order k. We can thus represent a video $\mathbf{v}$ as the contribution of all classes to the composition of an *act descriptor* $\Phi_k = [\phi_k^1; \cdots; \phi_k^c; \cdots; \phi_k^N]$. This feature is important because allows us to express shared features between classes. Finally, in order to retrieve the temporal relationship between key-sequences of the video, we define a function to create an *inter-temporal acts descriptor*. The *inter-temporal acts descriptor* of a video $\mathbf{v}$ is defined by concatenating each *act descriptor* from each ordering as $\Phi(\mathbf{v}) = [\Phi_1; \ldots; \Phi_K]$.

2.3 Classification Strategy

The high-level features from the previous step can be used in any supervised classification approach. Again, we chose to use a classification based on sparse coding. Let β^c be a dictionary learned from the *inter-temporal acts descriptors* of the class c in the train stage. Let $\beta = [\beta^1 \ldots \beta^c \ldots \beta^N]$ be a concatenated overcomplete dictionary. Let $\Phi(\hat{\mathbf{v}})$ be the matrix containing the *inter-temporal acts descriptor* of the query video $\hat{\mathbf{v}}$. The classification consists of identifying a sparse representation called α for the *inter-temporal acts descriptor* of the test sample. This sparse representation is found using OMP [19]:

$$\min_{\alpha} ||\Phi(\hat{\mathbf{v}}) - \beta\alpha||_F^2 \text{ subject to } ||\alpha_l||_0 \leq \lambda_3 \tag{4}$$

Again the sparse representation α can be seen as a block matrix of the classes. Thus, it is possible to calculate the contribution of each class by applying the sum pooling operator SP. Finally, we choose $\hat{c}$, the class with the highest contribution.

3 Experiments and Results

In order to validate the method outlined in Section 2, in this section, we describe the experimental settings and report the results obtained in three well-known datasets of actions: KTH, UCF-Sports, and Olympic.

3.1 Experimental Settings

We configure the training and testing parameters for each dataset as follows:

Decomposition in Key-Sequences: We believe that a key-sequence should contain a short number of frames for two reasons. First, short sequences can capture atomic motion. Second, short sequences can be processed quickly. Then, we take a fixed group of $t = 7$ frames to form a sequence. In short videos, choosing many key-sequences may imply a high overlap. Specifically, the key-sequences of periodic actions can capture similar information because these actions are highly repetitive. For example, the action 'run' is a monotone action (arms and legs have a cyclic motion), and hence their key-sequences may be similar. A reasonable strategy is thus to select a few key-sequences in order to avoid providing the same information. We select a number of $K = 3$ key-sequences to represent a video. For each key-sequence and for each body-part, we select 5 random body part positions to select 5 patches of 20×20 pixels. Around each of these patches we select another 8 patches of the same size to complete a total of 45 patches to cover each of the 10 body-parts. Thus, each key-sequence produces 450 spatio-temporal sub-cuboids with size $20 \times 20 \times 7$. Each sub-cuboid is described using HOG3D (300 dimensions). In order to deal with uninformative sub-cuboids, we apply a threshold to the magnitude of the descriptor to filter them out. The values of the threshold are 1.8, 1 and 2 to UCF-Sports, KTH and Olympic dataset, respectively. Afterwards, the remaining descriptors are normalized.

Temporal Dictionaries: We create the class-based dictionaries using $P = 600$ atoms (*i.e.* with redundancy $\mu = 2^1$). For each concatenated temporal dictionary, we set $\mu = 2$ and $P = \mu \times N \times K$. In particular, the number of atoms for KTH, Olympic and UCF-Sports are $36, 96$ and 54, respectively. The parameter of sparsity is set to the 10% of the number of atoms in both levels ($\lambda_1 = \lambda_2$) in accordance with [10]. Finally, the dimension of our *inter-temporal acts descriptor* is $N \times K$. Therefore, the dimension of the final descriptors in KTH, Olympic dataset and UCF-Sports are 36, 48 and 27, respectively.

Classification Strategy: We create a concatenated temporal dictionary for classification containing $P = \mu \times N$ atoms ($\mu = 2$) and set λ_3 to the 10% of the number of atoms. Thus, the number of atoms in KTH, Olympic dataset and UCF-Sports are 12, 32 and 18.

3.2   Results

• *KTH Dataset:* The dataset contains 2391 sequences from six types of human actions. Each action is performed by 25 actors in four different scenarios with view point changes and variations in scale, lighting and appearance (clothes). We use the original setup [22], *i.e.* splitting the data in training and testing. In order to engage in a fair comparison, we selected methods that use the same testing protocol. Table 1 shows a summary of the comparison. We obtained 95.7 % accuracy in the recognition compared to other state-of-the-art methods. Regarding the confusion matrix (see Fig. 4), actions such as boxing, clapping and waving are confused. We anticipated these findings because these actions are characterized by similar hand motions. The same situation is observable with actions

---

[1] The redundancy indicates the folds of basis vectors that are to be identified with respect to the dimension of the descriptor.

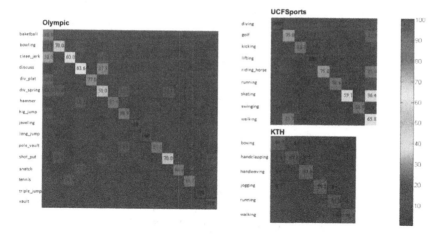

Fig. 4. Confusion matrix on the tested datasets using proposed method

Table 1. Comparison of accuracy using KTH dataset

Method	Year	Acc.(%)
Laptev et al. [15]	2008	91.8
Niebles et al. [18]	2010	91.3
Zang et al. [27]	2012	94.0
Our method		95.7

jogging, running and walking, due to the leg-centered motion. Nevertheless, our method obtains high accuracy in all classes.

• *Olympic Dataset:* The Olympic Sports Dataset contains 16 actions and about 783 videos of athletes practicing different sports from Youtube [18]. This dataset is challenging because it contains camera motion and several views. Unlike the KTH and UCF-Sports datasets, the bounding boxes are not available. Due to the complexity of the scenes, applying the body-part model may produce errors in the actor detection. Therefore, we use the raw frames from each key-sequence to extract 450 random sub-cuboids. These sub-cuboids are used to obtain the temporal dictionaries. Table 2 shows the results where we obtain an overall performance of 81.3%.

We noted from the confusion matrix (see Fig. 4) that the actions associated with javeling, long jump, triple jump and vault are perfectly classified. These actions are characterized by a similar start and a different ending. In this case, it seems that key-sequences are important for breaking the actions down into atomic acts, which implies a good classification. However, actions that involve moderate motion and short duration such as clean and jerk, discus throwing, diving springboard and shot put have a lower recognition rate.

Table 2. Comparison of accuracy using Olympic dataset

Method	Year	Acc.(%)
Niebles et al. [18]	2010	72.1
Liu et al. [17]	2011	74.4
Jiang et al. [12]	2012	80.6
Our method		81.3

Table 3. Comparison of accuracy using UCF-Sports dataset

Method	Year	Acc.(%)
Rodríguez et al. [20]	2008	69.2
Wang et al. [24]	2009	85.6
Guha et al. [10]	2012	83.8
Our method		80.4

• *UCF-Sports Dataset:* This data set consists of 150 videos of several sports obtained from several sources. We decided to present results in 9 actions: diving, golf, kicking, lifting, riding horse, running, skateboarding, swinging and walking. This dataset present many challenges, including dynamic backgrounds, camera motion, scale changes, and variations in lighting and appearance. We increased the amount of data samples by adding a vertically flipped version of each video. We trained and tested all sequences (original and flipped version) and obtain an overall performance of 80.4 %. Table 3 shows the comparison our results using a leave-one-out setup.

Diving, lifting, kicking, running and swinging are correctly classified because they were broken down into differentiable acts. In addition, our method notably differentiates between running and kicking despite the fact that they involve similar acts. Other actions such as golf, riding horse and skate boarding, which involve objects and moderate body motions, present issues of misclassification. However, we believe that this is due to the fact that the key-sequence may contain similar information (due to the short duration of videos) and the lack of context information (see Fig. 4).

4   Conclusions

We proposed a non-supervised method to extract key-sequences that potentially contain the acts to summarize a video. Also, our method describes the video key-sequences as a mixture of different classes and different times called *inter-temporal acts descriptor*. Our approach achieved a robust representation to face the inner-class variations and several video lengths. The experiments have shown that our approach is effective and it obtains a good performance compared to other methods in the state-of-the-art in standard and challenging datasets. In a future work, we plan to integrated the overall process of our method using sparse dictionary learning.

Acknowledgement. The work of Analí Alfaro has been supported by Mecesup Program for Doctoral Scholarship.

References

1. Aharon, M., Elad, M., Bruckstein, A.: K-SVD: An Algorithm for Designing Overcomplete Dictionaries for Sparse Representation. IEEE Trans. on Signal Processing 54, 4311–4322 (2006)
2. Andriluka, M., Roth, S., Schiele, B.: Pictorial Structures Revisited: People Detection and Articulated Pose Estimation. In: Proc. in Computer Vision and Pattern Recognition (2009)
3. Bobick, A., Davis, J.: The Recognition of Human Movement Using Temporal Templates. IEEE Trans. on Pattern Analysis and Machine Intelligence 23, 257–267 (2001)
4. Carlsson, S., Sullivan, J.: Action Recognition by Shape Matching to Key Frames. In: Workshop on Models versus Exemplars in Computer Vision (2001)
5. Dollar, P., Rabaud, V., Cottrell, G., Belongie, S.: Behavior Recognition via Sparse Spatio-Temporal Features. In: VS-PETS (2005)
6. Efros, A., Berg, A., Berg, E., Mori, G., Malik, J.: Recognizing Action at a Distance. In: Proc. in International Conference on Computer Vision (2003)
7. Fathi, A., Mori, G.: Action recognition by learning mid-level motion features. In: Proc. in Computer Vision and Pattern Recognition (2008)
8. Gaidon, A., Harchaoui, Z., Schmid, C.: Actom sequence models for efficient action detection. In: Proc. in Computer Vision and Pattern Recognition (2011)
9. Gorelick, L., Blank, M., Shechtman, E., Irani, M., Basri, R.: Actions as space-time shapes. In: Proc. in International Conference on Computer Vision (2005)
10. Guha, T., Ward, R.: Learning Sparse Representations for Human Action Recognition. IEEE Trans. on Pattern Analysis and Machine Intelligence 34, 1576–1588 (2012)
11. Guo, K., Ishwar, P., Konrad, J.: Action Recognition in Video by Sparse Representation on Covariance Manifolds of Silhouette Tunnels. In: Proc. in International Conference on Pattern Recognition (2010)
12. Jiang, Y.-G., Dai, Q., Xue, X., Liu, W., Ngo, C.-W.: Trajectory-Based Modeling of Human Actions with Motion Reference Points. In: Fitzgibbon, A., Lazebnik, S., Perona, P., Sato, Y., Schmid, C. (eds.) ECCV 2012, Part V. LNCS, vol. 7576, pp. 425–438. Springer, Heidelberg (2012)
13. Kläser, A., Marszalek, M., Schmid, C.: A spatio-temporal descriptor based on 3d-gradients. In: Proc. in British Machine Vision Conference (2008)
14. Laptev, I., Lindeberg, T.: Space-time interest points. In: Proc. in International Conference on Computer Vision (2003)
15. Laptev, I., Marszalek, M., Schmid, C., Rozenfeld, B.: Learning realistic human actions from movies. In: Proc. in Computer Vision and Pattern Recognition (2008)
16. Liu, J., Ali, S., Shah, M.: Recognizing human actions using multiple features. In: Proc. in Computer Vision and Pattern Recognition (2008)
17. Liu, J., Kuipers, B., Savarese, S.: Recognizing human actions by attributes. In: Proc. in Computer Vision and Pattern Recognition (2011)

18. Niebles, J.C., Chen, C.-W., Fei-Fei, L.: Modeling Temporal Structure of Decomposable Motion Segments for Activity Classification. In: Daniilidis, K., Maragos, P., Paragios, N. (eds.) ECCV 2010, Part II. LNCS, vol. 6312, pp. 392–405. Springer, Heidelberg (2010)
19. Pati, Y., Rezaiifar, R., Krishnaprasad, P.: Orthogonal Matching Pursuit: Recursive Function Approximation with Applications to Wavelet Decomposition. In: Proceedings of the 27th Annual Asilomar Conference on Signals, Systems, and Computers (1993)
20. Rodriguez, M., Ahmed, J., Shah, M.: Action MACH a spatio-temporal Maximum Average Correlation Height filter for action recognition. In: Proc. In: Computer Vision and Pattern Recognition (2008)
21. Schindler, K., Van Gool, L.: Action Snippets: How many frames does human action recognition require? In: Proc. in Computer Vision and Pattern Recognition (2008)
22. Schüldt, C., Laptev, I., Caputo, B.: Recognizing human actions: A local SVM approach. In: Proc. in International Conference on Pattern Recognition (2004)
23. Tran, K., Kakadiaris, I., Shah, S.: Modeling Motion of Body Parts for Action Recognition. In: Proc. in British Machine Vision Conference (2011)
24. Wang, H., Ullah, M., Kläser, A., Laptev, I., Schmid, C.: Evaluation of local spatio-temporal features for action recognition. In: Proc. in British Machine Vision Conference (2009)
25. Yao, A., Gall, U., Van Gool, L.: A Hough transform-based voting framework for action recognition. In: Proc. in Computer Vision and Pattern Recognition (2010)
26. Yu, T., Kim, T., Cipolla, R.: Real-time Action Recognition by Spatiotemporal Semantic and Structural Forest. In: Proc. in British Machine Vision Conference (2010)
27. Zhang, Y., Liu, X., Chang, M.-C., Ge, W., Chen, T.: Spatio-Temporal Phrases for Activity Recognition. In: Fitzgibbon, A., Lazebnik, S., Perona, P., Sato, Y., Schmid, C. (eds.) ECCV 2012, Part III. LNCS, vol. 7574, pp. 707–721. Springer, Heidelberg (2012)

Summarization of Egocentric Moving Videos for Generating Walking Route Guidance

Masaya Okamoto* and Keiji Yanai

Department of Informatics, The University of Electro-Communications
1-5-1 Chofugaoka, Chofu-shi, Tokyo 182-8585 Japan
{okamoto-m,yanai}@mm.cs.uec.ac.jp

Abstract. In this paper, we propose a method to summarize an ego-centric moving video (a video recorded by a moving wearable camera) for generating a walking route guidance video. To summarize an ego-centric video, we analyze it by applying pedestrian crosswalk detection as well as ego-motion classification, and estimate an importance score of each section of the given video. Based on the estimated importance scores, we dynamically control video playing speed instead of generating a summarized video file in advance. In the experiments, we prepared an egocentric moving video dataset including more than one-hour-long videos totally, and evaluated crosswalk detection and ego-motion classification methods. Evaluation of the whole system by user study has been proved that the proposed method is much better than a simple baseline summarization method without video analysis.

Keywords: Egocentric Vision, Video Summarization, Walking Route Guidance.

1 Introduction

In this paper, we propose a system to summarize an egocentric moving video. The goal of summarization of an egocentric moving video in this work is to produce a compact summary video, assuming that an input video is an egocentric video recorded continuously from a departure place to a destination by a wearable camera that a walking person is wearing. Therefore, the generated summary video can be used as a guidance video which explains the walking route from a departure place to a destination. In general, making a route guidance video manually is a time-consuming job. With this system, we can generate compact guidance videos on walking path routes very easily by walking the routes with a wearable camera.

To produce a summarized video, we make use of ego-motion (motion of the person wearing a wearable camera) and detection of a pedestrian crosswalk as cues. Ego-motion is estimated based on optical flow of the scene, while crosswalks

---

* He is currently a graduate student at Graduate School of Information Science and Technology, The University of Tokyo.

R. Klette, M. Rivera, and S. Satoh (Eds.): PSIVT 2013, LNCS 8333, pp. 431–442, 2014.
© Springer-Verlag Berlin Heidelberg 2014

are detected by Geometric Context [1] and a standard object recognition method based on bag-of-features representation and non-linear SVM classifier. Based on these cues, the system estimates importance of each section in the given video.

Actually, in the proposed system, summarized video files are not generated. Instead, a playing scenario is generated which instructs relative playing speed on each video section according to the importance scores of video sections. Basically, we play important scenes at a normal speed, while we play less important scenes at a high speed or skip them. With the playing scenario, the system dynamically controls video playing speeds. Since HTML5 video player can control video playing speeds even while playing a video, we implemented a viewing system on the Web in HTML5. That is, the proposed system does not generate a summary video in advance, but generates a summery video dynamically. Therefore, a user can adjust a total playing time of a summary video, when watching. This is the biggest difference from the previous works.

In the rest of this paper, we describe related work in Section 2. In Section 3, we describe the overview of the proposed system, and explain the methods to classify ego-motion, to detect crosswalks and to evaluate importance scores of video sections in Section 4. Section 5 shows experimental results and user study. We conclude this paper in Section 6.

2   Related Work

In this section, we review some works on video summarization related to egocentric vision and ego-motion classification.

To summarize a video, it is common to divide a given video into some shots, select important shots from them, and concatenate selected shots for generating a summarized video [2,3]. In contrast to them, our goal is to generate a route guidance video, and it does not erase any video shots from an original video because lack of shots confuse people who watch the video regarding a current location of the video. To achieve video summarization for route guidance, we control video playing speed according to the importance scores of video sections, and unrelated scenes for route guiding are fast-forwarded.

Some works on egocentric video summarization have been proposed so far. One of the works which is similar to ours is Lee et al.'s work [4]. In their work, they used no GPS or other sensors, and focuses on image-based detection of the most important objects and people with which the person wearing a camera interacts. The proposed method selects some important frames to create storyboards to explain the recorded egocentric video shortly. In contrast to our work, its targets are any kinds of egocentric videos, and they used not motion cues but only static image features. The results are represented by a set of selected frame images as a storyboard, while our objective is summarizing an egocentric video into a shorter video.

On the other hand, some other works used auxiliary information such as GPS and motion sensor logs to summarize life-log videos. Datchakorn et al. [5] proposed a system which summarizes life-log videos based on some sensor logs including gyro, acceleration and GPS. In contrast to this work, we use only visual features extracted from videos, and need no GPS records.

As a method to analyze egocentric videos, ego-motion classification is common. For example, Kitani et al. [6] proposed a method to classify motions in several kinds of sports videos such as surfing and skiing employing non-parametric Bayesian model in a unsupervised way. In this work, as a feature to classify ego-motion, optical flow is used. In our work, we also use only optical flow to classify ego-motions as a visual motion feature. As another work on first-person activity analysis, Ogaki et al. [7] proposed a method on ego-motion recognition for an "inside-out" camera, which can capture both frontal view and eye movement of the person at the same time. In their work, they use the first-person eye movement as well as ego-motion in order to recognize indoor activities. In our work, we use normal wearable camera which can capture only frontal view, and target outdoor videos.

3   Overview of the Proposed System

In this section, we explain an overview of the proposed system. In the proposed system, we estimate importance of each video section of the given egocentric video based on ego-motion and existence of crosswalks, and generate playing scenario off-line. Based on the scenario, we summarize the given video dynamically by controlling playing speed of the HTML5 video player on-line. The off-line processing to generate a playing scenario is as follows:

1. Ego-motion classification based on optical flow with SVM.
2. Detection of pedestrian crosswalks with bag-of-features and non-linear SVM after estimation of road areas by Geometric Context [1].
3. Estimation of importance of each video section (The duration of each section is four second long.)

4   Method

In this section, we explain the detail of each processing step.

4.1   Ego-motion Classification

In general, a video taken by a wearable camera is called "an egocentric video" or "a first-person video". The most basic analysis on such a video is estimation of the motion of people wearing a camera, which is called "ego-motion".

Since we assume that the given video is taken while walking in this work, we classify ego-motion of each section of the given video into one of the following four moving conditions: (1) moving forward (2) stopping (3) turning right (4) turning left.

Because we treat with only walking egocentric videos, we assume that the videos contain only forward, right and left moves, and do not contain backward moves. If several kinds of moves are included in a unit shot, it will be classified into the majority move.

To classify ego-motion, firstly we extract twelve frame images per second from the given video for every four seconds, and secondly estimate optical flows for each interval of frame images using the Lucas-Kanade method [8], and then we convert them into histogram-based representation.

Figure 1 shows an example of calculating feature vector. We calculate coordinates of the feature points on the current video frame given the coordinates on the previous frame. The function finds the coordinates with sub-pixel accuracy. The red lines in (A) represent the obtained optical flows. To convert raw optical flows into a feature vector, we divide an image into 4×4 grids (B), and extract a 18-bin directional histogram from each block with dividing the optical flow direction by 20 degrees (C). Since we set temporal window size for motion feature extraction as four second long, we average feature vectors for four seconds and L1-normalize the averaged feature vector. Finally we obtain a 288-dim optical flow feature vector for every four-second sections of the given video.

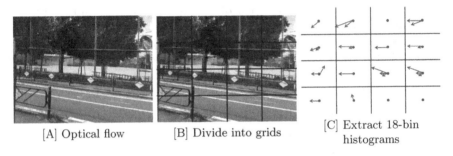

[A] Optical flow   [B] Divide into grids   [C] Extract 18-bin histograms

Fig. 1. Calculating feature vector

To classify ego-motion of each four-second video section into one of the above-mentioned four kinds of the ego-motion conditions, we use SVM as a classifier for the extracted ego-motion feature vectors. In this work, we use LIBSVM library and RBF kernel. We train four SVM classifiers in the one-vs-all way. We prepare hand-labeled training data for training in the experiment. In the step to estimate video section importance, we use the pseudo-probability values obtained by applying a sigmoid function to the output values of SVMs.

4.2   Crosswalk Detection

For walking route guidance in cities, crosswalk is an important and remarkable cue to explain walking routes. To prevent the scenes containing crosswalks from being skipped or played in a high speed, we detect pedestrian crosswalks in the given egocentric video as well as ego-motion conditions.

For crosswalk detection, we extract three frames per second, and detect the frames including crosswalks after road region estimation for each extracted frame.

We estimate road regions for each extracted frame. To do that, we use Geometric Context [1]. This work provides a multiple hypothesis framework for robustly estimating scene structure from a single image and obtaining confidences for each geometric label (See Figure 2). We regard ground regions as road regions which may contain crosswalks. The right figure in Figure 2 shows a final output of the Geometric Context method where ground (green), sky (blue) and vertical (red) regions are classified, subdivided into planar orientation (arrows) and non-planar solid ('x') and porous ('o').

We use results of boosted decision trees for main class, "support"(ground). The pixels that its likelihood is higher than the pre-defined threshold are regarded as spatial support pixels. In our work, the threshold is set 0.4.

Input   Surface Layout

Fig. 2. Geometric context method

Ground regions estimated by Geometric Context method tend to fragment and have holes of non-ground regions. We integrate these regions and fill up the holes because fragmentation and holes make bad influence on the following feature extraction. We apply the closing method of morphological operations to input regions. Figure 3 shows an example of ground region integration. Green regions in these images correspond to the estimated ground regions. The regions applied the integration method are estimated as ground regions finally.

[A] Input   [B] Ground Region   [C] Output

Fig. 3. An example of ground region integration

We use a bag-of-features vector (BoF) with SIFT as an image feature for crosswalk detection. First, we extract keypoints using the default keypoint detector of SIFT which is the difference of Gaussian (DoG) from the ground region estimated in the previous step, and describe local patterns around the keypoints with SIFT descriptor. Next, we vector-quantize extracted SIFT features against the pre-specified codebook and generate a bag-of-features (BoF) vector regarding each of the extracted frames. After that, all the BoF vectors are L1-normalized. In the experiments, we built a 500-dim codebook by k-means clustering with SIFT features sampled from training data.

We use non-linear SVM as classifier to examine if the given frame contains a crosswalk or not. In the experiments, we trained SVM with 80 positive images and 160 negative images.

4.3   Estimation of Importance of Video Sections

Based on the results of ego-motion classification and crosswalk detection, we estimate a importance score of each video section of the given egocentric video. We divide the given video into video sections every four seconds. The importance score varies between 0.0 and 1.0, which decides playing speed of the corresponding video section.

The importance scores of the i-th video section S_i in terms of ego-motion is calculated in the following equation:

$$S_i = c_f v_{f[i]} + c_s v_{s[i]} + c_r v_{r[i]} + c_l v_{l[i]}, \tag{1}$$

where $v_{f[i]}$ $v_{s[i]}$, $v_{r[i]}$ and $v_{l[i]}$, are the sigmoid function values of the SVM outputs regarding "moving forward", "stopping", "turning right" and "turning left", respectively. c_f, c_s, c_r and c_l represent weighting factors. We set those constants as follows: $c_f = -2$, $c_s = 1$, $c_r = 2$, and $c_l = 2$. Because we regard the scenes classified as "turning right or left" as being important, c_r and c_l are positive values. Because the scene classified as "moving forward" is less important, we set c_f as a negative value.

After S_i is obtained, we normalized it so that it varies between 0 to 1 by using maximum S_{max} and minimum S_{min} within the given video in the following equation:

$$S_i' = \frac{S_i - S_{min}}{S_{max} - S_{min}} \tag{2}$$

The sections where crosswalks are detected are important cues for walking route guidance. We sum all the outputs of the SVM classifiers for crosswalk detection in each video section. The sections where total output values become more than the pre-defined threshold are regarded as being crosswalk sections. In the experiments, we set the threshold as 7, which are decided in the preliminary experiment. The normalized importance scores of the crosswalk sections are added 0.5 by the following equation:

$$S_i'' = min(S_i' + 0.5, 1.0) \tag{3}$$

Note that the scores of the first and last four sections are set as 1.0 regardless of ego-motion and crosswalk, since the sections representing the starting place and destination are important.

The list containing importance scores on each video section over the given video is called as "play scenario".

4.4   Calculation of Playing Speed

Finally, we decide speeds of playing video sections based on play scenario. Only this step is carried out on-line when playing, since a user can provide the maximum playing speed. We define playing speed of the i-th section s_i using the following equation:

$$s[i] = \frac{1}{S_i''(1 - (1/(s_{max} - 1))) + (1/(s_{max} - 1))} + 1, \tag{4}$$

where s_{max} is a scaling factor which is expected to be given by a user when playing. s_{max} defines the maximum speed of playing video. s_{max} is set as 7 in the experiments.

When playing practically, the smoothing regarding playing speed is carried out except for the first and last section by the following equation:

$$s'[i] = 0.1(s[i-1] + s[i+1]) + 0.8s[i] \tag{5}$$

5   Experiments

5.1   Data Collection

To collect egocentric videos, we used Looxcie2 (Figure 4). We can wear it on an ear like Figure 5. Figure 6 shows an example of the recorded egocentric video frame.

Fig. 4. Looxcie2   **Fig. 5.** Video recording style

We collected nine egocentric videos for the experiments as shown in Table 1.

Fig. 6. Examples of the video frame

Table 1. Data collection

Activity	Num	Average duration (min.)
walk	9	9:12

5.2   Evaluation on Ego-motion Classification

First, we evaluate performance of ego-motion classification. To learn four kinds of SVM classifiers, we extract hand-labeled sections from four videos for training. The detail of training data is shown in Table 2. The values in the Table represent the number of video sections.

For this experiment, we extract video sections for test from three videos. The results are shown in Table 3. Figure 7 shows the recall-precision curves of four-kinds of ego-motion classification. The classification rate over four-kinds of ego-motion was 83.8%.

Figure 8 shows a typical failure of ego-motion classification. Since it is a scene of waiting for a traffic light, its video section should be classified as "Stop". However, it was classified as "Go right" under the influence of optical flows from motions of the car. Ego-classification tends to fail in the video sections including many moving objects such as people or bikes.

5.3   Evaluation on Crosswalk Detection Performance

In this subsection, we evaluate the performance of crosswalk detection. For this experiment, we selected four videos for training and five videos for test from

Table 2. Training data for ego-motion classification

Motion	Positive	Negative	Num
Move forward	512	216	728
Stop	74	146	220
Turn right	70	147	217
Turn left	68	131	119

Table 3. Ego-motion classification result

Motion	# section	recall	precision	F-number
Forward	244	0.943	0.697	0.801
Stop	72	0.694	0.893	0.781
Go right	84	0.738	0.969	0.838
Go left	88	0.795	0.972	0.875

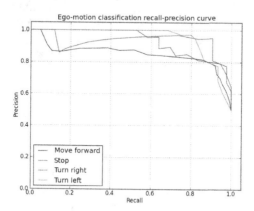

Fig. 7. Recall-Precision curves of ego-motion classification

datasets. We extract 250 images from the learning videos, and extract 200 images from the testing videos. To evaluate the effectiveness of ground region estimation based on Geometric Context, we compared the results with and without ground region estimation. In case of the method without ground estimation, we extracted SIFT keypoints from whole a frame image.

Figure 9 shows the recall-precision curves of crosswalk detection with and without ground region estimation. These results proved that ground estimation could improve the crosswalk detection performance.

Figure 10 shows typical success and failure examples on crosswalk detection. Green regions in these images correspond to the estimated ground regions. In the case of [A], a crosswalk was recognized successfully with ground estimation, while it failed without ground estimation. In this case, ground estimation correctly removed noise regions on the upper part of the given image. On the other hand, in the case of [B], a crosswalk detection failed with ground estimation, while it succeeded without ground estimation. This is because ground estimation recognized a part of the crosswalk region as a vertical region incorrectly.

5.4   User Study

In this subsection, we show the results of user study employing ten subjects. To evaluate the proposed method on walking egocentric video summarization,

Fig. 8. A typical failure of ego-motion classification

we compared the proposed summarization method with two baseline methods. The first baseline is just playing videos in fast-forwarding at a uniform speed. The second one is a storyboard-style summarization which displays uniformly sampled frames from the video. The numbers of storyboard frames are proportional to the length of the given video. We sampled a frame every five second from the given video. To evaluate the effectiveness of crosswalk detection, we carried out a method using only ego-motion classification without crosswalk detection as well. The summarization methods are experimented as follows:

1. Ego-motion classification only
2. Crosswalk detection + ego-motion classification
3. Baseline 1 (fast-forwarding at a uniform speed)
4. Baseline 2 (storyboard-style (sampled frames at even interval))

We asked the subjects to vote the best summary as a walking route guidance among the storyboard and the videos generated by three kinds of summarization methods for each of the egocentric video. The maximum playing speed s_{max} of an input summary video are fix to 7. The details of input and summary video are shown in Table 4.

We obtain 30 votes from 10 subjects. The experimental results are shown in Table 5. The proposed method gathered the best votes on average over three test videos, which means the proposed method based on ego-motion and crosswalk detection was effective compared to the two baselines and the method without crosswalk detection. The method with only ego-motion received some votes for A and B videos. It means the method based on only ego-motion was some effective. The two baseline methods received few votes for all the videos.

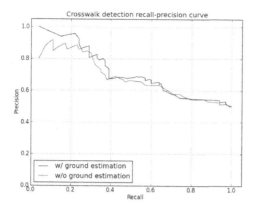

Fig. 9. Recall-Precision curves of crosswalk detection

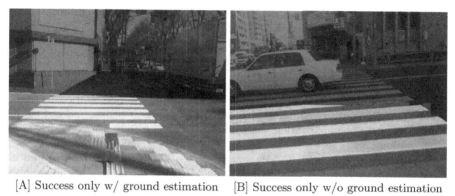

[A] Success only w/ ground estimation   [B] Success only w/o ground estimation

Fig. 10. Crosswalk detection examples of success and failure

Table 4. User study dataset

Video	Duration	After duration	Average speed	Storyboard size
Video A	7:47	1:45	4.5	21
Video B	9:17	2:20	3.9	28
Video C	11:26	2:40	4.3	32

Table 5. User study result

Video	Ego-motion	Ego. + crosswalk	baseline	storyboard
Video A	4	6	0	0
Video B	3	6	1	0
Video C	1	7	1	1
total	8	19	2	1

6   Conclusions and Future Work

In this paper, we proposed a new method to summarize walking ego-centric video for generating walking route guidance. From the user study, it has been proved that the proposed method is better than simple summarization method. About ego-motion classification, it has achieved the classification rate 83.8%. About crosswalk detection, the proposed system has achieved the 63.5% detection rate with ground region estimation.

For future work, we plan to extend target egocentric videos. Although we focused on only walking egocentric video in this paper, we plan to treat with a bike and a car egocentric video. In such cases, other object cues are expected to be importance for egocentric video summarization. We plan to add detection methods on other important objects to the system.

References

1. Hoiem, D., Efros, A., Hebert, M.: Recovering surface layout from an image. International Journal of Computer Vision (2006)
2. Chong-Wah, N., Yu-Fei, M., Hong-Jiang, Z.: Video Summarization and Scene Detection by Graph Modeling. IEEE Transactions on Circuits and Systems for Video Technology 15 (2005)
3. Arthur, G., Harry, A.: Video summarization: A conceptual framework and survey of the state of the art. Visual Communication and Image Representation 19 (2008)
4. Lee, Y.J., Ghosh, J., Grauman, K.: Discovering important people and objects for egocentric video summarization. In: Proc. of IEEE Computer Vision and Pattern Recognition (2012)
5. Tancharoen, D., Yamasaki, T., Aizawa, K.: Practical experience recording and indexing of life log video. In: Proc. of ACM SIGMM Workshop on Continuous Archival and Retrieval of Personal Experiences (2005)
6. Kitani, K.M., Okabe, T., Sato, Y., Sugimoto, A.: Fast unsupervised ego-action learning for first-person sports videos. In: Proc. of IEEE Computer Vision and Pattern Recognition, pp. 3241–3248 (2011)
7. Ogaki, K., Kitani, K.M., Sugano, Y., Sato, Y.: Coupling eye-motion and ego-motion features for first-person activity recognition. In: Proc. of CVPR Workshop on Egocentric Vision (2012)
8. Lucas, B., Kanade, T.: An iterative image registration technique with an application to stereo vision. In: International Joint Conference on Artificial Intelligence, pp. 674–679 (1981)

A Robust Integrated Framework
for Segmentation and Tracking

Prabhu Kaliamoorthi and Ramakrishna Kakarala

Nanyang Technological University,
Singapore
{prab0009,ramakrishna}@ntu.edu.sg

Abstract. Recent studies on human motion capture (HMC) indicate the need for
a likelihood model that does not rely on a static background. In this paper, we
present an approach to human motion capture using a robust version of the oriented chamfer matching scheme. Our method relies on an MRF based segmentation to isolate the subject from the background, and therefore does not require a
static background. Furthermore, we use robust statistics and make the likelihood
robust to outliers. We compare the proposed approach to the alternative methods
used in recent studies in HMC using the Human Eva I dataset. We show that our
method performs significantly better than the alternatives despite of not assuming
a static background.

1 Introduction

Human motion capture (HMC) is a challenging and an important area of research
in the vision community. Though there is a large body of literature on HMC
[18,7,22,1,21,19,8,15,12], most recent methods on HMC [20,7,8] rely on either chroma
keying or a static background for background subtraction. Consequently, they are not
suitable for outdoor motion capture where lighting change and non static background
makes the assumptions invalid. This is observed to be a critical problem for HMC in
recent studies [20]. In order to overcome this limitation, some studies augment the visual data with other sensors such as IMU's [16]. Recent studies [20] indicate that these
problems can be mitigated by designing a suitable cost function that does not make
strong assumptions about a static background and yet would enable tracking with an
acceptable computational overhead. We address this aspect of HMC systems in this
paper.

Our approach draws inspiration from oriented chamfer matching (OCM) in object
recognition [17] and exemplar based pose estimation [14]. Shotton et al. [17] note that
OCM has high discriminative properties for articulated objects and it is robust to noise.
Though these properties have been exploited in areas such as exemplar based pose estimation [14] and articulated hand tracking [23], these techniques have not been applied
to model based HMC.

In this paper, we formulate a cost function for HMC using robust oriented chamfer
matching. The analysis by synthesis framework that is widely used for HMC minimizes
an energy functional that measures the disparity between the observed image and the
synthesized output. The energy functional is generally [8,20] composed of a model to

R. Klette, M. Rivera, and S. Satoh (Eds.): PSIVT 2013, LNCS 8333, pp. 443–453, 2014.

Fig. 1. Edge fragments from the observed image (red) and synthesized output (green) superimposed on the observed image.

observation and an observation to model matching (bidirectional) terms. Our method extracts a set of edge fragments from the observation and the synthesized output, and minimizes a bidirectional oriented chamfer distance between the two. Since our observation is a general set of oriented edge fragments, our method does not make any assumption about a static background. Furthermore, since the observation could include significant noise, we extend the standard oriented chamfer distance with a robust function. This is combined with an MRF based shape prior which segments out the subject from the background to ensure an acceptable computational overhead.

Our approach is compared with the alternative approaches used in recent publications [20,8] using the data from the Human Eva I dataset. We demonstrate with quantitative results, that our method on an average reduces the tracking error by up to 15%, despite of not making limiting assumptions such as a static background.

2   Previous Work

Local optimization and optical flow is used for HMC by studies such as [6,3]. These methods are known to get stuck in incorrect hypothesis [9]. Hence they are not suitable for situations where the model is not exact, or the image observation is uncertain. Some studies [1,4] directly infer the human pose from a set of image features. However, these methods are known to be sensitive to the appearance of the subject and to require extensive training. Exemplar based methods [15,14] have been in use for pose estimation. However, they are not accurate enough for motion capture. Model free approaches to HMC [2,21], loosely assemble human parts to a plausible pose. However, anatomically correct reconstruction of the human motion cannot be ensured by these methods.

Widely used methods such as [7] rely on a kinematic skeleton fleshed with parametric surfaces and achieve motion capture using stochastic search. Gall et al. [8] describe a multi-pass solution that performs initial tracking with a stochastic search method, which is refined with a smoothing filter and local optimization. They use a deformable surface model of the human for tracking. Sidenbladh et al. [18] describe a complete generative framework to model based human motion capture using sequential Monte Carlo tracker. Our method can be incorporated within their framework.

Kohli et al. [13] present an integrated framework for segmentation and pose estimation. The MRF based shape prior we use in this work is similar to [13]. However, their approach uses background and foreground statistics. Hence their approach is not suitable for outdoor situations where the statistics are expected to change due to lighting changes. Since we don't explicitly use background and foreground statistics for segmentation, our approach is insensitive to lighting changes that are expected in outdoor situations such as those considered in [16].

3   Oriented Chamfer Matching

3.1   Overview

Oriented chamfer matching is a technique used in object recognition for matching edge fragments [17,14,11]. Let $\mathcal{P}$ be the space $\mathbb{R}^2 \times [0, \pi)$ that denote the coordinates of an edge fragment along with the edge orientation. Let the respective sets of observation and synthesized edge fragments be $O = \{o_i \in \mathcal{P}\}$ and $S = \{s_i \in \mathcal{P}\}$. The oriented chamfer distance between the two is defined as

$$d_{OCM}(O, S) = \frac{1}{|O|} \sum_{o_i \in O} \min_{s_i \in S} d_{\mathcal{P}}(o_i, s_i) \tag{1}$$

where $|O|$ is the cardinality of the set O, and $d_{\mathcal{P}} : \mathcal{P} \times \mathcal{P} \to \mathbb{R}$, is a distance metric on $\mathcal{P}$ described below

$$d_{\mathcal{P}}(A, B) = \sqrt{\frac{\| A_x - B_x \|_2^2}{\lambda} + \| A_a - B_a \|_a^2} \tag{2}$$

where $\| A_a - B_a \|_a = \min(|A_a - B_a|, \pi - |A_a - B_a|)$ is a distance metric for the angular component. Let W be a warping function parametrized by x, then the optimal parameter $\hat{x}$ that aligns the synthesized edge fragments S with the observation O can be obtained by minimizing the distance d_{OCM} as below

$$\hat{x} = \arg\min_x d_{OCM}(O, W(S; x)) \tag{3}$$

When matching edge fragments, the warping function W is generally a planar affine warp, for example, $x \in SE(2)$. In this paper, we consider the warp W to be a nonlinear map that assembles the articulated model in its pose in $\mathbb{R}^3$ and projects it to calibrated cameras to obtain the synthesized output S. We treat x to be the parameters of the articulated model.

Furthermore, as observed in earlier studies [10], human pose tracking requires a bidirectional matching. Hence we extend the oriented chamfer matching scheme for HMC by defining a bidirectional likelihood term for the camera C as below

$$\begin{aligned} -lnP(O; X, C) &= d_{OCM}(O, W(X, C)) \\ &+ d_{OCM}(W(X, C), O) \end{aligned} \tag{4}$$

The overall likelihood is expressed as the mean from all the cameras used by the multi-view HMC system. The above formulation of the likelihood performs well for HMC. In this paper, we extend this with a robust formulation which is described next.

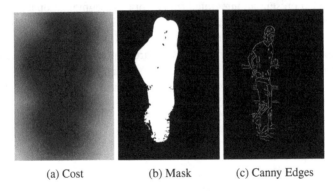

(a) Cost   (b) Mask   (c) Canny Edges

Fig. 2. Segmentation using oriented chamfer distance. The sub-figure a) shows the likelihood term used by the MRF based segmentation technique, b) shows the segmented foreground region, and c) shows the Canny edges extracted from the foreground region that are used for tracking.

Fig. 3. Canny edge fragments obtained by the MRF based segmentation for the Subject 1 walking sequence superimposed on the input image. It can be observed that the subject and a small region around the subject is carved out of the input.

3.2   Robust OCM

The likelihood described in last section assumes that an error free observation O representing the subject is available. This could be achieved in practice by using a silhouette obtained by background subtraction. However, this would result in a method that does not work well in outdoor situations. Hence in this work we use an MRF based segmentation technique that isolates the subject from the background, which we describe next.

Let Z_i ($i \in \{1, \ldots, n\}$) represent the random variables corresponding to the individual pixels. The segmentation task is formulated as the problem of classifying the pixels into two coherent regions represented by the labels $\mathcal{L} \in \{f, b\}$. Spatial coherency between the segmented regions is ensured by a neighborhood influence function. Let $\mathcal{N}_i$ represent a set of neighbors of Z_i, which we consider to be the four adjacent pixels. The posterior probability of the set of pixels in the image Z taking a configuration $z \in \mathcal{L}^n$, is expressed as

$$Pr(Z = z) \propto \prod_{i \in \{1,\dots,n\}} \left(\phi(z_i) \prod_{j \in \mathcal{N}_i} \psi(z_i, z_j) \right) \qquad (5)$$

where $\phi(z_i)$ is the data likelihood term that indicates how likely is a given pixel to belong to a specific label, and $\psi(z_i, z_j)$ is the prior term that enforces spatial coherency.

It can be shown [5] that finding the MAP configuration is equivalent to finding the minimum energy configuration

$$E(z) = \sum_{i \in \{1,\dots,n\}} -log\, \phi(z_i) + \sum_{\substack{i \in \{1,\dots,n\} \\ j \in \mathcal{N}_i}} -log\, \psi(z_i, z_j) \qquad (6)$$

The minimum energy configuration of Z can be efficiently obtained using graph cuts [5]. In this paper, we consider the prior term $\psi(z_i, z_j)$ to be the generalized Potts model [13]. The likelihood using the oriented chamfer distance can be expressed as

$$-log\, \phi(z_i = f) = \min_{y \in \Pi(X_{t-1})} d_{\mathcal{P}}(\mathcal{P}(z_i), y) \qquad (7)$$

where $\Pi(X_{t-1})$ is the synthesized model from the previous time frame, and the operator $\mathcal{P}(z_i)$ returns the 3-tuple $\in \mathcal{P}$ for the pixel z_i. We fix $\phi(z_i = b)$ to be a constant in this work. It should be noted that our framework does not make use of the appearance for the segmentation and it only makes use of the oriented chamfer distance. As a result, our segmentation is robust to lighting changes that are expected to happen in outdoor scenario.

Figure 2 shows the segmentation using the MRF. The cost $-log\, \phi(z_i = f)$ is shown in Figure 2a. The mask obtained using graph cut is shown in Figure 2b. Figure 2c shows the Canny edge segments in the foreground region. Figure 3 shows the segmented Canny edge fragments for the Subject 1 walking sequence.

3.3   Robust Likelihood

It can be observed from Figure 2c, that the edge fragments obtained from segmentation include considerable noise. Consequently, the likelihood described in Section 3.1 can be biased by the noise. We extend the likelihood model in order to overcome this. The likelihood described in Section 3.1 is composed of two parts. The first part measures the fit of the observation to the synthesized model, and the second term measures the fit of the synthesized model to the observation. The observation edge fragments O include substantial noise as a result of the segmentation. However, synthesized edge fragments remain the same as before. Hence we modify the first term to use a robust function that is less sensitive to noise than the squared error. Formally,

$$d_{ROCM}(O, S) = \frac{1}{|O|} \sum_{o_i \in O} \rho \left(\inf_{s_i \in S} d_{\mathcal{P}}(o_i, s_i) \right) \qquad (8)$$

where $\rho(x)$ is the Geman-McClure error function described below.

$$\rho(x) = \frac{x^2}{x^2 + \alpha^2} \qquad (9)$$

The robust likelihood is formally expressed as

$$
\begin{aligned}
-lnP(O; X, C) = & \, d_{ROCM}(O, W(X, C)) \\
& + d_{OCM}(W(X, C), O)
\end{aligned} \tag{10}
$$

We refer to the oriented chamfer matching scheme that uses the above likelihood and the MRF based segmentation described in Section 3.2 as robust oriented chamfer matching (**ROCM**).

4   Experiments and Results

In this section, we compare the proposed method with the alternative methods used for HMC in recent publications [16,8,20]. The Human Eva I dataset that provides video and motion capture data was used for validating the proposed approach. We used input from 3 RGB cameras and 2 grayscale cameras in all the sequences except the Subject 3 jogging and walking sequence. For the Subject 3 jogging and walking sequence, we used an additional camera input, since we found the segmented video had a blind spot near a corner, where nearly 60% of the foreground was invisible, resulting in a tracking failure.

Initialization was performed with the ground truth provided with the Human Eva I dataset as commonly done [20] in recent work. We registered a set of markers provided by the ground truth to the model in the first frame in order to measure the tracking error. Mean Euclidean distance (in mm) between the registered markers and the ground truth in subsequent frames are reported as the tracking error. A constant position model [7] was used as a motion prediction strategy for tracking. We used a kinematic model with 25 degrees of freedom and 10 links. The rigid links were fleshed with truncated cones with elliptical cross section [20].

We obtained silhouettes by background subtraction using the background statistics provided with the Human Eva I dataset. The likelihoods used in current methods [20,8] require the silhouettes. However, our method **ROCM** does not need the silhouettes. Our method was compared with two common likelihoods used with model based motion capture systems. The study in [20] finds bidirectional silhouette (**BiS**) based likelihood to produce the best results. We briefly describe the method here, **BiS** is composed of two terms,

$$
\begin{aligned}
-lnP_{\mathbf{BiS}}(Sil; X, C) = & \, \frac{1}{|\sum_p Sil(p)|} \sum_p Sil(p)(1 - \Pi(p)) \\
& + \frac{1}{|p \in \Pi(X)|} \sum_{p \in \Pi(X)} (1 - Sil(p))
\end{aligned} \tag{11}
$$

where Sil is the smoothed silhouette and $\Pi(X)$ is the synthesized projection. The first terms in Eq. (11) penalizes the set of pixels in the silhouette that are not explained by the synthesized projection and the second term penalizes the set of pixels in the synthetic projection that are not explained by the silhouette. This is similar to the bidirectional matching we perform.

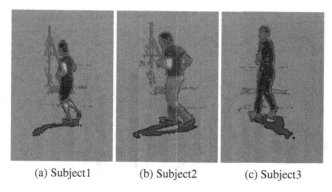

(a) Subject1   (b) Subject2   (c) Subject3

Fig. 4. Image features used for tracking. The silhouette of the subjects are shown as the foreground region, appearance is shown by the intensity values and the oriented edge fragments are shown as red dots.

Appearance (**App**) based likelihood [16,8] is used in recent studies, since it is more informative than likelihoods such as **BiS**. It uses appearance cues in addition to the silhouette (**BiS**). The likelihood requires the segmentation of the projection $\Pi(X)$ into those of the individual body parts $\Pi_i(X)$, which takes occlusion into consideration. The subscript i in $\Pi_i(X)$ indicates that it is the projection for the part i. In the initial frame, the statistics for the part i, Ψ_i is extracted and is assumed to remain unchanged. The appearance based likelihood is formally expressed as below using the statistics for the parts Ψ_i

$$-lnP_{\text{App}}(I; X, C) = \frac{1}{|parts|} \sum_{i \in parts} D_B(\Psi_i || \Psi(\Pi_i(X), I)) \qquad (12)$$

where $D_B(X || Y)$ is the Bhattacharya distance between the two distributions, and $\Psi(\Pi_i(X), I)$ is the statistics extracted from the image I in the region corresponding to $\Pi_i(X)$. The appearance statistics were represented as histograms. In order to make the likelihood invariant to lighting change, similar to [8], we use the statistics from the a and b channels alone of the CIELab representation of the image.

Figure 4 shows the image features used for tracking for the three subjects in Human Eva I. The silhouette of the subjects are shown by the foreground region. It can be observed that the shadow of the subject is part of the silhouette region. The appearance is shown by the intensity values. The set O of observation edge fragments are shown as red dots.

Figure 5 shows the time and ensemble averaged tracking error and deviation of 5 different runs for each sequence. It can be noticed that for Subject 1, in general **BiS** has a very high error. We found the reason for this to be the poor model fit for the subject, which results in a highly multimodal likelihood. Using appearance cues (**App**), improves the tracking performance. Our method (**ROCM**) has the least tracking error. The tracking performance of Subject 2 is equally good with **BiS** and **App**, since Subject 2 is well segmented from the background. Our method performs better than the other

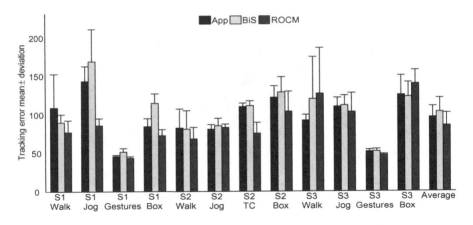

Fig. 5. Tracking error for the twelve sequences compared. Overall mean error for all the sequences compared is shown in the last group. It can be observed that ROCM has the least overall error and it perform better than the other configurations in 9 out of 12 sequences.

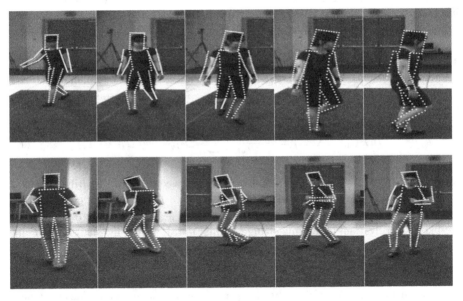

Fig. 6. Tracking results for the Subjects 1 (top row) and 2 (bottom row) using the configuration **ROCM** (without using silhouettes). The best result out of five runs for each sequence is shown.

two methods for this subject too. Silhouettes obtained from Subject 3 are highly reliable, but the subject is completely dressed in black. As a result there are hardly any edges visible due to depth discontinuity (as observed in 4c). Hence, for this subject our method performs worse for two sequences.

Table 1. Runtime and overall error for the three configurations compared. It can be observed that the proposed method has a lower error and runtime.

	App	**BiS**	**ROCM**
Runtime per frame (sec)	29.3	26	13 (+3.3)
Overall error (mm) mean ± std	96 ± 14	103 ± 18	85 ± 16

The configuration **ROCM** has a lower error than **BiS** and **App** in 9 out of 12 sequences. Overall mean error for **ROCM** (shown in Table 1) is more than 15% and 10% lower than that of **BiS** and **App** respectively. The best tracking results for the Subject 1 walking and the Subject 2 jogging sequences, obtained using the configuration **ROCM** is shown in Figure 6. Figure 7 shows two situations where the proposed method switches to an incorrect hypothesis. It can be observed that ROCM at times gets misled by edges that appear to be from the subject. However, it did not result in a complete tracking failure. We believe that such problems can be reduced by using a more accurate model of the subject.

Our HMC framework is currently implemented in Matlab. However, critical computational blocks such as the evaluation of the cost function are implemented in C. We further use data structures such as KD trees [23] to reduce the complexity of the robust oriented chamfer matching scheme. We ran the code on a standard PC and the processing time. It can be observed that our method is significantly faster than the other two methods. The preprocessing time necessary for the MRF segmentation of the proposed method is shown separately (3.3 seconds).

Fig. 7. Incorrect tracking results obtained by using ROCM. It can be observed that ROCM gets misled by the presence of edges that are similar to those from the human subject.

5   Conclusion

In this paper, we describe a robust oriented chamfer matching scheme for human motion capture. The method relies on an MRF based segmentation technique to segment out the subject from the background. Furthermore, we extend the well-known OCM scheme with robust statistics. We compare our approach to the alternative methods used in HMC in recent studies, and show that our method reduces the tracking error by up to 15%, despite of not using background statistics. In the future, we hope to extend our method to scenarios where multiple subjects interact.

References

1. Agarwal, A., Triggs, B.: 3d human pose from silhouettes by relevance vector regression. In: CVPR, pp. 882–888 (2004)
2. Andriluka, M., Roth, S., Schiele, B.: Monocular 3d pose estimation and tracking by detection. In: CVPR, pp. 623–630 (2010)
3. Ballan, L., Cortelazzo, G.M.: Marker-less motion capture of skinned models in a four camera set-up using optical flow and silhouettes. In: 3DPVT (June 2008)
4. Bo, L., Sminchisescu, C.: Twin Gaussian processes for structured prediction. IJCV 87, 28–52 (2010)
5. Boykov, Y., Funka-Lea, G.: Graph cuts and efficient n-d image segmentation. IJCV 70, 109–131 (2006)
6. Bregler, C., Malik, J.: Tracking people with twists and exponential maps. In: CVPR, pp. 8–15 (1998)
7. Deutscher, J., Reid, I.: Articulated body motion capture by stochastic search. IJCV 61, 185–205 (2005)
8. Gall, J., Rosenhahn, B., Brox, T., Seidel, H.-P.: Optimization and filtering for human motion capture. IJCV 87, 75–92 (2010)
9. Gall, J., Stoll, C., de Aguiar, E., Theobalt, C., Rosenhahn, B., Seidel, H.-P.: Motion capture using joint skeleton tracking and surface estimation. In: CVPR, pp. 1746–1753 (2009)
10. Gavrila, D.M., Davis, L.S.: 3-d model-based tracking of humans in action: a multi-view approach. In: CVPR, pp. 73–80 (1996)
11. Kaliamoorthi, P., Kakarala, R.: Directional chamfer matching in 2.5 dimensions. IEEE Signal Processing Letters, 1–4 (in press, 2013)
12. Kaliamoorthi, P., Kakarala, R.: Parametric annealing: A stochastic search method for human pose tracking. Pattern Recognition 46, 1501–1510 (2013)
13. Kohli, P., Rihan, J., Bray, M., Torr, P.H.: Simultaneous segmentation and pose estimation of humans using dynamic graph cuts. IJCV 79, 285–298 (2008)
14. Liu, M.-Y., Tuzel, O., Veeraraghavan, A., Chellappa, R.: Fast directional chamfer matching. In: CVPR, pp. 1696–1703 (2010)
15. Mori, G., Malik, J.: Estimating human body configurations using shape context matching. In: Heyden, A., Sparr, G., Nielsen, M., Johansen, P. (eds.) ECCV 2002, Part III. LNCS, vol. 2352, pp. 666–680. Springer, Heidelberg (2002)
16. Pons-Moll, G., Baak, A., Gall, J., Leal-Taixé, L., Müller, M., Seidel, H.-P., Rosenhahn, B.: Outdoor human motion capture using inverse kinematics and von Mises-Fisher sampling. In: ICCV, pp. 1243–1250 (2011)
17. Shotton, J., Blake, A., Cipolla, R.: Multiscale categorical object recognition using contour fragments. TPAMI 30, 1270–1281 (2008)
18. Sidenbladh, H., Black, M.J., Fleet, D.J.: Stochastic tracking of 3D human figures using 2D image motion. In: Vernon, D. (ed.) ECCV 2000. LNCS, vol. 1843, pp. 702–718. Springer, Heidelberg (2000)
19. Sigal, L., Balan, A.O., Black, M.J.: Combined discriminative and generative articulated pose and non-rigid shape estimation. In: NIPS, pp. 1337–1344 (2007)

20. Sigal, L., Balan, A.O., Black, M.J.: HumanEva: Synchronized video and motion capture dataset and baseline algorithm for evaluation of articulated human motion. IJCV 87, 4–27 (2010)
21. Sigal, L., Isard, M., Haussecker, H.W., Black, M.J.: Loose-limbed people: Estimating 3d human pose and motion using non-parametric belief propagation. IJCV 98, 15–48 (2012)
22. Sminchisescu, C., Triggs, B.: Estimating articulated human motion with covariance scaled sampling. IJRR 22, 371–392 (2003)
23. Sudderth, E.B., Mandel, M.I., Freeman, W.T., Willsky, A.S.: Visual hand tracking using nonparametric belief propagation. In: IEEE Workshop on Generative Model Based Vision, p. 189 (2004)

Video Error Concealment Based on Data Hiding for the Emerging Video Technologies

Francisco Aguirre-Ramos, Claudia Feregrino-Uribe, and Rene Cumplido

Coordinación de Ciencias Computacionales,
Instituto Nacional de Astrofísica, Óptica y Electrónica.
Luis Enrique Erro no. 1, 72840 Tonantzintla, Puebla, Mexico
{fjaguirre,cferegrino,rcumplido}@inaoep.mx
http://www.inaoep.mx

Abstract. The new high efficiency video coding standard (HEVC) includes structures and tools that were not available in previous standards. The macrobock concept was replaced by a quad-tree structure that includes: coding units, prediction units and transform units; also, new parallelization tools are now available. Video transmissions over error prone environments have the need of reliable and efficient error concealment methods. Unfortunately, most of the existent error concealment methods interfere, or do not take advantage of the new structures and tools.

In this work, a data hiding based error concealment method is proposed for the HEVC. During encoding, information is embedded into the residual transform coefficients; this information, is later retrieved and used during the error concealment process. The performed experiments and results show a superior performance when compared against the non-normative error concealment method included in the H.264/AVC joint model.

Keywords: Error concealment, Data hiding, HEVC, Quad-tree, H.264.

1 Introduction

Video technologies constantly evolve, new applications emerge everyday and the video compression technologies have to be capable of following the same evolution rhythm to provide compression solutions to the new video applications. Recently, in a combined effort, the ITU-T Video Coding Experts Group and the ISO/IEC Moving Picture Experts Group, created the Joint Collaborative Team on Video Coding (JCT-VC) with the aim of developing the new video coding standard High Efficiency Video Coding (HEVC) [5].

It is predicted that in some years, HEVC will replace H.264/AVC [12] in most video applications. HEVC introduces some new characteristics such as the quad-tree structure and parallel encoding/decoding tools. Also, some characteristics that were available in previous standards are taken away; one of them, flexible macroblock ordering (FMO), was the basis of many error concealment (EC) methods [15, 19].

R. Klette, M. Rivera, and S. Satoh (Eds.): PSIVT 2013, LNCS 8333, pp. 454–467, 2014.
© Springer-Verlag Berlin Heidelberg 2014

EC methods are designed to deal with lost parts of video that are the product of a failure in the storage media or packet losses during transmission of the coded bit-string. These methods can recover inter coded frames, intra coded frames, or both; in previous standards, intra frames were notably more important than inter frames. In HEVC the inter frames have an increased importance due to the redesign made to the open group of pictures (GOP) and random access features.

There are many approaches for inter EC (also named temporal EC), some of them [14, 13, 19, 17, 15, 18] create a set of candidate motion vectors (MVs) to replace the lost block and select the best candidate by using some distortion measure, these candidates can belong to neighboring blocks [14, 17] or be artificially created [13, 19, 15, 18]. Some other authors have proposed to perform the concealment using a reduced block size [20, 17, 16], instead of the basic block size (16×16 in H.264/AVC and 64×64 in HEVC) they use smaller partitions to achieve better approximations in areas with complex motion or high detail.

The previously mentioned methods had an acceptable performance when working in H.264/AVC but, to achieve their results, they mostly rely on two features that are no longer available in HEVC. First, the block size, in H.264/AVC and previous standards, had been 16×16 samples; now, in HEVC the size was increased to 64×64 and linked to a complex quad-tree structure. The other feature that is not longer available in HEVC is the FMO, this tool was useful to increase the resiliency of slices when transmitted over error prone environments and allowed the possibility of correctly receiving the top, left, bottom and right block neighbors. Also, new structures were introduced to allow parallel encoding/decoding; this interferes with the slice interleaving schemes used in most of the EC methods in the literature.

In this work, an inter error concealment method, based on reversible data embedding is proposed. Information is embedded in the video during the encoding process, this information is retrieved and used in the decoding stage to conceal lost parts of video; the proposal takes into account the newly introduced features in HEVC such as quad-tree partitioning, coding units, prediction units, transform units, and parallel structures. Experimental results show an increase over the widely known inter error concealment method present in the H.264/AVC joint model.

The paper is organized as follows; in section 2, the embedded information and the details of the reversible embedding scheme are given. In section 3, the information retrieval process and the concealment process is presented. The experiments, results, and comparisons are included in section 4. Finally, in section 5, conclusions of the present work are presented.

1.1   The HEVC Standard

The Joint Collaborative Team on Video Coding (JCT-VC) is in charge of the creation and standardization of the new HEVC, which in January 2013 was in the first stage of approval [3]. HEVC, named H.265 by the ITU-T and MPEG-H part 2 by the ISO/IEC, is designed to provide up to 50% of increased coding efficiency when compared to the H.264/AVC video coding standard.

The compression efficiency gain in HEVC is the result of many optimizations that report small gains in the coding process. Also, HEVC encoder has an
increased complexity of about 10 times when compared with H.264/AVC [4].

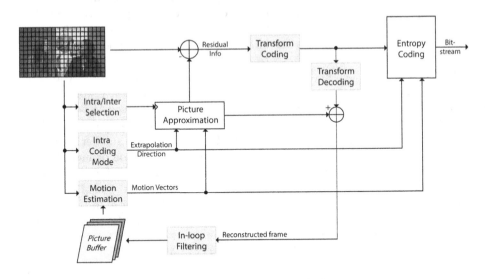

Fig. 1. Basic HEVC encoder block diagram

A basic diagram of the HEVC encoding process is shown in figure 1, broadly
explained, the process includes:

- Partitioning. As a first step, each frame is partitioned into the basic block
  unit, now named coding unit (CU); coding units can be as small (SCU) as
  8×8 or as large (LCU) as 64×64 samples, depending on the encoding configurations. In previous standards, the basic block unit was the macroblock
  (MB) with a maximum size of 16×16 pixels. Also, each LCU can be recursively partitioned into smaller CUs; this process generates tree-like structures
  named quad-tree structures. The quad-tree structure is one of the most relevant characteristics of HEVC and helps to provide better approximations
  to the object shapes in frame.
- Intra/Inter coding. A block level decision of the coding mode is carried out
  based on distortion measures, the idea is to achieve the minimum distortion
  (at LCU-level) while keeping the bit rate within a defined constrained level.
  Once the coding mode has been defined, the intra or inter coding information
  is calculated.
  - Intra information. For intra coding, similar to H.264/AVC, an intra cod-
    ing mode is calculated; many modes are calculated per LCU and there
    are 35 different intra modes to chose from (for luma) [5]. Each CU has a
    prediction unit (PU) shape assigned. PUs are another sub-partitioning
    structure introduced in HEVC, they help to approximate more closely

the shape of objects in the image. There are different PUs available for each coding mode (intra and inter) and each of them has its own coding restrictions [4].

- Inter information. Inter coding requires of the calculation of motion-vectors (MVs), the motion-estimation process is carried out at PU partition level. There is a higher number of PU shapes available for inter coding than for intra coding; up to two MVs are calculated per PU partition, increasing the accuracy of the motion-estimation process and reducing significantly the residuals.

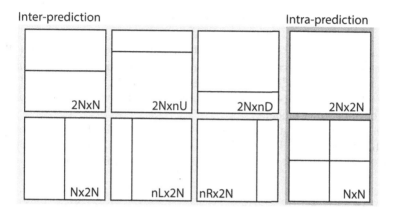

Fig. 2. Allowed PUs shapes in HEVC, all the shown PUs are available for inter coding but only the last two ($2N \times 2N$ and $N \times N$) are alowed for intra coding

In figure 2, the available PUs shapes for each of the coding modes are shown. Notice that some asymmetrical PUs were introduced for inter coding, allowing better approximations in the motion-estimation process than in previous standards.

- Residual calculation. The residuals are calculated between the original block and its approximation at CU level. For some inter coding modes, residuals are not coded.
- Transform coding. The residual block is transform-coded, this is achieved by sub-partitioning each CU residual block into transform units (TU). The partitioning scheme can be recursive, similar to the CU partitioning. There are different sizes of TUs, they can be as large as 32×32 or as small as 4×4, this allows an increased efficiency in residual coding.
- Entropy coding. All the required reconstruction information is coded using context-adaptive binary arithmetic coding (CABAC) in any of its operating modes: regular and bypass [6].
- Reconstruction and buffering. The transmitted picture is reconstructed at encoder. This includes all in-loop filtering process, the resulting picture is a reproduction of the one reconstructed at decoder's side. The reproduced

frame is buffered and used later as a reference picture during the inter coding process.

Many different features were added to HEVC, some of them aim at creating error resilient bit-strings; allowing the decoding of damaged sequences and avoiding error propagation at bit-string level. Nonetheless, sequences decoded from damaged bit-strings keep having the same issues related to error propagation due to inter and intra coding. In fact, the problem is worst because of the increased block size in HEVC; most of the state of the art error concealment techniques do not perform well with the new size.

2   Proposed Method: Encoder

The operations performed by the proposed data hiding error concealment (DHEC) method can be divided according to where they are carried out: encoding or decoding stage. In the encoder, the information that will be used to conceal the lost parts in each frame during decoding, is embedded into the video using the proposed multi-level embedding scheme.

The information is embedded exclusively into the DCT coefficients of the residual blocks, the embedding technique is fully reversible, so the original media can be recovered at decoder if the sequence was successfully transmitted without errors.

2.1   Information to Embed

During the design of a DHEC method, many important decisions are taken, maybe the most important, is which information will be embedded into the media. This information has to be carefully selected to be lightweight but useful during the error concealment stage. An excess in the amount of embedded information will cause a considerable increment in the video bit rate; on the other hand, if the information is lightweight but not useful enough, its embedding will only represent a disadvantage.

The proposed method embeds the complete LCU partitioning structure, including the PU partitions. This information is available during the encoding stage and can be used to improve the reconstruction during concealment of damaged areas in frame.

The coding scheme is simple, each partitioning level in the LCU structure is coded using '1'; when the maximum depth in the partition branch has been reached, '0' is coded. After each '0', the corresponding PU structure is coded using the same variable-length codes that are used during the encoding stage in the Test Model under Consideration (TMuC) of HEVC [7], with a maximum requirement of 5 bits per PU shape. In figure 3, a graphical example of a LCU partitioning structure and its associated Tree-CU (TCU) is shown, the bit-string that represents the LCU structure is: 1110000100000011000000100001000010000. In the example bit-string, the PU codes are missing; as it was aforementioned, PU codes should be located after each '0' in the bit-string.

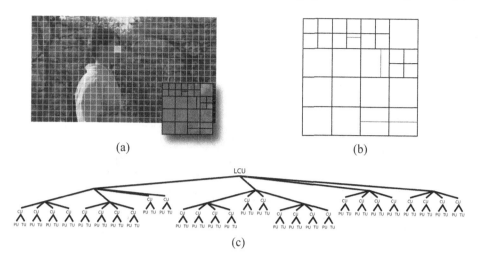

Fig. 3. Frame partitioning example in HEVC. (a) Frame partitioned into 64×64 LCUs, at the same time each LCU has its own structure. (b) Example of a LCU partitioning structure. (c) TCU of the structure shown in (b).

In the worst case, a maximum of 85 bits are needed to codify the most complex CU structure, and 320 bits to describe the same structure using the longest PU codes. This structure would be difficult to find in a real case because it involves the smallest CU partition size and two asymmetrical PU shapes.

Even in the worst case, where 320 bits are embedded, using an insertion rate of one bit per coefficient, in a 64 × 64 block with 4,096 transform coefficients, less than 10% of them will be needed for embedding.

2.2 Multilevel Embedding Scheme

Information is embedded into the DCT transform coefficients. Those coefficients belong to the block residuals generated during the motion compensation process. Thanks to the new structures introduced in HEVC, most of the transform coefficients are zero, this due to object shapes are closely approximated by using quad-tree structures and asymmetrical PUs; also, the transform process is carried out more efficiently by the newly introduced TUs. These zeros represent an excellent environment to implement a reversible embedding scheme.

The proposed method includes a multi-level embedding scheme where each LCU is evaluated previous to its modification, to decide if the information will be embedded into the first or second level, with the latter having more embedding space than the former but also introducing a higher distortion; if even the second level is not enough to embed the information, the embedding process is omitted. The EC method is prepared to perform concealment even when no information is available for the lost block. This embedding scheme is implemented to distribute the *synthetic coefficients* (created by embedding information into zero-coefficients) in a better way, and to avoid embedding the information only in the first TUs of the LCU. The number and amount of embedded information per level, is adjustable according to the application distortion constraints; in this work a two-level embedding scheme is used.

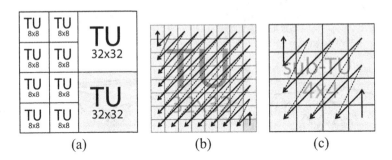

      (a)   (b)   (c)

Fig. 4. Embedding scheme order. (a) CU partitioned into TUs for coding. (b) Each TU is divided into 4×4 blocks to perform embedding. The inverse diagonal order is used also at block level. (c) Embedding is performed in a inverse diagonal order at coefficient level.

Multilevel embedding scheme is described in figure 4, 4×4 transform coefficient blocks are used as embedding space in an inverse diagonal order (figure 4(c)). Exclusively zero-coefficients are used for embedding, and the last zero-coefficient of each block is used as flag to indicate if the block contains any information to be retrieved. A number of 4×4 blocks is assigned to each level according to the transform unit size (except by the 4×4 TU size), this is directly related to the amount of embedded information allowed per level. Table 1 reflects the number of blocks per level and transform sizes used in this work.

Table 1. Two-level embedding scheme configuration

TU Size	Level 1	Level 2
4×4	4 coefficients	4 coefficients
8×8	1 block	3 blocks
16×16	4 blocks	12 blocks
32×32	16 blocks	48 blocks

The embedding scheme aims at introducing only a small distortion by embedding the information in the last 4×4 block coefficients of each TU. Those coefficients represent high frequency information, the *human visual system* is less sensitive to high frequency distortions than to those in low frequency [8], so, most of the introduced distortion is not visible when the sequence is decoded using a normal decoder without the proposed DHEC feature.

2.3 Embedding Algorithm

To achieve reversibility two rules are followed, first, only zero-coefficients are modified, and second, all the non-zero coefficient values are incremented by one. Over the zero-coefficients, even-odd signaling is used to embed the bit value. The embedding procedure is described by the flow chart in figure 5(a), the algorithm is applied starting from the last coefficients in each TU block, following the aforementioned inverse diagonal order.

There is no need to verify for overflow in the coefficient values, this is, because the complete process is performed after the quantization procedure. If lossless compression mode is used, it is necessary to add a verification step to avoid increasing the maximum coefficient values.

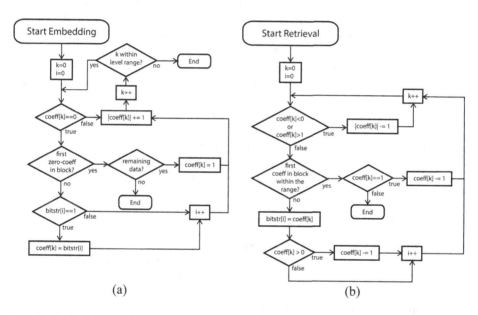

(a)   (b)

Fig. 5. Embedding and retrieval process flow charts; $coeff[k]$ and $bitstr[i]$ refer to the current coefficient and bit-string element, respectively. (a) Embedding process applied at TU level. (b) Retrieval process shown at TU level.

The embedding is carried out using an inverse diagonal order, during this process, each transform unit is partitioned into 4×4 blocks; the first zero-coefficient of each 4×4 block (in embedding order) is used as flag to signal if information was or not embedded, this coefficient might not be the first (last in HEVC coding order and first in embedding order) to be found but the first zero-coefficient. As an example, the embedding order at block level into a 32×32 TU is shown in figure 4(b) and the order at coefficient level is shown in figure 4(c).

In the proposed method, any complex slice interleaving scheme is avoided; those schemes interfere with the parallel encoding tools available in HEVC. Instead, the information belonging to a LCU is embedded within the LCU in the same position into the next slice, making it compatible with the wavefront parallel processing (WPP) feature in HEVC [5].

3   Proposed Method: Decoder

As it was mentioned in section 2.2, in some cases no information is embedded. The proposed scheme assigns a generic structure to the lost blocks whose concealment information is also lost or was not embedded due to lack of embedding space. The information retrieval process in the proposed method is integrated in the decoding stage; the information of each block is retrieved previously to the dequantization process, in this way, the host block is decoded without added distortions. This characteristic helps to make the embedding technique fully reversible, being capable of recovering the original block generated at encoder side, avoiding impairments between the decoded frame and the reference frame used during encoding. Obviously, this happens only when no errors occurred during transmission.

The original LCU structure, including its PUs is recovered from the retrieved information and assigned to the lost block; then, an outer boundary matching algorithm (OBMA), based on the mean of absolute differences (MAD) measure, is used to evaluate and choose the best replacement from a defined set of motion candidates, this process is carried out at PU level.

3.1   Multilevel Retrieval Scheme

The information retrieval process is simple and relies on flags that indicate if the 4×4 transform coefficient blocks contain or not embedded information. The retrieval process is described by the flow chart in figure 5(b); notice how the process is a mirrored version of the embedding algorithm, but without taking into account the levels it is fully guided by the block flags.

3.2   Selecting the Best Neighbor

The process of evaluating the best candidate is independent from the block structure origin, the structure can be the one generated from the retrieved information, or a generic one assigned to all the lost blocks whose information was lost or not embedded. The best neighbor selection has two main characteristics: the candidate list and the MAD calculation. These two characteristics are explained next:

- Candidate list. The candidate list includes the top, top-left, left, bottom-left, bottom, right and top-right neighboring PUs within the same frame. It also includes zero-motion and collocated neighbors in both the next and previous frames. Anyway, not all candidates are evaluated; a maximum of 4 neighbors, plus the zero-motion case, are evaluated per PU partition. Also, each PU partition has its own candidates depending on its shape and position. The PU partition shapes, position, and their possible neighboring candidates are shown in figure 6; all the presented shapes can use the collocated and zero-motion candidates.

In figure 6, each partition has an arrow, this arrow signals the called *most important neighbor* (MIN); this means, that the partition is more likely to share motion information with that specific partition than with any other. It is common to some neighboring partitions not to be available, this is due to the concealment order (up-down, left-right). To improve concealment, a reach-forward scheme is implemented; this means that if the neighboring PU is not available, and it is the case of a MIN, the next PU along the same direction is reached and taken as a candidate. This technique is not always useful and its use is mostly restricted to cases when only one LCU is coded per slice.

– OBMA based on MAD. The MAD between the outer pixels of each PU partition and the outer pixels of each candidate is used to select the best replacement. The pixels involved in the calculation of MAD depend on the partition shape and position; in figure 7, each partition and the pixels involved in the MAD calculation are signaled. This selection is based on the way the partitioning scheme works in HEVC; if two partitions within the same CU share the same motion information, there is no reason of the partition to exist, a bigger partition would had been coded instead. Therefore, PU partitions withing the same CU are ignored in the motion candidate list creation and in the MAD calculation.

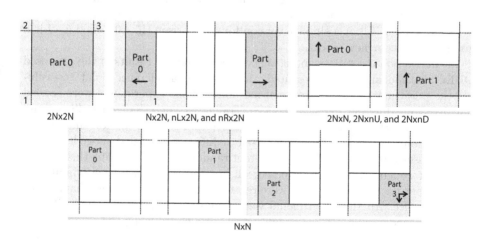

Fig. 6. Different PUs and their candidates. The partition number and its neighboring motion candidates are shown in a darker color, arrows signal the direction over which the reach-forward technique is used.

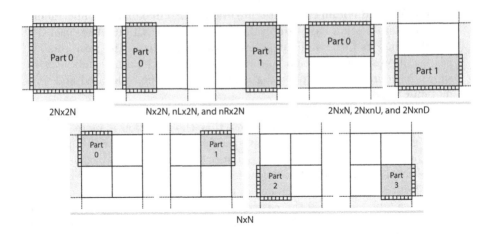

Fig. 7. Different PU shapes and the pixels involved in the calculation of the MAD measure, used to select the best replacement for the lost part

4   Experiments and Results

Achieving a fair comparison between the proposed DHEC method and the state of the art approaches is not an easy task. Due to the new features introduced in HEVC and those that were removed in comparison with H.264/AVC, the direct implementation of most of the previous methods is not possible. A widely known temporal error concealment (TEC) method was proposed by Wang et al. [9], it is based on candidate evaluation using boundary matching algorithm (BMA) [14]. The concealment results achieved with [9] are fair, so, it was adopted as the non-normative TEC method in the H.264/AVC joint model (JM); many different works use BMA [14] or a simpler version for comparison [15–20], making of it a good reference for new works.

In this section a comparison between the concealment results of the proposed DHEC method and [9] is presented; this provides a reference point to evaluate the performance of the proposed method. All the experiments were carried out over four different video sequences: Traffic, Kimono, KristenAndSara, and RaceHorses; they were chosen based on their resolution and motion characteristics. The four test sequences were exposed to different random damage levels, i.e. packet losses were simulated using different random patterns, during this process only inter coded frames were affected; all losses were at slice level (simulating one slice per packet in a scenario were retransmission is not feasible), having one LCU per slice. All the experiments were performed using the HEVC's TMuC in its HM9.1rc1 version [11], also, all videos were coded using the recommendations given in [10], using the *Low-delay B - Main* configuration, and disabling the Sample Adaptive Offset (SAO) and Sign Hiding features.

Table 2. Error concealment results with a 1% of random loss; values in bold represent the best result for each experiment. The PSNR [2] and the SSIM [1] metrics are used to evaluate and compare the quality of the concealed sequences

Sequence	Resolution	HM9.1rc1 - Zero		Wang, et al. [9]		Proposed DHEC	
		PSNR (dB)	SSIM	PSNR (dB)	SSIM	PSNR (dB)	SSIM
Traffic	2560x1600	22.2249	0.8677	29.8122	0.9639	**33.2031**	**0.9841**
Kimono	1920x1080	24.0473	0.8861	32.5780	0.9543	**34.1789**	**0.9669**
KristenAndSara	1280x720	16.2563	0.6866	34.5961	0.9755	**35.3161**	**0.9800**
RaceHorses	832x480	20.0839	0.7855	26.4078	0.8825	**28.7902**	**0.9217**

Table 3. Error concealment results with 5% of random loss; values in bold represent the best result for each experiment. The PSNR [2] and the SSIM [1] metrics are used to evaluate and compare the quality of the concealed sequences

Sequence	Resolution	HM9.1rc1 - Zero		Wang, et al. [9]		Proposed DHEC	
		PSNR (dB)	SSIM	PSNR (dB)	SSIM	PSNR (dB)	SSIM
Traffic	2560x1600	16.2081	0.5772	24.5597	0.8819	**27.5680**	**0.9354**
Kimono	1920x1080	18.1355	0.6355	27.3605	0.8363	**28.7508**	**0.8782**
KristenAndSara	1280x720	11.2851	0.4034	29.7259	0.9287	**29.8487**	**0.9385**
RaceHorses	832x480	14.5185	0.4709	21.4956	0.6879	**23.5374**	**0.7660**

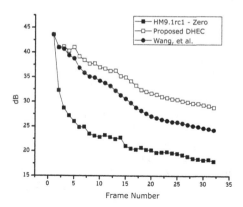

Fig. 8. Error propagation through frames due to inter-prediction coding with 1% of damage. Low quality concealment in a current frame introduces distortions into following frames due to inter prediction, this effect heavily degrades the sequence quality

Table 2 shows the comparison between the results of the proposed method, the method proposed by Wang et al. [9], and zero substitution (lost blocks are substituted by black areas). It can be seen that the proposed method performs better in the sequences Traffic and RaceHorses, both classified as high motion, with a maximum PSNR gain of 3.39 dB over [9]; it is noticeable that the same result pattern is maintained in the SSIM measurements. In table 3 the proposed method achieves better concealment results in the same two sequences. Nonetheless, it has to be mentioned that the proposed method introduced an average increment of 3.83% in the bit rate of the sequences; the increment has a strong relation with the video motion characteristics and image detail.

One of the main reasons to perform concealment over damaged frames is to avoid the error propagation due to inter and intra prediction. In figure 8, the error propagation through frames is shown, notice how the proposed method helps to control the propagation better than Wang et al. [9].

5   Conclusions

New features were included in the new HEVC standard; these features are not compatible with most of the state of the art video error concealment methods. In this work we presented a data hiding based error concealment approach; with the aid of information available during encoding stage such as the LCU structure, and performing the concealment at PU level, it is possible to obtain superior results to [9], especially in high motion videos. The presented method was specially designed to be compatible with the new features in HEVC, and can be used to provide error concealment to the new generation of video applications.

Acknowledgments. The authors would like to thank to CONACYT for the grant number 261243.

References

1. Wang, Z., Bovik, A.C., Sheikh, H.R., Simoncelli, E.P.: Image quality assessment: from error visibility to structural similarity. IEEE Transactions on Image Processing 13(4), 600–612 (2004)
2. ITU-T.: J.247: Objective perceptual multimedia video quality measurement in the presence of a full reference (2008) (online) http://www.itu.int/
3. New video codec to ease pressure on global networks - press release, http://www.itu.int/net/pressoffice/press/_releases/2013/01.aspx
4. Pourazad, M., Doutre, C., Azimi, M., Nasiopoulos, P.: HEVC: The New Gold Standard for Video Compression: How Does HEVC Compare with H.264/AVC? IEEE Consumer Electronics Magazine 1(3), 36–46 (2012)
5. Sullivan, G.J., Ohm, J., Han, W., Wiegand, T.: Overview of the High Efficiency Video Coding (HEVC) Standard. IEEE Transactions on Circuits and Systems for Video Technology 22(12), 1649–1668 (2012)
6. Sole, J., Joshi, R., Nguyen, N., Ji, T., et al.: Transform Coefficient Coding in HEVC. IEEE Transactions on Circuits and Systems for Video Technology 22(12), 1765–1777 (2012)
7. Kim, I.-K., McCann, K., Sugimoto, K., Bross, B., Han, W.: High Efficiency Video Coding (HEVC) Test Model 9 Encoder Description. Document of Joint Collaborative Team on Video Coding, JCTVC-K1002v2 (2012)
8. Richardson, I.E.G.: Video Codec Design, Developing Image and Video Compression System. John Wiley & Sons Ltd., England (2002)
9. Wang, Y.-K., Hannuksela, M.M., Varsa, V., Hourunranta, A., Gabbouj, M.: The error concealment feature in the H.26L test model. In: International Conference on Image Processing, vol. 2, pp. II-729–II-732. IEEE (2002)

10. Bossen, F.: Common test conditions and software reference configurations. Document of Joint Collaborative Team on Video Coding, JCTVC-K1100 (2012)
11. HEVC's Test Model under Consideration, Software Repository,
    `https://hevc.hhi.fraunhofer.de/svn/svn_HEVCSoftware/tags/HM-9.1rc1/`
12. Wiegand, T., Sullivan, G.J., Bjontegaard, G., Luthra, A.: Overview of the H.264/AVC video coding standard. IEEE Transactions on Circuits and Systems for Video Technology 13(7), 560–576 (2003)
13. Pyun, J.-Y., Lee, J.-S., Jeong, J.-W., Jeong, J.-H., Ko, S.-J.: Robust error concealment for visual communications in burst-packet-loss networks. IEEE Transactions on Consumer Electronics 49(4), 1013–1019 (2003)
14. Lam, W.-M., Reibman, A.R., Liu, B.: Recovery of lost or erroneously received motion vectors. In: IEEE International Conference on Acoustics, Speech, and Signal Processing, vol. 5, pp. 417–420. IEEE (1993)
15. Seth, K., Kamakoti, V., Srinivasan, S.: Efficient Motion Vector Recovery Algorithm for H.264 Using B-Spline Approximation. IEEE Transactions on Broadcasting 56(4), 467–480 (2010)
16. Kim, D., Yang, S., Jeong, J.: A new temporal error concealment method for H.264 using adaptive block sizes. In: IEEE International Conference on Image Processing, vol. 3, pp. III-928–III-931. IEEE (2005)
17. Xu, Y., Zhou, Y.: H.264 video communication based refined error concealment schemes. IEEE Transactions on Consumer Electronics 50(4), 1135–1141 (2004)
18. Zheng, J., Chau, L.-P.: Efficient motion vector recovery algorithm for H.264 based on a polynomial model. IEEE Transactions on Multimedia 7(3), 507–513 (2005)
19. Zhou, J., Yan, B., Gharavi, H.: Efficient Motion Vector Interpolation for Error Concealment of H.264/AVC. IEEE Transactions on Broadcasting 57(1), 75–80 (2011)
20. Chen, T., Zhang, X., Shi, Y.-Q.: Error concealment using refined boundary matching algorithm. In: International Conference on Information Technology: Research and Education, pp. 55–59. IEEE (2003)

Incorporating Audio Signals into Constructing a Visual Saliency Map

Jiro Nakajima[1], Akihiro Sugimoto[2], and Kazuhiko Kawamoto[1]

[1] Chiba University, Chiba, Japan
nakajima13@chiba-u.jp, kawa@faculty.chiba-u.jp
[2] National Institute of Informatics, Tokyo, Japan
sugimoto@nii.ac.jp

Abstract. The saliency map has been proposed to identify regions that draw human visual attention. Differences of features from the surroundings are hierarchially computed for an image or an image sequence in multiple resolutions and they are fused in a fully bottom-up manner to obtain a saliency map. A video usually contains sounds, and not only visual stimuli but also auditory stimuli attract human attention. Nevertheless, most conventional methods discard auditory information and image information alone is used in computing a saliency map. This paper presents a method for constructing a visual saliency map by integrating image features with auditory features. We assume a single moving sound source in a video and introduce a sound source feature. Our method detects the sound source feature using the correlation between audio signals and sound source motion, and computes its importance in each frame in a video using an auditory saliency map. The importance is used to fuse the sound source feature with image features to construct a visual saliency map. Experiments using subjects demonstrate that a saliency map by our proposed method reflects human's visual attention more accurately than that by a conventional method.

Keywords: gaze, visual attention, visual saliency, auditory saliency, audio signal, video, sound source feature.

1 Introduction

Visual focus of attention can be an important cue for understanding human behaviors or supporting human activities [17]. To estimate human visual focus of attention, a computational model of visual saliency map, which identifies image regions that draw more human attention, was proposed by Itti *et al.* [9]. The saliency map is computed based on center-surround contrast of image features such as color, intensity or orientation in an image in a fully bottom-up manner.

Following a method computing a saliency map of a still image [9], many types of saliency maps have been intensively studied. Itti *et al.* [8] employed a feature-integration theory [16] and incorporated low-level dynamic features such as motions or flickers to extend the model to be applicable to a video. Harel *et al.* [6] introduced a graph structure over image maps that arise in

R. Klette, M. Rivera, and S. Satoh (Eds.): PSIVT 2013, LNCS 8333, pp. 468–480, 2014.
© Springer-Verlag Berlin Heidelberg 2014

saliency computation to improve the accuracy of a saliency map. Bruce *et al.*[2] used Shannon's self-information in measuring saliency to construct a model of bottom-up overt attention. Cerf *et al.* [3] proposed combining face detection with a saliency map computed from contrasts of image features. Taking into account the difference between central (fovea) and peripheral areas in computing a saliency map was proposed by Kubota *et al.* [12]. Saliency computation from an ego-centric video was proposed by Yamada *et al.* [17].

Eye movements are indeed affected by visual stimuli and visual attention is drawn accordingly. Human attention, however, is attracted by auditory stimuli as well. When we hear an extraordinary sound, we tends to look at the direction of the sound source even if it is not visually salient. A video usually contains sounds and auditory stimuli are available. Nevertheless, most existing methods for computing saliency from a video discard such sounds and use image features alone. Combining image features with sounds in saliency computation is promising to significantly improve the accuracy of a saliency map.

In contrast to visual saliency, few models to determine salient audio signals have been proposed [11,14,10]. Kayer *et al.* [11] proposed an auditory saliency map model to detect salient sounds embedded in noisy backgrounds. In that work, the sound wave is converted to a time-frequency representation to have an intensity image and then important auditory features (intensity, frequency contrast and temporal contrast) are extracted on different scales. An auditory saliency map is computed using the center-surround contrast of the features in the same way of computing a visual saliency map.

In the context of human-machine interaction, there are a few attempts in which audio signals are taken into account to construct a visual saliency map [7,14]. Since they focus on real-time performance for the interaction, the accuracy of constructed saliency maps is not deeply investigated; how to control the system in real time is more important. In [7], for example, a microphone array is used as a device to estimate high salient auditory stimuli in real time. Visual saliency map and auditory saliency map are fused by a weighted linear combination into a single audio-visual saliency map, which is used for robot head control. This method, however, cannot be applicable without any microphone array. Moreover, it cannot deal with recorded videos.

This paper presents a method for constructing a visual saliency map for a video[1] by incorporating sounds in its computation. We assume a single moving sound source. To treat sounds like image features, we introduce a sound source feature which represents the location of a sound source in each frame. The location of a sound source is computed using the correlation with audio signals and sound source motion by [18]. Our method then computes the importance of the sound source feature in each frame using an auditory saliency map by [11]. The importance is then used to fuse the sound source feature with image features. By this way, we obtain a visual saliency map that reflects sounds contained in

---

[1] Hereafter, we discriminate an image sequence from a video to highlight the existence/non-existence of sounds. In this paper, a video contains audio signals while an image sequence does not.

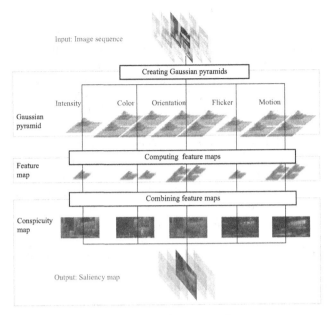

Fig. 1. Computation flow of a saliency map

a video. Experiments using subjects confirm that our proposed saliency map outperforms a saliency map computed using image features alone.

2   Visual Saliency Map

We here present a brief overview on how to compute a bottom-up visual saliency map [8]. The core concept in computational visual saliency is extracting regions with vastly different image features than their surrounding regions. Figure 1 depicts the computation flow. An input frame is decomposed into a set of multi-scale feature maps which extract local spatial discontinuities in the modalities of color, intensity, orientation, motion and flicker. All feature maps are then combined into a unique scalar saliency map which encodes for the salience of a location in the scene irrespectively of the particular feature which detected this location as conspicuous.

Gaussian pyramids [5], hierarchical images in multi-scales, are first created from an input frame. For color and intensity, five base images are first generated using an input RGB channels, denoted by R, G and B, of a frame: $i = (R + G + B)/3, r = R - (G + B)/2, g = G - (R + B)/2, b = B - (R + G)/2$ and $y = (R+G)/2 - |R-G|/2 - B$. Four base images r, g, b and y are then individually normalized by i and small values (for example, less than $1/10$) are set to zero. Next, Gaussian pyramids of each image are created by iteratively applying the pair of smoothing with a Gaussian filter and down-sampling. We denote the pyramids by $i(\sigma), r(\sigma), g(\sigma), b(\sigma)$ and $y(\sigma)$ where $\sigma = 0, 1, \ldots, 8$ represents the

---

Algorithm 1. The max-lacal normalization $N(\cdot)$

---

1. Normalizing the values in the map to a fixed range $[0, M]$.
2. Set $\bar{M}$ as the average of the local maximal values over the map, each of which is strictly less than M.
3. Multiply $(M - \bar{M})^2$ to all the values in the map.

---

scale. Gaussian pyramid $i(\sigma)$ is used as the intensity feature while Gaussian pyramids $r(\sigma), g(\sigma), b(\sigma)$ and $y(\sigma)$ are as the color features. For orientation, on the other hand, four Gabor pyramids $o(\sigma, \theta)$ ($\theta = 1, 2, 3, 4$) are created from base image i [5]. For the modalities of dynamic features (motion and flicker), orientation and intensity are used for creating pyramids. Four motion pyramids $m(\sigma, \theta)$ are created from $o(\sigma, \theta)$ and its shift while flicker pyramid $f(\sigma)$ is created by taking the absolute difference of $i(\sigma)$'s between two successive frames.

Feature maps are computed in a center-surround structure akin to visual receptive fields from the Gaussian pyramids of image features. Center-surround operations are implemented by the absolute across-scale subtraction, i.e., absolute difference between a fine and a coarse scales in a pyramid in concern. When two images at different scales in a pyramid are given, the bilinear interpolation [4] is first applied to a smaller image so that the two images have the same size. The corresponding pixel-wise subtraction between the two images is then computed. We note that color feature maps follow the opponent color theory (we thus have two color-opponent feature maps). We first compute the subtraction in each pair of opponent color and then apply the absolute across-scale subtraction.

For each feature, its corresponding feature maps are individually normalized and then combined to have a single conspicuity map. The max-local normalization[2][9], denoted by $N(\cdot)$, highlights the most discriminative features in each feature map. Algorithm 1 shows the detail of this normalization. The across-scale addition is applied to normalized feature maps, which results in a conspicuity map. We remark that two color-opponent feature maps are combined into a color conspicuity map. We denote the conspicuity map for each feature (intensity, color, orientation, flicker, and motion) by $\bar{i}(\boldsymbol{x}, t), \bar{c}(\boldsymbol{x}, t), \bar{o}(\boldsymbol{x}, t), \bar{f}(\boldsymbol{x}, t)$, and $\bar{m}(\boldsymbol{x}, t) \in \mathbb{R}$, where $\boldsymbol{x}$ is the coordinates of a point in a frame and $t \in \{0, 1, ..., T - 1\}$ is the frame number.

Finally, the normalized conspicuity maps are all linearly combined to have a single saliency map for the frame:

$$s_v(\boldsymbol{x}, t) = \frac{1}{5} \left\{ N(\bar{i}(\boldsymbol{x}, t)) + N(\bar{c}(\boldsymbol{x}, t)) + N(\bar{o}(\boldsymbol{x}, t)) \right.$$
$$\left. + N(\bar{f}(\boldsymbol{x}, t)) + N(\bar{m}(\boldsymbol{x}, t)) \right\}. \tag{1}$$

If a point has a large value, the point highly attracts the visual focus of attention. A point with a low value, on the other hand, tends not to attract attention.

---

[2] The range becomes $[0, M]$ after this normalization. M is a given constant value. We set M to 1.0 in our experiments.

3   Saliency Map with Audio Signals

We design a visual saliency map model that reflects saliency of the spatial location of a sound source. To treat sounds like image features, we introduce a sound source feature which represents the location of the sound source in each frame. We also compute an importance of the sound source feature in each frame.

3.1   Detecting a Sound Source Feature

As we assume a single moving sound source, we have to identify the location of the sound source to use the sound source feature. Motion of a sound source can be detected using image features in a video. Therefore, the correlation between sound source motion and audio signals can be used to identify the location of the sound source.

We employ a method [18] to detect the sound source location where the location of a sound source is detected by using a correlation with sound source motion and audio signals. This method computes a visual inconsistency feature representing motion changes at each point in a frame, and an audio inconsistency feature representing audio changes at each frame in a video. From these features, an audiovisual correlation at each point at each frame is computed by tracking points that maximizing the correlation between the visual and audio features using a beam search. This audiovisual correlation represents synchronization of motion changes and audio changes in a video. Assuming that human visual attention is attracted by motions that synchronize with audio signals, it is reasonable to use this audiovisual correlation as our sound source feature. We denote the sound source feature by $h(x, t)$ where x is the coordinates of a point in a frame and t is the frame number.

3.2   Computing Weights for Frames

The sound source feature does not account for changes in audio signal because the correlation between sound source motion and audio signals cannot capture changes of audio signals. When we hear a loud sound, our attention is attracted by the sound at the beginning. Such attention, however, is not preserved if we keep listening to the same loud sound. Therefore, in order to reflect changes of audio signals into a saliency map, we have to assign a weight to each frame which represents discriminative changes of audio signals over frames. We use auditory saliency to measure this weight according to the insight that human attention is attracted by salient sounds.

The auditory saliency map is a model to analyze saliency of audio signals. We employ an auditory saliency map [11] to compute auditory saliency. The auditory saliency map is computed by converting audio signals to a two-dimensional image, i.e., a sound spectrogram, which is a time-frequency representation of a sound. Sound intensity, frequency contrast, and temporal contrast are extracted as image features from the sound spectrogram. The auditory saliency map is

obtained by hierarchially computing differences of these features from the surroundings in multiple resolutions and fusing them in a fully bottom-up manner
like a visual saliency map. We denote the auditory saliency map by $s_a(t, f)$ where
f is frequency.

For each frame, we compute its weight $w(t)$ of the sound source feature from
the auditory saliency map $s_a(t, f)$. Since the dimension of $s_a(t, f)$ is two and that
of $w(t)$ is one, dimension reduction is required. Assuming that human attention
is attracted by a sound derived from a single sound source and that human
turns attention to the most salient sound in each frame, we extract the most
high salient frequency in each frame as the weight of the frame. This selection of
frequency allows us to reduce the effect of audio noises as well. The most salient
sound at frame t is defined as

$$w(t) = \max_f s_a(t, f). \tag{2}$$

$w(t)$ is normalized the range of $[0, W]$. As we see in the experiments, W depends
on the video. We experimentally determine W.

3.3   Constructing a Saliency Map with Audio Signals

We incorporate the sound source feature $h(\boldsymbol{x}, t)$ and its weight $w(t)$ into constructing a visual saliency map. Since $h(\boldsymbol{x}, t)$ is not a conspicuity map, $h(\boldsymbol{x}, t)$
cannot be directly combined with conspicuity maps $\bar{i}(\boldsymbol{x}, t), \bar{c}(\boldsymbol{x}, t), \bar{o}(\boldsymbol{x}, t), \bar{f}(\boldsymbol{x}, t)$
and $\bar{m}(\boldsymbol{x}, t)$, each of which is derived from an image feature. According to the
feature integration theory by Treisman [16], each feature is independently processed in parallel and fused in the end. In our case, independently of the image
features, $h(\boldsymbol{x}, t)$ is computed as the sound source location that is synchronized
with audio signals in a video. We can thus deal with $h(\boldsymbol{x}, t)$ like other image
features and construct a conspicuity map for $h(\boldsymbol{x}, t)$ in the same way as those
for the image features.

The process to construct the conspicuity map for $h(\boldsymbol{x}, t)$ is as follows:

1. create a sound source Gaussian pyramid $h(\sigma)$ from the audiovisual correlation in each scale of the intensity Gaussian pyramid $i(\sigma)$,
2. compute sound source feature maps based on the mechanisms of center-
   surround,
3. compute a sound source conspicuity map $\bar{h}(\boldsymbol{x}, t)$ by normalizing and combing
   the sound source feature maps.

We construct our proposed saliency map for a video by linearly combining $\bar{h}(\boldsymbol{x}, t)$
with the conspicuity maps derived from static image features (intensity, color,
orientation) and dynamic image features (flicker and motion) using weight $w(t)$.

$$s(\boldsymbol{x}, t) = \frac{1}{5 + W} \left\{ N(\bar{i}(\boldsymbol{x}, t)) + N(\bar{c}(\boldsymbol{x}, t)) + N(\bar{o}(\boldsymbol{x}, t)) \right.$$
$$\left. + N(\bar{f}(\boldsymbol{x}, t)) + N(\bar{m}(\boldsymbol{x}, t)) + w(t)N(\bar{h}(\boldsymbol{x}, t)) \right\}. \tag{3}$$

Table 1. Details of videos

Video	♯frames	fps	sound source location
A	121	25	left
B	115	25	right
C	112	25	right

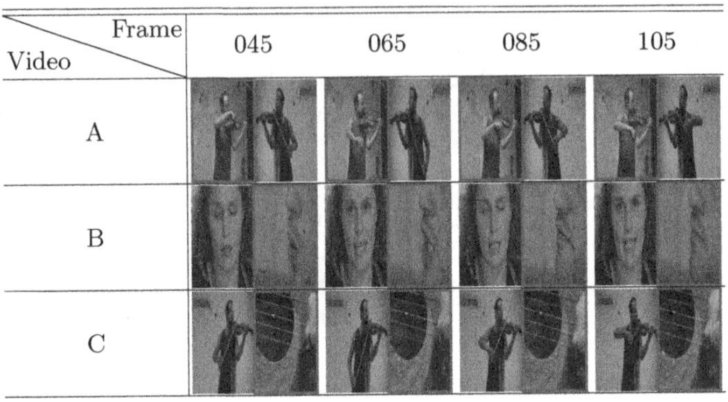

Fig. 2. Example of the input videos. Image sequences surrounded in red indicate the sound source locations.

4 Experiments

The proposed saliency map was evaluated in terms of how much scan-path data fit human visual attention. We compute the conventional saliency map s_v (Eq. (1)) and our proposed saliency map s (Eq. (3)) from input videos, and compared their performances and found that our proposed saliency map outperformed the conventional saliency map.

4.1 Experiment Set-Up

We used three pairs of an image sequence and its corresponding audio signals: videos A, B, and C [1]. Table 1 shows the details of the videos A, B, and C, and some example frames are illustrated in Fig. 2. Each video used in our experiment consists of combined two image sequences aligned in the right and left, and the audio signal sound is attached to the sequence in only one side. We say right if the sound is attached to the image sequence in right-hand side and left if the sound is attached in left-hand side (cf. Table 1). The color feature c was not used in our experiments since all the frames of the videos are monochrome.

We used an eye tracker Tobii TX300[3] to detect scan-pathes of 10 subjects. The scan-path data were used as the ground truth for evaluation. We used a chin

---

[3] Tobii TX300 eye tracker. http://www.tobii.com/en/eye-tracking-research/global/products/hardware/tobii-tx300-eye-tracker/

support to restrict subjects' head movements. With this restriction, the accuracy of eye tracking is increased and stable scan-path data become available. We used speakers that are built in the eye tracker to output audio signals. We obtained 10 scan-path data by displaying the videos to the subjects. We identified as gaze points the points among the scan-path data whose movements are not greater than 2.12 pixels per 0.1 seconds.

4.2   Evaluation Criteria

We used a Receiver Operating Characteristic (ROC) curve [15] and a Normalized Scanpath Saliency (NSS) [13] as evaluation criteria of the saliency map. This is because these criteria are known to be better suited to scan-path evaluation.

The ROC is a curve that plots a false detection rate (labelling a non-gazed location as fixed) as a function of a detection rate (labelling gazed locations as fixed). The more the ROC curve is located at an upper left, the higher the accuracy of the saliency map becomes. Moreover, we calculated an Area Under the Curve (AUC) value of the ROC curve. The closer the AUC value is 1.0, the higher the accuracy of the saliency map becomes.

The NSS measures significant difference from a random scan-path movement. The NSS value is calculated as the average of saliency over the entire saliency map that is normalized into mean 0.0 and variance 1.0. If the NSS value is greater than 0.0, the saliency map is significant compared with a random case.

4.3   Results and Discussion

As mentioned above, W depends on the video. This is because W affects the balance between the sound source feature and the image features. To find an appropriate W for each video, we changed W by 1.0 from 0.0 to 10.0 and evaluated the saliency map of each video using our evaluation criteria[4] (we also tested the cases of $W = 15.0$ and 20.0). Figures 3 and 4 show AUC values and NSS values under different Ws.

From Figs. 3 and 4, as the overall tendency, we observe that as W increases, both AUC and NSS increase at the beginning, then decrease and finally become almost constant. This observation suggests that the accuracy of our proposed saliency map depends on W and that an appropriate W exists that achieves the most accurate saliency map: as W increases, the accuracy is improved at the beginning and then degraded to converge at a constant. The reason for this property comes from the following facts. (1) Saliency of gaze points is increased by incorporating the sound source feature at the beginning. (2) Such tendency continues until the image features and the sound source feature are balanced. (3) Once the sound source feature is overweighted, saliency of gaze points starts decreasing. (4) The sound source feature gradually dominates saliency values (and image features are almost neglected finally). We remark that if the accuracy

---

[4] Note that $W = 0.0$ indicates $s = s_v$. The case of $W = 0.0$ corresponds to the method without using auditory feature.

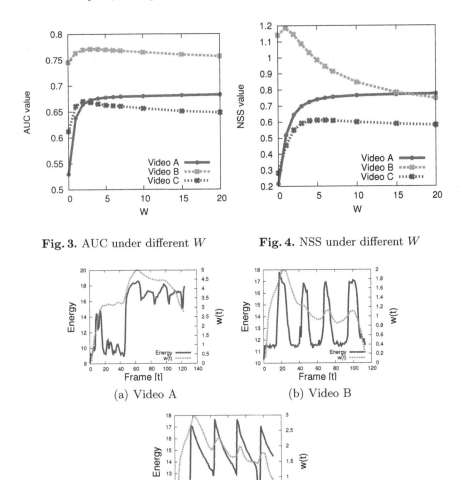

Fig. 3. AUC under different W **Fig. 4.** NSS under different W

(a) Video A   (b) Video B

(c) Video C

Fig. 5. Audio energy and $w(t)$

of sound source feature detection is poor, saliency of a wrong region, i.e., a region incorrectly identified as the sound source location, is increased by incorporating the sound source feature. The accuracy of the saliency map is degraded in such a case. Indeed, in Figs. 3 and 4, there are cases where the accuracy of the saliency map greatly decreases. We selected and fixed the most effective value of W for each video: $W = 5.0$ (video A), $W = 2.0$ (video B) and $W = 3.0$ (video C). These Ws were used to obtain the results below.

Figure 5 shows an audio energy calculated by audio signals and $w(t)$. We observe that $w(t)$ becomes large at frames when the audio energy greatly changes.

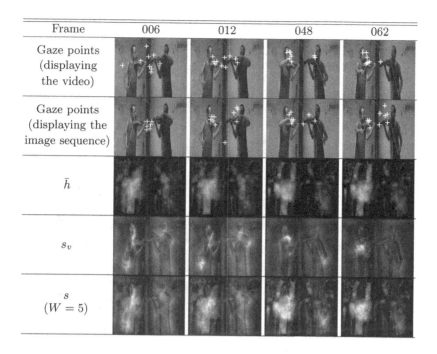

Frame	006	012	048	062
Gaze points (displaying the video)				
Gaze points (displaying the image sequence)				
$\bar{h}$				
s_v				
s ($W = 5$)				

Fig. 6. Examples of images and saliency maps of Video A

Frame	003	022	033	094
Gaze points (displaying the video)				
Gaze points (displaying the image sequence)				
$\bar{h}$				
s_v				
s ($W = 2$)				

Fig. 7. Examples of images and saliency maps of Video B

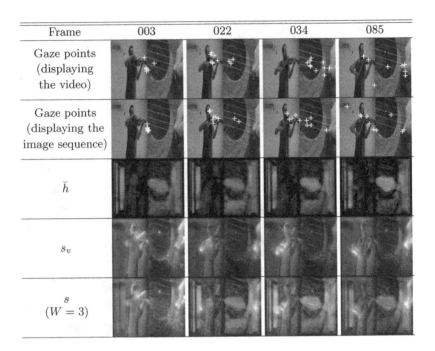

Frame	003	022	034	085
Gaze points (displaying the video)				
Gaze points (displaying the image sequence)				
$\bar{h}$				
s_v				
s $(W = 3)$				

Fig. 8. Examples of images and saliency maps of Video C

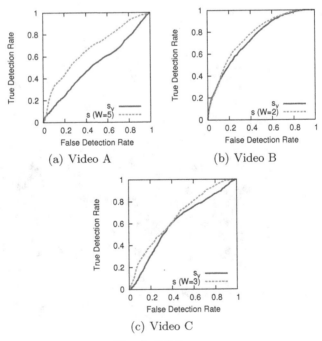

(a) Video A

(b) Video B

(c) Video C

Fig. 9. ROC curve

Thus, it is possible to reflect discriminative changes of audio signals over frames by using $w(t)$.

Figures 6, 7, and 8 show examples of images and saliency maps of videos A, B, and C, respectively. In each figure, gaze points obtained by displaying the video, gaze points obtained by displaying only the image sequence, the conspicuity map of the sound source feature $\bar{h}$, the conventional visual saliency map s_v, and our proposed saliency map s are illustrated in this order. We remark that gaze points are represented as white crosses. In the saliency maps, high salient regions are displayed in white. If the white crosses fall into the white regions, the saliency map is highly accurate. We observe that gaze points are affected by the existence/non-existence of audio signals and the gaze points are drawn to the sound source (left or right) depending on the frame. This indicates that human gazes are attracted by not only visual stimuli but also auditory stimuli. We also observe that (1) $\bar{h}$ is indeed reflected in s_v, and (2) how much $\bar{h}$ is reflected in s_v depends on the frame. Therefore, we can conclude that the proposed saliency map appropriately reflects changes of audio signals in terms of $w(t)$.

Figure 9 shows the ROC curves of videos A, B, and C. The ROC curve of s is located in a more upper left than s_v for all the videos. Therefore, the accuracy of the saliency map increases by incorporating sound source feature $\bar{h}$. This confirms that incorporating audio signals significantly improves a saliency map.

5 Conclusions

This paper presented a method for constructing a visual saliency map for a video by incorporating sounds in its computation. To deal with sounds like image features, we introduced a sound source feature which represents the location of a sound source in each frame. The location of a sound source was computed using the correlation with audio signals and sound source motion. Our method then computed the importance of the feature in each frame using an auditory saliency map. The importance was then used to fuse the sound source feature with image features. By this way, we obtained a visual saliency map that reflects sounds contained in a video. Experiments using subjects confirmed that our proposed saliency map outperforms a saliency map computed using image features alone.

Acknowledgments. This work was in part supported by CREST.

References

1. Barzelay, Z., Schechner, Y.Y.: Harmony in motion. In: IEEE Conference on Computer Vision and Pattern Recognition, CVPR 2007, pp. 1–8 (2007)
2. Bruce, N.D.B., Tsotsos, J.K.: Saliency based on information maximization. In: NIPS (2005)
3. Cerf, M., Harel, J., Einhäuser, W., Koch, C.: Predicting human gaze using low-level saliency combined with face detection. In: NIPS (2007)

4. Gangnet, M., Perny, D., Coueignoux, P.: Perspective mapping of planar textures. Computers & Graphics 8(2), 115–123 (1984)
5. Greenspan, H., Belongie, S., Goodman, R., Perona, P., Rakshit, S., Anderson, C.H.: Overcomplete steerable pyramid filters and rotation invariance. In: Proceedings of the IEEE Conference on Computer Vision and Pattern Recognition, pp. 222–228 (1994)
6. Harel, J., Koch, C., Perona, P.: Graph-based visual saliency. In: Advances in Neural Information Processing Systems 19, Proceedings of the Twentieth Annual Conference on Neural Information Processing Systems, Vancouver, British Columbia, Canada, December 4-7, pp. 545–552 (2006)
7. Huber, D.J., Khosla, D., Dow, P.A.: Fusion of multi-sensory saliency maps for automated perception and control. In: Proceedings of the SPIE (2009)
8. Itti, L., Dhavale, N., Pighin, F.: Realistic avatar eye and head animation using a neurobiological model of visual attention. In: Bosacchi, B., Fogel, D.B., Bezdek, J.C. (eds.) Proceedings of the SPIE 48th Annual International Symposium on Optical Science and Technology, vol. 5200, pp. 64–78. SPIE Press (2003)
9. Itti, L., Koch, C., Niebur, E.: A model of saliency-based visual attention for rapid scene analysis. IEEE Trans. Pattern Anal. Mach. Intell. 20(11), 1254–1259 (1998)
10. Kalinli, O., Narayanan, S.S.: Prominence detection using auditory attention cues and task-dependent high level information. IEEE Transactions on Audio, Speech & Language Processing 17, 1009–1024 (2009)
11. Kayser, C., Petkov, C.I., Lippert, M., Logothetis, N.K.: Mechanisms for Allocating Auditory Attention: An Auditory Saliency Map. Current Biology 15(21), 1943–1947 (2005)
12. Kubota, H., Sugano, Y., Okabe, T., Sato, Y., Sugimoto, A., Hiraki, K.: Incorporating visual field characteristics into a saliency map. In: Proceedings of the Symposium on Eye Tracking Research and Applications, ETRA 2012, pp. 333–336. ACM (2012)
13. Peters, R.J., Iyer, A., Itti, L., Koch, C.: Components of bottom-up gaze allocation in natural images. Vision Research 45(8), 2397–2416 (2005)
14. Schauerte, B., Kühn, B., Kroschel, K., Stiefelhagen, R.: Multimodal saliency-based attention for object-based scene analysis. In: Proceedings of the 24th International Conference on Intelligent Robots and Systems (IROS). IEEE/RSJ (2011)
15. Tatler, B.W., Baddeley, R.J., Gilchrist, I.D.: Visual correlates of fixation selection: effects of scale and time. Vision Research 45(5), 643–659 (2005)
16. Treisman, A.M., Gelade, G.: A feature-integration theory of attention. Cognitive Psychology 12(1), 97–136 (1980)
17. Yamada, K., Sugano, Y., Okabe, T., Sato, Y., Sugimoto, A., Hiraki, K.: Attention prediction in egocentric video using motion and visual saliency. In: Ho, Y.-S. (ed.) PSIVT 2011, Part I. LNCS, vol. 7087, pp. 277–288. Springer, Heidelberg (2011)
18. Yuyu, L., Sato, Y.: Visual localization of non-stationary sound sources. In: Proceedings of the 17th ACM International Conference on Multimedia, pp. 513–516. ACM (2009)

Generation of Animated Stereo Panoramic Images for Image-Based Virtual Reality Systems

Fay Huang*, Chih-Kai Chang, and Zi-Xuan Lin

Department of Computer Science and Information Engineering,
National Ilan University, Yi-Lan, Taiwan, R.O.C.

Abstract. Panoramic image-based representation of real world environments has received much attention in virtual/augmented reality applications due to advantages such as shorter generation times, faster rendering speeds, higher photorealism, and less storage needed when compared to the 3D modeling approaches. In this paper, a novel approach is proposed for generating animated stereo panoramic images based on a single video sequence captured by a panning camera. The techniques involved include generating seamless stereo video textures, inpainting the unsatisfactory regions, and embedding video textures into stereo panoramic images. A player is also developed to provide user stereo visualization and real-time navigation of the image-based virtual environment that are featured with seamlessly-looping animated scenes. The quality of the generated animated stereo panoramic image is satisfactory for virtual reality applications and the computation time is acceptable for practical use.

Keywords: Image-based virtual reality, stereo panoramic imaging, video inpainting, video textures.

1   Introduction

Stereo imaging has been an active research topic due to the rapidly evolving and improving of stereoscopic display technology. Panoramic images have been widely used in various virtual reality (VR) applications, such as virtual touring and navigation, to achieve realistic rendering in real-time. The goal of the developed program is to combine those two features into an image-based virtual reality system. In this paper, the generated output images are referred to animated stereo panoramic images. There are several forms of panoramic images, such as spherical, cubic, or cylindrical panoramas. Among them, only cylindrical form can provide non-contradictionary relative depth perception of any given view within the captured scene. In other words, representing the virtual environment by a pair of cylindrical panoramic images is the only solution which allows stereoscopic visualization [7]. Therefore this paper aims to generate a pair of stereo cylindrical panoramic images featured with animated scenes from a video sequence acquired by an off-the-shelf digital camera. Figure 1 illustrates the concept of the proposed approach.

* Research funded by NSC Taiwan. (NSC 102-2221-E-197 -025 -)

R. Klette, M. Rivera, and S. Satoh (Eds.): PSIVT 2013, LNCS 8333, pp. 481–492, 2014.

Fig. 1. The concept of the proposed approach

A 360° cylindrical panoramic image can be generated by various techniques, such as mosaicing or stitching [2,15], or can also be acquired using specialized sensors such as catadioptric [11]. In particular, stitching is an efficient method if taking only camera panning motion into account. Therefore, panoramic image stitcher has become a standard built-in feature for many models of digital cameras. Many cameras' built-in image stitchers or commercially available panorama makers would automatically estimate all the parameters required for generating the panoramic image based on the provided set of sequential images. The underlying calculations include feature detection, matching, warping, and color blending. Their performances, in terms of the resulting panoramic image and the stitching speed, are in general satisfactory, but none of them are able to generate stereo panoramic images.

Generating a cylindrical panoramic image from a rotating video camera is an alternative approach [5,13]. Ideally the camera should be supported by a special designed rotating platform and only a narrow vertical image region from each capturing position is used to compose the final panoramic image. By this approach, it can naturally bypass camera parameter estimation and image warping processes. Image warping is a process highly depends on the accuracy of the estimated camera parameters. The resulting panoramic images would suffer from "double-image" effects if incorrect warping has been performed. Another major advantage of this rotating camera approach is its ability of generating the stereo panoramic images. However, it can only produce static stereo panoramic images.

Our program adopts the advantages from both methods. It accepts a video sequence captured by a rotating camera (on a tripod) as input, thus no special equipment is needed. The final stereo panoramic images are generated by combining side-by-side image columns from different video frames without image warping. Moreover, during the video capturing process, it is often unavoidable to have walking pedestrians or moving vehicles in the scene, which will then appear in the resulting panoramic images. The program provides a simple user interface, which allows users to specify the undesired object to be removed and then fills the hole with the available background scene by video inpainting technique. The concept of the inpainting algorithm used in the program is similar to [3,16].

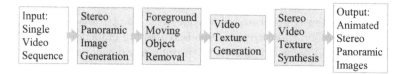

Fig. 2. The flowchart of the proposed framework for generating a pair of animated stereo panoramic images

In order to increase the realistic impression while navigating in a panoramic-image-based virtual reality platform, various hybrid image or video approaches have been proposed [4,8,9,12]. The goal is to preserve and illustrate the moving objects in the scene caused by nature or man-made forces, such as waving trees, fountains or streams, to enhance the realism of the virtual environment. Video data often contains spatial and temporal redundancy, especially for the above-mentioned object motions, information is highly repetitive or quasi-repetitive. The concept of video textures [14] is to create an impression that a video can be played continuously and infinitely based on a given sample video. Panoramic video textures [1] inherit the same concept and allow generating a wide field-of-view video texture. It employs graph-cut algorithms to generate the video textures, which is very time consuming.

The aim of this paper is to achieve a comparable quality of animation effects within a practically acceptable time. The animated stereo panoramic images are a pair of cylindrical panoramic images embedded with multiple stereo video textures. A virtual reality navigation tool (i.e., a player) has been implemented, which is capable of playing such format of animated stereo panoramic images and supports stereo visualization.

2   Program Framework

The framework of the proposed approach is illustrated in Fig. 2. The developed program accepts a single MPG video file and converts it to a set of JPG images for the subsequent tasks. First, a pair of still stereo panoramic images in cylindrical form is generated by image stitching technique. At this point, users are already able to visualize the result through mouse interaction. This is the same as many other commercially available panoramic image viewers/players, except that two panoramic images (one for the left and the other for the right eye) instead of a single image are displayed at the same time. Within the image displaying window, users are able to specify image regions containing undesired moving objects. Then, those regions will be inpainted by copying background patches from other image frames. This procedure can be performed repeatedly until a satisfactory result is achieved. Next, for those background image regions containing dynamic objects, upon user's selection, individual (single-view) video texture will be generated. Solely based on the single input video sequence, it is impossible to construct a "geometrically-correct" stereo video textures. Hence, the last step of the framework is to synthesize another left/right video texture for each of the previously generated video textures. The parallax is estimated by stereo analysis. Finally, those stereo video textures are embedded on the stereo panoramic images while visualizing them through the developed player.

3   Stereo Panoramic Image Generation

The task is to generate two cylindrical panoramic images containing parallax information from a finite sequence of video frames captured by a single rotating camera. The method for generating the stereo panoramic images used in this paper can be considered similar to approaches reported in [7,13]. Peleg and Ben-Ezra firstly proposed the idea of generating a stereo panorama using a single camera. However, the selection of image strips and the determination of image strip[1] width have not been taken into concern. In Huang et al.'s approach, a special designed rotating camera was used to capture a cylindrical panoramic image. The camera rotation speed was assumed constant during image adequation. There was no discussion on the situation when the camera is rotated manually, and as a result, constant rotation speed is on longer possible. For a manually controlled motion, it is possible to intentionally slow down the camera rotation speed or even pause the rotation a bit to capture dynamic features within the scene. Approaches to the above-mentioned issues will be addressed in this section.

3.1   Image Acquisition

The image acquisition approach can be considered as an approximation to the method presented in [7]. Instead of the special designed rotating rig and a line-camera, a video camera mounted on a standard rotatable tripod were used to simplify the image acquisition process. In order to generate a pair of stereo-viewable panoramic images, the camera should be placed away from the rotation axis during capturing, and two symmetric[2] portions of image columns are used to compose left and right images, respectively. The proof that this approach can deliver a pair of stereo-viewable panoramic images is given in [7]. The imaging geometry is depicted in Fig. 3 and an example of a pair of stereo panoramic images is illustrated in Fig. 4. Moreover, it is highly recommended to use leveler to minimize geometrical distortion in the resulting panoramic images. From our experiences, the scan time for a 360 degree rotation between 70 to 100 seconds is the optimal speed to balance the image quality and the processing time.

The video camera is rotated with respect to a fixed rotation axis as shown in Fig. 3. For a 360 degree rotation, the camera's trajectory form a circle. The radius and the center of the circle are denoted as R and $\mathbf{O}$, respectively. Camera's projection center is denoted as $\mathbf{C}_i$, where index i is used to indicate different

---

[1] In [13], image strip is referred to a set of adjacent image columns.
[2] Two image stripes are symmetric with respect to the normal of the camera trajectory.

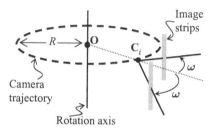

Fig. 3. The imaging geometry of a pair of stereo panoramic images

camera positions along the trajectory. This index will be used also corresponding to individual image frame. Later in the paper, an image frame captured at
position $\mathbf{C}_i$ will be denoted as E_i. The two image strips are formed by a set of
image columns (or vertical lines) with angular distance ω away from the optical
axis of the camera (i.e., dashed line).

3.2   Determination of Image Strips

Due to that the rotation speed of the video camera varies during recording,
each frame should contribute different numbers of image columns to compose
the final panorama. Before determine the image strip in each frame, a quick
image preprocess is performed to identify image frames captured at the same
location $\mathbf{C}_i$. There are two purposes for this process: First, those frames should
be ignored while determining the optimal width of the image strips. Second,
those frames are needed for video texture generation. The pseudocode of the
algorithm is presented in Algorithm 1.

In particular, function *Sampling*() in the algorithm is to resample all image
frames. The original image resolution has been set to 480(width) $\times$ 720 (height)
pixels, and the resampled images have resolution of 90$\times$ 120 pixels. This would
reduce the preprocessing time. After function *CannyEdge*(), images were also
binarized. Therefore, function *Thresholding*() is able to consider the resulting D_j
as an one-dimensional curve, and the values represent the similarity information
of two adjacent frames calculated by function *Difference*(). While the similarity

Fig. 4. An example of a pair of stereo panoramic images

Algorithm 1 : Removing paused image frames

Input: Image frames E_j for $j = 1, 2, ..., m$.
Output: Image frames E_i for $i = 1, 2, ..., n$.

for $j = 1$ to m **do**
    $S_j = Sampling(E_j)$, $S_j = CannyEdge(S_j)$, $S_j = Dilation(S_j)$.
end
for $j = 1$ to m-1 **do**
    $D_j = Difference(S_{j+1} - S_j)$.
end
$I = Thresholding(D_j$ for all $j)$ *% I is an 1D array recording indexes*
                                               % associated to the paused image frames
$E_i = Updateting(I, E_j$ for all $j)$ *% paused image frames have been eliminated*
                                               % from resulting E_i, where $n \leq m$.

---

value is above a given threshold (i.e., 90%), it is to assume that those images were captured at the same location and thus are referred to the "paused image frames". In the remaining contents, n will be used to denote the number of image frames after the removal of the paused image frames.

Next, it is necessary to determine which image columns are to be used to generate the panoramic images. This is equivalent to computing the value of ω (in Fig. 3). A larger value of ω would provide greater depth resolution for stereo-viewing. However, in some cases, especially for the indoor scenes where some objects are relatively close to the camera, a large ω value might cause difficult or impossible for your eyes to fuse the stereo images. The determination of the optimal value of ω requires the knowledge of scene range of interest, the value of R, and the maximum angular image disparity. The scene range of interest defines a near and a far distances of the interested scene, which is to say that users would like to make sure stereo fusion is possible for all objects lie within this range. Let D_1 and D_2 denote these two distances, where $D_1 < D_2$. The maximum angular image disparity, denoted as θ, may vary depending on the applied stereoscopic visualization method. The relation among the optimal value of ω and all other variables defined above is given by Equation (1).

$$\frac{\theta}{2} = \sin^{-1}\left(\frac{R\sin\omega}{D_1}\right) - \sin^{-1}\left(\frac{R\sin\omega}{D_2}\right) \tag{1}$$

To calculate ω given R, D_1, D_2, and θ is not straightforward. Therefore, an approximation formula was derived for this purpose as shown in Equation (2).

$$\omega = \sin^{-1}\left(\frac{0.0078\theta}{R(\frac{1}{D_1} - \frac{1}{D_2})}\right) \tag{2}$$

In the equation, all the distance measurements are given in meters, and angles are given in degrees. It gives a good approximation while the values of R is below 0.5 meters, which is practically true due to the limitation of the extension slider.

The last step in this subsection is to obtain a suitable image strip width. Starting from the left panoramic image, let l_i denote the number of image columns contributed from the ith frame to generate the panoramic image. Further, let

w denote the expected average number of image columns contributed from all frames. Ideally, $w = \frac{1}{n}\sum_{i=1}^{n} l_i$, where n is the total number of frames. If the camera's intrinsic parameters are known, then it is possible to estimate w by the following equation:

$$w = \frac{2f\pi}{\tau n},$$

where f and τ denote the focal length of the camera and the pixel size (assuming squared pixels), respectively. Again, this formula gives a good approximation while the values of R is below 0.5 meters. The value of w is to be rounded to the neatest integer for later calculations. The image strips used for generating the left panoramic image are calculated based on the estimated w.

Let W denote the width of an image frame in pixels. Image strips bounded by columns c_s through c_e in each frame are gathered by the program to perform image stitching calculations. The formulas for obtaining c_s and c_e are as follows:

$$c_s = max\{1, round\left(\frac{W-w}{2} - \frac{f\tan\omega}{\tau}\right) - 3\},$$

$$c_e = round\left(\frac{W+w}{2} - \frac{f\tan\omega}{\tau}\right) + 3.$$

If users have no information of camera intrinsic parameters, then by default, program would select left image strip from column $\lfloor\frac{W}{20}\rfloor$ to column $\lfloor\frac{W}{5}\rfloor$. For the right image strips, symmetric image regions are selected with respect to the central image column.

The value of l_i for each $i \in \{1, 2, \ldots, n\}$ is determined by the result of image stitching, which will be discussed in the next subsection. Finally, let r_i denote the number of image columns contributed from the ith frame to generate the right panoramic image. An important key in generating a pair of stereo panoramic images is to make sure the resulting left and right images have the same number of columns (i.e., equal image width). Although l_i is not necessarily equals to r_i for each i as they are stitched separately, the following constraint has been proposed in this paper to ensure $\sum_{i=1}^{N} l_i = \sum_{i=1}^{N} r_i$. We assume that $l_i = r_j$, where

$$j = i + \frac{n}{\pi}\left[\omega - \sin^{-1}\left(\frac{2R\sin\omega}{D_1 + D_2}\right)\right].$$

3.3   Image Stitching

There have been many algorithms developed for video registration for different purposes. Here, the task is to generate a pair of stereo panoramic images. Base on the proposed camera setup, registration problem is relatively simple due to the constrained camera motion. The selected image strips are used for accelerating the video registration speed. All successive image strips from two adjacent frames are to be registered to form a panoramic image. This process is also referred to as image stitching.

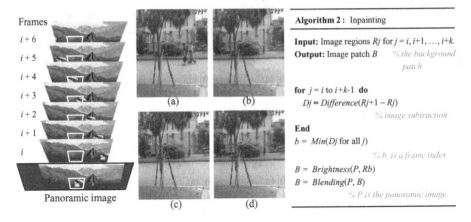

Fig. 5. Left: The concept of foreground moving objects removal. Middle: An example of inpainting result. (a) is the original resulting panoramic image, (b) is an intermediate result after the region has been replaced, (c) is the result after brightness correction, and (d) is the result after blending. Right: Inpainting algorithm.

For each pair of successive image strips, a similarity measure is defined as the average pixel intensity difference within the overlapping region. Image strips are stitched based on the obtained minimum similarity value. For instance, if the left strips from the the ith and the $(i+1)$th frames have been determined having o_i columns overlapping. Then we have $l_i = w - o_i$. The resulting left panoramic image is composed by stitching together l_i image columns from the ith frame, for all $i \in \{1, 2, \ldots, n\}$. An example of image stitching result is illustrated in Fig. 4.

3.4   Moving Object Removal

An image refinement feature has been implemented, that has the ability to remove the undesired foreground moving objects. This makes the developed program more advance than other existing panoramic image makers or stitchers, such as Panorama Maker, PixMaker, Panorama Factory, AutoPano, and PT-Gui. The program provides an interface which allows users to specify regions to be refined, and the specified regions will then be replaced with background scene by exemplar-based image inpainting technique.

Figure 5(left) shows the concept of our inpainting approach, where the undesired object in the panoramic image (at the bottom) has been enclosed by a white rectangle. The available source image frames from i to $i+6$ are displayed above the panoramic image. The actual number of available source image frames depends on the camera rotation speed and the detected paused frames. In each source image frames, the corresponding image regions (also enclosed by white rectangles) are then determined based on the previously obtained l_i and r_i. The program automatically replaces the specified region in the panoramic image with the determined region among the source image frames. The inpainting algorithm is given in Algorithm 2.

It is naturally that the brightness of the panoramic image and the replacement batch R_b (obtained by the algorithm) are different due to that they were captured at different time instant. A brightness correction function, $Brightness()$, has been implemented to reduce the visibility of the seam. Pixel-wise color similarity test was perform between the user selected rectangular region, denoted as U, and the obtained image region R_b from the bth frame. For each pixel position, if the color similarity of two pixels in U and R_b is above a threshold, then the intensity value of the pixel in U will be taken into account. An average intensity value can be obtained through this process. Then, the intensity of image region R_b will be adjusted according to the obtained average intensity value. The output of function $Brightness()$, is the result after intensity adjustment.

Finally, a linear blending scheme is also applied to further reduce the rectangular artifact. An image border region of B (obtained by the algorithm) is defined to perform the color blending. The width of the border was set to five pixels. A linear color blending function is used to adjust the pixels' colors within the border region. Figure 5(middle) illustrates an example where the moving pedestrians have been removed. (a) shows the original panoramic image, (b) shows an intermediate result after the region has been replaced, (c) is the result after brightness correction, and (d) is the result after color blending. The process can be done repeatedly, each time enclosing a different region, until the refinement result is satisfactory.

4   Stereo Video Texture Synthesis

The method for generating a video texture based on a single image sequence has been reported in [6]. Due to page limitation, this section focuses on synthesizing the 'stereo' video texture. Because it is impossible by any way to construct a pair of "geometrically-correct" stereo video textures from a single video sequence acquired by rotating a camera. Therefore, once the left/right video texture has been created, another video texture (for stereo views) must be generated by image synthesis technique.

Given the left video texture, the algorithm used to synthesize the right video texture is presented in Algorithm 3. Assuming that the left video texture consists of k frames, and they are denoted as L_i for $i = 1, 2, \ldots, k$. A function $DynamicArea()$ has been performed to partition the image region into two subregions. One is still background region and the other is dynamic object region. Function $DynamicArea()$ analyzes the intensity variation of each pixel among L_i for all i. If the intensity variation of the considered pixel is below a threshold, then it is assigned as a background region pixel, otherwise, it is assigned as a dynamic object region pixel. The resulting mask M is a binarized image.

Algorithm 3 : Video texture synthesis

Input: Image frames L_i for i = 1, 2, ..., k.
Output: Image frames R_i for i = 1, 2, ..., k.

$M = DynamicArea(L_i$ for all i),   *% M is a mask*
$[L, R] = Cropping(L_1, P_l, P_r),$ *% P_l and P_r are the left and the right panoramic images*
$A = Parallax(L, R),$ *% A is a 2D array storing the parallax information*
for i = 1 to k **do**
   $L_i = UpdatingLeftFrame(L_i, M, L),$
   $R_i = CreatingRightFrame(R),$
   $R_i = UpdatingRightFrame(L_i, R_i, M, A),$
end

Next, a left and a right images are cropped from the left and the right panoramic images, respectively, based on the given left video texture location. These two images L and R are used for calculating the image parallax (or disparity) information. The first step in the function $Parallax()$ is to apply the SIFT (Scale-invariant Feature Transform) feature detection on the two input images. Then, the SIFT-based matching is used to obtain the image disparity values. The result is stored in a 2D array A.

Before generating the right video textures, the input left video textures goes through an updating function, called $UpdatingLeftFrame()$. The reason for this updating is to avoid image "shaking" effect while visualizing them through the developed player. For each frame L_i, image pixels outside of the determined mask M will be replaced by the pixel at the same coordinates in image L. Each frame of the right video texture, R_i, is first created by an identical image from image R. Then, the function $UpdatingRightFrame()$ will be performed to synthesize the parallax for the dynamic object regions. For each R_i, image pixels within the mask M will be replaced by the pixel at the same coordinates in image L_i taking into account the disparity information in A. The procedures and example are illustrated in Fig. 6.

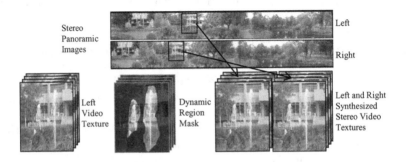

Fig. 6. The procedures of stereo video texture generation.

Table 1. Information of the input videos for generating the video textures

	Original sequence	Video texture	Image size	Computation time
Fountain 1	105 frames	27 frames	382×209 pixels	136 seconds
Straws	80 frames	22 frames	180×210 pixels	121 seconds
Fig. 6	223 frames	25 frames	181×289 pixels	132 seconds
Fountain 2	124 frames	28 frames	255×115 pixels	38 seconds
Leaves	165 frames	24 frames	158×111 pixels	83 seconds

Fountain 2   Leaves

Fountain 1   Straws

Fig. 7. Four video texture examples. The video size and the computation time are given in Table 1.

5   Experimental Results

The program was written in Borland C++ Builder 6.0. The experiments were performed on Windows XP (Service Pack 3) operating system running on a Intel(R) Core(TM) i7 CPU 920 2.67 GHz with 3G of RAM. The image resolution has been set to 480(width) × 720 (height) pixels with frame rate equal to 30 frames per second. The computation time for video registration and stereo panoramic image generation together is between 5 and 9 minutes depending on width of image strips assigned to perform registration. This is considered acceptable if comparing to panoramic video texture [1], which would take hours to process.

We have tested the algorithm on dynamic scene objects such as waves trees or leaves and water fountains. Examples used for experiments are shown in Fig. 7. The original fountain 1 sequence extracted from the input video consists of 105 frames of size 382 × 209 pixels. The resulting video texture has 27 frames. The video texture computation time for this example is 136 seconds. The video information of these examples and the computation times are summarized in Table 1. The aim is to produce video textures consisting of small number of image frames unless user has specified a preferred minimum video texture length. All these examples demonstrate the capability of the proposed approach to generate video textures that are consist of small number of image frames. In comparison to the panoramic video, the proposed approach requires much less memory storage to represent the animated scenes. Some results are also included in supplementary material.

6   Conclusion

This paper presented an approach for generating a pair of animated stereo panoramic images based on a single video sequence. The developed program has the following novel features: First, the input video sequence can be captured by a standard digital recorder, no special equipment or stereo camera is required. Second, it provides an user interface for eliminating the undesired moving foreground objects. Finally, the dynamic sceneries can be represented by seamless-looping stereo video textures to enhance the realistic impression of the virtual environment.

References

1. Agarwala, A., Zheng, C., Pal, C., Agrawala, M., Cohen, M., Curless, B., Salesin, D., Szeliski, R.: Panoramic video textures. In: Proc. SIGGRAPH 2005, Los Angeles, USA, pp. 821–827 (August 2005)
2. Chen, S.E.: QuickTimeVR - an image-based approach to virtual environment navigation. In: Proc. SIGGRAPH 1995, Los Angeles, California, USA, pp. 29–38 (August 1995)
3. Criminisi, A., Perez, P., Toyama, K.: Region filling and object removal by exemplar-based image inpainting. EEE Trans. Image Process. 13 (2004)
4. Finkelstein, A., Jacobs, C., Salesin, D.: Multiresolution video. In: Proc. SIGGRAPH 1996, New Orleans, Louisiana, USA, pp. 281–290 (August 1996)
5. Huang, F., Klette, R.: Astereo panorama acquisition and automatic image disparity adjustment for stereoscopic visualization. Multimedia Tools and Applications 47(3), 353–377 (2010)
6. Huang, F., Yang, K.-M., Wei, Z.-J., Tsai, A., Tsai, J.-Y.: Animated Panorama from a Panning Video Sequence. In: Proc. IVCNZ 2010, Queenstown, New Zealand (November 2010)
7. Huang, F., Klette, R., Scheibe, K.: Panoramic Imaging: Sensor-Line Cameras and Laser Range-Finders. Wiley, West Sussex (2008)
8. Irani, M., Anandan, P.: Video indexing based on mosaic representation. In: Proc. IEEE 1986 (1986)
9. Kimber, D., Foote, J., Lertsithichai, S.: Flyabout: spatially indexed panoramic video. In: Proc. ACM MULTIMEDIA 2001, New York, NY, USA, pp. 339–347 (2001)
10. Kwatra, V., Schodl, A., Essa, I., Turk, G., Bobick, A.: Graphcut textures: image and video synthesis using graph cuts. In: Proc. SIGGRAPH 2003, San Diego, California, USA, pp. 277–286 (July 2003)
11. Nayar, S.: Catadioptic omnidirectional cameras. In: Proc. CVPR 1997, San Jaun, Puerto Rico, USA, pp. 482–488 (June 1997)
12. Neumann, U., Pintaric, T., Rizzo, A.: Immersive panoramic video. In: Proc. ACM MULTIMEDIA 2000, New York, NY, USA, pp. 493–494 (2000)
13. Peleg, S., Ben-Ezra, M.: Stereo panorama with a single camera. In: Proc. CVPR 1999, Fort Collins, Colorado, USA, pp. 395–401 (June 1999)
14. Schödl, A., Szeliski, R., Salesin, D.H., Essa, I.: Video textures. In: Proc. SIGGRAPH 2000, New Orleans, Louisiana, USA, pp. 489–498 (July 2000)
15. Shum, H.-Y., He, L.-W.: Rendering with concentric mosaics. In: Proc. SIGGRAPH 1999, Los Angeles, California, USA, pp. 299–306 (August 1999)
16. Wexler, Y., Shechtman, E., Irani, M.: Space-time completion of video. IEEE Trans. Pattern Anal. Mach. Intell. 29 (2007)

Gray-World Assumption on Perceptual Color Spaces

Jonathan Cepeda-Negrete and Raul E. Sanchez-Yanez

Universidad de Guanajuato DICIS
Salamanca, Guanajuato, Mexico
jonathancn@laviria.org, sanchezy@ugto.mx

Abstract. In this paper, the estimation of the illuminant in color constancy issues is analysed in two perceptual color spaces, and a variation of a well-known methodology is presented. Such approach is based on the Gray-World assumption, here particularly applied on the chromatic components in the CIELAB and CIELUV color spaces. A comparison is made between the outcomes on imagery for each color model considered. Reference images from the Gray-Ball dataset are considered for experimental tests. The performance of the approach is evaluated with the angular error, a metric well accepted in this field. The experimental results show that operating on perceptual color spaces improves the illuminant estimation, in comparison with the results obtained using the standard approach in RGB.

Keywords: Gray-World algorithm, color constancy, CIELAB, CIELUV.

1 Introduction

Color is an important feature for pattern recognition and computer vision fields. Typical applications include feature extraction [1], image classification [2], object recognition [3,4], scene categorization [5,6], human-computer interaction [7] and color appearance models [8]. Colors observed in images are determined by the intrinsic properties of objects and surfaces, as well as by the color of the illuminant. For a robust color-based system, effects generated by the illumination should be removed [9].

The ability of a system to recognize the correct colors, independently of the color source present in a scene, is known as color constancy [10]. Remarkably, the human visual system has a natural capability to correct the color effects of the light source. However, the factors that are involved in this capability is not yet fully understood. The same process is not trivial to machine vision systems in an unconstrained scene [11].

Most color constancy algorithms use assumptions to simplify the computational estimation of the illuminant. The Gray-World (GW) [12] is one of the well-known approaches. This assumes that the average illumination reflected by the objects (reflectance) in a scene under a white light source, is achromatic.

R. Klette, M. Rivera, and S. Satoh (Eds.): PSIVT 2013, LNCS 8333, pp. 493–504, 2014.

White Patch (WP) is another algorithm commonly used. It is based on the assumption that the maximum response in the channels of the RGB space is caused by a perfect reflectance [13]. Some other methods rely on simple statistics of the images, like the Shades-of-Gray algorithm [14], the Gray-Edges (GE) algorithm [15] and the Local Color Space Average [16].

Originally the GW approach was proposed on the non-perceptual RGB color space, despite that color is a property of the human vision that depends on individual perception. Actually, most color constancy algorithms have been proposed and implemented in the RGB color space [17], and, in spite of the existence of a considerable number of methods, there is not a general solution for the color constancy problem.

Among the few research works addressing on the estimation of the illuminant on perceptual color spaces we can mention the study by Kloss [18], where the illuminant was estimated using WP and GW algorithms on CIELAB. Even though this method succeeds for chromatic adaptation purposes, the performance of the approach is not evaluated using the computed illuminant, leaving the accuracy of the estimation unverified. Similarly, experiments on the WP were done for image enhancement issues [19].

In this study, we propose the estimation of the illuminant directly on a perceptual color space. Thus, we focus on solving the color constancy problem. The GW assumption is analysed in two perceptual color spaces. Specifically, the well-known CIE 1976 $L^*a^*b^*$ (CIELAB) and the CIE 1976 $L^*u^*v^*$ (CIELUV) in order to provide a simple and fast transformation. For these two spaces, the Euclidean distance between two points in the space is proportionally uniform to the perceptual difference of the corresponding colors at the points [8]. The performance of the method is evaluated computing the accuracy between the estimated illuminant and a known reference value. Also, the outcomes using the standard GW approach on the non-perceptual RGB color space, are included for reference purposes. In addition, the GE algorithm is included in the comparison because of its outstanding performance [15].

The rest of this paper is organized as follows. In Section 2, the GW algorithm, the color space transformations and our approach, are presented. Section 3 includes the experimental results in the test series, and the observations from the data obtained. Finally, the concluding remarks are given in Section 4.

2   Methodology

In this paper, the outcomes of GW approach in two perceptual color spaces are compared with those obtained using the standard GW, as depicted in Figure 1.

Basically, the methodology consists in the next modules:

- Illuminant estimation using the Gray-World algorithm, for all images in RGB.
- Illuminant estimation using the Gray-World algorithm proposed, for all images in CIELAB.

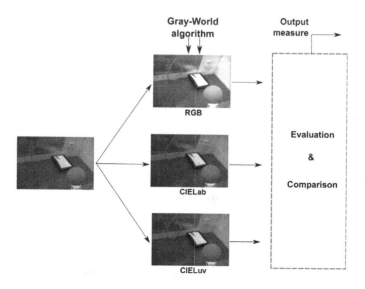

Fig. 1. Methodology for the experimental tests

- Illuminant estimation using the Gray-World algorithm proposed, for all images in CIELUV.
- The evaluation of the accuracy by the angular error between the illuminant estimated and its corresponding ground truth, for each approach.
- The comparison of the outcomes and the measures obtained.

The implementation of these modules requires the study of the image transformation from RGB to the CIELAB or CIELUV, and the corresponding inverse. Also, the assumption particular to the GW method must be given. These issues are addressed now.

2.1 Image Transformation

The algorithm considered throughout this work assumes that the illumination is uniform across the scene. Equation (1) gives the relationship for the color intensity,

$$f_i(x, y) = G(x, y)R_i(x, y)I_i, \tag{1}$$

where, $f_i(x, y)$ is the pixel intensity at the position (x, y) in an image or a frame, $G(x, y)$ is a factor that depends on the scene geometry, $R_i(x, y)$ is the reflectance of the object point displayed at position (x, y) in the image and, I_i is the illuminant in the scene. Index i denotes the corresponding color channel in the image.

Once a color constancy algorithm is applied over an image $f_i(x, y)$, the outcome, $o_i(x, y)$, only depends on $G(x, y)$ and $R_i(x, y)$ assuming that $I_i = 1$, that is, there is a white source illuminating the scene. In this case,

$$o_i(x, y) = \frac{f_i(x, y)}{I_i} = G(x, y)R_i(x, y). \tag{2}$$

2.2   Gray-World Assumption

The GW assumption is the most popular algorithm for color constancy. Proposed by Buchsbaum [12], it is used as reference for other algorithms. The GW is based on the assumption that, on average, the real world tends to gray, and estimates the illuminant using the average color of all pixels. It is assumed that the information given by the average of each channel of the image is representative of the gray level.

The first step in the GW algorithm, is to compute the average a_i, as indicated in (3),

$$a_i = \frac{1}{MN} \sum_{x=0}^{M-1} \sum_{y=0}^{N-1} \{f_i(x, y)\}, \tag{3}$$

where M and N are the number of columns and rows, respectively. Likewise, a_i can be represented by

$$a_i = \frac{1}{MN} \sum_{x=0}^{M-1} \sum_{y=0}^{N-1} G(x, y)R_i(x, y)I_i, \tag{4}$$

$$a_i = I_i \frac{1}{MN} \sum_{x=0}^{M-1} \sum_{y=0}^{N-1} G(x, y)R_i(x, y), \tag{5}$$

$$a_i \approx I_i E[GR_i] = I_i E[G]E[R_i]. \tag{6}$$

The function $E[GR_i]$ is the expected value of the geometry factor G multiplied by the reflectance R_i. Both can be considered as independent random variables, as there is no correlation between the color and the shape of an object. Assuming that many different colors are present in the scene and each color is equally likely, the reflectance can be considered to be a random variable drawn from the range $[0, 1]$, and

$$E[G]E[R_i] = E[G] \left(\int_0^1 x\,dx \right) = E[G]\frac{1}{2}, \tag{7}$$

$$a_i \approx I_i E[G]\frac{1}{2}, \tag{8}$$

$$I_i \approx \frac{2}{E[G]} a_i. \tag{9}$$

Once this global value is known, the illuminant I_i is computed. Assuming that there is a perpendicular orientation between the object and the camera, $E[G] = 1$.

$$I_i \approx 2a_i. \tag{10}$$

Since $f_i(x, y) = G(x, y)R_i(x, y)I_i$, the outcome image is given by

$$o_i(x, y) = \frac{f_i(x, y)}{I_i} = \frac{f_i(x, y)}{2a_i}. \tag{11}$$

2.3 Color Transformations

The perceptual space transformations used in this study are applied to the CIEXYZ color space [20]. In order to transform an image from RGB to CIEXYZ, the RGB space needs to be determined. Here, sRGB is used because it is based in a colorimetric RGB calibrated space [21]. All images need to be transformed from sRGB to CIEXYZ, applying (12) where $\{r, g, b\} \in [0, 1]$ are the normalized color components

$$
\begin{bmatrix} X \\ Y \\ Z \end{bmatrix} = \begin{bmatrix} 0.4124 & 0.3576 & 0.1805 \\ 0.2126 & 0.7152 & 0.0722 \\ 0.0193 & 0.1192 & 0.9505 \end{bmatrix} \begin{bmatrix} r \\ g \\ b \end{bmatrix}, \tag{12}
$$

whereas the inverse transformation is given by (13),

$$
\begin{bmatrix} r \\ g \\ b \end{bmatrix} = \begin{bmatrix} 3.2410 & -1.5374 & -0.4986 \\ -0.9692 & 1.8760 & 0.0416 \\ 0.0556 & -0.2040 & 1.0570 \end{bmatrix} \begin{bmatrix} X \\ Y \\ Z \end{bmatrix}. \tag{13}
$$

The color space CIELAB is computed from CIEXYZ using (14)-(17), obtaining the components of this space.

$$
L^* = 116 f(Y/Y_n) - 16, \tag{14}
$$

$$
a^* = 500 \left[f(X/X_n) - f(Y/Y_n) \right], \tag{15}
$$

$$
b^* = 200 \left[f(Y/Y_n) - f(Z/Z_n) \right], \tag{16}
$$

$$
f(t) = \begin{cases} t^{1/3} & \text{if } t > \sigma^3 \\ t/(3\sigma^2) + 16/116 & \text{otherwise,} \end{cases} \tag{17}
$$

where X_n, Y_n and Z_n are the coordinates of the reference white for the scene in CIEXYZ, t can be X/X_n, Y/Y_n or Z/Z_n, and $\sigma = 6/29$.

For the inverse transformation, three intermediate variables are required, f_Y, f_X and f_Z, shown in (18)-(20),

$$
f_Y = (L^* + 16)/166, \tag{18}
$$

$$
f_X = f_Y + (a^*/500), \tag{19}
$$

$$
f_Z = f_Y - (b^*/200). \tag{20}
$$

Finally, (21)-(23) are used to obtain the inverse transformation.

$$
Y = \begin{cases} Y_n f_Y^3 & \text{if } f_Y > \sigma \\ f_Y - 16/116 & \text{otherwise} \end{cases} \tag{21}
$$

$$
X = \begin{cases} X_n f_X^3 & \text{if } f_X > \sigma \\ f_X - 16/116 & \text{otherwise} \end{cases} \tag{22}
$$

$$
Z = \begin{cases} Z_n f_Z^3 & \text{if } f_Z > \sigma \\ f_Z - 16/116 & \text{otherwise} \end{cases} \tag{23}
$$

The transformation from XYZ to CIELUV begins by computing two intermediate variables, u' and v', given by

$$u' = \frac{4X}{X + 15Y + 3Z},$$ (24)

$$v' = \frac{9Y}{X + 15Y + 3Z}.$$ (25)

Also, it is necessary to obtain the variables u'_n and v'_n, which are given by the coordinates for the reference white $(X_n, Y_n$ and $Z_n)$, using the same set of equations. Finally, the L^*, u^* and v^* components are computed applying the following equations

$$L^* = \begin{cases} (2/\sigma)^3 Y/Y_n & \text{if } Y/Y_n \leq \sigma^3 \\ 116(Y/Y_n)^3 - 16 & \text{otherwise,} \end{cases}$$ (26)

$$u^* = 13L^*(u' - u'_n),$$ (27)

$$v^* = 13L^*(v' - v'_n),$$ (28)

where $\sigma = 6/29$. The inverse transformation is given by Equations (29)-(33).

$$u' = \frac{u^*}{13L^*} + u'_n$$ (29)

$$v' = \frac{v^*}{13L^*} + v'_n$$ (30)

$$Y = \begin{cases} Y_n L^*(\sigma/2)^3 & \text{if } L^* \leq 8 \\ Y_n \left(\frac{L^*+16}{116}\right)^3 & \text{otherwise} \end{cases}$$ (31)

$$X = Y \left(\frac{9u'}{4v'}\right)$$ (32)

$$Z = Y \left(\frac{12 - 3u' - 20v'}{4v'}\right)$$ (33)

2.4   Gray-World Assumption on Perceptual Color Spaces

The Gray-World theory assumes that the average color in an image tends to a gray color. In other words, the mean of each chromatic component tends to this gray color. This assumption, originally was applied to the RGB color space, which has three color components. We propose to apply this assumption on two perceptual color spaces.

The reason for transforming the input image into a perceptual color space is the estimation of the illuminant. Perceptual color spaces are conformed by two chromatic components, additionally to lightness. These two chromatic components are used in our approach while the lighting information is omitted.

CIELAB is the first perceptual color space taking into account. This space is perceptually uniform, and the chromatic components, a^* and b^*, are not correlated with the lightness component L^*. This last, corresponding to a perceptual scale of brightness and excluding any color information. Given an image $f_i(x, y)$, where $i \in \{R, G, B\}$, we compute the component of each pixel, L^*, a^*, and b^*, of the corresponding image on the CIELAB space, using Eqs. (12) and (14)-(17). Following the Gray-World assumption, the average value for each chromatic component is then computed as

$$I_{a^*} = \frac{1}{MN} \sum_{y=0}^{M-1} \sum_{x=0}^{N-1} a^*(x, y), \tag{34}$$

$$I_{b^*} = \frac{1}{MN} \sum_{y=0}^{M-1} \sum_{x=0}^{N-1} b^*(x, y), \tag{35}$$

where M and N are the number of columns and rows in the image, respectively. These two values are very important because they represent the color of the illuminant in this perceptual space.

In order to increase the lighting in the outcome image, for completing the illuminant estimation we suggest the use of $I_{L^*} = \max\{L^*(x, y)\}$ as a third component. That is, we assume that the lightness value for the approximate gray is the highest possible in the image. Experimental tests support this assumption. Therefore, we can consider this approach as a combination between the White-Patch and the Gray-World methods.

Now, the output image will be that obtained using the calculated illuminant. For this purpose, such illuminant must be in the RGB space. For the computation of $I_{i \in \{R,G,B\}}$, the $I_{j \in \{L^*,a^*,b^*\}}$ illuminant is mapped by the sequential inverse transformations from CIELAB to XYZ using (18)-(23), and then from XYZ to RGB using Eq. (13). Finally, the accuracy for the illuminant I_i is evaluated and the outcome image is computed using (2).

CIELUV is the second perceptual color space considered in this study. Although it has some similar properties than CIELAB (two chromatic components and lightness), CIELUV incorporates a different formulation for the chromatic adaptation. Transformations in this space are performed using Equations (24)-(33), applied in a manner similar to the aforementioned process.

3   Experimental Results

In order to test our approaches, we compare their performance with the corresponding outcomes using the standard approach in RGB. We use the Gray-Ball [22] benchmark image set for the experiments. This image set is commonly used for the evaluation of color constancy algorithms as it is labeled with ground truth illuminants. More than 11000 images belong to this image set, however most of these images are highly correlated. Thus, Bianco et al. [5] propose the use of a subset containing approximately the 10% of the complete set. We use this subset, which includes 1135 images.

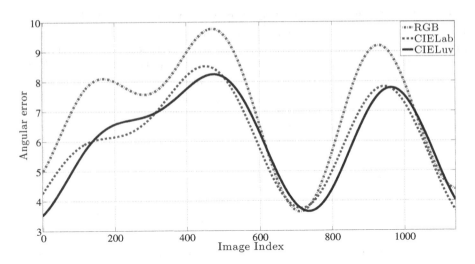

Fig. 2. Curve fitting for each approach showing the trend of the angular errors given by the outcomes. The lower the angular error is, the better the estimation is.

Table 1. Statistical angular errors for the different approaches

Algorithm	Mean	Median	Max
Gray-World (RGB)	7.2	6.0	33.3
Gray-World (CIELAB)	6.5	5.7	25.9
Gray-World (CIELUV)	6.2	5.5	27.1
2nd order Gray-Edge	6.1	5.1	24.0
1st order Gray-Edge	6.0	4.9	23.7

3.1   Performance Evaluation

In order to evaluate the performance of the color constancy algorithms, a metric of performance must be considered. In this case, color constancy must be evaluated according to the estimated color of the illuminant. Hordley and Finlayson [23] proposed a metric well suited for the evaluation of the color constancy, the angular error. In such study, they discussed three good descriptors for the angular error distribution, which are the mean, median and maximum error values. This metric is given by

$$e_{ang} = \cos^{-1}\left(\frac{\mathbf{I}_r\mathbf{I}_e}{|\mathbf{I}_r||\mathbf{I}_e|}\right), \tag{36}$$

where $\mathbf{I}_r$ is the known illuminant in the scene (ground truth) and $\mathbf{I}_e$ is the illuminant estimated by an algorithm under test. It is important to note that for the evaluation of the color constancy, a ground truth is always necessary. These reference values should be provided by the authors of the image dataset. We must note that the lower the angular error is, the better the estimation is.

Fig. 3. Three examples out of the 1135 images where the angular error is shown in the gray ball. The ideal image is included. a) ApacheTrial frame no. 01520, b) CIC2002 frame no. 10150, c) DeerLake frame no. 00140.

Table 2. Computing time for each approach

Algorithm	Time (ms)
Gray-World (RGB)	0.57
Gray-World (CIELUV)	15.73
Gray-World (CIELAB)	31.22
1st Gray-Edge	130.44
2nd Gray-Edge	216.20

3.2   Data Obtained and Comparison

The experiment was conducted on a comparative analysis between the outcomes from our approaches and the outcomes from the classical approach using RGB discussed in Section 2. Therefore, 1135 illuminants were obtained, and the angular error was calculated for these outcomes. In order to clarify the behavior of the outcomes, the angular errors obtained were approximated by curve fitting. This approximation was computed using three terms of the Fourier Series, such that the fitted curve describes the trend of the particular approach, as shown in Fig. 2.

Three examples of outcomes using the algorithms under evaluation are shown in Fig. 3. Each image is presented under diverse light conditions and is processed using the three approaches. In addition, the corresponding ideal image is shown. An ideal image is one that is corrected using the ground truth illuminant. GW applied in RGB, generally introduces a saturation which is not found in the source images. In contrast, this algorithm applied on perceptual color spaces preserves better the relation of the colors. We can appreciate this in Fig. 3.

Table 1 shows the three descriptors for the angular error distribution suggested in Section 4.1. According to these descriptors, the application of GW on any perceptual color space is significantly better than using RGB. However, the GW algorithm applied on CIELUV is marginally better than the algorithm on CIELAB. The Gray-Edge (GE) algorithm is included in the experiments for comparison purposes. This algorithm has shown the best performance for this image set [5], and belongs to the group of static color constancy algorithms. However, this has the particular disadvantage of requiring a tuning process using training images. Particularly, the method depends of three parameters, which must be correctly chosen to improve the performance. For this work, GE operates using the parameters proposed by Bianco *et al.* [24]. Nevertheless, the difference in performance between GW using a perceptual space and GE is very small. The main difference is that the GW algorithm in any color space does not require any tuning process.

Table 2 shows the processing time taken by each approach. The specifications of the computer are the following: iMac Apple, 2.5 GHz Intel Core i5, 4GB ram 1333MHz DDR3. We can appreciate that the difference in computing time between GE and GWs approaches is significant. The GW algorithm using CIELUV was the best in performance, except in comparison with GE. However, GW is about 8.3 times faster than the 1st order GE, and 13.7 times faster than the 2nd order GE.

4   Conclusion

A variation of the method using the GW assumption for color constancy has been analyzed in the CIELAB and CIELUV color spaces. Given a test image, the illuminant is estimated and then compared against a reference value. Experimental tests are conducted comparing the outcomes of the proposed methods with outcomes using the standard GW in RGB and the GE algorithm. According to the results, we conclude that outcomes from our approach, a GW assumption in a perceptual color space, are better than those obtained using the standard procedure in RGB. Despite that the outcomes using the GE algorithm are slightly better than those using our approach, for practical applications we can choose the latter, because it is significantly faster and does not require a tuning process. Also, we can appreciate that GW on CIELUV is marginally better than on CIELAB according to the accuracy of the estimated illuminant. Moreover, the processing time is considerably faster on CIELUV. For these reasons, our approaches, particularly the GW using CIELUV, can be considered well-suited preprocessing methods for real-time applications in the pattern recognition and computer vision fields.

Acknowledgments. Jonathan Cepeda-Negrete thanks to the Mexican National Council on Science and Technology, CONACyT, for the financial support provided via the scholarship 290747 (Grant No. 388681/254884), to the University of Guanajuato for the financial support provided via the PIFI-2012 program and the DAIP FJI scholarship.

References

1. Gevers, T., Smeulders, A.W.M.: PicToSeek: Combining Color and Shape Invariant Features for Image Retrieval. IEEE Trans. Image Process. 9(1), 102–119 (2000)
2. Schroeder, M., Moser, S.: Automatic Color Correction Based on Generic Content-Based Image Analysis. In: Proc. of Color Imaging Conference, pp. 41–45 (2001)
3. Gasparini, F., Schettini, R.: Color balancing of digital photos using simple image statistics. Pattern Recognition 37(6), 1201–1217 (2004)
4. van de Weijer, J., Schmid, C., Verbeek, J.: Using High-Level Visual Information for Color Constancy. In: Proc. of the Inter. Conf. on Computer Vision, pp. 1–8 (2007)
5. Bianco, S., Ciocca, G., Cusano, C., Schettini, R.: Improving Color Constancy Using Indoor-Outdoor Image Classification. IEEE Trans. Image Process. 17(12), 2381–2392 (2008)
6. Gijsenij, A., Gevers, T.: Color Constancy using Natural Image Statistics. In: IEEE Conf. on Computer Vision and Pattern Recogn., pp. 1–8 (2007)
7. Yang, J., Stiefelhagen, R., Meier, U., Waibel, A.: Visual tracking for multimodal human computer interaction. In: Proc. of the Conference on Human Factors in Computing Systems, pp. 140–147 (1998)
8. Fairchild, M.D.: Color Appearance Models, 2nd edn. John Wiley & Sons (2005)
9. Gijsenij, A., Gevers, T., van de Weijer, J.: Computational Color Constancy: Survey and Experiments. IEEE Trans. Image Process. 20(9), 2475–2489 (2011)
10. Zeki, S.: A vision of the brain. John Wiley & Sons (1993)
11. Agarwal, V., Abidi, B.R., Koshan, A., Abidi, M.A.: An Overview of Color Constancy Algorithms. J. Pattern Recogn. Res. 1, 42–54 (2006)
12. Buchsbaum, G.: A spatial processor model for object colour perception. Journal of the Franklin Institute 310, 1–26 (1980)
13. Land, E.H., McCann, J.J.: Lightness and Retinex Theory. J. Opt. Soc. Am. 61(1), 1–11 (1971)

14. Finlayson, G.D., Trezzi, E.: Shades of Gray and Colour Constancy. In: Proc. of Color Imaging Conf., pp. 37–41 (2004)
15. van de Weijer, J., Gevers, T., Gijsenij, A.: Edge-Based Color Constancy. IEEE Trans. Image Process. 16(9), 2207–2214 (2007)
16. Ebner, M.: Color constancy based on local space average color. Machine Vision and Applications 20, 283–301 (2009)
17. Ebner, M.: Color Constancy. John Wiley & Sons (2007)
18. Kloss, G.K.: Colour Constancy using von Kries Transformations Colour Constancy goes to the Lab. Res. Lett. Inf. Math. Sci. 13, 19–33 (2009)
19. Cepeda-Negrete, J., Sanchez-Yanez, R.E.: Experiments on the White Patch Retinex in RGB and CIELAB color spaces. Acta Universitaria 22(NE-1), 21–26 (2012)
20. Colorimetry, S.J.: Understanding the CIE System. John Wiley & Sons (2007)
21. Stokes, M., Anderson, M., Chandrasekar, S., Motta, R.: A Standard Default Color Space for the Internet - sRGB. Hewlett-Packard, Microsoft (1996)
22. Ciurea, F., Funt, B.: A Large Image Database for Color Constancy Research. In: Proc. of the IS&T/SID Eleventh Color Imaging Conf., pp. 160–164 (2003)
23. Hordley, S.D., Finlayson, G.A.: A Re-evaluation of Colour Constancy Algorithms. In: Proc. of 17th Inter. Conf. on Pattern Recog (ICPR), pp. 76–79 (2004)
24. Bianco, S., Ciocca, G., Cusano, C., Schettini, R.: Automatic color constancy algorithm selection and combination. Pattern Recogn. 43(3), 695–705 (2010)

A Variational Method for the Optimization of Tone Mapping Operators

Praveen Cyriac, Thomas Batard, and Marcelo Bertalmío

Department on Information and Communication Technologies,
Universitat Pompeu Fabra, Barcelona, Spain
{praveen.cyriac,thomas.batard,marcelo.bertalmio}@upf.edu

Abstract. Given any metric that compares images of different dynamic range, we propose a method to reduce their distance with respect to this metric. The key idea is to consider the metric as a non local operator. Then, we transform the problem of distance reduction into a non local variational problem. In this context, the low dynamic range image having the smallest distance with a given high dynamic range is the minimum of a suitable energy, and can be reached through a gradient descent algorithm. Dealing with an appropriate metric, we present an application to Tone Mapping Operator (TMO) optimization. We apply our gradient descent algorithm, where the initial conditions are Tone Mapped (TM) images. Experiments show that our algorithm does reduce the distance of the TM images with the high dynamic range source images, meaning that our method improves the corresponding TMOs.

Keywords: Tone mapping, Dynamic range independent metric, Contrast distortion, Variational methods.

1 Introduction

The vast range of light intensities of the real world span many orders of magnitude. The human visual system can handle intensities from about 10^{-6} to 10^8 [18], because it continuously adjusts to the light in any viewed scene. High Dynamic Range (HDR) images constitute a powerful tool to store those intensities. However, they cannot be reproduced in common display devices and printers, as these usually span only two orders of magnitude. So an operation called "tone mapping" is performed on the HDR image to scale down the dynamic range in order to obtain a Low Dynamic Range (LDR) image. A good TMO should produce in the observer a sensation as close as possible to the perception produced by the real-world scene. In particular, it should neither introduce nor lose details.

As mentioned in Ferradans et al. [9], TMOs might be classified into two categories. There is a category of TMOs inspired by vision models, like Retinex theory [10], anchoring theory [11], Naka-Rushton formula ([18],[20],[12]), Weber-Fechner's law ([2],[25]). There exists a second category, called gradient-based

R. Klette, M. Rivera, and S. Satoh (Eds.): PSIVT 2013, LNCS 8333, pp. 505–516, 2014.

TMOs, which rely on the idea of shrinking large intensity gradients while preserving small fluctuations, corresponding to fine details ([6],[8],[14],[23]). We refer to [19] for more details about tone mapping and HDR imaging.

An accurate evaluation of TMOs requires a measure of comparison of color sensation and detail visibility between the source (an HDR image) and the output (an LDR image). To the best of our knowledge, there exists no perceptual based measure that compares color appearance between HDR and LDR images. On the other hand, metrics comparing detail visibility or contrast between HDR and LDR images have been investigated (see e.g. [3],[22]). In particular, an objective tone mapping evaluation tool has been proposed by Smith et al. [22], based on the measure of suprathreshold contrast distortion between the source HDR image and its TM LDR version. However, the contrast measure holds only for neighboring pixels, meaning that its sensitivity is limited to high frequency details. More recently, Aydin et al. [3] proposed a metric (DRIM) independent of the dynamic range whose contrast measure is not limited to neighboring pixels (see Sect. 3.1 for a description of the metric DRIM).

Our contribution is two-fold. We first introduce a general framework to reduce the distance (with respect to a given metric) between two images of any dynamic range. Then, we make use of this dynamic range independence to optimize any existing TMO with respect to a given metric. In this paper, we focus on the metric DRIM [3], however we would like to point out that our method is very general and may be applied to any metric. Considering the metric as a non local operator, we are led to a non local variational problem where the quantity to be minimized is a distance associated to the metric. We test our method on the TMOs of Drago et al. [5], Ferradans et al. [9], Mantiuk et al. [15], Reinhard et al. [20]. Experiments show that our method appreciably reduces contrast distortion in the results of the aforementioned TMOs.

The paper is organized as follows. In Sect. 2, we introduce the variational problem, that consists in minimizing a distance between images. We show that this approach is very generic since we only require the metric to be a non local operator. We discuss both continuous and discrete cases. In Sect. 3, we treat the special case where the metric involved is the metric DRIM. We first remind the main properties of this metric. Then, we provide applications to TMOs optimization. We detail a preprocessing that we apply on the TM image we aim at modifying. Finally, we show results of our minimization algorithm applied on the output of the preprocessing, and compare with the initial TM images.

2 Minimization of the Distance between Images

2.1 Image Quality Metrics as Non Local Operators

Many tasks in image processing and computer vision require a validation by comparing the result with the original data, e.g. optical flow estimation, image denoising, tone mapping. Whereas measures based on pixel-wise comparisons (e.g. MSE, SNR, PSNR) are suitable to evaluate image denoising and optical flow estimation algorithms, they are not adapted to evaluate tone mapping.

Tone mapping evaluation requires a measure that compares color sensation and detail visibility (contrast), which are not pixel-wise neither local concepts. This leads us to the following definitions.

Definition 1 (metric). *Let* $L, H: \Omega \longrightarrow \mathbb{R}$ *be two images. We call **metric** an operator **met** such that* $met(L, H)$ *is of the form* $met(L, H): \Omega \longrightarrow \mathbb{R}^n, n \geq 1$.

*We say that a metric is **non local** if the quantities*

$$\frac{\partial met(L, H)(x)}{\partial L(y)}, \frac{\partial met(L, H)(x)}{\partial H(y)} \tag{1}$$

do not vanish for some points $y \neq x$.

The two terms in (1) are infinite dimensional extensions of the notion of derivation with respect to the n-th component. For instance, the first term means that we compute the variations of the functional $L \longmapsto met(L, H)(x)$ with respect to the variations of the function L at the point y.

In this context, we can classify image quality measures into three categories. The first one is the class of metrics that are not non local, like MSE, PSNR and SNR measures. Indeed, the term (1) vanishes since such metrics are based on pixel-wise differences. The second category gathers the metrics that are non local and compare images of same dynamic range (see e.g. [4] for LDR images, [13],[16] for HDR images, and [24] for images of any dynamic range). The last category contains the metrics that are non local and compare images of different dynamic range (see e.g. [3],[22]). In particular, the metric DRIM [3] belongs to both second and third categories since it is independent of the dynamic range of the images it compares.

Definition 2 (distance between images). *A **distance** associated to the metric met is an energy E of the form*

$$E: (L, H) \longmapsto \frac{1}{|\Omega|} \int_{\Omega} \Phi(met(L, H)(x)) \, dx \tag{2}$$

where $\Phi: \mathbb{R}^n \longrightarrow \mathbb{R}^+$ *is a differentiable map.*

2.2   Minimization of the Distance: Continuous Formulation

From now on, we assume that H is fixed and met is a non local metric. We aim at finding the images L that minimize the distance with H. A necessary condition for L to be a minimum of the energy (2) is that L is a critical point of (2), i.e. the differential of the energy at this point in every direction is 0.

Proposition 1. *The images L which are critical points of the energy (2) satisfy*

$$\int_{\Omega} \partial \Phi \left(met(L, H)(x); \frac{\partial met(L, H)(x)}{\partial L(y)} \right) dx = 0 \qquad \forall y \in \Omega$$

Proof. Let $\psi\colon \Omega \longrightarrow \mathbb{R}$ be a compact support function. We compute the differential ∂E of the energy (2) at a point (L, H) in the direction $(\psi, 0)$. We have

$$\partial E((L, H); (\psi, 0)) = \frac{1}{|\Omega|} \int_\Omega \partial \left(\Phi \circ met\right)((L, H); (\psi, 0))(x)\, dx$$

$$= \frac{1}{|\Omega|} \int_\Omega \partial\Phi \left(met(L, H)(x); \partial met\left((L, H); (\psi, 0)\right)(x)\right) dx$$

by the composition law in differential calculus.

Then,

$$\partial met\left((L, H); (\psi, 0)(x)\right) = \int_\Omega \frac{\partial met(L, H)(x)}{\partial L(y)} \psi(y)\, dy \qquad (3)$$

Finally we have

$$\partial E((L, H); (\psi, 0)) = \frac{1}{|\Omega|} \int_\Omega \int_\Omega \partial\Phi \left(met(L, H)(x); \frac{\partial met(L, H)(x)}{\partial L(y)}\right) \psi(y) dx dy$$

At last, as ψ has compact support, $\partial E((L, H); (\psi, 0)) = 0 \Longrightarrow$

$$\int_\Omega \partial\Phi \left(met(L, H)(x); \frac{\partial met(L, H)(x)}{\partial L(y)}\right) dx = 0 \qquad \forall y \in \Omega \qquad (4)$$

□

The term

$$y \colon \longmapsto \frac{1}{|\Omega|} \int_\Omega \partial\Phi \left(met(L, H)(x); \frac{\partial met(L, H)(x)}{\partial L(y)}\right) dx \qquad (5)$$

is the gradient $\nabla(E)$ of the functional $L \colon \longmapsto E(L, H)$.

It is not trivial to obtain mathematical properties of functionals (2) because of the nature of the operators *met*. Hence, it is hard to establish accurate numerical schemes in order to get the minima of the energy (2). For this reason, we deal in this paper with the gradient descent algorithm, which has the property of being applicable to a large class of functionals. Given an image L_0, we consider the scheme

$$L_{k+1} = L_k - \alpha_k \nabla(E)(L_k), \qquad L_{|t=0} = L_0 \qquad (6)$$

However, such a method may reach critical points that are local minima and not global minima. Hence, the initial condition has to be carefully chosen.

2.3   Minimization of the Distance: Discrete Formulation

We assume that L and H are of size $M \times N$. Following Sect.2.2, we define the (discrete) distance between L and H as

$$E(L, H) = \frac{1}{MN} \sum_{m=1}^{M} \sum_{n=1}^{N} \Phi(met(L, H)(m, n)) \qquad (7)$$

In this section, we construct a discrete counterpart of the gradient (5). The main task is to define a discrete counterpart of the term (1). In particular, the term $\partial L(y)$ yields the construction of pixel-wise intensity increments.

Pixel-wise Intensity Increments. There is not a unique choice to compute pixel-wise intensity increments. The trivial approach consists in considering the value $L_+(i,j) := L(i,j) + k$ as forward increment and $L_-(i,j) := L(i,j) - k$ as backward increment at a pixel (i,j), for a fixed $k \in \mathbb{R}^{+*}$. However we claim that such an approach is not adapted to the problem addressed here. Indeed, because the metric *met* in (1) involves perceptual concepts, we intuit that the increments should involve perceptual concepts too.

In [21], a perceptual distance between pixels that takes into account the Weber law principle has been constructed. In particular, the authors construct a "perceptual gradient"

$$\nabla_W I := \frac{\nabla I}{I} \tag{8}$$

for image denoising purposes.

Then, we define the backward $L_-(i,j)$ and forward $L_+(i,j)$ increment at the pixel (i,j) by requiring their perceptual distance (in the sense of Shen) with $L(i,j)$ to be equal, i.e.

$$\frac{L_+(i,j) - L(i,j)}{L(i,j)} = \frac{L(i,j) - L_-(i,j)}{L(i,j)} = k$$

for some $k > 0$.

Expression of the Discrete Gradient. Given a constant $\lambda \in]0,1[$, we construct for each pixel (i,j) two images $L_+(i,j)$ and $L_-(i,j)$ defined as follows

$$L_+(i,j): (m,n) \longmapsto L(m,n)\Big(1 + \min(1/L(i,j) - 1, \lambda)\, \delta((m,n) - (i,j))\Big)$$

$$L_-(i,j): (m,n) \longmapsto L(m,n)\Big(1 - \min(1/L(i,j) - 1, \lambda)\, \delta((m,n) - (i,j))\Big)$$

where δ is the Dirac delta function.

Remark 1. By the use of the increment $k = \min(1/L(i,j) - 1, \lambda)$, we impose that the values of the images $L_+(i,j)$ do not exceed 1. Moreover, the assumption $\lambda \in]0,1[$ imposes that the values of the images $L_-(i,j)$ do not become negative.

Then, we define the discrete version of the term (1) as

$$\frac{\partial met(L,H)(m,n)}{\partial L(i,j)} := \frac{met(L_+(i,j), H)(m,n) - met(L_-(i,j), H)(m,n)}{2\min(1/L(i,j) - 1, \lambda)} \tag{9}$$

from which we derive each component (i,j) of the discrete gradient:

$$\frac{1}{MN} \sum_{m=1}^{M} \sum_{n=1}^{N} \partial\Phi\left(met(L,H)(m,n); \frac{[met(L_+(i,j), H) - met(L_-(i,j), H)](m,n)}{2\min(1/L(i,j) - 1, \lambda)}\right) \tag{10}$$

Finally, we perform the gradient descent (6) where $\nabla(E)(L_k)$ is given by (10).

3   Optimization of Tone Mapping Operators

In this Section, we make use of the minimization approach of Sect. 2 in order to improve TMOs relatively to a given metric. This is a general approach which can be applied to any TMO. Whereas any dynamic range independent metric that can be defined as a non local metric in the sense of Def.1 (see Sect. 2.1) can be used, we focus in our experiments on the metric DRIM [3].

3.1   Dynamic Range Independent Metrics (DRIM)

The metric DRIM compares images of any dynamic range. For applications to tone mapping evaluation, the inputs are a HDR reference image H and its LDR tone-mapped image L. The purpose of the metric is to consider the perception that a viewer would have of both scenes relying on psychophysical data, and to estimate at each pixel the probabilities that distortions appear. The distortions are based on the detection and classification of visible changes in the image structure. Three types of distortion are considered: Loss of Visible Contrast (LVC), contrast visible in the HDR image and not in the LDR image; Amplification of Invisible Contrast (AIC), details that appear in LDR image that were not in the HDR image; and contrast reversal (INV), contrast visible both in the HDR and LDR images with different polarity.

Each type of distortion can be represented as a $[0,1]$-valued function on the image domain $\Omega \subset \mathbb{R}^2$. Then, we define a metric met (in the sense of Def.1) between HDR and tone mapped LDR images by

$$met\,(L, H) := (LVC, AIC, INV) \tag{11}$$

from which we define the distance $E(L, H)$ between L and H associated to met as

$$E\,(L, H) = \frac{1}{MN} \sum_{m=1}^{M} \sum_{n=1}^{N} \sqrt{LVC\,(m, n)^2 + AIC\,(m, n)^2 + INV\,(m, n)^2} \tag{12}$$

Note that the function ϕ of Def.2 we take in the expression of (12) is the Euclidean norm on $\mathbb{R}^3$. Applying formula (10) to the energy (12), we obtain the expression of the gradient of the functional $L \longmapsto E(L, H)$

$$\nabla\,(E\,(L, H))\,(i, j) = \frac{1}{MN} \sum_{m=1}^{M} \sum_{n=1}^{N} \frac{\langle met\,(L, H\,(m, n)), \frac{\partial met(L,H)}{\partial L(i,j)}\,(m, n)\rangle}{\phi\,(met\,(L, H)\,(m, n))} \tag{13}$$

where the term $\frac{\partial met(L,H)}{\partial L(i,j)}$ is given by (9). Then we perform the gradient descent method (6) in order to reduce the distance (12) between the TM image L and the HDR source H.

The existence of global extrema of the energy (12) is ensured. Indeed, the energy is bounded below by 0 and above by $\sqrt{3}$ since the metric met is bounded below by 0 and above by $\sqrt{3}$. Moreover, the set $L^2(\Omega; [0, 1])$ on which we minimize the energy is closed and bounded.

However, local extrema might exist because we do not have information about the convexity of the energy. Hence, the gradient descent method we apply may converge to a local minimum that is not global.

Remark 2. Even if the theoretical lower bound of the energy is 0, it is barely conceivable that this bound might be reached. Indeed, experiments show that we have $E(L, L) > 0$ and $E(H, H) > 0$ when we test the metric DRIM on any LDR image L or HDR image H of non constant intensity values. Hence, we claim that the situation $E(L, H) = 0$ does not occur with the DRIM metric. As a consequence, we do not know if the critical point our algorithm reaches is a local or global minimum.

3.2   Preprocessing

To increase the chance that the algorithm converges to an image that has the smallest distance to H, i.e. a global minimum, we apply a preprocessing on the original TM image L in order to get an initial condition of our algorithm that is closer (in terms of distance) to H than L. The method we propose relies on the intuition that high values of LVC might be reduced by application of local sharpening whereas high values of AIC might be reduced by local Gaussian blurring. Hence we perform local Gaussian blurring and unsharp masking [1] to the initial LDR image depending on the values of the function $LVC - AIC$.

Denoting by L_{smooth} a blurred version of L and defining L_{sharp} as

$$L_{sharp} = L + \alpha \left(L - L_{smooth}\right) \tag{14}$$

for some constant α, we define the image L_{new} as

$$L_{new}(i, j) = \begin{cases} L_{sharp}(i, j) & \text{if } LVC(i, j) - AIC(i, j) > 0 \\ (1 - \beta)L(i, j) + \beta L_{smooth}(i, j) & \text{if } LVC(i, j) - AIC(i, j) < 0 \end{cases} \tag{15}$$

Experiments (see Table 1) show that we do have $E(L_{new}, H) < E(L, H)$.

3.3   Experiments

As the metric DRIM only takes into account the luminance information of the images, we first convert the LDR color image into a luminance map. It is performed by mapping its RGB values into the Lab color space and extracting the L-channel. Then inverse gamma correction is applied.

We perform the preprocessing described in Sect. 3.2 with the following parameters: the parameter σ of the Gaussian smoothing kernel is set to 0.62, and the constants α, β are respectively 0.7 and 0.5. These values provide good results and have been fixed for all the experiments in this paper.

Fig. 1. The preprocessing stage. From left to right: input TM image (distance =0.717), output image (distance =0.682), distortion map of the input, distortion map of the output.In this case, the preprocessing reduces the TM error by 5%.

Then, we apply the gradient descent algorithm of Sect. 3.1, where the initial condition is the output of the preprocessing. Because the variational problem we propose is non local, the gradient descent algorithm is very time-consuming. In order to decrease the execution time of the algorithm, rather than computing the sum in eq. (10) over the whole image, we only consider 50×50 neighbourhoods. The algorithm stops when a local minimum is reached, i.e. when the energy does not decrease anymore.

The output LDR color image is obtained by adding the components a,b of the initial TM image to the output LDR luminance map.

The evaluation of our algorithm is two-fold: global and pixel-wise. As a global measure, we consider the total energy (7) of the output (see Table 1). As a pixel-wise measure, we make use of the distortion map in [3]. The basic idea is to encode contrast distortions by colors: green hue represents LVC, blue hue stands for AIC and red hue indicates INV, the saturation encoding the magnitude of the corresponding distortion, whereas the intensity corresponds to the intensity of the HDR source image (up to rounding). At each pixel, the maximum of the three distortions is computed, and the corresponding color is displayed. If the maximum is lower than 0.5, then the saturation is set to 0.

The first experiment consists in evaluating the preprocessing. In Fig. 1 we show an output color image of the preprocessing, as well as its distortion map. We have applied the formula (15) to a TM image obtained with the method of Ferradans et al. [9]. The HDR source image is taken from the MPI database [17]. We observe that the LVC distortion has been reduced, whereas the INV distortion has increased a bit. As we can see in formula (15), the preprocessing is only devoted to reduce the LVC and AIC distortions, and does not take into account the INV distortion. This might explain why the INV distortion tends to increase. On Table 1, we present results of the preprocessing tested on images of the Fairchild database [7] for different TMOs, i.e. Ferradans et al. [9], Drago et al. [5], Reinhard et al. [20], Mantiuk et al. [15]. The images have been rescaled to 200×200 pixels in order to speed the algorithm up. Average results have been computed over 5 images of the dataset. The results confirm that the preprocessing reduces the distance with the HDR source image.

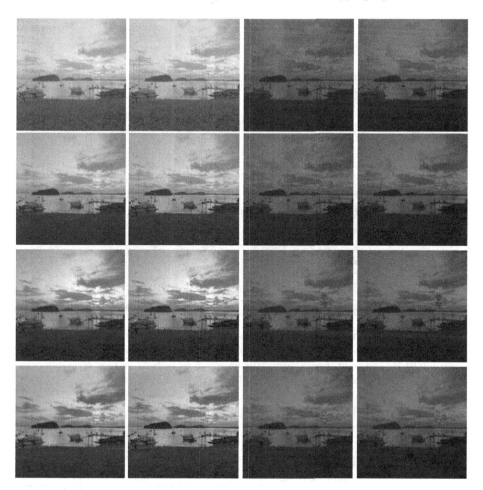

Fig. 2. The final output. First column: input TM images (from top to bottom: Drago et al.[5], Reinhard et al.[20], Mantiuk et al.[15], Ferradans et al. [9] TMOs). Second column: final output images. Third column: distortion maps of input TM images. Fourth column: distortion maps of final outputs. See Table. 1 (image "BarharborPresun") for the corresponding distances.

In the second experiment, we evaluate the final output of our method described above. In Fig. 2 we show some results of our algorithm tested on the different TMOs mentioned above. The HDR source is the image "BarharborPresun" taken from Fairchild database. The distortion maps show that the algorithm reduces drastically the distortion LVC, but the INV tends to remain. Table 1 shows the distances of the initial TM images and output images with the HDR source image, as well as for other images of the Fairchild dataset. As expected, the final distance is lower than the initial distance. An other interesting point is the observation in Fig. 2 that the contrast in the output color images is higher than the one in the initial TM images.

Fig. 3. Comparison between the preprocessing stage and the final output. Top left: input TM image (distance = 0.708). Top middle: output of preprocessing stage (distance = 0.615). Top right: final output (distance = 0.533). Bottom row: corresponding distortion maps. For this image our method reduces the TM error by 25%.

Table 1. Distance at each stage of our method computed with DRIM[3]

Image	TMO	Initial	Preprocessing	Final	Improvement(%)
BarharborPresun	Drago et al.	0.681	0.608	0.502	26.25
	Reinhard et al.	0.676	0.607	0.493	27.05
	Mantiuk et al.	0.528	0.487	0.424	19.75
	Ferradans et al.	0.560	0.509	0.438	21.46
AmikBeavDamPM1	Drago et al.	0.767	0.682	0.584	23.90
	Reinhard et al.	0.708	0.615	0.533	24.70
	Mantiuk et al.	0.726	0.649	0.564	22.25
	Ferradans et al.	0.691	0.630	0.542	21.50
Average	Drago et al.	0.672	0.606	0.525	21.91
	Reinhard et al.	0.636	0.564	0.464	27.09
	Mantiuk et al.	0.619	0.564	0.493	20.40
	Ferradans et al.	0.609	0.566	0.491	19.39

At last, we compare the output of the preprocessing stage with the final output of our method. In Fig. 3, we compare distortion maps. The HDR source is the image "AmikeusBeaverDamPM1" from the Fairchild database. The input TM image is provided by the TMO of Reinhard et al. [20]. The corresponding distortion map shows a high loss of contrast. We observe that the preprocessing stage reduces it to a great extent, and the gradient descent algorithm applied to the output of the preprocessing reduces it more. However, we see that neither the preprocessing nor the gradient descent algorithm achieves to reduce the INV distortion. The results on Table 1 confirm that applying the gradient descent algorithm to the output of the preprocessing provides better results than applying only the preprocessing.

4 Conclusion

We proposed a variational method to reduce the distance between two images of any dynamic range based on a non local metric. Then, dealing with the dynamic range independent metric DRIM, we presented an application to TMOs optimization. We tested our method on different TMOs of the literature. Experiments confirmed that our method substantially reduces the perceptual distance with the HDR source image, providing an average improvement of more than 20% for several state of the art TMOs.

Current work is devoted to improve the preprocessing stage by taking into account the INV distortion. Whereas the gradient term was approximated on 50×50 neighbourhoods in our experiments, we intend to decrease the execution time of our algorithm in order to compute the whole gradient term, which will probably improve our results. Finally, because our approach is a generic method that can be applied to images of any dynamic range and any non local metric, other applications might be envisaged in the future.

Acknowledgement. The authors would like to express their utmost gratitude to Tunc Aydin, Karol Myszkowski, Rafal Mantiuk and Hans-Peter Seidel for their help. This work was supported by the European Research Council, Starting Grant ref. 306337, and by Spanish grants ref. TIN2011-15954-E and ref. TIN2012-38112.

References

1. Adams, J.E., Deever, A.T., Morales, E.O., Pillman, B.H.: Perceptually based Image Processing Algorithm Design. Perceptual Digital Imaging: Methods and Applications 6, 123 (2012)
2. Ashikhmin, M.: A Tone Mapping Algorithm for High Contrast Images. In: Proc. Eurographics Workshop Rendering, pp. 1–11 (2002)
3. Aydin, T.O., Mantiuk, R., Myszkowski, K., Seidel, H.-P.: Dynamic Range Independent Image Quality Assessment. In: Proc. ACM SIGGRAPH, pp. 1–10 (2008)
4. Daly, S.: The Visible Differences Predictor: An Algorithm for the Assessment of Image Fidelity. In: Watson, A.B. (ed.) Digital Images and Human Vision, pp. 179–206. MIT Press (1993)
5. Drago, F., Myszkowski, K., Annen, T., Chiba, N.: Adaptive Logarithmic Mapping for Displaying High Contrast Scenes. Computer Graphics Forum 22(3), 419–426 (2003)
6. Durand, F., Dorsey, J.: Fast Bilateral Filtering for the Display of High Dynamic Range Images. In: Proc. ACM SIGGRAPH, pp. 257–266 (2002)

7. Fairchild, M.: http://www.cis.rit.edu/fairchild/HDRPS/HDRthumbs.html
8. Fattal, R., Lischinski, D., Werman, M.: Gradient Domain High Dynamic Range Compression. In: Proc. ACM SIGGRAPH, pp. 249–256 (2002)
9. Ferradans, S., Bertalmío, M., Provenzi, E., Caselles, V.: An Analysis of Visual Adaptation and Contrast Perception for Tone Mapping. IEEE Trans. on Pattern Analysis and Machine Intelligence 33(10), 2002–2012 (2011)
10. Jobson, D., Rahman, Z., Woodell, G.: A Multiscale Retinex for Bridging the Gap between Color Images and the Human Observation of Scenes. IEEE Trans. Image Processing 6(7), 965–976 (1997)
11. Krawczyk, G., Myszkowski, K., Seidel, H.-P.: Lightness Perception in Tone Reproduction for High Dynamic Range Images. Computer Graphics Forum 24(3), 635–645 (2005)
12. Kuang, J., Johnson, G.M., Fairchild, M.: iCAM06: A Refined Image Appearance Model for HDR Image Rendering. J. Visual Comm. and Image Representation 18, 406–414 (2007)
13. Mantiuk, R., Daly, S., Myszkowski, K., Seidel, H.-P.: Predicting Visible Differences in High Dynamic Range Images - Model and its Calibration. In: Human Vision and Electronic Imaging X. SPIE Proceedings Serie, vol. 5666, pp. 204–214 (2005)
14. Mantiuk, R., Myszkowski, K., Seidel, H.-P.: A Perceptual Framework for Contrast Processing of High Dynamic Range Images. ACM Trans. Applied Perception 3(3), 286–308 (2006)
15. Mantiuk, R., Daly, S., Kerofsky, L.: Display Adaptative Tone Mapping. In: Proc. ACM SIGGRAPH, vol. 68 (2008)
16. Mantiuk, R., Kim, K.J., Rempel, A.G., Heidrich, W.: HDR-VDP-2: A Calibrated Visual Metric for Visibility and Quality Predictions in all Luminance Conditions. In: Proc. ACM SIGGRAPH, vol. 40 (2011)
17. MPI database, http://www.mpi-inf.mpg.de/resources/hdr/gallery.html
18. Pattanaik, S., Tumblin, J., Yee, H., Greenberg, D.: Time-Dependent Visual Adaptation for Fast Realistic Image Display. In: Proc. ACM SIGGRAPH, pp. 47–54 (2000)
19. Reinhard, E., Ward, G., Pattanaik, S., Debevec, P.: High Dynamic Range Imaging, Acquisition, Display, and Image-Based Lighting. Morgan Kaufmann (2005)
20. Reinhard, E., Devlin, K.: Dynamic Range Reduction Inspired by Photoreceptor Physiology. IEEE Trans. Visualization and Computer Graphics 11(1), 13–24 (2005)
21. Shen, J.: On the Foundations of Vision Modeling, I. Weber's law and Weberized TV (Total Variation) Restoration. Phys. D 175, 241–251 (2003)
22. Smith, K., Krawczyk, G., Myszkowski, K., Seidel, H.-P.: Beyond Tone Mapping: Enhanced Depiction of Tone Mapped HDR Images. Computer Graphics Forum 25(3), 427–438 (2006)
23. Tumblin, J., Turk, G.: Lcis: A Boundary Hierarchy for Detail-Preserving Contrast Reduction. In: Proc. ACM SIGGRAPH, pp. 83–90 (1999)
24. Wang, Z., Bovik, A.C.: A Universal Image Quality Index. IEEE Signal Processing Letters 9(3), 81–84 (2002)
25. Ward, G., Rushmeier, H., Piatko, C.: A Visibility Matching Tone Reproduction Operator for High Dynamic Range Scenes. IEEE Trans. Visualization and Computer Graphics 3(4), 291–306 (1997)

Author Index